CANADIAN COMPETITION LAW AND POLICY

UPDATED FIRST EDITION

Other Books in the *Essentials of Canadian Law* Series

International Trade Law

Family Law

Copyright Law

The Law of Sentencing

Administrative Law

Computer Law 2/e

International Human Rights Law

Franchise Law

Legal Ethics and Professional Responsibility 2/e

Public International Law 2/e

Individual Employment Law 2/e

Civil Litigation

Canadian Telecommunications Law

Intellectual Property Law 2/e

Animals and the Law

Income Tax Law 2/e

Personal Property Security Law 2/e

Youth Criminal Justice Law 3/e

Bank and Customer Law in Canada 2/e

The Law of Equitable Remedies 2/e

Pension Law 2/e

Remedies: The Law of Damages 3/e

Freedom of Conscience and Religion 2/e

The Law of Trusts 3/e

Ethics and Criminal Law 2/e

Insurance Law 2/e

Immigration Law 2/e

Bankruptcy and Insolvency Law 2/e

Legal Research and Writing 4/e

Canadian Maritime Law 2/e

Public Lands and Resources in Canada

Conflict of Laws 2/e

Statutory Interpretation 3/e

The Charter of Rights and Freedoms 6/e

Constitutional Law 5/e

Land-Use Planning

Detention and Arrest 2/e

Refugee Law 2/e

Religious Institutions and the Law 4/e

Securities Law 2/e

Criminal Law 7/e

The Law of Partnerships and Corporations 4/e

Environmental Law 5/e

Fundamental Justice 2/e

International and Transnational Criminal Law 3/e

The Law of Torts 6/e

Mergers, Acquisitions, and Other Changes of Corporate Control 3/e

Criminal Procedure 4/e

Information and Privacy Law in Canada

The Law of Evidence 8/e

The Law of Contracts 3/e

National Security Law 2/e

The Law of Property

ESSENTIALS OF
CANADIAN LAW

CANADIAN COMPETITION LAW AND POLICY

UPDATED FIRST EDITION

JOHN S. TYHURST
BA (Econ), LLB, LLM
Member of the Ontario and BC Bars

UNIVERSITY OF TORONTO PRESS
Toronto Buffalo London

Irwin Law
An imprint of University of Toronto Press
Toronto Buffalo London
utorontopress.com
Printed and bound by CPI Group (UK) Ltd, Croydon, CR0 4YY

ISBN 978-1-4875-7114-6 (paper) ISBN 978-1-4875-7115-3 (PDF)
ISBN 978-1-4875-7116-0 (EPUB)

Cataloguing in Publication available from Library and Archives Canada

---

We wish to acknowledge the land on which the University of Toronto Press operates. This land is the traditional territory of the Wendat, the Anishnaabeg, the Haudenosaunee, the Métis, and the Mississaugas of the Credit First Nation.

University of Toronto Press acknowledges the financial support of the Government of Canada and the Ontario Arts Council, an agency of the Government of Ontario, for its publishing activities.

Canada Council for the Arts Conseil des Arts du Canada

ONTARIO ARTS COUNCIL
CONSEIL DES ARTS DE L'ONTARIO
an Ontario government agency
un organisme du gouvernement de l'Ontario

Funded by the Government of Canada Financé par le gouvernement du Canada | Canada

To our beloved son Mark.
Love you forever - to the moon and back

SUMMARY TABLE OF CONTENTS

DETAILED TABLE OF CONTENTS

CHAPTER 6:
AGREEMENTS BETWEEN COMPETITORS *265*

LIST OF TABLES AND FIGURES

PREFACE

Competition law is centred on an important and deceptively simple idea: that competitive markets can efficiently and effectively deliver the goods, services, and economic growth which society desires. The power of this idea is reflected in the predominance of mixed, market-reliant economies around the world, and the adoption of competition laws in more than 125 countries.[1]

Competitive markets are, however, complex and seldom resemble the economists' models. Digital and data markets illustrate the point. These markets have many new entrants, are incredibly innovative, swift to change, and are growing quickly. Nonetheless, certain market segments have seen the emergence of dominant players. Some commentators have made comparisons to the railways and trusts which spawned competition and antitrust laws in North America in the late 1800s. Others see the leading firms as vibrant competitors, merely delivering what consumers want: low prices and innovative products or services. Should the emergence of these large digital players be a concern for competition law? The assessment of such market structures and conduct often requires the balancing of beneficial against harmful effects. It also requires consideration of the goals of the law, and how they may (or may not) be served by alternative remedies.

The foregoing are among the reasons why competition law and policy is not only a highly relevant, but also a fascinating and challenging area,

1 OECD (2020), *OECD Competition Trends 2020*, online: www.oecd.org/competition/oecd-competition-trends.htm.

and one that demands a flexible and interdisciplinary approach. In this light, the objective of this book is to offer students, lawyers, and others with an interest in the subject a practical guide, not only to the law, but also to its broader context, its objectives, and its evolution. In addition to setting out the elements of the relevant statutory provisions and their treatment in the caselaw, the book seeks to provide

- an overview of the jurisprudential and legislative history of the current provisions;
- an approachable outline of the key economic concepts upon which Canadian competition law and policy analysis is founded; and
- a review of methods and approaches applied by economists and lawyers to the analysis of competition law problems.

This updated version of the book tracks three rounds of important amendments made to the *Competition Act* in the period 2022-24. These are the most significant changes to the Act since the major rounds of amendments which occurred in 1986 and 2009. The most recent changes did not modify the institutional and adjudicative structure of the legislative scheme, but they do reflect a change in direction away from an emphasis on efficiency as the central objective of the legislation. Examples in the areas of merger review are the addition of a structural presumption and the repeal of the efficiencies defence. In the area of abuse of dominance, the test was modified to provide a remedy for anti-competitive conduct even where no substantial lessening of competition is found. At the time of writing, the Competition Bureau had not yet completed its revisions to the various Guidelines which set out guidance on its enforcement approach in light of the amendments. A Second Edition of the book is planned following the completion of those Guidelines.

ACKNOWLEDGEMENTS

This is an updated version of the book originally published by Irwin Law in 2021. I would like to acknowledge the contribution of Jeff Miller, Irwin Publisher, without whom the book would never have been produced. Jeff recently retired, and passed the torch of the Irwin *Essentials of Canadian Law* series to the U of T Press. Jeff's passion for independent Canadian publishing was reflected in his close attention to the production and quality of the series. He was always accessible to discuss any issues that arose, and made a personal call when the decision to move the series to U of T Press was made.

My sincere thanks to the staff at U of T Press who worked with me on this updated version following the recent amendments to the *Competition Act*. I look forward to working with them on a forthcoming Second Edition, which will incorporate Bureau's updated *Guidelines*, currently under revision, and further updates in the case law.

John S Tyhurst
Ottawa
December 2024

CHAPTER 1

INTRODUCTION

A. COMPETITION LAW AND POLICY

This book is about Canadian competition law, which is found primarily in the provisions of the federal *Competition Act* and related jurisprudence addressing competitive behaviour in the economy.[1] While this book is focused on the law, the discussion also touches on topics related to the broader subject of competition policy, which is a branch of economic policy concerned with the way competition legislation is designed and implemented, how market competition can play a role in the operation of regulatory schemes, the manner in which other government policies may affect the competitive market system, and competition issues arising in international fora.

Competition law and policy raise a fascinating blend of business, consumer, economic, and legal issues. The legal issues may involve criminal, constitutional, administrative, commercial, corporate, tort, and contract law. It is an area where consumers, businesspeople, lawyers, economists, and policy makers often engage in a multi-disciplinary dialogue. That exchange may occur in the hearing room in the context of a contested case, in the boardroom as part of an advisory or planning process for commercial or competitive action, or in a legislative or

1 *Competition Act*, RSC 1985, c C-34 [Act]; also re civil adjudication, procedure, and remedies, see the *Competition Tribunal Act*, RSC 1985, c 19 (2nd Supp) and regulations thereunder.

policy context related to modifications or reform of laws, regulations or enforcement practices and procedures. The dynamic nature of the issues raised, as well as their practical relevance and importance to the prices, choice, and quality of the products and services we all use or consume on a daily basis, make this a stimulating and ever-changing area.

In essence, competition law seeks to promote the proper functioning of competitive markets in order to deliver such benefits as low prices, consumer choice, and innovative products. Competitive markets can lower product costs, increase international competitiveness, and create incentives to innovate. Competition law and policy thus focus on ensuring the efficient operation of competitive markets. On the other hand, industry-specific or sectoral regulation may be employed where market competition does not deliver desired outcomes. Other government policy tools may be needed to address such important matters as public safety, workers' rights, environmental protection, or privacy. Even in such areas, however, competition policy can provide a reminder that regulation can be relaxed or dispensed with when markets are sufficiently robust to deliver sought-after competitive prices, quality, and product choice.

This chapter provides an overview of the book after a brief discussion of how competition law and policy interrelate with sectoral regulation and other economic policies.

B. THE ROLE OF COMPETITION LAW AND POLICY IN THE ECONOMY

Market-based competition plays a role as part of a country's economic policy. It can provide a less intrusive method, in comparison to direct forms of regulation or government control of the economy, for the achievement of certain policy goals. This was explained in the watershed 1969 *Interim Report on Competition Policy* by the Economic Council of Canada:

> [C]ompetitive market forces are potentially capable of allocating resources better and more cheaply, with a less cumbersome administrative overhead, than any alternative arrangement such as wholesale public ownership and control, detailed government regulation of enterprises, or self-regulation by large industrial units within a corporate state.[2]

Competition law and policy are among other "business framework" laws and policies which set the broad parameters within which business

---

2 Economic Council of Canada, *Interim Report on Competition Policy* (Ottawa: Queen's Printer, 1969) at 8.

operates in the Canadian economy. Other examples include rules governing intellectual property, international trade, corporate governance, and capital markets. These can be contrasted with industry-specific regulation. These "framework" policies play a role in determining national economic growth rates. They affect incentives for efficient capital accumulation, technological diffusion and the modernization of production processes and marketing arrangements. They influence attitudes and conduct affecting innovation and adjustment to change.[3]

As part of such a framework policy, the *Competition Act* is a law of "general application" — it applies across industries and economic activity. Unlike industry-specific regulation, which often seeks to prescribe particular levels of price, service, or other outcomes, competition law seeks to ensure that *the operation of the market* is able to deliver competitive prices, quality of service, and choice. Thus, it is competition which performs the primary regulating function. Competition law enforcement functions somewhat like a referee in a hockey game — it is largely invisible until a problem which impedes the smooth functioning of the "game" — the market — arises. To do this, competition law enforcement applies criminal offences, civil prohibitions, and other remedies intended to encourage competitive conditions and conduct, so that *the competitive process itself* can produce desirable outcomes for consumers.

In this vein, the Competition Tribunal has held that it "is not a rate-setting body. The implications of rate-setting . . . [are] the antithesis of competition policy."[4] In *Commissioner of Competition v VISA/MasterCard* the Tribunal went even further, stating, "[t]he powers of the Tribunal to effectively fashion a remedy are limited. Ongoing monitoring and enforcement are impossible."[5] Through such statements we see that "competition authorities are generally reluctant to seek orders which require continuous supervision or frequent adjustments. Indeed, their main goal is to establish or restore a situation where the market can function competitively with a minimum further intervention or even surveillance on their part."[6]

Where competition is sufficiently strong, industry-specific regulation may no longer be necessary and the "framework" rules of competition

---

3 Industry Canada, *Competition Policy as a Dimension of Economic Policy: A Comparative Perspective*, Occasional Paper Number 7 (May 1995) at 3–4, online: www.ic.gc.ca/eic/site/eas-aes.nsf/vwapj/op07e.pdf/$file/op07e.pdf.

4 *Canada (Competition Act, Director of Investigation and Research) v Tele-Direct (Publications) Inc*, [1997] CCTD 8 at para 533.

5 *Canada (Commissioner of Competition) v Visa Canada Corp*, [2013] CCTD 10 at para 397.

6 Robert D Anderson et al, "Competition Policy and Regulatory Reform in Canada, 1986–1997" (1998) 13 *Review of Industrial Organization* 177 at 185.

law can be applied. Industries that have been deregulated, in whole or in part, given the presence of increased competition and liberalized entry rules include airlines, railways, and electricity.[7]

In the telecommunications sector, the regulator, the Canadian Radio-television and Telecommunications Commission (CRTC), was given the power in the *Telecommunications Act* to withdraw regulation when it found that this would be consistent with Canadian telecommunications policy objectives. The statute also provided that the CRTC "shall" forbear where the service in question "is or will be subject to competition sufficient to protect the interests of users."[8] As competition has emerged over time in telecommunications markets, the Commission has applied this forbearance power to numerous services, from long distance to wireless.[9] This has progressed to the point that by 2018, approximately 96 percent of telecommunications revenues in Canada were generated from forborne services.[10] Competition in markets such as mobile wireless services is still evolving, and calls for regulatory remedies persisting, given such factors as significant barriers to entry and the potential for coordinated pricing among the handful of large, facilities-based competitors.[11]

While increasing competition can result in the removal of the underlying rationale for regulation in whole or part, the opposite may also be true: when a market's structure or performance changes to the point that it is determined that competition and hence competition law cannot address public policy concerns, there may be a call for greater regulation. In the case of digital markets, for example, the dominance of companies such as Facebook, Google, and Amazon have led to calls for specialized rules and additional regulatory resources to govern such matters as consumer data mobility, access to data for emerging competitors, and the protection of privacy. In the United Kingdom, several government

7 For an overview, see Andrew J Roman, "Electricity Deregulation in Canada: An Idea Which Has Yet to Be Tried" (2002) 40 *Alberta Law Review* 97; Edward Iacobucci, Michel Trebilcock & Ralph A Winter, "The Canadian Experience with Deregulation" (2006) 56 *University of Toronto Law Journal* 1.

8 *Telecommunications Act*, SC 1993, c 38, s 34.

9 For an historical overview, see John S Tyhurst, "Monopoly Lost: The Legal and Regulatory Path to Canadian Telecommunications Competition 1979–2002" (2001–2002) 33 *Ottawa Law Review* 385 at 419–24.

10 Canadian Radio-television and Telecommunications Commission, *Telecommunications Monitoring Report 2019* (Ottawa: CRTC, 2020) at 227.

11 See, e.g., Competition Bureau, "Comments of the Competition Bureau, Telecom Notice of Consultation 2019-57, *Review of Mobile Wireless Services*" (15 May 2019), and Competition Bureau, "Final Comments of the Competition Bureau, Telecom Notice of Consultation 2019-57, *Review of Mobile Wireless Services*" (15 July 2020) at 21: "there is a market power problem in most Canadian markets."

reports have expressed the view, in proposing more digital platform regulation, that competition law is not sufficiently swift or otherwise capable of dealing with problems such as "making it easier for consumers to move and control their data, and for new digital businesses to interoperate with established platforms."[12] The European Union has put into effect regulations governing how digital marketplaces and search engines (e.g., Amazon, eBay, Google) must treat online businesses' services and proposed a Digital Markets Act to regulate any "core platform service" in areas such as social media and search engines.[13]

On the other hand, regulatory approaches have been criticized by those who take the view that data and digital markets are suitable for governance by strengthened competition law oversight, and that recourse to detailed regulation may be harmful to the dynamic nature of those markets.[14] The appropriate mix of competition law and regulatory

---

12 UK, *Report of the Digital Competition Expert Panel* (HM Treasury: London, 2019) at 5, online: https://assets.publishing.service.gov.uk/government/uploads/system/uploads/attachment_data/file/785547/unlocking_digital_competition_furman_review_web.pdf. See also the final report by the Competition and Markets Authority, *Online Platforms and Digital Advertising* (1 July 2020), online: www.gov.uk/cma-cases/online-platforms-and-digital-advertising-market-study#final-report at 329–30: "Competition law, consumer law and data protection law is principally used to correct or stop conduct after that conduct has occurred, often with a penal element. The current enforcement models typically require lengthy investigations and/or litigation before the illegality of the conduct is finally determined. The code would enable behaviour to be challenged and changed much more rapidly than is possible through existing laws and before it has harmed competition"; US House of Representatives, Subcommittee on Antitrust Commercial and Administrative Law of The Committee on The Judiciary, *Investigation of Competition in Digital Markets Majority Staff Report and Recommendations* (6 October 2020) at 387 "It is unclear whether the antitrust agencies are presently equipped to block anti-competitive mergers in digital markets. The record of the Federal Trade Commission and the Justice Department in this area shows significant missteps and repeat enforcement failures. . . . These concerns are especially acute today, given the combined national health and economic crises, which have widened the gap between the dominant platforms and businesses across the rest of the economy."

13 EU, *Regulation (EU) 2019/1150 of the European Parliament and of The Council of 20 June 2019 on promoting fairness and transparency for business users of online intermediation services*; European Commission, "Digital Markets Act: Ensuring Fair and Open Digital Markets" (15 December 2020).

14 John Pecman, Paul A Johnson & Justine Reisler, "Essential Facilities Fallacy: Big Tech, Winner-Take-All Markets, and Anticompetitive Effects" (Winter 2020) 2:2 *CPI Antitrust Chronicle* 1 at 4–5 and 11:

> The benefit to using the traditional antitrust framework is that it avoids micro-managing the technology sector, a complex and rapidly evolving sector of the economy. . . . [T]raditionally regulation is only imposed in industries

approaches for addressing the policy issues raised in digital markets will be the subject of continuing public debate as competition law enforcement actions unfold[15] and remedies such as steps pursuant to privacy regulations[16] are taken.

In recent decades, competition laws have been adopted in numerous economies transitioning from central or state control. By 1996, less than a decade after the fall of the Berlin Wall, twenty-two of twenty-six economies in Central and Eastern Europe and the former Soviet Union had adopted competition laws.[17] While the effectiveness of these new regimes has varied, this widespread deployment of competition law shows its importance as a policy tool for most economies, which now overwhelmingly rely upon free markets to deliver goods and services. The adoption of competition laws has occurred in other state-dominated economies. For example, in 2008, China adopted competition laws to address certain kinds of anti-competitive conduct, and created administration and enforcement institutions, including an Anti-monopoly Commission.[18]

In Canada, the competition law regime has been strengthened substantially in the last several decades, with, *inter alia*, the creation of the Competition Tribunal, a specialized civil tribunal for mergers, abuse of dominance, and other practices requiring a case-by-case assessment, and by focusing the criminal provisions on clearly harmful conduct (such as price fixing) which does not require such an assessment. Further improvements are possible. These include strengthening the independent role of the Competition Bureau (or perhaps some other

---

> where the cost of entry is so great, or the duplication of facilities would be so wasteful, that some degree of monopoly is considered unavoidable. . . . [I]mproving current competition law enforcement is valuable because it provides a tangible response to widespread calls for potentially dramatic change. Calls to regulate big tech companies like we do a municipal utility are indeed dramatic and, we believe, are likely to be harmful on balance. Instead, we believe that a better path forward is to give competition — and antitrust enforcement — a shot.

15 See, e.g., *US et al v Google LLC, Complaint* (20 October 2020); *Federal Trade Commission v Facebook Inc*, Complaint (9 December 2020).

16 See, e.g., Privacy Commissioner of Canada, *Joint Investigation of Facebook by the Privacy Commissioner of Canada and the Information and Privacy Commissioner for British Columbia*, PIPEDA Report of Findings #2019-002 (25 April 2019).

17 Mark A Dutz & Maria Vagliasindi, "Competition Policy Implementation in Transition Economies: An Empirical Assessment" (2000) 44:4 *European Economic Review* 762 at 763, online: www.oecd.org/daf/competition/prosecutionandlawenforcement/39990968.pdf.

18 Organization for Economic Cooperation and Development (OECD), *Competition Laws in the Asia-Pacific, A Guide to Selected Jurisdictions* (2018) at 37, online: www.oecd.org/daf/competition/Competition-Law-in-Asia-Pacific-Guide-2018.pdf.

organization[19]) as an advocate for competition policy in Canada,[20] and measures such as permitting private applications to the Competition Tribunal in merger and abuse of dominance cases[21] to complement limited public enforcement resources and to increase jurisprudential guidance on the application of the legislation. Nonetheless, after three major rounds of reform beginning in 1976 (and several more minor ones during this period), the *Competition Act* provides an advanced and comprehensive legal framework for the promotion of competitive markets in Canada.

C. OVERVIEW OF THE BOOK

Chapters 2 and 3 begin with introductory and background topics before the discussion turns to the substantive law in chapters 4 through 10. Chapter 2 examines the historical evolution and current structure of the enforcement and adjudication institutions for Canadian competition law. Canada has the distinction of being the first jurisdiction in the world to adopt a competition law statute, in 1890. However, the legislation was largely ineffective, lacking a permanent agency to carry out investigation and enforcement. While this improved by the early decades of the twentieth century with the creation of a dedicated enforcement agency, the exclusive reliance on the criminal law (largely due to constitutional constraints) was problematic. Criminal law proved to be ill-adapted to such matters as merger and monopoly, which require an economic analysis of competitive effects. As a result, enforcement in those areas was, in large measure, ineffectual for most of the law's first century. Through several rounds of amendments beginning in 1976, the law moved away from criminal enforcement for merger, abuse of dominance, and other practices requiring a case-by-case assessment of economic effect. The creation of the specialized civil Competition Tribunal in 1986 was a major advance in modernizing the law. Private enforcement through civil damages actions for breaches of the criminal provisions, added

19 Competition Policy Review Panel, *Compete to Win: Final Report* (Ottawa: Industry Canada, 2008) at 99.

20 John Pecman, "Unleash Canada's Competition Watchdog: Improving the Effectiveness and Ensuring the Independence of Canada's Competition Bureau" (2018) 31:1 *Can Competition L Rev* 5 at 30–39.

21 *Ibid* at 39; House of Commons, Standing Committee on Industry, Science and Technology, *A Plan to Modernize Canada's Competition Regime* (April 2002) (Chair: Walt Lastewka) at 33, online: www.ourcommons.ca/Content/Committee/371/INST/Reports/RP1032077/indurp08/indurp08-e.pdf.

in 1976, provided a complement to public enforcement. Such actions gained momentum, particularly in the area of price fixing and other collusive behaviour, with the liberalization of class action procedures in the 1990s. Recent decisions from the Supreme Court of Canada on competition law class actions also provide the potential for an increased role of this avenue for compensation of those harmed, and for deterrence of anti-competitive conduct. Limited private enforcement of certain civil provisions was also provided for in 2002, but this has not led to many significant private applications to the Competition Tribunal.

Chapter 2 also provides an overview of the roles and structure of the various players involved in competition law: the Commissioner of Competition, the Competition Bureau, the Minister of Industry, Science and Economic Development, the Competition Tribunal, the criminal and civil courts, the Department and Minister of Justice, the Attorney General of Canada, the Director of Public Prosecutions, and the Public Prosecution Service of Canada.

Chapter 3 covers the objectives of Canadian competition law and certain foundational economic concepts. The objectives of any law are a central aspect of the modern approach to statutory interpretation. Competition law provides particularly fertile ground for a discussion of objectives, given the disparate range of goals and interests at play during the development and amendment of Canadian competition legislation since 1890. The purpose clause of the *Competition Act*, added in 1986, reveals that the promotion of competition is only a means to achieving other objectives: efficiency, competitive prices and choice for consumers, small and medium-sized business equity, and international competitiveness. A review of the evolution of these and other objectives discloses an increasing emphasis on the economic and efficiency-oriented goals of the legislation over time. Other objectives, such as the promotion of small and medium-sized business equity, remain part of the fabric of the law, but recent amendments have moved away from provisions (such as the criminal prohibition of price discrimination, which was repealed in 2009), which assigned a substantial level of importance to such objectives.

Chapter 3 also provides an overview of some of the key concepts drawn from economics which are part of the analytical tools of competition law and policy today. The discussion starts by examining the concept of economic efficiency and its three principal dimensions: allocative, productive, and dynamic efficiency. It then turns to the paradigms of perfect competition and monopoly as developed by economists, and their predictions about the kind of competitive conduct which may be harmful. Such models provide a helpful foundation or starting point for understanding competitive markets, but given that most of the economy is neither perfectly competitive nor completely monopolistic, additional analysis must be brought to bear. The discussion thus turns to various models and approaches used by economists to analyze intermediate competitive markets. Significant changes in approach followed the birth of the Chicago school of antitrust analysis in the United States, beginning in the middle of the last century. This led to the reform, and in some cases, the reversal, of how economists, lawyers, judges, and policy makers viewed the benefits and costs of certain competitive practices, such as resale price maintenance, predatory pricing, and tied selling. Flowing from this discussion we see areas of consensus, where competition analysis has concluded that certain core competition law rules should be relied upon to promote efficient markets: the control over mergers between firms involving substantial market power, the prohibition of naked price fixing and other collusive behaviour and the review of practices by dominant firms which exclude competitors. These areas form the main pillars of competition law not only in Canada, but also in most of the numerous jurisdictions worldwide that have adopted competition laws. Less consensus has developed on how to treat vertical practices put in place between players in the chain of supply, or collusive behaviour between competitors which involves tacit coordination falling short of express agreement. As the understanding of these and other practices evolves, we can expect to see further adaptation or change in the legal tests or analytical framework covering them.

Having discussed the historical background, objectives and key economic concepts, Chapter 4 turns to what is usually the first substantive step in the analysis of a competition law case requiring an assessment of competitive effect: market definition. Market definition is only a tool to determine whether a given firm or firms possess market power. Market power refers to the ability of a firm to raise prices or change non-price variables from the conditions prevailing in a competitive market. The discussion begins with an examination of the nature of market power and how it is measured. Where there are direct indicators of market power, market definition may not be needed, or can be more cursory. Nonetheless, in most cases, the Competition Bureau and Competition Tribunal will commence an assessment of competitive behaviour by examining the dimensions of the product and geographic market in which the firm or firms being studied compete. Where market definition reveals an unconcentrated market (e.g., many competitors, each with small market share), it may be a basis to conclude that no competition issues are raised, and the file may be closed, or the case dismissed on that basis. Market definition focuses on the degree to which products are competitive substitutes and the scope of the geographic area within which consumers can practicably look for supplies. Direct data on substitutability can be examined, if available, but often practical indicia are relied upon, such as: end use, pricing, industry views, switching costs, and buyer views. The resulting market definition may be only an approximation of the competitive dynamic in the market, but will provide a basis to begin to infer the existence of market power by examining market shares, barriers to entry, remaining competition, and other indicia. It is important to recall that market definition is only a step in the assessment of market power and not an end in itself.

Chapter 4 also touches on some emerging issues in the area of market definition. Several have arisen in the context of examining digital and data-driven markets. They include: how to assess markets involving a two-sided delivery platform such as social media, which serve both consumers and advertisers as clients; how to assess "zero price" markets such as internet search engines; and what measures or approaches can be used to infer market power directly, without recourse to market definition.

Merger review is the topic of Chapter 5. The assessment of mergers is a useful place to start a discussion of the analytic process used to assess competition law problems for a number of reasons. First, the Competition Bureau's *Merger Enforcement Guidelines*,[22] while a non-binding statement of the general approach used in assessing mergers and not a statement of law, provide a useful and detailed framework to assist understanding how competitive effects are examined. Second, many of the issues addressed in merger review, and covered in the *Guidelines*, including market definition, assessment of market concentration, barriers to entry, remaining competition, and vertical effects, are also encountered under the abuse of dominance, civil horizontal agreement and vertical restraint provisions of the Act.

Other issues arising in the context of merger review include the failing firm factor and the efficiencies defence. The presence of the efficiencies defence in section 96 of the legislation reflects Parliament's desire to permit firms to realize scale and other economies so that they may perform efficiently and be internationally competitive. The provision has been praised by some as putting Canada on the leading edge of modern merger analysis, and decried by others as overly complex, a source of considerable uncertainty, and a barrier to controlling mergers which may harm a dynamic and innovative economy. The Supreme Court's decision

22 Canada, Competition Bureau, *Merger Enforcement Guidelines* (6 October 2011), online: www.competitionbureau.gc.ca/eic/site/cb-bc.nsf/vwapj/cb-meg-2011-e.pdf/$FILE/cb-meg-2011-e.pdf.

in *Tervita Corp v Canada (Commissioner of Competition)*[23] has fuelled this debate, by imposing an onus to quantify anti-competitive effects on the Commissioner as part of the efficiencies defence.

The examination of merger review also canvasses procedural matters, including the various remedies available to the Commissioner before the Tribunal in challenging a merger, and the requirement that parties to very large transactions notify the Competition Bureau prior to closing, providing a package of information which can be supplemented if the Bureau deems necessary. Only a small number of mergers reviewed by the Bureau raise competition concerns, given that the ultimate test is whether the transaction is likely to create, maintain, or enhance the ability of the merged entity to exercise market power. This test means that only transactions in markets involving high concentration and significant barriers to entry are likely to raise issues under the Act.

The area of horizontal (competitor to competitor) agreements is discussed in Chapter 6. Such agreements cover a spectrum, from clearly harmful conspiracies (such as price fixing cartels) subject to criminal prohibition, to beneficial joint ventures (such as research and development agreements), which may be subject to civil review if competition issues are raised. Significant amendments in 2009 narrowed the criminal conspiracy prohibition to cover three *per se* illegal categories of agreement (price fixing, market sharing, and production limitation) and created a civil provision permitting the review before the civil Competition Tribunal of agreements which may substantially prevent or lessen competition. This scheme represents a significant improvement over the previous all-criminal regime, which turned on the application of the vague standard of "undue lessening of competition." The chapter examines the policy rationale for a criminal prohibition of certain types of naked agreements to restrict competition, the history of the conspiracy provision, and the question of how agreement is proven, which can be challenging given the absence of direct evidence in many cases.

The discussion of the criminal conspiracy provision then turns to the defences available, including the ancillary restraints defence, which is applicable where a *per se* restraint is merely ancillary to a broader agreement. Also examined are the export defence, the "regulated conduct defence," and the exemption for affiliated companies. Additional criminal provisions covering the implementation of foreign conspiracies, bid-rigging, professional sports agreements, and agreements between financial institutions are considered. Finally, penalties and other remedies associated with the criminal agreement provisions are reviewed.

23 *Tervita Corp v Canada (Commissioner of Competition)*, [2015] 1 SCR 161.

Chapter 6 concludes with a review of the civil agreements provision in section 90.1 and a number of miscellaneous exemptions. The former provision is available to review agreements (such as product swap agreements or exchanges of information between competitors), which may lessen competition but which do not fall within the criminal prohibition. The various exemptions include agreements concerning collective bargaining, cooperative action by copyright holders, and certain specific types of sectoral agreements covering ocean shipping, supply managed agriculture, and between financial institutions and airlines.

Chapter 7 examines abuse of dominance, which involves a firm or firms with market power engaging in a practice of anti-competitive acts preserving or adding to that market power. The relevant provisions have assumed greater profile in light of issues arising in the digital or online economy. Under these provisions, the mere possession or exercise of market power does not provide the basis for an order of the Tribunal; there must also be a practice of acts which are predatory, exclusionary, or disciplinary in nature and which has the requisite anti-competitive effect. This approach is intended to avoid competition law inadvertently discouraging legitimate competitive behaviour by large firms. The requirement for a practice of anti-competitive acts has proven to be a challenging aspect of abuse of dominance, as it requires the screening of legitimate business behaviour (like a policy by a supplier to encourage exclusive dealing in its products to ensure better service or a broader selection of parts) from exclusionary conduct (such as using that exclusivity to create a barrier to entry for new competitors seeking to distribute their products).

Other aspects of the abuse of dominance provisions examined include the exemption of the mere exercise of rights derived from intellectual property statutes, joint dominance (which may encompass collusive practices falling short of an express agreement), and regulated conduct. Finally, remedies available to address abuse of dominance are reviewed.

Chapters 8 and 9 address two categories of conduct which can also fall within the abuse of dominance provisions as anti-competitive acts: vertical restraints (those between parties in the chain of supply) and pricing practices: predatory pricing, price discrimination, and resale price maintenance. In the case of the former, the Act contains specific provisions covering exclusive dealing, market restriction, tied selling, and refusals to supply. The first three involve elements that are very similar to those arising in abuse of dominance, and have often been raised alongside the latter in the caselaw. Refusals to supply are subject to a complex multi-part test, which has narrowed its application in recent years. Price discrimination and predatory pricing were, until 2009, criminal offences, when they were repealed; they now fall within abuse of dominance. Resale price maintenance was also a criminal offence until 2009; since then it has been subject to its own civil provision.

The understanding of these vertical and pricing practices by economics has evolved substantially in the last half-century. Many of them are now widely seen as being pro-competitive in most circumstances. For example, resale price maintenance may be a method used by a supplier to increase the dedication of, or service levels offered by, its dealers or franchisees. The dealers' increased selling effort will tend to increase competition between competing branded products or services. Similarly, predatory pricing is viewed as unlikely to raise issues unless practised by a firm with market power and undertaken in a market subject to high barriers to entry. At the same time, predatory pricing can be a strategy to eliminate competitors or discourage them from entry in certain circumstances. As a result, a case-by-case assessment of such practices is adopted in the Canadian law.

Chapter 10 concludes by examining the unfair and deceptive marketing practices provisions. These provisions cover a range of conduct that often visibly and directly affects consumers, from deceptive contests and telemarketing to misleading electronic messages. The enforcement of the provisions has been advanced by the availability of a range of civil remedies, including monetary penalties and restitution. Recent cases have involved consent remedies against such companies as the Hudson's Bay Company, Amazon, and Live Nation.

CHAPTER 2

ENFORCEMENT AND ADJUDICATION: HISTORICAL EVOLUTION AND CURRENT STRUCTURE

A. INTRODUCTION

Canada has had competition law since 1889, a year before the first antitrust legislation was passed in the United States. However, there was soon a marked divergence between America's forceful embrace of antitrust and Canada's rather anaemic scheme. The reasons for this included Canada's weak initial legislation, Canada's smaller and trade-dependent economy, a differing business and economic culture, and the constitutional structure of the two countries. By the 1960s, it was clear that Canada's "combines" regime was badly broken, largely ineffective, and in need of overhaul. Constitutional limitations had frustrated efforts to move away from the ineffective criminal law enforcement that lay at the centre of the problems facing the Canadian law. Reform was, however, a slow and incremental process. Major rounds of amendments took place in 1976, 1986, and 2009. With those changes, Canada's legislative scheme moved to the forefront of competition law regimes in the world, armed with the enforcement tools, adjudicative structure, and substantive tests which make it possible to promote strong and dynamic competition in the economy. For example, Canada was described in one journal article as "the leading jurisdiction" in dealing with efficiencies in merger assessment.[1]

1 Roger Ware & Ralph A Winter, "Merger Efficiencies in Canada: Lessons for the Integration of Economics into Antitrust Law" (2016) 61:3 *Antitrust Bulletin* 365 at 366.

This chapter examines the historical evolution of enforcement and adjudication of Canadian competition law, and describes the current structure. The emphasis will be on the institutions governing investigation and adjudication, and the reasons for their evolution over time. The major changes to the substantive law will be touched upon, but discussed in greater detail in later chapters. **Table 2.1** below provides a chronological overview.

Table 2.1. Enforcement and Adjudication of Competition Law: 1889–Present

Period	Provisions	Investigation	Adjudication
1889–1910	**Criminal:** • conspiracy	AG of Province (crown prosecutor)	Courts
1910–1919	**Criminal:** • conspiracy • combines breaching a Board order	AG of Province (crown prosecutor)	Courts
	Civil: • combines: inquiry and report only	Ad Hoc Board	
1919–1923	**Civil:** • combines: inquiry, remedial orders	Board of Commerce	Board of Commerce
1923–1935	**Criminal:** • combines (merger, monopoly, etc.), conspiracy	Registrar or Ad Hoc Commissioners	Courts
1935–1937	**Criminal:** • conspiracy , price discrimination, predation	AG of Province (crown prosecutor)	Courts
	Civil: • exemption of agreements	Dominion Trade and Industry Commission	Dominion Trade and Industry Commission
1937–1952	**Criminal:** • conspiracy, combines, price discrimination, predation	Commissioner or Ad Hoc Commissioners	Courts
1952–1976	**Criminal:** • combines (until 1960) • merger/monopoly (from 1960) • conspiracy, price discrimination/predation, resale price maintenance, trade practices	Director of Investigation and Research	Courts

(Continued)

Table 2.1. Enforcement and Adjudication of Competition Law: 1889–Present (*Continued*)

Period	Provisions	Investigation	Adjudication
Regimes declared unconstitutional on division of powers grounds			
1976–1986	**Criminal:** • conspiracy, price discrimination/predation, price maintenance, trade practices, merger/monopoly	Director of Investigation and Research	Courts
	Civil: • refusal to supply, consignment selling, exclusive dealing, tied selling, etc.	Director of Investigation and Research	Restrictive Trade Practices Commission
	Civil (private actions): actions for damages	Plaintiff	Courts
1986–present	**Criminal:** • conspiracy, trade practices • price discrimination/predation (until 2009) • price maintenance (until 2009)	• Director of Investigation and Research (until 1999) • Commissioner of Competition (from 1999)	Courts
	Civil: • merger, abuse of dominance • refusal to supply, exclusive dealing, tied selling, trade practices, etc. • consignment selling (until 2009) • resale price maintenance (from 2009)	• Director of Investigation and Research (until 1999) • Commissioner of Competition (from 1999)	Competition Tribunal
	Civil (private actions/applications): • actions for damages • leave applications to the Tribunal (from 2002)	Plaintiff/Applicant	Courts , Competition Tribunal

Three main themes will be explored in this chapter:

1) During the first half-century of competition law in Canada, there was an evolution of enforcement toward a specialized agency with increasing resources, powers, and expertise.

2) Since the 1970s, there has been a gradual movement away from the criminal courts and criminal offences and toward a specialized civil tribunal to adjudicate a growing number of civilly reviewable practices.
3) Private enforcement avenues have become increasingly available through a statutory cause of action for damages (for breach of the criminal prohibitions) and private access to the Competition Tribunal (to obtain remedies for certain civilly reviewable practices). Since the advent of class actions reform, and recent Supreme Court jurisprudence, the civil damages action has shown the promise of becoming a more important companion to public enforcement.

B. HISTORY OF ENFORCEMENT AND ADJUDICATION

1) The First Legislation, 1889: A Paper Tiger

Canada's first competition legislation had its roots in events which occurred in the first decades after Confederation.[2] During this period, the Canadian economy experienced several ups and downs in the business cycle between growth and recession. Years of growth in heavy industry, transportation, and other sectors of the North American economy were matched by recessions in the 1870s and then 1880s. Some businesses reacted to market downturns with price cutting, then to the drop in prices with consolidation and restrictive agreements.[3] In the United States, great fortunes were gathered by the "trusts" in railways, oil, whiskey, meat, nails, lead, copper, steel rail, iron nuts and washers, barbed fence wire, slate-pencils, nickel, zinc, jute bags, castor oil, linseed oil, cottonseed oil, and other products.[4]

In Canada, the effect of similar combines and restrictive arrangements was magnified by the National Policy, the economic policy of Prime Minister Sir John A Macdonald which centred on the erection of high tariffs to help develop manufacturing industry in central Canada.

---

2 Described in generous terms by one commentator as "the world's first modern competition statute": Charles Paul Hoffman, "A Reappraisal of the Canadian Anti-Combines Act of 1889" (2013) 39 *Queen's Law Journal* 127 at 128 [Hoffman].

3 William T Easterbrook & Hugh Aitken, *Canadian Economic History* (Toronto: MacMillan, 1975) at 387–400.

4 Robin Carey, "The Sherman Act: What Did Congress Intend?" (1989) 34:2 *Antitrust Bulletin* 337 and 338–41; Carman D Baggaley, "Tariffs, Combines and Politics: The Beginning of Canadian Competition Policy, 1888-1900" [Baggaley] in RS Khemani & William T Stanbury, eds, *Historical Perspectives on Canadian Competition Policy* (Halifax: IRPP, 1991) at 9 [Khemani & Stanbury, *Historical Perspectives*].

Under the Policy, for example, duties on textiles and footwear were raised to approximately 30 percent and 25 percent, respectively. Such tariffs promoted domestic industry and provided funds to finance projects such as the transcontinental railway, but they also insulated Canadian business from foreign competition. (See **Figure 2.1.**)

THE CONSUMER CONSUMED.

FIGURE 2.1. *Grip* magazine, Toronto, 21 January 1888
Prime Minister John A Macdonald looks on as the consumer feeds monopolistic industries with high tariffs and taxation

In 1888, increased visibility in the press and in political debate concerning private combines which controlled supply or fixed prices of sugar, coal, and other products led to a "Select Committee on Combinations" being appointed by Parliament to examine the nature, extent, and effect of business combinations in Canada. The Committee's Report concluded that the "injurious tendencies" of such combinations of competing sellers in industries such as sugar and stoves, groceries, coal, coffins, biscuits, barbed wire, and binder twine "justify legislative action arising from these and similar combinations and monopolies."[5] One combine of Ottawa coal suppliers, for example, channelled the product through a single jointly-controlled company, which carried out delivery to customers at a common price and distributed substantial profits back to the "competitors."

FIGURE 2.2. A cartoon supporting the National Policy depicts the benefit of the tariff as a dam holding back "American competition" (National Archives, LAC item 2989918)

5 Canada, *Report of the Select Committee appointed 29th February, 1888, to Investigate and Report upon alleged combinations in Manufacturing, Trade and Insurance in Canada* by NC Wallace in 51-52 Vict, Sessional Papers, 6th Parl, 2d Sess (16 May 1888) at 10; see also John M Magwood, *Competition Law of Canada* (Toronto: Carswell, 1981) at 42.

FIGURE 2.3.
N Clarke Wallace, MP

N Clarke Wallace, a back-bench Member of Parliament and small businessman from the Toronto area, chaired the Select Committee. Shortly after the release of the Committee's report, he tabled a private member's bill, proposing to create an offence of combining, agreeing, or arranging to prevent or restrict competition in various ways.[6] While public statements by Wallace described the bill as providing "prompt and decisive action" to the evil of combines,[7] there are differing views on what motivations were at play. Some commentators have viewed the bill as "part of a calculated Conservative manoeuvre to deflect criticism from the combines-creating effects of the protective tariff";[8] others as "a genuine attempt to resolve the combines problem in its incipiency."[9]

Wallace's Conservative government colleagues did not wholeheartedly embrace his proposal: "the lukewarm, almost disinterested, attitude of the government afforded little aid to the measure's parliamentary progress."[10] When reviewed by a Parliamentary Committee the following year, the statutory language was watered down by requiring that the conduct in question be carried out "unlawfully," "unreasonably," or "unduly." These words found their way into the final legislation, *An Act for the Prevention and Suppression of Combinations Formed in Restraint of Trade*.[11] The *Act* created a misdemeanour with a maximum penalty of $4,000 or two years' imprisonment for "[e]very person who conspires, combines, agrees or arranges with any other person . . . *unlawfully* . . . [t]o *unduly* prevent or lessen competition" or "to *unreasonably* enhance" prices.[12] The offence was incorporated into the *Criminal Code* in 1892.[13]

6 Richard Gosse, *The Law on Competition in Canada* (Toronto: Carswell, 1962) at 70.

7 Baggaley, above note 4 at 22.

8 Michael Bliss, "Another Anti-Trust Tradition: Canadian Anti-Combines Policy, 1889–1910" (1973) 47 *Business History Review* 177 at 180. See also Lloyd G Reynolds, *The Control of Competition in Canada* (Cambridge, MA: Harvard University Press, 1940) at 134.

9 Hoffman, above note 2 at 173.

10 Maxwell Cohen, "The Canadian Anti-Trust Laws — Doctrinal and Legislative Beginnings" (1938) 16:6 *Canadian Bar Review* 439 at 455 [Cohen].

11 (1889) 52 Vict, c 41 [*Canada Anti-Combines Act* 1889]; Cohen, above note 10 at 455–58; Baggaley, above note 4 at 24–25.

12 *Canada Anti-Combines Act* 1889, s 1. In 1892, the section was placed in the *Criminal Code*, SC 1892, c 29 as s 520 [*Criminal Code* 1892]; in 1900, as s 498 of the *Criminal Code*, RSC 1927, c 36.

13 *Criminal Code* 1892, above note 12, s 520.

The word "unlawfully" incorporated the existing common law jurisprudence, leaving the law effectively unchanged.[14] This reflected the view of the then Minister of Justice, who said in the House that "the Bill . . . will not create any new offence."[15] The common law at the time provided only a weak foundation to attack restrictions on competition, as the relevant test was oriented toward protecting the fairness of the bargain between the parties, not the anti-competitive effects of restrictive agreements on the general public.[16] Justice Osler of the Ontario Court of Appeal summed the situation up well when he held that this convoluted language "made the section unintelligible and innocuous by attaching a penalty only to a conspiracy to do an unlawful act unduly."[17] A prominent Canadian business historian aptly described the 1889 Act as "utterly useless."[18] After a series of attempts, Parliament finally removed the word "unlawfully" in 1900.[19] However, the words "unduly" and "unreasonably" remained, reducing the effectiveness of the prohibition.

The New Scourge of the North-West.
NOW IN PROCESS OF HATCHING AT OTTAWA.
FIGURE 2.4. *Grip* magazine, Toronto, 1880

The unwillingness of Canadian legislators to embrace forceful competition law and enforcement is a theme repeated throughout subsequent decades, including after the Economic Council of Canada had recommended wholesale reform in 1969.[20] Thus, while Canada's competition legislation shares historical roots, at least in terms of its initial timing, with its American counterparts (the first US antitrust legislation being passed in 1890[21]), these roots were not, for a significant period, nurtured in Canada.

---

14 Cohen, above note 10 at 461–63, citing *R v American Tobacco Company of Canada* (1897) 3 *Rev de Jur* 453, the first reported prosecution under the legislation.

15 *House of Commons Debates*, 6th Parl, 3d Sess (8 April 1889) at 1438 (Sir John Thompson).

16 Cohen, above note 10 at 440–53.

17 *R v Elliott, [1905] OJ No 162 (CA) at para 55.*

18 Michael Bliss, *A Living Profit* (Toronto: McClelland & Stewart, 1974) at 39.

19 Baggaley, above note 4 at 41; *An Act to further amend the Criminal Code*, SC 1900, c 46, s 3. In fact, "unduly" and "unreasonably" were briefly removed (and then re-inserted) before "unlawfully" was removed: *ibid*, s 1.

20 Canada, Bureau of Competition Policy, *Competition Policy in Canada: The First Hundred Years* (Ottawa: Consumer and Corporate Affairs Canada, 1989) at 19–20 [*Competition Policy in Canada*].

21 *Sherman Act*, 26 US Stat 209 (1890).

Over most of its early history, Canada's combines policy and enforcement reflected an historic British tendency to tolerate the possession of economic power.[22] For almost a century in Canada after the passage of the first legislation in 1889, a combination of historical circumstances, political culture and economic conditions led to a weak response to anti-competitive practices, merger, and monopoly. This flowed from both the lack of effective legislation and its weak enforcement. British influences and institutions, starting with the monopoly granted to the Hudson's Bay Company in 1670, have shaped Canadian economic development. The relatively small size of the Canadian economy and the periodic need for nation-building projects led to reliance on economic power in the form of Crown or other monopolies in sectors such as transcontinental railway, energy, or broadcasting. Lacking a revolutionary history or civil war, and with a different frontier tradition, Canadians demonstrated a greater degree of deference to sources of authority of various kinds, whether king, country, or company.[23] Author Peter C Newman has described an "early attitude of obedience and fear of distant authority" in Canada, which was quite different from that prevailing south of the border:

> [The] tendency to defer to corporate authority . . . was one of the most significant differences between the Canadian and American frontiers. Lacking any corporate infrastructure, the American Wild West developed in exactly the opposite direction. There, rugged individualism became the way of life, enforced with the fabled six-shooter. Every man and woman was on his or her own, challenging or escaping authority, never catering to it.[24]

Canada's constitutional structure also significantly affected the development of competition law. Substantial economic powers were granted to the provinces in the *British North America Act, 1867*.[25] Early

---

22 Frederic M Scherer, *Industrial Market Structure and Economic Performance* (Boston: Houghton-Mifflin, 1980) at 512, citing AD Neale, *Antitrust Laws and the United States* (London: Cambridge University Press, 1967) at 475–76, who wrote: "In general, the possession of power by established authorities arouses a much lesser degree of anxiety or resentment in Britain, where emphasis is much more on the use of power."

23 Bruce Dunlop, Michael J Trebilcock & David McQueen, *Canadian Competition Policy: A Legal and Economic Analysis* (Toronto: Canada Law Book, 1987) at 20–22 [Dunlop, Trebilcock & McQueen].

24 Peter C Newman, *The Canadian Revolution 1985-1995: From Deference to Defiance* (Toronto: Viking, 1997) at 8.

25 Now *The Constitution Act, 1867* (UK), 30 & 31 Vict, c 3.

constitutional jurisprudence narrowly interpreted the scope of federal legislative authority over trade and commerce.[26] As a result, competition laws remained shackled to the criminal law as an enforcement vehicle, with constitutional uncertainty leading to hesitation to adopt another approach for more than half a century, from the 1930s through to the 1980s.[27]

For these reasons, Canadian competition law and enforcement had weak beginnings and a slow development. The differences between the competition law regimes in the United States and Canada, however, have narrowed with the growing integration of the North American economy, a change in direction of Canadian constitutional jurisprudence, and several rounds of amendments to the Canadian legislation, which began in the mid-1970s.

Looking back on the origins of the Canadian law, it is evident that the first legislation cannot be characterized as a part of some unified or carefully planned framework of economic policies. Rather, its development was reactive rather than proactive. Limited and ineffective legislation was passed in response to public, and political, concern over the "combines problem" and the unintended side-effects of a high tariffs policy. This reactive character continued until more recent decades, when circumstances and growing economic learning helped competition policy take a more central place among other economic and regulatory policies.

2) Evolution of the Enforcement Role

Over the decades, competition legislation has gone through a series of changes which created the bureaucratic and legal infrastructure for investigation, collection of evidence and statistics, searching premises, and compelling oral evidence, and bringing matters to adjudication. The present legislation contains few remnants of the enforcement machinery put in place in the early 1900s. An example is the ability of six citizens to initiate an inquiry, found in section 9 of today's *Competition Act*,

---

26 See, e.g., *Canada (Attorney General) v Alberta (Attorney General)* (1921), 60 DLR 513 (UKPC) [*Reference re Board of Commerce Act, 1919*].

27 Canada, Committee to Study Combines Legislation, *Report of the Committee to Study Combines Legislation and Interim Report on Resale Price Maintenance* (Ottawa: Queen's Printer, 1952) at 7: "There has been a widely held view that the jurisdiction of the Federal Government did not extend beyond the criminal field. This partly explains why other types of action, which have been adopted in other countries, have not been used in Canada."

which dates from the 1910 *Combines Investigation Act*.[28] In general terms, there has been a slow and steady evolution toward a more independent, sophisticated, and better-resourced enforcement authority for competition law in Canada.

In addition to weaknesses in the substantive law, the first legislation contained no formal investigative processes or permanent enforcement agency. The enforcement function was left to the provincial Attorneys General, reacting to public complaints; a mechanism described in an early text as "lethargic."[29] Only ten prosecutions were brought in the period 1889–1910 (nine after the word "unlawfully" was removed in 1900), and seven convictions were obtained.[30]

Complaints by individuals, who generally lack the information, knowledge, or incentive to bring forward cases, are an ineffective avenue for initiating investigations and prosecutions of matters such as price fixing. In spite of the severe harm that may be caused to the economy at large, the effects of such conduct are often broadly spread across a market, and an individual consumer is unlikely to experience sufficient economic loss or outrage to believe that it justifies the time and personal exposure to file and to pursue a complaint. Furthermore, the disclosure, investigation, and proof of such practices often requires the marshalling of data and economic evidence which requires specialized knowledge, and "falls more in the realm of the economist than the police detective."[31] Conspiratorial behaviour is also usually clandestine, and uncovering evidence often requires special powers for the search, seizure, or compulsion of the production of business and financial records. The possession of such powers is insufficient unless their holder also possesses the knowledge of where to look, and what to look for.

Over the period 1889–1952, there were four identifiable periods in the evolution of the enforcement function governing competition law in Canada (the following omits the regimes found unconstitutional in 1921 and 1937[32]):

---

28 *Competition Act*, RSC 1985, c C-34 [*Competition Act*]; *Combines Investigation Act*, SC 1910, c 9, s 5 [*Combines Investigation Act* 1910].

29 John A Ball, *Canadian Anti-Trust Legislation* (Baltimore: William & Wilkins, 1934) at 23; see also Paul K Gorecki & William T Stanbury, "The Administration and Enforcement of Competition Policy in Canada, 1889 to 1952," ch 2 of Khemani & Stanbury, *Historical Perspectives*, above note 4 at 61 [Gorecki & Stanbury, "The Administration and Enforcement of Competition Policy in Canada"].

30 *Competition Policy in Canada*, above note 20 at 7, Table 4.

31 Dunlop, Trebilcock & McQueen, above note 23 at 45.

32 *Ibid* at 46–48. See also Table 2.1 above.

Table 2.2. Evolution of the Enforcement Function 1889–1952

1. 1889–1910[33] In this period, there was no formal enforcement agency. The prosecution of cases was left to complaints by the public to prosecutors. Competition law offences were treated as any other criminal prohibition. Few cases were brought forward.
2. 1910–1923[34] A process for the referral of complaints from six citizens to an *ad hoc* Board for the preparation of a report[35] was put in place. Formal powers of inquiry to assist the production of evidence were made available. Only one case was brought using this structure.[36]
3. 1923–1952[37] A permanent enforcement official, the "Registrar" (renamed the "Commissioner" in 1937) was given the task of carrying out investigations and making reports, along with investigative powers.[38] The Registrar could initiate investigations, or rely upon six citizens or the Minister. Enforcement activities increased.
4. 1952 onward[39] The permanent enforcement official was renamed the "Director of Investigation and Research" in 1952 and the preparation of reports was assigned to the Restrictive Trade Practices Commission. The Director's enforcement role was limited to carrying out investigations as opposed to preparing reports assessing conduct.

While there was only one investigation from 1910 to 1919,[40] and no prosecutions during that period,[41] from 1923 to 1952 there were forty-one reports prepared from investigations carried out under the legislation; all but thirteen were made public. The vast majority of the reports

33 *Proprietary Articles Trade Association v Canada (Attorney General)*, [1931] 2 DLR 1 (UKPC) at paras 9–10 [*Proprietary Articles Trade Association*] sets out the history of this enforcement regime.

34 *Combines Investigation Act* 1910, above note 28.

35 *Competition Policy in Canada*, above note 20 at 7–8. "Reports" were summaries of the anti-competitive behaviour which were to be made public on the belief that "publicity is more effective than penalty": William Lyon Mackenzie King, then Minister of Labour, 1912; *ibid* at 8.

36 The case involved the United Shoe Machinery Company. See Ball, above note 29, ch 5, "Combines Investigation Act of 1910."

37 *Combines Investigation Act*, SC 1923, c 9.

38 *Ibid*; in particular, see the new investigative powers in ss 8–18.

39 *Combines Investigation Act*, RSC 1952, c 314.

40 Until the advent of the Board of Commerce, which was found unconstitutional in 1923.

41 Gorecki & Stanbury, "The Administration and Enforcement of Competition Policy in Canada," above note 29 at 69–70.

related to price fixing; a handful to merger, monopoly, and other practices.[42] Eighteen prosecutions were brought, with fourteen convictions, all for price fixing.[43]

From 1952 until the mid-1970s, the Restrictive Trade Practices Commission (RTPC) was referred numerous matters for the purposes of conducting an inquiry. In this period, it prepared seventy-seven reports from its inquiries, all of which were public.[44] The inquiry reports related to alleged anti-competitive conduct and created a rich legacy of information about industry structure and practices.[45] The reports provide some of the only "jurisprudence" in the areas of merger and monopoly in that time period. Some matters were referred to the Commission as so-called research inquiries, leading to recommendations to reform or to amend the legislation. An example was the Commission's 1962 report from an inquiry into petroleum industry distribution practices.[46] The report from that inquiry recommended the adoption of provisions relating to exclusive dealing and tied selling, which were added to the legislation in 1976.[47]

By the late 1970s, however, the RTPC was no longer being referred case-specific investigations for inquiry and report,[48] and in 1986 these functions were eliminated, the Commission was disbanded, and the Competition Tribunal was created (see below). The investigation function was thereafter solely the responsibility of the Director of Investigation and Research and the public report function ceased to exist.

The level of enforcement activity is a reflection, to a degree, of the budget of competition law enforcement officials. That budget also demonstrates the resources Parliament had been willing to devote to this task. The average yearly expenditures did not exceed $100,000 (in current dollars) until the period 1946–1950. From 1966 to 1970, they exceeded $1 million; during 1986 to 1988 this had grown to more than

---

42 *Ibid*, Table 5 at 135.

43 *Ibid*, Table 11 at 142–43.

44 JJ Quinlan, "The Restrictive Trade Practices Commission: Its Functions and Duties" (1975) 44 *Antitrust Law Journal* 492 at 502.

45 See, e.g., the cases reviewed in G Rosenbluth, "Monopoly and Monopolization," ch 13 of Robert S Pritchard, William T Stanbury & Thomas Wilson, eds, *Canadian Competition Policy: Essays in Law and Economics* (Toronto: Butterworths, 1979) at 331–35 [Pritchard, Stanbury & Wilson].

46 Canada, Restrictive Trade Practices Commission, *Report on the Distribution and Sale of Automotive Oils, Greases, Anti-Freeze, Additives, Tires, Batteries and Accessories and Related Products* (Ottawa: Queen's Printer, 1962).

47 See Chapter 9.

48 Paul K Gorecki & William T Stanbury, "Canada's *Combines Investigation Act*, The Record of Public Law Enforcement, 1889-1976," in ch 13 of Pritchard, Stanbury & Wilson, above note 45 at 153.

$15 million.[49] The Director of Investigation and Research was renamed the Commissioner of Competition in 1999.[50] As noted in Chapter 1, the Commissioner heads the Competition Bureau, which had more than 350 employees and a budget of $52.5 million in 2018–19.[51] The Bureau's budget was increased in 2021 by an additional $96 million over the following five years and $27.5 million more per year after that.[52] As a result, the Bureau's budget rose to $65.3 million in 2022-23.[53]

The rationale for special investigatory powers in the enforcement of competition legislation was well summarized in the *Guide* which accompanied the 1986 amendments:

> In addition to the difficulties of detection, competition matters are characterized by unique enforcement problems. Because inquiries under the Act often involve assessing a firm's behaviour against the probable economic effects of the conduct, the analysis is unusually complex and often prospective. Sufficient information, including documentary information, must be available for the enforcement agency to make informed decisions. . . . [E]nforcement of legislation involving these critical factors requires effective investigatory powers. These include the powers to search premises and seize documents, require written return of information and affidavit evidence and subpoena witnesses to give oral testimony or produce documents.[54]

The 1986 amendments included changes to ensure compliance with the *Charter of Rights and Freedoms*[55] in respect of the search and seizure powers in the legislation. The Supreme Court had held in *Hunter v Southam Inc* that the RTPC, given its investigative role, could not act judicially to provide prior authorization of search warrants.[56] In 1990, in *Thomson Newspapers Ltd v Canada (Director of Investigation and Research, Restrictive Trade Practices Commission)*, the Supreme Court upheld the amended

49 *Competition Policy in Canada*, above note 20, Table 1 at 58.

50 *An Act to amend the Competition Act and to make consequential and related amendments to other Acts*, SC 1999, c 2, s 4 [*An Act to amend the Competition Act* 1999].

51 Canada, Competition Bureau, *2018-19 Annual Plan: Building Trust to Advance Competition in the Marketplace* (3 May 2018), online: www.competitionbureau.gc.ca/eic/site/cb-bc.nsf/eng/04356.html.

52 Canada, Competition Bureau, *2021-22 Annual Report at 3, online:* https://publications.gc.ca/collections/collection_2023/isde-ised/Iu50-2022-eng.pdf.

53 Canada, Competition Bureau, *2022-23 Annual Report at 20, online: https://publications.gc.ca/collections/collection_2023/isde-ised/Iu50-2023-eng.pdf.*

54 Canada, Department of Consumer and Corporate Affairs, *Competition Law Amendments, A Guide* (Ottawa: Minister of Supply and Services, 1985) at 13.

55 The *Constitution Act, 1982*, being Schedule B to the *Canada Act 1982* (UK), 1982, c 11 [*Charter*].

56 *Hunter v Southam Inc*, [1984] 2 SCR 145 [*Hunter v Southam*].

procedures for compelling evidence and documents in the legislative scheme. Justice La Forest explained the need for special powers possessed by competition authorities to compel oral and documentary evidence:

> [B]ecause of the nature of the conduct regulated by the *Act*, there will in many cases be no way of determining whether proscribed conduct has been engaged in, short of studying the process by which a suspected corporation or business has made and implemented its decisions. . . . Investigatory mechanisms which force corporations and other businesses to divulge what they and only they can know about their internal affairs are part of the state's interest in the enforcement of combines legislation. The power to subpoena books, records and documents is obviously one such investigatory mechanism.[57]

In addition to *Charter* compliance, investigative powers and programs have had to adapt to changing times and conditions, for example:

- In 1999, wiretapping was permitted for investigations into the conspiracy, bid-rigging, and deceptive telemarketing offences.[58]
- Provisions to protect whistleblowers (any person who has reasonable grounds to believe that another person has committed or intends to commit an offence) were also added in 1999.[59]
- In 2002, amendments were made to facilitate cooperation with foreign competition authorities for the enforcement of competition and fair trade practices laws.[60]
- In 2009, in merger cases, the Commissioner was given the power to make supplementary requests for information. Such requests automatically delay the closing of a transaction until thirty days after receipt by the Commissioner of the information requested, facilitating the completion of the Commissioner's investigation.[61]
- In 2022, authority to seek written returns of information (in addition to production of records) from affiliates, whether or not located in Canada, was added to the Commissioner's arsenal of evidence gathering powers.[62]

---

57 *Thomson Newspapers Ltd v Canada (Director of Investigation and Research, Restrictive Trade Practices Commission), [1990] 1 SCR 425 at para 153.*

58 *An Act to amend the Competition Act* 1999, above note 50, s 47.

59 *Ibid*, s 19.

60 *An Act to amend the Competition Act and the Competition Tribunal Act*, SC 2002, c 16, s 3 [*An Act to amend the Competition Act* 2002].

61 *Budget Implementation Act, 2009*, SC 2009, c 2, s 439 [*Budget Implementation Act, 2009*].

62 *An Act to implement certain provisions of the budget tables in Parliament April 7, 2022 and other measures*, SC 2022, c 10, s 256 [*Bill C-19 2022*].

- In 2023, the Commissioner was empowered to carry out a "market or industry inquiry" into "the state of competition in a market or industry" and to issue a public report.[63]
- In 2024, remedies against reprisal actions taken against those who communicate or cooperate with the Bureau were provided for.[64]

From the foregoing, we see that Canadian competition law enforcement has evolved over the decades since 1889 toward a permanent enforcement agency, with specialized powers and increasing resources to analyze and to marshal the evidence produced. The early years demonstrated that this area of the law requires the expertise of a full-time enforcement agency which has specialized investigative knowledge and the authority to compel production of evidence. An increasing enforcement sophistication has occurred over time. The Commissioner now possesses powers to compel the production, interception, and seizure of evidence and other investigative tools. Specialized powers have been developed to cope with the unique problems posed by economic evidence, transnational anti-competitive behaviour, clandestine conspiratorial conduct, and electronic business records.

3) Moving from Criminal Toward Civil Law Adjudication

a) The Constitutional Division of Powers: Reliance on the Criminal Law Power

As noted earlier, during the first century of Canadian combines laws, attempts to move beyond the criminal law for enforcement were limited by constitutional uncertainty. Legislation giving a civil tribunal the authority to make final orders was struck down by the Judicial Committee of the Privy Council in the *Board of Commerce* case in 1921[65] and by the Supreme Court in the *Reference re Dominion Trade and Industry Commission* in 1936.[66] The Privy Council in the *Board of Commerce* case took a narrow view of federal trade and commerce authority, holding that the power to regulate "trade and commerce [does] not, by itself, enable

63 *An Act to amend the Excise Act and the Competition Act*, SC 2023, c 31, s 3 [*Bill C-56 2023*].

64 *Fall Economic Statement Implementation Act, 2023*, SC 2024, c 15, s 260 [*Bill C-59 2024*].

65 *Reference re Board of Commerce Act, 1919*, *above note 26*.

66 *Reference re legislative jurisdiction of Parliament of Canada to enact the Dominion Trade and Industry Commission Act, 1935, [1936] SCR 379 [Dominion Trade and Industry Commission* SCC], aff'd [1937] AC 405 (UKPC) [*Dominion Trade and Industry Commission* UKPC].

interference with particular trades."[67] This contrasted with the situation in the United States, where the interstate commerce jurisdiction had long been recognized as a foundation for federal antitrust law.[68]

On the other hand, the Canadian courts consistently confirmed the constitutionality of Parliament's criminal law authority as a basis for competition law. The criminal enforcement regime put in place under the *Combines Investigation Act* of 1923 was confirmed in *Proprietary Articles Trade Association v Canada (Attorney General)*.[69] The Privy Council had no difficulty with the proposition that commercial activities found by Parliament to be against the public interest could be made crimes. In the *Dominion Trade and Industry* decision, the Supreme Court and Privy Council upheld the investigative powers given the Commission as within the federal criminal law power.[70] The price discrimination and predatory pricing provisions added in 1935 were sustained under the criminal law power in *British Columbia (Attorney General) v Canada (Attorney General)*.[71] In 1956, the Supreme Court (which had by then become Canada's highest appellate court) similarly sustained a section in the *Combines Investigation Act* providing for the making of prohibition orders as criminal law.[72] Prohibitions of resale price maintenance,[73] conspiracy,[74] and pyramid selling[75] were also held to be within federal competence based on the criminal law power.

b) Enforcement Problems in the Criminal Courts

In 1957, the Supreme Court of Canada heard an appeal in *R v Howard Smith Paper Mills*, a prosecution for price fixing in the production and distribution of fine papers, which raised the question of when a conspiracy to fix prices would be considered "undue" under the criminal conspiracy prohibition. Justice Cartwright, concurring, held:

> [A]n agreement to prevent or lessen competition in commercial activities of the sort described in the section becomes criminal when the prevention or lessening agreed upon reaches the point at which the

67 *Reference re Board of Commerce Act*, above note 26 at 517.

68 US Constitution, art I, § 8, cl 3.

69 *Proprietary Articles Trade Association*, above note 33.

70 *Dominion Trade and Industry Commission* SCC, above note 66, aff'd *Dominion Trade and Industry Commission* UKPC, above note 66.

71 *British Columbia (Attorney General) v Canada (Attorney General)*, [1937] 1 DLR 688 (UKPC).

72 *Goodyear Tire & Rubber Co v R* (1956), 2 DLR (2d) 11 (SCC).

73 *R v Campbell* (1966), 58 DLR (2d) 673n (SCC), aff'g (1964), 46 DLR (2d) 83 (Ont CA).

74 *Canada (Attorney General) v CN Transportation Ltd*, [1983] 2 SCR 206 [*CN Transportation*].

75 *Canada v Shaklee Canada Inc*, [1985] 1 FC 593 (CA).

> participants in the agreement become free to carry on these activities *virtually unaffected by the influence of competition* . . . that is, it is the arrogation to the members of the combination of the power to carry on their activities *without competition* which is rendered unlawful.[76]

The italicized text implied that a virtual monopoly among the conspirators was required before the agreement would violate the Act. This was a much higher standard than had previously been applied. While Cartwright J did not speak for a majority of the Court, his judgment created confusion,[77] and a troubling trend in the law.

Other setbacks came in two criminal prosecutions of mergers decided in 1960, *R v Canadian Breweries Ltd*[78] and *R v British Columbia Sugar Refining Co.*[79] (These cases are discussed in more detail in Chapter 5.) At that time, under the *Combines Investigation Act*, mergers fell within the criminal prohibition of "the formation or operation of a combine"[80] where the merger "operated or is likely to operate to the detriment or against the interest of the public, whether consumers, producers or others."[81] In both cases, the mergers had resulted in substantial control of the markets in question, but the trial courts were not satisfied that the necessary "detriment to the public" had been shown beyond a reasonable doubt. These cases suggested that the criminal law was ill-adapted to sanctioning certain types of anti-competitive conduct. Several reasons can be identified:

- The courts were reluctant to brand as criminal business conduct, such as mergers and acquisitions, subject to a case-by-case assessment based upon a "detriment to the public" standard. Given the need to balance myriad economic considerations under this standard—a "polycentric" inquiry—such conduct often lacks the character to justify the moral condemnation and the proof to result in a criminal conviction.[82] The criminal law *mens rea* requirement shifts the inquiry toward moral blameworthiness, rather than an assessment of whether

76 *R v Howard Smith Paper Mills*, [1957] SCR 403 at 426 [emphasis added].

77 Dunlop, Trebilcock & McQueen, above note 23 at 125. See, e.g., *R v Aetna Insurance Co, [1978] 1 SCR 731 at 740–41.*

78 *R v Canadian Breweries Ltd, [1960] OR 601 (HCJ) [Canadian Breweries].*

79 *R v British Columbia Sugar Refining Co* (1960), 129 CCC 7 (Man QB) [*BC Sugar*].

80 *Combines Investigation Act*, RSC 1952, c 314, s 32.

81 *Ibid*, s 2(a)(vi).

82 Michael J Trebilcock, "The Supreme Court and Strengthening the Conditions for Effective Competition in the Canadian Economy" (2001) 80 *Canadian Bar Review* 542 at 588; Bruce C McDonald, "Criminality and the Canadian Anti-combines Laws" (1965) 4 *Alberta Law Review* 67 at 74–75 [McDonald].

the public interest has been prejudiced by the *effects* of the conduct, which is the principal concern of competition law.

- The criminal law presents a number of procedural difficulties for the presentation of economic evidence and concepts. Strict rules of evidence make the tendering of a wide range of data more difficult. The "beyond a reasonable doubt" burden of proof is difficult to meet where the assessment of such matters as the *likely* future impact of a practice on markets and competition is at issue.[83] Criminal remedies are also usually directed toward punishment rather than market restructuring and remedial action.
- Economic expertise is uncommon on the bench, particularly for courts hearing criminal matters. Economic evidence and assessment is unfamiliar territory for many judges.[84] In *R v McGavin Bakeries*, for example, a price fixing prosecution, the trial judge, cited *R v Container Materials* as follows:

> Hope J. at p. 296 points out that: "Our lady of the common law is not a professed economist," and in my opinion the same is true of our statute law . . . in the apt language of Hope J. . . . of which I approve and with respect adopt, in view of the fact that economics are not by any means an exact science I do not feel I am justified in the circumstances of this case in developing any new jurisprudence based on alleged new or fashionable economic theories.[85]

Reviewing the combines decisions in 1965, a leading member of the bar questioned the institutional competence of the criminal courts to decide competition cases:

> The demands of 1889 are not the demands of the 1960's, and the combines cases illustrate contortions through which the courts have been going in their attempts to accommodate the change absent any fundamental overhaul of the statute. The object of the statute has changed, and increasingly the control of combines is recognized as a sophisticated problem requiring analysis of economic data. The Canadian courts, aware of their deficiencies in the training need for such evaluations, resist as much as possible any debate over or inquiry into economic data or theory.[86]

83 McDonald, *ibid* at 87.

84 Irving Brecher, *Canada's Competition Policy Revisited: Some New Thoughts on an Old Story* (Montreal: IRPP, 1982) at 13 [Brecher], commenting on the merger decisions: "an unsophisticated judiciary, overwhelmed by strict criminal law tests, had come very close to rendering the merger offence meaningless."

85 *R v McGavin Bakeries Limited, [1952] 13 CR 63 (Alta QB) at para 50, citing R v Container Materials*, [1940] 4 DLR 293 at 296 (Ont SCJ).

86 McDonald, above note 82 at 92.

The criminal monopoly provision was also subject to the same requirement of operating "to the detriment or against the interests of the public" and therefore to the high thresholds applied by the courts in *Canadian Breweries* and *BC Sugar*. There was only one conviction for the offence of monopoly throughout the criminal law's lifespan[87] and as a result of the test applied by the courts, it "was widely perceived as ineffective in dealing with anti-competitive conduct by dominant firms."[88]

By the 1960s, Canadian combines law was an awkward jumble of sometimes conflicting prohibitions, all uneasily enforced under the banner of the criminal law. For example, even though the Supreme Court, in reference to the legislation's central conspiracy prohibition, had held that "[t]he enactment before us ... was passed for the protection of the specific public interest in free competition,"[89] provisions such as predatory pricing and price discrimination (enacted in 1935) were directed as much at protecting competitors as promoting competition.[90] The tide was turning however; competition policy was finally being viewed as having a central place among other economic and regulatory policies.

In 1966, the Liberal government decided to refer "the whole question of combines, mergers, monopolies and restraint to trade" to the Economic Council of Canada along with other issues such as intellectual property. It stated that it did not want to make "piecemeal" changes to the *Combines Investigation Act*. Changes would only be undertaken "in the context of the whole review and any revisions that may take place in light of the findings of the Economic Council."[91] The government thus saw competition policy as an element of broader economic policy. This, itself, represented a more modern view, and an evolution of thinking in comparison to the reactive nature of the early law.

87 *R v Eddy Match Company Limited* (1953), 109 CCC 1 (Que CA).

88 D Jeffrey Brown, ed, *Competition Act and Commentary* (Markham: LexisNexis, 2016) at 123 [Brown, ed].

89 *R v Container Materials*, [1942] SCR 147 at 152.

90 Lawrence A Skeoch & Bruce C McDonald, *Dynamic Change and Accountability in a Canadian Market Economy* (Ottawa, Consumer and Corporate Affairs, 1976) at 223 [*Skeoch-McDonald Report*], observing that predatory pricing "can be construed as protecting competitors, regardless of the overall effect on competition or efficiency. To this extent, the provision is in conflict with the economic analysis of predation." See also Chapter 9.

91 Economic Council of Canada, *Interim Report on Competition Policy* (Ottawa: Queen's Printer, 1969) at 200 [*Interim Report* 1969].

FIGURE 2.5. The *Interim Report on Competition Policy*

c) The *Interim Report on Competition Policy*

The *Interim Report on Competition Policy* of the Economic Council of Canada was released in July 1969 (**Figure 2.5**).[92] (In spite of its title, there was no further, or *final*, report.[93]) The Chairman of the Council described the *Report* as "a consensus among twenty-eight people reflecting a very broad cross-section of views and interests in different parts of the country and different sectors of the economy."[94]

The *Report* began by noting how much the country had changed, in terms of industrialization and urbanization, in the preceding years. It noted that the government had requested a fundamental re-examination of the role of competition policy in the economy in light of these changes.[95] The Council's assessment was that competition legislation had historically had little more than a "modest" or "uneven" impact on the economy. In the area of corporate mergers, for example, the Report concluded bluntly that "the Act has been all but inoperative."[96] It stated that "it has proved impossible, within the confines of the criminal court procedure, to provide the sort of examination of complex economic phenomena that would adequately satisfy the protection of the public interest."[97]

---

92 For further background, see John S Tyhurst, "50 Years On: The Influence of the Economic Council of Canada's Interim Report on Competition Policy" (2019) 32 *Canadian Competition Law Review* 122.

93 The Council released two other "interim" reports (also final); its first, released in 1967, resulted in legislation to create the Department of Consumer and Corporate Affairs, transferring supervision of the Director of Investigation and Research, the predecessor to the Commissioner of Competition, to that Department from the Registrar General. See William T Stanbury, *Business Interests and Reform of Canadian Competition Policy, 1971-1975* (Toronto: Carswell/Methuen, 1977) at 61 [Stanbury].

94 *Ibid* at 63. Under its 1963 enabling legislation, *An Act to establish the Economic Council of Canada Act*, 12 Eliz II, c 11, s 3, as repealed 1993, c 1, s 23, the Council was composed of "a chairman, two directors and not more than twenty-five other members, to be appointed by the Governor in Council": The members were drawn from a broad cross-section of society—from business and agriculture to academe. See D McQueen, "Revising Competition Law: Overview by a Participant," ch 1 in Prichard, Stanbury & Wilson, above note 45 at 6.

95 *Interim Report* 1969, above note 91 at 1–4.

96 *Ibid* at 64.

97 *Ibid* at 70.

The *Report* contained two powerful, and as it turned out, persuasive, ideas.

First, the *Report's* second chapter, "Philosophy and Problems" proposed that "the main objective of competition policy should be that of obtaining the most efficient possible performance from the economy."[98] The Report explained that historically, "popular thinking about competition policy" had emphasized the "income distribution" objective—the transfer of income which occurs, for example, when a monopoly seller raises prices to the consumer.[99] It explained, however, that other policies, such as taxation and direct subsidies would be more effective in achieving distributive goals; that elevating efficiency as the main objective was likely to lead to a more consistent application of competition policy.[100] The Report's emphasis was on pursuing "the most efficient performance from the economy" in terms of optimal resource use (i.e., allocative efficiency)[101] as well as "the recognition of the importance of research, invention and innovation" (i.e., dynamic efficiency).[102]

Second, the Council recommended moving away from criminal law enforcement of competition law. The Council argued that conduct which could be prohibited outright, such as bid rigging, price fixing, market allocation, resale price maintenance, and misleading advertising, should continue to be dealt with under the criminal law.[103] However, other practices, such as mergers and monopoly, require an assessment of their economic effects based on the facts of a particular case, and should be adjudicated by a new, independent, expert, "Competitive Practices Tribunal."[104] The rationale was explained as follows:

> The basic reason for seeking to place some of the federal government's competition policy on a civil law basis would be to improve its relevance to economic goals, its effectiveness, and its acceptability to the general public. The greater flexibility afforded by the civil law is especially to be desired in those areas of the policy that do not lend themselves to relatively unqualified prohibitions and that may in addition call for some case-by-case consideration of the likely economic effects of particular business structures or practices.[105]

98 *Ibid* at 19.
99 *Ibid* at 6–7.
100 *Ibid* at 20.
101 *Ibid* at 19.
102 *Ibid* at 19 and 12–15.
103 *Ibid* at 101–2.
104 *Ibid* at 188, referring to the "crucial requirement of independence."
105 *Ibid* at 109.

An expert civil tribunal, the Council believed, would be able to distil the complex data and other evidence required to assess competition law issues, while retaining "some of the characteristics of a court," such as affording the parties before it the right to be heard and other aspects of procedural fairness.[106] It would also provide a range of remedies suited to practices such as mergers.[107] At the same time, the tribunal would have flexible procedures and expertise, permitting it to analyze and to decide technical economic questions: "[t]he prevailing atmosphere would ideally be one of a collective search for understanding of business practice and its economic effects."[108]

The *Report* noted that reliance on civil law remedies and adjudication for federal competition law required their constitutionality on division of powers grounds, although it accepted that there was "no certainty" in this respect until the issue was pronounced upon by the courts.[109] The *Report* did provide factual support for federal authority, however, in Appendix IV, entitled "The Interdependency of the Canadian Economy," which concluded that "an effective competition policy in Canada must be organized, at least in part, on a national basis."[110] One commentator noted several "firsts" found in the Council's *Report*:

> [T]he earliest displacement of the term "anti-combines policy" by a positive-sounding "competition policy"; the first government attempt at in-depth analysis of its economic roots; the first real effort to explore the implications of competition policy for efficiency in government regulation and ownership.[111]

d) The Process of Reform: Taking up the Council's Mantle

Over a period of almost two decades after the Economic Council's *Report*, there were numerous initiatives to amend the law. Success was finally achieved in two main stages, in 1976 and 1986. These amendments shifted Canadian competition law toward a more consistent focus on the economic and efficiency-related effects of anti-competitive practices, and toward the use of civil remedies adjudicated before an expert tribunal, as the Council had recommended. More recently, amendments in 2002 adding a requirement for an "adverse effect on competition" to the refusal to supply provision and a right of private access to the Tribunal for certain provisions, and those of 2009, addressing conspiracy

106 *Ibid* at 110.
107 *Ibid* at 114–15.
108 *Ibid* at 110.
109 *Ibid* at 107.
110 *Ibid* at 232.
111 Brecher, above note 84 at 13.

and other anti-competitive agreements and pricing practices, carried on the process of decriminalization and increased the consistency of the economic focus for the law.

The initial effort to achieve reform in one package was Bill C-256, tabled in June 1971. It was described by one commentator as "the most significant pro-competition, pro-consumer legislation in Canadian history."[112] The Council's Chairman noted that the proposals followed "closely the Economic Council's general approach."[113] Indeed, the responsible Minister had instructed officials that he wanted the draft legislation to reflect the Council's recommendations.[114] The proposed Competitive Practices Tribunal contained in the bill would have had an inquisitorial role and broad powers to restructure Canadian industry.

The bill encountered a strong adverse reaction from the business community:[115] "[i]n the eyes of some, the proposals . . . went far beyond the Council's recommendations in the extent of its advocacy for consumer interests."[116] To move matters forward, the reform proposals were split into Stage I and Stage II, with the more controversial matters, such as merger and monopoly law reform, and the recommended new tribunal, deferred to Stage II.[117]

i) 1976 Amendments: Civil Reviewable Practices and the RTPC

The Stage I proposals were first introduced in November 1973. They were finally passed into law in late 1975 and came into effect in January 1976.[118] One significant amendment was giving the existing Restrictive Trade Practices Commission (RTPC) the authority to make final decisions, and issue binding orders, in respect of a number of new "civilly reviewable matters." These were mainly "vertical" practices (i.e., seller to buyer, as opposed to "horizontal," competitor to competitor, conduct), such as refusal to supply and exclusive dealing. The RTPC had hitherto been tasked with investigations and "research inquiries," rather than conducting trial-like proceedings. Its expanded mandate implemented the Council's recommendation that a specialized tribunal be used for cases which involved a case-by-case assessment of economic effects.

112 Stanbury, above note 93 at 95.

113 *Ibid* at 98.

114 *Ibid* at 70.

115 For a detailed discussion, see Stanbury, above note 93, ch 8.

116 I Clark, "Legislative Reform and the Policy Process: The Case of the Competition Act," ch 6 [Clark] in Khemani & Stanbury, *Historical Perspectives*, above note 4 at 228.

117 Stanbury, above 88 at 133.

118 *An Act to amend the Combines Investigation Act and the Bank Act*, SC 1974-75-76, c 76.

Another important innovation in the 1976 amendments was the addition of a civil right of action for violations of the criminal provisions of the Act, and breaches of orders of the RTPC. This provision will be discussed in detail below.

It can be seen from the foregoing that Parliament took a partial step in 1976 toward moving the law away from its previously exclusive criminal law foundation, as the Economic Council had recommended. This step was taken in spite of the uncertain constitutional basis for such action in the jurisprudence as it then stood.

ii) 1976–86: Continued Resistance to Change

In 1976, the government commissioned and received a report from an advisory committee led by Dr Lawrence Skeoch (an economist) and Bruce McDonald (a lawyer).[119] The *Skeoch-McDonald Report* (*Dynamic Change and Accountability in a Canadian Market Economy*, **Figure 2.6**) continued to recommend the creation of a new expert civil tribunal and a shift away from criminal law for merger and monopoly review, as the Economic Council had done. There was also a subtle shift in the approach. It placed an emphasis on ensuring that too-vigorous enforcement using structural tests would not stymie critical dynamic forces, such as innovation. The authors viewed such forces as a key driver of competitive markets. On adjudicative matters, it recommended that the new tribunal be subject to the "supervisory jurisdiction of the Federal Court of Canada"[120] and that Cabinet should have the ability to rescind or vary any order of the new civil tribunal because "[t]he Canadian economy is not as uniformly vigorous as some other economies and there is a greater need at times to compromise between public policy objectives."[121] The suggested need to reign in the authority of the proposed tribunal on substance and procedure gave ammunition to critics of subsequent proposals for a civil tribunal.[122] Thus, the Report had a mixed effect in terms of advancing the urgently needed legislative changes.

FIGURE 2.6.
The *Skeoch-McDonald Report*

---

119 *Skeoch-McDonald Report*, above note 90.

120 *Ibid* at 309.

121 *Ibid* at 314–15.

122 Brecher, above note 84 at 31.

Bill C-42, introduced in March 1977, represented a blend of the recommendations of the Economic Council's *Report*, the *Skeoch-MacDonald Report*, and other proposals. It continued to propose that merger and monopoly law be shifted to a new civil tribunal. It also introduced controversial proposals for class actions to recover damages from anti-competitive practices.[123] Witnesses before the House of Commons Committee were generally critical.[124] The bill died after second reading. Its successor, Bill C-13, was introduced in November 1977. It contained substantial revisions to the language and tests in the earlier bill. Completely new was a Cabinet power to override decisions of a new civil tribunal on merger, monopoly, and other matters (as recommended in the *Skeoch-MacDonald Report*). In spite of such changes designed to deal with many of the criticisms that had emerged, Bill C-13 was never given second reading or referred to Committee.

In May 1981, the government released a discussion paper proposing, yet again, new civil-law based provisions dealing with merger and monopoly, but this time to be adjudicated by the civil courts. No draft legislation flowed from these proposals, but they initiated a slow process of further consultation between government officials and interested groups.[125] Eventually this led to Bill C-29, introduced in 1984. However, the bill was not enacted before the general election in the fall of that year.

iii) The 1986 Competition Act

The new (Conservative) government took up the legislative torch where the previous (Liberal) government had left off. Proposals for reform of competition law were introduced as Bill C-91 in December 1985. The bill was passed into law as the *Competition Act* in June 1986.[126]

Table 2.3 summarizes the principal changes in the existing structure of enforcement and adjudication made in the 1986 amendments.

---

123 *Ibid* at 31–36.

124 *Ibid* at 34–36: "[T]he islands of support were barely visible in an ocean of demands for exemption, deletion and 'clarification.'"

125 Consultations focused on what became known as the "Gang of Three"—The Canadian Manufacturer's Association, Canadian Chamber of Commerce, and Business Council on National Issues. They were later broadened to include the Grocery Products Manufacturers of Canada, the Canadian Bar Association, the Consumers' Association of Canada, and the academic community. See Clark, above note 116 at 232.

126 *Competition Tribunal Act*, RSC 1985, c 19 (2d Supp); enacted by *An Act to establish the Competition Tribunal*, SC 1986, c 26, assented to 17 June 1986 [*Competition Tribunal Act*].

Table 2.3. Major Legislative Changes in the 1986 Amendments

1. **Creation of the Competition Tribunal** The Restrictive Trade Practices Commission (RTPC) was abolished and the Competition Tribunal, composed of judges from the Federal Court of Canada and lay members, was created. (More will be said about the structure of the Tribunal below.)
2. **Civil Merger and Monopoly Laws** The criminal merger and monopoly prohibition was abolished and new civil law provisions were enacted, reviewable by the Competition Tribunal. As with the civilly reviewable practices enacted in 1976, applications to the Tribunal based upon these provisions had to be brought by the Director of Investigation and Research.
3. **Changes to Inquiry/Report and Search Authorization Functions** Changes were needed to accommodate the findings in *Hunter v Southam*.[127] The RTPC was abolished and applications for the exercise of search and seizure powers transferred to the regular courts in the new Act. Investigative inquiries leading to a public report and research inquiry function were also abolished.[128]

e) Confirmation of a Non-criminal Constitutional Foundation for Competition Law

The 1986 *Competition Act* put into effect one of the principal recommendations for reform dating back to the Economic Council's 1969 *Interim Report*, with the creation of the civil-law Competition Tribunal to adjudicate such matters as mergers, abuse of dominance, and other restrictive practices. The first reliance on a civil tribunal dated to the 1976 Stage I amendments, which had given the RTPC jurisdiction over civilly reviewable practices.

In 1986, however, the Supreme Court had still not spoken definitively on the ability of Parliament to legislate to create competition laws not founded on a criminal law basis. The governing jurisprudence continued to be the *Board of Commerce* and *Re Dominion Trade and Industry Commission* decisions which, as seen above, had struck down two federal attempts to create civil law tribunals adjudicating competition law-related standards. The uncertain legal foundation of the federal jurisdiction over competition law led the 1985 *MacDonald Royal Commission* to state:

> Effective competition policy is essential to developing the full benefits that can occur from an economic union. Canada has not been very

127 *Hunter v Southam*, above note 56.

128 These amendments caused little practical change, as the Director had already virtually ceased to bring such inquiries forward in any case.

aggressive in encouraging competition, and one reason for this may be our constitutional structure.[129]

Authority for a constitutional structure more favourable to national competition law was potentially present in section 91(2) of the *Constitution Act, 1867*, the federal trade and commerce power. That source did not show promise until Privy Council appeals were abolished in 1949 and the Supreme Court of Canada became the final authority on Canada's division of powers. First the "international and interprovincial" branch of the trade and commerce power,[130] and then the "general" branch, were given content by the Supreme Court.[131] Justice Dickson (as he then was) picked up this line of authority in a concurring judgment in *Canada (Attorney General) v CN Transportation*,[132] in which he held that competition law could be supported on the basis of the federal trade and commerce power.

Chief Justice Dickson then authored the 1989 decision in *General Motors of Canada Ltd v City National Leasing*,[133] in which a unanimous court confirmed that competition law could be supported under the general branch of the trade and commerce power, sustaining the civil damages action in the *Combines Investigation Act* on that basis. Although the decision addressed the civil damages action and not the substantive civil provisions or the Competition Tribunal, it provided support for the constitutionality of the latter provisions, which have been upheld in challenges to date before the Tribunal and lower courts.[134] The Supreme Court's more recent decision upholding a federal scheme of securities regulation provides additional support, comparing the constitutional competence of federal securities and competition regulation as follows:

> [B]oth are aimed at stamping out risks and practices that are unhealthy to the Canadian economy. That Parliament's trade and commerce power

---

129 *Royal Commission on the Economic Union and Development Prospects for Canada* (Ottawa: Minister of Supply and Services Canada, 1985), vol III at 168.

130 *Re The Farm Products Marketing Act*, [1957] SCR 198 at 265; *R v Klassen* (1959), 20 DLR (2d) 406 (Man CA), leave to appeal to SCC refused [1959] SCR ix.

131 *Re Anti-Inflation Act*, [1976] 2 SCR 373; *MacDonald v Vapour Canada* (1977), 66 DLR (3d) 1 (SCC).

132 *CN Transportation*, above note 74.

133 *General Motors of Canada Ltd v City National Leasing*, [1989] 1 SCR 641 [*General Motors*].

134 See *Alex Couture Inc v Canada (Procureur général)* (1990), 41 QAC 1, leave to appeal to SCC ref'd, [1992] 2 SCR v; *Canada (Director of Investigation and Research, Competition Act) v Xerox Canada Inc* (1990), 33 CPR (3d) 83 (CCT); see also *Canada (Director of Investigation and Research, Competition Act) v Nutra-Sweet Co (1990), 32 CPR (3d) 1 (CCT).*

is exercised in a way that affects particular industries is not inherently objectionable, so long as the focus of that exercise is on matters that affect trade as a whole.[135]

C. THE CURRENT ENFORCEMENT AND ADJUDICATIVE STRUCTURE

1) Public Enforcement

The following describes the roles and authorities of those involved in the public investigation, enforcement, prosecution, and adjudication of competition law matters.

a) The Commissioner of Competition

The Commissioner of Competition is appointed by the Governor in Council as the public official responsible for the administration and enforcement of the *Competition Act*.[136] The current Commissioner was appointed in 2019 to serve "during pleasure for a term of five years."[137] The *Competition Act* specifies the various enforcement powers and responsibilities of the Commissioner, such as the ability to apply to the courts to compel the production of records and oral evidence as part of the investigative process,[138] to seek remedial orders against mergers, abuse of dominance or other civilly reviewable practices from the Competition Tribunal,[139] and to refer criminal matters for prosecution to the Attorney General of Canada.[140] In late 2023, the Commissioner was given the authority to conduct inquiries into the general "state of competition in a market or industry" at the Commissioner's own initiative or if directed by the Minister, with the power to compel the production of evidence relevant to the inquiry.[141]

---

135 *Reference re Pan-Canadian Securities Regulation, [2018] 3 SCR 189 at para 111.*

136 *Competition Act*, above note 28, s 7(1). The Commissioner is also responsible for the administration and enforcement of the *Consumer Packaging and Labelling Act*, RSC 1985, c C-38, the *Precious Metals Marking Act*, RSC 1985, c P-19, and the *Textile Labelling Act*, RSC 1985, c T-10.

137 Order in Council PC 2019-0107, 27 February 2019.

138 *Competition Act*, above note 28, ss 11–20.

139 *Ibid*, pt VIII, ss 75–92.

140 *Ibid*, s 23(1).

141 *Bill C-56 2023*, above note 63, s 3; *Competition Act*, above note 28, s 10.1. The Commissioner must first consult the Minister before proceeding with an inquiry, and the Minister must consult the Commissioner before making a direction to the Commissioner: see ss 10.1(1) and

Finally, the Commissioner produces an annual report which describes enforcement and other activities in the past year, which the Minister tables in Parliament.[142]

b) The Competition Bureau

The Commissioner is the head of the Competition Bureau, made up of several hundred personnel trained in business, economics, and law who enforce the *Competition Act* and carry out other competition policy-related functions. The Bureau is self-described as "an independent law enforcement agency, [which] ensures that Canadian businesses and consumers prosper in a competitive and innovative marketplace."[143] The Bureau's budget in 2017–18 was $49.6 million and it had a staff of 361.[144] It is divided into Branches dealing with Mergers and Monopolistic Practices, Cartel and Deceptive Marketing Practices, Competition Promotion, and Corporate Services. In 2021, the Digital Enforcement and Intelligence Branch was added as a "a centre of expertise on technology and data and [to] act as an early-warning system for potential competition issues in the digital and traditional economies."[145] These branches are headed by Senior Deputy and Deputy Commissioners.

The Branches are divided into directorates. See **Figure 2.7** below:[146]

10.1(2). The first such inquiry was initiated by the Commissioner into the state of competition in the Canadian airline industry in July 2024. See Canada, Competition Bureau, "Market Study Notice: Competition in Canada's Airline industry" (29 July 2024), online: https://competition-bureau.canada.ca/how-we-foster-competition/promotion-and-advocacy/market-study-notice-competition-canadas-airline-industry-0.

142 *Competition Act*, above note 28, s 127. See Canada, Competition Bureau, *Annual Report of the Commissioner of Competition for the Year Ended March 31, 2018* (26 February 2020), online: www.competitionbureau.gc.ca/eic/site/cb-bc.nsf/eng/04380.html [*Annual Report 2018*].

143 Canada, Competition Bureau, *Competition Bureau Canada*, online: www.competitionbureau.gc.ca/eic/site/cb-bc.nsf/eng/home.

144 *Annual Report 2018*, above note 142 at 2. The 361 are FTEs or "full time equivalent" positions.

145 Matthew Boswell, Commissioner of Competition, Remarks to the Canadian Bar Association Competition Law Fall Conference (20 October 2021), online: https://www.canada.ca/en/competition-bureau/news/2021/10/canada-needs-more-competition.html.

146 Canada, Competition Bureau, online: https://competition-bureau.canada.ca/how-we-foster-competition/our-organization/our-structure.

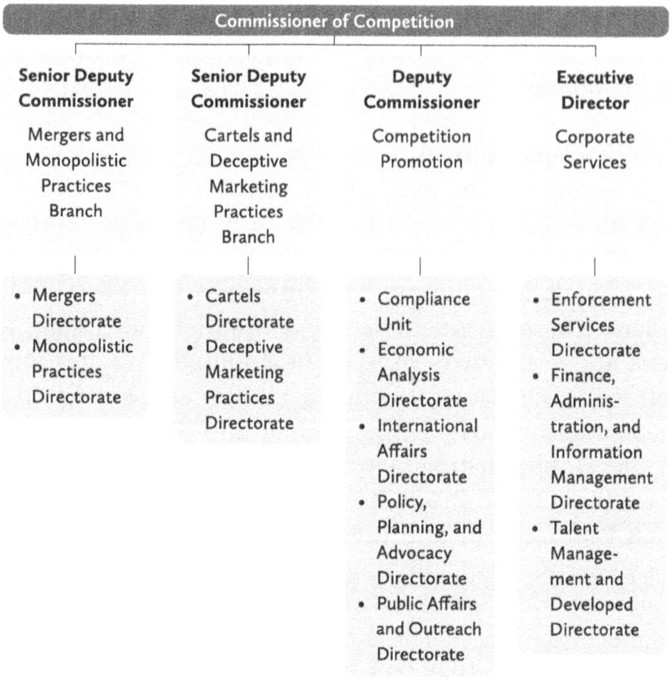

FIGURE 2.7.

c) The Minister of Industry

The Minister of Industry is responsible in Parliament for the *Competition Act* and has certain discrete powers under it. The Minister -- can direct the Commissioner to carry out an inquiry into potential violations of the Act;[147] receives a report from the Commissioner on the reasons for discontinuing an inquiry,[148] signalling that such applications were envisioned by Parliament as an effective means to bring a matter forward; may "require the Commissioner to submit an interim report with respect to any inquiry;"[149] and may "review any decision of the Commissioner to discontinue an inquiry . . . and may, if in the Minister's opinion the circumstances warrant, instruct the Commissioner to make further inquiry."[150] These powers have seldom been used. If the Minister directs an inquiry to occur, the Commissioner still has the discretion to take, or not to take, the steps that he or she sees fit in view of the circumstances.[151]

---

147 *Competition Act*, above note 28, s 10(1)(c).
148 *Ibid*, s 22(2).
149 *Ibid*, s 28.
150 *Ibid*, s 22(4).
151 *Ibid*, s 10(1).

d) The Minister of Justice and Attorney General of Canada

These two roles, which in Canada are held by the same member of Cabinet, are assigned discrete responsibilities in the Act. The statute provides that the Attorney General of Canada may appoint and instruct counsel when requested by the Commissioner to assist in an inquiry.[152] Counsel from the Department of Justice are assigned to a Legal Services Unit which provides ongoing advice and other legal support to the Competition Bureau during all stages of the investigative process, including acting as civil litigation counsel. Private sector agents may also be retained by the Attorney General to act on behalf of the Commissioner.

The Attorney General also has carriage of matters referred by the Commissioner for possible criminal prosecution.[153] Under the *Director of Public Prosecutions Act*, the Director of Public Prosecutions (DPP) has the authority to initiate and conduct criminal prosecutions on behalf of the Crown that are under the jurisdiction of the Attorney General of Canada.[154] The Attorney General also has authority to apply to the courts for remedies for the misuse of intellectual property rights,[155] injunctive relief,[156] and prohibition orders in criminal matters.[157]

The Minister of Justice has certain specific responsibilities in respect of mutual legal assistance agreements and requests for mutual legal assistance from foreign states.[158]

2) Private Enforcement

There are three potential avenues for private parties to play a role in the enforcement of the Act: complaints to the Competition Bureau, private damage applications, and applications to the Competition Tribunal. All of these offer the potential to complement the enforcement efforts of the Bureau and promote greater deterrence and compliance with the legislation. Private actions also offer an avenue for injured parties to obtain compensation and damages.

a) Complaints to the Bureau and Formal Inquiries

The Competition Bureau receives thousands of complaints annually.[159] The Bureau must sift through them to identify those which raise serious

152 *Ibid*, s 21.
153 *Ibid*, ss 23, 73.
154 SC 2006, c 9, pt 3.
155 *Competition Act*, above note 28, s 32.
156 *Ibid*, s 33.
157 *Ibid*, s 34; the latter two powers also possessed by provincial Attorneys General.
158 *Ibid*, pt III.
159 See, e.g. 8,715 complaints and information requests in the fiscal year 2022-23: Canada, Competition Bureau, *Performance Measures and Statistics Report 2023-24* (28 March 2024), online:

issues under the Act and justify a further investigation or a formal inquiry. A formal inquiry under section 10 of the Act can be commenced if the Commissioner has reason to believe that there is the basis to obtain a civil remedy, or that there has been a breach of the criminal provision of the Act or of an order of the courts or Tribunal.[160] Commencing a formal inquiry opens the way for the Commissioner to apply to a judge for an order permitting the use of formal powers under the Act to compel the production of records, to obtain a search warrant, or to conduct oral examination of witnesses.[161] Evidence may also be collected without the use of these formal powers.

As noted above, the Act retains, in section 9, an avenue first added in 1910 permitting six residents of Canada over 18 years of age to compel the initiation of a formal inquiry into alleged breaches of the criminal and civil provisions of the Act.[162] The six residents must comply with certain formalities in the required supporting material, which include "a statement in the form of a solemn or statutory declaration" setting out the basis for their complaint, including "a concise statement of the evidence" in support.[163] If these formalities are met, the statute specifies that the Commissioner "shall . . . cause an inquiry to be made."[164]

Despite this mandatory language, the Federal Court of Appeal held that "the Commissioner is not required to initiate a formal inquiry under paragraph 10(1)(a) into complaints which he has already thoroughly investigated and found not to warrant a formal inquiry." In that case, the matter had already been investigated and the complaint provided no new information. The Court held that nothing would be accomplished by ordering that an inquiry occur.[165]

Once a formal inquiry is started, the Commissioner has discretion to determine what steps to take. The Commissioner need only examine "such matters as . . . necessary to inquire into with the view of determining the facts."[166] The Act contains nothing "that clearly requires the Commissioner to complete any inquiry [based on the request of six residents]. On the contrary, [it] recognizes the Commissioner's

---

https://competition-bureau.canada.ca/how-we-foster-competition/education-and-outreach/competition-bureau-performance-measurement-statistics-report-2023-2024.

160 *Competition Act*, above note 28, s 10(1)(b); also on a six residents' complaint (s 10(1)(a)) and where directed by the Minister (s 10(1)(c)).

161 *Ibid*, ss 11–20.

162 *Ibid*, s 9(1).

163 *Ibid*, s 9(2).

164 *Ibid*, s 10.

165 *Charette v Canada (Commissioner of Competition)*, 2003 FCA 426 at para 50.

166 *Ibid*.

discretion to not continue an inquiry."[167] It has been held that this creates little scope for judicial review because the Commissioner "in conducting [an] inquiry is performing a purely administrative function" and such a function cannot be made subject to a mandatory order of the court.[168]

The initiation of a formal "inquiry" under section 10 thus may change little in terms of the position of a six residents' complaint versus an "informal" complaint to the Bureau.[169] A six residents' complaint does oblige the Commissioner to inform the party under inquiry and the six residents of progress, if they so request.[170] On discontinuance of the inquiry, the Commissioner is required to "make a report in writing to the Minister showing the information obtained and the reason for discontinuing the inquiry."[171] Both steps provide some accountability. However, if the Commissioner has examined the facts and decided the matter has no merit, there is little latitude for further recourse.

As noted above, the Minister has certain limited powers in respect of inquiries. In addition to initiating an inquiry and receiving a report on discontinuance, "[t]he Minister may, on the written request of applicants under section 9 or on the Minister's own motion, review any decision of the Commissioner to discontinue an inquiry under section 10, and may, if in the Minister's opinion the circumstances warrant, instruct the Commissioner to make further inquiry."[172] However, the Minister cannot initiate, or direct the initiation of, enforcement action. The limited scope for Ministerial direction at the enforcement level highlights the status of the Commissioner as an independent law enforcement official in this respect.

b) Section 36—Statutory Cause of Action for Damages

i) History

A civil damages action has been a long-standing feature of the American law, as a complement to public enforcement.[173] In fact, given the incentive

---

167 *Ashley v Canada (Commissioner of Competition), 2006 FC 459 (TD) at para 45. See the power to discontinue in s 22(1): "At any stage of an inquiry under section 10, if the Commissioner is of the opinion that the matter being inquired into does not justify further inquiry."*

168 *Ibid* at paras 27 and 48–49, citing *Gauthier v Canada (Director of Investigation and Research)*, [1991] FCJ 1002 (CA). See also *Cinémas Guzzo Inc v Canada (Attorney General), 2005 FC 691 (TD), aff'd 2006 FCA 160.*

169 The process for filing a complaint is described at Canada, Competition Bureau, *Filing a Complaint* (5 November 2015), online: www.competitionbureau.gc.ca/eic/site/cb-bc.nsf/eng/02930.html.

170 *Competition Act*, above note 28, s 10(2).

171 *Ibid*, s 20(2).

172 *Ibid*, s 22(4).

173 *Clayton Act*, 15 USC §§ 12–27, 29 USC §§ 52–53.

created by the ability to recover treble damages for any loss proven under the applicable statutory cause of action in the United States, the American private plaintiff has been described as "the primary enforcer of antitrust laws,"[174] and the private action there "the strongest pillar of antitrust."[175]

In Canada, there was no such statutory action passed as a companion to the initial law. In fact, the courts rejected attempts to use criminal competition law provisions as a foundation for a civil cause of action. In *Transport Oil*, the Ontario Court of Appeal said in 1935, "it is plain that the Parliament of Canada in passing this Act intended it to be an exercise by it of the power to legislate with respect to crime and criminal law, and that it did not intend to interfere with the Provincial jurisdiction over property and civil rights."[176] In *Direct Lumber*, the Supreme Court held in respect of the *Criminal Code* price discrimination prohibition, "this legislation creating a new crime was enacted solely for the protection of the public interest and . . . does not create a civil cause of action."[177]

In the reports and materials leading to the development of the 1976 amendments, a civil action was seen as substantially furthering certain policy objectives, such as compensation and deterrence. The Department of Consumer and Corporate Affairs cited compensation as a central rationale for the original proposals in 1973. The Department stated, "although [the civil damages action] is expected to be of particular value to small businessmen who have been hurt by conduct contrary to the Act, [it] will be equally available to consumers and to any other members of the public who have been so damaged."[178] Furthering deterrence was also identified as an objective. The Competition Bureau's *Background Papers* to the 1976 amendments stated, "we are hopeful that the inclusion of a private damage action will be a significant deterrent to violations of the *Act* and also prevent unjust enrichment."[179]

In 1989, in sustaining the constitutionality of the civil damages action in section 36 as within federal authority, the Supreme Court of Canada held that it "is clearly as much a part of the legislative scheme regulating competition throughout Canada as is the criminal action for fines and

174 Note, "The Antitrust Treble Damages Remedy" (1983) 9 *William Mitchell Law Review* 435 at 436.

175 Lee Loevinger, "Private Action — The Strongest Pillar of Antitrust" 3 *Antitrust Bulletin* 167 (1958).

176 *Transport Oil Ltd v Imperial Oil Ltd*, [1935] 2 DLR 500 (Ont CA) at 501.

177 *Direct Lumber Co v Western Plywood Co*, [1962] SCR 646 at 648.

178 *Proposals for a New Competition Policy for Canada* (Ottawa: Consumer and Corp Affairs Canada, 1973) at 48–49; cited in *Pioneer Corp v Godfrey*, 2019 SCC 42 at para 68 [*Pioneer*].

179 Canada, Bureau of Competition Policy, *Stage I Competition Policy, Background Papers* (Ottawa, Consumer and Corporate Affairs, 1976) at 32 [*Stage I Competition Policy*].

imprisonment or the administrative action involving an inquiry or the reduction of customs duties."[180] The Court noted that the damages remedy in the United States had proven to be "an ever-present threat to deter anyone contemplating business behaviour in violation of the antitrust laws."[181]

ii) Section 36: Statutory Language

Subsection 36(1) creates a statutory cause of action for breaches of the criminal prohibitions in Part VI of the Act or of an order of the Tribunal or other court under the Act. It states:

> 36(1) Any person who has suffered loss or damage as a result of
> (a) conduct that is contrary to any provision of Part VI, or
> (b) the failure of any person to comply with an order of the Tribunal or another court under this Act,
>
> may, in any court of competent jurisdiction, sue for and recover from the person who engaged in the conduct or failed to comply with the order an amount equal to the loss or damage proved to have been suffered by him, together with any additional amount that the court may allow not exceeding the full cost to him of any investigation in connection with the matter and of proceedings under this section.

a. "Loss or Damage" Needed for the Cause of Action

Under the subsection, the plaintiff may recover "an amount equal to the loss or damage proved to have been suffered by him." The Supreme Court has given a plain reading to the "loss or damage" requirement. In a trilogy of decisions in 2013, it permitted class actions by indirect purchasers affected by an alleged price fixing overcharge.[182] "Indirect" purchasers are "consumers who have not purchased a product directly from the alleged overcharger, but who have purchased it either from one of the overcharger's direct purchasers, or from some other intermediary in the chain of distribution."[183] This includes situations where the prod-

---

180 *General Motors*, above note 133 at para 70.

181 *Ibid* at para 74. See also M Trebilcock & M Sanderson, "Competition Class Actions: An Evaluation of Deterrence and Corrective Justice Rationales" and E Iacobucci, "Imperfect Information and Conspiracy Class Actions" in S Pitel, *Litigating Conspiracy: An Analysis of Competition Class Actions* (Toronto: Irwin Law, 2006) [*Litigating Conspiracy*].

182 *Pro-Sys Consultants Ltd v Microsoft Corporation*, 2013 SCC 57 [*Microsoft*]; *Sun-Rype Products Ltd v Archer Daniels Midland Company*, 2013 SCC 58; and *Infineon Technologies v Option Consommateurs*, 2013 SCC 59. For background, see JJ Camp, "A Historical Perspective of a Made-in-Canada Remedy for Anticompetitive Behaviour" (2018) 31:1 *Canadian Competition Law Review* 85.

183 *Microsoft*, above note 182 at para 16.

uct (such as a computer chip) is only a component of a manufactured product. In spite of the potential remoteness of this interest, and the spectre of double recovery, the Court accepted that any proven loss or damage may fall within the section:

> Practically, the risk of duplicate or multiple recoveries can be managed by the courts.
>
> Indirect purchaser actions, especially in the antitrust context, will often involve large amounts of evidence, complex economic theories and multiple parties in a chain of distribution, making the tracing of the overcharges to their ultimate end an unenviable task. However . . . these same concerns can be raised in most antitrust cases, and should not stand in the way of allowing indirect purchasers an opportunity to make their case.[184]

The Court saw such actions as serving the compensation objective, "because it allows for compensating the parties who have actually suffered the harm rather than merely reserving these actions for direct purchasers who may have in fact passed on the overcharge."[185] It also viewed permitting the action to proceed as furthering deterrence, noting that "the Competition Bureau in this case has said that it will not be pursuing any action against Microsoft. Accordingly, if the class action does not proceed, the objectives of deterrence and behaviour modification will not be addressed at all. On this issue, the class action is not only the preferable procedure but the only procedure available to serve these objectives."[186]

The Court has more recently permitted actions by another remote class of plaintiff, so-called umbrella purchasers. These are purchasers who have allegedly suffered damage based on the theory that "the defendants' anti-competitive cartel activity creates an 'umbrella' of supra-competitive prices, causing non-cartel manufacturers to raise their prices."[187] The Court again cited the plain words of section 36 in finding that the provision does not exclude such plaintiffs:

> Section 36(1)(a) provides a cause of action to *any person* who has *suffered loss or damage* as a result of conduct contrary to s. 45. Significantly, Parliament's use of "any person" does not narrow the realm of possible claimants. Rather, it empowers *any* claimant who can demonstrate that loss or damage was incurred as a result of the defendant's

184 *Ibid* at paras 37 and 44.

185 *Ibid* at para 50.

186 *Ibid* at para 141.

187 *Pioneer*, above note 178 at para 58.

conduct to bring a claim. On this point, the following paragraph from the Court of Appeal for Ontario's decision in *Shah (ONCA)* (at para. 34) is apposite, and I adopt it as mine:

> ... the umbrella purchasers' right of recovery is limited only by their ability to demonstrate two things: (1) that the respondents conspired within the meaning of s. 45; and (2) that the losses or damages suffered by the appellants resulted from that conspiracy.[188]

The Court held, referring to the objectives of the legislation:

> [T]he purpose of the *Competition Act* is to "maintain and encourage competition in Canada" with a view to providing consumers with "competitive prices and product choices" (s. 1.1). A conspiracy to price-fix is the "very antithesis of the *Competition Act*'s objective." ... Monetary sanctions for such anti-competitive conduct therefore further the *Competition Act*'s purpose. This Court has also recognized two other objectives of the *Competition Act* of particular relevance here, being deterrence of anti-competitive behaviour, and compensation for the victims of such behaviour.... Interpreting s. 36(1)(a) so as to permit umbrella purchaser actions furthers both of these objectives.[189]

The Court explained that this result "furthers deterrence because it increases the potential liability falling upon those who engage in anti-competitive behaviour."[190]

While indirect and umbrella purchasers may assert claims, they still must prove they have incurred "loss or damage." This can pose challenges. In a price fixing case, for example, it will be necessary to connect a price increase or "overcharge" flowing from the conspiracy to harm to the plaintiff. It must be shown that the overcharge was paid, in whole or part, by the plaintiff. This is an area that is yet to be subject to extensive contested litigation, with most of the jurisprudence arising in the context of consent settlements.[191]

b. Other Relief

A section 36 plaintiff may also recover "any additional amount that the court may allow not exceeding the full cost to him of any investigation

188 *Ibid* at para 64 [emphasis in original].
189 *Ibid* at para 65 [citations omitted].
190 *Ibid* at para 66.
191 Eliot Kolers & Danielle Royal, "Canada," ch 7 in Ilene K Gotts, ed, *The Private Competition Enforcement Review*, 7th ed (London: Law Business Research, 2014) at 94.

in connection with the matter and of proceedings under this section." This amounts to a bolstered costs authority given that it expressly refers to "the full cost . . . of any investigation," an amount that would not flow simply from a right to recover litigation costs.

Section 36 does not provide for punitive damages. Such damages may be the subject, however, of concurrent tort claims, such as for intentional interference with economic relations or conspiracy to carry out an unlawful act. The Supreme Court has held that section 36 does not preclude a tort claim which relies upon the breach of the Act as the "unlawful act," which is a required element in tort. The Court reasoned:

> [Section] 62 of the *Competition Act* . . . contemplates the subsistence of common law and equitable rights of action by providing that "nothing in this Part [which includes s. 45(1), in respect of which s. 36(1) creates a statutory right of action] shall be construed as depriving any person of any civil right of action."[192]

c. *Conduct Contrary to the Criminal Prohibitions; Onus*

Subparagraph 36(1)(a) provides for an action in respect of "conduct that is contrary to" the criminal prohibitions the Act. The bulk of the actions brought under the section have been alleged breaches of three prohibitions, of conspiracy (section 45), of bid-rigging (section 47), and of knowingly false or misleading representations (section 52).

It is noteworthy that while the legislation creates a private cause of action for breach of *criminal* prohibitions, no cause of action for damages is available for breach of the *civil* prohibitions which are subject to review by the Competition Tribunal, except for breaches of civil orders made by the Tribunal.[193] As we will see below, a limited right to challenge certain practices is made available before the Tribunal, but damages are not an available remedy.

The reference to "conduct contrary to" the criminal prohibitions in section 36(1)(a) requires the plaintiff to prove that the defendant carried out the elements of the underlying offence. For example, for price fixing, the plaintiff must prove both the *actus reus* of agreement to fix prices and the necessary *mens rea* to carry out the agreement.[194] The Supreme Court has made it clear that in a civil action, each of these requisite elements need only be proven on a balance of probabilities, not beyond a reasonable doubt. In *FH v McDougall*, the Court held:

---

192 *Pioneer*, above note 178 at para 88.

193 *Competition Act*, above note 28, s 36(1)(b).

194 *Watson v Bank of America Corp*, 2015 BCCA 362 at para 72.

> I think it is time to say, once and for all in Canada, that there is only one civil standard of proof at common law and that is proof on a balance of probabilities. Of course, context is all important and a judge should not be unmindful, where appropriate, of inherent probabilities or improbabilities or the seriousness of the allegations or consequences. However, these considerations do not change the standard of proof.[195]

Subsection 36(2) assists a plaintiff with the burden of proof where there has been a prior criminal conviction. It supplies *prima facie* proof in the damages action that an offence was committed:

> [T]he record of proceedings in any court in which that person was convicted of an offence under Part VI . . . is, in the absence of any evidence to the contrary, proof that the person against whom the action is brought engaged in conduct that was contrary to a provision of Part VI . . . and any evidence given in those proceedings as to the effect of those acts or omissions on the person bringing the action is evidence thereof in an action.

Reflecting the value of this provision, a substantial portion of the actions commenced under section 36 have been brought after criminal proceedings were filed, and in many cases after guilty pleas were obtained. Difficulties are raised for plaintiffs when there is settlement of criminal proceedings prior to prosecution but no public record of the resolution, because "even where there is evidence of criminal activity, the Commissioner will not necessarily refer the matter for prosecution but may settle it through negotiation. The terms of such settlement are kept confidential and no consent order is usually sought from the court."[196]

Even where the matter is contested and proceeds to trial, a plaintiff cannot necessarily expect the enforcement authorities to provide them free and open access to the investigative file. The Bureau's position is that it "will not voluntarily provide information to persons contemplating or initiating a private action under section 36 of the Act" and will "oppose subpoenas for production of information if compliance with them would potentially interfere with an ongoing examination or

---

195 *FH v McDougall*, 2008 SCC 53 at para 40. A standard of "high preponderance of possibilities" was applied in *Distrimedic Inc v Dispill Inc*, 2013 FC 1043 (TD) at para 270, citing *Janelle Pharmacy Ltd v Blue Cross of Atlantic Canada*, 2003 NSSC 179; *Pentagon Investments Ltd v Canadian Surety Co*, [1992] NSJ No 402 (CA).

196 House of Commons, Standing Committee on Industry, *Interim Report on the Competition Act* (June 2000) (Chair: Susan Whelan), online: www.ourcommons.ca/DocumentViewer/en/36-2/INDU/report-7/page-78 [Standing Committee *Interim Report*].

inquiry." If opposition is unsuccessful, the Bureau will seek protective orders to maintain the confidentiality of the information in question.[197]

The Bureau has successfully resisted attempts to compel production of investigative evidence.[198] Furthermore, third party discovery is not available from the Competition Bureau under the provisions of the *Crown Liability and Proceedings Act*.[199]

d. Class Actions

As the recent jurisprudence from the Supreme Court indicates, class actions have become a leading vehicle for the pursuit of section 36 damages claims. Their potential importance in furthering the effectiveness of civil damages actions was recognized at the time of the 1976 amendments, but the issue was deferred for further study.[200] A 1977 report recommended that further amendments "provide for class and substitute actions and the procedure in relation to them."[201] Citing the recently added civil damages action, it noted that "only in situations involving large sums of money would suits normally be brought . . . . Those whose damages are small would not individually bring suit because their individual recoveries would be small and they would be bound to incur legal fees and costs of a prohibitive size if they were to lose."[202] The report referred to a study by an Osgoode Hall Law School law professor, which concluded that class actions were particularly effective means by which "the economically disadvantaged, consumers, tenants, small businessmen and others, can secure collective redress in the courts for injury, actual or threatened, inflicted by government or industry."[203]

---

197 Canada, Competition Bureau, "Submission to the OECD Competition Committee Roundtable on the Relationship between Public and Private Antitrust Enforcement," (10 June 2015), online: www.competitionbureau.gc.ca/eic/site/cb-bc.nsf/eng/03926.html.

198 *Pro-Sys Consultants Ltd v Microsoft Corporation*, 2016 BCSC 97; however, a class privilege was not recognized in *Vancouver Airport Authority v Commissioner of Competition*, 2018 FCA 24; see also Mohsen Seddigh, "Section 36 Requests for Access to Information and the Competition Bureau: Hast Thou Forsaken Me?" (2018) 31 *Canadian Competition Law Review* 233.

199 RSC 1985, c C-50, as am; *Canada (Attorney General) v Thouin*, [2017] 2 SCR 184.

200 *Stage I Competition Policy*, above note 179 at 33.

201 Consumer and Corporate Affairs Canada, *Proposals for a New Competition Policy for Canada Second Stage* (Ottawa: Consumer and Corporate Affairs Canada, 1977) at 73.

202 *Ibid*.

203 *Ibid* at 72.

A class actions regime was proposed in two bills tabled in 1977.[204] The initiative proved controversial[205] and the amendments were shelved. When the Stage II amendments finally went ahead a decade later, class actions provisions were not part of the amendments.[206]

With the institution of class actions regimes under provincial legislation in all provinces but PEI (beginning with Quebec in 1978),[207] the recognition of a common law foundation for class proceedings by the Supreme Court in 2001,[208] and the adoption of class actions rules in the Federal Court,[209] there has been a steady escalation of recourse to this procedure in Canada.[210] The overall number of class actions in Ontario was recently profiled by the Law Commission of Ontario (see **Figure 2.8**):[211]

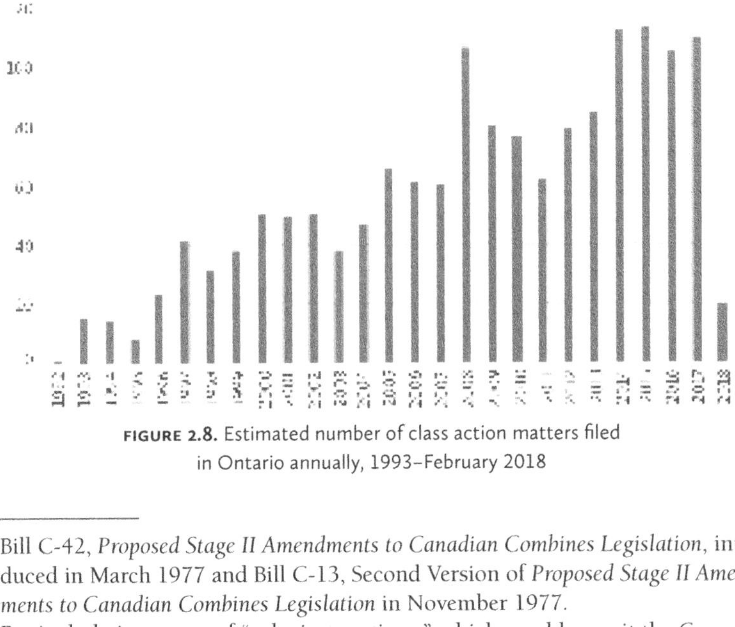

FIGURE 2.8. Estimated number of class action matters filed in Ontario annually, 1993–February 2018

204 Bill C-42, *Proposed Stage II Amendments to Canadian Combines Legislation*, introduced in March 1977 and Bill C-13, Second Version of *Proposed Stage II Amendments to Canadian Combines Legislation* in November 1977.

205 Particularly in respect of "substitute actions," which would permit the Competition Policy Advocate to bring an action when certification was denied. See William T Stanbury, "The Stage II Amendments: An Overview," ch 3 in Prichard, Stanbury & Wilson, above note 45 at 68–70.

206 *Competition Tribunal Act*, above note 126.

207 *Code of Civil Procedure*, CQLR c C-25.01.

208 *Western Canadian Shopping Centres v Dutton*, [2001] 2 SCR 534.

209 *Federal Courts Rules*, SOR/98-106, pt 5.1.

210 Law Commission of Ontario, *Class Actions: Objectives, Experiences and Reforms: Final Report* (Toronto: Law Commission of Ontario, 2019), online: www.lco-cdo.org/wp-content/uploads/2019/07/LCO-Class-Actions-Report-FINAL-July-17-2019.pdf at 5: "The number of class action matters filed in recent years has clearly increased, averaging more than 100 class actions per year for the last several years."

211 *Ibid* at 14.

Class actions provide a vehicle well-suited for claims such as price fixing, which often feature broadly spread impacts on a large number of parties. An Ontario court observed the following in this respect:

> Price-fixing conspiracy cases by their nature, deal with common legal and factual questions about the existence, scope and effect of an alleged conspiracy. Putative class members have a common interest in any proof of a concerted action, conspiracy and of agreement with the aim and result of restricting trade.
>
> If each class member in the subject class actions proceeded individually against the Defendants, each would have to prove the existence and impact of the identical conspiracy to fix prices and allocate markets. Therefore, in each of these actions the common issue satisfies the test of advancing the proceeding and avoiding duplication of the fact-finding and legal analysis.
>
> A class proceeding is the preferable procedure because it provides a fair, efficient and manageable method of determining the common issues and because it will advance the actions in accordance with the goals of judicial economy, access to justice and behaviour modification. In the absence of these class actions, it is unlikely that the majority of claims would be advanced at all.[212]

One of the challenges posed in *Competition Act*-based class actions relating to such matters as price fixing is the need for the plaintiff to show that some loss can be proven on a class-wide basis, rather than the need for numerous individual damage assessments. This issue is heightened where indirect purchasers are the claimants. For certification, the Supreme Court held in *Microsoft* that the plaintiff must at least lay the foundation to prove class-wide loss:

> It is not necessary at the certification stage that the methodology establish the actual loss to the class, as long as the plaintiff has demonstrated that there is a methodology capable of doing so. In indirect purchaser actions, this means that the methodology must be able to establish that the overcharges have been passed on to the indirect-purchaser level in the distribution chain.[213]

212 *Vitapharm Canada Ltd v F Hoffmann-La Roche Ltd* (2005), 74 OR (2d) 758 (SC) at paras 34 and 36. See however *Shah v LG Chem Ltd*, 2015 ONSC 6148 at paras 132–37, rev'd 2018 ONCA 819 to the effect that this statement should not be taken as determinative as to the requirements for certification based on common issues.

213 *Microsoft*, above note 182 at para 115. See also the assessment of damages methodology by Perell J and certification of class claims made against certain banks for conspiracy to fix or unreasonably enhance the prices of currency purchased in the

The Court explained the nature of the evidence required in *Pioneer*:

> [F]or a court to certify loss-related questions as common issues in a price-fixing class proceeding, it must be satisfied that the plaintiff has shown a plausible methodology to establish that loss reached one or more purchasers—that is, claimants at the "purchaser *level*." For indirect purchasers, this would involve demonstrating that the direct purchasers passed on the overcharge.[214]

In terms of the strength of the evidence required, the Court held that the methodology must demonstrate only "a realistic prospect of establishing loss on a class-wide basis."[215]

The recent jurisprudence from the Supreme Court provides helpful guidance for the certification of competition law class proceedings. While methodology for proof of loss has not been tested extensively in the courts to date, and other challenges, such as access to evidence, may face plaintiffs, the recent decisions may bolster further actions under section 36.

e. *Limitation Period*

Subsection 36(4) provides a two-year limitation period for private damages actions in respect of breaches of the criminal provisions:

> (4) No action may be brought under subsection (1),
> (a) in the case of an action based on conduct that is contrary to any provision of Part VI, after two years from
> (i) a day on which the conduct was engaged in, or
> (ii) the day on which any criminal proceedings relating thereto were finally disposed of,
> whichever is the later.

The Supreme Court in *Pioneer* held the subparagraph (i) limitation period above is subject to the "discoverability" principle—meaning that it does not begin to run until "the material facts on which [the cause of action] is based have been discovered or ought to have been discovered by the plaintiff by the exercise of reasonable diligence."[216] The majority noted that anti-competitive agreements "are invariably conducted

---

foreign exchange foreign currency market in *Mancinelli v Royal Bank of Canada et al*, 2020 ONSC 1646.

214 *Pioneer*, above note 178 at para 107 [emphasis in original].

215 *Ibid* at para 118. Re proof of damage methodology, see also James A Brander & Thomas W Ross, "Estimating Damages from Price-Fixing," in *Litigating Conspiracy*, above note 181.

216 *Pioneer*, above note 178 at para 31, citing *Central Trust Co v Rafuse*, [1986] 2 SCR 147 at 224.

through secrecy and deception . . . meaning that they are, by their very nature, *unknown* to s. 36(1)(a) claimants."[217] They concluded:

> It would therefore be absurd, and would render the cause of action granted by s. 36(1)(a) almost meaningless, to state that Parliament did not intend for discoverability to apply, such that the plaintiff's right of action would expire prior to his or her acquiring knowledge of the anti-competitive behaviour. I agree with the Court of Appeal that "it cannot be said that Parliament intended to accord such little weight to the interests of injured plaintiffs in the context of alleged conspiracies so as to exclude the availability of the discoverability rule in s. 36(4)."[218]

In terms of what may constitute discoverability, publicity and general public notoriety of conspiratorial conduct has been found to be sufficient to satisfy this requirement, given the interest of businesspeople in being informed of matters within their commercial interest. In upholding discoverability, the BC Court of Appeal held "[i]t strains credulity to find that those purchasing several hundreds of thousands of dollars' worth of a product annually would not make it their business to know all of the sources of supply and how the prices were determined."[219]

The limitation period is also delayed under the statute until the conclusion of any criminal prosecution relating to the conduct. This may extend the limitation period significantly, given that it may take several years for charges to be laid, and the matter brought to trial. In the case of the lysine conspiracy in the United States, for example, class proceedings were still being dealt with at the certification stage in Canada almost two decades after the period of the conspiracy in question.[220]

c) Section 103.1 Applications to the Competition Tribunal

i) *History*

Only the Commissioner (or the predecessor, Director of Investigation and Research) was permitted to seek a remedy under the original civil practices provisions added to the legislation in 1976. Private access to civil adjudication had, however, been recommended by the Economic Council's 1969 *Interim Report on Competition Policy*. The Council proposed that applications before a new civil tribunal could be initiated both

---

217 *Pioneer*, above note 178 at para 46 [emphasis in original].
218 *Ibid.*
219 *Sun-Rype Products Ltd v Archer Daniels Midland Co, 2008 BCCA 278 at para 129.*
220 See, e.g., *Mura v Archer Daniels Midland Co, 2003 BCSC 727.*

by a Crown official (the "Director of Legal Proceedings") and by "private parties deeming themselves affected by the practice." Applications by the latter would have been subject to a screening process before the tribunal to determine whether "there appeared to be public interest grounds for subjecting the practice to a full hearing."[221]

In 1995, a consultation paper was issued by the Competition Bureau proposing a private right of action to supplement the Bureau's limited resources in bringing vertical restraints (refusals to deal, market restriction, exclusive dealing, tied selling) matters.[222] A 1996 Consultative Panel report was divided over this proposal.[223] The Bureau then funded further studies, two of which supported this change,[224] but no amendments were brought forward at that time.

A further consultation process on the proposal of expanded private access was initiated in 2000.[225] Concerns in respect of the potential tactical use of applications to the Tribunal by competitors were raised before the House of Commons Committee studying the proposal. However, the Committee concluded that the cost and time required to bring such applications would mitigate such concerns, stating: "[t]he mere cost of bringing a case to the Tribunal [provides] a disincentive to spurious litigation."[226] Noting that there had been few applications to the Tribunal by the Commissioner in the first decade after the *Competition Act* was enacted,[227] the House Committee concluded in its *Interim Report*: "the Act is currently under-enforced by the Commissioner of Competition and . . . the Canadian competitive environment would benefit from having more cases brought to the Competition Tribunal."[228] The Committee put forward the following rationales for extending private access to the Tribunal:[229]

---

221 *Interim Report* 1969, above note 91 at 121.

222 Canada, Bureau of Competition Policy, *Competition Act Amendments* (Ottawa: Industry Canada, 1995) at 21–23.

223 Canada, *Report of the Consultative Panel on Amendments to the Competition Act* (Ottawa: Industry Canada, 1996). See also A Neil Campbell, "Distribution Freedom: The Evolution of Vertical Distribution Practices under the Competition Act" (2012) 25:2 *Canadian Competition Law Review* 377.

224 Kent Roach & Michael Trebilcock, *Private Party Access to the Competition Tribunal* (Ottawa: Competition Bureau, 1996); Kent Roach & Michael Trebilcock, "Private Enforcement of Competition Laws" (1997) 34:3 *Osgoode Hall Law Journal* 461.

225 Canada, Competition Bureau, *Amending the Competition Act: Discussion Paper on Meeting the Challenges of the Global Economy* (Ottawa: Industry Canada, 2000).

226 Standing Committee *Interim Report*, above note 196.

227 *Ibid*.

228 *Ibid*.

229 *Ibid*, Exhibit 6.1.

Reasons for a Right of Private Access to the Competition Tribunal

Studies suggest that the private sector is more able than the government in detecting anticompetitive conduct that has an immediate impact on participants in a specific market.

Private actions would free up Bureau resources, and allow it to focus upon higher-level anticompetitive conduct that is not readily detectable, owing to its covert nature.

The Competition Tribunal is currently underutilized.

The possibility of private action might deter firms from undertaking anticompetitive activity.

The private sector could be an effective partner in achieving compliance with competition law if interim injunctive relief or cease and desist orders were made available to it on a relatively inexpensive, expedited basis.

Private actions would result in judicial decisions providing guidance to the business community on its responsibilities under competition law.

An increase in cases would provide new opportunities for more lawyers to specialize in competition law practice, contributing to the development of a more diverse bar reflecting broader socio-economic interests.

Similarly, increased opportunities for economists and other experts to provide evidence in proceedings would promote the development of theoretical constructs unique to the Canadian experience, and reduce the degree of reliance on the experience of foreign jurisdictions.

In the Committee's final report in 2002, which followed additional consultations, it noted that there was "broad agreement on the principle of granting private access to the Tribunal" among interested parties.[230] It recommended permitting the Tribunal to: (1) impose administrative monetary penalties in cases involving refusal to deal, consignment selling, tied selling, market restriction, exclusive dealing, abuse of dominant position, and delivered pricing; and (2) entertain private proceedings involving the bulk of the foregoing provisions, including abuse of dominance, as well as expanding the Tribunal's authority to award damages

230 House of Commons, Standing Committee on Industry, Science and Technology, *A Plan to Modernize Canada's Competition Regime* (April 2002) (Chair: Walt Lastewka) at 33, online: www.ourcommons.ca/Content/Committee/371/INST/Reports/RP1032077/indurp08/indurp08-e.pdf [*A Plan to Modernize Canada's Competition Regime*].

in such applications.[231] The Committee considered that damages would provide greater deterrence of anti-competitive behaviour.[232]

In the amendments that followed the Report, only the private applications in respect of vertical restraints were added.[233] The Commissioner thus remained the gatekeeper to the Tribunal for applications in respect of mergers and abuse of dominance, and no damages were made available. The government left the door open to broadening access, stating in its response to the House Committee Report, "[a] review of the amendments relating to private access . . . will take place two years after it comes into force. At that time, the Government will be in a better position to assess whether rights of private access should be extended to" abuse of dominance.[234] However, no such changes were made at that time.

The 2008 *Compete to Win* panel recommended against extension of private access to the Tribunal for the abuse of dominance and merger provisions.[235] A modest expansion in private access occurred in 2009, when resale price maintenance was decriminalized, and private applications were permitted to enforce that provision.[236]

In the period following the 2009 amendments, commentators periodically renewed the call for the enlargement of private applications to

---

231 *Ibid* at 50, Recommendation 8: "That the Government of Canada amend the *Competition Act* and the *Competition Tribunal Act* to extend the private right of action in the case of abuse of dominant position (section 79) and to permit the Competition Tribunal to award damages in private action proceedings (sections 75, 77 and 79)."

232 *Ibid* at 48.

233 *An Act to amend the Competition Act* 2002, above note 60.

234 Canada, Competition Bureau, "Government Response to the Report of the House of Commons Standing Committee on Industry, Science and Technology '*A Plan to Modernize Canada's Competition Regime*'" (1 October 2002) at 9, online: www.competitionbureau.gc.ca/eic/site/iccat.nsf/eng/03282.html.

235 Canada, Competition Policy Review Panel, *Compete to Win, Final Report* (Public Works and Government Services Canada: Ottawa, 2008) at 59. The Panel's Report stated:

> [T]here is a concern that extending private access to the abuse of dominance or merger provisions would serve to promote unmeritorious litigation between competitors that would not enhance the competitiveness of Canadian industry or markets. The Panel is of the view that empowering the Competition Tribunal to award damages should not be pursued for similar reasons.

On the issue of expanding such remedies, see Paul Erik Veel, "Private Party Access to the Competition Tribunal: A Critical Evaluation of the Section 103.1 Experiment" (2009) 18:1 *Dalhousie Journal of Legal Studies* 1; Calvin S Goldman & Navin Joneja, "The Institutional Design of Canadian Competition Law: The Evolving Role of the Commissioner" (2010) 41:3 *Loyola University Chicago Law Journal* 535.

236 *Budget Implementation Act, 2009*, above note 61, ss 426 and 431.

cover abuse of dominance, as well as the recovery of damages, as a way of increasing the effectiveness and enforcement of the legislation.[237] With the momentum for legislative change building in 2021, in 2022 the Bureau itself called for private access to be expanded to abuse of dominance,[238] and this was included in the amendments tabled as part of the Spring Budget omnibus legislation (Bill C-19) passed by Parliament in June, 2022.[239] Remedies available to both the Commissioner and private applicants for abuse of dominance were expanded in 2022 and 2023 to include administrative monetary penalties not exceeding the greater of $25 million[240] or "three times the value of the benefit derived from the anti-competitive practice, or, if that amount cannot be reasonably determined, 3% of the person's annual worldwide gross revenues."[241]

Private applications were further expanded to cover the civil deceptive marketing and the civil agreements provisions in 2024 as part of the Government's omnibus *Fall Economic Statement Implementation Act, 2023*.[242] The test for leave to bring such applications was modified to add a public interest test, described below. At the same time, the Tribunal was given the authority in the case of well-founded private applications to order the respondent supplier to pay "an amount, not exceeding the value of the benefit derived from the conduct that is the subject of the order." This amount may be "distributed among the applicant and any other person affected by the conduct," on terms which include how the payment is to be administered and distributed.[243]

---

237 See, e.g. C.D. Howe Institute Competition Policy Council, "Damage Control: Abuse of Dominance and the State of Private Remedies in the *Competition Act*," 20 October 2016; Ducci, Francesco and Michael Trebilcock, "The Evolution of Canadian Competition Policy: A Retrospective" (2018) 60 Canadian Business Law Journal 171 at 193.

238 Competition Bureau Canada, "Examining the Canadian *Competition Act* in the Digital Era, Submission by the Competition Bureau" (8 February 2022) [Bureau Submissions 2022] at s 3.4, online: https://ised-isde.canada.ca/site/competition-bureau-canada/en/how-we-foster-competition/promotion-and-advocacy/regulatory-adviceinterventions-competition-bureau/examining-canadian-competition-act-digital-era.

239 *Bill C-19 2022*, above note 62, s 266.

240 *Bill C-56, 2023*, above note 63, s 7.1.

241 *Ibid*, s 262.

242 *Bill C-59 2024*, above note 64, s 254. This change comes into force on June 20, 2025.

243 *Ibid*, s 244(2). The authority to make this kind of monetary award also comes into force on June 20, 2025.

ii) Screens for Bringing Private Applications

The Tribunal may screen out and refuse a private party's leave application if

- the matter is already the subject of an inquiry being carried out by the Commissioner;
- the Commissioner has reached a settlement with the person against whom an order is sought and discontinued a related inquiry as a result;
- the matter was already the subject of an application by the Commissioner[244] or
- it is an agreement or arrangement for the purpose of protecting the environment covered by an exemption certificate issued by the Commissioner.[245]

iii) The Test for Leave

Subsections 103.1(6.1),(7) and (7.1) provide that leave may be granted to a private party to bring an application

- under section 75 (refusal to supply), section 77 (exclusive dealing, market restriction, tied selling) or section 79 (abuse of dominance) if the Tribunal "has reason to believe that the applicant is directly and substantially affected in the whole or part of the applicant's business[246] by any conduct referred to in one of those sections that could be subject to an order under that section or if it is satisfied that it is in the public interest to do so";
- under section 74.1 (deceptive marketing practices) if the Tribunal "is satisfied that it is in the public interest to do so"; and
- under section 76 (resale price maintenance), if the Tribunal has reason to believe that "the applicant is directly affected" by any conduct referred to in that section that could be subject to an order.

The public interest test was added in the 2024 amendments alongside enlargement of the practices which can be the subject to private enforcement.[247] In interpreting this test, the Tribunal may have regard to the common law test for public interest standing, which has three requirements: "whether the case raises a serious justiciable issue, whether the party bringing the action has a real stake or a genuine interest in its outcome and whether, having regard to a number of

244 *Competition Act*, above note 28, s 103.1(4), (5).

245 *Ibid*, s 103.1(7.2).

246 The words "in the whole or part of" come into force June 20, 2025.

247 *Bill C-59 2024*, above note 64, s 254.

factors, the proposed suit is a reasonable and effective means to bring the case to court."[248] That test will require adaptation to the context of *Competition Act* private applications. For example, the third component may be less relevant given that this is a statutory private proceeding created by Parliament to provide for recourse against anti-competitive behaviour and as a complement to public enforcement, signalling that this is what was deemed by Parliament to be the most effective means to bring the matter forward.

The test applied by the Tribunal for standing based on substantial impact on the applicant's business is "whether the leave application is supported by sufficient credible evidence to give rise to a bona fide belief that the applicant may have been directly and substantially affected in the applicant's business by a reviewable practice, and that the practice in question could be subject to an order."[249] Justice Rothstein of the Federal Court of Appeal (as he then was) noted with respect to the latter part of the test:

> The threshold for an applicant obtaining leave is not a difficult one to meet. It need only provide sufficient credible evidence of what is alleged to give rise to a bona fide belief by the Tribunal. This is a lower standard of proof than proof on a balance of probabilities which will be the standard applicable to the decision on the merits.[250]

New entrants to the market face a challenge in cases such as refusal to supply, because they lack a track record from which to prove a substantial effect on their existing business. While projections can provide a foundation for an application, they must be based on credible evidence. The Court of Appeal upheld the Tribunal's rejection of projections when they disclosed only the "mere possibility" of substantial effect, were "speculative" and not sufficiently supported by "background or explanation as to how [they] were established."[251]

While the most active provision for applications to the Tribunal for leave under section 103.1 has been refusal to supply, such difficulties have made the leave requirement a significant hurdle. The success rate

---

248 *Canada (Attorney General) v Downtown Eastside Sex Workers United Against Violence Society*, 2012 SCC 45 at para 2.

249 *Symbol Technologies Canada ULC v Barcode Systems Inc*, 2004 FCA 339 at para 16, citing *National Capital News Canada v Canada (Speaker House of Commons)* (2002), 23 CPR (4th) 77 (CCT).

250 *Ibid* at para 17. See also *Safa Enterprises Inc v Imperial Tobacco Company Limited*, 2013 CACT 19 at para 15; *Stargrove Entertainment Inc v Universal Music Publishing Group Canada, [2015] CCTD 26.*

251 *CarGurus, Inc v Trader Corp*, 2017 FCA 181 at para 27, aff'g [2016] CCTD 15.

of leave applications in refusal to supply cases has historically been less than 50 percent.[252]

iv) Costs

As part of the 2002 amendments, the Tribunal was given the power to award costs.[253] The Tribunal has held that it has broad discretion under this provision consistent with the costs requirements of the *Federal Courts Rules* and has awarded costs against an unsuccessful section 103.1 applicant.[254]

v) Impact of Civil Actions on Tribunal Proceedings

In *B-Filer Inc v Bank of Nova Scotia*, the Tribunal held that the prior dismissal of a tort claim for the same conduct did not render a Tribunal application for refusal to supply *res judicata*, finding "the issues before the Tribunal are not the same as the issues that were before the Alberta court." The Tribunal also found that the claim was not subject to estoppel or an abuse of process because of the Tribunal's exclusive jurisdiction to deal with issues under the refusal to supply and vertical restraints provisions of the *Competition Act*.[255]

vi) Consent Orders

As in the case of applications brought by the Commissioner, private applicants can obtain an order from the Tribunal where the respondents consent, simply by filing the agreed terms for registration.[256] The 2024 amendments added provisions requiring any such agreement to be served on the Commissioner and permitting the Commissioner to apply to the Tribunal to vary or to rescind the agreement, which the Tribunal may do if it finds that the agreement "has or is likely to have anti-competitive effects."[257] This provides the Commissioner some ability to ensure that agreements reached to settle a private application do not, in resolving the dispute between the parties to the agreement, have broader anti-competitive effects which could prejudice the public interest. This is an important function, given that the Tribunal has no (since amendments in 2022) no supervisory role to refuse registration of a consent agreement as an order when the private applicant and respondent reach a settlement which they wish to register.

---

252 Brown, ed, above note 88 at 96 indicates that, to the year 2016, twenty refusal to supply applications for leave were filed and seven were successful.

253 *Competition Tribunal Act*, above note 126, s 8.1.

254 See, e.g., *B-Filer Inc v Bank of Nova Scotia*, [2007] CCTD 32.

255 *Ibid* at para 13.

256 *Competition Act*, above note 28, s 106.1.

257 *Bill C-59 2024*, above note 64, s 259. This authority comes into effect June 20, 2025.

3) Adjudication

a) The Courts

The federal and provincial courts, *inter alia*, receive requests for investigative orders and may hear and try criminal matters.[258] The Federal Court may also receive requests for judicial review; the Federal Court of Appeal hears appeals from the Federal Court and from the Competition Tribunal.[259] Private actions for damages under the statutory cause of action in section 36 of the Act may be brought in any court of competent jurisdiction, which includes the Federal Court.[260]

b) The Competition Tribunal

i) Jurisdiction

The Tribunal's jurisdiction covers the civil practices provisions in Part VIII of the *Competition Act*. Under those provisions, including such matters as mergers, abuse of dominant position, and vertical restraints, the Commissioner of Competition may challenge conduct and bring forward a case to the Tribunal. As discussed above, private parties can also initiate proceedings in respect of refusals to supply, resale price maintenance and other vertical practices with leave of the Tribunal.

The Tribunal is given the powers of a superior court of record in respect of proceedings before it, including the compulsion of evidence and witnesses. In *Chrysler Canada Ltd v Competition Tribunal*,[261] the Supreme Court confirmed that these powers include the power to sanction for contempt of the Tribunal's orders. The Court found that the Tribunal's powers extended to the enforcement of an order against Chrysler Canada related to Chrysler's refusal to supply automotive parts.

The Competition Tribunal's jurisdiction was enlarged by the 2009 amendments creating new civil practices. A new civil agreements provision permits a case-by-case analysis by the Tribunal to determine whether an agreement results in a "substantial prevention or lessening of competition."[262] The criminal predatory pricing provision was repealed and left

---

258 *Competition Act*, above note 28, ss 67 and 73.

259 *Federal Courts Act*, RSC 1985, c F-7, ss 18 and 28; *Competition Tribunal Act*, above note 126, s 13.

260 *Competition Act*, above note 28, s 36(1), (3).

261 *Chrysler Canada Ltd v Canada (Competition Tribunal)*, [1992] 2 SCR 394 [*Chrysler Canada*].

262 Bill C-10, *An Act to implement certain provisions of the budget tabled in Parliament on January 27, 2009 and related fiscal measures*, 40th Parl, 2d Sess, 2009; passed as *Budget Implementation Act, 2009*, above note 61. See chapters 6, 8, and 9.

to consideration under the existing abuse of dominance provision on the same "substantial prevention or lessening of competition" standard.[263] Resale price maintenance was decriminalized and made subject to a new civil practice, reviewable by the Tribunal where it is "likely to have an adverse effect on competition in a market."[264] The 2009 amendments therefore carried on the trend of having those provisions which require a case-by-case economic assessment addressed before the expert Competition Tribunal, and removing or simplifying the criminal provisions.

The 2022 amendments permitted private enforcement of the abuse of dominance provision, as noted above,[265] with remedies available expanded in 2022 and 2023 to include administrative monetary penalties of the greater of $25,000,000 or "three times the value of the benefit derived from the anti-competitive practice, or, if that amount cannot be reasonably determined, 3% of the person's annual worldwide gross revenues."[266] The 2024 amendments added awards to recover the benefits derived from the conduct at issue by the private applicants and, potentially, other persons affected.[267] In 2024, private applications were also made possible in the case of the civil deceptive marketing and the civil agreements provisions.[268]

Costs against the Commissioner were prohibited in 2024, except when "necessary to maintain confidence in the administration of justice" or where failure to award such costs "would have a substantial adverse effect on the other party's ability to carry on business."[269]

ii) Structure

The Competition Tribunal is a specialized civil tribunal with the expertise and other tools enabling it to conduct a weighing and analysis of economic factors. The *Competition Tribunal Act* lays out the structure of the Tribunal. It is composed of up to six judges of the Federal Court and eight lay members. Both groups are appointed by the Governor in Council.[270] No particular background is specified for the lay members, although the Tribunal website notes that current members "provide

263 See Canada, Competition Bureau, *Abuse of Dominance Enforcement Guidelines* (7 March 2019) at paras 59–61, online: www.competitionbureau.gc.ca/eic/site/cb-bc.nsf/eng/04420.html.

264 *Competition Act*, above note 28, s 76.

265 *Bill C-19 2022*, above note 62, s 266.

266 *Ibid*, s 262.

267 *Bill C-59 2024*, above note 64, s 244 effective June 20, 2025.

268 *Bill C-59 2024*, above note 64, s 254, effective June 20, 2025.

269 *Bill C-59 2024*, above note 64, s 266.

270 See *Competition Tribunal Act*, above note 126, s 3(2).

expertise based on their individual backgrounds in economics, business, finance, accounting or marketing."[271]

The Chairperson of the Tribunal is designated by the Governor in Council from among the judicial members. Only judicial members may make determinations of questions of law in proceedings before the Tribunal. On the other hand, questions of fact and mixed fact and law may be determined by all members.[272] The scheme ensures judicial expertise is brought to the legal issues before the Tribunal. Lay members are involved in those matters for which their expertise qualifies them most strongly: fact-related determinations, which may involve an appreciation of economic evidence, statistics, and particular analytical approaches.[273]

Hearings are presided over by judicial members. Hearing panels for applications are composed of three to five members, with at least one lay member.[274] Reflecting a Parliamentary desire that the Tribunal's rules of evidence be more flexible than those of the criminal courts (which were perceived to have created problems for proof and enforcement of the law), the *Competition Tribunal Act* states in subsection 9(2):

> All proceedings before the Tribunal shall be dealt with as informally and expeditiously as the circumstances and considerations of fairness permit.[275]

Hearings before the Competition Tribunal have in general more closely resembled those of a civil trial than a hearing before an administrative tribunal, such as the Canadian Radio-television and Telecommunications Commission (CRTC). The Competition Tribunal is a more

---

271 Canada, Competition Tribunal, *Member Appointments* (20 March 2020), online: www.ct-tc.gc.ca/en/tribunal/members.html. The *Competition Tribunal Act*, above note 126, s 3(3) provides for an "advisory council to advise the Minister with respect to appointment of lay members," which council is to be "knowledgeable in economics, industry or public affairs." However, the appointment of the council is discretionary and based upon a review of Orders in Council (Canada, Orders in Council Division, *Orders in Council Search*, online: https://orders-in-council.canada.ca), no such council had been appointed as of 1 July 2020.

272 *Competition Tribunal Act*, above note 126, s 12.

273 *Canada (Director of Investigation and Research) v Southam Inc*, [1997] 1 SCR 748 at para 53: "over questions of fact and of mixed law and fact, the judicial members share their jurisdiction with the lay members. . . . This makes sense because, as I have observed, the expertise of the lay members is invaluable in the application of the principles of competition law" [*Southam*].

274 *Competition Tribunal Act*, above note 126, s 10.

275 The Tribunal has made *Rules* by regulation pursuant to the Act: *Competition Tribunal Rules*, SOR/2008-141.

court-like body than the one envisaged by the Economic Council in 1969. For example, while suggesting that it retain some resemblance to a court, the Council recommended a tribunal possessing a "small expert staff of its own . . . to provide factual information and analysis . . . which was not forthcoming from any other source."[276] It was also to have a role in "education and persuasion" through such means as "issuing general guidelines . . . in respect of certain types of merger or trade practices."[277] These functions have more in common with a regulatory agency (such as the CRTC) or inquisitorial body (such as the European Commission Directorate-General for Competition) than a court. These are not the kinds of functions currently carried out by the Competition Tribunal.

iii) Appeals and Standard of Review

Appeals from the Tribunal are made to the Federal Court of Appeal. Leave from the Court of Appeal is required from appeals raising questions of fact.[278] In *Canada (Director of Investigation and Research) v Southam Inc*, the Tribunal's determination of whether or not the Vancouver daily newspapers were in the same competitive market as regional newspapers was characterized as a "question of mixed fact and law."[279] The Supreme Court of Canada had to decide to what extent judicial deference should be accorded to the Tribunal's decisions. Justice Iacobucci held that a court hearing an appeal from the Tribunal should not intervene on a question such as the assessment of market definition unless the decision is unreasonable. That standard "instructs reviewing courts to accord considerable weight to the views of tribunals about matters with respect to which they have significant expertise."[280] Under its more recent formulation by the Supreme Court, a reasonable decision evidences "an internally coherent and rational chain of analysis" and "is justified in relation to the facts and law that constrain the decision maker."[281] In applying the reasonableness standard in *Southam*, the Court made it clear that it did not consider that it had to agree with the Tribunal's conclusions to sustain its decision.

Determinations of law by the Tribunal, such as statutory interpretation, are subject to appeal to the Federal Court of Appeal.[282] The standard

276 *Interim Report* 1969, above note 91 at 111.
277 *Ibid* at 192.
278 *Competition Tribunal Act*, above note 126, s 13(2).
279 *Southam*, above note 273.
280 *Ibid* at para 62.
281 *Canada (Minister of Citizenship and Immigration) v Vavilov*, 2019 SCC 65 at para 85.
282 *Competition Tribunal Act*, above note 126, s 13(1).

is correctness, meaning that the appellate court accords no deference to the decision under review.[283]

iv) Explaining the Tribunal's Structure

Why is the Competition Tribunal structured as it is, essentially a hybrid somewhere between a civil court and an administrative tribunal? In considering this question, it is useful to think of a spectrum of alternative structures for adjudication or final determination, with institutions which most closely resemble the ordinary courts at one end, and those which involve more political decision making on the other.

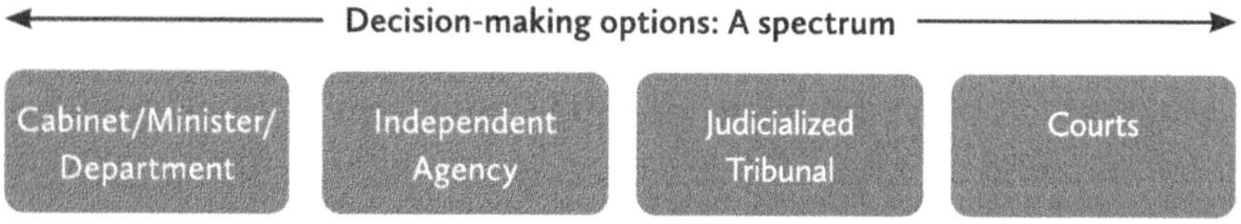

FIGURE 2.9.

At the judicial end of the spectrum are the regular courts, with decisions made by judges, full procedural rights afforded to parties, the strict application of the rule of law and precedent, and judicial review or appeal confined to errors of law or palpable and overriding errors of fact. At the other end, decisions are made by, or through, politically accountable persons or their staff, there are few procedural rights, and precedents are not binding. In between are a range of possible models which mix some or all of these features. An agency such as the CRTC, for example, is independent from any government department, but has a large specialized staff and Commissioners drawn from a range of expertise relevant to its mandate and thus bears some similarity to a department.

One of the key factors mentioned by the Economic Council of Canada in its 1969 *Interim Report* which affects the position on this spectrum of a competition law tribunal was the need to leave certain conduct, such as mergers and abuse of dominance, to a case-by-case assessment governed by tests that involve balancing sometimes complex economic evidence. The applicable tests, such as "substantial lessening of competition," are written in flexible language to permit the adjudicator to screen out mergers or other conduct which are *de minimis* or which have a beneficial impact on competition. These tests must also tolerate the differing assessments necessary when applied across varying industries. The *Competition Act* is a law of general application and therefore can

283 *Tervita Corp v Canada (Commissioner of Competition)*, [2015] 1 SCR 161 at para 34 [*Tervita*]. Justice Abella dissented on this point; see paras 169–80.

apply to virtually any market, product, or service. For these reasons, it is simply not possible to spell out in advance or in great detail precisely what conduct may be harmful; it is the effect of the conduct, based on structural and behavioural analysis in a given case, which must be assessed.

The current merger provisions also require the Tribunal to assess whether a merger with a clearly anti-competitive impact should nonetheless be permitted because of counterbalancing efficiencies. The greater procedural flexibility and expertise of a specialized tribunal may accommodate this kind of balancing test better than the regular courts. An expert tribunal can use its judgment in the reception of economic evidence and its familiarity with specialized concepts and terminology to assist at getting at the facts more quickly, efficiently, and accurately. The Supreme Court of Canada confirmed the specialized nature of the legislative scheme in an appeal from a merger determination by the Tribunal in *Southam*:

> The aims of the Act are more "economic" than strictly "legal." The "efficiency and adaptability of the Canadian economy" and the relationship among Canadian companies and their foreign competitors are matters that business women and men and economists are better able to understand than is a typical judge. Perhaps recognizing this, Parliament created a specialized Competition Tribunal and invested it with responsibility for the administration of the civil part of the *Competition Tribunal Act*.[284]

The Competition Tribunal seeks to marry the benefits of a specialized body with lay membership chosen for its expertise with the greater certainty, known procedures, and judicial decision making found in the Federal Court. The government's *Guide* accompanying the 1986 amendments explained the rationale for a judicialized tribunal in a passage worth citing at length:

> The Economic Council of Canada's 1969 Interim Report on Competition Policy stated that any shift of competition policy legislation out of the criminal law should be accompanied by the formation of a specialized tribunal to adjudicate these matters.
>
> The issue of adjudication of competition matters has been the subject of much discussion over the long history of competition law reform. Many interested parties have proposed reliance on the ordinary courts to adjudicate competition matters. One factor often cited in support of

---

284 *Southam*, above note 273 at para 48. See also *Chrysler Canada*, above note 261 at 406.

> the courts is their ability to produce consistent results with clear and full rights of appeal. Others have expressed a preference for the use of a specialized tribunal because it would provide greater potential for expertise in economics and business, and would permit more scope for response by the decision maker to social and economic change. In particular, lay experts are better able to reflect the reality of the business world.
>
> On balance, the Government believes it is more appropriate that these matters be adjudicated by a highly judicialized tribunal. This hybrid will allow the use of expert lay persons as well as judges in the decision-making process. Nevertheless, the Government agrees that it is very important to have in the law an adjudication system that ensures the impartiality, due process and certainty which is associated with the courts.[285]

The Competition Tribunal's court-like structure and processes have led to questions and concerns concerning the cost and delay required to obtain a final ruling.[286] For example, the prospect of spending several years and substantial legal costs in litigation can lead businesses to abandon transactions when challenged by the Commissioner, regardless of the merits of a challenge under the Act.[287] This has contributed to the lack of contested cases being heard before the Tribunal.[288] The level of case load has in turn fuelled concern that the Tribunal may not easily develop or refine its expertise in competition law matters.[289]

The difficulty is finding an alternative adjudicative structure which can achieve greater expedition while supplying the fairness and certainty

---

285 Canada, Consumer and Corporate Affairs, *Competition Law Amendment, A Guide* (Ottawa, Consumer and Corporate Affairs, 1985) at 10–11.

286 See Neil A Campbell, Hudson N Janisch & Michael J Trebilcock, "Rethinking the Role of the Competition Tribunal" (1997) 76 *Canadian Bar Review* 297.

287 See, e.g., William T Stanbury, "The Merger Review Process in Canada: Information and the Structure of Incentives" (1995) 16 *Canadian Competition Record* (no 3) 73.

288 Edward M Iacobucci & Michael J Trebilcock, "Critical Reflections on the Institutional Design of Canadian Competition Policy" (2011) 24 *Canadian Competition Law Review* 39 at 42 [Iacobucci & Trebilcock, "Critical Reflections"]:

> The consensus among interviewees, however, is that timeliness of disposition is still a major concern with Tribunal proceedings in contested cases. It is possible, for example, that parties are especially reluctant to take more complex cases to the Tribunal because of doubts about timeliness, which may explain the continued consensus concern about timeliness despite the clearly observed improvement in the timeliness of Tribunal decision-making recently.

289 Michael Trebilcock & Edward Iacobucci, "Designing Competition Law Institutions" (2002) 25 *World Competition* 361; Iacobucci & Trebilcock, "Critical Reflections," above note 288.

that a judicialized body offers.[290] If the authority to approve conduct was given to a body capable of dispensing speedy summary justice, but without according the procedural safeguards, evidentiary rules, and appeal rights available through the Tribunal,[291] other concerns, such as arbitrariness or lack of procedural fairness, would inevitably be raised.[292] A move toward an "integrated agency model" along the lines of the European Commission, in which investigation and first-level adjudication are married in the same body,[293] may lead to a greater body of published decisions but could raise the kinds of concerns, such as predictability, which surfaced in the 1970s in Canada with the business community's rejection of a more inquisitorial civil tribunal in Bill C-256.[294] It is also not clear that an inquisitorial system, with added appeals of first-level administrative decisions to the courts, would lead to faster final determinations.[295] Giving the Tribunal a more proactive role to issue guidelines or to

---

290 Iacobucci & Trebilcock, "Critical Reflections," above note 288 at 46:

> The difficulty for reform is that while there is a consensus on the shortcomings of the *status quo*, there is no such agreement over fundamental aspects of reform. In particular, while our interviews suggest that there is general support for the idea of a multi-person commission, there is division over its particular role, as well as the institutional framework for review of its decisions.

291 As noted above, appeal may be brought on questions of law to the Federal Court of Appeal on a correctness standard of review. Appeals on questions of fact and mixed fact and law require leave; reasonableness is the standard of review in such appeals (*Tervita*, above note 283, paras 34–39).

292 See, e.g., the kind of challenge made, and rejected, in *Canada (Commissioner of Competition) v Canada Pipe Company Ltd*, [2003] CCTD 24.

293 The European Commission, through the initiation of the Competition Directorate, investigates, enforces, and adjudicates all issues relating to competition law within its jurisdiction (hence an integrated agency model). The case team writes the draft of the decision, albeit usually after a hearing and after much vetting within the Competition directorate, by the directorate's Legal Service, and by a committee of member-state experts. The Commission does not sit as an adjudicating body. Appeal lies to the European General Court, and further to the European Court of Justice on matters of law.

294 See Section B(3)(d)(ii), above in this chapter.

295 In reviewing policy options for competition issues in digital markets, the UK Competition and Markets Authority observed in *Online Platforms and Digital Advertising* (1 July 2020), online: www.gov.uk/cma-cases/online-platforms-and-digital-advertising-market-study#final-report at 330:

> Of those cases that have been brought by the European Commission against Google in recent years, *Android* took more than five years, *Shopping* took more than seven years and *AdSense* took nine years, not including their appeal processes. The CMA's most complex competition enforcement cases also tend to take several years to reach a final decision. Such timescales create a material risk that, even if a platform is ultimately found to have acted

participate in evidentiary collection and assembly, as the Economic Council suggested, may also affect its perceived independence and impartiality as a fact finder. Thus, it may be hard to improve on the compromise reflected in the structure of the Competition Tribunal, even though it is a more judicialized body than the Economic Council envisioned in 1969.

The Tribunal has taken steps both to streamline its rules of procedure and to adopt an expedited timetable for hearing matters.[296] Permitting a streamlined consent order process through a 2002 amendment has also introduced greater expedition and certainty, and some transparency, to settlements achieved between the Commissioner and respondents.[297] Efforts toward procedural and other improvements are likely to be ongoing, as the complexity of the issues in this area of the law will continue to create tensions between the goals of expedition and fairness under the current adjudicative structure.[298]

D. CONCLUSION

For almost a century from the first legislation in 1889, Canadian competition law was confined to the constitutional straightjacket of the criminal law. Criminal prohibitions governed not only conduct seen as morally reprehensible, such as price fixing, but other commercial behaviour, such as mergers and monopoly, which required a case-by-case

---

anti-competitively, the harm to competition and consumers will have become irreversible before such a conclusion is reached.

296 Canada, Competition Tribunal, *Practice Direction Regarding an Expedited Proceeding Process Before the Tribunal* (January 2019), online: https://ct-tc.gc.ca/en/procedure/practice/expedited-proceeding.html:

> The Tribunal considers that a period of five (5) to six (6) months between the filing of a Notice of Application ("NOA") and the commencement of the hearing on the merits will typically be a reasonable timeline for the Expedited Process, subject in each case to the nature of the particular application.

297 See Chapter 5, Section F(2)(c). Transparency is limited to the filing of the agreed-upon consent order and publication on the Tribunal's website, and any public statement or backgrounder released by the Commissioner.

298 In *Canada (Commissioner of Competition) v Parrish & Heimbecker, Limited*, [2020] CCTD 1, the parties to a merger opposed an expedited schedule, and the Tribunal held:

> [T]he Commissioner has not persuaded the Tribunal that using the Expedited Process is a reasonable and advisable option in light of the circumstances of this specific matter and the considerations of fairness, or that the period of three to four months that could be gained with the Expedited Process option justifies imposing the Expedited Process against the strong objection of P&H.

assessment of their prejudicial impact on the economy to determine whether a remedy was justified. Such an assessment was unsuited to the criminal law courts, which lack economic expertise and flexible remedial powers. The result was an ineffective regime that provided little protection against increasing concentration of the economy or abusive or exclusionary practices by dominant firms.

While there was a gradual improvement in the authority and sophistication of competition law enforcement with the first permanent agency created in the 1920s, followed by greater enforcement powers and resources in the 1950s, federal authority to pass competition prohibitions on a non-criminal law foundation remained uncertain into the 1980s. It was only after the Economic Council of Canada issued a comprehensive set of recommendations for reform in 1969 that Parliament in 1976 took the first tentative steps by adopting provisions for civilly reviewable practices, including refusal to supply, exclusive dealing, and tied selling. A more comprehensive package followed in 1986, making mergers and abuse of dominance reviewable before the new civil Competition Tribunal, using flexible tests focused on the impacts of these practices in competition. The Supreme Court finally placed civil competition laws on a firm constitutional foundation in *General Motors of Canada Ltd v City National Leasing* in 1989. A further important step in implementing the Economic Council's template occurred with the 2009 amendments, which repealed the criminal predatory pricing, price discrimination, and resale price maintenance offences and expanded the civilly reviewable practices. Significantly, the criminal conspiracy prohibition was simplified to remove the need for the courts to engage in any economic assessment of price fixing, market sharing, or supply limitation agreements.

With reduced reliance on the criminal law and greater use of civil provisions reviewable before an expert tribunal, the current *Competition Act* prohibitions are better tailored to assessment by the adjudicative bodies that enforce them. Tensions and areas of potential improvement, however, remain. For example, the trial-focused adjudicative model adopted in the quasi-judicial Competition Tribunal (a hybrid body composed of Federal Court judges and lay members) continues to raise concerns, as it does in other areas of civil litigation, relating to the time and cost needed to obtain a resolution. On the other hand, efforts to adopt a more expeditious agency-based model in the 1970s were forcefully rejected by the business community as likely to produce uncertainty and an unpredictable business climate, suggesting that any improvements may require changes within the existing adjudicative architecture rather than moving toward a European-style agency model.

An emerging area of enforcement is private civil damages actions. Aided by advances in the important procedural tool of class proceedings, which permits groups of plaintiffs such as consumers harmed by price fixing or misleading representations to seek redress, such actions hold the promise of providing a helpful complement to public enforcement. Recent decisions by the Supreme Court permitting class actions by indirect and umbrella purchasers may facilitate such proceedings.

Since their first limited introduction in 2002, private applications to the Competition Tribunal have not generated the hoped-for body of jurisprudence or remedies for private parties. This has been due to a number of factors, including fairly stringent leave requirements, and the tests in the underlying substantive law, which mean that relief is either uncertain or that remedies are limited (confined as they were to a remedial order rather than compensatory damages).

As recommended by a House of Commons Committee in 2002,[299] private applications were finally expanded in 2022 to cover abuse of dominance[300] and in 2024 to permit applications addressing deceptive marketing and anti-competitive agreements.[301] These amendments also provided the Tribunal authority to make various monetary awards. The leave requirement was also modified in the 2024 amendments to introduce a public interest test and to lessen the alternative leave test to require that the alleged anti-competitive conduct only affect *part of* the applicant's business. These changes may incent private enforcement, yield more work for and further jurisprudence from the Tribunal and provide additional remedies to promote dynamic markets. If this occurs, private applications would provide an important complement to enforcement by the Competition Bureau.

---

299 *A Plan to Modernize Canada's Competition Regime*, above note 230 at 50.
300 *Bill C-19 2022*, above note 62, s 266.
301 *Bill C-59 2024*, above note 64, s 254.

CHAPTER 3

CANADIAN COMPETITION LAW OBJECTIVES AND FOUNDATIONAL ECONOMIC CONCEPTS

> The purpose of this Act is to maintain and encourage competition in Canada in order to promote the efficiency and adaptability of the Canadian economy, in order to expand opportunities for Canadian participation in world markets while at the same time recognizing the role of foreign competition in Canada, in order to ensure that small and medium-sized enterprises have an equitable opportunity to participate in the Canadian economy and in order to provide consumers with competitive prices and product choices.
>
> —Section 1.1 of the *Competition Act*

A. INTRODUCTION

This chapter examines the objectives of Canadian competition law, their origins, their content and their implications. It begins by considering the legislative "pole star," the purpose clause, above. The discussion turns to a brief survey of the main historical objectives. The modern objectives are then reviewed, beginning with economic efficiency, a central focus in the current legislation. That review provides an opportunity to examine the concept of efficiency, as well as to provide an overview of some of the key economic models and concepts which are applied or referred to in later chapters. The chapter then closes by looking into two clusters of objectives, distribution of wealth and concern for economic power/

business equity, which have played a diminishing role with the evolution of Canadian competition law over time, but which are still part of its fabric, content, and context.

B. THE PURPOSE CLAUSE

1) Interpretative Role of a Purpose Clause and Objectives

The Supreme Court of Canada has stated that in construing a statutory provision, one must read its words "in their entire context and in their grammatical and ordinary sense harmoniously with the scheme of the Act, the object of the Act, and the intention of Parliament."[1] A purpose clause provides interpretative guidance which carries "the authority and weight of duly enacted law," and context for the entire Act.[2] In *Canada (Commissioner of Competition) v Superior Propane Inc*, the Federal Court of Appeal examined section 1.1 and observed that such clauses "are integral to the statute and can carry as much weight as its other sections."[3] The Court noted, however, that "the wording of a particular provision in a statute may be so clear and precise that it must be regarded as overriding an ambiguous purpose clause."

A purpose clause, like that found in the *Competition Act*, may contain a number of disparate objectives. In *Superior Propane*, Evans JA of the Federal Court of Appeal observed, "[a]s is not uncommon in such clauses, not all of the stated purposes or objectives can be served at the same time, nor are all necessarily consistent." The objectives must thus be weighed and balanced in applying the legislation to particular cases.[4]

Even if we cannot identify a single, unifying objective for a particular provision, we may be able to refine our understanding of how a given interpretation has an impact on the realization of different goals and objectives, to develop greater clarity in assessing the outcomes available, and the nature or content of the trade-offs between objectives that may sometimes be necessary. As Robert Bork noted in his influential treatise on antitrust:

---

1 *R v Sharpe*, [2001] 1 SCR 45 at para 33; *Canadian Foundation for Children, Youth and the Law v Canada (Attorney General)*, [2004] 1 SCR 76 at para 20. See also *Re Rizzo and Rizzo Shoes Ltd*, [1998] 1 SCR 27 at para 21.

2 Ruth Sullivan, *Sullivan on the Construction of Statutes*, 6th ed (Toronto: LexisNexis, 2014) at §§14.39, 14.41.

3 *Canada (Commissioner of Competition) v Superior Propane Inc*, 2001 FCA 104 at paras 106–7 [*Propane FCA1*], leave to appeal to SCC refused [2001] SCCA 252.

4 *Propane FCA1*, above note 3 at para 105.

Only when the issue of goals has been settled is it possible to frame a coherent body of substantive rules.[5]

Examining the objectives of legislation can also provide parameters which may help guide the design or application of a legislative provision or rule. In the case of competition law, economics is the discipline that has increasingly provided a framework for determining how the guiding principles and rules should be designed and applied.

During the *Competition Act* amendment process that gathered steam in 2021, differing views were expressed on whether the purpose clause was in need of reform. One commentator suggested that section 1.1. "is both overinclusive, in that it includes a grab-bag of occasionally conflicting and sometimes puzzling goals, and underinclusive, in that it includes specific concern for some matters but not others, despite their similarity on relevant dimensions." He advocated making efficiency the sole purpose of the Act, on the basis that it would make it "clear and more predictable, [leaving] the promotion of non-economic objectives to other regimes."[6] Other views expressed during the consultation process "ranged from general calls to consider 'fairness,' 'inclusive growth,' and 'political and social problems,' to more specific requests to include mention of items such as the environment, climate change and labour."[7]

The Bureau favoured leaving section 1.1 unchanged on the basis that "[i]t makes sense for the Act's purpose clause to be cast broadly. This is because competition law embodies a broader range of economic values than just efficiency."[8] In the end, no changes were made to the clause.

5 Robert H Bork, *The Antitrust Paradox: A Policy at War with Itself* (New York: Basic Books, 1978) at 50 [Bork].

6 Edward M Iacobucci, "Examining the Canadian Competition Act in the Digital Era" (27 September 2021) at 49 and 72.

7 Canada, ISED, *Future of Canada's Competition Policy Consultation – What We Heard Report*, 20 Sept 2023 at s. 9–10, online: https://ised-isde.canada.ca/site/strategic-policy-sector/en/marketplace-framework-policy/competition-policy/consultation-future-competition-policy-canada/future-canadas-competition-policy-consultation-what-we-heard-report.

8 Competition Bureau Canada, "Examining the Canadian *Competition Act* in the Digital Era, Submission by the Competition Bureau" (8 February 2022) [Bureau Submissions 2022] at s. 1.1, online: https://ised-isde.canada.ca/site/competition-bureau-canada/en/how-we-foster-competition/promotion-and-advocacy/regulatory-adviceinterventions-competition-bureau/examining-canadian-competition-act-digital-era.

2) Content of the Purpose Clause

a) The Meaning of "Competition"

A glance at section 1.1 of the *Competition Act* above reveals that the legislation's overall purpose is "to maintain and encourage competition in Canada"—something that comes as no surprise in an Act with this title. But what does "competition" mean? The Supreme Court of Canada in the 1997 decision *Canada (Director of Investigation and Research) v Southam Inc*, considered the purpose clause of the Act in the context of an appeal from the Competition Tribunal's assessment of a merger of Vancouver newspapers and concluded that "[t]he aims of this Act are more 'economic' than they are strictly 'legal.'"[9] Even taking into account this economic context, the word "competition" can still have a range of meanings. While others are possible, three meanings of the term which appear most relevant in this context are: (1) competition as a form of *behaviour or process*, (2) competition as a *market structure or economic outcome*, and (3) competition viewed through the lens of *economic freedom*.

First, "competition" can refer to "rivalry"[10] or "a striving for the custom and business of people in the marketplace,"[11] i.e., a form of *behaviour*. Rivalry involves the jockeying for competitive position, carried out by independent players in an attempt to gain a competitive advantage over others. American Justice Learned Hand wrote in *United States v Aluminum Co of America* that "immunity from competition is a narcotic, and rivalry is a stimulant, to industrial progress."[12] Adam Smith in *The Wealth of Nations* in 1776 referred to "a competition" for trade, which would result in a market achieving a natural price to which commodities "are continually gravitating."[13] In this sense, competition is a *process* which

9 *Canada (Director of Investigation and Research) v Southam Inc*, [1997] 1 SCR 748 at para 48 [*Southam*].

10 *The Shorter Oxford English Dictionary* (Oxford: Oxford University Press, 1973) at 382.

11 Richard Whish & David Bailey, *Competition Law*, 9th ed (Oxford: Oxford University Press, 2018) at 4. See also Harry S Gerla, "Restoring Rivalry as a Central Concept in Antitrust Law" (1996) 75:2 *Nebraska Law Review* 209.

12 *United States v Aluminum Co of America*, 148 F2d 416 (2d Cir 1945) at 427 [*Alcoa*].

13 Adam Smith, *An Inquiry into the Nature and Causes of the Wealth of Nations* (London: Dent & Sons, 1910), vol 1 at 51 and 48–55; Figure 3.1 is the title page of that work. As Mark Blaug, "Is Competition Such a Good Thing? Static Efficiency versus Dynamic Efficiency" (2001) 19 *Review of Industrial Organization* 37 at 38 points out, Smith used the word "competition" with the article "a" or "the," in the sense of a "behavioural activity"; a "race."

can yield benefits, such as lower prices and better quality products.[14] The process of competition, which includes change brought about through innovation, is sometimes described with the amorphous term "dynamic competition."[15]

Second, the idea of "competition" can involve a competitive *market structure or economic outcome*.[16] As examined in the next section, economics has developed models or paradigms, including the polar opposites of the "perfectly competitive" market and "monopoly," to assess performance in terms of such measures as efficiency and the impact on social welfare.[17] These models are usually framed using static or short-term time horizons, in contrast to the more long-term or fluid time periods used in the conception of competition as a dynamic process mentioned above. One important measure used by economists to evaluate these market structures and their impacts on society is the benchmark of "market power." Market power (discussed at greater length in chapters 4 and 5[18]) refers to the ability to raise prices and alter other terms of trade from those prevailing in a competitive market. American antitrust scholar Robert Bork saw competition in these terms, as a "state of affairs" involving "low prices, innovation, [and] choice among different products."[19]

FIGURE 3.1. The title page of *An Inquiry into the Nature and Causes of the Wealth of Nations* (1910)

---

14 See, e.g., *Morrison v Murray Biscuit Co*, 797 F2d 1430 (7th Cir 1986) at 1437, Posner J: "The purpose of antitrust law, at least as articulated in the modern cases, is to protect the competitive process as a means of promoting economic efficiency."

15 Maurice E Stucke, "What is Competition?," ch 2 in Daniel Zimmer, ed, *The Goals of Competition Law* (Cheltenham: Edward Elgar, 2012) at 33; for an overview of the different meanings of dynamic competition, starting with Schumpeter, see J Ellig & D Lin, "A Taxonomy of Dynamic Competition Theories," ch 1 in Jerry Ellig, ed, *Dynamic Competition and Public Policy* (Cambridge: Cambridge University Press, 2001).

16 Christopher Green, *Canadian Industrial Organization and Policy*, 3d ed (Toronto: McGraw-Hill, 1990) at 58 [Green].

17 See the discussion below in this chapter at Section 2(b).

18 See Chapter 4, Section B and Chapter 5, Section C.

19 Bork, above note 5 at 61. Bork saw competition as furthering "consumer welfare" in the sense of "social welfare": see Herbert J Hovenkamp, "On the Meaning of Antitrust's Consumer Welfare Principle" [2020] *Faculty Scholarship at Penn Law* 2152, online: https://scholarship.law.upenn.edu/faculty_scholarship/2152.

Finally, the promotion of competition can invoke the protection of *economic freedom*—consumers' freedom to choose, businesses' freedom to trade and to compete without undue restraint, and free access to markets, for example.[20] Focusing on competition in this sense can lead to an examination of the impact of the accumulation, use, or abuse of economic power on such freedoms.

All three conceptions of competition have played a role in the history and development of competition law in Canada to some degree. In recent decades, there has been a greater emphasis on the view that competition is primarily a means for promoting economic welfare and efficiency, and for addressing market power. The concept of dynamic competition and the role of innovation have also assumed importance in terms of how competition is understood and analyzed.

b) Competition Is a Means to Realize Other Objectives

Competition is, however, not the ultimate purpose of the legislation. It is only a means for achieving the four further objectives set out in section 1.1. As held by Sexton J in *Premier Career Management*, a case dealing with the misleading marketing provisions, "the goal of the Act is not to foster competition for its own sake, but rather to promote derivative economic objectives, such as efficiency, global participation, high quality products, and competitive prices."[21] The four ultimate objectives bear repeating in full, with some emphasis on key terms:

1) "to promote the ***efficiency and adaptability*** of the Canadian economy";
2) "to ***expand opportunities for Canadian participation in world markets*** while at the same time recognizing the role of foreign competition in Canada";
3) "to ensure that ***small and medium-sized enterprises have an equitable opportunity*** to participate in the Canadian economy"; and
4) "to provide consumers with ***competitive prices and product choices***."

These are varied objectives. Tensions may be created in applying them in certain situations. An example is a merger that (1) results in

---

20 *United States v Topco Associates, Inc*, 405 US 596 (1972) at 610 [*Topco*]: antitrust laws are "as important to the preservation of economic freedom and our free-enterprise system as the *Bill of Rights* is to the protection of our fundamental personal freedoms." See also Tim Hazeldine, "Rationalism Rebuffed? Lessons from Modern Canadian and New Zealand Competition Policy" (1998) 13 *Review of Industrial Organization* 243 at 254–55 [Hazeldine]; Thomas B Leary, "Freedom as the Core Value of Antitrust in the New Millennium" (2001) 68 *Antitrust Law Journal* 545.

21 *Canada (Commissioner of Competition) v Premier Career Management Group Corp*, 2009 FCA 295 at para 60.

efficiencies which lower the merged firms' costs, but also (2) increases prices to, and reduces choice for, consumers. How should competition law deal with such a merger if, for example, the bulk of the wealth received from the efficiencies is collected by the owners of the merging companies, and consumers are faced with a substantial price increase? Does permitting such a transaction for the sake of efficiency further the overall objectives of the legislation?

Recognizing that Canada's relatively small and open economy may benefit from transactions which permit firms to take advantage of scale and other economies, Parliament inserted an "efficiencies defence" into the merger provisions which mandates a balancing of efficiencies against the anti-competitive effects of a merger.[22] The Federal Court of Appeal interpreted the provision in *Canada (Commissioner of Competition) v Superior Propane Inc*,[23] a case involving a nation-wide merger of Canada's two largest propane suppliers, Superior and ICG. The Court concluded that the Competition Tribunal could not, as a matter of law, completely exclude the impacts of the merger on consumer income from the balancing exercise, and overruled the Tribunal for having done so. On a re-hearing by the Tribunal, the merger was nonetheless permitted to proceed. The Tribunal held that the efficiencies still outweighed the anti-competitive effects, even taking into account the impact of price increases from the merger on identified vulnerable consumers.

The fact that such a merger was permitted, even though it was found to reduce competition substantially and create monopoly conditions in a large number of local markets across Canada, shows that the interpretation and application of the legislation may sometimes involve difficult trade-offs among differing objectives and interests.

Not all anti-competitive conduct involves these kinds of tensions between objectives. An example is "naked" price fixing, which merely restricts output and raises prices. A price-fixing cartel will also often increase costs where its members expend resources to manage it or to police compliance.[24] Recognizing their clearly prejudicial nature, Parliament in 2009 amended the criminal conspiracy provision to prohibit agreements to fix prices, to share markets, and to limit production, removing the need for any case-specific assessment of their anti-competitive effect.[25]

---

22 *Competition Act*, RSC 1985, c C-34, s 96 [*Competition Act* or Act].

23 *Propane FCA1*, above note 3.

24 See Chapter 6.

25 The amended conspiracy provision covers collusion, which is "naked" price fixing, market sharing, or production limitation; that is, agreements on such matters that are not ancillary to a broader agreement or arrangement.

These examples illustrate that the objectives set out in the purpose clause may come into play in different ways for different provisions and different conduct. The level of legislative guidance also varies between provisions. The Act often permits considerable interpretative scope. There remains room for debate about what certain objectives mean, whether they are complete, and which ones should be given priority.[26] Canada's distinct history, geography, and our relatively small economy are among the factors that have influenced, and will continue to influence, the evolution and application of the objectives of the legislation.

C. HISTORICAL CANADIAN COMPETITION LAW OBJECTIVES

1) Shifting Objectives over Time

As seen in Chapter 2, Canada's first anti-combines legislation was first adopted in 1889, but the initial legislation was largely ineffective. It took almost a hundred years until a process of meaningful substantive reform took place. Several rounds of amendments since 1976 shifted the direction of Canadian competition law toward a more consistent focus on the economic and efficiency-related effects of anti-competitive practices, consistent with the guidance of the Economic Council of Canada in its seminal *Interim Report on Competition Policy*.[27]

The 1986 amendments added the purpose clause. The government's 1985 *Guide* to those amendments noted at its outset that the *Interim Report* 1969 had fostered a sixteen-year-long "debate on the substance and form of amendments necessary to strengthen and modernize the law." It went on to note that given the increasing competitiveness of the world economy since the 1960s, "the need for a comprehensive reform of Canada's outmoded competition law has become even more pressing."[28] The purpose clause made it clearer what the legislation is *for:* promoting competition, but as noted above, as a means of advancing four ultimate goals.

26 See Hazeldine, above note 20; in the United States, see, e.g., Lina M Khan, "The Ideological Roots of America's Market Power Problem" (2018) 127 *Yale Law Journal Forum* 960; Jonathan B Baker & Steven C Salop, "Antitrust, Competition Policy, and Inequality" (2015) 104 *Georgetown Law Journal Online* 1; Carl Shapiro, "Antitrust in a Time of Populism" (2018) 61 *International Journal of Industrial Organization* 714.

27 Economic Council of Canada, *Interim Report on Competition Policy* (Ottawa: Queen's Printer, 1969) at 19 [*Interim Report* 1969].

28 Canada, Department of Consumer and Corporate Affairs, *Competition Law Amendment, A Guide* (Ottawa, Consumer and Corporate Affairs, 1985) at 2–3.

These modern goals represent a refinement of the range of objectives pursued during the legislation's earlier history. The historical objectives, however, remain part of the overall legislative context which may inform the interpretation of particular sections of the legislation.

2) Three Major Historical Themes

A comprehensive historical analysis in 1984 by Gorecki and Stanbury identified "three main themes" from a larger group of objectives raised during the first hundred years of the legislation: (1) preventing abuses of economic power, (2) maintaining free competition, and (3) achieving economic efficiency.[29]

a) Preventing the Abuse of Economic Power by Trade Combinations or "Combines"

Concern for the impact of corporate power played a major role in the initial legislation, directed as it was to addressing perceived high profits, price increases, and quality problems produced by the so-called combines prevalent in North America in the late nineteenth century. Combines ("trusts" in the United States) were anti-competitive agreements and arrangements between competing firms which afforded monopolistic control of goods or commodities. As we saw in Chapter 2, Canada's 1889 anti-combines legislation, like the 1890 US *Sherman Antitrust Act*, was born out of a populist backlash against the profiteering and abuses of these large combinations of capital in the late 1800s.

FIGURE 3.2.
Chic, *The Moon*, 1902, p 390

The same legislative motivation continued at the time of 1910 and 1923 amendments to the legislation. Those amendments bolstered the investigative machinery by creating a more permanent enforcement regime. In 1910, William Lyon Mackenzie King, then Minister of Labour, stated in the Parliamentary debates that "[t]he one end and purpose of this legislation is to prevent the mean

29 Paul K Gorecki & William T Stanbury, *The Objectives of Canadian Competition Policy 1888-1983* (Montreal: IRPP, 1984) [Gorecki & Stanbury].

man from profiting in virtue of his meanness."[30] In 1923, Mackenzie King, by then Prime Minister, stated that "the government recognizes that some restraint must be placed on the possible abuse of great power" by "large combinations of capital."[31] The Canadian legislation in this era was thus directed primarily at addressing "developments in the economy that ... people were against," i.e., combinations and agreements permitting companies to raise prices or dictate terms of trade. [32]

b) Maintaining Free Competition

In 1912, the Supreme Court of Canada heard *Weidman v Shragge*, the first case considering Canadian anti-combines legislation.[33] The case concerned the enforceability of an agreement between two "junk" dealers who purchased bottles and other used material in Western Canada and shipped them to Chicago. The agreement set the maximum prices to be paid to sources of supply. The Supreme Court saw the criminal prohibition of agreements which "unduly lessen competition" as an indicator of what was "unreasonable in the public interest" and therefore unenforceable under contract law. Justice Anglin noted that the parties to the agreement "controlled from 90% to 95% of the junk business in the territory in which they operated" and that the agreement "would tend to destroy in that territory all substantial competition ... and to leave the public as to the market price for these articles entirely at the mercy of the contracting parties."[34] The agreement was therefore found to be unreasonable and unenforceable. He noted:

> [T]he prime question certainly must be, does it, however advantageous or even necessary for the protection of the business interests of the parties, impose improper, inordinate, excessive, or oppressive restrictions *upon that competition the benefit of which is the right of every one?*[35]

The idea that the legislation was directed to provide the public the benefit of "free competition" was repeated by the Supreme Court in two subsequent price fixing cases, *R v Stinson-Reeb Builders Supply Co* (1929),[36]

30 *Ibid* at 22.

31 *Ibid* at 26.

32 J Bruce Dunlop, David McQueen & Michael J Trebilcock, *Canadian Competition Policy: A Legal and Economic Analysis* (Toronto: Canada Law Book, 1987) at 58 [Dunlop, McQueen & Trebilcock].

33 *Weidman v Shragge* (1912), 46 SCR 1.

34 *Ibid* at 40.

35 *Ibid* at 42–43 [emphasis added].

36 *R v Stinson-Reeb Builders Supply Co*, [1929] SCR 276 at 280: "[i]njury to the public by the hindering or suppressing of free competition, notwithstanding any advantage which may accrue to the business interests of the members of the

involving a cartel of gypsum manufacturers and dealers who had secured "a monopoly of the trade in Montreal in gypsum products" and *R v Container Materials Ltd* (1942), a prosecution of the members of an organization which at trial was found to have "substantially controlled throughout Canada . . . the manufacture and sale" of "corrugated and fibre board shipping containers." [37] The next price fixing prosecution to reach the Court was *Howard Smith Paper Mills Ltd v The Queen* (1957), involving a conspiracy among mills producing, and merchants selling, fine papers in Ontario and Quebec. Justice Taschereau held: "[t]he public is entitled to the benefit of free competition, and prohibitions of the *Act* cannot be evaded by good motives."[38] He concluded:

> [M]anufacturers and producers cannot, as the law now stands, monopolize a substantial part of the markets of the country in given industries, to promote their own business interests, and then set themselves up as public benefactors, by saying to the Courts that the conspiracy was organized in order to achieve the stabilization of prices and production.[39]

Later decisions of the Supreme Court echoed the early jurisprudence. In 1989, in *General Motors of Canada Ltd v City National Leasing*, Dickson CJ wrote for the Court, "the Act as a whole embodies a complex scheme of economic regulation. The purpose of the Act is to eliminate activities that reduce competition in the market-place. The entire Act is geared to achieving this objective."[40] The Court examined the consistency of the conspiracy provision with the *Charter* in the 1992 *R v Nova Scotia Pharmaceutical Society* decision. After a review of the jurisprudence under the section, the Court concluded "[c]ompetition is presumed by the Act to be in the public benefit. The only issue is whether the agreement impairs competition to the extent that it will attract liability."[41]

From these cases, it can be seen that Canadian courts, for almost 100 years, identified the pursuit of "free competition" as a core value of the legislation. The term appears to have been used in the sense of "rivalrous behaviour" rather than the economists' conception of a particular

---

combine, is what brings an agreement or a combination under the ban of section 498 Cr. C." The Court held that the fact that the agreement may have provided the conspirators benefits was irrelevant to whether it was illegal.

37 *R v Container Materials Ltd*, [1942] SCR 147 at 150. In upholding the conviction, Lyman Duff CJ rejected the argument of the accused that to constitute an "undue lessening of competition" under the statute, some specific public injury beyond the impact on competition needed to be shown.

38 *R v Howard Smith Paper Mills Ltd*, [1957] SCR 403 at 407.

39 *Ibid.*

40 *General Motors of Canada Ltd v City National Leasing*, [1989] 1 SCR 641 at 676.

41 *R v Nova Scotia Pharmaceutical Society*, [1992] 2 SCR 606 at para 88.

competitive market structure. The latter meaning has been given greater emphasis as the focus of the legislation shifted in recent decades toward the importance and value of economic efficiency.

c) Economic Efficiency

Economic efficiency does not appear explicitly in the early jurisprudence. Although it can be traced to certain policy papers and speeches by officials and politicians in the 1940s and 1950s,[42] it was only in the period since the 1960s, particularly since the publication of the Economic Council of Canada's *Interim Report on Competition Policy* in 1969, that the legislation began to shift direction toward a more consistent emphasis on efficiency as a central objective. Section 1.1 now lists among the ultimate objectives of the legislation, "to promote the efficiency and adaptability of the Canadian economy."

The Supreme Court noted in *Tervita v Commissioner of Competition* in examining the efficiency defence contained in the merger provisions of the *Competition Act*:

> The process of reforming Canada's competition laws began in 1966 when the federal government requested a study from the Economic Council of Canada. The Council's 1969 report "identified economic efficiency as the overriding policy objective" of legislative reform.[43]

Since then, through the three major rounds of amendments that followed, the economic focus of the legislation has strengthened. This can be seen in provisions governing the assessment of mergers and dominant firm behaviour, which require the assessment of their economic effect using a "substantial lessening of competition" standard. This has been interpreted to require conduct which preserves or adds to "market power." The provisions containing this market power requirement are subject to adjudication before the Competition Tribunal, which, as discussed in Chapter 2, is a specialized civil tribunal with the expertise and other tools enabling it to conduct a weighing of economic factors.

Promoting market efficiency by regulating the distribution of misleading or incomplete information was also cited as a rationale for the amendments which expanded the misleading trade promotion prohibitions in the Act in 1975.[44] The Competition Bureau noted in respect of

---

42 Gorecki & Stanbury, above note 29 at 84–87.

43 *Tervita Corporation v Commissioner of Competition*, [2015] 1 SCR 161at para 65 [*Tervita*], citing Andrew Neil Campbell, *Merger Law and Practice: The Regulation of Mergers Under the Competition Act* (Toronto: Carswell, 1997) at 21.

44 Canada, Bureau of Competition Policy, *Stage I Competition Policy, Background Papers* (Ottawa, Consumer and Corporate Affairs, 1976) at 38 [*Stage I Competition Policy*].

these amendments that "[i]t can be shown where there is a lack of complete information or where distorted information in relation to a product is fed into the marketplace, its function will be seriously affected and the distortion will be injurious to honest competitors."[45]

Given its importance, the concept of efficiency is explored in greater detail in Section D below in this chapter.

3) Lesser Objectives

Certain objectives appeared over the years that were less consistently emphasized or more transient in their importance to policy discussion, legislative debate, or jurisprudence. Three of the most significant objectives were protecting small business, controlling inflation and ensuring marketplace fairness and honesty. Each of these can be linked to particular amendments or periods in the legislation's history, although they were often relied upon alongside other objectives as a rationale for specific provisions.

a) Protecting Small Business

The purpose clause refers to the objective of ensuring "that small and medium-sized enterprises have an equitable opportunity to participate in the Canadian economy." Provisions added to the legislation dealing with price discrimination and predatory pricing (1935), resale price maintenance (1951), and refusal to deal (1976) reflected this objective in whole or part. Over time, the changing focus of the legislation resulted in the repeal or amendment of all these provisions, and a diminished emphasis on this objective.

- **Price discrimination and predatory pricing:**[46] Widespread business failures during and after the Great Depression led to a legislative policy agenda in the 1930s favouring the protection of competitors and individual businesses. In 1935, Parliament added criminal prohibitions of predatory pricing and price discrimination.[47] The purpose of the legislation has been described as discouraging price reductions and the "protection of certain groups from injury inflicted by deep depression at home and abroad." [48] While these provisions did not generate

45 *Ibid.*

46 See also Chapter 9 for a more detailed discussion of the reform of these provisions.

47 In response to Canada, *Report of the Royal Commission on Price Spreads* (Ottawa: King's Printer, 1935), Parliament enacted s 489A of the *Criminal Code* in SC 1935, c 56, s 9; SC 1952, c 39, s 11. The provision became s 412 in SC 1953-54, c 51. It was transferred to the *Combines Investigation Act* as s 33A (SC 1960, c 45, s 13).

48 Lawrence A Skeoch & Bruce C McDonald, *Dynamic Change and Accountability in the Canadian Economy* (Ottawa, Consumer and Corporate Affairs, 1976) at 204–5 [Skeoch & McDonald].

significant enforcement activity, they remained in the legislation for more than sixty years, until their removal in 2009.[49]

- **Resale price maintenance:** In 1951, another provision with a populist flavour, a criminal prohibition of resale price maintenance, was added. It prohibited suppliers from coercing a downstream seller of its products not to discount by various means, including by refusing to supply. Over time, economists came to regard resale price maintenance as neutral or even beneficial because it may stimulate greater competition by, for example, encouraging enhanced services by retailers or assisting the entry of new suppliers.[50] In 2009, the *per se* criminal prohibition of price maintenance was replaced by a civil prohibition requiring the practice to have some "adverse effect" on competition.[51]
- **Refusal to deal:** The amendments of 1976 included a new civil provision relating to refusals to deal (refusals to supply with a substantial effect on a business).[52] It was introduced after the Competition Bureau received "many complaints from businessmen who have been unable to get supplies needed for their operations on ordinary trade terms."[53] The provision initially did not require that there be any impact on competition from the refusal. In 2002, amendments to the section required the practice to have at least an "adverse effect on competition," again reflecting the legislation's changed focus toward providing remedies only where behaviour affects the broader competitive process.[54]

b) Controlling Inflation

The passage of the resale price maintenance provision in the 1950s reflected, in part, the "high rate of inflation at the time."[55] The Minister of Justice stated when the amending legislation was passed that the *Combines Investigation Act* was a tool "to prevent . . . high prices."[56] Concern overinflation dominated the national policy agenda in Canada in the 1970s. In 1973, Herb Gray, then Minister responsible for the legislation stated that "[c]ontinued enforcement of the legislation . . . [can] inhibit restraints on competitive market forces and thus exercise downward

---

49 *Budget Implementation Act, 2009*, SC 2009, c 2, s 413 [*BIA, 2009*].

50 See, e.g., J Anthony VanDuzer, "Assessing the Canadian Law and Practice on Predatory Pricing, Price Discrimination and Price Maintenance 2000-2001" 32:2 *Ottawa Law Review* 179 at 226–27.

51 *BIA, 2009*, above note 49, ss 417 and 426.

52 Now s 75 of the *Competition Act*, above note 22. See also Chapter 8.

53 *Stage I Competition Policy*, above note 44 at 4.

54 *An Act to Amend the Competition Act and Competition Tribunal Act*, SC 2002, c 16, royal assent granted 4 June 2002, s 11.1.

55 Gorecki & Stanbury, above note 29 at 127.

56 *Ibid* at 119.

pressure on prices."[57] In the House of Commons that year, he also cited "the importance of competition as a policy instrument that can have a key role to play in maintaining cost-effective markets for food in Canada."[58]

It has been observed that "the empirical evidence of a connection between inflation and competition policy is fairly thin."[59] Nonetheless, the references to impacts on inflation were sometimes seen as a way to garner support for competition legislation and its reform when inflationary concerns were prevalent.

c) Ensuring Marketplace Fairness and Honesty

This theme was cited in the 1970s by the minister responsible for competition legislation in support of amendments to the misleading advertising provisions. Prohibitions against misleading price advertising were initially added to the *Combines Investigation Act* in 1960 and 1969; they were bolstered by the Stage I amendments, enacted in 1975, with a number of additional deceptive practice offences, covering such matters as misleading performance guarantees, "bait and switch" advertising, pyramid schemes, misleading promotional contests, and sale above advertising prices.[60] Minister André Ouellet stated in support of the amendments in 1975 that their purposes included establishing rules to encourage the private sector to conduct business in an "orderly fashion" and "restor[e] public confidence in the effectiveness of the market system."[61] As will be seen below, reducing misleading commercial behaviour can also further the efficient operation of markets.

D. OBJECTIVES OF MODERN CANADIAN COMPETITION LAW

1) Economic Efficiency and Related Concepts

> Economics is "the science of human choice in a world in which resources are limited in relation to human wants."
>
> — R Posner, *Economic Analysis of Law* (Boston: Little Brown and Company, 1977) at 3.

57 *Ibid* at 119–20.

58 Canada, Consumer and Corporate Affairs, *Proposals for a New Competition Policy for Canada, First Stage* (Ottawa, Consumer and Corporate Affairs, 1973) at 2; comments during a debate on a motion to support the *Food Prices Committee Report*, *House of Commons Debates*, 29th Parl, 1st Sess (10 April 1973) at 3155 (Hon Herb Gray).

59 Gorecki & Stanbury, above note 29 at 121.

60 *An Act to amend the Combines Investigation Act and the Bank Act*, SC 1974-75-76, c 76.

61 Gorecki & Stanbury, above note 29 at 137.

a) Introduction

Modern Canadian competition laws, both in their design and in their application, involve rules for assessing market structures and competitive behaviour which often employ analytical tools based upon learning drawn from economics. As a result, certain underlying economic concepts are central to this area of the law. These include market power, barriers to entry, and economies of scale. Such concepts are part of the day-to-day tools used by counsel in advising clients, acting as an advocate, or in contributing to the process of policy development.

The areas of economics which have been most important to the development of competition laws include microeconomics, industrial organization, and price theory—which involve the study of markets and industry structures, of how prices and output levels are determined, and of how products and resources are allocated in an economy. A concept central to all of these areas of economics is that of efficiency.

b) *Caveats:* Assumptions in, and Limitations of, Economic Models

Economics is a social science. It may rely upon methodologies that generate some important qualifications which should be kept in mind in the discussion of economic theory that follows.

First, attempting to deal with the complexities of human behaviour, economics often employs assumptions which simplify the real world to permit a reasoned examination of a problem or activity. These assumptions may sometimes be baked into economic models used to examine market outcomes. It is important that any assumptions be transparent, so that their impact or limitations on real world applications can be factored in. It has been pointed out that sometimes a failure to declare or to weigh the impact of critical assumptions can reveal ideological biases or blatant simplifications which can put into question the conclusions drawn from the models built around them. This critique is not uncommon in the area of competition and antitrust policy.[62] While a detailed evaluation of such considerations is not possible in the overview offered below, the need to examine and to question assumptions made, and their impacts, remains an active and important area of inquiry. A discerning application of economics to competition law is prudent. Thus, the critical assumptions employed should be kept in mind when economists, lawyers, and judges apply

62 See, e.g., Christopher R Leslie, "Antitrust Made (Too) Simple" (2014) 79:3 *Antitrust Law Journal* 917; Reza Dibadj, "Saving Antitrust" (2004) 75:3 *University of Colorado Law Review* 745; Herbert Hovenkamp, "Post-Chicago Antitrust: A Review and Critique" [2001] *Columbia Business Law Review* 257.

the theoretical models and learning of economics to competition law issues in the real world. American scholar Lawrence Sullivan decades ago put it well, in the introductory chapter to his antitrust text:

> The great thing is to understand the power of economics and its potential, but also its limits – to draw upon it not as one who borrows, or imposes, but as one possessing a tool; to use it selectively, both wisely and well.[63]

Second, economics treats efficiency as a separate question from the issue of how wealth, or economic power, should be distributed or controlled. Distribution of wealth (e.g., price impacts on consumers' incomes) and business equity (opportunities for small and medium-sized businesses) are objectives reflected in the purpose clause of the Act, alongside efficiency and adaptability of the economy. In keeping with their treatment by economics, the nature and role of these non-efficiency related objectives are discussed separately below after consideration of the efficiency-oriented aspects.

c) The Three Aspects of Economic Efficiency

Economic efficiency has been described as "exploiting economic resources in such a way that 'value'—human satisfaction as measured by aggregate consumer willingness to pay for goods and services—is maximized."[64] Economic efficiency is thus about yielding the greatest human satisfaction or "welfare" possible within the constraints of existing resources. Three different aspects of efficiency are often considered by economists and lawyers in the context of a discussion of competition policy: **allocative**, **productive**, and **dynamic efficiency**.[65] These are considered in turn below.

i) Allocative Efficiency

Allocative efficiency relates to how society's scarce resources are employed, or allocated, in the production, use, and consumption of goods and services in an economy. Resources are said to be allocated efficiently when the manner in which they are employed maximizes total welfare for society. The Supreme Court in *Tervita* noted that allocative efficiency "is achieved when the existing stock of goods and productive output is allocated throughout the price system to those buyers who

---

63 Lawrence A Sullivan, *Handbook of the Law of Antitrust* (St Paul: West Publishing, 1977) at 9 and 4–10.

64 Richard A Posner, *Economic Analysis of Law* (Boston: Little Brown, 1977) at 10 [Posner].

65 See, e.g., Dunlop, McQueen & Trebilcock, above note 32 at 63; Gorecki & Stanbury, above note 29 at 81–82; Richard Whish, *Competition Law*, 6th ed (Oxford: Oxford University Press, 2008), ch 1 [Whish].

value them most in terms of willingness to pay, such that 'resources available to society are allocated to their most valuable use.'"[66]

Allocative efficiency is promoted when resources in competitive markets are priced so they reflect their "true" cost to society. That will occur when prices for different commodities are a reliable reflection of their relative scarcities and relative demand.[67] When prices do not reflect real, relative resource costs ("social cost"), society may consume less of a commodity (because its price is relatively too high), and more of a less desirable substitute commodity (because its price is relatively too low) that is more expensive for society to produce. This leads to a distortion in the efficient use of resources, and what economists term a "deadweight loss" for society. The Supreme Court described this concept as follows in *Tervita* in the context of assessment of a merger:

> Deadweight loss "results from the fall in demand for the merged entities' products following a post-merger increase in price, and the inefficient allocation of resources that occurs when, as prices rise, consumers purchase a less suitable substitute."[68]

In reflecting on the concept of deadweight loss, it is helpful first to examine how consumer demand changes in response to changes in price. Demand for a given commodity usually increases when the price is reduced and decreases when the price is raised (all else remaining equal). This relationship can be depicted on a "demand curve"—a line plotted with the price of the commodity on the vertical axis, and the quantity demanded or consumed on the horizontal axis. In the typical

---

66 *Tervita*, above note 43 at para 65, citing Brian A Facey & Cassandra Brown, *Competition and Antitrust Laws in Canada: Mergers, Joint Ventures and Competitor Collaborations* (Toronto: LexisNexis, 2013) at 253–55. If efficiency in this sense is achieved, the level of relative use of each good or service is what is "just right" to maximize benefits for all. Resources are allocated efficiently when it is not possible to make anyone better off without making someone else worse off. Economists term this a "Pareto optimal" result, after the Italian/French economist Vilfredo D Pareto (1848–1923), a founder of modern welfare economics. See Graham Bannock, RE Baxter & Ray Rees, eds, *The Penguin Dictionary of Economics* (Middlesex: Penguin, 1974) at 132 [Bannock, Baxter & Rees, eds].

67 This idea has been summarized as follows:

> Ideally, and taking as given for now whatever prior distribution of wealth the past has bequeathed us, we would like the determination of who gets what in the economy, over some subsequent production period, to be an accurate reflection of the real, relative resource costs of producing goods and services in each sector of the economy, and of the relative utility or satisfaction to each consuming unit of the various goods and services on offer.

Dunlop, McQueen & Trebilcock, above note 32 at 63.

68 *Tervita*, above note 43 at para 94.

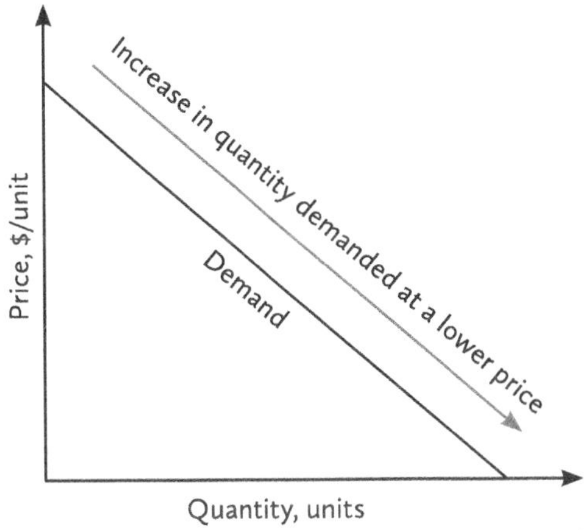

FIGURE 3.3. A demand curve shows the price per unit of a product that consumers are willing to pay for (on the vertical axis) plotted against the quantity of the product demanded at any given price (horizontal axis). More of the product is consumed as the price falls, making the line ("curve") downward-sloping

relationship, a lowering of prices produces an increase in demand, and thus "downward sloping demand." This is depicted in **Figure 3.3** below. For simplification, the demand curve below is linear — it is a straight line, reflecting the fact that the quantity demanded of this hypothetical product changes by the same amount in response to a given price change over the entire demand curve. However, the demand curve need not be linear. Its shape will vary depending on the way in which demand for a given product changes in response to price changes.

The presence of downward sloping demand is an important assumption underlying the discussion of allocative inefficiency below.

Buyers of different commodities have differing responses to price changes. Demand is said to be "elastic" if the quantity demanded is very responsive to price changes, and "inelastic" if there is relatively little change in demand with changes in price.[69] For example, demand for moderately priced restaurant food is probably quite price elastic — for the sake of convenience, consumers will eat at restaurants more (up to a point) when prices fall rather than prepare food at home. Consumer demand for electricity is, in contrast, more inelastic. At least in the short run, most consumers have no alternative to turn to in the case of a price increase, although they may use electricity more sparingly over time if prices rise significantly.

The following example illustrates the impact of a price increase on allocative efficiency. It examines what happens when the price for a given commodity is raised above its social cost. In a competitive market, assume product X is priced at $100 per unit, which is also its social cost.[70] Entry

69 See Chapter 4, Section C(c)(i) for a further discussion of demand elasticity.

70 Even in a competitive market, prices may not equate to social costs. For example, if there are what economists term consumption externalities (e.g., pollution caused by the product in question) then the social cost will exceed the price.

is easy and there are lots of competitors. Suppliers are forced to price at cost (plus a reasonable market return) to survive.

Because of downward sloping demand, at a competitive price of $100 per unit, there are some consumers who would have paid more for product X, but did not have to, because of the prevailing competitive price. For illustrative purposes, let us assume that some consumers would have paid $130 per unit, so that they kept the extra $30 per unit in their pockets at the $100 market price. This $30 difference represents what economists refer to as "consumer surplus," which is the amount a consumer would have been willing to pay for something, less what they actually had to pay in the marketplace.[71]

Table 3.1. Impacts of Monopoly Pricing

Market conditions for product X	Social cost per unit	Price per unit	Notes
Competitive market	$100	$100	A consumer who would have paid $130 keeps the $30 difference ("consumer surplus").
Monopoly	$100	$125	Loss of $25 in consumer surplus for those consumers who would have paid $130 before the price increase and continue to purchase good X afterward. This is a "wealth transfer" to producers with no effect on allocative efficiency. Loss of $15 in consumer surplus from those consumers who would have paid up to $115 for good X and switch to another good "Y" for which they paid $115. This also results in allocative inefficiency ("deadweight loss") of $15 per unit if good Y costs $115 per unit for society to make.

The bottom row above illustrates what happens when the market price for product X is raised under conditions of monopoly. The

However, in a perfectly competitive market, price will be the same as social cost if there are no externalities.

71 Bannock, Baxter & Rees, eds, above note 66 at 81 defines consumer surplus as: "[t]he difference between the total amount of money an individual would be prepared to pay for some quantity of a good, and the amount he [or she] actually has to pay."

monopolist is not constrained by competition and raises the price to a point which maximizes profits. This example specifies that the price charged is raised to $125 per unit, $25 above the social cost of $100. In this scenario, several impacts on the economy as a whole can be observed.

First, those consumers who would have paid $130 still consume the good (since it is priced below their maximum tolerable price of $130), but they pay $25 more per unit. They are still consuming the same amount of the good, but they have less money to spend on other goods and services. This loss to consumers is a transfer of wealth to suppliers. While this transfer may create policy issues relating to fairness or income distribution, it does not make society worse off as a whole: the transferred wealth remains in the economy. It has merely gone from one social pocket to another. In other words, this transfer represents a loss to consumers and may create equity concerns, but it is efficiency-neutral and is not included in the deadweight loss.

Second, some consumers who were willing to pay up to $115, given their income, circumstances, and preferences, have stopped consuming product X altogether at the new higher price. They switch in this example to a product Y, for which the consumers have the same willingness to pay as for product X and which sells for $115. In such circumstances, they are worse off after the price increase, because they are paying $15 more of their income per unit for a product that provides them the same value as product X. If product Y is competitively supplied and the social cost per unit to produce it is $115, society as a whole is also worse off—this is not just an income transfer. This is because $15 more per unit in social resources are being used to satisfy the same consumer demand at the new price of product X. In other words, "[t]he effect of monopoly is to make some consumers satisfy their demand by switching to goods that cost society more to produce than the monopolized good. The cost increment is a waste to society."[72]

As a practical example, one might think of product X as propane used by consumers for home heating in remote areas and product Y as electricity used for the same purpose. If the price of propane rises in conditions of monopoly, some consumers may turn to electricity for their heating needs. If electricity uses more social resources to produce for the same amount of heating value in that area, this would mean that, not only are some consumers transferring more of their wealth to energy suppliers at the monopoly price, but society's overall wealth is being reduced due to a misallocation of resources toward the production

72 Posner, above note 64 at 201.

of additional, higher-cost electricity. The result is that "[n]ot enough of the monopolized good is produced, from a social point of view, and too much of the other good is produced."[73] The monopoly price, in other words, gives rise to allocative inefficiency.

Another source of allocative inefficiency results in the above example if electricity is a less desirable substitute for consumers (because, for example, it is susceptible to power outages or does not heat a home evenly). If that is true, consumers will lose some welfare as they shift to that less preferred substitute product, which delivers less consumer surplus to them because of its characteristics. This loss of welfare is also a deadweight loss to society, because it is not recovered through a transfer to another group.[74]

The effects on society we see from the above example as a result of the monopolist's price increase are that (1) more resources are being used to satisfy the same social needs and the social "pie" of resources has actually shrunken; and (2) consumers have shifted to a less desirable substitute product, reducing social welfare. These are the sources of the deadweight loss to society from this increase in price.

The price increase may also result in an additional loss of "producer surplus" (the difference between revenue received by the producer and the cost of producing the product) if the price being charged for product X before the price increase was already above cost. The graphical explanation of this, which also illustrates the loss of consumer surplus, is provided below in this chapter at Appendix 3.1.

ii) Productive Efficiency

While allocative efficiency considers the impact on the economy as a whole in terms of resource allocation, productive efficiency focuses on the efficiency of individual firms or businesses. Productive efficiency considers whether any given level of output is being produced at least cost, or alternatively, whether a given amount of inputs (e.g., labour,

73 Stephen Martin, *Industrial Economics* (New York: Macmillan, 1988) at 31 [Martin].

74 In *Canada (Director of Investigation and Research) v Hillsdown Holdings (Canada) Ltd*, [1992] CCTD 4 at para 143, Reed J in examining the merger efficiency defence described this loss:

> Detriment to society as a whole is said to arise, for example, when consumers because of the higher prices choose an alternate and less appropriate substitute product for the use they have in mind. They substitute a product which would have been their second choice in a competitive market. This inefficient substitution is seen as a misallocation of resources; it is seen as a loss to society as a whole. It is referred to as allocative inefficiency or the deadweight loss.

parts, machinery) is yielding the maximum possible output.[75] Productive efficiency occurs where the cost per unit produced by a firm is at its lowest point.

We can illustrate this through examining a firm's "average cost curve," which is a line plotting the per-unit cost of production (vertical axis) with changes in output (horizontal axis). In the chart below, the firm's average cost per unit is in the $250 to $300 per unit range at the lowest level of production, but drops to approximately $50 per unit at output of 2,000 to 2,500 units, the level of output involving the greatest productive efficiency.

This kind of structure is typical of industries such as manufacturing, in which some significant costs (e.g., administrative overhead, plant, or equipment) are fixed. Fixed costs cannot be changed in the short to medium term. They cannot be adjusted to permit an increase in output without significant time delays. Other costs, such as labour and parts, are variable in the short run, and change in response to increases or decreases in the number of units produced.

A factory making plastic cup lids, for example, must invest in the heat-molding plant and machinery needed, whether the facility makes 100 units or 100,000. The firm will also incur other fixed costs, such as management salaries, a human resources department, debt payments, and insurance. None of these items vary with output, at least in the short run. The U-shaped cost curve above (which shows the situation in static or short-run terms) reflects the typical situation in which there are economies of scale: average cost per unit (total cost divided by output) falls as output expands. While variable cost per unit (at least initially) doesn't change, average fixed costs per unit fall as output increases. At some point, diseconomies of scale may set in, such as reduced assembly line efficiency due to crowding on the shop floor, or a level of output which outstrips management's ability to ensure quality control or efficient production practices. At that point, average costs per unit begin to rise because of an increase in average variable costs and the curve turns upward.

Productive and allocative efficiency may come into conflict. For example, a merger of competing business may permit the continuing firm to eliminate duplication, reduce administrative overhead, or take advantage of economies of scale, lowering its average costs of production (increasing productive efficiency). However, if the merged entity acquires a monopoly position permitting a price increase above competitive levels, this results in a reduction of allocative efficiency.

---

75 Dunlop, McQueen & Trebilcock, above note 32 at 51.

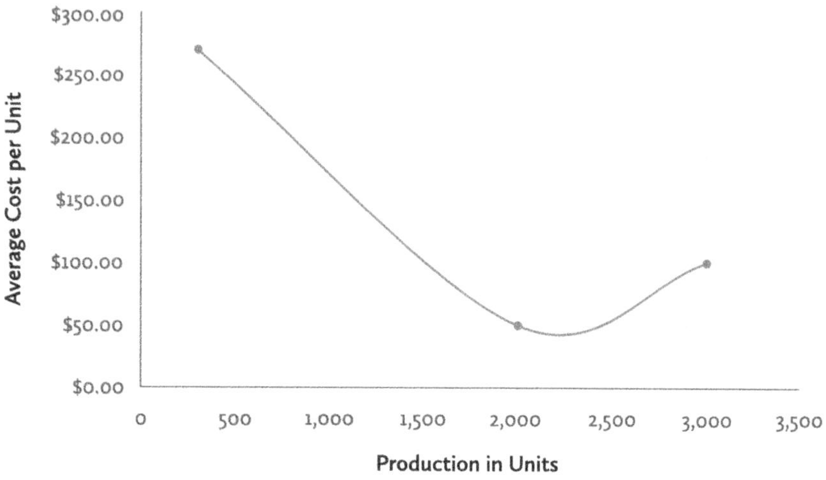

FIGURE 3.4. Cost curve

iii) Dynamic Efficiency

As noted above, the average cost curve in **Figure** 3.4 is "static" in the sense that it represents a snapshot of operations and production methods in a defined, short-run time period. If, over a longer time frame, there is an efficiency-enhancing technological change such as robotics, or an improvement in labour productivity, the cost curve may shift downward to reflect a reduction in cost per unit. The concept of dynamic efficiency considers such changes by examining how efficiency may vary over time in light of changing incentives to reduce costs through innovation or other change. The *Skeoch-MacDonald*, or "Dynamic Change" *Report*, prepared for the government in 1976 in the context of proposals to amend the legislation, viewed dynamic efficiency as the most important objective for competition law:

> The primary thrust of policy in our view should be to promote adaptability and flexibility in the economy, and to provide both pressures and incentives to develop new products and services, as well as new methods of production and distribution, which will more effectively meet the needs and desires of society.[76]

There has been a building recognition of the importance of competition in stimulating innovation and dynamic change. It is well known that technological and other innovations introduced by firms such as Microsoft, Google, Apple, Netflix, Amazon, Zoom, Uber, Lyft, Shopify, and others have become a key driver of economic growth in recent

---

76 Skeoch & McDonald, above note 48 at 205.

years.[77] The scholarship has studied the relationship among competition, innovation, and growth in both theoretical and empirical terms.[78] The theoretical analysis has examined the effect of competitive pressures on the incentives of management to innovate. One observed outcome is that "competition promotes innovation."[79] Empirical analysis has linked higher productivity to more competitive markets.[80] Other research and scholarship argue that competition laws play an important role in encouraging product changes and other forms of innovation, which in turn increase productivity and economic growth.[81]

A contrary view of the relationship between monopoly power and dynamic efficiency, often attributed to economist Joseph Schumpeter, holds that the profits available from market power are what provide the incentive, and the resources, to engage in innovative activity. Schumpeter termed innovation "the perennial gale of creative destruction," which is driven by "the competition from the new commodity, the new technology, the new source of supply, the new type of organization (the largest-scale unit of control for instance) — competition which commands a decisive cost or quality advantage." In his view, the incentive to

---

77 John Pecman, "Remarks by John Pecman, Commissioner of Competition" (Speech delivered at the Innovation and Antitrust Workshop, Ottawa, 4 November 2014), online: www.competitionbureau.gc.ca/eic/site/cb-bc.nsf/eng/03834.html: "Economic research has shown that technological innovation is the primary driver of economic growth. In fact, growth theory pioneered by Nobel laureate Robert Solow has found that the vast majority of output growth in an economy occurs from technological progress, as opposed to increased use of labor and capital." See also David J Teece, "Pivoting toward Schumpeter: Makan Delrahim and the Recasting of U.S. Antitrust towards Innovation, Competitiveness, and Growth" (2018) 32 *Antitrust* 32.

78 For a review, see Matthew Chiasson & Paul A Johnson, "Canada's (In)Efficiency Defence: Why Section 96 May Do More Harm than Good for Economic Efficiency and Innovation" (2019) 32:1 *Canadian Competition Law Review* 1 at 7–13.

79 See, e.g., Thomas A Holmes & James A Schmitz, "Competition and Productivity, A Review of Evidence" (2010) 2 *Annual Review of Economics* 619; Andrew I Gavil, William E Kovacic & Jonathan B Baker, *Antitrust Law in Perspective: Cases, Concepts and Problems in Competition Policy* (St Paul: West Group, 2002) at 1093–96 [Gavil, Kovacic & Baker].

80 See, e.g., Chad Syverson, "Market Structure and Productivity: A Concrete Example" (2004) 112 *Journal of Political Economy* 1181; Michael E Porter, "Competition and Antitrust: Toward a Productivity-Based Approach to Evaluating Mergers and Joint Ventures" (2001) 46:4 *Antitrust Bulletin* 919 [Porter].

81 See the research cited in Jonathan B Baker, "Beyond Schumpeter vs. Arrow: How Antitrust Fosters Innovation" (2007) 74 *Antitrust Law Journal* 575 at footnotes 8 and 9 and following; see also Gregory Day, "Innovative Antitrust and the Patent System" (2018) 96:4 *Nebraska Law Review* 829.

innovate would ensure that any monopoly power would be only transient.[82] The idea that a monopoly position increases dynamic efficiency is embraced in the patent system, which is a legal regime protecting novel inventions from competition, potentially giving rise to increased profits which will reward and incentivize innovation.

Michael Porter, who has embraced the role of innovation for productivity growth, takes a more middle-ground view that "[h]igh profits are fine, provided competition is healthy and there are strong pressures for dynamic improvement."[83] Rivalry and new entry are seen, for example, as key to ensuring that markets remain competitive and dynamically efficient. Porter emphasized the importance of an effective competition law review of mergers, for example, in ensuring the continued dynamic nature of an industry.

Innovation has played a role in competition law analysis of mergers and abuse of dominance. For example, the Competition Tribunal in its 2017 *Toronto Real Estate Board* decision prohibited certain restrictions on the use of multiple listings data as a substantial lessening of competition because they "have stifled innovation in the supply of Internet-based real estate brokerage services."[84] Similarly, the European Commission, in the context of a merger between chemical manufacturing giants, Dow and DuPont, assessed the impact of the transaction on innovation. Although the parties had argued the contrary, the Commission's review of the literature in the area concluded that "[a] merger between two significant and close competitors is . . . likely to reduce the level of innovation by each of the merging parties."[85] The merger was permitted, although certain conditions were imposed which were intended to reduce impacts on innovation. The presence of innovation may affect whether market power is likely to endure in view of the dynamic state of an industry in terms of change, market growth, or the entry and expansion of new competitors.

---

82 Joseph Schumpeter, *Capitalism, Socialism, and Democracy* (New York: Routledge, 2003) at 84–85.

83 Porter, above note 80 at 941.

84 *Canada (Commissioner of Competition) v Toronto Real Estate Board*, [2016] CCTD No 7 at para 672, aff'd 2017 FCA 236. A report on efficiencies in merger assessment commissioned for the Competition Bureau concluded, "The effects of a merger on dynamic efficiency must be assessed case by case." Marcel Côté, Jalynn H Bennett & Roger Gibbons, "Report of the Advisory Panel on Efficiencies" (2005), online: www.ic.gc.ca/eic/site/cb-bc.nsf/eng/01954.html at 43.

85 EC, Commission Decision of 27.3.2017 "Declaring a Concentration to Be Compatible with the Internal Market and the EEA Agreement" (Case M.7932—Dow/Dupont), Annex 4 to the Commission Decision, "Implications of the Economic Theory on Mergers, Competition and Innovation in Light of the Features of the Transaction" at para 59, online: https://ec.europa.eu/competition/mergers/cases/decisions/m7932_13668_3.pdf.

Summary: The Supreme Court on Types of Efficiency

The Supreme Court of Canada in *Tervita* succinctly summarized the three categories of efficiency as follows:

> (1) production efficiency . . . "is achieved when output is produced using the most cost-effective combination of productive resources available under existing technology"; (2) innovation or dynamic efficiency . . . "is achieved through the invention, development and diffusion of new products and production processes"; and (3) allocative efficiency, . . . "is achieved when the existing stock of goods and productive output is allocated throughout the price system to those buyers who value them most in terms of willingness to pay, such that 'resources available to society are allocated to their most valuable use'."
>
> —*Tervita Corp v Canada (Commissioner of Competition)*, 2015 SCC 3 at para 102.

d) Market Analysis and Paradigms

i) *Market Structure Classification*

To examine how these three different kinds of efficiency relate to competitive market conditions, we can look to the outcomes economists predict from the polar extremes of perfect competition and monopoly. Their basic structural conditions, and those of other intermediate market structures, are set out in simplified form in the table below.[86] The top heading shows conditions of entry into an industry or market (e.g,. how long it takes for a viable competitor to enter). The left column sets out the number of competitors in the market in question.

Table 3.2. Market Structure Classification

Number of sellers ↓ / Conditions of entry →	ENTRY BLOCKED or LIMITED	EASY ENTRY
ONE SELLER	Monopoly	Contestable Monopoly
FEW SELLERS	Duopoly (2) or Oligopoly	Contestable Oligopoly
MANY SELLERS	Monopolistic Competition	Perfect Competition

86 Adapted from Green, above note 16 at 49, Table 3-1, "Market Structure Taxonomy."

In a monopoly, there is one seller, entry is blocked (perhaps by regulatory rules), or entry barriers are very high. An example is a city-owned residential water utility, where competitive entry is barred by municipal bylaws. Customers have no choice but to obtain their water supply from the utility. Entry barriers may also arise from economies of scale—due, for example, to the fact that production costs fall up to a level of output which makes up a substantial portion of the market.[87]

At the other extreme is perfect competition, where there is easy entry (or costless entry and exit), and many sellers. In perfect competition, there are so many sellers that any one firm's change in production has no impact on the market price. The product sold by each supplier is qualitatively the same or "standardized." For example, a particular type of grain sold by individual prairie farmers into the world market may approach conditions of perfect competition. There are many sellers. An individual farmer would not be able to change the price received in the market by changing his or her output. Entry can be relatively swift and easy, as farms can change what they plant and produce from season to season.

Another important variable, not depicted in this diagram, is the nature of the product sold and the extent of "product differentiation." Products offered by different firms have different qualitative or other performance characteristics, or otherwise provide different levels of value, or perceived value, to consumers. A so-called commodity product such as a particular grade of iron ore or grain is an undifferentiated product. It is sold according to specifications which are unlikely to vary significantly between suppliers. Complex manufactured goods, such as cars, are differentiated products. There are many different characteristics—colours, size, engine performance, comfort, safety, speed—which distinguish automobiles from one another. A product may be differentiated by its unique characteristics and performance, by the services offered with it (such as repair or customer support), and even by a brand or image created by marketing.

The presence of product differentiation, even in markets featuring a large number of sellers, can provide the seller some power over price which changes how competitive conditions may operate. Product differentiation is a key variable, for example, in distinguishing some structures examined by economists, such as "monopolistic competition," from a competitive market. [88]

Conditions of true monopoly and perfect competition are rare in the economy. Most economic activity falls into the other categories in the

87 *Ibid* at 67–87; Jeffrey R Church & Roger Ware, *Industrial Organization: A Strategic Approach* (Boston: McGraw-Hill, 2000) at 54–58 and 514–15.

88 See *ibid*, ch 11.

table. We see structures involving or approaching duopoly, for example, in national scheduled airlines (Air Canada and WestJet) and in rail services (CN and Canadian Pacific). Oligopoly, involving only a handful of sellers, is a common structure in the Canadian economy and a feature of the supply of many goods and services. For example, the three top suppliers of wireless mobile services in Canada (Bell, Rogers, and Telus) had 90.7 percent of revenues in 2018.[89] Many manufactured consumer goods such as computers, televisions, appliances, and automobiles feature only a handful of suppliers. In retail markets, in any given local area there are often only a few competing players among the gas stations, supermarkets, office supply stores, and building supply outlets providing options for consumers within a reasonable driving distance.

ii) Results from Perfect Competition[90]

The assessment of perfectly competitive markets by economics typically assumes: (1) many buyers and sellers; (2) free entry and exit; (3) perfect knowledge, i.e., firms making rational choices between available goods and services; (4) undifferentiated or homogeneous products; and (5) firms which act independently and strive to profit-maximize.[91]

What efficiency outcomes are predicted from this market structure? As noted above, the case of perfect competition, low entry barriers, numerous competitors, and a homogenous product means that suppliers are "price-takers"; that is, they cannot profitably raise their selling price because their customers would simply switch to other suppliers, or move to new or more efficient entrants who appear in response to any increase in the prevailing price. If demand expands, entry may occur, and once entry occurs, supply will expand to the point at which the price falls because there will be too much product chasing too little demand. As the price falls, firms will curtail production and some firms will leave the market. If the price falls below a certain point, so many firms will exit or fail that industry output will fall and scarcity will occur, which will again drive the price upward.

These different upward and downward pressures on price from changes in demand and supply will cause a movement, over time,

89 Canadian Radio-television and Telecommunications Commission (CRTC), *Telecommunications Monitoring Report 2019* (Ottawa, CRTC, 2020) at 237, online: https://crtc.gc.ca/pubs/cmr2019-en.pdf.

90 For a more detailed treatment, see E Thomas Sullivan & Jeffrey L Harrison, *Understanding Antitrust and Its Economic Implications*, 4th ed (Newark: Matthew Bender, 2003) at 10–20.

91 John Lipczynski & John OS Wilson, *Industrial Organisation: An Analysis of Competitive Markets* (Harlow, Essex: Pearson Education, 2001) at 2.

toward what economists refer to as an equilibrium price: firms make just enough money to cover their costs plus a reasonable return on capital, but no more. This results in all three kinds of economic efficiency being achieved in perfectly competitive markets:

Allocative efficiency: Because firms are forced to charge prices in competitive markets which reflect their costs (plus a reasonable return on capital), perfect competition achieves allocative efficiency: "consumers can obtain the amount of goods or services they require at the price they are prepared to pay: resources are allocated precisely according to their wishes."[92]

Productive efficiency: Firms will also be forced by the competitive pressure of entry and the rivalry of competing suppliers to be productively efficient over the long run. If they are not, and their costs drift upward, they will not earn a profit, and they will fail, because the prevailing price will be driven down to the level of the costs of an efficient firm.

Dynamic efficiency: Firms will have an incentive, given continuing entry and rivalry from competitors, to strive to adopt novel methods of production and unique services or otherwise to innovate, i.e., to be dynamically efficient.[93]

iii) Results from Monopoly

In contrast, under conditions of monopoly, the monopolist is the sole seller, controls all market output, and therefore can affect the market price by changing output levels. Additional assumptions in the typical "pure monopoly" model include: (1) a large number of buyers, (2) no close substitutes for the product sold by the monopolist, (3) demand for the product is downward-sloping, and (4) other markets in the economy are perfectly competitive.

The monopolist is selling to the entire market, or to put it another way, is faced by the entire market demand curve. Thus, if the monopolist's output is reduced, the prevailing price will rise. Unlike a firm in a perfectly competitive market, in raising its price above cost, a monopolist's sales are not cut to zero, because there are no other firms selling the product to which consumers can shift their demand. Sales will be reduced by a price increase, for a product with downward-sloping demand; however, up to a point the gain in profit to the monopolist on retained sales will exceed the loss in profits from lost sales (as long as

92 Whish, above note 65, ch 1.

93 As noted above, this conclusion was challenged by Austrian economist Joseph Schumpeter and his disciples.

it doesn't increase price by too much), and as a result the monopolist's profit increases with a higher price.

Through an examination of the impact of increasing prices on a monopolist's costs, revenues and profit, in the general case, economists can show that a monopolist will maximize profits by reducing output from what would prevail in competitive conditions and raising the price above cost.[94] There are implications of this in terms of the three aspects of efficiency discussed.

Allocative inefficiency: A monopolist will set prices at a level that is above social cost and below a socially optimal output. The monopolist restricts output from that prevailing in a competitive market in order to raise prices to its profit-maximizing level. The result is allocative inefficiency.

Productive inefficiency: Because a monopolist is not forced by competitive pressure to produce at the point where costs are at their lowest possible level, costs may tend to drift upward and productive efficiency sacrificed. As one economist put it, monopolists "are likely to exploit their advantage much more by not bothering to get very near the position of maximum profit, than by straining themselves to get very close to it. The best of all monopoly profits is a quiet life."[95]

Another source of productive inefficiency occurs if resources are expended by sellers in the quest to obtain a monopoly position. An example is a firm that expends resources in forming or gaining admission to a cartel in order to be in a position to charge a monopoly price.[96]

Dynamic inefficiency: Again, given the lack of competitive pressure and rivalry, there may be less incentive to innovate, to invest in research and

---

94 For a graphical explanation, see, e.g., Michael J Brennan, *The Theory of Economic Statics*, 2d ed (Englewoods Cliffs, NJ: Prentice-Hall, 1970) at 225–42; see also Dunlop, McQueen & Trebilcock, above note 32 at 50–57; Martin, above note 70 at 25–29; Posner, above note 64 at 195–201.

95 Robert H Lande, "Wealth Transfers as the Original and Primary Concern of Antitrust: The Efficiency Interpretation Challenged" (1982) 34:1 *Hastings Law Journal* 65 at 78, citing JR Hicks, "Annual Survey of Economic Theory: The Theory of Monopoly" (1935) 3 *Econometrica* 1 at 8, and Harvey Liebenstein, "Allocative Efficiency vs. 'X-Efficiency'" (1966) 56 *American Economic Review* 392. See also Mark J Roe, "Rents and Their Corporate Consequences" (2001) 53:6 *Stanford Law Review* 1463 at 1468–73; Albert Foer, "On the Inefficiencies of Efficiency as the Single-Minded Goad of Antitrust" (2015) 60:2 *Antitrust Bulletin* 103 at 122. This view has been contentious; see, e.g., Richard A Posner, *Antitrust Law, An Economic Perspective* (Chicago: University of Chicago Press, 1976) at 12.

96 *Ibid* at 11–12.

development, to introduce lower-cost methods, and generally to become a more efficient or effective competitor.

Having described the structural extremes of perfect competition and monopoly and their predicted outcomes in efficiency terms, a remaining question is: what value do the results of these models have for the real world and for design of competition law rules? The next sections examine some tools economists have used to answer this question.

iv) Models of Market and Industry Performance

Market structure (concentration ratios and market shares, barriers to entry, and growth, among other indicators) is sometimes used in competition law as a *prima facie* indicator of the extent to which a market may be subject to monopoly power, and as an entry point to determining whether particular conduct raises competition concerns.[97] The rationales for this approach include the predicted efficiency results of monopoly and perfect competition seen above, which suggest, all else equal, that society as a whole will be better off if competitive markets can be promoted or favoured over monopolistic ones. The benefits of competition arising from the outcomes above include greater overall output of goods and services, lower prices, more product choices, and faster and potentially more robust change and innovation. This is a foundation for the "standard industrial organization paradigm," which expresses the relationship between a particular industry's structure (i.e., number and relative size of competitors, and nature of barriers to entry), its competitive conduct (pricing and other competitive behaviour such as collusion), and its economic performance (e.g., achievement of the three types of efficiency) as follows (burgundy arrows) (**Figure 3.5**):[98]

Under this paradigm, market structure is seen as influencing firms' behaviour, and the firms' behaviour to affect industry performance. For example, collusion and coordinated behaviour is seen as more easily facilitated in an industry which is highly concentrated and where barriers to entry are high, than where there are many competitors and barriers are low. A dominant firm (a firm with large market share and not faced with significant competition or likely entry thereof)

97 See, e.g., Canada, Competition Bureau, *Merger Enforcement Guidelines* (6 October 2011), online: www.competitionbureau.gc.ca/eic/site/cb-bc.nsf/eng/03420.html [*Merger Enforcement Guidelines*] and Canada, Competition Bureau, *Abuse of Dominance Enforcement Guidelines* (7 March 2019), online: www.competitionbureau.gc.ca/eic/site/cb-bc.nsf/eng/04420.html, discussed in chapters 5 and 7.

98 For a more detailed examination of the paradigm, see Martin, above note 73 at 2–8; Lipczynski & Wilson, above note 91 at 7–10.

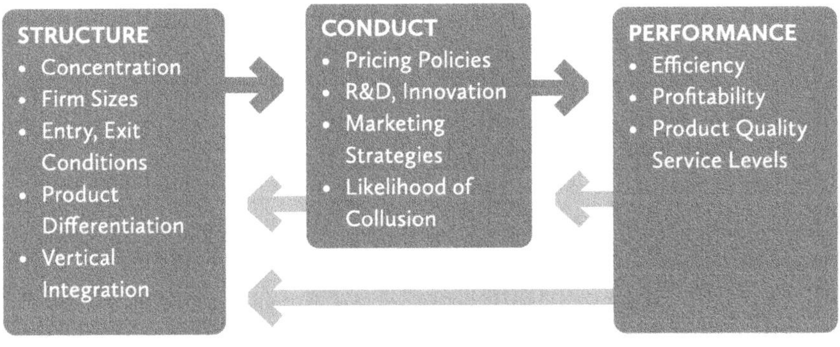

FIGURE 3.5. The structure-conduct-performance paradigm

is similarly presumed to have the ability to raise prices and restrict output.[99]

"Concentration" in this context refers to the relative size and distribution of the market shares of the firms in the market. Various measures are used, but one typical measure is the "concentration ratio" for a particular number of firms. The "four-firm concentration ratio" or CR4, calculates the sum of the market shares of the four largest firms in the industry; the CR3 encompasses the three largest firms. For example, the CR3 in Canadian wireless mobile service in 2018 was 90.7 percent, reflecting a high level of industry concentration.

The structure-conduct-performance paradigm had its origins in the work of Harvard University economists in the 1950s and 1960s.[100] It strongly influenced American antitrust jurisprudence in the period,[101] resulting in a so-called structuralist approach, which advocated the use of trends in concentration and concentration ratios as at least a *prima facie* indicator of whether, for example, mergers between competitors should be considered problematic. In 1966, in *Von's Grocery*, the US Supreme Court cited a trend of increasing concentration and blocked a merger between two grocery chains which collectively held just a 7.5 percent share of the revenues from groceries in the Los Angeles area. Justice Black, for the majority, described the purpose of the merger law

---

99 Green, above note 16 at 48–49.

100 See, e.g., *ibid*, notes 2 and 3; Gavil, Kovacic & Baker, above note 79 at 61–62; Eleanor M Fox & Lawrence A Sullivan, "Antitrust — Retrospective and Prospective: Where Are We Coming From? Where Are We Going?" (1987) 62 *New York University Law Review* 916 at 942–44.

101 See, e.g., *United States v Von's Grocery Co*, 384 US 270 (1966) [*Von's Grocery*]; *United States v Philadelphia National Bank*, 374 US 321 (1963) [*Philadelphia National Bank*]; *Brown Shoe Co v United States*, 370 US 294 (1962).

as "to prevent economic concentration in the American economy by keeping a large number of small competitors in business."[102]

The grey arrows above (which point in the opposite direction) reflect the fact that the relationships between structure, conduct, and performance are complex. A more interactive diagram would be more accurate. Other variables such as demand conditions and technology could also be added in terms of their influence on structure and conduct.[103] Economists point out that conduct and performance have feedbacks on industry structure, so that the lines of causation in the paradigm can operate in the opposite direction. The Chicago view, discussed further below, posits that efficiency may cause or be reflected in high profitability, which can stimulate or spark innovation or other competitive conduct and lead to high market share.[104] Proponents of the importance of "dynamic competition" underline the feedback between how a firm is organized internally and its ability to stimulate innovative behaviour and conduct.[105] Others employing game theory have developed models showing competitive strategies (i.e., conduct) of firms influencing industry structure.[106] The lessons from these disparate approaches include that generalizations in economics are difficult; how tendencies play out in practice will turn on the particular market conditions influencing a given set of facts.

v) *The Harvard, Chicago, and Post-Chicago Schools and Their Impact*

The Harvard "structuralist" approach was called into question by Chicago school academics, who argued, for example, that more concentrated markets may reflect superior performance and efficiency, attributes which, the latter suggested, should be favoured rather than

---

102 *Von's Grocery Co*, above note 101 at 277.

103 Martin, above note 73 at 7, Figure 1-2.

104 Green, above note 16 at 55–56, notes 14 and 15.

105 J Gregory Sidak & David J Teece, "Dynamic Competition in Antitrust Law" 5 *Journal of Competition Law & Economics* 581 at 611:

> In stark contrast to the neoclassical assumption of the structure-conduct-performance paradigm, in dynamic contexts conduct in this framework is not a function of market structure. Market conduct is driven more by internal organizational factors: standard operating procedures, investment strategies, and improvement routines. Performance depends on the (relative) organizational capabilities and behavioral traits of the enterprise. Enhanced industrial performance also stems from improvement in individual technologies and expanded use of more productive technologies.

106 Lipczynski & Wilson, above note 91 at 9–10, referring to Jean Tirole, *Theory of Industrial Organization* (Cambridge: Cambridge University Press, 1988). See also below.

attacked.[107] They criticized the application of structure-focused antitrust rules. The Chicago perspective also held that concentrated markets can be competitive, that market power is likely to be transient due to new entry, and that barriers to entry are typically no greater for new entrants than those faced by an incumbent. Chicago school adherents took the view that "markets were far more robust than people had previously imagined, and nearly always work themselves toward the competitive solution."[108] In their view, economic efficiency should be the exclusive goal of antitrust policy.[109]

In the United States, Chicago School learning fostered a shift in antitrust law in the 1970s and 1980s toward greater concern for the inefficient allocation of resources. This reflected a move away from more populist goals, such as furthering entrepreneurial independence and market participation by individual competitors, or attacking large firms due to concern over the influence they may have on policy or democratic values.[110] In spite of this shift, key aspects consistent with the structuralist approach, such as the presumption of illegality in US merger review which is triggered once high market shares and a substantial increase in concentration are proven,[111] have been retained in the American jurisprudence. This approach has been bolstered by analysis of empirical data from past mergers supporting a link between high market concentration and anti-competitive effects such as prices increases.[112]

---

107 Yale Brozen, "The Antitrust Task Force Deconcentration Recommendation" (1970) 13 *Journal of Law & Economics* 279 at 292; Bork, above note 5; Richard A Posner, "The Chicago School of Antitrust Analysis" (1979) 127 *University of Pennsylvania Law Review* 925, online: https://scholarship.law.upenn.edu/penn_law_review/vol127/iss4/15.

108 Herbert Hovenkamp, "Post-Chicago Antitrust: A Review and Critique" [2001] *Columbia Business Law Review* 257 at 266 [Hovenkamp, "Post-Chicago Antitrust"].

109 Michael J Trebilcock et al, *The Law and Economics of Canadian Competition Policy* (Toronto: University of Toronto Press, 2003) at 33–34.

110 Herbert Hovenkamp & Carl Shapiro, "Horizontal Mergers, Market Structure, and Burdens of Proof" (2018) 127 *Yale Law Journal* 1996 at 2001: "[M]odern industrial organization economics strongly supports the view that antitrust policy must always be careful not to discourage firms, even large firms, from competing on the merits to attract more customers. This idea is captured well by what has become the mantra of modern antitrust policy: the goal of antitrust is 'the protection of *competition, not competitors*.'"

111 *Philadelphia National Bank*, above note 101 at 363; Steven C Salop, "The Evolution and Vitality of Merger Presumptions: A Decision Theoretic Approach" (2015) 80 *Antitrust Law Journal* 269.

112 John Kwoka, "The Structural Presumption and the Safe Harbor in Merger Review: False Positives or Unwarranted Concerns?" (2017) 81 *Antitrust Law Journal* 837 at 837–72.

Post-Chicago scholarship has been directed at showing that markets are not as simple or seamless as the Chicago school would suggest, or that Chicago's conclusions rest on assumptions, such as perfect information, which are not a realistic portrayal of modern-day market conditions. Some post-Chicago ideas have gained wide acceptance. An example is the concept of "raising rivals' costs" as an anti-competitive strategy. It posits that exclusion of competitors using vertical practices may occur through anti-competitive strategies, such as refusal to deal or exclusive dealing arrangements, which make production or distribution more costly for competitors by denying them inputs or making it harder for them to find distribution channels.[113]

The result of the influences of these schools of thought on the judiciary in the United States has been pendulum swings in the law, with the periodic digestion of their respective ideas into the American antitrust jurisprudence. This has induced a blending of the "intellectual DNA of modern US antitrust doctrine" as it has been described by one scholar, into "a double helix . . . of two intertwined chains of ideas, one drawn from the Chicago School . . . and the other drawn from the Harvard School."[114]

In Canada, the modern legislative tests provide more statutory guidance and leave less room for judicial interpretation than in the United States. The evolution of economic thinking over the last half-century has translated into gradual legislative change toward a more efficiency-oriented competition law statute, alongside other objectives reflected in the purpose clause and legislative history.

e) Competitive Dynamics in Theory and Practice

i) *Qualifications on Perfect Competition: Workable Competition, Contestable Markets*

A difficulty with reliance on the results of the perfect competition and monopoly paradigms as a basis for guiding competition policy approaches and standards is that, as already noted, neither of these "pure" extremes reflect the reality of the modern marketplace. The Canadian economy, like most other advanced economies, is found somewhere in between, whether due to product differentiation, economies of scale, entry barriers, or imperfect information possessed by market

113 Hovenkamp, "Post-Chicago Antitrust," above note 108 at 321; Thomas G Krattenmaker & Steven C Salop, "Anticompetitive Exclusion: Raising Rivals' Costs to Achieve Power Over Price" (1986) 96 *Yale Law Journal* 209.

114 William E Kovacic, "The Intellectual DNA of Modern US Competition Law for Dominant Firm Conduct: The Chicago/Harvard Double Helix" [2007] *Columbia Business Law Review* 1 at 14.

players. In fact, much of the Canadian economy likely falls into the category of oligopoly—a few sellers and some barriers to entry created by such factors as brand loyalty, regulatory requirements, or scale economies. What does this reality mean for the design of competition laws? For example, if we cannot achieve perfect competition, or some facsimile of it, is it still worth striving to increase competition, and if so, in what fashion? Economists have developed a number of approaches to provide guidance in response to these questions.

As a practical improvement on the theoretical constructs of perfect competition and monopoly, and the complexities and ambiguities of the various models of monopolistic competition and oligopoly, economists developed the concept of "workable competition," setting out certain minimal criteria for determining when a market structure may produce results which are beneficial to the public.[115] These criteria recognize that perfectly competitive markets cannot be achieved in most cases. They seek to provide guidance on what conditions may at least approximate, or permit one to move a market toward, the results of perfect competition.

Structural criteria for workable competition include that the number of suppliers be at least as large as economies of scale will permit, and that there be no artificial limits on entry or exit. Conduct criteria include that there be independent rivalry among market participants, free of collusion, that there be no "unfair, exclusionary, predatory or coercive tactics," and that sales promotion be informative, or not misleading.[116]

Even where a market structure is highly concentrated, the theory of "contestable markets" suggests that the market performance may approach, or at least move in the direction of, that of perfect competition as long as entry and exit conditions are easy (including not subject to "sunk" costs which cannot be recovered on exit) and there is some lag time in the ability of the incumbent to respond to an entrant's price or contract offer to buyers.[117] The "contestability" theory[118] argues that even a monopolist will not have the power to raise prices above competitive levels if price increases are likely to quickly stimulate new entry which will drive prices back down to cost. Whether this entry is permanent or "hit and run," the theory posits that the threat of entry can cause industry performance to approach that predicted in a perfectly competitive market. While it has been questioned whether this theory adds a

115 Frederic M Scherer, *Industrial Market Structure and Economic Performance* (Boston: Houghton Mifflin, 1980) at 42.

116 *Ibid.*

117 Trebilcock et al, above note 109 at 138.

118 William J Baumol, John C Panzar & Robert D Willig, *Contestable Markets and the Theory of Industry Structure* (San Diego: Harcourt Brace Jovanovich, 1982).

great deal to the theoretical foundations discussed above,[119] it advocates an emphasis on the value of examining of the presence or absence of entry barriers and the effects of firm conduct which might raise barriers to entry.

ii) Oligopoly and Its Brethren: The Middle Kingdom

Considerable scholarship has been devoted by economists to the question of the performance of the intermediate market structures of monopolistic competition and oligopoly. The various models and their predicted outcomes are complex and depend on the particular market conditions affecting the participants.[120] French economists Cournot (1838) and Bertrand (1883) developed the two basic models of non-cooperative oligopoly pricing which have endured and been applied, for example to the assessment of the likelihood of coordinated or collusive behaviour.[121] Suppliers in oligopolistic markets possess a critical aspect: unlike players in perfectly competitive markets, whose output is so small relative to the market size that they cannot affect market price, oligopolists can have some impact on market price through changes in their output or other adjustment in other product attributes. They also recognize that their returns are affected by the actions of their competitors—so-called interdependence recognized. Such actions may include the initiation of, and response to, price, output, and other competitive changes. This leads, for example, to incentives to engage in forms of collusive behaviour, whether expressly or through various forms of tacit conduct or signalling.[122]

The study of the operation of oligopolistic markets—markets with few sellers—has yielded useful insights which can assist in the assessment of competitive behaviour. For example, certain conditions such as the ability of co-conspirators to monitor competitors' behaviour, to detect cheating, and the ability to retaliate, make collusion more likely to be successful.[123] These insights led to a shift in attention by econo-

---

119 See, e.g., Whish & Bailey, above note 11 at 17.

120 See, e.g., the discussion in Martin, above note 73 at ch 5 and 6.

121 William J Kolasky, "Coordinated Effects in Merger Review: From Dead Frenchmen to Beautiful Minds and Mavericks" (Address delivered at the ABA Section of Antitrust Law Spring Meeting, Washington, DC, 24 April 2002) at Section II A, online: www.justice.gov/atr/speech/coordinated-effects-merger-review-dead-frenchmen-beautiful-minds-and-mavericks [Kolasky]; Lipczynski & Wilson, above note 91 at 19–25; Church & Ware, above note 87, ch 8.

122 Church & Ware, above note 87, ch 6.

123 George J Stigler, "A Theory of Oligopoly" (1964) 72 *Journal of Political Economy* 44; Martin, above note 73, ch 6; Donald G McFetridge, "Economics and Canadian Competition Policy" (2012) 25:2 *Canadian Competition Law Review* 540; Thomas

mists away from concern with market concentration alone and toward other market factors that may serve to facilitate reaching and enforcing collusive agreements, such as buyer size, frequency of purchases, and transparency of price and other terms.[124] These kinds of considerations have practical value; they are adopted, for example, in the Competition Bureau's *Merger Enforcement Guidelines* as factors in the assessment of when a merger is more likely to be of concern based upon its effect on future coordinated behaviour.[125] They have played a role in the Tribunal's assessment of the likelihood of a merger lessening competition. In a case involving a merger of gasoline retailers, such conditions contributed to the Tribunal finding that a lessening of competition from collusion was likely to result in certain geographic markets.[126]

Economists also apply various models of oligopolistic behaviour to predict the unilateral impacts of mergers between firms with differentiated products (unilateral effects occur when a merger eliminates competition between two merging firms but does not alter the manner in which the other firms in the market compete).[127] Applying these models, unilateral effects are seen to be influenced by the extent of direct competition, or "diversion," between the merging firms, rather than the overall level of market concentration in the pre-merger market. The Bureau's *Merger Guidelines* operationalize these models by taking the view that a price increase is more likely between firms with differentiated products when those products are viewed by consumers as each other's closest substitutes.[128] This approach was adopted in the Tribunal's decision in *Canada (Commissioner of Competition) v Superior Propane Inc*, where the fact that consumers viewed the merging parties as close substitutes was seen a factor in finding that the merger resulted in a substantial lessening of competition.[129]

W Ross & Andy Baziliauskas, "Lessening of Competition in Mergers under the Competition Act: Unilateral and Interdependence Effects" (2000) 33 *Canadian Business Law Journal* 373 [Ross & Baziliauskas].

124 Kolasky, above note 121.

125 *Merger Enforcement Guidelines*, above note 97, paras 6.31–6.32.

126 *Canada (Commissioner of Competition) v Parkland Industries Ltd*, [2015] CCTD No 4 at para 98.

127 See, e.g., Carl Shapiro, "Mergers with Differentiated Products" (1996) 10:2 *Antitrust* 23.

128 *Merger Enforcement Guidelines*, above note 97, para 6.13.

129 *Canada (Commissioner of Competition) v Superior Propane Inc* (2000), 7 CPR (4th) 385 at para 247 [*Propane CCT1*].

iii) Game Theory

Game theory is a tool used in the context of competition economics to analyze strategic behaviour by competitors in oligopolistic markets, where each competitor takes into account how it expects others to behave, given that each competitor's optimal strategy (and ultimate payoff) depends on the strategies of all other players in the game. For example, each competitor may be assumed to believe that its profit-maximizing price depends on the prices chosen by other competitors. Game theory assesses the optimal outcome for each player from a set of choices by analyzing the costs and benefits to players as they compete with each other. The "solution" to the game is the set of strategies in which each competitor maximizes its payoff given the strategies of all other players (a "Nash equilibrium").[130] Game theory relies upon certain critical assumptions, such as rationality (players have a desire to maximize their own payoffs) and common knowledge (players know the structure and rules of the game).[131] These assumptions may or may not apply in certain real world applications. As a result, there has been some criticism of game theory models as being unable to accurately predict the results in real-world situations.[132]

Game theory can be useful in modelling markets with a small number of players who are aware that their competitive moves will affect the other and influence the prevailing price or other competitive variables.[133] In such circumstances, competitors' choices, for example, about whether to "cheat" on a cartel by reducing a price below the agreed-upon collusive price, can resemble those of the players in the classic game theory interaction in the "prisoner's dilemma." This can mean that a small

130 For an overview of game theory methodology see Church & Ware, above note 87 at 211–30 and 283–303.

131 *Ibid* at 216:

> 1. *Rationality.* Game theory assumes that players are interested in maximizing their payoffs. We often assume that a player's preferences can be represented by a utility function. . . . In game theory it is common to refer to a player's utility function as her payoff function. Payoffs for firms, the predominant players in this book, are simply profits or expected profits. We assume that firms, for the most part, are interested in maximizing profits. 2. *Common Knowledge.* Common knowledge means that all players know the structure of the game and that their opponents are rational, that all players know that all players know the structure of the game and that their opponents are rational, and so on.

132 Bruce H Kobayashi, "Game Theory and Antitrust: A Post-Mortem" (1997) 5:3 *George Mason Law Review* 41 at 415: "there exists little evidence that game theoretic models of interactions between firms can more accurately describe the behavior of complex organizations in markets."

133 Gregory J Werden, "Economic Evidence on the Existence of Collusion: Reconciling Antitrust Law with Oligopoly Theory" (2004) 71:3 *Antitrust Law Journal* 719.

number of competitors can sustain higher prices without an express agreement through a form of "tacit collusion" which resembles the game theory model of a Nash equilibrium. Models drawn from game theory have been combined with those drawn from oligopoly theory to help identify a range of market and firm characteristics which are conducive to coordinated or collusive behaviour, such as:

> (i) a limited number of competitors or, conversely high shares of market sales and capacities of the firms in question; (ii) a high degree of homogeneity in terms of products and cost structures; (iii) a high level of market transparency; (iv) significant barriers to entry; (v) the absence of significant buyer power; (vi) a low probability of detection and legal sanctions; (vii) multi-market contacts; (viii) past experience with coordination and (ix) a stable economic environment.[134]

Such models may also be used in assessing the impact of a merger on future competition and market prices, taking into account such variables as the number of competitors, their relative size, capacity, and cost structures.[135]

f) Conclusion: Areas of Economic Consensus; Core Competition Law Provisions

The foundational concerns with the reduction in efficiency and economic welfare from monopoly remains the base upon which competition law architecture is constructed. The determination of how to promote or encourage increased competition and efficient markets and analyze conduct has evolved from that basic framework with various economic models and approaches. With the development of more tools, such as game theory models, in the economists' toolbox, the conventional market structure-conduct-performance has been qualified to place less weight on market shares and industry structure and more on particular market characteristics that may permit firms to raise prices.

The translation of these evolving concepts drawn from economics into legal analysis and standards is a gradual process.[136] Ideas and models drawn from economics and related disciplines have been incorporated

---

134 See, e.g., Gisela Aigner, Oliver Budzinski & Arndt Christiansen, "Analysis of Coordinated Effects in EU Merger Control: Where Do We Stand after Sony/BMG and Impala?" (2006) 2 *European Competition Journal* 311 at 313.

135 See Ross & Baziliauskas, above note 123 at 388–95; Malcolm B Coate, "Unilateral Effects Analysis in Merger Review: Limits and Opportunities" (2014) 10:2 *European Competition Journal* 231.

136 Daniel Zimmer, "The Emancipation of Antitrust from Market-Share-Based Approaches" (2016) 61:1 *Antitrust Bulletin* 133.

into the elements of modern competition law over time. These concepts have informed the fashioning of the main pillars of competition law regimes around the globe, including in Canada. The following core provisions are found in most modern competition laws and reflect a broad consensus in economic thinking about those areas that raise policy concerns:

- prohibitions of price fixing and other collusive behaviour that reduce or eliminate rivalry between competitors;
- review of mergers which reduce the number of competitors, substantially increase concentration or the probability of coordinated behaviour; and
- remedies to address the behaviour of dominant firms that increases barriers to entry or that targets the ability of emerging competitors to compete.

Another area in which there is a general consensus that a type of conduct can be anti-competitive, but not necessarily a consistent approach in the rules developed across jurisdictions, is that of coordinated behaviour falling short of an express agreement. Economic theory has provided insights into approaches useful in combatting the anti-competitive effects of tacit collusion by, for example, identifying as potentially problematic those practices falling short of express agreement that can facilitate price or other coordination among firms in concentrated markets, such as "most favoured nation clauses" (whereby a seller agrees that a buyer will benefit from terms that are at least as favourable as those offered by the seller to any other buyer[137]) and termination penalties in customer contracts. However, designing ex ante rules for addressing such conduct is difficult, because the conduct can often be benign. In Canada, while such conduct is not subject to a specifically targeted prohibition, it may be addressed under provisions such as abuse of dominance or as a factor in merger review.

More unsettled still in terms of economic analysis is the assessment of practices between suppliers and customers, such as franchise restrictions, and other so-called vertical practices applying between parties in the chain of supply. These include such matters as refusals to supply, territorial restraints, resale price maintenance, and tied selling. Such conduct may promote or hinder competition depending on the circumstances, and the policy case for intervention is thus more mixed or controversial. The competition law treatment of various jurisdictions varies

137 See Francisco Enrique Gonzalez-Diaz & Matthew Bennett, "The Law and Economics of Most-Favoured Nation Clauses" (2015) 1:3 *Competition Law & Policy Debate* 26 at 36–39.

more widely, reflecting the evolving economic thinking surrounding these practices. In Canada, these practices are subject to a case-by-case assessment of their competitive effects, but in other jurisdictions some have been prohibited applying a *per se* standard, i.e., irrespective of their effect on competition.

The integration of economics into competition law remains challenging because law requires a manageable and understandable set of rules that can govern business behaviour and be applied consistently.[138] It is likely that competition laws will continue to evolve as economics influences our understanding of the effects of various kinds of competitive conduct and industry structures. At the same time, certain non-efficiency-related objectives continue to play a role in the law. The discussion now turns to those objectives.

2) Distributive Concerns and Consumer Welfare

a) Introduction

While economic efficiency is concerned with the size of the economic pie and, in the context of competition policy, how competitive actions or market structures may make public wealth greater or smaller over time, distributive concerns relate to how wealth is distributed among various groups in society, such as consumers, producers, labour, and small business. Among these groups, competition policy focuses most often on distributive impacts on consumers. "Consumers" in this sense are those who are made subject to a price increase or reduction in quality due to market power or a monopolistic practice. These parties may not be individual families or end product consumers. They may be businesses which buy inputs for further manufacture, or retailers which acquire goods for resale. They may also be *sellers* of goods which are subject to market power among purchasers (or "monopsony" power). The term "consumers" is thus used below as a flexible catch-all to reflect that broad group of interests.[139] The distributive concern as discussed below

138 As has been noted, "a fundamental challenge for antitrust is the existence of too many theories without methodological commitments from regulators and courts on how to select among them . . . this model selection problem threatens to strip the disciplining force that economics has placed on antitrust law." Geoffrey A Manne & Joshua D Wright, "Google and the Limits of Antitrust: The Case against the Case against Google" (2011) 34:1 *Harvard Journal of Law & Public Policy* 171 at 182.

139 Herbert J Hovenkamp, "Is Antitrust's Consumer Welfare Principle Imperiled?" (2019) *Faculty Scholarship at Penn Law* 1985 at 17–19, online: https://scholarship.law.upenn.edu/faculty_scholarship/1985 [Hovenkamp, *Penn Law*, "Consumer Welfare Principle"].

addresses the extent to which there are transfers of wealth between producers and these consumers arising from anti-competitive practices.

The concept of consumer welfare in competition policy has been described by a senior American scholar as follows:

> [T]he consumer welfare principle favors consumers. If a practice leads to lower output and higher prices the consumer welfare principle disfavors it even though the gains to producers might be larger than any losses to consumers.[140]

The consumer welfare standard in competition law does not seek to distribute income from the "wealthy producer" to the "impoverished consumer" in an unlimited fashion or for its own sake. It is directed at addressing the impacts of *price increases* and other changes resulting from the exercise of market power to ensure that consumers are not prejudiced. Concern for consumer welfare finds expression in the purpose clause of the Act, in the objective "to provide consumers with competitive prices and product choices."

The consumer welfare standard can be contrasted with a "total welfare" (also called "total surplus") approach, which would favour permitting a practice even if consumers pay higher prices, as long as producer gains (e.g., from cost savings and transfers of income from consumers) are larger than any allocative efficiency losses resulting from the price increase, so that overall social welfare is increased. The logic of this approach is that if the societal pie is increased by greater efficiency, everyone will eventually share in the benefits. As noted earlier, economists generally view redistribution of income caused by monopoly pricing as neutral from an efficiency perspective because it represents simply a transfer from one pocket to another within the overall economy: "transformation of benefits from one form (consumers' surplus) to another (profit) is treated as a wash under the conventional welfare economics model."[141]

Whether competition law should pursue a total welfare versus consumer welfare approach has been the subject of extensive debate; one that surfaced, as will be seen below, in the interpretation of the merger efficiency defence in the *Competition Act*. The Federal Court of Appeal

140 *Ibid* at 2; also Herbert J Hovenkamp, "Is Antitrust's Consumer Welfare Principle Imperiled?" (2019) 45 *Journal of Corporation Law* 65 at 66: "the consumer welfare [('CW') principle, as most people understand it today] antitrust policy encourages markets to produce output as high as is consistent with sustainable competition, and prices that are accordingly as low."

141 See, e.g., Oliver E Williamson, "Economies as an Antitrust Defense Revisited" (1977) 125 *University of Pennsylvania Law Review* 699 at 711.

held that the efficiency defence did not mandate a total welfare approach and that the Tribunal erred when it completely excluded income distribution effects in the assessment of the merger efficiencies defence under section 96 of the Act.

b) Historical Background

As we have seen already, distributive concerns motivated many of those who advocated for anti-combines legislation in Canada in the 1880s. The perceived monopoly profits of manufacturers and railroads were regarded as "a privately imposed tax" on consumers and farmers; an objective was "to recover some of the income which they believed had been transferred from themselves to the tariff-protected and in some cases quite highly concentrated" industries.[142] The Select Committee of the House of Commons appointed to examine trade combinations in 1888 revealed combinations and agreements among firms supplying such things as sugar, coal, biscuits, undertaking services, and oatmeal milling.[143] During debate on second reading of the bill to address the effects of these combinations in 1889, Conservative MP Clarke Wallace, the bill's sponsor, placed the spotlight on the monopoly profits extracted by members of an Ottawa coal combine: "three men . . . divided amongst themselves, on a capital of $15,000, after paying all expenses of management, and all the expenses of the combination, $33,000."[144]

The Economic Council's 1969 *Interim Report on Competition Policy* recognized that distributive concerns, including what it called "an equitable distribution" of income, had been part of the historical rationale for early competition legislation in Canada. Similarly, in the United States, although the early objectives of antitrust laws remain controversial,[145] one commentator concluded that "Congress passed the antitrust laws to further economic objectives, but primarily objectives of a distributive rather than of an efficiency nature."[146] The case for continued reliance

142 *Interim Report* 1969, above note 27 at 6–7.

143 Carman D Baggaley, "Tariffs, Combines and Politics: The Beginning of Canadian Competition Policy, 1888–1900," ch 1 in RS Khemani & William T Stanbury, eds, *Historical Perspectives on Canadian Competition Policy* (IRPP: Halifax, 1991) at 12–17.

144 *House of Commons Debates*, 6th Parl, 3d Sess (8 April 1889) at 1111 (Clarke Wallace).

145 Daniel A Crane, "Rationales for Antitrust: Economics and Other Bases" in Roger D Blair & D Daniel Sokol, eds, *The Oxford Handbook of International Antitrust Economics* (Oxford: Oxford University Press, 2014), vol 1 at 3 [Crane].

146 Robert H Lande, "Wealth Transfers as the Original and Primary Concern of Antitrust: The Efficiency Interpretation Challenged" (1982) 34:1 *Hastings Law Journal* 65 at 68.

on a consideration of distributive effects on consumers as part of competition law is bolstered by the view that the transfer of income caused by monopoly pricing may outweigh the allocative inefficiency impacts by a wide margin:

> Under market conditions most likely to be encountered . . . the transferred wealth usually will be between two and forty times as great as the accompanying allocative inefficiency. Thus, the redistributive effects of market power generally exceed the allocative inefficiency effects by a substantial amount.[147]

In the Economic Council's view, in most cases, pursuing economic efficiency as the primary goal of the legislation would also further other objectives, including "more equal income distribution."[148] Thus, addressing price fixing or conduct by dominant firms that excludes competitors will both advance efficient market operation and produce more competitive prices for consumers. Matters become more complicated where a practice—a merger, exclusive arrangement by a dominant firm or joint venture agreement among competitors—may raise consumer prices but also create substantial efficiencies which lower costs. That issue was raised in the *Canada (Commissioner of Competition) v Superior Propane Inc* merger.

c) *Superior Propane:* Differing Views of the Objectives and the Efficiency Defence

Superior Propane involved a merger between two nation-wide suppliers of propane. The customers affected included hospitals, small businesses, and residential consumers. For some of these parties, propane was the only viable energy source. The Competition Tribunal found that the merger was likely to lessen competition substantially in dozens of cities and towns, and to raise prices by an average of 8 percent. In spite of that finding, the Tribunal did not block the merger, due to efficiency gains from the transaction, applying the then-existing[149] "efficiencies defence" to the merger provisions.[150] On appeal, the Federal Court of Appeal found the Tribunal had erred in law in its interpretation of the section.[151]

The Tribunal's and Court of Appeal's interpretations of the scope of section 96, the efficiency defence, turned on different conceptions of that section's objectives. Justice Nadon in the Competition Tribunal took the

147 *Ibid* at 75.
148 *Interim Report* 1969, above note 27 at 20.
149 As discussed further in Chapter 5, the defence was repealed in 2023.
150 *Propane CCT1*, above note 129.
151 *Propane FCA1*, above note 3.

view that economic efficiency was "Parliament's paramount objective in passing the merger provisions of the Act." As noted at the outset of the chapter, one of the objectives listed in section 1.1 of the Act is "to promote the efficiency and adaptability of the Canadian economy." Justice Nadon held that the pursuit of efficiency meant that the only anti-competitive effects which should be balanced against a merger's efficiency gains under section 96 are efficiency losses: the deadweight loss due to allocative inefficiency caused by the price increase.[152] He adopted a "total welfare" approach to interpretation of the provision. Effects from the mere transfer of wealth from propane producers to consumers due to higher prices were deemed irrelevant because they were regarded as having no efficiency implications. Justice Nadon concluded that "nothing in the Act allows us to consider distributional goals in merger review."[153]

The Court of Appeal majority per Evans JA found that the Tribunal erred in law when it excluded wealth transfers completely from the effects of a merger balanced against efficiency gains. The Appeal Court noted the purpose clause also refers, for example, to the goal of providing "consumers with competitive prices and product choices." In its earlier decision in *Hillsdown Holdings*, the Tribunal per Reed J had held in reviewing the efficiency defence:

> The Tribunal has not been referred to any jurisprudence which indicates that in a listing of objectives in the purpose clause of a statute that which is listed first is to be given greater weight than those which follow. Also, there is nothing in the text of the purpose section which indicates that such preference is to be given. Indeed, in debates in the House of Commons, the Minister responsible for the Act indicated that it was the fourth objective which was of overriding concern:
>
>> The fourth but not the least objective is to provide consumers with competitive prices and product choices. As such, this objective becomes the common denominator in what we are trying to achieve. This is the ultimate objective of the Bill.[154]

Justice Evans cited Reed J's analysis of the legislative history of section 96, which noted that versions of the efficiency defence contained in two earlier bills would have adopted a total welfare approach. He concluded that the balancing approach ultimately enacted as section 96 did not take

---

152 Such as the fact that prices may lead some consumers to substitute products that cost more for society to produce than the products of the merged entity.

153 *Propane CCT1*, above note 129 at para 426.

154 *Canada (Director of Investigation and Research, Competition Act) v Hillsdown Holdings (Canada) Ltd*, [1992] CCTD No 4 at para 151.

that approach, and therefore that wealth transfers may not be excluded *per se* from the effects of the merger to be weighed under the efficiency defence.[155]

The Competition Tribunal reheard the case in light of the guidance of the Court of Appeal, and considered the evidence of wealth transfers as it was directed to do. However, it permitted the merger, finding that the efficiencies still outweighed the anti-competitive effects, even taking into account the transfers which it found relevant. The Tribunal determined that the only wealth transfers deserving of weight were those imposed on low income or vulnerable propane customers. A further appeal was dismissed. The Federal Court of Appeal found that the Tribunal was free to fashion a weighing test as it had done, that it had not excluded potentially relevant factors, and had committed no reviewable error in weighing the available evidence.[156]

d) Challenges in Applying Distributive Considerations

A number of issues have been identified with respect to giving income distribution a leading role in competition law decision making:

- The precise income impacts on the public of anti-competitive conduct such as price increases may be difficult to gauge. Consumers may also be shareholders, or beneficiaries of pension plans and therefore benefit from higher producer prices and profits. Consumers can also be intermediate purchasers, such as small business operators, who can pass on any price increase to their customers.[157] Some consumers, particularly of luxury goods, may not have low incomes. In *Superior Propane*, the Tribunal addressed such concerns by only taking into account distributive effects on "captive" consumers in the balancing test under the efficiencies defence.[158]
- Income effects on the producer side of the ledger are similarly hard to evaluate. Businesses are run by individuals who are themselves consumers.[159] Producers also reflect a range of varied interests, such as small or medium-sized business owners. Higher producer prices may be shared by labour, especially when a company is unionized.

---

155 *Propane FCA1*, above note 3 at paras 149–51 and 159.

156 *Canada (Commissioner of Competition) v Superior Propane Inc* (2002), 18 CPR (4th) 417 (CCT) [*Propane CCT2*], aff'd 2003 FCA 53.

157 See Dunlop, McQueen & Trebilcock, above note 32 at 65.

158 See *Propane CCT2*, above note 156 at paras 333–65.

159 Francesco Ducci & Michael Trebilcock, "The Revival of Fairness Discourse in Competition Policy" (2019) 64 *Antitrust Bulletin* 79 at 87 [Ducci & Trebilcock]; Dunlop, McQueen & Trebilcock, above note 32 at 65.

Some empirical evidence suggests, for example, that employees tend to earn higher wages in more concentrated markets.[160]

- The challenges created by applying distributive considerations include having to answer questions such as: "distribution of income from whom in favour of whom?" To answer such a question may raise a subjective and potentially value-laden assessment about which interests in society are more deserving than others. Such determinations are difficult to reduce to a comprehensible legal rule or standard, particularly one free from complaints of a lack of predictable application, or arbitrariness.[161] Robert Bork opined in *The Antitrust Paradox*, "the shift in income distribution does not lessen total wealth, and a decision about it requires a choice between two groups of consumers that should be made by the legislature rather than by the judiciary."[162]
- Excessive or above-cost pricing says little about the underlying competitive conduct which may have produced it and therefore can provide a weak foundation, alone, for competition law intervention.[163] High prices may be the product of the dynamic and competitive behaviour that competition policy seeks to promote. Addressing such pricing which does not occur in the context of anti-competitive or exclusionary conduct "would turn competition agencies into price regulators, a task they are not generally well equipped to perform."[164]

Other policy tools are also generally seen as more effective or direct ways to address income distribution issues.[165] One scholar opined, "[a]ntitrust

160 Crane, above note 145 at 4.

161 See, e.g., Daniel A Crane, "Antitrust and Wealth Inequality" (2016) 101 *Cornell Law Review* 1171 at 1228:

> Antitrust law works best as a set of objective principles regarding measurable economic effects in commercial markets. Concrete proof of progressivity or regressivity from changes in market power is usually unavailable and admitting efforts to prove them could lead to systemic error. While there may be an occasional need for flexibility in antitrust doctrine or practice to accommodate civil society initiatives focused on redistributing wealth or achieving related social justice objectives, the scope of any such exemption should remain narrow.

162 Bork, above note 5 at 111.

163 See Chapter 9, Section D(2).

164 Ducci & Trebilcock, above note 153 at 88.

165 Louis Kaplow, "On the Choice of Welfare Standards in Competition Law," ch 1 in Daniel Zimmer, ed, *The Goals of Competition Law* (Cheltenham: Edward Elgar, 2012) at 26: "it is more efficient to confine competition law to the maximization of total welfare and achieve redistribution solely through the tax and transfer system. The same redistribution can be achieved at less cost, or more redistribution at the same cost; in general, all income groups can be made better off."

... is poorly suited to address issues of income inequality. Many other public policies are far superior for this purpose."[166] The same point was made by the Economic Council of Canada in 1969: "deliberate changes in the distribution of income are best brought about by relying mainly on policies other than competition policy," such as taxation.[167]

e) Conclusion

There are many situations where the promotion of competition and efficiency also promotes consumer welfare; for example, stopping a merger that raises prices paid by consumers, when the merger does not bring about significant beneficial efficiencies, will promote competition, efficiency, and avoid a transfer of income to the merging parties from their customers. Outside the merger context, the situations in which Canadian competition law must integrate, or balance, considerations of income distribution as a potentially explicit or decisive factor against efficiency, as occurred in *Superior Propane*, may be fairly limited, but two examples can be cited. An efficiency defence containing the same balancing framework as in section 96 was included in the civil agreements provision. That section has to date, however, generated little litigation or even consent resolutions.[168] In the area of dominant firm practices, the Tribunal has also recognized efficiency considerations may be a factor in assessing whether a practice should be found "anti-competitive." In this assessment there can be a balancing of the pro-competitive or efficiency-based justifications against the anti-competitive effect.[169] The jurisprudence under abuse of dominance has not thus far directly assessed the balancing of consumer wealth transfers against efficiency, but the issue may arise in a future case.

How distributional concerns may play out in these other contexts remains to be seen. One journal article has suggested, in weighing the opposing arguments, that there is "limited room for achieving distributive goals through the choice of welfare standard, which cannot be a direct and consistent instrument for advancing distributive goals, except

166 Carl Shapiro, "Antitrust in a Time of Populism" (2018) 61 *International Journal of Industrial Organization* 714 at 717 [Shapiro]:

> Tax policy, government programs such as Medicaid, disability insurance, and Social Security, and a whole range of policies relating to education and training spring immediately to mind. So, while stronger antitrust enforcement will modestly help address income inequality, explicitly bringing income distribution into antitrust analysis would be unwise.

167 *Interim Report* 1969, above note 27 at 23.

168 See Chapter 6, Section E(3)(a).

169 See Chapter 7, Section C(2)(b)(ii)(e).

for avoiding some specific cases of regressive effects that may be felt by poorer consumers."[170] Nonetheless, as *Superior Propane* holds, distributive considerations have played an historical role as part of the context of Canadian competition legislation. Consumer welfare concerns are reflected in the purpose clause and feature in competition law rules applied in many other jurisdictions. The Federal Court of Appeal in *Superior Propane* left it to the Competition Tribunal to adopt an appropriate methodology for weighing distributional considerations where relevant. The decision counsels that as a matter of law, this element cannot be excluded from the calculus where anti-competitive effects must be weighed against efficiencies as part of the applicable test.

3) Concerns with the Accumulation and Use of Economic Power and Business Equity

a) Introduction

As noted above, the abuse of economic power was a rationale for the first anti-combines law in the late 1880s. Concerns about economic power raised at the time and subsequently reflect a range of disparate considerations. These will be examined below, including one aspect specifically found in the purpose class: small and medium-sized business equity.

b) Populist or Political Goals Relating to the Exercise of Economic Power

While controlling the negative effects of the accumulation of economic power was a factor in the passage of Canada's first competition legislation, this consideration did not assume the profile in Canada that it did in the United States in later decades. From time to time, however, calls for a policy response to increased corporate concentration in the Canadian economy have arisen. For example, in the 1970s, the proposed takeover by Power Corporation of Argus Corporation (two large corporate conglomerates) led to the appointment of the Royal Commission on Corporate Concentration. The Commission's 1978 report advocated vigorous enforcement of competition laws in respect of collusion and to address "attempts to build or maintain barriers to entry and attempts by dominant firms in mature industries to monopolize markets." The Commission saw this as a route to "workable competition."[171] However,

---

170 Ducci & Trebilcock, above note 159 at 88.

171 Canada, *Report of the Royal Commission on Corporate Concentration* (Ottawa: Queen's Printer, 1978) at 216.

the Report devoted little discussion to policy problems associated with the presence of corporate power *per se*.

In the United States, concerns about economic power have more frequently motivated legislative change and informed judicial interpretation. Such considerations were cited as a foundational rationale for the passage of the first antitrust statute, the *Sherman Act*. President Grover Cleveland said in his State of the Union speech in 1888, prior to the passage of the legislation:

> As we view the achievements of aggregated capital, we discover the existence of trusts, combinations and monopolies, while the citizen is struggling in the rear or is trampled to death beneath an iron heel. Corporations, which should be the carefully restrained creatures of the law and servants of the people, are fast becoming the people's masters.[172]

In 1946, Learned Hand J wrote the following in holding that Alcoa had illegally monopolized US aluminum markets under the *Sherman Act*:

> [A]mong the purposes of Congress in 1890 was a desire to put an end to great aggregations of capital because of the helplessness of the individual before them. . . . Throughout the history of these statutes it has been constantly assumed that one of their purposes was to perpetuate and preserve, for its own sake and in spite of possible cost, an organization of industry in small units which can effectively compete with each other.[173]

In 1947, in another monopolization case, *United States v EI Du Pont de Nemours and Co*, the US Supreme Court summarized the origins of the *Sherman Act* as follows:

> [F]ear of the power of rapid accumulations of individual and corporate wealth from the trade and industry of a developing national economy caused its passage. Units of traders and producers snowballed by combining into so-called "trusts." Competition was threatened. Control of prices was feared. Individual initiative was dampened.[174]

---

172 As cited by Donald I Baker & William Blumenthal, "Ideological Cycles and Unstable Antitrust Rules" (1986) 31 *Antitrust Bulletin* 323 at 326 [Baker & Blumenthal].

173 *Alcoa*, above note 12 at 429.

174 *United States v EI Du Pont de Nemours and Co*, 351 US 377 (1947) at 386. In dissent in *United States v Columbia Steel Co*, 334 US 495 (1948) at 536, Douglas J wrote that the *Sherman Act* "is founded on a theory of hostility to the concentration in private hands of power so great that only a government of the people should have it."

The foregoing passages reflect a number of overlapping concerns which have been described as the "populist"[175] or "political"[176] goals of competition or antitrust laws. They include themes that often overlap.

- Concerns for democratic values: "[C]oncentrated economic power is generally accompanied by centralized political power, which is seen as dangerous to a democratic polity"; "[A]ntitrust is a semi-constitutional tool for maintaining a certain vision of democracy, akin to the fundamental political concepts of separation of powers, checks-and-balances, and federalism."[177]
- "Jeffersonian" values: "[S]mall, local, responsible businesses"[178] are not only more democratic but have "the assumed moral superiority of rural life and small scale institutions."[179]
- Equity: Certain American commentators have called for a greater role for equity concerns in antitrust. Equity can mean more than addressing income distribution; it can cover freedom of market access: "Equity in antitrust means tilting the scales away from powerful business and [towards] powerless people; away from protecting the (freedom of) the incumbent and towards protecting the access and opportunity of young challengers. Safeguarding opportunity for outsiders is a far cry from handing them money. It has obvious efficiency properties."[180]
- Freedom: This can mean "the freedom of producers to sell and the freedom of consumers to buy."[181] For consumers, this includes freedom of choice; for producers, the freedom to enter a market and compete without artificial constraints. With respect to the latter, the US Supreme Court stated in 1972 in *Topco,* in assessing a restriction placed on the territories within which supermarkets could sell, that antitrust laws are "as important to the preservation of economic freedom and our free-enterprise system as the Bill of Rights is to the protection of our fundamental personal freedoms. And the freedom guaranteed each and every business, no matter how small, is the

175 See, e.g., Baker & Blumenthal, above note 172; Shapiro, above note 166.

176 Dunlop, McQueen & Trebilcock, above note 32 at 67–68; Albert Foer, "The Goals of Antitrust: Thoughts on Consumer Welfare in the U.S." (31 August 2005), American Antitrust Institute Working Paper No 05-09 at 15 [Foer].

177 *Ibid* at 15; Robert Pitofsky, "The Political Content of Antitrust" (1979) 127 *University of Pennsylvania Law Review* 1051.

178 Baker & Blumenthal, above note 172 at 325.

179 Foer, above note 176 at 16.

180 Eleanor M Fox, "Competition Policy at the Intersection of Equity and Efficiency: The Developed and Developing Worlds" (2018) 63 *Antitrust Bulletin* 3 at 5.

181 Thomas B Leary, "Freedom as the Core Value of Antitrust in the New Millennium" (2001) 68:2 *Antitrust Law Journal* 545 at 546.

freedom to compete — to assert with vigor, imagination, devotion, and ingenuity whatever economic muscle it can muster."[182] This viewpoint is similar to that taken by the European Ordoliberal school, which developed in Germany and Austria in the 1950s. It saw the ultimate objective of competition law as maintaining the freedom of individual market actors to compete.[183]

Competition law is also sometimes seen as a way of reducing demand for regulation or other forms of state intervention. It has been argued in Canada, for example, that without effective competition laws, "the likely result will be an economy so dominated by a few corporate giants that it will be politically impossible for the State not to play a more intrusive role in economic affairs."[184] In the United States, Senator Kefauver said in advocating amendments to the antitrust laws in the Cold War context of 1950:

> A point is eventually reached, and we are rapidly reaching that point in this country, where the public steps in to take over when concentration and monopoly gain too much power. . . . It either results in a Fascist

182 *Topco*, above note 20 at 610. See also US House of Representatives, Subcommittee on Antitrust Commercial and Administrative Law of The Committee on The Judiciary, *Investigation of Competition in Digital Markets Majority Staff Report and Recommendations* (6 October 2020) Chair's Foreword at 7, calling antitrust laws a "charter of economic liberty" [US House Digital Markets Report 2020].

183 Frank Maier-Rigaud, "On the Normative Foundations of Competition Law — Efficiency, Political Freedom and the Freedom to Compete," ch 8 in Daniel Zimmer, ed, *The Goals of Competition Law* (Cheltenham: Edward Elgar, 2012) at 135; Daniel Zimmer, "The Emancipation of Antitrust from Market-Share-Based Approaches" (2016) 61:1 *Antitrust Bulletin* 133 at 135. See also Ben Van Rompuy, *Economic Efficiency: The Sole Concern of Modern Antitrust Policy? Non-efficiency Considerations within Article 101 TFEU* (Alphen aan den Rijn: Kluwer Law International, 2012) at 86–87:

> The Ordoliberal view of competition shares the basic starting points of traditional liberalism, namely that a competitive economic system is necessary for a prosperous, free, and equitable society and that economic freedom is a corollary to political freedom. Yet it is distinctive in the essential role it attributes to the legal institutional framework in developing such a society. According to Ordoliberals, safeguarding the freedom of the individual demands protection not only from the power of government but also from economic power. This position was strongly influenced by the view that the accumulation of private economic power was the main cause of Germany's economic and political disintegration between the two World Wars.

184 Dunlop, McQueen & Trebilcock, above note 32 at 67; see also Gorecki & Stanbury, above note 29 at 129, referring, *inter alia*, to a speech by Minister of Justice Davie Fulton in 1959.

state or the nationalization of industries and thereafter a Socialist or Communist state.[185]

More recently in the United States, fueled by data suggesting increasing corporate concentration and rising profits,[186] as well as the dominance of firms such as Google and Amazon in emerging digital markets, there has been a call for reinvigorated enforcement of antitrust laws.[187] It is claimed that lax enforcement since the 1980s, for example, is among the factors that have "increased the prevalence of market power,"[188] leading to calls for "[r]estoring a theory of power that accords with the original values of antitrust—including a distrust of concentrated private power."[189]

c) Challenges Posed by Economic Power as a Criterion for Competition Law Intervention

Whether the data supports concerns about the state of competition in light of trends toward increased concentration remains controversial. One leading American economist's review of the available evidence concluded that "it is far from clear that the reported changes in concentration over time are informative regarding changes in competition."[190] While calling for a number of changes which could bolster enforcement, he issued the following cautionary view on the use of antitrust to address concerns for the growth of corporate political power: "antitrust is poorly suited to address problems associated with the excessive political power of large corporations. . . . Indeed, introducing issues of political power into antitrust enforcement decisions . . . could dangerously politicize antitrust enforcement."[191] A US government submission to the OECD in respect of the objectives of competition law in 2003 similarly

---

185 See, e.g., Lina M Khan, "The Ideological Roots of America's Market Power Problem" (2018) 127 *Yale Law Journal Forum* 960 at 966, citing 96 Cong Rec 16,452 (1950) [Khan].

186 See American Antitrust Institute, Statement: "A National Competition Policy: Unpacking the Problem of Declining Competition and Setting Priorities Moving Forward" (28 September 2016) at 11: "The dominant antitrust enforcement ideology over the last several decades has likely contributed to higher concentration, higher prices, higher profits to relatively few firms, and growing inequality," online: www.antitrustinstitute.org/wp-content/uploads/2018/08/AAINatlComp-Policy-1.pdf.

187 See, e.g., Khan, above note 185; US House Digital Markets Report 2020 note 179

188 Jonathan B Baker & Steven C Salop, "Antitrust, Competition Policy, and Inequality" (2015) 104 *Georgetown Law Journal Online* 1 at 11.

189 Khan, above note 185 at 979.

190 Shapiro, above note 166 at 716.

191 *Ibid.*

summarized that, "[i]n the United States, the practical conflicts generated between pursuit of so many varied and often vague goals gave rise to the modern consensus . . . that economic efficiency and consumer welfare is in fact the appropriate basis for U.S. antitrust policy."[192]

There are other targeted policy means, such as lobbying rules, political contribution regulation, and general corruption laws that can be used to address more directly the concerns arising from the presence of excessive economic power. Employing such tools avoids difficulties which have been identified from trying to use competition laws as a primary method of controlling economic power. These include the following.

- Writing a legal rule or standard to address "excessive" economic power, particularly a rule that would be justiciable by a court or tribunal, may be difficult or impossible.[193]
- The application of any such standard would draw the courts or the Tribunal into what could be equated to a political assessment of when economic or political power has been exceeded beyond acceptable limits. This could lead to unpredictable outcomes and erode respect for such institutions and the rule of law.[194]
- Trying to integrate concerns for excessive economic power as a primary driver of the enforcement of competition laws may cause such

192 OECD, Global Forum on Competition, CCNM/GF/COMP/WD(2003)34, Submission of the United States, "The Objectives of Competition Law and Policy" (31 January 2003) at 5, online:www.ftc.gov/system/files/attachments/us-submissions-oecd-2000-2009/2003-the_objectives_of_competition_law_and_policy.pdf.

193 Foer, above note 176 at 23.

194 See, e.g., John Pecman, "Populism, Public Interest and Competition" (Speech delivered at the CD Howe Institute, Toronto, April 27, 2018), online: www.canada.ca/en/competition-bureau/news/2018/05/john-pecman-commissioner-of-competition---populism-public-interest-and-competition.html:

> The right question is whether antitrust is the appropriate tool to remedy social issues like inequality and unemployment. And I am greatly concerned by any suggestion that competition law should transition away from an economics-based, consumer welfare standard toward a value-based public interest standard. The rationale for my concern is simple: competition law is most effective when it operates with clear and objective criteria and injecting public interest concerns into competition law prevents that from happening. Moreover, doing so injects politics into the process and politics, as we know, is best left to the people we elect to do that job—politicians. Competition authorities—as unelected bodies—are particularly unsuited to making value judgments; in fact, it's the very antithesis of our role, which is to perform objective, rigorous analysis. There are other policy instruments that are far better suited to addressing social and cultural objectives.

laws to conflict with, and to compromise, their ability to be effective in achieving key objectives such as economic efficiency and lower consumer prices.[195] For example, a large firm like Amazon has dominated certain market segments and has driven some retailers out of business; however, it offers consumers low prices and additional choices. While other public policy responses may be appropriate to address the privacy concerns and dislocation created in the wake of the rise of such tech and other giants,[196] tackling these issues using competition laws may conflict with the core objective of such laws, i.e., to promote competition and efficiency.

In Canada, it has been argued, furthermore, that a connection between corporate concentration and political influence may be difficult to demonstrate.[197] While expressions of concern in this area arise from time to time, the foregoing discussion suggests that to the extent such considerations may play a role in competition law, they sit more comfortably in a secondary or supportive capacity, given that they may conflict in some situations with core objectives. In this sense, the law can perhaps best be thought of as employing a hierarchy of objectives, depending on the provision under consideration, with the predominant objectives under the modern law being the promotion of competition, consumer welfare and economic efficiency, and other objectives playing an informing role depending on the nature, history, and purpose of the provision being applied.

d) Small and Medium-Sized Business Equity

A particular thread within the broad concerns for the possession and exercise of economic power relates to competitive impacts on small businesses and their freedom to compete. The purpose clause includes the objective "to ensure that small and medium-sized enterprises have an equitable opportunity to participate in the Canadian economy." What role should this factor play in the application of the modern law?

As seen above, concern for the role of small business played a prominent role in the incorporation of price discrimination, predatory pricing, and resale price maintenance laws into the Canadian competition law in 1935 and 1951 respectively. In the period after the Great Depression, for

195 Foer, above note 176 at 24.

196 See, e.g., Angela Daly, "Beyond 'Hipster Antitrust': A Critical Perspective on the European Commission's Google Decision" (2017) 1:3 *European Competition and Regulation Law Review* 188.

197 Dunlop, McQueen & Trebilcock, above note 32 at 67.

example, there were concerns that small businesses could not survive unless products were made available to them at the same prices also available to large enterprises. Similarly, the refusal to supply provision was added in 1976, after a large number of complaints were made by businesses seeking product supply for which there was no available remedy.[198] The objectives of the section were considered by the Competition Tribunal in *Director of Investigation and Research v Xerox*. The respondent had cut off small third-party companies (including the complainant, Exdos) from supplies of replacement parts. Exdos serviced and repaired Xerox copiers for a range of clients, including charities and hospitals. In determining that an order requiring Xerox to supply was justified, the Tribunal held:

> Section 1.1 describes the purposes of the *Competition Act* as including "to ensure that small and medium-sized enterprises have an equitable opportunity to participate in the Canadian economy" and "to provide consumers with competitive prices and product choices." Both these purposes would be served by granting an order in favour of Exdos as sought by the Director. Exdos will continue to have an "equitable opportunity to participate" and consumers will have price and product choices available which they would not otherwise have.[199]

As this passage indicates, providing a remedy to promote small businesses' participation in markets can also increase competition, and promote competitive prices and choices for consumers. In such circumstances, several objectives in the purpose clause can be advanced in a complementary fashion. However, small and medium-sized businesses may be less efficient than larger players. Promoting their participation can also lead to a conflict with the pursuit of either consumer or total welfare, or both:

> Protecting less efficient producers disregards the advantages of economies of scale enjoyed by larger suppliers, which benefit consumers with lower prices. Protecting competitors for their own sake also sacrifices efficient resource allocation by reducing the positive incentives created by competitive dynamics in order to protect less efficient rivals from market forces.[200]

In *Canada (Commissioner of Competition) v Canada Pipe*, the Federal Court of Appeal held that for a practice engaged in by a dominant

198 See Chapter 8, Section E(1).

199 *Canada (Director of Investigation & Research) v Xerox Canada Inc* (1990), 33 CPR (3d) 83 (CCT) at para 92.

200 Ducci & Trebilcock, above note 159 at 96.

firm to be found anti-competitive, "there must be evidence linking the impugned practice to the requisite intended negative effect *on a competitor*."[201] This formulation of the test for an anti-competitive practice (which was placed in doubt by the Court of Appeal's subsequent decision in *Canada (Commissioner of Competition) v Toronto Real Estate Board* (*TREB*)[202]) has been criticized for elevating the protection of individual competitors above the protection of competition:

> It is unfortunate to have on the record the statement that an act taken with the purpose of having a "negative effect on a competitor" is by definition anticompetitive. Such an interpretation reinforces the idea that the purpose of competition policy is to protect competitors. All sorts of acts hurt competitors, primarily offering lower prices and offering better service. On that account, firms would and should be acting anti-competitively all the time.[203]

The Economic Council of Canada also noted in 1969 that while a practice such as predatory pricing may harm individual competitors, it also reduces prices for consumers and can weed out inefficient small firms, leading to the promotion of competition and efficiency.[204] The Council also noted that pursuing economic efficiency would often promote the participation of small and medium-sized businesses, because "such a policy would be very much concerned with eliminating barriers to the entry of new enterprises, some of which would often be relatively small enterprises."[205]

Over the decades following the Economic Council's report, there was a growing recognition that the criminal price discrimination and predatory pricing provisions were not compatible with the

---

201 *Canada (Commissioner of Competition) v Canada Pipe, 2006 FCA 233 at para 284 [emphasis added].*

202 See Chapter 7, Section C(b)(ii)(b).

203 Timothy Brennan & Alan Gunderson, "2006 in Competition Policy and Enforcement: An Economic Perspective" [2007] *Canadian Competition Record* 22 at 77.

204 *Interim Report* 1969, above note 27 at 20:

> [I]f the squeezing out of competitors appears to be part of a process likely to produce increased efficiency and lower costs and prices (if, for instance, a number of small corner stores are being forced out of business by the entry of new, low-cost, mass distributors) then a dilemma is faced. The economic efficiency goal might well suggest letting the process work itself out; the goal of diffusing economic power would call for intervention. By recommending that efficiency be the sole objective of competition policy, we are in effect saying that no individual competitor, corporate or otherwise, has an inherent right to stay in business.

205 *Ibid.*

predominant thrust of the Act in promoting competition and efficiency. A process of amendment finally took hold after various proposals and studies in the 1990s and 2000s.[206] In 2002, the refusal to supply provision was amended to add an "adverse effect on competition" test, making it more consistent with the pursuit of competition rather than the mere protection of competitors. Most significantly, the 2009 amendments repealed the criminal price discrimination and predatory pricing prohibitions, making those practices subject to review as abuse of dominance under a lessening of competition standard. Thus, the *Competition Act* has, with these changes, moved away from provisions which have as a central rationale the protection of individual competitors.

Even though these provisions, which were more specifically directed at protection of individual competitors, have been repealed, Canadian competition law has not wholly abandoned concerns for business equity or small business participation. Various provisions such as abuse of dominance and the vertical practices provisions, while applying a substantial lessening of competition test, can still play a role in providing remedies against practices by large firms that exclude smaller competitors, where there is a broader impact on market power. By addressing barriers to entry and exclusionary conduct, these provisions provide a framework which can increase opportunities for competitors to enter markets and potentially displace incumbents by applying rivalry and competitive pressure.

At minimum, the acceptance of the promotion of small and medium-sized business as an objective complicates the application of an efficiency or consumer welfare standard in competition law enforcement in some cases. In some situations, it presents the potential for an outright conflict with the promotion of the efficient practices of large players. To address such conflicts, the Economic Council, in 1969, and many economists since have advocated that promoting efficiency should be the dominant or leading objective of competition policy. To date, however, Parliament has retained the small and medium-sized business equity objective, and it remains at play in the interpretation of the legislation. Given the occasional inconsistencies with the pursuit of competition, consumer welfare, and efficiency, this objective may sometimes, by necessity, be assigned a secondary status in the hierarchy of objectives in the legislation. It may also take on the role of the "tiebreaker" in close cases, or might come into play in the exercise of the Tribunal's discretion about

206 See Chapter 9, Section B(1)(b).

whether to issue an order which could serve multiple objectives of the legislation.[207]

4) An International Perspective

The Organization for Economic Cooperation and Development (OECD) is a Paris-based international body made up of representatives from three dozen market economies, including Canada, the United States, the EC, and its member countries. In 1992, it held a round table discussion on the objectives of competition policy through its Competition Committee. The conclusions from this review are self-explanatory and worth quoting at some length:

> This *overview* of the objectives of competition policy across different countries indicates that in most jurisdictions, the basic objectives are to maintain and encourage the process of competition in order to promote efficient use of resources while protecting the freedom of economic action of various market participants. Competition policy has been generally viewed to achieve or preserve a number of other objectives as well: pluralism, de-centralisation of economic decision-making, preventing abuses of economic power, promoting small business, fairness and equity and other socio-political values. It has been noted that these "supplementary" objectives tend to vary across jurisdictions and over time. The latter reflects the changing nature and adaptability of competition policy so as to address current concerns of society while remaining steadfast to the basic objectives.
>
> The inclusion of multiple objectives, however, increases the risks of conflicts and inconsistent application of competition policy. The interests of different stakeholders may severely constrain the independence of competition policy authorities, lead to political intervention and compromise and, adversely affect one of the major benefits of the competitive process namely, economic efficiency.[208]

In 2003, the topic of the objectives of competition law and policy was again raised as part of the OECD's Annual Global Forum on Competition, which included representatives from both OECD and non-OECD countries. The OECD Secretariat cited the above conclusion as remaining accurate and went on to review the results of a new questionnaire

---

207 On the presence of such discretion, see *Canada (Commissioner of Competition) v Visa Canada Corp, [2013] CCTD No 10* at paras 393–401.

208 OECD, Global Forum on Competition, CCNM/GF/COMP/WD(2003)34, Note by the Secretariat, "The Objectives of Competition Law and Policy" (29 January 2003) at para 3 [emphasis in original] [OECD, "Note by the Secretariat"].

which was answered by thirty-five jurisdictions; sixteen OECD and nineteen non-OECD. The main conclusions were as follows:

- Since 1992, there has been a "shift away from the use of competition laws to promote what might be characterized as broad public interest objectives" such as "the promotion of employment, regional development, national champions . . . national ownership, economic stability, anti-inflation policies" toward the "core objectives" of promoting the competitive process and efficiency.[209]
- No similar shift was observed away from so-called grey zone objectives—such as ensuring fair competition or equitable opportunities for small and medium-sized businesses—which "continue to be embraced by many countries."[210]
- The shift away from public interest objectives "suggests a consensus may be emerging that it is sub-optimal . . . to use competition law and policy to promote such goals." Reasons given by member countries included:
  - » broadly and vaguely specified public interest objectives (such as regional development) can be "hijacked" by "the politically strongest private interests, usually those of producers or workers," meaning that such "public interest" objectives wind up, in fact, serving narrow private interests; and
  - » "non-competition policy mechanisms are generally superior for achieving non-competition policy objectives."[211]
- Developing and transitional countries[212] are those which tend to embrace public interest objectives, either as factors expressly written into the law, or through the discretion given to political actors, such as the responsible Minister, in deciding appeals from the competition authority. This may be due to the "greater influence of vested business interests" or the perceived pressing need "to promote one or more public interest objectives given the stage of economic development in such countries."

In Canada, one finds examples of regulatory regimes in the areas of broadcasting and foreign investment review which, in contrast to competition law, are centred on what is termed above as "public interest"

209 *Ibid* at para 4.
210 *Ibid* at para 5.
211 *Ibid* at para 6.
212 Countries cited were China, Brazil, Russia, Ukraine, Pakistan, Chinese Taipei, Romania, Macedonia, Morocco, Tunisia, Cameroon, Gabon, Ivory Coast, Kenya, Zambia, Sri Lanka, and Jamaica; *ibid*, para 7.

objectives. In the case of broadcasting, under the *Broadcasting Act*, the criteria in the statute are very broad for assessing whether approval of the Canadian Radio-television and Telecommunications Commission (CRTC) should be granted for changes of control or ownership of licensed undertakings. Under the statute, "the onus is on the applicant to demonstrate that approval is in the public interest, that the benefits of the transaction are commensurate with the size and nature of the transaction and that the application represents the best possible proposal under the circumstances."[213] The Commission is required to take into account the objectives included in section 3(1) of the Act, which include favouring Canadian ownership and disparate cultural objectives. Decisions by the CRTC can be appealed to the federal Cabinet.

In the case of foreign investment, the *Investment Canada Act* provides the framework for conducting reviews of acquisitions of control of Canadian businesses by non-Canadians. Reviewable foreign investments can be approved only if the Minister of Industry is satisfied that the transaction is likely to be of "net benefit" to Canada. The Act sets out a list of criteria for consideration that includes such matters as the degree of Canadian participation in the business, and impacts on productivity, efficiency and Canada's international competitiveness.[214]

In contrast, the test governing merger review under the *Competition Act* is restricted to whether the transaction "substantially prevents or lessens competition." This is just one of the factors taken into account in the broadcasting and foreign investment regimes. Furthermore, merger challenges are adjudicated by the Competition Tribunal, and not Cabinet or Ministerial appeal, and no political review is available. The contrasting tests and structure of these regimes illustrate that while Canadian competition law has a range of goals, they remain quite narrowly focused on competition-related matters, and are subject to legal tests fashioned and applied by the Tribunal and the courts.

With respect to the issue of the role of efficiency as an objective of competition law, an observation by the OECD Secretariat from its Global Forum is of interest:

> Most countries which focus on efficiency and promoting competition still include the consideration of impacts on consumer welfare. Thus "it is extremely rare, if not unheard of, in those jurisdictions to allow

213 *MTS Inc — Terrestrial broadcasting distribution undertaking serving Winnipeg and surrounding areas — Change of effective control* (20 December 2016), Broadcasting Decision CRTC 20167-487.

214 *Investment Canada Act*, RSC 1985, c 28 (1st Supp), s 20.

> an anti-competitive merger that is likely to increase total welfare, unless gains in efficiency are likely to be shared with consumers."[215]

The conclusions of the OECD analysis highlight that while efficiency has played a greater role over time as an objective of the competition laws of most developed economies, it is seldom the sole objective pursued. Most competition laws, like the *Competition Act* in Canada, give some weight to other values, such as competitive prices for consumers and equity in small business participation. These values do not pose as great a potential for tension or outright conflict with the promotion of competition as do what the OECD refers to as "public interest" objectives. As noted earlier, in many cases, stopping an anti-competitive merger or prohibiting entry-limiting behaviour by a dominant firm will promote competition and efficiency, as well as open markets to small business and lower prices to consumers. In other situations, application of the law may require a weighing of values, depending on how these different objectives interact.

Finally, consumer welfare ranked ahead of efficiency in a 2007 survey by the International Competition Network (ICN), on the objectives of the law relating to unilateral conduct (i.e., dominant firm behaviour).[216] The ICN is a group of more than 130 competition enforcement agencies from every continent in the world.[217] Its survey of agencies in 2007 was responded to by thirty-three competition agencies.[218] The results were as follows:

215 OECD, "Note by the Secretariat," above note 208 at para 9.

216 Described as "unilateral conduct of dominant firms and firms with substantial market power": International Competition Network, *Unilateral Conduct Working Group 2019-2022 Work Plan* (2018), "Mission," online: www.internationalcompetitionnetwork.org/wp-content/uploads/2019/07/Work-Plan2019-22UCWG.pdf.

217 Self-described as "network of established and newer agencies, enriched by the participation of non-governmental advisors (representatives from business, consumer groups, academics, and the legal and economic professions), with the common aim of addressing practical antitrust enforcement and policy issues." International Competition Network, *ICN Factsheet and Key Messages* (April 2009), online: www.internationalcompetitionnetwork.org/wp-content/uploads/2018/09/Factsheet2009.pdf.

218 Responding agencies were from Australia, Brazil, Bulgaria, Canada, Chile, Czech Republic, European Union, France, Germany, Hungary, Ireland, Israel, Italy, Jamaica, Japan, Jersey, Korea, Latvia, Mexico, Netherlands, New Zealand, Pakistan, Romania, Russia, Serbia, Singapore, Slovak Republic, South Africa, Spain, Sweden, Switzerland, Turkey, Ukraine, United Kingdom, and United States. See International Competition Network, *Report on the Objectives of Unilateral Conduct Laws, Assessment of Dominance/Substantial Market Power, and State-Created Monopolies* (May 2007), online: www.internationalcompetitionnetwork.org/wp-content/uploads/2018/07/UCWG_SR_Objectives.pdf, Annex A.

Table 3.3. ICN 2007 Survey—Objectives of Unilateral Conduct Laws Identified in Agency Responses

Objective	Number of Responses
Ensure an effective competitive process as a goal and/or a means	32
Promote consumer welfare	30
Maximize efficiency	20
Ensure economic freedom	13
Ensure a level playing field for small and medium-sized enterprises	7
Promote fairness and equality	6
Promote consumer choice	5
Achieve market integration	4
Facilitate privatization and market liberalization	2
Promote competitiveness in international markets	2

These responses are broadly consistent with the OECD analyses, and confirm the trend to the elimination or marginalization of public interest objectives such as promoting national champions, employment, and regional development as competition law objectives, and to greater emphasis on the promotion of the competitive process, efficiency, and consumer welfare.

E. CONCLUSION

This examination of the objectives of Canadian competition law discloses a clear trend in the legislative changes in this country over the last several decades toward a more economic and efficiency-oriented law. Competition laws were born in North America near the end of the nineteenth century out of a populist reaction to the economic power and abuses of large enterprises and cartels. Today, the law faces some of the same pressures to address the large accumulations of capital and wealth that have emerged from the digital economy and globalization. However, our understanding of the role of competition law as a policy tool has evolved since the 1880s. Competition law is now understood as a branch of economic policy that is centred on the goal of stimulating the effective functioning of markets and promoting efficient practices and innovations that will enhance social welfare. In addition to economic efficiency, other ultimate objectives include providing opportunities for small and medium-sized businesses, low prices and greater choice for consumers, and international competitiveness. Applying these disparate objectives in a specific case can sometimes present challenges where tensions or, in certain circumstances, outright conflicts arise between them. The content and context of the provision under consideration will affect the appropriate balance among, and the weight to be given to, the relevant objectives on the facts of a particular case.

APPENDIX 3.1

Deadweight Loss from Monopoly Pricing

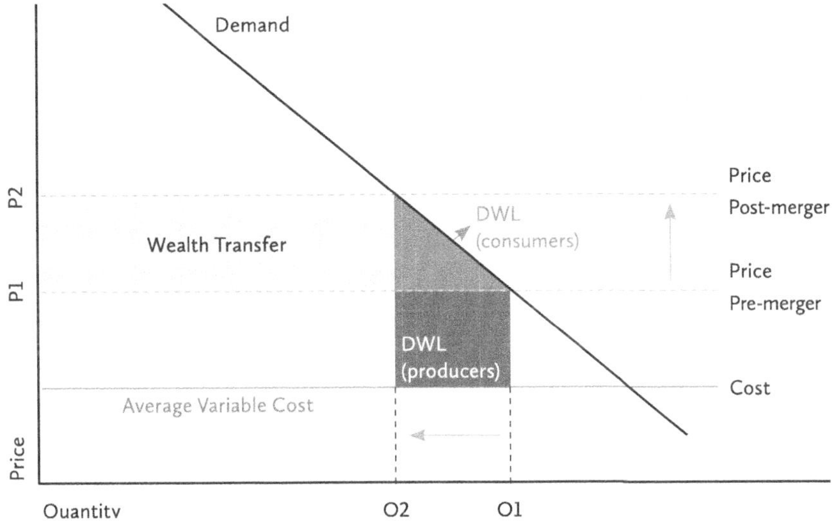

The above diagram depicts the welfare loss from monopoly pricing. A firm prior to a merger was pricing at P1. The demand curve (black line) determines how much will be sold at price P1, which is Q1 units (where the pre-merger price line intersects with the demand curve.)

Post-merger, the firm is able to increase the price from P1 to P2. Consumption now drops from Q1 to Q2.

The triangle labelled "DWL (consumers)" reflects the deadweight welfare loss that occurs because a portion of consumers' surplus (the difference between what consumers paid and what they were willing to pay) has been lost, reflected by the triangular area above the line at P1 which has been eliminated, but not transferred to producers. This is a loss not only to consumers, but to society because it is not collected by anyone. It reflects the reduced satisfaction and increased social cost from the shifting of consumption away from this product at the higher price.

The rectangle labelled "Wealth Transfer" reflects a loss of consumers' surplus at the higher price, but this amount is collected by the producer after the price increase. It is a transfer of wealth from consumers to producers. It is not part of the deadweight loss because it is surplus that has simply changed hands within the economy.

The rectangle "DWL (producers)" reflects a loss of producer surplus (the difference between revenue received by the producer and the cost of producing — essentially profit over variable cost). In this example producers were already pricing above cost, but their producer surplus has been reduced due to the increase in price from P1 to P2 and the reduction in demand from Q1 to Q2, and this amount is not recovered by another party and is therefore lost to society, and a deadweight loss.

CHAPTER 4

MARKET DEFINITION AND MARKET POWER

A. INTRODUCTION

Market definition is usually a threshold, and sometimes a decisive, issue in competition law cases. In the *Canada (Director of Investigation and Research) v Southam Inc* merger case, for example, the central issue before the Supreme Court of Canada was whether the acquired community newspapers were in the same "relevant market" as two daily newspapers, the Vancouver Sun and Vancouver Province.[1] Southam owned the two daily newspapers. In 1989, it acquired thirteen community newspapers and certain other publishing concerns. In 1990, an application was filed under section 92 of the *Competition Act* by the Director (now Commissioner of Competition) seeking to have Southam divest the largest community papers in the Greater Vancouver area, the North Shore News and Vancouver Courier, as well as the Real Estate Weekly, on the basis that those acquisitions were "likely to prevent or lessen competition substantially" in the retail print advertising and real estate print advertising markets in the Lower Mainland area of Vancouver.

The Competition Tribunal found that the community newspapers were not in the same market as the dailies, on the basis that they served different print advertising markets. It held that the dailies appealed to large national advertisers (like banks and automobile companies) seeking

1 *Canada (Director of Investigation and Research) v Southam Inc*, [1997] 1 SCR 748 [*Southam* SCC], overturning [1995] 3 FC 557 (CA) [*Southam* FCA].

coverage throughout a metropolitan area, while the community papers appealed to local advertisers (such as smaller retailers), whose customers live within a certain district.[2] The acquisition by Southam of the two community newspapers was permitted because they were found not to compete in the same market. That finding was ultimately upheld by the Supreme Court. The Supreme Court overturned the Federal Court of Appeal, finding that the Tribunal's determination on the relevant market was reasonable and should have been shown deference by the appeal court.[3]

A price fixing case which turned on market definition was *R v Clarke Transport Inc*. An agreement to fix prices and allocate customers was proven. The trial judge, Moldaver J (as he then was), found that "I am satisfied beyond any reasonable doubt that the five corporate accused conspired amongst themselves and with others in respect of prices for the delivery of freight by rail from Toronto to various destinations in Western Canada."[4] However, prior to amendments to the Act in 2009, the Crown had to prove that the conspiracy resulted in an "undue lessening of competition." This required that the co-conspirators possess some market power in a relevant market. Justice Moldaver was not satisfied that the relevant market was restricted to freight transportation by railway "pool" car, as the Crown alleged. He concluded that "pool car operators, truckers and intermodal operators were equally capable of moving and indeed did move the identical kinds of freight on behalf of shipper/customers from Ontario to points west."[5] He was unable to conclude that the pool car conspirators had market power in the broader market for freight transportation. They were acquitted.

An example of market definition playing a decisive role in a monopolization case under the American *Sherman Act* was the 1947 *Du Pont* case.[6] Du Pont produced almost 75 percent of the cellophane sold in the United States at that time, but cellophane constituted less than 20 percent of the sales of all "flexible packaging material" (including wax paper, aluminum foil, etc.). While the US Supreme Court found that Du Pont had a monopoly in cellophane by virtue of its patent protection and licensing agreements, it noted that "[t]he court below held that the 'great sensitivity of customers in the flexible packaging markets to price or quality changes'

2 *Canada (Director of Investigation and Research) v Southam Inc* (1992), 43 CPR (3d) 161 (CCT) [*Southam* CCT].

3 *Southam* SCC, above note 1.

4 *R v Clarke Transport Canada Inc* (1995), 130 DLR (4th) 500 (Ont Gen Div) at para 45.

5 *Ibid* at para 133.

6 *United States v EI du Pont de Nemours and Co*, 351 US 377 (1947).

prevented du Pont from possessing monopoly control over price."[7] It held (consistent with the lower court's determination): "du Pont should not be found to monopolize cellophane when that product has the competition and interchangeability with other wrappings that this record shows."[8] While the result has been criticized because the Court failed to take into account that Du Pont's prices were already elevated by, and more price sensitive due to, its existing cellophane monopoly (the so-called cellophane fallacy discussed below), the case illustrates again how market definition can be a decisive threshold issue in competition law.

B. MARKET DEFINITION AS A STEP IN ASSESSING MARKET POWER

1) The Meaning and Relevance of "Market Power"

Market definition was required in the three cases discussed above because the applicable legal tests involved a determination of the impact of the conduct in question on competition. Market definition provides a framework within which to assess competitive effects. The *Competition Act* requires that the Competition Tribunal assess whether or not the party's or parties' conduct has had, or would have, the following effect:

- "substantial prevention or lessening of competition" (for mergers, vertical practices, abuse of dominance, anti-competitive agreements)[9] and
- "adverse effect on competition in a market" (for refusal to supply, resale price maintenance).[10]

These tests have been held to require some degree of impact on market power. "Market power" was defined by the Supreme Court in *Tervita* as follows:

> Market power is the ability to "profitably influence price, quality, variety, service, advertising, innovation or other dimensions of competition." . . . Or, in other words, market power is "the ability to maintain prices above the competitive level for a considerable period of time without such action being unprofitable" . . . where "price" is "generally used as shorthand for all aspects of a firm's actions that have an impact on buyers."[11]

---

7 *Ibid* at 400.

8 *Ibid* at 404.

9 *Competition Act*, RSC 1985, c C-34, ss 77, 79, and 82.

10 *Ibid*, ss 75 & 76.

11 *Tervita Corp v Canada (Commissioner of Competition)*, [2015] 1 SCR 161 at para 44.

One seminal American article similarly defined market power as: "the ability of a firm (or a group of firms, acting jointly) to raise price above the competitive level without losing so many sales so rapidly that the price increase is unprofitable and must be rescinded."[12] Another useful definition of market power which introduces other competitive dimensions is: "the ability profitably to raise prices over a period of time, or to behave analogously, for example, by restricting output or limiting consumer choice."[13]

A measure of market power is the Lerner Index, which assesses a firm's ability to raise prices above those charged in perfectly competitive conditions.[14] In competitive market conditions, firms will be forced to set the price at marginal cost. The Index calculates the difference between the firm's profit maximizing price (P) and marginal cost (MC) divided by the profit maximizing price. Mathematically this is expressed as:

$$\text{Lerner Index (L)} = \frac{(P - MC)}{P}$$

For a firm in a perfectly competitive market charging a price equal to marginal cost, L = 0. If a firm possesses some market power and is charging P = $12 per unit, where its marginal cost is say, $10 per unit, L = 0.20. L increases with increased market power and cannot exceed 1.0.

On a practical level, the Lerner Index is difficult to measure because the marginal cost of a particular product is not routinely recorded in accounting records. Market power must therefore usually be inferred from more indirect indicators. One such indicator is market share.

By examining additional variables relating to the degree to which demand changes with changes in price (demand elasticity) and the supply response of competing firms to a price increase (supply elasticity), it can be shown that L, or the market power of a firm, generally increases with the firm's market share. The higher the market share, the smaller the competitive constraint imposed by the supply response of competing suppliers, for example.[15] Thus a firm with 90 percent of the market is

---

12 William M Landes & Richard A Posner, "Market Power in Antitrust Cases" (1981) 94:5 *Harvard Law Review* 937 at 937 [Landes & Posner].

13 Richard Whish & David Bailey, *Competition Law*, 9th ed (Oxford: Oxford University Press, 2018) at 42 [Whish & Bailey].

14 See Chapter 3, Section D(1)(d)(ii) for the assumptions surrounding perfectly competitive markets.

15 See Paul Collins, Michael Trebilcock & Ralph A Winter, *The Law and Economics of Canadian Competition Policy* (Toronto: University of Toronto Press, 2003) at 78–81, citing Landes & Posner, above note 12 [Collins, Trebilcock & Winter].

more likely to be able to sustain high prices without a substantial decline in sales than a firm with 10 percent. A firm's market power also increases when its competitors have lower supply elasticity or when demand for the firm's product is less elastic. Market share must therefore be considered in conjunction with other market conditions to yield a more reliable picture of the likelihood of market power.

2) A Market Power Assessment May Be Possible Without Market Definition

Market definition is used as a means to infer the existence of market power from market share and other indicators calculated based upon the defined market. However, in a given case there may be other methodologies which can be used to measure market power more directly, which do not require the definition of a relevant market.

In abuse of dominance cases, for example, the market power of the allegedly dominant firm can sometimes be inferred directly without market definition. The Competition Tribunal held that market power can be demonstrated from such evidence as "performance results (e.g., profits) or observed patterns of conduct (e.g., pricing policy)."[16] In the United States, evidence of detrimental effects from anti-competitive conduct has been relied upon by the Supreme Court as a telltale sign of the possession of market power without the need for market definition. The Court held:

> Since the purpose of the inquiries into market definition and market power is to determine whether an arrangement has the potential for genuine adverse effects on competition, "proof of actual detrimental effects, such as a reduction of output," can obviate the need for an inquiry into market power, which is but a "surrogate for detrimental effects."[17]

In merger cases, determining market power directly may also be possible in the assessment of so-called unilateral effects (effects

---

16 *Canada (Competition Act, Director of Investigation and Research) v Tele-Direct (Publications) Inc* (1997), 73 CPR (3d) 1 (CCT) at para 226 [*Tele-Direct*].

17 *FTC v Indiana Federation of Dentists*, 476 US 447 (1986) at 460–61: "we conclude that the finding of actual, sustained adverse effects on competition in those areas where IFD dentists predominated . . . is legally sufficient to support a finding that the challenged restraint was unreasonable even in the absence of elaborate market analysis; J Shaw, 'Avoiding Market Definition under Section 1 of the Sherman Act' (2019) 88:3 *Fordham L Rev* 1133 at 1154-56; Louis Kaplow, 'Why (Ever) Define Markets' (2010) 124:2 *Harv L Rev* 437." See also Chapter 7, Section C(1)(d).

flowing from the reduction of competition between the merging parties only). Methodologies have been developed which focus on whether, and to what extent, the merging firms will be able to increase prices. An example is a merger between manufacturers of differentiated goods (such as automobiles) when the products of the merging parties are the closest substitutes for one another, and the non-merging competitors are not close substitutes. For illustration, take a merger between the makers of two luxury automobiles (say, BMW and Audi), where a significant fraction of the customers purchasing BMWs view Audis as their next-best choice. In such circumstances, if sufficient data are available about the extent to which consumers would switch between the products of the merging parties in the face of a pre-merger price increase, an assessment of the potential for a price increase post-merger may be possible directly, without defining a market.[18] The postulated price increase will then have to be assessed against other competitive conditions beyond those prevailing between the merging parties.[19]

Another approach used in merger cases is "merger simulation," which is used to predict the effects of mergers on market prices and quantity. Tools drawn from game theory and other disciplines are used to construct a model based on data and assumptions about demand and market conditions, the number of competitors, and their future behaviour.[20] Such models or methodologies may not be definitive, however, and may be used to supplement an assessment of market

---

18 See, e.g., US, Department of Justice and Federal Trade Commission, *Horizontal Merger Guidelines* (19 August 2010) at 6.1 [*Horizontal Merger Guidelines*], online: www.ftc.gov/sites/default/files/attachments/merger-review/100819hmg.pdf:

> In some cases, where sufficient information is available, the Agencies assess the value of diverted sales, which can serve as an indicator of the upward pricing pressure on the first product resulting from the merger. Diagnosing unilateral price effects based on the value of diverted sales need not rely on market definition or the calculation of market shares and concentration.

See also Daniel Zimmer, "The Emancipation of Antitrust from Market-Share-Based Approaches" (2016) 61:1 *Antitrust Bulletin* 133 at 139–40.

19 Herbert Hovenkamp, "Markets in Merger Analysis" 57 *Antitrust Bulletin* 887 at 912:

> Merger analysis under such an approach is fundamentally a two stage inquiry. First one looks at the expected price impact of the proposed merger based on present product and geographic conditions. Second, one must consider the likelihood and effect of the responses that nonmerging firms are likely to make, with the likelihood question determined by profitability.

20 *Ibid* at 140–41; Jeffrey Church & Roger Ware, *Industrial Organization; A Strategic Approach* (Boston: McGraw-Hill, 2000) at 732–34.

power based on more conventional market structure indicators considered below.[21]

3) Inference of Market Power from Market Structure Indicators

The Competition Tribunal in *Hillsdown*, in assessing a merger between meat rendering companies, cited with approval the following passage from the monograph *Horizontal Mergers: Law and Policy*:

> For purposes of assessing the likelihood that a merger will create or enhance single-firm market power, market definition has been characterized as "an analytical construct enabling us to compensate for our inability to measure market power directly." Areeda and Turner explain:
>
>> Market definition becomes crucial only when there are no other discoverable facts establishing the existence and degree of market power more directly and with tolerable accuracy. One would never need to define the market if he could accurately establish the firm's demand and cost curves—the quantities that could be sold at various prices, and the costs of producing those quantities. That information would directly establish both the presence of market power and the magnitude of potential monopoly profits. . . .
>
> Because direct measurement of a firm's market power is extraordinarily difficult, a two-step indirect measurement process has evolved: first define the relevant market, and then infer power within the market through the use of proxies such as market shares and other factors.[22]

The Tribunal in that case described the purpose of market definition as: "to allow for identification of the competitors to the merged firm and the calculation of the respective market shares of the market participants."[23]

---

21 Thomas W Ross & Andy Baziliauskas, "Lessening of Competition in Mergers under the Competition Act: Unilateral and Interdependence Effects" (2000) 33:3 *Canadian Business Law Journal* 373 at 385–86.

22 *Canada (Director of Investigation and Research) v Hillsdown Holdings (Canada) Ltd* (1992), 41 CPR (3d) 289 (CCT) at para 24 [*Hillsdown*], quoting from William Blumenthal, *Horizontal Mergers: Law and Policy* (Chicago: ABA Antitrust Section, Monograph No 12, 1986) at 62–63.

23 *Ibid* at para 66; see also *Canada (Commissioner of Competition) v Superior Propane Inc* (2000), 7 CPR (4th) 385 (CCT) at para 56 [*Propane CCT1*]: "[T]he delineation of competition markets is one way of demonstrating the likely competitive

In a merger case, for example, defining a relevant market makes it possible to identify who the competitors to the merging firms are and where they are located. Once that occurs, it is possible to move on to assess various indicia of market power, based on factors such as:

- market shares or concentration ratios with the defined market;
- the number of competitors in the market;
- relative firm size, dominant firm(s); and
- barriers to entry into the market.

Potential indicia of market power include high market share, a small number of competitors (or viable competitors), the presence of a dominant firm, and high barriers to entry. The Competition Tribunal held in *Canada (Commissioner of Competition) v Canada Pipe*: "Market share can be a significant indicator of market power, absent evidence of ease of entry for competitors (*Tele-Direct*). What needs to be considered, therefore, is whether the barriers to entry or other factors preclude other competitors from entering the market."[24]

Market definition can be a decisive step, which may result in competition authorities closing a file at an early stage where industry concentration data are determined, for example, to be below thresholds set out in the Bureau's enforcement guidelines.[25]

4) Market Definition Is Just an Analytical Step

It is important to emphasize that the determination of the relevant market is just one step in the process of assessing market power. Market definition is not an exact science—it is an exercise in judgment and may require adjustment at later stages of the assessment of market power depending on the approach taken. The Tribunal noted this in *Hillsdown*:

> [M]arket boundaries cannot and will not in many instances be precise. They can only be approximations. As long as market share statistics are

---

effect of a merger and that, where such an approach is valid, the competition market adopted must be relevant to the purposes and goals of the merger provisions of the Act, which focus on the creation or enhancement of market power."

24 *Canada (Commissioner of Competition) v Canada Pipe*, [2005] CCTD No 3 at para 140, rev'd on other grounds 2006 FCA 236, leave to appeal to SCC refused, [2006] SCCA No 366 [*Canada Pipe*].

25 Canada, Competition Bureau, *Merger Enforcement Guidelines* (6 October 2011), online: www.competitionbureau.gc.ca/eic/site/cb-bc.nsf/eng/03420.html at para 5.9 [*Merger Enforcement Guidelines*]; Canada, Competition Bureau, *Abuse of Dominance Provisions Enforcement Guidelines* (7 March 2019) at para 34, online: www.competitionbureau.gc.ca/eic/site/cb-bc.nsf/eng/04420.html.

> not taken as the only indicators of the existence of market power, the exact location of those boundaries becomes less important. Restraints on a merged firm's (alleged) market power can come from both inside and outside the market as defined.[26]

In an abuse of dominance case, *Toronto Real Estate Board*, the Competition Tribunal noted:

> [I]t should be recognized that it will often neither be possible nor necessary to define the product and geographic dimensions of the relevant market(s) with precision. However, an assessment must ultimately be made . . . of the extent to which products and supply locations that have not been included in the relevant market provide or would likely provide competition to the products and locations that have been included in the market.[27]

Professor Sullivan made a similar point in his *Antitrust* text: "To define a market is to take a step toward gauging market power; to evaluate a seller's strength within a market as defined is to complete the inquiry—to determine whether the . . . firm sufficiently controls the supply within the market so that it can at its election raise prices within a substantial range."[28]

The somewhat fluid nature of the market definition process means that competitive constraints which exist outside the relevant market can still be taken into account at the later stage of evaluation of market power. As such, market definition does not create a watertight structure that excludes the consideration of other relevant evidence during the market power assessment.

5) Dimensions of Relevant Markets

The Tribunal stated in *Hillsdown*:

> The identification of the relevant market in which it is alleged a substantial lessening of competition is likely to occur is normally assessed from two perspectives: the product or products with respect to which a merged firm acting alone or in concert with others is likely to be able

26 *Hillsdown*, above note 22 at para 61.

27 *Canada (Commissioner of Competition) v Toronto Real Estate Board*, [2016] CCTD No 7 (CCT) at para 132 [*TREB*], aff'd 2017 FCA 236, leave to appeal to SCC ref'd, [2018] SCCA No 24.

28 Lawrence A Sullivan, *Handbook on the Law of Antitrust* (New York: West, 1977) at 41–42 [Sullivan].

> to exercise market power and the geographic area within which such power is likely to be exercised.[29]

The two principal dimensions of market definition are the product market and the geographic market.

- The **product** market: what are the products (or services) which compete with those of the subject firm or firms?
- The **geographic** market: what geographic area(s) does the subject firm (or do the subject firms) compete in?

Another dimension which applies to both product and geographic markets is *time*: over what period does one assess the competitive reaction to price changes made by the subject firm(s) in determining what product(s) or geographic area(s) are within the market? For example, in assessing the geographic market, using a two-year rather than a one-year time horizon to determine where competitors reside may result in including firms from further away who require more time to set up operations or to deliver product into the subject firm's market. The Competition Bureau generally uses a *one-year* time horizon, in response to a 5 percent price increase by the subject firm, in assessing product and geographic markets.[30]

With respect to the product and geographic dimensions of the market, there is both a demand and a supply aspect. The issues raised in respect of these aspects are as follows:

- Product market
  - » Demand side: What product(s) do customers see as substitutable?
  - » Supply side: What firms can produce the competitive product(s) in question?
- Geographic market
  - » Demand side: How far are customers willing to go to obtain the product(s)?
  - » Supply side: Which suppliers are willing/able to provide the product(s) and from what locations?

The Bureau's 2011 *Merger Enforcement Guidelines* exclude consideration of the supply side at the market definition stage. They state:

> The ability of competitive suppliers to respond to a price increase is also important when assessing the potential for the exercise of market power, but the Bureau examines such responses later in the

29 *Hillsdown*, above note 22 at para 25.
30 *Merger Enforcement Guidelines*, above note 25 at para 4.3.

analysis—either when identifying the participants in the relevant market or when examining entry into the relevant market.[31]

The same approach is taken in the US *Merger Guidelines*, under which the market analysis "focuses solely on demand substitution factors, i.e., on customers' ability and willingness to substitute away from one product to another in response to a price increase or a corresponding non-price change such as a reduction in product quality or service."[32] Supply-side factors are taken into account later, as part of assessing competitive effects and entry.

The Competition Tribunal has varied in its approach, considering only demand-side factors in product market definition in *Hillsdown*, but including a consideration of supply elasticity in *Southam*.[33] This highlights that the process of market power assessment is a continuum, and that the stage at which factors are considered is of secondary importance, as long as the relevant factors are weighed at some point in the process.

The methodology for assessing product and geographic markets is considered in turn below. The discussion is patterned after that in the Bureau's *Merger Enforcement Guidelines*. The Bureau's *Guidelines*, while adopted in certain respects by the Competition Tribunal, "are not law because they are not made under a grant of statutory authority, and cannot determine the meaning of the Act."[34] They are a non-binding expression of the enforcement approach generally taken by the Competition Bureau in its decision making.[35] The Bureau has on occasion departed

---

31 *Ibid* at para 4.2.

32 *Horizontal Merger Guidelines* above note 18 at 7. The same approach is taken in the EC: see Whish & Bailey, above note 13 at 30.

33 See the discussion in Collins, Trebilcock & Winter, above note 15 at 33–34.

34 *Canada (Commissioner of Competition) v Superior Propane Inc*, 2001 FCA 104 at paras 144 and 146 [*Propane FCA1*]:

> [T]he possibility that a reviewing court may not agree with an agency's view of the law is an inevitable risk associated with the administrative practice of issuing non-binding guidelines and other policy documents to shed light on agency thinking and to assist those subject to the regulatory regime that it administers. This risk should deter neither the courts from deciding what the law is, nor agencies from engaging in the often useful exercise of administrative rule making.

35 *Merger Enforcement Guidelines*, above note 25, Foreword:

> The guidelines describe, to the extent possible, how the Bureau analyzes merger transactions. Given that merger law applies to a wide variety of factual circumstances, these guidelines are not applied rigidly. As such, this document sets out the Bureau's general approach to merger review and is not a binding

in its approach from its own *Guidelines*.[36] Nonetheless, they remain a useful framework, providing factors to consider in assessing elements of the legal test set out in the legislation.

6) The Hypothetical Monopolist Test

This conceptual test is set out in the Bureau's *Merger Enforcement Guidelines* as follows:

> Conceptually, a relevant market is defined as the smallest group of products, including at least one product of the merging parties, and the smallest geographic area, in which a sole profit-maximizing seller (a "*hypothetical monopolist*") would impose and sustain a small but significant and non-transitory increase in price ("SSNIP") above levels that would likely exist in the absence of the merger.[37]

The test has been adopted by the Competition Tribunal,[38] and is employed in other competition law jurisdictions.[39] While the general approach is similar in the case of conduct other than mergers, there are differences, particularly for abuse of dominance cases, which will be highlighted below. While the hypothetical monopolist test provides a helpful conceptual framework for market definition, the market definition assessment usually relies on a number of practical indicia of buyer and supply responses.

statement of how the analysis is carried out in any particular case. The specific facts of a case, as well as the nature of the information and data available, determine how the Bureau assesses a proposed transaction and may sometimes require methodologies other than those noted here.

36 *Propane FCA1*, above note 34 at paras 140–46 and para 144: "it may do little to inspire public confidence in the administration of the Competition Act that, in the context of the merger of Superior and ICG, the present Commissioner has apparently disavowed the interpretation of section 96 advanced in the *MEGs*"; see also *Propane CCT1*, above note 23 at paras 392–97.

37 *Merger Enforcement Guidelines*, above note 25 at para 4.4.

38 See, e.g., *Canada (Commissioner of Competition) v CCS Corp*, [2012] CCTD No 14 at para 58 [*CCS Corp*]; reversed on other grounds 2015 SCC 3; *Canada (Commissioner of Competition) v Visa Canada Corp*, [2013] CCTD No 10 [*Visa Canada Corp*] at para 173.

39 See, e.g., *Horizontal Merger Guidelines*, above note 18 at 7; EU, *Notice on the Definition of the Relevant Market for the Purposes of Competition Law*, OJ [1997] C 372/5.

C. THE PRODUCT MARKET

1) Hypothetical Monopolist: Product Market

In assessing the *product* side of the relevant market, the hypothetical monopolist test involves the following steps:

1) **Choose** the candidate product (e.g., a product made by one or both of the merging parties) — start with a fairly narrow product line.
2) **Ask**: "would a hypothetical monopolist selling that product be able to profitably sustain a small but significant and non-transitory increase in price (SSNIP)?"
3) **If** buyers would switch a sufficient quantity of demand to other products outside the candidate market to make the price increase unprofitable, the next-best substitute is added to the candidate market.
4) **Repeat 1–3** until the hypothetical monopolist *could* profitably impose and sustain the price increase for all products in the candidate market.
5) The smallest set of products for which the price increase can profitably be sustained is defined as the relevant product market.

As noted earlier, the Competition Bureau generally uses 5 percent as the small but significant price increase and one year as a non-transitory time frame in order to gauge the demand response to the SSNIP. While the Competition Tribunal stated in *Hillsdown* that it did "not find it useful to apply rigid numerical criteria,"[40] that framework has been referred to with approval more recently as supplying "objective benchmarks."[41]

As a practical example, consider a proposed merger of soft drink and fruit juice suppliers. To define the relevant market, we first choose a candidate product such as soft drinks (step 1). We then ask: what would happen if a hypothetical monopolist supplying soft drinks were to implement a small but significant and non-transitory price increase (step 2)? If the supplier could implement such an increase profitably, we define the market as soft drinks. If not, and buyers would switch to the next best substitute, fruit and other juices, to such an extent to constrain that price increase, we ask whether a monopolist supplying *both* soft drinks and fruit juices would be able to sustain a SSNIP (step 3). We continue adding next best substitutes, such as bottled water, to the point where the price increase *could* be sustained profitably (step 4).

---

40 *Hillsdown*, above note 22 at para 119.

41 *TREB*, above note 27 at para 124; see also *Visa Canada Corp*, above note 38 at para 173.

(It is worth noting that *some* substitution to bottled water would not be sufficient to consider it a constraint unless the substitution is in quantities sufficient to make the price increase unprofitable.) If the price increase is sustainable profitably, the products supplied by the hypothetical monopolist constitute the relevant market, and we are in a position to analyse market shares, number of competitors, etc., within that market (**Figure 4.1**).

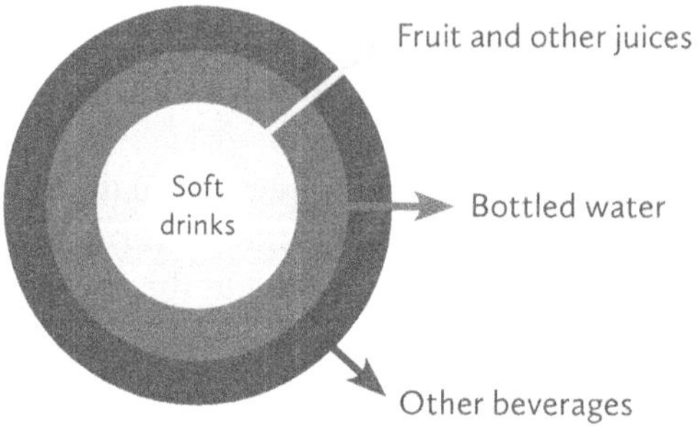

FIGURE 4.1. The hypothetical monopolist test: The candidate substitutes are represented as circles of greater and greater size emanating from the target product under consideration, soft drinks

2) Qualifications on the Hypothetical Monopolist Test: Assessing the Base Price

The hypothetical monopolist test measures the impact on substitution of a price increase in order to determine what candidate substitute product or products to include in the relevant market. But what "base price" does one use on which to add the hypothesized price increase? In the case of a merger alleged to lessen competition from the acquisition of an existing competitor, the prevailing market price prior to the merger is generally the appropriate base price from which to assess that price increase. This is because we want the relevant market to be a framework in which to examine the increases in market shares and other changes in structural variables resulting from the acquisition. Conversely, in the case of a merger alleged to prevent competition, such as by the acquisition of a potential new entrant, the prices likely to result from the competitive presence of the foreclosed entrant provide the benchmark. The *Merger Enforcement Guidelines* reflect this approach:

> The base price used to postulate a price increase is typically the prevailing price in the relevant market. The Bureau may elect not to use the prevailing price when market conditions (absent the merger) would likely result in a lower or higher price in the future.

> In general, the base price used to postulate a price increase is whatever is ordinarily considered to be the price of the product in the sector of the industry (e.g., manufacturing, wholesale, retail) being examined.[42]

Of course, determining the base price, particularly when it involves a projection of the impact of a potential competitor or new entrant, may be difficult.[43] The Tribunal has recognized that when the base price cannot be predicted with certainty "it may be sufficient for the Commissioner to demonstrate a range in which the likely future price would have fallen."[44]

If the pre-merger price is non-competitive, this may not supply the appropriate base price. For example, if prior to a merger between two firms, the firms were colluding to raise prices, the elevated prices could lead to a mistaken assessment of substitutability at those already-higher prices. At the higher prices, buyers will have a greater tendency to shift to substitutes than they would have at a competitive price. In *Canadian Waste Services* the Competition Tribunal agreed that "using distorted prevailing prices as the base in reviewing such a merger could well lead to an over-broad definition of the market. The correct approach in such cases is . . . to use the future lower price 'if it is determined that prices were to fall, but for the merger.'"[45]

In an abuse of dominance case, the problem of the prevailing price is also present. As we will see in Chapter 7, in an abuse of dominance case, the subject firm will usually already possess market power, and will have engaged in a practice of anti-competitive acts *to preserve or to add to* its existing market power. In such circumstances, the prevailing price will often not be competitive.

This analytical problem has been termed the "cellophane fallacy," arising from criticism of the US Supreme Court's findings in the *Du Pont* case, cited at the start of the chapter. It will be recalled that in that case, the Court held that all flexible wrapping materials were the appropriate product market rather than only cellophane, because of evidence of substitution for cellophane of other wrapping materials by consumers. But if Du Pont possessed a monopoly, the evidence of price sensitivity was misleading because consumers were already paying monopoly prices. Those

---

42 *Merger Enforcement Guidelines*, above note 25 at paras 4.6 & 4.7.

43 See Jonathan B Baker, "Market Definition: An Analytical Overview" (2007) 74:1 *Antitrust Law Journal* 129 at 162–65.

44 *CCS Corp*, above note 38 at para 58; *Canada (Commissioner of Competition) v Canadian Waste Services Holdings Inc*, [2001] CCTD No 3 at para 92 [*Canadian Waste Services*].

45 *Ibid* at para 91.

prices would reflect greater demand sensitivity to price than would be observed if prices were at competitive levels.[46] Without the elevated price resulting from Du Pont's existing market power, substitution due to a hypothesized price increase might be less frequent, and the market more narrowly defined. As the Tribunal held in *Visa Canada Corp*:

> The hypothetical monopolist test may define the relevant market too broadly in the presence of what is known as the cellophane fallacy. The cellophane fallacy can lead to an overly broad market definition if the price to which the SSNIP is applied is already above the competitive level.[47]

This problem led the Tribunal in *Tele-Direct* to reject evidence that substitution for Yellow Pages advertising in response to a hypothetical price increase was relevant to market definition. The Tribunal held:

> Their inability to raise their prices without buyer switching "at the margin" is, in these circumstances, because they have already exercised their market power not because they have no market power because of the presence of close substitutes.[48]

The cellophane fallacy means that the prevailing price would have to be adjusted to deduct the effects of monopoly power to determine a base price for the purposes of the hypothetical monopolist test. As noted above, this can be a difficult exercise given the need to postulate or model competitive conditions. Calculating a base price for the purposes of the hypothetical monopolist test may therefore be challenging due to the need to address the market power effects arising from the cellophane fallacy or other problems. As a result, the Competition Tribunal has held that in an abuse of dominance case, "the practical challenges associated with applying the iterative exercise contemplated by the hypothetical monopolist approach may be insurmountable" and therefore "proceedings will largely involve assessing indirect evidence of substitutability."[49] We return to the nature of indirect evidence in a moment, after a discussion of direct evidence.

---

46 This results from "the well-known proposition in economies that in order to maximize profits, a firm with market power will price at a level where their demand for its product is elastic." *Canada (Competition Act, Director of Investigation and Research) v The D&B Companies of Canada Ltd* (1995), 64 CPR (3d) 216 (CCT) at para 109.

47 *Visa Canada Corp*, above note 38 at para 206.

48 *Tele-Direct*, above note 16 at para 130.

49 *TREB*, above note 27 at para 129.

3) Direct Evidence of Substitutability

Direct evidence of substitutability, if available, should be considered first in the process of market definition.[50] Such evidence would include, for example, data from suppliers on how the quantity demanded for a product has responded to historic price increases. Economists use the concept of "price elasticity" to describe how demand of a given product changes in response to changes in price.

a) Own-Price Elasticity

"Own-price elasticity" (or simply "demand elasticity") of a product is a measure of how its own demand changes in response to price.[51] The Competition Tribunal in *Superior Propane* defined it as follows:

> The own price elasticity of demand is the percentage change in quantity of the product consumed that results from a one percent price increase in its price.[52]

Own-price elasticity is expressed as follows:

$$\text{Own-price elasticity or demand elasticity} = \frac{\text{Percentage change in quantity demanded}}{\text{Percentage change in price}}$$

Where the percentage quantity demanded is less than the percentage change in price, the above number will be less than one. In such circumstances, demand is referred to as "inelastic."[53] If it is greater than the percentage change in price, it will be greater than one and demand is described as "elastic," suggesting that demand responds quite significantly to price changes. If the percentage change is the same, it is referred to as "unitary." In summary:

Inelastic demand = Elasticity less than one

Unitary demand = Elasticity equal to one

Elastic demand = Elasticity greater than one

---

50 *Tele-Direct*, above note 16 at para 78.

51 Generally, see Gregory J Werden, "Demand Elasticities in Antitrust Analysis" (1998) 66:2 *Antitrust Law Journal* 363.

52 *Propane CCT1*, above note 23 at para 34.

53 Given that an increase in price for most commodities results in a reduction of demand (i.e., "downward sloping demand" as seen in Chapter 3) price elasticity is generally a negative number. However, the minus sign is often ignored by economists for ease of expression. That practice will be followed here. See, e.g., Michael J Brennan, *Theory of Economic Statics*, 2d ed (Englewood Cliffs, NJ: Prentice Hall, 1970) at 77 [Brennan].

For example, if the price elasticity of soft drinks is 1.5, demand is elastic—a 1 percent increase in the price of soft drinks results in demand going down 1.5 percent. (A 2010 Mexican study concluded that "sugar sweetened beverages" have a demand elasticity in the range of 1.06 to 1.16, supporting the view that in fact soft drink demand is elastic.[54])

If the price elasticity is 0.5, it means a 1 percent increase in price results in a 0.5 percent reduction in demand and demand is inelastic.

For the purposes of market definition, in addition to elasticity, the impact of the demand changes on profitability must be factored in. This requires some knowledge of the firm's cost structure. The question to be asked for market definition is whether "on a price increase by a firm, enough of its sales would be lost to all competing products, regardless of their number or identity, to make the price increase unprofitable."[55]

b) Cross-Price Elasticity (or Cross-Elasticity)

The Competition Tribunal stated in *Superior Propane:*

> The cross-price elasticity of demand concept is frequently used in market definition. This measure identifies a product as a substitute if its quantity demanded rises when the price of the good in question rises. For any pair of products A and B there will be two such elasticities (the percentage change in consumption of product A when the price of product B increases by one percent, and the percentage change in the consumption of product B when the price of product A increases by one percent).[56]

The two cross-price elasticities of demand in respect of soft drinks (SD) and fruit juices (FJ) are:

$$\text{Cross-elasticity of SD with respect to the price of FJ} = \frac{\text{Percentage change in quantity of SD demanded}}{\text{Percentage change in price of FJ}}$$

$$\text{Cross-elasticity of FJ with respect to the price of SD} = \frac{\text{Percentage change in quantity of FJ demanded}}{\text{Percentage change in price of SD}}$$

54 MA Colchero et al, "Price Elasticity of the Demand for Sugar Sweetened Beverages and Soft Drinks in Mexico" (2015) 19 *Economics & Human Biology* 129.

55 *Propane CCT1*, above note 23 at para 61.

56 *Ibid* at para 59.

Cross-elasticity is a measure of the responsiveness of the quantity of a particular product's demand to changes in the price of another product (rather than in its own price). When two products are substitutes for one another, their cross-elasticity is positive. For example, if soft drinks and fruit juices are substitutes, a reduction in the price of fruit juices will draw away demand from soft drink consumption. The top and bottom percentages in the above fraction will both be negative, meaning that the elasticity will be positive.[57]

When two products are complements—for example products that are consumed in conjunction with each other, such as shoes and shoelaces—the cross-elasticity is negative.

The Tribunal has noted that, while cross-elasticity data are helpful, for example, in identifying a next-best substitute, own price elasticity is what ultimately assists in measuring the ability to increase price in the face of all available substitutes:

> The more important limitation on the use of the concept of cross-price elasticity of demand to delineate markets is its indirect relevance to the exercise of market power. The definition of the relevant competition market does not depend on identifying particular substitutes in some pairwise fashion. Rather, the important question is whether, on a price increase by a firm, enough of its sales would be lost to all competing products, regardless of their number or identity, to make the price increase unprofitable. . . . A cross elasticity estimate may identify a substitute and can be helpful in delineating a market, but it does not directly measure the ability of a firm to raise the price.[58]

On the evidence, the Tribunal held that propane and natural gas were not substitutes given the lack of cross-elasticity.[59]

The *Merger Enforcement Guidelines* recognize the value of cross-elasticity data, where available, in identifying potential substitutes:

> While cross-price elasticities do not in themselves directly measure the ability of a firm to profitably raise prices, they are particularly useful when determining whether differentiated products are substitutes for one another and whether such products are part of the same relevant market.[60]

---

57 See the discussion in Brennan, above note 53 at 89–91.

58 *Propane CCT1*, above note 23 at para 61. See also Collins, Trebilcock & Winter, above note 15 at 243.

59 *Propane CCT1*, above note 23 at para 60. The correctness of the Tribunal's statement that "reciprocal substitutability must be demonstrated" has been questioned: Collins, Trebilcock & Winter, above note 15 at 242–43.

60 *Merger Enforcement Guidelines*, above note 25 at para 4.11.

Sometimes economists are able to rely upon the results of what is termed a natural experiment as a source of direct evidence of elasticity. A natural experiment involves the use of data or results from a naturally occurring event or events as a basis to test certain hypotheses. In the *Visa Canada Corp* case, for example, the response of customers to the conversion of portfolios of credit cards by MasterCard to "premium designations" with higher card fees was referred to in the process of determining that the relevant market was "the supply of Credit Card Network Services to Acquirers."[61] Natural experiments which test the boundaries of a relevant market may also examine competitive responses to new entry, changes in marketing strategies, or changes in output.[62]

c) Impact of Substitution on Profitability

The hypothetical monopolist test asks whether substitution away from the candidate product in response to a SSNIP would be sufficiently great that the price increase would be unprofitable. To assess the transaction volume a hypothetical monopolist would have to lose before a SSNIP became unprofitable, economists sometimes apply a "critical loss" analysis, which estimates the loss in demand that would make a SSNIP unprofitable given the variable profit margins of firms in the candidate market. Direct and indirect evidence can be used to assess whether the actual loss from the price increase is likely to exceed the critical loss.[63] The Tribunal has considered such an analysis in assessing market definition.[64]

4) Practical Indicia Used for Product Market Definition

In many cases, reliable data or other direct evidence of demand elasticity are not available. Even when sufficient data are available to allow for the estimation of demand elasticities, and the base price issue can be overcome, recourse to practical indicia or factors is usually made by the Bureau[65] or by the Competition Tribunal in defining the market. The

---

61 *Visa Canada Corp*, above note 38 at paras 206–12.

62 Malcolm B Coate & Jeffrey H Fischer, "A Practical Guide to the Hypothetical Monopolist Test for Market Definition" (2008) 4 *Journal of Competition Law & Economics* 1031 at 1045–46.

63 "Critical loss analyses involve measuring the minimum amount of sales a hypothetical monopolist would need to lose to make a 5–10% price increase unprofitable": Renée M Duplantis, Canada, Competition Bureau, "Economic Analysis of Retail Mergers at the Competition Bureau" (14 September 2014), online: www.competitionbureau.gc.ca/eic/site/cb-bc.nsf/eng/03796.html at footnote 8.

64 *Visa Canada Corp*, above note 38 at paras 210–25.

65 *Merger Enforcement Guidelines*, above note 25 at para 4.12.

Federal Court of Appeal in *Southam* recognized the value of practical indicia of substitutability:

> Direct evidence of substitutability includes both statistical evidence of buyer price sensitivity and anecdotal evidence, such as the testimony of buyers on past or hypothetical responses to price changes. However, since direct evidence may be difficult to obtain, it is also possible to measure substitutability and thereby infer price sensitivity through indirect means. Such indirect evidence focusses on certain practical indicia, such as functional interchangeability and industry views/behaviour, to show that products are close substitutes.[66]

As the foregoing indicates, the practical analysis involves an assessment of which products are sufficiently close substitutes that they should be included in the relevant market. In *TREB*, the Tribunal referred to substitutability in the context of an abuse of dominance case:

> In defining relevant markets in proceedings brought under section 79 of the Act [abuse of dominance], the Tribunal has focused upon whether there are close substitutes for the product "at issue" . . . "close substitutes" have been defined in terms of whether "buyers are willing to switch from one product to another in response to a relative change in price, i.e., if there is buyer price sensitivity."[67]

The Tribunal in *Canada Pipe*, for example, assessed indirect evidence of substitutability in determining whether cast iron drain, waste, and ventilation (DWV) pipes were in the same market as plastic or concrete pipes:

> In determining the relevant product market one considers substitutability—in other words, whether there exist sufficiently close substitutes to the product at issue, such that the market for that product includes those substitutes.
>
> In the absence of direct evidence about price elasticity and given the importance of determining whether other products would constrain price increases of cast iron DWV products, the Tribunal considered the indirect evidence on the topics enumerated in the Guidelines.[68]

---

66 *Southam* FCA, above note 1 at 632–33; applied in *Tele-Direct*, above note 16 at para 76.

67 *TREB*, above note 27 at paras 117–18; citing *Canada Pipe*, above note 24 at paras 12–16, and *Tele-Direct*, above note 16 at 35, both citing the test adopted by the Federal Court of Appeal in *Southam* FCA, above note 1.

68 *Canada Pipe*, above note 24 at paras 68 and 71.

This indirect evidence, as set out by the *Merger Enforcement Guidelines* and considered in the caselaw, includes the following main areas:

- end use/functional interchangeability
- physical and technical characteristics
- buyer views and behaviour
- trade views and behaviour
- switching costs
- price relationships and relative price levels
- cost of adapting or constructing production processes, distribution and marketing

These will now be considered in turn.

a) End Use/Functional Interchangeability

The fact that a product has the same end use as another one is a necessary, but not sufficient, condition for them to be found to be in the same relevant market. For example, fruit juices and soft drinks both quench thirst, but that alone is not decisive that fruit juices provide a sufficiently strong competitive constraint on soft drinks to be in the same market. The Competition Tribunal held in *Tele-Direct*:

> A finding that the products alleged to be in the same market serve the same relevant purpose is a necessary first step in the analysis. A finding of functional interchangeability, however, is not alone sufficient to place the products in the same market.[69]

Given that it is only one factor, the Supreme Court in *Southam* noted that "[i]t cannot be said as a matter of law that evidence of functional interchangeability should weigh more heavily in the balance than other kinds of evidence."[70] A difficulty in determining what weight to give the fact that two products are interchangeable for a particular use or purpose is whether the purpose in question is important enough to make the products true substitutes. The Supreme Court pointed out in *Southam*:

> [I]t is unhelpful to suggest that once a purpose has been identified, all those products that serve that purpose should be considered to fall within a single market. It is the *correct* or *relevant* purpose that must be found, which is to say the broadest purpose that is consistent with a high cross-elasticity of demand.[71]

---

69 *Tele-Direct*, above note 16 at para 87.

70 *Southam* SCC, above note 1 at para 67.

71 *Ibid* at para 72 [emphasis in original].

That cars and tanks provide transportation is at such a "high level of generality" that it says little about market definition and is therefore unhelpful in that analysis.[72] One must search for a relevant and potentially probative purpose. The Supreme Court held that the Competition Tribunal had not erred in finding that community newspapers and dailies were in different markets even though they both served as media for "multiple price/product" advertising. The Tribunal found that providing price/product advertising was not the sole or decisive relevant purpose and that the additional purpose of targeting local versus national consumers placed local newspapers in different markets. The Supreme Court held that this was a reasonable factor for the Tribunal to rely upon and one to which the Court of Appeal should have shown deference.

In *Tele-Direct*, the Tribunal held that Yellow Pages advertising was in a different market from newspaper and electronic media because these media served different functions. The print media create awareness or stimulate demand for goods, while directories like Yellow Pages operate at a later point in the buying cycle, when a customer has made a purchase decision and needs to be directed to a supplier.[73]

In *TREB*, the fact that both the internet and the Multiple Listing Service (MLS) provide information on real estate listings to home buyers was held to be insufficient to make those sources interchangeable. The Tribunal held that the latter supplied a "broad range of the information" about real estate which "customers would not likely seek or be able to readily obtain . . . from alternative sources."[74]

b) Physical and Technical Characteristics

Closely tied to a product's end use are its physical characteristics, which may provide some indication (although often not decisive) about substitutability. It is a question of determining what physical characteristics may affect the practical use or consumption of the product in question in a way that affects substitutability.

The *Merger Enforcement Guidelines* note that "when buyers place a high value on the actual or perceived unique physical or technical characteristics of a product (including warranties, post-sales service and order turnaround time), it may be necessary to define distinct relevant markets based on these characteristics."[75] In *Canada Pipe*, for example, this factor played a relatively large role in distinguishing cast iron drain, waste, and ventilation (DWV) pipes from plastic pipes in their construction

---

72 *Tele-Direct*, above note 16 at para 98.

73 *Ibid* at para 101.

74 *TREB*, above note 27 at paras 144–45.

75 *Merger Enforcement Guidelines*, above note 25 at para 4.14.

applications. Factors considered included: cast iron is non-combustible and therefore more widely approved in building codes; it is less noisy than plastic in drain applications within apartments and residences; it has a lower thermal expansion rate; and, it offers strength and load bearing properties that plastic does not. Thus, even though plastic was lower cost, lighter, and offered greater ease of installation, the Tribunal held that "it still cannot replace cast iron in all its applications, nor does it offer the same characteristics."[76]

Certain technical characteristics distinguished directory advertising from other advertising media in *Tele-Direct*. These included: that it was a less time-sensitive medium (published annually); that it provided a comprehensive listing of suppliers; and, that it did not permit pricing information to be displayed.[77] As a result, the Tribunal concluded "[t]he existence of significant . . . differences between Yellow Pages and other media would lead to the inference that other media are not close substitutes to the Yellow Pages."[78]

c) Views, Strategies, Behaviour, and Identity of Buyers

Evidence from buyers on what they view as substitutes can be very informative about which products exercise a competitive constraint on the product under examination, and how they would respond to a price increase. This evidence may be anecdotal (i.e., what individual buyers or users say) or based on surveys or interviews taken from a population or sample group. The representativeness of the sample or survey will depend on the methodology for study design, sampling, and other variables. The weight given this evidence will turn on the conclusions of the trier of fact about its usefulness and whether it is representative.

For example, in *Southam*, the Tribunal noted that the Competition Bureau put forward "evidence of the buyers or consumers of the product [which] takes the form of anecdotal evidence (as opposed to survey results or statistical studies) from selected retail advertisers carrying on business in the Lower Mainland."[79] The Tribunal went through what the Supreme Court described as a "painstaking review" of this evidence. The consumer evidence was not found to be decisive; for example, the Tribunal observed that "[i]n a few cases the witnesses are very explicit as to why they have chosen a particular mix of advertising channels. In most others the rationale is unclear"; "[a] number of witnesses were asked about their likely response to hypothetical price increases in the

---

76 *Canada Pipe*, above note 24 at paras 86–87 and 94.

77 *Tele-Direct*, above note 16 at paras 120–24.

78 *Ibid* at para 125.

79 *Southam* CCT, above note 2 at 37.

community newspapers or the dailies but there was no systematic pursuit of this line of questioning."[80] In the end, it concluded that there was "no evidence before the Tribunal that advertisers are highly sensitive to the relative prices of the dailies and the community newspapers."[81]

On the other hand, "the respondents commissioned a survey of advertisers in the Lower Mainland from the Angus Reid Group, Inc. . . . Advertisers currently using newspapers were . . . asked how they might respond to a hypothetical increase in the price of newspaper advertising." However, the survey results fared no better than the Bureau's anecdotal witness evidence. Tribunal held that the sampling process used in the survey was so flawed "that any dependence on it became impossible."[82]

In *Canada Pipe*, the Tribunal relied on anecdotal evidence from buyers that cast iron was not substitutable: "[c]ontractor requirements or building code specifications may dictate the choice of cast iron over other materials. . . . When options are provided to contractors by mechanical engineers, the evidence of some contractors was that they opt for cast iron for certain applications."[83]

d) Trade Views, Strategies, and Behaviour (Inter-industry Competition)

The evidence of industry players such as suppliers, competitors, retired executives, and industry experts can provide insights into whether products compete and should be considered to be in the same market. In *Canada Pipe*, the Commissioner called a building code consultant who testified that "the current regulatory restrictions favour and will continue to favour the use of cast iron for DWV applications." The Tribunal concluded from this that cast iron was not substitutable in certain applications, such as for high-rise buildings.[84]

The parties themselves may supply very probative evidence in their own documents, on issues such as who they consider competitors. Key internal documents include marketing and planning documents, presentations to the Board or senior management on competitive strategies, presentations on the merits of proposed acquisitions, and research and other documents underlying pricing decisions.

The factors that go into pricing decisions, and what prices are monitored for competitive decision making, are key pieces of evidence that

80 *Ibid* at 43 and 47.

81 *Ibid* at 69.

82 *Ibid* at 55.

83 *Canada Pipe*, above note 24 at paras 72 and 74.

84 *Ibid* at paras 80–82.

often disclose where the real competition is coming from. For example, in *Canada Pipe* the Tribunal noted in finding cast iron pipe a separate market, "Bibby devotes considerable effort to promoting the physical characteristics of cast iron products as compared to plastics, but these efforts do not lead to a reduction in price for cast iron products."[85] Similarly, the fact that Tele-Direct's own documents showed "no effort" on the company's part "to track revenues, prices, features or circulation in a comprehensive and detailed a fashion" with respect to media other than directories was given great weight by the Tribunal in concluding that directories formed a separate advertising market.[86]

In *TREB*, the Tribunal noted that "industry documentation reflects a view that industry participants consider that there is a single and distinct market for MLS-based residential real estate brokerage services."[87]

Statements made in other contexts by industry players may also be of value. In the *VISA Canada Corp* decision, the Tribunal referred to the testimony of the president of MasterCard Canada made before the Standing Senate Committee on Banking, Trade and Commerce to the effect that the use of debit and credit cards involve "completely different transactions" because, for example, "a credit card transaction has features that simply do not exist for a debit purchase, like fraud monitoring, charge-back protection, zero liability, and so on."[88] This supported the view that retailers did not have a substitute for credit cards if fees were increased by the credit card companies.

e) Price Relationships and Relative Price Levels

The fact that the prices of two products move in tandem is a supportive,[89] but not decisive, factor in determining that they are in the same market. The common movement may be the product of other factors, such as that they share common inputs, or that their pricing reflects changes in other market conditions. The Tribunal held in *Tele-Direct*:

> Given that there are common economic forces driving prices even in very disparate industries, one would expect to see some correlation in overall price movement. An attenuated correlation in price movement does not indicate close substitutes. Even a high correlation between two sets of prices is only a necessary condition for the two products to

85 *Ibid* at para 101.
86 *Tele-Direct*, above note 16 at paras 179 and 186.
87 *TREB*, above note 27 at para 146.
88 *Visa Canada Corp*, above note 38 at para 229.
89 This follows from the fact that the prices of products in the same market should tend toward equality, after accounting for arbitrage costs (the costs of moving the product from the high-cost to the low-cost market), such as transportation costs.

> be considered to be in the same market. But, it is not a sufficient condition to prove they are in the same market because other factors than substitutability may be responsible for the correlation.[90]

In that case, the Tribunal rejected evidence of average annual price increases of different media as helpful evidence of substitutability, given the "common economic forces" driving them, and that there was no link from this evidence to strategies in the companies' internal documents.

On the other hand, the absence of price correlation between two products can be evidence that they are in separate markets. In *Canada Pipe*, the Commissioner relied upon "evidence that pricing for other products is independent of price movements in the cast iron products sector." The Tribunal reviewed the evidence and concluded that while competition from cast iron suppliers had elicited a price response, the same was not true of alleged substitutes such as plastic pipe.[91] This factored into its finding that cast iron pipe was a separate market.

f) Switching Costs

If customers face costs to switch between products this may reduce the potential for substitution. Switching costs may include both monetary outlays such as costs to retool, repackage, adapt marketing, or replace a full line of products, as well as other obstacles such as time or contractual restrictions. In some cases, suppliers may attempt to increase switching costs and differentiate their products through strategies such as loyalty or points programs, or the use of proprietary parts and software not available from other sources.

When linked to the ability to substitute between products or services, switching costs are relevant to market definition. In *Superior Propane*, the Tribunal held that certain national accounts handled by one firm would be unlikely to switch to multiple suppliers, so that "national account coordination services" should be considered as a product market distinct from the general supply of propane.[92]

g) Price Discrimination

A narrower market may be defined based upon so-called targeted customers or price discrimination. Price discrimination involves charging customers different prices when price differences are not related to cost differences. Price discrimination is profitable for a supplier when

---

90 *Tele-Direct*, above note 16 at para 221.

91 *Canada Pipe*, above note 24 at paras 96–101.

92 *Propane CCT1*, above note 23 at paras 80–81.

some consumers are prepared to pay higher prices than others. It is only feasible when consumers are unable to arbitrage—that is, when consumers who are charged the lower price cannot profitably resell the product to consumers who are charged a higher price from the supplier. The US *Horizontal Merger Guidelines* give as an example of price discrimination a glass jar manufacturer who is able to charge a baby food processor higher prices because (unlike other customers) it cannot substitute metal containers. In such circumstances, it may be possible to "define a distinct market for glass containers used to package baby food."[93] Those *Guidelines* also indicate that groups of targeted customers sharing the same characteristics may form a distinct market.[94]

Similarly, the Canadian *Merger Enforcement Guidelines* signal that it may be possible to define relevant markets when "targeted buyers cannot effectively switch to other products or geographic locations, and cannot engage in arbitrage with other buyers by taking advantage of price differences."[95]

In *FTC v Staples*, the targeted buyers were so-called business-to-business (B-to-B) clients who procured large volumes of office supplies from the parties to the proposed merger, Staples and Office Depot. The US District Court held that B-to-B customers comprise "a targeted customer market for procurement of consumable office supplies. There is overwhelming evidence in this case that large B-to-B customers constitute a market that Defendants could target for price increases if they are allowed to merge. Significantly, Defendants themselves used the proposed merger to pressure B-to-B customers to lock in prices based on the expectation that they would lose negotiating leverage if the merger were approved."[96] The Court cited the following evidence to support this target market of B-to-B customers:

> (a) industry or public recognition of the market as a separate economic entity; (b) B-to-B customers demand distinct prices and demonstrate a high sensitivity to price changes; and (c) B-to-B customers require specialized vendors that offer value-added services, including: (i) sophisticated information technology (IT) services; (ii) high quality customer service; and (iii) expedited delivery.[97]

---

93 *Horizontal Merger Guidelines*, above note 18 at 13.

94 *Ibid*.

95 *Merger Enforcement Guidelines*, above note 25 at para 4.8.

96 *FTC v Staples, Inc*, 190 F Supp 3d 100 (DC Cir 2016) at 127 [*Staples*].

97 *Ibid* at 123.

h) Product Cluster Markets

It has been noted that "products can also be 'clustered' together if the 'cluster' is itself an object of consumer demand."[98] For example, "[i]f consumers strongly prefer to purchase a group of goods from a single firm, firms selling only part of this group will not compete effectively with firms supplying the full line."[99]

The *Merger Enforcement Guidelines* explain that a product market may be defined around "a group of diverse products that are not themselves substitutes for each other" where buyers would face "significant transactions costs" from trying to source the products from multiple sellers.[100]

In *FTC v Staples*, for example, the court accepted a product cluster market of "consumable office supplies" which included such diverse products as pens, file folders, Post-it notes, binder clips, and paper for copiers and printers. It held that "[a]lthough a pen is not a functional substitute for a paperclip, it is possible to cluster consumable office supplies into one market for analytical convenience."[101] The merging parties alleged that this market was overly narrow and gerrymandered because it excluded other products such as ink and toner. The court stated, however, that "the critical question that must be answered when determining whether a particular product should be included in a cluster market: are the items subject to the same competitive conditions?"[102] Because there were competitive options for ink and toner, it held that those products were properly excluded from the product cluster.

i) Two-Sided Markets

Some firms sell products or supply services using what is termed a "double-sided platform": product delivery which engages two different customers groups at the same time. These groups may interact with each other directly or indirectly. For example, newspapers have been identified as a double-sided platform, given that they bring together readers and advertisers. Newspapers supply both content for readers (the readership market) and space for advertisers (the advertising market). The quality of the content affects readership levels, which increases the value of the newspaper in the eyes of advertisers. The nature and scope of advertising also affects readers' valuations.

---

98 *FTC v Advocate Health Care Network*, 841 F3d 460 (7th Cir Ill 2016) at 468.

99 Ian Ayres, "Rationalizing Antitrust Cluster Markets" (1985) 95 *Yale Law Journal* 109 at 114.

100 *Merger Enforcement Guidelines*, above note 25 at para 4.16.

101 *Staples*, above note 96 at 117.

102 *Ibid* at 123.

How does one define such separate but interrelated markets? Is there one market? Two? Three? The Competition Bureau, in approving a merger of two large newspaper chains, Postmedia and Sun Media (Quebecor) conducted a separate assessment of the advertising and readership markets, finding a newspaper-specific market in both cases. It also noted "a strong interaction between the advertising and readership sides of the newspaper markets."[103] The Bureau recognized the importance of this interaction in a draft discussion paper on Big Data:

> While one side of a platform may constitute a properly defined market using the hypothetical monopolist test, a clear appreciation of the interaction between all sides of the market is required when defining markets involving platforms. For example, a newspaper may have less incentive to raise price to readers because of the resulting loss of advertising revenue.[104]

In the *Visa Canada Corp* case, the Tribunal identified credit cards as a platform featuring a two-sided market.[105] On one side of the market are cardholders—consumers who make payments with their cards. On the other side are merchants who accept cards as a payment vehicle for consumers. The value of the card for both sides is affected by the extent and nature of use by the other side. The more merchants accept the card, the more customers value the card; the more customers have the card, the more potential business merchants get from accepting the card for payment. Given these interactions, the Tribunal concluded that both separate and interconnected assessments were appropriate:

> Given the evidence before us, we find that one side of the platform can be a candidate relevant product market for the purposes of the hypothetical monopolist test and that the SSNIP can be applied to the price charged to customers on that side of the platform provided both the interdependence of demand, feedback effects and ultimately changes in profit on both sides of the platform are taken into account.[106]

---

103 Canada, Competition Bureau, "Position Statement Regarding the Proposed Acquisition by Postmedia Network Inc. of the English-language newspapers of Quebecor Media Inc." (25 March 2015), online: www.competitionbureau.gc.ca/eic/site/cb-bc.Nsf/eng/03899.html.

104 Canada, Competition Bureau, Draft Discussion Paper, "Big Data and Innovation: Implications for Competition Policy in Canada" (18 September 2017) at 13, online: www.competitionbureau.gc.ca/eic/site/cb-bc.nsf/vwapj/Big-Data-e.pdf/$file/Big-Data-e.pdf.

105 *Visa Canada Corp*, above note 38 at paras 174–76.

106 *Ibid* at para 189.

A different approach was taken by the majority of the US Supreme Court in *Ohio v American Express Co.*[107] The majority identified the credit card market as two-sided, and because the market involves a joint transaction, held that both sides of the market need to be taken into account in market definition: "[t]ransaction platforms are thus better understood as 'suppl[ying] only one product'— transactions."[108]

In defining the market by taking into account competitive effects on both sides of the platform, the majority determined that American Express's "anti-steering" rules, which prohibited merchants from favouring other credit cards over its own, were not illegal under section 1 of the *Sherman Act* on a rule of reason assessment. The majority considered that American Express did not possess market power simply because it raised credit card fees. The court weighed increases in card fees on the merchant side against beneficial effects on the customer side, such as "a more robust rewards program, which is necessary to maintain cardholder loyalty and encourage the level of spending that makes Amex valuable to merchants."[109] In a strong dissent, Breyer J disagreed with this approach, saying it was unprecedented and arguing that customer and merchant credit card services are complements, not substitutes, and therefore should be assessed separately in any market definition.[110]

Digital and data-driven markets are often two-sided and provide fertile ground for analysis and the development of novel approaches to market definition.[111] A key aspect of analyzing data is that it is often an input (as Google consumer browsing data is an input into its targeted advertising). A growing literature and caselaw in different jurisdictions has led to an evolution in methodology on how to approach market definition in data and two-sided markets given the ultimate purpose is to assess the degree of market power which may be present in a given market.[112]

---

107 *Ohio v American Express Co*, 138 S Ct 2274 (2018).

108 *Ibid* at 2286. The majority noted that "it is not always necessary to consider both sides of a two-sided platform" in the course of market definition.

109 *Ibid* at 2288.

110 *Ibid* at 2295–96: "An example of complements is gasoline and tires. A driver needs both gasoline and tires to drive, but they are not substitutes for each other, and so the sale price of tires does not check the ability of a gasoline firm (say a gasoline monopolist) to raise the price of gasoline above competitive levels."

111 See Michael Katz & Jonathan Sallet, "Multisided Platforms and Antitrust Enforcement" (2018) 127 *Yale Law Journal* 2142 at 2151–62.

112 See, e.g., Lapo Filistrucchi et al, "Market Definition in Two-Sided Markets: Theory and Practice" (2014) 10 *Journal of Competition Law & Economics* 293; Liang Li, "Data and Market Definition of Internet-Based Businesses" (2019) 20 *Competition and Regulation in Network Industries* 54.

j) Zero-Priced Product Markets

Challenges are raised by how to treat products that have a zero price. For example, Facebook does not charge for the use of its social media platform; Google does not charge for internet search services. In assessing the relevant market, the application of the hypothetical monopolist test employing a small (but significant) non-transitory price increase is not possible. The mere fact of a "zero price" does not mean, however, that there is no market and no competition law issues that can be raised from mergers, conspiratorial conduct, dominant firm behaviour, etc., with respect to such products.[113] The dimensions of competition in such markets may be non-price related. For example, some have argued that an approach to market definition in these markets is to focus on quality. Reductions in the quality of "free" services (e.g., in privacy protections on a social network) can be treated as increases in the quality-adjusted prices of those services. Market power by a firm offering "free" goods or services would be demonstrated by the ability to profitably raise quality-adjusted prices significantly above competitive levels.[114] Others have suggested, noticing that many of the digital and other media platforms compete by attracting consumer attention to their services in order to gain advertisers, that these markets be defined by focusing on consumer time spent on the platform or attention time as the "currency" by which to define markets, rather than price.[115] Another approach to market assessment here is to examine the practical indicia of the qualitative aspects of various services defining a market. Under this approach, one would assess the practical product or service functionalities and their interchangeability.[116]

If the foregoing approaches are unsatisfactory, or as a complement to them, market power can also be inferred directly (as discussed above). For example, it has been suggested that changes by Facebook to degrade its privacy protections following acquisitions of emerging competitors can be taken as an indicator of its market power.[117] Thus, there are

---

113 Makan Delrahim, "'I'm Free': Platforms and Antitrust Enforcement in the Zero-Price Economy" (Speech delivered at the Silicon Flatirons Annual Technology Policy Conference at the University of Colorado Law School, 11 February 2019), online: www.justice.gov/opa/speech/assistant-attorney-general-makan-delrahim-delivers-keynote-addresssilicon-flatirons.

114 In other words, "a 'small but significant non-transitory decrease in quality' (SSNDQ) test." Daniel L Rubinfeld & Michal S Gal, "The Hidden Costs of Free Goods: Implications for Antitrust Enforcement" (2016) 80 *Antitrust Law Journal* 521 at 551.

115 Tim Wu, "Blind Spot: The Attention Economy and the Law" (2019) 82 *Antitrust Law Journal* 771 at 772.

116 Jacques Crémer, Yves-Alexandre de Montjoye & Heike Schweitzer, *Competition Policy for the Digital Era* (Brussels: European Commission, 2019) at 45.

117 Wilson C Freeman & Jay B Sykes, *Antitrust and "Big Tech"* (Washington: Congressional Research Service, 2019) at 31, online: https://fas.org/sgp/crs/misc/R45910.pdf.

various tools with which to assess zero-price product markets even when the traditional hypothetical monopolist approach cannot be relied upon.

k) Other Unique Product Markets

Other product markets may have particular characteristics that raise unique issues. For example, do replacement parts for Xerox copiers constitute a separate product market even though there is plenty of competition in the copier market? In the particular context of an application alleging refusal to supply, albeit before amendments that introduced a market power requirement into the relevant legal test, the Tribunal said "yes."[118] A similar result was reached in the United States in the *Kodak* case.[119]

Other product markets that raise particular issues are procurement and so-called innovation markets.[120]

D. GEOGRAPHIC MARKET

1) Introduction

Geographic markets may be as narrow as a neighbourhood or as broad as the world. For some products, consumers will generally not travel large distances to make a purchase—groceries or gasoline are examples. Other products like commercial jets and armaments are sourced on a world-wide basis.

In *Hillsdown*, the central issue was whether the geographic market for meat rendering firms (companies that process meat by-products) extended beyond southern Ontario to include firms based in areas such as Buffalo and Detroit. If that were so, the market shares of the Ontario firms would be substantially reduced and the merger would not likely result in a lessening of competition. The Tribunal described the general parameters surrounding geographic market definition as follows:

> Determining the geographic dimensions of the relevant market is similar to determining the product dimensions; one asks whether there is a geographic area within which the merged firm either alone or in concert with others is likely to have market power. This requires identifying some area such that the merged firm has an advantage based on

---

118 *Canada (Director of Investigation and Research, Competition Act) v Xerox Canada Inc* (1990), 33 CPR (3d) 83 (CCT); see also *Canada (Director of Investigation and Research, Competition Act) v Chrysler Canada Ltd*, [1989] CCTD No 49.

119 *Eastman Kodak Co v Image Technical Services, Inc*, 504 US 451 (1992).

120 Whish & Bailey, above note 13 at 37–38.

> geographic considerations over firms not inside that area. Frequently this advantage results from transportation costs but often other factors may also be relevant, such as differing labour costs in the two areas or governmental restrictions and regulations.[121]

To perform geographic market definition, an assessment is required of the extent to which consumers within a candidate geographic area can turn to suppliers outside that area who could act as effective competition to firms within that area. As the Tribunal noted, "geographic boundaries of adjacent markets overlap and they are neither static nor precise,"[122] signalling that, like product market definition, geographic markets require the exercise of judgment and must be viewed as simply a step in the assessment of market power.

2) Hypothetical Monopolist: Geographic Market

The hypothetical monopolist test supplies a conceptual framework for assessing the geographic market, as it does for product markets. In assessing the *geographic* side of the relevant market, the hypothetical monopolist test involves the following steps for products supplied from a particular location:[123]

1) Start with a candidate area (neighbourhood, city, county, province, etc.) that includes a supply location of the merging firms and assume a small but significant non-transitory price increase (SSNIP).
2) If buyers would shift sufficient demand to sellers in more distant locations in sufficient quantities to render a SSNIP by a hypothetical monopolist unprofitable, "the location that is the next-best substitute is added to the candidate market."[124]
3) Then ask whether a firm operating at both locations could profitably sustain a price increase.

---

121 *Hillsdown*, above note 22 at para 35.

122 *Ibid.*

123 As the US *Horizontal Merger Guidelines* note:

> Geographic markets based on the locations of suppliers encompass the region from which sales are made. Geographic markets of this type often apply when customers receive goods or services at suppliers' locations. Competitors in the market are firms with relevant production, sales, or service facilities in that region. Some customers who buy from these firms may be located outside the boundaries of the geographic market.

Horizontal Merger Guidelines, above note 18 at 13. Geographic markets can also be defined around the locations of customers where the hypothetical monopolist can discriminate between customers based on location. See *ibid* at 14–15.

124 *Merger Enforcement Guidelines*, above note 25 at §4.5.

4) If the answer to the question in 3 is "no," repeat 1–3 by adding locations to the hypothetical firm until a price increase can be sustained. "This process continues until the smallest set of areas over which a hypothetical monopolist would impose and sustain the price increase is identified."[125]

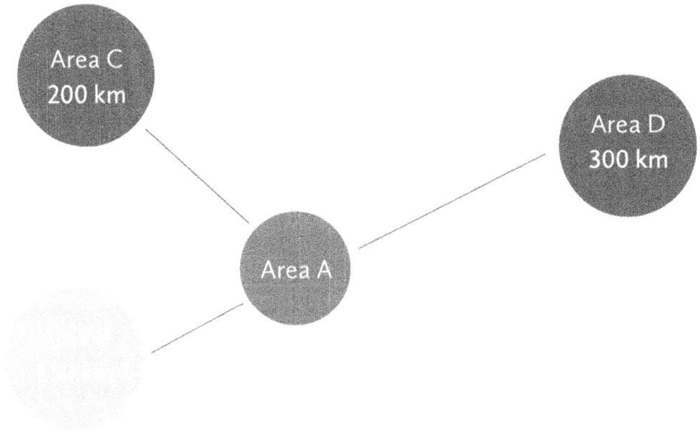

FIGURE 4.2. Steps in geographic market definition

Using the above example (see **Figure 4.2**), we would choose an area containing a location of the merging parties (Area A), and ask the question: would the hypothetical monopolist operating in this area be able to profitably sustain a SSNIP? If so, that area defines the market. If not, we would add the "location which attracts the largest percentage of the volume of lost sales of the relevant product."[126] If that location is in Area B, we would ask whether a firm operating at *both* these locations could profitably sustain a SSNIP. If that price increase *can* be profitably sustained, the market is defined to be those two areas. If not, we add the next closest location(s) and perform the same exercise of asking whether a monopolist operating at the several locations could sustain a SSNIP until the price increase *can* be profitably sustained.

3) Direct Evidence of Geographic Substitutability

As in the case of the product market, geographic substitutability can be measured by demand and supply elasticities. This was explained in *Hillsdown*:

125 *Ibid.*

126 Collins, Trebilcock & Winter, above note 15 at 243.

> An assessment of geographic boundaries requires an assessment as to whether a significant number of consumers within the alleged area are willing to turn to suppliers outside of that area to obtain, in this case, rendering services and whether there are suppliers outside the proposed boundary who could supply consumers within that area with rendering services, as effective competitors to the merged firm (indicators of demand elasticity and supply elasticity respectively).[127]

4) Practical Indicia Used for Geographic Market Definition

As in the case of product markets, reliable data or other direct evidence of elasticity is often not available for geographic markets, and practical indicia are used in order to assess the boundaries of the market. As a practical test, the US Supreme Court described the geographic market inquiry as focusing on the "area of effective competition . . . in which the seller operates, and to which the purchaser can practicably turn for supplies."[128] That test reflects that there are two main sides to the inquiry; first, where are the sellers operating in competition with each other, and second, as a practical matter, how far afield are customers prepared to travel or to seek sources of supply?

In *Laidlaw*, the Tribunal posed the relevant question this way: "what are the boundaries of the geographic area within which competitors must be based if they are to provide effective competition to Laidlaw? Effective competition means that the competitor provides a significant restraint on Laidlaw's ability to raise prices above the competitive level."[129] In that case, the Tribunal defined the geographic markets for Laidlaw's waste disposal services on Vancouver Island by taking into account a number of considerations, including that "providers of lift-on-board service generally . . . do not . . . provide service to customers located more than 50 km from the base of operation at which their trucks are parked," as well as past patterns of pricing, the local geography, and customer density.[130] The Tribunal determined that the Courtney-Comox-Cumberland area was not part of the same geographic market as Campbell River, given evidence that the area between the two regions had little population and therefore consumers would be unlikely to use a provider operating in another area, and that suppliers in that other area could therefore not provide price discipline.

---

127 *Hillsdown*, above note 22 at para 36.

128 *United States v Philadelphia National Bank*, 374 US 321 (1963) at 359.

129 *Canada (Director of Investigation and Research, Competition Act) v Laidlaw Waste Systems Ltd*, [1992] CCTD No 1 at para 66.

130 *Ibid* at para 93.

The main practical criteria referred to in the *Merger Enforcement Guidelines* and the caselaw, and discussed in more detail below, are:

- views, strategies, behaviour and identity of buyers
- trade views, strategies and behaviour
- transportation costs
- local set-up costs
- particular characteristics of the product
- price relationships and relative price levels
- shipment patterns

a) Views, Strategies, Behaviour, and Identity of Buyers

Evidence from buyers on where they are able, or prefer, to source the product or service in question can play a significant role in determining the scope of the geographic market. In *TREB*, a "consumer demand for local expertise" among users of real estate brokerage services supported a market "at the local level"—i.e., within a 20 to 30 kilometre radius of a real estate agent's base of operations.[131] A broader geographic market was not supported by the buyer evidence: "[n]o evidence was adduced to suggest that home buyers or home sellers in the GTA retain the services of agents whose principal base of operations is located outside the GTA."[132]

The need for a reliable and convenient source of supply close at hand can suggest a narrower geographic market area, particularly when there are frequent pick-ups or deliveries involved in the course of patronage. In *Hillsdown*, it was argued that there was a customer preference for a local source of rendering services on the basis that "renderable materials must be removed on a daily basis, [so] there is a need for reliable service."[133] However, the Tribunal was not convinced by this, given patterns of trade that often extended beyond the local area.

b) Trade Views, Strategies, and Behaviour

Views on the scope of the geographic market from existing business operators, retired executives, or industry experts, can assist geographic market assessment. Real estate agents testified in *TREB*, for example, "that agents tend to specialize at the local level."[134]

The *Merger Enforcement Guidelines* note that "[i]ndustry surveys and the views, strategies and behaviour of industry participants also inform the analysis by providing information on how buyers of a relevant

131 *TREB*, above note 27 at para 155–56.
132 *Ibid* at para 157.
133 *Hillsdown*, above note 22 at para 60.
134 *TREB*, above note 27 at para 156.

product in one geographic area respond or have responded to changes in the price, packaging or servicing of the relevant product in another geographic area."[135] In *Superior Propane*, Superior's internal documents provided evidence of the scope of the geographic market for the delivery of propane. Its Annual Report stated "[t]he further propane is transported, the higher the delivered cost, therefore, the competitive operating area is limited to a reasonable radius" which varied between 70 and 400 kilometres from a supply location.[136] The Commissioner called an expert who conducted an assessment of each of the merging parties' 240 branches and satellite locations from which they shipped propane. The Tribunal accepted his detailed analysis, applying "a buffer zone of 100 kilometers" around locations that translated into seventy-four separate geographic markets across Canada.[137]

c) Transportation and Related Costs

The cost of transporting the product in question is a key driver of geographic market definition. Products with low value to weight or to volume, such as gravel or cement, have high transportation costs as a portion of their value, and this tends to reduce the geographic market to a more local area.

In *Hillsdown*, the costs of transportation, regulatory delay, and uncertainty from crossing borders all played a role in the scope of the collection area served by red meat renderers. The Tribunal held that "transportation and other costs related to operating at a distance are such that a renderer located over 200–250 miles from Rothsay-Orenco should not be included in the relevant market." While crossing the border meant "additional costs for renderers . . . as a result of required paper work and possible delays," the Tribunal concluded that "renderers located within the United States but close to the border could provide effective competition to the merged firm."[138]

The *Merger Enforcement Guidelines* refer to the insights that can be gained from comparing historic prices in the area under consideration (area A) with prices in a distant location which is a candidate for inclusion in the geographic market (area B) plus transportation cost. If the price of the relevant product in area B plus the cost of transporting it to area A materially exceeds the price in the candidate market including a SSNIP, the Bureau would not include area B in the geographic market. If price in area B has historically exceeded or been lower than prices in

---

135 *Merger Enforcement Guidelines*, above note 25 at para 4.19.

136 *Propane CCT1*, above note 23 at paras 94–95.

137 *Ibid* at paras 90–91.

138 *Hillsdown*, above note 22 at para 64.

area A by more than the transportation costs, this suggests these areas are not in the same market, but there is still a need to examine whether the postulated price increase (under a SSNIP) will make area B competitive. If so, it could be included.[139]

On the other hand, if the price in area A has historically exceeded area B prices by *less* than the transportation cost plus a SSNIP, this suggests the areas may be in the same market. However, there is still a need to ask if there are other reasons that limit competition between those areas (such as a border, regulatory limitations, etc.).

d) Particular Characteristics of the Product

Examples of product characteristics that affect the ability to transport large distances include fragility and perishability.[140] The need for refrigeration, special delivery equipment (such as cement trucks), and the requirement for just-in-time delivery may also affect the scope of the geographic market.

e) Price Relationships and Relative Price Levels

A factor given substantial weight in many cases, because it is a reflection of actual market conditions, is the prevailing and historical price level in different geographic areas. The presence of price differences between areas over time is a strong indicator that competitive conditions differ and that the areas are in different geographic markets. For example, *NutraSweet* considered whether the market for aspartame (an artificial sweetener) was international or national. NutraSweet argued that the market was worldwide, on the basis "that transportation costs are low, that there are no Canadian tariff or non-tariff barriers and that . . . minimal required infrastructure for distribution makes entry easy."[141] The Tribunal examined price levels, however, and concluded that "[c]ountry-specific clauses in multi-country contracts along with these average price differences indicate that market conditions in Canada . . . can and have produced prices that differ significantly from those in other regions of competition."[142] As a result, it found that Canada was the applicable geographic market.

Similarly, in *Canada Pipe*, the respondent manufacturer of cast iron pipe argued for a national or North American market based on historic

---

139 *Merger Enforcement Guidelines*, above note 25 at para 4.23.

140 *Ibid* at para 4.22.

141 *Canada (Director of Investigation and Research, Competition Act) v NutraSweet Co*, [1990] CCTD No 17 at 12.

142 *Ibid* at 13.

shipments within Canada and from the United States. However, the Tribunal noted:

> The price of the relevant product may act as an indicator of geographic market. If prices show homogeneity in a given region as compared to another region, each of these regions could be considered a separate geographic market; in an integrated geographic market, lower-price goods will simply move into the areas where higher prices are charged, thus providing effective price discipline.[143]

The Tribunal found that the "very significant price differences from one region to the next"[144] reflected differing competitive conditions in those areas. This was the result of the presence of different competitive players in certain areas like Ontario and the influence of imports in the west, with the result that "[t]he different regions react to their own competitive factors."[145] As a result, the Tribunal concluded that there were six geographic markets: Atlantic Canada, Quebec, Ontario, the Prairies, Alberta, and British Columbia.

f) Shipment Patterns

The *Merger Enforcement Guidelines* note that historical shipments between the candidate and a distant area "may suggest that the distant area is in the relevant geographic market."[146] However, such evidence is not conclusive because this still must be tested against what would happen in the face of a price increase (SSNIP). Furthermore, it must be determined if shipment patterns reflect competitive conditions or something else.

In *Canadian Waste Services*, the Tribunal determined that shipments of waste to Michigan by integrated waste collectors, which were the result of internal company decisions to free up space in Southern Ontario disposal sites, were not a helpful indicator of the boundaries of the geographic market. The Tribunal noted that areas of trade "established by managers for operational purposes" are not always an indicator of the scope of the geographic market.[147]

g) Price Discrimination

As in the case of the product market, the existence of price discrimination can justify narrowing geographic markets. The Tribunal noted in

143 *Canada Pipe*, above note 24 at para 104.
144 *Ibid* at para 108.
145 *Ibid* at para 111.
146 *Merger Enforcement Guidelines*, above note 25 at para 4.24.
147 *Canadian Waste Services*, above note 44 at para 72.

Canadian Waste Services that "where price discrimination is possible, it is appropriate to delineate additional smaller markets based on the location of customers against whom price discrimination would be exercised."[148] It held that the presence of price discrimination was a factor supporting a narrower market area for waste disposal, which was defined as "that area of Southern Ontario containing disposal sites capable of accepting ICI Waste from the GTA," i.e., excluding New York and Michigan.[149]

E. CONCLUSION

The extent of market power is a central and often a decisive factor in competition law cases, whether the case involves an alleged exclusionary act by a dominant firm, a merger between competitors, or some other conduct. The most common method for assessing market power is to define the relevant market and measure the firm's market share in that market, or to measure the collective market shares of the firms involved in a merger or agreement. Finally, one infers from this share and other factors the degree of market power, and assesses the result according to the applicable legal standard. Markets are analyzed from both product and geographic perspectives.

The methodology for assessing relevant markets in most cases uses a number of proxies for substitutability, because direct evidence such as demand elasticity is often not available. At the end of the day, two important qualifications must be kept in mind about this process, relying as it does on practical indicia. First, the conclusions achieved are often approximations, and some flexibility must be retained in how the results of this inquiry are used in the process of assessing market power. Second, market definition is not an end in itself; it is only a step on the way to assessing market power. It been wisely noted that "[t]here is not for any product a single real 'market' waiting to be discovered."[150] Market boundaries are not firmly etched, but a matter of subtle contours. Factors left outside a relevant market, for example, can be brought back into the assessment of market power at a later stage to ensure that a full picture of the competitive conditions is obtained. As the Supreme Court's decision in *Southam* makes clear, market definition is largely a fact-driven process of weighing a number of differing indicators, rather than the mere application of a strict set of legal principles or rules.

---

148 *Ibid* at para 78.
149 *Ibid* at paras 94 and 100.
150 Sullivan, above note 28 at 41.

The *Hillsdown* case offers a useful example of the fluid nature of market definition. In that case, the Tribunal concluded that the geographic market for meat rendering firms should be limited to competitors within 320 to 400 kilometres from the merging parties. It calculated the pre-merger market share of the merging firms at 62–63 percent (in terms of material processed) and 56–66 percent (in terms of capacity). In spite of these high market shares, the Tribunal noted that "[t]he excess capacity of firms both within and outside the relevant market will provide a degree of competitive pressure on the merged firm and restrain to a considerable extent its ability to raise prices."[151] Competition outside the market was a key factor, in addition to the shrinking nature of the red meat rendering market and resulting excess capacity, in the Tribunal's assessment that the merger was *not* likely to substantially lessen competition. It concluded, "a significant source of competitive discipline will exist from those firms which border geographically on the relevant market and which would be prepared to expand their area of collection in the face of a price rise by the merged firm."[152] The boundary of the geographic market as defined did not create an analytical limit: it properly did not confine the Tribunal's assessment of how competitors might affect future market power. At the end of the day, as Professor Sullivan has pointed out:

> Though the law's need is for norms sufficiently specific for courts to apply, it cannot be too forcefully emphasized that there are no absolutes in the analysis. Power is always a matter of degree, and market definition is always a matter of judgment.[153]

Because market definition can usually only yield an approximation of market boundaries, and because of the significant resources and effort that it can take, it has become increasingly common for competition authorities, economists, and lawyers to seek to assess market power through direct means, in an attempt to bring greater empirical precision, or objectivity, into its measurement. Certain empirical methodologies developed by economists assess market power, for example, by measuring customer responses directly, by asking how many sales or how much revenue would be lost if a firm increases its prices. This can yield an indication of an individual firm's power over price, or of the effects of a merger, without defining a relevant market. These approaches are a useful reminder that market definition is a mere tool for, not a goal of, competition law assessment.

---

151 *Hillsdown*, above note 22 at para 94.

152 *Ibid.*

153 Sullivan, above note 28 at 42.

CHAPTER 5

MERGER REVIEW

A. INTRODUCTION

1) Why Review Mergers?

The *Competition Act* gives the Commissioner of Competition authority to apply to the Competition Tribunal to block a proposed merger, or to seek to dismantle a completed merger, on the basis that the merger would be likely to substantially prevent or lessen competition.[1] The legislative scheme also requires parties to any acquisition[2] over defined size thresholds (regardless of its effect on competition) to notify the Competition Bureau of the transaction and to provide prescribed information before the merger can be closed.

The applicable legal test is focused on the effects of a merger on competition. In addition to the effects of a merger on competition, other policy concerns, such as the impact of foreign investment, the effects of a plant closure on employment, or impacts on minority shareholders, may be raised. While these are evidently legitimate considerations, they are not the concern of competition law *per se*,[3] although a competition-

1 Section 92 of the *Competition Act*, RSC 1985, c C-34 [*Competition Act* or Act].

2 As referred to in s 110 of the *Competition Act*, *ibid*, and as prescribed in applicable regulations.

3 See Chapter 3. In *Imperial Oil*, the Tribunal stated the following:

> It is clear that there is a social value in keeping the refinery running. It is common knowledge that employment opportunities are not as numerous in the

FIGURE 5.1. ABOVE, The Toronto Brewing & Malting Company (from 1932, renamed Canadian Bud Breweries Ltd), north of Dundas Street, west of University Ave, Toronto, and **FIGURE 5.2.** BELOW, The O'Keefe Toronto Brewery, 11–17 Gould Street (near Yonge and Dundas), Toronto, were acquired by Canadian Breweries Ltd in 1934 and 1937, respectively

focused scheme may have an impact in these areas. Other regimes, such as foreign investment review, industrial policy, or securities and corporate law, may apply to address them.

Why is this competition-focused regime necessary? Mergers may often have beneficial effects through the overhaul of management, product improvements, or cost reductions from consolidation and economies of scale. Given the potential for such benefits, why not permit mergers simply to proceed, and deal with any undesirable effects after the fact, if they ever occur? Available remedies in competition law include review of anti-competitive practices by dominant firms, or if coordinated behaviour occurs, application of the Act's prohibitions against collusion and anti-competitive agreements.

There are a number of reasons for a merger review regime. First, as the Economic Council's 1969 *Interim Report* explained, a merger between competing firms, or the acquisition of an emerging competitor by a dominant firm, may cause an immediate adverse effect on competition:

> [T]he basic reason for public policy to be concerned with mergers is that in the majority of cases they result in permanent changes in the structure of industry—changes which can have important implications for the future performance of the economy.[4]

Mergers which prevent or reduce competition may result in price increases, eliminate the potential for future price reductions, or harm service or other competitive terms of trade. These are akin to the effects of a horizontal conspiracy, and with a more enduring impact on industry structure. As reviewed in Chapter 3, such combinations, when resulting in the creation or enhancement of market power, can adversely affect allocative, productive, and dynamic efficiency, as rivalry is lost between competing firms, or as an emerging disruptive competitive force is stifled by a takeover. In data-related markets, for example, concerns have been

---

> Atlantic region as elsewhere in the country. At the same time the focus of the Tribunal's attention could not be primarily on that consideration, if competition concerns could equally be met by use of the terminaling facilities. There was some concrete evidence that this might be the case. The primary concerns of the Tribunal have to be factors such as those listed in section 93 of the *Competition Act*, with a view to the issues which Professor Trebilcock indicated should be the focus of attention in any merger case: possible emergence of a dominant firm; enhanced ability for tacit collusion.

Canada (Director of Investigation and Research, Competition Act) v Imperial Oil Limited, [1990] CCTD No 1 at para 79.

4 Economic Council of Canada, *Interim Report on Competition Policy* (Ottawa: Queen's Printer, 1969) at 113.

raised about past mergers and acquisitions of the leading players such as Google, Facebook, and Microsoft—which some have linked to the present structure involving the hegemony of a few large firms.[5]

Furthermore, tackling the impact of dominance after the fact is not simple, quick, or cheap. The use of dominance law to address the practices of larger firms often involves lengthy and complex proceedings which may not yield a remedy until years after the competitive harm has already occurred.

The law must therefore be equipped to address mergers and acquisitions which adversely alter industry structure, and to provide remedies in a timely fashion. As stated in the *Guide* published with the 1986 amendments, "[w]ithout an effective law on merger, the performance of the economy, over the long run, suffers."[6]

Another rationale for merger review is addressing acquisitions which increase the likelihood of coordinated action. The takeover, for example, of a price discounting rival or "maverick" innovator in an already-concentrated market may permit the remaining firms to quell competitive and innovative behaviour, to adopt follow-the-leader pricing, or to engage in other coordinated tactics. These may flow from a tacit arrangement, which is not easily addressed by the conspiracy or anti-competitive agreement provisions of the Act, given the lack of evidence of an explicit agreement. At the same time, the conduct may achieve many of the same undesirable results as a formal cartel. Merger law can therefore be an important tool in keeping markets rivalrous and dynamic.[7]

---

5 See US House of Representatives, Subcommittee on Antitrust Commercial and Administrative Law of the Committee on the Judiciary, *Investigation of Competition in Digital Markets Majority Staff Report and Recommendations* (6 October 2020) at 392; Carl Shapiro, "Antitrust in a Time of Populism" (2018) 61 *International Journal of Industrial Organization* 714 at 740:

> One common fact pattern that can involve a loss of future competition occurs when a large incumbent firm acquires a highly capable firm operating in an adjacent space. This happens frequently in the technology sector. Prominent examples include Google's acquisition of YouTube in 2006 and DoubleClick in 2007, Facebook's acquisition of Instagram in 2012 and of the virtual reality firm Oculus VR in 2014, and Microsoft's acquisition of LinkedIn in 2016.

6 Canada, Department of Consumer and Corporate Affairs, *Competition Law Amendments, A Guide* (Ottawa: Minister of Supply and Services, 1985) at 15, online: www.competitionbureau.gc.ca/eic/site/cb-bc.nsf/eng/03045.html [*Competition Law Amendments, A Guide*, the *Guide*].

7 See, e.g., Canada, Competition Bureau, "Big Data and Innovation: Key Themes for Competition Policy in Canada" (19 February 2018) at 9, online: www.competitionbureau.gc.ca/eic/site/cb-bc.nsf/eng/04342.html: "Mergers can lessen competition through *coordinated effects*. Big data could facilitate coordinated interaction; big data could also facilitate vigorous competition. Thus, in any particular case,

The review of mergers in advance of consummation also avoids the need to seek often-ineffective or inefficient after-the-fact remedies.[8] Once competitive information, trade secrets or other know-how is shared with the acquiring firm, an acquired plant is closed, or employees are laid off, it may be difficult or impossible to remedy the anti-competitive effects. In such circumstances, divestitures may have only a limited benefit in restoring the competitive *status quo ante*. Thus, a legal regime permitting powerful legal tools to block mergers in advance of their completion is a critical aspect of any competition law.

2) Historical Background

As discussed in Chapter 2, prior to 1986, mergers in Canada were subject to a criminal prohibition in the *Combines Investigation Act*, which stated in stark terms:

> 33. Every person who is party or privy to or knowingly assists in, or in the formation of, a merger . . . is guilty of an indictable offence and is liable to imprisonment for two years.[9]

A "merger" was in turn defined as an acquisition "whereby competition . . . is or is likely to be lessened to the detriment or against the interest of the public, whether consumers, producers or others."[10] This vague language provided no legislative guidance to the courts on the meaning of "public detriment" or the "public interest." Given that it was found in a criminal prohibition, it led to an understandable reluctance to convict businesses and individuals of conduct which could in many circumstances be beneficial or benign.

Prior to the 1986 amendments to the merger provisions, there had never been a conviction in a contested merger case in Canada. Only eight cases had been brought to the courts in the time since the first provisions addressing mergers were passed in 1910.[11] The lack of cases and convictions was linked to several factors, including the initially cumbersome

---

the use of big data may increase or decrease the likelihood of coordinated interaction among competitors" [emphasis in original].

8 *Competition Law Amendments, A Guide*, above note 6 at 19. Sometimes termed "the scrambling of the eggs," the Federal Court of Appeal expressed doubt about this concern in situations where divestitures can restore competition: *Canada (Commissioner of Competition) v Superior Propane Inc*, 2001 FCA 104 at paras 41–42 [*Propane FCA1*].

9 *Combines Investigation Act*, RSC 1970, c C-23, s 33.

10 *Ibid*, s 2.

11 *Competition Law Amendments, A Guide*, above note 6 at 16.

investigative process[12] and the burden of proof (beyond a reasonable doubt) that was "not suited to the examination of complex economic evidence and the determination of effects, which are often prospective in nature."[13] After a brief attempt to rely upon a post–WWI civil law regime under the Board of Commerce that was struck down as unconstitutional by the Judicial Committee of the Privy Council in 1921, the criminal law regime was reinstated in 1923.[14]

Three cases in particular, touched on in Chapter 2, illustrated the need to move away from the criminal law.[15] Two were trial decisions (*R v Canadian Breweries Ltd* (1960) and *R v British Columbia Sugar Refining Co* (1960)); the third was an appeal to the Supreme of Canada (*R v KC Irving Ltd* (1976)). In all three cases, the courts, trial and appellate, struggled with the application of the concept of "public detriment" contained in the criminal prohibition.

---

12 The *Combines Investigation Act*, SC 1910, c 9 only addressed continuing practices by a combine, which included a merger, not past actions. Section 2 defined a combine as "any contract, agreement, arrangement or combination which has, or is designed to have, the effect of . . . restricting competition . . . to the detriment of consumers or producers of such article of trade or commerce, and includes the . . . obtaining by any person to the end aforesaid, of any control over or interest in the business, or any portion of the business, of any other person, and also includes what is known as a trust, monopoly or merger." A combine could be subject to investigation on application by six persons to a judge (s 5). If the judge ordered an investigation, the minister was required to appoint a three-person board (s 9). The board was required to make a report to the minister, which was made public by various means, including in the *Canada Gazette* (ss 18–20). Anyone found in a report to have committed conduct including "unduly preventing or lessening competition in the production, manufacture, purchase, barter, sale, transportation, storage or supply of any . . . article" and "who thereafter continues so to offend" was "guilty of an indictable offence" and a "penalty of one thousand dollars and costs for each day after the expiration of ten days, or such further extension of time as in the opinion of the Board may be necessary, from the date of the publication of the report of the Board in *The Canada Gazette* during which such person so continues to offend" (s 23).

13 *Competition Law Amendments, A Guide*, above note 6 at 16.

14 The *Combines and Fair Prices Act*, SC 1919, c 45 was found unconstitutional in 1921 (*Reference re Board of Commerce Act, 1919* (1921), 60 DLR 513 (JCPC)). Parliament enacted the *Combines Investigation Act*, SC 1923, c 9, which made it an offence to be a party or privy to combines which, *inter alia*, "operated or are likely to operate to the detriment of or against the interest of the public": ss 2(a) and 26. See John A Ball, *Canadian Anti-Trust Legislation* (Baltimore: William & Wilkins, 1934) at ch 8, "*The Combines Investigation Act* of 1923."

15 Canada, Consumer and Corporate Affairs, *Amendments to the Combines Investigation Act, Background Information and Explanatory Notes* (Ottawa: Minister of Supply and Services, 1984) at 16.

R v Canadian Breweries Ltd was "the first case based solely on the operations of the accused as a merger to come before any Court in Canada."[16] The accused corporation was the leading manufacturer of beer in Ontario. Its market share had increased from 11.2 percent in 1930 to 60.9 percent in 1958. During that period, twenty-three plants were acquired, six of which were closed "very shortly after their acquisition."[17] Among the companies acquired were the following (**Figure 5.3**):[18]

- The Brading Breweries (Ottawa) (merged 1930) (FIGURE 5.4., RIGHT)
- Kuntz Brewery (Waterloo) (merged 1930)
- Grant's Spring (Hamilton) (merger 1930, closed 1932)
- Budweiser Brewery of Canada (Belleville) (acquired 1930, closed 1936)
- Taylor & Bate (St Catharines) (acquired 1930, closed 1938)
- Regal Brewing (Hamilton) (merger 1930, closed 1938)
- Dominion Brewery (Toronto) (acquired 1930, closed 1936)
- British American Brewing Company (Windsor) (acquired 1930)
- Carling Brewing (London) (acquired 1930)
- Rock Brewery, Geo Bernhardt, Preston, Ont
- O'Keefe (Toronto) (acquired 1934)
- Cosgrave Export Brewery (Toronto) (acquired 1934)
- Welland Brewery (Welland) (acquired and closed 1934)
- Riverside Brewery (Windsor) (acquired and closed 1935)
- Canada Bud Breweries Ltd (Toronto) (stock control 1936, closed 1943 and merged into O'Keefe) (FIGURE 5.5., RIGHT)
- Capital Brewing (Ottawa) (acquired 1944, merged into Brading)
- Bixel Brewery (acquired 1944)
- Walkerville Brewery (acquired 1944)

FIGURE 5.3. Some of the competitors acquired by Canadian Breweries Ltd

The Crown argued at trial that the acquisitions and other conduct justified criminal conviction on the basis, *inter alia*, of evidence showing that "the purpose of acquiring competing plants was to destroy

16 *R v British Columbia Sugar Refining Co (1960)*, 129 CCC 7 (Man QB) at para 3 [*BC Sugar*].

17 *R v Canadian Breweries Ltd, [1960] OR 601 (HCJ) [Canadian Breweries]*.

18 Table source: "Canadian Breweries," Wikipedia, online: https://en.wikipedia.org/wiki/Canadian_Breweries.

the competition that arose from price-cutting activities of some of the plants acquired."[19] The trial judge, McRuer CJ, rejected this argument and acquitted, finding that "I do not think it is an offence against the Act for one corporation to acquire the business of another merely because it wishes to extinguish a competitor."[20] He found that the Crown had to show "the power of the merger to so extinguish competition as to affect prices by monopolistic control."[21] This was an extremely high threshold for the Crown to satisfy—essentially merger to monopoly. Because other competitors remained in the beer market, it could not be met. Other factors were at play, such as provincial regulation of beer prices. The Court acquitted the accused. There was no appeal.

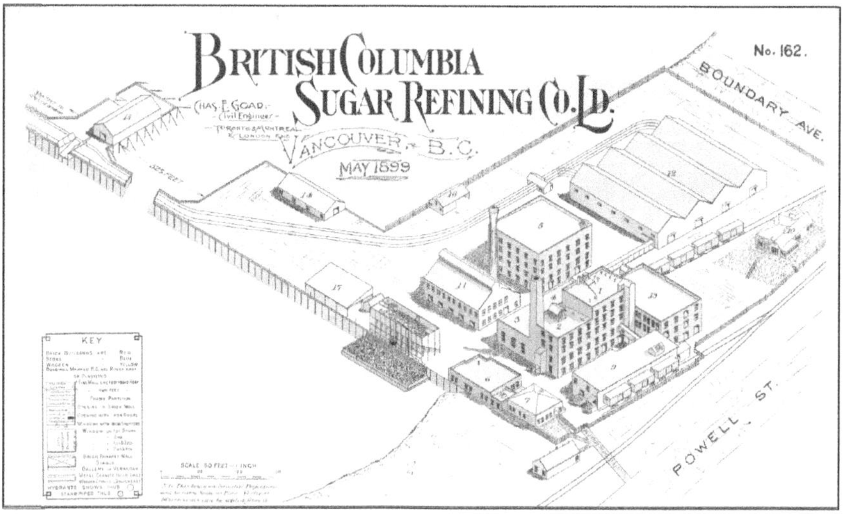

FIGURE 5.6. BC Sugar, which operated the only sugar plants in British Columbia (ABOVE) and in Alberta, acquired the only plant in Manitoba, giving it a monopoly in sugar production in Western Canada

In *BC Sugar* there had been a series of mergers from the 1930s to the 1950s whereby the accused became the sole sugar refiner in Western Canada. The Crown argued that the transactions gave the accused the power "to exercise a complete monopoly of the sugar business in Western Canada [and that] detriment to the public, etc., therefore resulted or was likely to result from this merger."[22] The trial judge, Manitoba's

19 *Canadian Breweries*, above note 17 at 620–21.

20 *Ibid* at 621.

21 *Ibid* at 624.

22 *BC Sugar*, above note 16 at para 253. Figure 5.6: Vancouver Archives, BC Sugar, Fonds: 2011-092.066, British Columbia Sugar Refining Co Ltd, Vancouver, BC 1921.

Esten Kenneth Williams CJ, held that the Crown needed not only to show a "virtual monopoly," but that in addition "it must also establish excessive or exorbitant profits or prices."[23] He held that the Crown had not shown this, noting the possibility of competition being provided by sugar refineries based in Eastern Canada. Another acquittal was entered; again, the Crown did not appeal.

In *R v KC Irving Ltd*, the accused were convicted at trial before the New Brunswick Supreme Court on criminal charges of merger and monopoly under section 33 of the *Combines Investigation Act*. The accused and its related corporations had acquired control of all five of the English-language newspapers in New Brunswick over the period 1944 to 1968. In 1968, KC Irving Limited, a conglomerate holding company owned and controlled by Mr KC Irving, his wife, and sons, acquired the fifth and remaining New Brunswick English language newspaper. Irving already controlled the *Telegraph Journal* and the *Evening Times Globe* (Saint John area), *The Times* (northeastern portion of the Province), and *The Transcript* (Moncton area). The fifth paper acquired in 1968 was the *Daily Gleaner* (Fredericton area).

The Crown argued, successfully at trial, that these acquisitions gave rise to a presumption of public detriment "upon proof of control of a business that excluded the possibility of any competition."[24] The trial decision was overturned by the New Brunswick Court of Appeal and the Crown appealed to the Supreme Court. The Court rejected the Crown's contention that any presumption arose from the acquisition of complete control and the absence of competition. Chief Justice Bora Laskin held that there was a need for additional evidence of public detriment, and that such evidence had not been forthcoming. For example, he noted that the individual newspapers had been granted "complete editorial autonomy," and that the trial judge had found "no actual detriment to the public by reason of the Irving acquisitions . . . either in respect of circulation rates, advertising content and rates, and improvement of quality and quantity of news."[25] One observer wrote that the case "hammered the last nail into the coffin of pre-1986 Canadian merger policy."[26]

---

23 *Ibid* at para 252.

24 *R v KC Irving Ltd, [1978] 1 SCR 408 at 421 [KC Irving]*.

25 *Ibid* at 417. Chief Justice Laskin held further at 425, "I do not think that it is open to a court in a criminal case to raise a presumption such as is contended for by the Crown in this case in the absence of legislative direction."

26 Christopher J Green, *Canadian Industrial Organization and Policy*, 3d ed (Toronto: McGraw-Hill, 1990) at 358. In the unreported decision of *R v Thomson Newspapers Ltd* (28 October 1983) [*Thomson Newspapers*], the Ontario Supreme Court, citing the authority of the Supreme Court of Canada in *KC Irving*, above note 24, acquitted the accused in another newspaper merger case.

In these three decisions, the courts did not regard the reduction or even elimination of competition as an indicator *per se* of public detriment flowing from a merger. As we have seen in Chapter 3, monopolistic conditions do harm the economy. Where a substantial lessening of competition is shown, insisting on further specific evidence of public detriment is unnecessary and redundant in view of effects such as the impact on efficiency—allocative, productive, and dynamic —which reduces wealth and harms public welfare.[27] It took until 1986, twenty-seven years after the Economic Council recommended it, for Parliament to remove the burden of the criminal law from these provisions and modernized the legal test by enacting a civil provision reviewable before a body with competition law expertise—the Competition Tribunal.

Significant changes were made to the merger provisions in the three amending Bills passed in the period 2022–24. Bill C-19 in 2022 added certain factors focused on digital markets to those the Tribunal may take into account in assessing the competitive effect of a merger.[28] Bill C-56 in 2023 repealed the efficiencies defence.[29] Bill C-59 in 2024 added a structural presumption, changed the remedies standard and made "interim interim" injunctions automatic on filing an application to enjoin a merger.[30]

B. THE DEFINITION OF A MERGER

The scheme introduced in 1986 begins with the definition of "merger" in section 91 of the Act, which states:

> 91 In sections 92 to 100, merger means the acquisition or establishment, direct or indirect, by one or more persons, whether by purchase or lease of shares or assets, by amalgamation or by combination or otherwise, of control over or significant interest in the whole or a part of a business of a competitor, supplier, customer or other person.

A merger may thus occur in two ways: through acquiring either "control over" or a "significant interest in" another business. The former is defined in section 2(4) of the Act. In the case of corporations, "control" is *de jure* or legal control—i.e., holding, directly or indirectly,

27 *Thomson Newspapers*, above note 26. See Chapter 3.

28 *An Act to implement certain provisions of the budget tables in Parliament April 7, 2022 and other measures*, SC 2022, c 10, s 262 [*Bill C-19 2022*].

29 *An Act to amend the Excise Act and the Competition Act*, SC 2023, c 31, s 10. [*Bill C-56 2023*].

30 *Fall Economic Statement Implementation Act, 2023*, SC 2024, c 15, ss 249, 253, 256 [*Bill C-59 2024*].

shares which permit "more than 50% of the votes that may be cast to elect directors of the corporation," which votes would elect a majority of the board.[31] In the case of partnerships and other unincorporated entities, "control" is based on entitlement "to receive more than 50% of the profits of that entity or more than 50% of its assets on dissolution."[32]

The concept of a "significant interest" is not defined in the Act and is potentially much more flexible. The Bureau's *Merger Enforcement Guidelines* take a broad view of this term, stating that it covers situations where the acquiring entity "obtains the ability to materially influence the economic behaviour of the target business, including but not limited to decisions relating to pricing, purchasing, distribution, marketing, investment, financing and the licensing of intellectual property rights."[33] The *Guidelines* go on to set out a list of factors which may be considered in determining whether such a "material interest" exists, including the nature of the interests acquired, the existence of profit sharing or other rights, and broadly the ability of the acquirer to "impose pressure on the business's decision making process."[34] These factors are consistent with the purposes of the legislation, focused as they are on the competitive effect of the transaction.

The *Merger Enforcement Guidelines* provide the Bureau's views on when a sufficient interest to trigger section 91 is acquired with respect to specific kinds of transactions. With respect to voting share acquisitions, for example, a significant interest can exist with holdings which permit the ability to "materially influence the board," or block resolutions of the corporation.[35] However, the Bureau's position is that on its own, "direct or indirect ownership of less than ten percent of the voting interests in a business does not generally constitute ownership of a significant interest."[36] Non-voting share interests are assessed based on whether they "can materially influence the economic behaviour of the business."[37]

---

31 *Competition Act*, above note 1, s 2(4)(a).

32 *Ibid*, s 2(4)(c). For Crown corporations without share capital, control is based on the ability to appoint a majority of the directors: s 2(4)(b).

33 Canada, Competition Bureau, *Merger Enforcement Guidelines* (6 October 2011), online: www.competitionbureau.gc.ca/eic/site/cb-bc.nsf/eng/03420.html at para 1.5 [*Merger Enforcement Guidelines*].

34 *Ibid* at para 1.6.

35 *Ibid* at para 1.9.

36 *Ibid* at para 1.10.

37 *Ibid* at para 1.11. Such a material influence might occur "where a shareholder holds a minority ownership in multiple competitors operating in the same product and geographic markets"—a situation termed "common ownership." The CD Howe Institute's Competition Policy Council in its communiqué "Should Merger Reviews Examine Common Ownership?" (2 November 2019) at 5, took the view that "potential anti-competitive effects from common ownership may

With respect to asset transactions, the importance of the assets in the ability "to carry on a separate business" is among the factors the Bureau considers in determining whether section 91 applies.[38]

Interlocking directorships occur where "a director of one firm is an employee, executive, partner, owner, or member of the board of directors of a second firm, or has another interest in the business of the second firm."[39] The *Guidelines* indicate that the acquisition of an interlocking directorship only raises issues under section 92 of the Act if the interlocked firms "are competitors, are vertically related, or produce complementary or related products." In such circumstances, the Bureau may examine whether the acquisition of an interlocking directorship may have the ability to materially influence the economic behaviour of those firm(s). Relevant facts include the nature of access by the director to confidential information, the director's voting and veto rights, and the board composition, quorum, voting rules, and historical voting patterns.[40]

Finally, even contractual, financing, or other arrangements may be considered a significant interest where they are found to meet the "materially influence" standard by virtue of factors, such as the nature of the relationship created, the ability to access confidential information, and "the acquirer's intentions to affect the behaviour of" the business involved.[41] For example, the Bureau took the position that a right of first refusal, obtained by Shell, in respect of sixty-six gas stations of discounting BC gasoline retailer Pay Less constituted a merger.[42]

There has not been significant jurisprudence on the issue of what constitutes a merger to date. The Competition Tribunal accepted in *Air Canada* that the contractual combination of two airlines' reservation systems in the so-called Gemini partnership constituted a merger.[43]

---

represent a valid concern for the competitiveness of the Canadian economy and that a preliminary consideration of the extent to which companies that compete in a relevant market exhibit common owners is relevant for the Bureau's review of mergers."

38 *Ibid* at para 1.13.

39 *Ibid* at para 1.17.

40 *Ibid* at para 1.17.

41 *Ibid* at paras 1.18–1.19.

42 Canada, Competition Bureau, Bureau Activities, "Proposed Transaction, November, 1989, Shell Canada Products Ltd./Pay Less Gas Co. (*Retail Gasoline*)," online: www.competitionbureau.gc.ca/eic/site/cb-bc.nsf/eng/03756.html#sec1989, accessed 12 September 2019; the Bureau ultimately concluded that the transaction was unlikely to substantially prevent or lessen competition.

43 *Canada (Director of Investigation and Research, Competition Act) v Air Canada, [1993] CCTD No 22* at para 7. The issue was not contested.

In *Tervita Corp v Canada (Commissioner of Competition)*,[44] the judicial members of the Tribunal split on the issue of whether the acquired firm need be competitive with the acquirer in a merger. The chair took the view that the business acquired must have at least the potential to compete with the acquiring firm for section 91 to apply.[45] Chief Justice Crampton disagreed, holding that "the term 'business' in section 91 is sufficiently broad to include any business in respect of which there is an acquisition or establishment of control or a significant interest" whether or not that business is a competitor.[46] As he noted, section 91 does not involve any substantive assessment of competitive effect; it is a mere gateway to such an assessment.[47] In support of this view, the section not only refers to the acquisition of competitors, but also to "the business of a . . . supplier, customer *or other person*" [emphasis added].

C. "SUBSTANTIAL PREVENTION OR LESSENING OF COMPETITION": THE MARKET POWER THRESHOLD

1) Introduction: A Focus on Market Power

Section 92 of the *Competition Act* provides the Commissioner with the ability to obtain a remedy against a merger in the following circumstances:

> 92(1) Where, on application by the Commissioner, the Tribunal finds *that a merger or proposed merger prevents or lessens, or is likely to prevent or lessen, competition substantially*
> (a) in a trade, industry or profession,
> (b) among the sources from which a trade, industry or profession obtains a product, including labour,
> (c) among the outlets through which a trade, industry or profession disposes of a product, including labour, or
> (d) otherwise than as described in paragraphs (a) to (c) [emphasis added].

The phrase "prevents or lessens, or is likely to prevent or lessen, competition substantially" defines the threshold for obtaining a remedy against a merger. In *Tervita*, the Supreme Court confirmed that the test is whether

44 *Tervita Corp v Canada (Commissioner of Competition)*, [2015] 1 SCR 161 [*Tervita*].
45 *Canada (Commissioner of Competition) v CCS Corp*, [2012] CCTD No 14 at paras 57 and 352–59 [*Tervita CT*].
46 *Ibid* at para 359.
47 *Ibid* at para 356.

the merger is "likely to create, maintain or enhance the ability of the merged entity to exercise market power, unilaterally or in coordination with other firms."[48] As noted above in the context of market definition, market power was defined by the Court as:

> [T]he ability to "profitably influence price, quality, variety, service, advertising, innovation or other dimensions of competition." . . . Or, in other words, market power is "the ability to maintain prices above the competitive level for a considerable period of time without such action being unprofitable" . . . ; where "price" is "generally used as shorthand for all aspects of a firm's actions that have an impact on buyers."[49]

2) The "Prevention" and "Lessening" Branches and the "But For" Test

Section 92 can be satisfied in two different ways: either by a *prevention* or by a *lessening* of competition. In both cases, the question is "whether the merged entity is likely to be able to exercise materially greater market power than in the absence of the merger" and it must be shown that the impact on market power is substantial.[50] The assessment required was described by the Supreme Court in *Tervita* as a "but for" inquiry: it involves a comparison of: (1) the ability of the merged entity after the merger to exercise market power, with (2) the level of competition in the pre-merger world or "but-for the merger" world.[51] One then asks whether the likely prevention or lessening of competition is "substantial."

Justice Rothstein for the majority in *Tervita* described the test as having a "forward looking" aspect, given that "the ordinary meaning of 'is likely to prevent or lessen' points to events in the future" with respect to both completed and proposed mergers.[52] The section also contemplates the potential for conducting an assessment based upon past or present performance, given that it uses the present tense "prevents or lessens" and refers to completed transactions as well as proposed ones.

The assessment of the impact of a proposed merger on competition requires a projection of how the merger is likely to affect the competitive conditions of the market in question. This requires the weighing of a range of economic indicators:

---

48 *Tervita*, above note 44 at para 44.

49 *Ibid* [citations omitted].

50 *Tervita*, above note 44 at para 54.

51 *Ibid* at paras 49–51.

52 *Ibid* at para 53.

> Merger review is now probably the most economics-intensive area of antitrust enforcement, in part because it is normally so prospective; that is, there are no existing effects to be observed and measured. Rather, economists must predict effects on competition and efficiencies based on an analysis that will normally require that they (i) define markets; (ii) assess the importance of barriers to entry; (iii) contemplate possible theories of harm; (iv) quantify the potential harm to competition; (v) quantify the potential efficiencies; (vi) combine harm and efficiencies into a net effect, allowing for various approaches to the trade-offs; and (vii) assess the potential impacts on the market of any proposed remedies, such as divestitures.[53]

3) The Onus and Standard of Proof Under Section 92

The onus is on the Commissioner under section 92 to prove on a balance of probabilities standard that there is or is likely to be a substantial prevention or lessening of competition. The Supreme Court in *Tervita*, a case founded on an alleged prevention of competition, framed the standard as follows:

> [T]he Tribunal must be of the view that it is more likely than not that the merger will result in a substantial prevention of competition. Mere possibilities are insufficient to meet this standard.[54]

In 2024, Parliament removed the limitation in s 92(2) against the Tribunal finding a substantial lessening or prevention of competition (SLPC) "solely on the basis of concentration or market share." This was replaced with a "structural presumption" whereby, if the Tribunal finds an increase in concentration or market share from the merger over certain thresholds defined in sections 92(3) and (4), the onus is shifted to the merging parties to disprove the SLPC on a balance of probabilities.[55] These provisions state as follows:

> *Evidence*
>
> (2) For the purpose of this section, if the Tribunal finds, on a balance of probabilities, that a merger or proposed merger results or is likely to result in a significant increase in concentration or market share, the Tribunal shall also find that the merger or proposed merger prevents or lessens, or is likely to prevent or lessen, competition substantially,

---

53 Marcel Boyer, Thomas W Ross & Ralph A Winter, *The Rise of Economics in Competition Policy: A Canadian Perspective, Working Paper 2017s-26* (Montreal: CIRANO, 2017), online: https://cirano.qc.ca/files/publications/2017s-26.pdf at 30–31.

54 *Tervita*, above note 44 at para 66.

55 *Bill C-59 2024*, above note 30, s 249(2).

unless the contrary is proved on a balance of probabilities by the parties to the merger or proposed merger.

Significant increase in concentration or market share
(3) A merger or proposed merger results or is likely to result in a significant increase in concentration or market share if, in any relevant market, as a result of the merger or proposed merger,

(a) the concentration index increases or is likely to increase by more than 100; and
(b) either

(i) the concentration index is or is likely to be more than 1,800, or
(ii) the market share of the parties to the merger or proposed merger is or is likely to be more than 30%.

Definition of concentration index
(4) In subsection (3), *concentration index* means, in any relevant market, the sum of the squares of the market shares of the suppliers or customers.

Regulations — different values
(5) The Governor in Council may by regulation prescribe different values than those provided in subsection (3).

The Commissioner advocated for a structural presumption during the course of the amendment process, stating that the American adoption of this approach since the 1960's is "not only logical, but also follows the economic conclusion that mergers in highly concentrated markets are more likely to be anti-competitive."[56] Views expressed during consultations were mixed, with those opposed arguing, for example, that "presumptions would lead to a lack of due process unless parties had more access to information held by the Bureau [and] that any market share presumptions simply reframe the legal battle as one of market definition instead of market effects."[57] The Commissioner nonetheless

56 Competition Bureau Canada, "Examining the Canadian *Competition Act* in the Digital Era, Submission by the Competition Bureau" (8 February 2022), [Bureau Submissions 2022] at s 2.2, online: https://ised-isde.canada.ca/site/competition-bureau-canada/en/how-we-foster-competition/promotion-and-advocacy/regulatory-adviceinterventions-competition-bureau/examining-canadian-competition-act-digital-era.

57 Canada, ISED, *Future of Canada's Competition Policy Consultation – What We Heard Report*, 20 Sept 2023 at s 9, online: https://ised-isde.canada.ca/site/strategic-policy-sector/en/marketplace-framework-policy/

continued to advocate for this change.[58] It was unanimously added by the House Committee studying the proposed legislation.[59] The intention as reflected in the submissions and evidence of the Bureau was to adopt the market share thresholds used for the presumption as developed in US antitrust jurisprudence and adopted in the US *Merger Guidelines*.[60] Unlike the US presumption, it is provided for in legislation, although the market share and concentration thresholds can be adjusted under s 92(5) by regulation.

4) Lessening of Competition

The majority of cases brought by the Commissioner to the Competition Tribunal have involved an alleged *lessening* of competition. In *Canada (Director of Investigation and Research) v Hillsdown Holdings (Canada) Ltd*, for example, the respondent Hillsdown Holdings controlled an existing meat-rendering business (Rothsay) and had acquired its main competitor (Orenco), giving it 62 to 63 percent of the southern Ontario red meat rendering market in terms of volume of material processed. The Tribunal held:

> A merger will lessen competition if it enhances the ability of the merging parties to exercise "market power" by either preserving, adding to or creating the power to raise prices above competitive levels for a significant period of time.[61]

In *Tervita*, the Supreme Court noted that the prevention and lessening branches differ in that "[i]n determining whether competition is substantially lessened, the focus is on whether the merged entity would increase its market power [while u]nder the 'prevention' branch, the

---

competition-policy/consultation-future-competition-policy-canada/future-canadas-competition-policy-consultation-what-we-heard-report.

58 Competition Bureau Canada, "The Future of Competition Policy in Canada, Submission by the Competition Bureau" (15 March 2023), [Bureau Submissions 2023] at s 1.4, online: https://competition-bureau.canada.ca/how-we-foster-competition/promotion-and-advocacy/regulatory-adviceinterventions-competition-bureau/future-competition-policy-canada; M Boswell, Letter to the Chair and Members of the House of Commons Standing Committee on Finance (March 1, 2024) [2024 Boswell Letter] at 6–10.

59 Canada, House of Commons, Standing Committee on Finance, *Evidence on Bill C-59*, 44th Parl. 1st Sess, No 140 (30 April 2024).

60 See 2024 Boswell Letter, above note 58 and US, Department of Justice and FTC, *Merger Guidelines* (18 Dec 2023) at 5–6, online: https://www.justice.gov/d9/2023-12/2023%20Merger%20Guidelines.pdf [US 2023 *Merger Guidelines*].

61 *Canada (Director of Investigation and Research) v Hillsdown Holdings (Canada) Ltd* (1992), 41 CPR (3d) 289 (CCT) at 16 [*Hillsdown*].

focus is on whether the merged entity would retain its existing market power." The Court referred to the judgment of Crampton CJ in the Tribunal below, where he noted that under the lessening branch, the assessment is "whether the merger is likely to facilitate the exercise of new or increased market power by the merged entity."[62]

A lessening of competition may occur through horizontal or vertical effects on competition.[63] *Horizontal* effects arise from transaction, such as by an acquisition or amalgamation between competing firms. *Vertical* effects occur through the acquisition of suppliers or customers. Such acquisitions can result in the foreclosure to competitors of access to their sources of supply (such as raw materials or parts needed for manufacture) or in the loss of markets and customers (who may refuse to buy competitors' products if those customers are now affiliated with the merged firm).[64]

5) Prevention of Competition

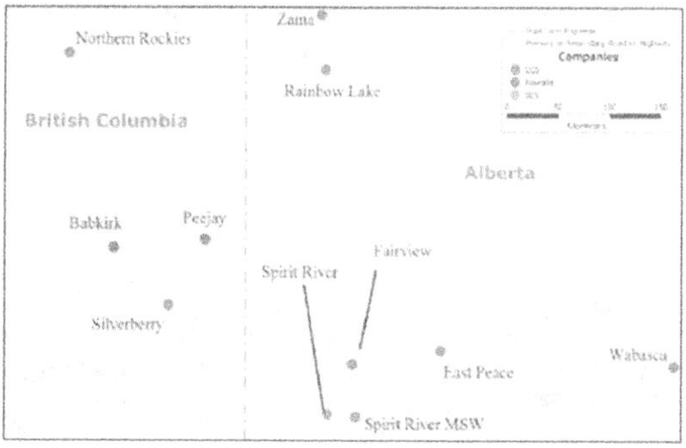

FIGURE 5.7. Schedule A from the Tribunal's *Tervita* decision shows the location of the merging firms' plants in NE BC

In *Tervita*, Tervita Corp operated the only two secure hazardous waste landfills in Northeastern BC (Northern Rockies and Silverberry). It acquired a potential competing site, Babkirk, in 2011. (The Peejay site, seen in **Figure 5.7**, was not yet developed.)[65] The Babkirk facility required additional investment to operate as a secure landfill, but the Tribunal concluded that its acquisition by Tervita "preserves a monopolistic market structure, and thereby prevents the emergence of potentially important competition."[66] Chief Justice Crampton (concurring) held that under the prevention branch, one assesses "whether the merger *is likely to preserve the existing market power of one or both of the merging parties*, by preventing the erosion of

62 *Tervita*, above note 44 at para 55.

63 There is also the potential for conglomerate mergers to affect competition, but such effects are rare. See *Merger Enforcement Guidelines*, above note 33 at paras 11.1 and 11.8.

64 See *ibid* at paras 11.1–11.9. See also below.

65 Map; *Tervita CT*, above note 45, Schedule A.

66 *Ibid* at para 297.

such market power that otherwise likely would have taken place if the merger did not occur."[67]

The Supreme Court identified the following steps in the prevention assessment:

1) **Identify the Potential Competitor:** "The first step is to identify the firm or firms the merger would prevent from independently entering the market, i.e. identifying the potential competitor. . . . Typically, the potential competitor will be one of the merged parties: the acquired firm or the acquiring firm."[68] The Court identified three scenarios:

    a) "potential entry of the acquired firm";
    b) "potential entry of the acquiring firm"; and
    c) "a third party entrant, one not involved in the merger . . . prevented from entering the market as a result of the merger."[69]

2) **Carry Out the "But For" Assessment:** Ask whether, "absent the merger, the potential competitor (usually one of the merging parties) would have likely entered the market and if so whether that entry would have decreased the market power of the acquiring firm."[70]
3) **Determine If the Effect Is "Substantial":** The entry of the potential competitor, which is prevented by the merger, "must be likely to have a substantial effect on the market" to satisfy section 92.[71]

In *Tervita*, the potential competitor was the acquired facility, Babkirk. The Tribunal held that, but for the merger, the site could have been profitably converted to a secure landfill, permitting it to "compete effectively" with Tervita, and that the effect of the loss of this potential competition was substantial.[72]

Before the Supreme Court, Tervita argued that the Tribunal's assessment of prevention was "speculative," and that it was improper to rely upon what may have occurred through conversion of the Babkirk facility years in the future. The Supreme Court disagreed, noting first that the prevention branch requires a forward-looking assessment, and that "there is no legal basis to restrict the evidence the Tribunal can look at" in assessing how entry by a potential competitor might have unfolded.[73]

---

67 Cited with approval by the SCC in *Tervita*, above note 44 at para 55 [emphasis added].
68 *Ibid* at paras 61–62.
69 *Ibid* at paras 62–63.
70 *Ibid* at para 64.
71 *Ibid* at para 78.
72 *Tervita CT*, above note 45 at para 208.
73 *Tervita*, above note 44 at para 69.

At the same time, the Court held: "'Likely' reflects the reality that merger review is an inherently predictive exercise, but it does not give the Tribunal license to speculate; its findings must be based on evidence."[74]

The Court held that the time frame for entry must be "discernable," meaning that "there must be evidence of when the merging party is realistically expected to enter the market in absence of the merger."[75] It noted that "the further into the future the Tribunal looks the more difficult it will be to meet" the "likely" standard.[76] The Court found that the Tribunal did not speculate and committed no error in its assessment of this issue. It concluded "there was sufficient . . . evidence upon which the Tribunal could find a substantial prevention of competition as a result of the merger."[77]

The *Merger Enforcement Guidelines* set out a number of potential scenarios under which a prevention may occur, including not only the acquisition of a likely future entrant (as in *Tervita*), but also:

- acquisition of a recent entrant;
- pre-emption of acquisition by a competitor; and
- prevention of geographic expansion, use of new capacity, or new product introduction.[78]

6) Substantial Prevention or Lessening of Competition

The word "substantial" in its plain and ordinary meaning has been described by the Tribunal in the (quite different) context of the deceptive marketing provisions as "something more than just *de minimus*."[79] The *Merger Enforcement Guidelines* more helpfully frame the Bureau's assessment of substantial effect around "the ability to *materially* influence price."[80] While this may seem like a simple substitution of one qualifier for another ("materially" for "substantially"), the *Merger Enforcement Guidelines* go on to break this benchmark down into two dimensions:

- magnitude (a "material price increase") and
- duration (that "sufficient entry" cannot occur "rapidly enough to prevent the material price increase").[81]

---

74 *Ibid* at para 65.
75 *Ibid* at para 68.
76 *Ibid* at para 75.
77 *Ibid* at para 82.
78 *Merger Enforcement Guidelines*, above note 33, para 2.12.
79 *Canada (Commissioner of Competition) v Sears Canada Inc*, [2005] CCTD No 1 at para 50.
80 *Merger Enforcement Guidelines*, above note 33 at para 2.13 [emphasis added].
81 *Ibid*.

Another potentially relevant factor is the *scope* of the price increase. This involves, for example, assessing whether or not the material price increase will occur in a "substantial part of the market."[82]

In *Tervita*, Crampton CJ concurring in the decision of the Tribunal stated, drawing a distinction between this standard and the "significant" price increase used in market definition, "the degree of market power used in assessing whether competition is likely to be prevented or lessened substantially . . . is a level of market power required to maintain prices *materially* higher, or to depress one or more forms of non-price competition to a level that is *materially* lower, than they likely would be in the absence of the merger."[83]

The Bureau "does not consider a numerical threshold for the material price increase"; its assessment is based on "market-specific factors." Where the merging firms have pre-existing market power, "smaller impacts on competition" may be deemed to meet the test.[84]

The approach confirmed in *Tervita* by the Supreme Court, based on the Tribunal's jurisprudence, parallels that in the *Merger Enforcement Guidelines*, although using slightly different terminology. Justice Rothstein held:

> The merger's likely effect on market power is what determines whether its effect on competition is likely to be "substantial." Two key components in assessing substantiality under the "lessening" branch are the degree and duration of the exercise of market power (*Hillsdown* at pp. 328-29). There is no reason why degree and duration should not also be considered under the "prevention" branch.
>
> What constitutes "substantial" will vary from case to case. The Tribunal has not found it useful to apply rigid numerical criteria:
>
> > What will constitute a likely "substantial" lessening will depend on the circumstances of each case . . . . Various tests have been proposed: a likely 5% price rise sustainable for one year; a 5% price rise sustainable over two years; a small but significant and non-transitory price rise. The tribunal does not find it useful to apply rigid numerical criteria although these may be useful for enforcement purposes. (*Hillsdown*, at pp. 328–29)[85]

---

82 Canada, Competition Bureau, *Merger Enforcement Guidelines* (1 September 2004) [*Merger Enforcement Guidelines* 2004] at para 2.13.

83 *Tervita CT*, above note 45 at para 377 [emphasis in original].

84 *Merger Enforcement Guidelines*, above note 33 at para 2.14.

85 *Tervita*, above note 44 at paras 45–46.

The two-year period for a sustainable price increase was referred to in the previous (2004) version of the *Merger Enforcement Guidelines* as being "typically used as a rule of thumb."[86] This has given way to a more flexible standard in the current version, consistent with the jurisprudence. In *Tervita*, although no specific time period for a material price increase was set out, the Tribunal found that in the face of the merger, competitive entry could not occur for at least thirty months, suggesting that a price increase by the merged entity could be sustained for at least that period.[87]

In *Hillsdown*, the Tribunal found a likely lessening of competition in red meat rendering from the merger of the two leading plants, but was unable to find this lessening "substantial." It concluded that in the future "a significant source of competitive discipline will exist from those firms which border geographically on the relevant market and which would be prepared to expand their area of collection in the face of a price rise by the merged firm."[88] It noted that "[t]his decision is very much a borderline one and the difficulty relates to the dynamic changes which are occurring in the market."[89] The changes included the contraction of red meat production and rendering, which meant that over time, excess capacity among the remaining competitors would increase, and enhance their ability to compete with the merged firm.

7) Mergers Affecting Labour: Monopsony Power

The 2024 amendments added the words "including labour" to sections 92(1)(b) and (c) as set out above. This was arguably not a substantive change, given that the effects of a merger on monopsony or purchaser power (i.e., the power of an employer as a purchaser of labour) could already be considered under the section.[90] However, consultations leading up to the amendments included the perspective that "effects on labour markets are simply not receiving due consideration in merger analysis, and [that] the Bureau ought to examine employment contracts to appreciate likely effects following a merger."[91] This amendment thus highlights this factor for the Tribunal's consideration.

---

86 *Merger Enforcement Guidelines* 2004, above note 82 at para 2.13, footnote 19.

87 *Tervita CT*, above note 42 at para 222; *Tervita*, above note 44 at para 81.

88 *Hillsdown*, above note 61 at 25.

89 *Ibid*.

90 See Susan M. Hutton et al., "When Should We Look out for the Little Guy? An Examination of the Inconsistencies in Antitrust Enforcement of Monopsony Power in Canada and the United States" (2022) 35:2 Can Competition L Rev 32.

91 Canada, ISED, *Future of Canada's Competition Policy Consultation – What We Heard Report*, 20 Sept 2023 at s 9, online: https://ised-isde.canada.ca/site/strategic-policy-sector/en/marketplace-framework-policy/

Under the US Merger Guidelines, labour effects may be raised in the course of merger review, on the basis that "[t]he same general concerns as in other markets apply to labor markets where employers are the buyers of labor and workers are the sellers. The Agencies will consider whether workers face a risk that the merger may substantially lessen competition for their labor in mergers in the United States."[92] In FTC v The Kroger Company and Albertsons Companies,,involving a proposed merger between supermarket chains, the FTC alleged that a "merger of competing buyers, including employers as buyers of labor, can substantially lessen competition between the merging buyers. The same tools used to assess the effects of a merger of sellers can be used to analyze a merger of employers as buyers of labor."[93] Competitive effects on the collective bargaining process with union grocery workers were among those adverse impacts alleged from the merger.

The monopsony power of publishers in their negotiations with authors of bestselling books was the foundation for blocking the proposed Penguin-Simon Schuster merger. The US District Court held that the relevant market at play was "the authors of anticipated top-selling books, [who] have unique needs and preferences, have fewer outlets that can satisfy their requirements, and therefore are vulnerable to anticompetitive behavior."[94] The Court concluded, in enjoining the merger, that it was "likely to substantially lessen competition in the market for the publishing rights to anticipated top-selling books."[95]

D. EVALUATION OF COMPETITIVE EFFECT

Section 93 of the *Competition Act* provides guidance to the Tribunal by setting out a non-exhaustive list of factors to consider in assessing the competitive effect of a merger:

> *Factors to be considered regarding prevention or lessening of competition*
> 93. In determining, for the purpose of section 92, whether or not a merger or proposed merger prevents or lessens, or is likely to prevent

competition-policy/consultation-future-competition-policy-canada/future-canadas-competition-policy-consultation-what-we-heard-report.

92 US 2023 *Merger Guidelines*, above note 60 at 26.

93 *FTC v The Kroger Company and Albertsons Companies*, Complaint, 26 Feb 2024 at para 57.

94 *United States v. Bertelsmann SE & Co.*, 646 F. Supp. 3d 1, (D.D.C. October 31, 2022) at 56.

95 *Ibid.*

or lessen, competition substantially, the Tribunal may have regard to the following factors:

(a) the extent to which foreign products or foreign competitors provide or are likely to provide effective competition to the businesses of the parties to the merger or proposed merger;

(b) whether the business, or a part of the business, of a party to the merger or proposed merger has failed or is likely to fail;

(c) the extent to which acceptable substitutes for products supplied by the parties to the merger or proposed merger are or are likely to be available;

(d) any barriers to entry into a market, including

(i) tariff and non-tariff barriers to international trade,

(ii) interprovincial barriers to trade, and

(iii) regulatory control over entry,

and any effect of the merger or proposed merger on such barriers;

(e) the extent to which effective competition remains or would remain in a market that is or would be affected by the merger or proposed merger;

(f) any likelihood that the merger or proposed merger will or would result in the removal of a vigorous and effective competitor;

(g) the nature and extent of change and innovation in a relevant market;

(g.1) network effects within the market;

(g.2) whether the agreement or arrangement would contribute to the entrenchment of the market position of leading incumbents;

(g.3) any effect of the agreement or arrangement on price or non-price competition, including quality, choice or consumer privacy;

(g.4) the change in concentration or market share that the merger or proposed merger has brought about or is likely to bring about

(g.5) any likelihood that the merger or proposed merger will or would result in express or tacit coordination between competitors in a market; and

(h) any other factor that is relevant to competition in a market that is or would be affected by the merger or proposed merger.

The final subparagraph (h) is clear that this list is not exhaustive. The factors listed in section 93 are grouped into the following areas in the discussion which follows. Also included are other factors identified in the *Merger Enforcement Guidelines* (MEGs) and case law:

1) *Market Definition Analysis* (MEGs 3.1, 4.1–4.28)
   a. Availability of acceptable substitute products (product market—s 93(c))
   b. Foreign competition (geographic market—s 93(a))

2) *Market Shares and Concentration*: Concentration and market shares of the merging parties and other players (s 92(2); MEGs 5.8–5.14)
3) *Barriers to Entry* (s 93(d); MEGs 7.1–7.17)
4) *Effects of the Merger on Competition*
   a. Theories of competitive harm
      i. Unilateral effects on competition (MEGs 6.10–6.22)
      ii. Coordinated effects (MEGs 6.23–6.39)
   b. Factors in assessing horizontal competitive effects
      i. Remaining competition (s 93(e); MEGs 6.2–6.4)
      ii. Removal of a vigorous and effective competitor (s 93(f); MEGs 6.5–6.6)
      iii. Impact of change and innovation (s 93(g); MEGs 6.7–6.9)
      iv. Factors focused on digital market issues (ss 93(g.1), (g.2), (g.3))
      v. Countervailing power (MEGs 8)
   c. Non-horizontal effects (MEGs 11)
5) *Failing Firm Assessment* (s 93(b); MEGs 13)
6) *Efficiencies* (s 96; MEGs 12)

1) Market Definition

The process of market definition was described in Chapter 4. The *Merger Enforcement Guidelines* describe market definition as an analytical tool, which can be imprecise.[96] They state that market definition "generally is undertaken."[97] The Tribunal in *Canada (Commissioner of Competition) v Superior Propane Inc* noted the importance of keeping in mind the ultimate objective of assessing the effects of the merger on competition and market power:

> While market definitions should be as precise as possible within the limit of reasonableness to provide a framework within which competition implications of a transaction can be analysed, the Tribunal should not be preoccupied with market definition to the point of losing sight of the purpose of the exercise under the Act which is to determine whether the merger is likely to lead to a substantial prevention or lessening of competition. As stated by the Supreme Court of Canada in *Director of Investigation and Research v. Southam Inc*:
>
> > . . . More generally, I notice that the Tribunal seems to have been preoccupied with the definition of the relevant market. It is possible that the members may occasionally have lost sight of the ultimate inquiry, which is whether the acquisition

96 *Merger Enforcement Guidelines*, above note 33 at para 3.2.
97 *Ibid* at para 3.1.

> of the community newspapers by Southam substantially lessened competition.[98]

Market definition may not be necessary where market power can be assessed or inferred in other ways, such as where it is "clear that anti-competitive effects would result under all plausible market definitions," or where a merger has already resulted in a material price increase, an indication that market power is present for the product at issue.[99] This accords with the views of a prominent American antitrust academic and jurist, who opined, "[m]arket definition is just a tool in the investigation of market power; it is an output of antitrust inquiry rather than an input into decisions, and it should be avoided whenever possible."[100]

In *Tervita*, however, Crampton CJ noted (in his separate concurring reasons) that market definition "has traditionally been a central part of merger analysis in Canada and abroad" in view of its value, for example, in identifying competitors, their locations and respective market shares. In his view, cases in which it would be unnecessary to define a relevant market would be "exceptional."[101]

2) Market Shares and Concentration

In *Hillsdown*, the Tribunal noted:

> The purpose of defining the relevant market is of course to facilitate identification of the merged firm's competitors and to assess the market share of the relevant market which each holds vis-à-vis the merged firm.[102]

Evidently, current sellers of the product are within the market. The determination of whether to include other "poised" competitors requires that some parameters define at what point they should be considered market participants. The *Merger Enforcement Guidelines* include "sellers that would begin selling the relevant product in the relevant geographic market" in response to a small but significant and non-transitory price

98 *Canada (Commissioner of Competition) v Superior Propane Inc* (2000), 7 CPR (4th) 385 at para 48 [*Propane CCT1*].

99 *Merger Enforcement Guidelines*, above note 33 at para 3.3.

100 Frank H Easterbrook, "The Limits of Antitrust" (1984) 63 *Texas Law Review* 2 at 22. He is a Circuit Judge of the United States Court of Appeals for the Seventh Circuit.

101 *Tervita CT*, above note 45 at paras 360–64.

102 *Hillsdown*, above note 61 at 15.

increase (SSNIP) — i.e., usually in response to a price increase of 5 percent and within a year.[103]

This assessment is aimed at ultimately drawing conclusions about the presence or absence of market power:

> Because direct measurement of a firm's market power is extraordinarily difficult, a two-step indirect measurement process has evolved: first define the relevant market, and then infer power within the market through the use of proxies such as market shares and other factors.[104]

The Tribunal has noted that market share is only a factor, but can provide a *prima facie* assessment of market power:

> Whether an enhancement of market power exists as a result of a merger and whether it is substantial is determined by reference to a number of factors. Market share data can give a prima facie indication as to whether such is the case.[105]

As noted above, in 2024 Parliament removed the limitation in section 92(2) that the Tribunal could not rely solely on evidence of concentration or market share in finding an SLPC and replaced it with a structural presumption.

a) Measures of Market Share

An initial issue that needs to be addressed is how to calculate market share. Market share may differ depending on the measure chosen (e.g., sales, unit production, capacity, reserves). The Tribunal noted in *Hillsdown*:

> The market concentration in the relevant market can be measured by reference to a number of different indicia. What measure will be chosen will depend upon the nature of the industry in question and the data available.[106]

In that case, the Tribunal considered data on both plant output and plant capacity.

The *Merger Enforcement Guidelines* indicate that the Bureau will use the market share measures that are "the best indicators of sellers' future

---

103 *Merger Enforcement Guidelines*, above note 33 at para 5.1.

104 *Hillsdown*, above note 61 at 7, relying on a passage from William Blumenthal, *Horizontal Mergers: Law and Policy* (Chicago: ABA Antitrust Section, Monograph No 12, 1986) at 62–63. See also *Canada (Commissioner of Competition) v Parkland Industries Ltd*, [2015] CCTD No 4 at para 70 [*Parkland*].

105 *Hillsdown*, above note 61 at 16.

106 *Hillsdown*, above note 61 at 17.

competitive significance." For example, for undifferentiated or homogeneous products, "dollar sales, unit sales and capacity should yield similar results." Where excess capacity is present, "market shares based on capacity may best reflect a firm's relative market position."[107] Where there are discounting sellers, dollar sales may be a better indicator of market position than capacity. The Bureau will also examine unit sales, as this may yield "important information about relative market positions."[108]

Once market share data are available, measures of industry concentration can be calculated. Two tools often used in the United States, and referred to in the *Hillsdown* decision, are the four-firm concentration ratio (CR4) and the Herfindahl-Hirschman Index (HHI). The Tribunal explained these measures as follows:

> The four-firm concentration ratio measures market concentration by adding together the market shares of the four largest firms in the market. If the post merger concentration is very high and the merged firm accounts for a significant proportion thereof, then the merger is one which if assessed solely by reference to market shares will be considered to lead to a substantial lessening of competition. The HHI is computed by adding together the squares of the market shares of all the firms in the market. The HHI can theoretically range from near zero to 10,000 (100 × 100) for a monopoly. In the context of anti-trust enforcement in the United States, it is generally thought that if a market has an HHI over 1,800 it is highly concentrated. An HHI between 1,000 and 1,800 is of medium concentration and below 1,000 relatively unconcentrated. If the increase in HHI as a result of the merger exceeds 100 and the post merger HHI for the market exceeds 1,800, according to the Director's expert, one should assume (at least on a prima facie basis) that the merger will substantially lessen competition.[109]

The Bureau's *Merger Enforcement Guidelines* refer to the CR4. It has been noted that pre-merger CR4 data may be unhelpful where the fifth or subsequent firms have significant share or where the merging parties are already both in the top four.[110] Thus, it will usually be important to look at other CR data, as well as the size and market share distribution of other industry players, to see what the data reveal about the size and distribution of sellers.

---

107 *Merger Enforcement Guidelines*, above note 33 at paras 5.3–5.4.

108 *Ibid* at para 5.5.

109 *Hillsdown*, above note 61 at 17.

110 Paul Collins, Michael Trebilcock & Ralph A Winter, *The Law and Economics of Canadian Competition Policy* (Toronto: University of Toronto Press, 2003) at 254 [Collins, Trebilcock & Winter].

In *Hillsdown*, the Tribunal examined the data from both the CR4 and HHI as part of its overall assessment of industry structure. Although it did not give any particular weight to a given indicator, it stated that HHI data on capacity did not "add much."[111] The Tribunal has not made extensive reference to these indicators in later decisions.[112]

The structural presumption in section 92(2) is triggered when the HHI (referred to as the "concentration index") increases or is likely to increase by more than 100 and either the post-merger market share is or is likely to be more than 30% or the HHI is or is likely to be more than 1800.[113] When the Tribunal finds that these conditions are met, the parties bear the onus of disproving an SLPC from the merger on a balance of probabilities.

b) "Safe Harbours" Under the *Merger Enforcement Guidelines*

The *Merger Enforcement Guidelines* provide the following statement about the thresholds below which mergers are less likely to raise competitive concerns:

- The Commissioner generally will not challenge a merger on the basis of a concern related to the unilateral exercise of market power when the post-merger market share of the merged firm would be less than 35 percent.
- The Commissioner generally will not challenge a merger on the basis of a concern related to a coordinated exercise of market power when:
  - » the post-merger market share accounted for by the four largest firms in the market (known as the four-firm concentration ratio or CR4) would be less than 65 percent; or
  - » the post-merger market share of the merged firm would be less than 10 percent.

Above these thresholds, the Bureau will examine the facts to see if indeed any issue is raised; market share and concentration data are again "only one part of the Bureau's analysis of competitive effects."[114] Below these thresholds, an issue may still be raised if there are other indicators of market power. For example, the Tribunal stated in *Canada (Commissioner of Competition) v Visa Canada Corp* (albeit in the context of an assessment of market power for the purposes of resale price maintenance):

---

111 *Hillsdown*, above note 61 at 18.

112 The Tribunal did refer to CR4 data in *Parkland*, above note 104 at para 64.

113 *Competition Act*, above note 1, ss 92(2), (3), (4).

114 *Merger Enforcement Guidelines*, above note 33 at paras 5.9 and 5.11.

> Given its one-third share of the relevant market and its apparent concern about whether a market share of this magnitude is sufficient for long-term viability, MasterCard might be regarded as being in a different situation. While it is true that the *Merger Enforcement Guidelines* state that a market share under 35% [does] not normally raise unilateral market power concerns, this does not mean that it can never do so. Taking into account MasterCard's pricing discretion, its margins and the very high barriers to entry, the Tribunal concludes that MasterCard also has market power in the relevant market.[115]

Another form of safe harbour is the presence of "effective remaining competition," a factor discussed in more detail below.[116] It is often a factor considered early in case analysis and may be a basis upon which the Bureau will close a case examination quickly when it finds the remaining competition is so vigorous that the transaction could not possibly prevent or lessen competition substantially.

3) Barriers to Entry

The assessment of barriers to entry is a critical aspect of analyzing the competitive effects of any merger. In *Tervita*, the Supreme Court majority stated that barriers to entry "relate to how easily a firm can commence business in the relevant market and establish itself as a viable competitor," citing *Laidlaw*.[117] The Tribunal in *Tervita* noted the importance of this factor:

> The conditions of entry into a relevant market can be a decisive factor in the Tribunal's assessment of whether a merger is likely to prevent or lessen competition substantially. This is because, "[i]n the absence of significant entry barriers it is unlikely that a merged firm, regardless of market share or concentration, could maintain supra-competitive pricing for any length of time".
>
> To be effective, entry must be timely, likely and sufficient to ensure that any prevention of future competition will not be substantial.[118]

The *Merger Enforcement Guidelines* elaborate on the factors of timeliness, likelihood, and sufficiency. Entry must occur "quickly enough

115 *Canada (Commissioner of Competition) v Visa Canada Corp, [2013] CCTD No 10 at para 267.*

116 See below in this chapter, Section D(4)(b)(i).

117 *Canada (Director of Investigation and Research, Competition Act) v Laidlaw Waste Systems Ltd* (1992), 40 CPR (3d) 289 (CCT) at para 118; *Tervita*, above note 44 at para 71.

118 *Tervita CT*, above note 45 at para 216 [citations omitted].

to deter or counteract any material price increase owing to the merger."[119] Likelihood of entry is assessed by examining who and where the entry candidates are, the history of entry and exit into the market, as well as the hurdles an entrant may face. This includes risks of incurring "sunk" costs (those which cannot be recovered on exit), incumbents' likely responses to entry, customers' willingness to support an entrant, and profitability.[120] Sufficiency relates to the scale and scope of entry needed to be a viable competitor and counteract a material price increase.[121]

The *Merger Enforcement Guidelines* and case law from the Tribunal identify a number of potential barriers to entry. The most significant ones are canvassed below.

a) Tariffs and Regulatory Barriers

Section 93(d) of the Act gives as examples of barriers to entry:

- tariff and non-tariff barriers to international trade
- interprovincial barriers to trade
- regulatory control over entry

With respect to the latter, in *Canada (Commissioner of Competition) v Canadian Waste Services Holdings Inc*, for example, the "numerous regulatory approvals" required for a new landfill involved a process consuming one to three years, and several million dollars in costs.[122] In *Hillsdown*, the Tribunal concluded with respect to potential entry by meat rendering plants, that "regulatory and environmental approvals which are required together with the construction time involved . . . would probably mean that approximately 18 months would be required to effect entry."[123] In *Tervita*, the Tribunal heard extensive evidence on the regulatory steps governing secure landfills in BC and concluded "this process would likely take at least 18–24 months and . . . a further 3 to 4 months are needed for construction."[124]

b) Sunk Costs

Capital costs are generally not recognized *alone* as a barrier to entry. The Tribunal explained in *Superior Propane*:

---

119 *Merger Enforcement Guidelines*, above note 33 at para 7.3.

120 *Ibid* at paras 7.4–7.6.

121 *Ibid* at para 7.7.

122 *Canada (Commissioner of Competition) v Canadian Waste Services Holdings Inc*, [2001] CCTD No 3 at paras 123–26 [*Canadian Waste Services*].

123 *Hillsdown*, above note 61 at 23.

124 *Tervita CT*, above note 44 at para 220.

> The Tribunal does not accept that high capital costs are inherently a barrier to entry. If a potential entrant's equity is insufficient to cover capital costs of entry at minimum efficient scale, then the balance can be obtained through credit markets providing that lenders are satisfied that the project is viable. In the event that lenders deny credit because of their assessment of the project, their reluctance to lend does not indicate that capital is not available.[125]

Costs that are not recoverable are sunk and a potential barrier to entry. The Tribunal concluded in *Superior Propane*: "the portion of costs that are not recoverable in the event of exit (the sunk costs) can, where they are significant, constitute a barrier to entry."[126] On the facts, it identified "market development costs, site-preparation costs, and the discounts to purchase price that would be incurred on asset disposals" as sunk costs constituting "a significant obstacle" facing new propane market entrants.[127]

Economists have used game theory to reinforce the importance of sunk costs as a barrier to entry. For example, an incumbent that enters a market by building a specialized plant is sending a signal to a rival contemplating entry that the rival must expect future competition from the incumbent, who is unlikely to exit the industry because the investment is sunk. The cost of building a highly specialized plant that has no use other than production of a particular product, is an example of a sunk cost. It is unlike investment in a non-specialized plant, for which exit is easy by converting the assets to other uses.[128]

Regulatory costs may be sunk costs. In *Canadian Waste Services*, the Tribunal found "the time and cost associated with the regulatory approval process, and the capital costs and time to develop new capacity represent significant barriers to entry into the waste disposal market to the extent that they represent sunk costs."[129] In *Hillsdown*, the Tribunal noted "[w]hile there is no direct evidence concerning the proportion of costs which would be sunk, it is clear that some must be involved, for example, the costs of obtaining regulatory approvals, the specialized equipment and building required which on resale would command a lower price than that for which they were bought."[130]

---

125 *Propane CCT1*, above note 98 at para 170.

126 *Ibid* at para 172.

127 *Ibid* at paras 173 and 175.

128 Dennis W Carlton, "The Relevance for Antitrust Policy of Theoretical and Empirical Advances in Industrial Organization" (2003) 12:1 *George Mason Law Review* 47 at 49.

129 *Canadian Waste Services, above note 122 at para 122.*

130 *Hillsdown*, above note 61 at 23.

Start-up and other initial entry costs may be sunk. These may include costs of "acquiring market information, developing and testing product designs, installing equipment, engaging personnel and setting up distribution systems" as well as marketing or other costs "to establish a reputation as a reliable or quality seller."[131]

c) Contractual Barriers

Barriers may be created where customers have signed long-term or exclusive contracts, or other contractual terms are present which delay, limit, or foreclose an entrant from obtaining new customers (such as termination penalties or "meet or release" clauses).[132] In *Superior Propane,* the Tribunal concluded that "the provisions in the contracts, including long-term exclusivity, automatic renewal, termination fees, right of first refusal . . . and tank ownership significantly raise the cost of entry and expansion and hence constitute a barrier to entry."[133]

d) Economies of Scale

Economies of scale are present if the long-run average cost of production of a product falls as output increases.[134] This will occur, for example, if there are substantial fixed costs (such as for an assembly line, central administration, or a plant) which do not vary with production in the short to medium run. Economies may also occur when division and specialization of labour, or more efficient use of space and equipment, is made possible as the scale of plant is enlarged or output expanded.[135]

The "minimum efficient scale" (MES), is the level of output at which average cost is minimized and economies of scale are exhausted.[136] If the MES is a large portion of total market output, it will be challenging for a new entrant to gain a foothold, because it will have to capture a significant share of the market relatively quickly in order to survive. The barrier this creates may be greater if combined with other limits on the ability to capture market share, such as the presence of long-term exclusive contracts. Thus, in *Superior Propane*, the Commissioner's expert opined that "a new entrant will have to acquire enough customers to achieve the minimum efficient scale of operation, failing which the

---

131 *Merger Enforcement Guidelines*, above note 33 at paras 7.11 and 7.13.

132 *Ibid* at para 7.14.

133 *Propane CCT1*, above note 98 at para 150.

134 Stephen Martin, *Industrial Economics* (New York: Macmillan, 1988) at 194.

135 Michael J Brennan, *The Theory of Economic Statics*, 2d ed (Englewoods Cliffs, NJ: Prentice-Hall Inc, 1970) at 160–61.

136 Jeffrey R Church & Roger Ware, *Industrial Organization, A Strategic Approach* (Englewood Cliffs: McGraw-Hill, 2000) at 54 [Church & Ware].

entrant will operate at a cost disadvantage compared to incumbents."[137] The Tribunal accepted that this contributed to high barriers to entry.

The *Merger Enforcement Guidelines* recognize that economies of scale may deter entry by small scale entrants "unless the entrant can successfully exploit a niche." Economies of scale may also deter large scale entry, because of the risk that such entry may "expand available capacity beyond market demand, depressing market prices."[138]

e) Market Maturity

Mature markets, featuring flat or declining demand, provide less "room" for new entrants than markets which are growing or creating new customers who are searching out new sources of supply. In *Hillsdown*, the Tribunal found that the decline in red meat renderable material made obtaining sufficient volumes to permit *de novo* entry into the rendering market unlikely.[139] In *Superior Propane*, the Tribunal found that the retail propane market was mature, experiencing flat or declining growth.[140] Similarly in *Canada (Commissioner of Competition) v Canada Pipe*, an abuse of dominance case, it held: "the Tribunal accepts that we are dealing with a mature market and that this constitutes a factor which may discourage more active entry."[141]

f) Incumbent Advantages

The *Merger Enforcement Guidelines* cite the following examples of entry-deterring cost advantages which may be held by incumbents: "transportation costs, control over access to scarce or non-duplicable resources such as technology, land, natural resources and distribution channels, network effects, and capital costs."[142]

An entrant's lack of a track record in a market when compared to that of an incumbent, may also pose a significant barrier, creating resistance to customer switching. This was true in *Superior Propane*, where the Tribunal found that reputation was "an important feature of propane suppliers to which customers attach value," increasing customer loyalty to incumbent suppliers. The Tribunal concluded that "the time to gain a

137 *Propane CCT1*, above note 98 at para 134.

138 *Merger Enforcement Guidelines*, above note 33 at para 7.15.

139 *Hillsdown*, above note 61 at 23. It held at 33: "[t]he Tribunal accepts the respondents' argument that the continued decline in red meat material together with other changes in the market make construction of a new plant in Hamilton less attractive."

140 *Propane CCT1*, above note 98 at paras 158–60.

141 *Canada (Commissioner of Competition) v Canada Pipe, [2005] CCTD No 3 at para 160.*

142 *Merger Enforcement Guidelines*, above note 33 at para 7.17.

reputation may make profitable entry more difficult and hence delays the competitive impact that an entrant would have in the marketplace."[143]

As noted above, reputation also gives rise to additional barriers, because "[t]he investment required to establish a reputation as a reliable or quality seller is also a sunk cost, constituting a barrier to entry when it is an important element in attracting buyers."[144]

g) The Track Record of Entry and Exit

The US *Horizontal Merger Guidelines* place significant weight on this factor, as previous entry efforts can yield great insight into the timeliness, scale and likelihood of successful entry:

> Recent examples of entry, whether successful or unsuccessful, generally provide the starting point for identifying the elements of practical entry efforts. They also can be informative regarding the scale necessary for an entrant to be successful, the presence or absence of entry barriers, the factors that influence the timing of entry, the costs and risk associated with entry, and the sales opportunities realistically available to entrants.[145]

In *Superior Propane*, the respondent sought to "demonstrate that barriers to entry are low by presenting evidence on actual entry over time by independent firms." However, on examining the evidence the Tribunal concluded that the bulk of the entry that had occurred had been on a small scale, that it had been accompanied by exit, and that the impact on the incumbents' market share was minimal.[146] The one example of large scale entry was by Imperial Oil Limited, a large well-resourced firm, and it was unsuccessful. The Tribunal concluded that this "demonstrates that even very large and sophisticated companies may not be able to enter the propane distribution business profitably,"[147] supporting the view that barriers were high.

h) Entry-Deterring Behaviour

The anticipated competitive response to a new entrant by an incumbent firm may deter entry. Incumbents may use various strategies to increase perceived entry barriers, such as pricing "in such a fashion as to signal

---

143 *Propane CCT1*, above note 98 at para 157.

144 *Merger Enforcement Guidelines*, above note 33 at para 7.13.

145 US, Department of Justice and FTC, *Horizontal Merger Guidelines* (19 August 2010) at 28, online: www.justice.gov/atr/horizontal-merger-guidelines-08192010 at 28 [US *Horizontal Merger Guidelines*].

146 *Propane CCT1*, above note 98 at paras 176–77.

147 *Ibid* at para 152.

false information about costs, thus deterring rivals who cannot meet the imagined costs of the dominant firm."[148]

In *Superior Propane*, the Tribunal noted "[a]n important component in the decision to enter the market is the assessment of the likelihood of a competitive response from the incumbents in the marketplace." On the facts, there was evidence of a "competitive response . . . generally in the form of intense price competition targeted at the entrant in order to affect its ability to compete in the market." Evidence from Imperial Oil was that it had experienced "a vigorous response from competitors following its attempt to enter the propane market . . . margins were 30 percent lower than planned and 45 percent lower than in 1991."[149] Such a competitive response can dramatically increase the perceived cost of, and hence substantially deter, new entry.

4) The Effects of the Merger on Competition

If it is determined that the merger passes the minimal market share thresholds in a properly defined market, and entry barriers are sufficiently high to raise concern about a potential material price increase, it is necessary to examine other indicators of the impact of the merger on competition, both between the merging parties and among the remaining market players.

a) Theories of Competitive Harm: Unilateral Versus Coordinated Effects

As indicated by the Supreme Court,[150] the assessment of market power proceeds on two possible theories of competitive effect:

1) the impact of the transaction on the ability of the parties to it to *unilaterally* exercise market power, and
2) its impact on the ability of those parties to raise prices through the *coordinated* exercise of market power with other competitors.

The former involves the ability of the merged entity profitably to sustain higher prices without relying upon the coordination of the non-merging competitors' responses. The latter assesses whether the merged entity and the other firms are able to raise prices due to an enhanced ability to coordinate their behaviour.[151]

---

148 Herbert Hovenkamp, "Post-Chicago Antitrust: A Review and Critique" (2001) 2001 *Columbia Business Law Review* 257 at 312.

149 *Propane CCT1*, above note 98 at paras 151–53.

150 *Tervita*, above note 44 at para 44.

151 *Merger Enforcement Guidelines*, above note 33 at paras 2.5–2.6.

In *Parkland*, which involved an injunction application to restrain aspects of a retail gasoline merger, the Tribunal accepted evidence from the Commissioner's expert, who had put forward both theories:

> Dr. Boyer states the concentration levels, combined with other factors such as barriers to entry and loss of pre-merger rivalry, raise the likelihood of unilateral effects and substantially raise the chances of coordinated price increases emerging. He states that the Proposed Merger poses serious risks to competition through unilateral effects and coordinated effects and that price overcharges would likely result from the transaction.[152]

i) Unilateral Effects

Unilateral effects arise from the elimination of the competition between two merging firms alone. The most obvious (but by no means only) example is a merger which creates a dominant firm in a relevant market. As a general matter, "unilateral exercise of market power occurs when the merged firm can profitably sustain a material price increase without effective discipline from competitive responses by rivals."[153]

Unilateral effects are assessed under the *Merger Enforcement Guidelines* slightly differently in differentiated versus homogeneous product markets. Product differentiation is the result of different product attributes or qualities that attract some brand or customer loyalty, giving the firm a measure of power over price. The *Merger Enforcement Guidelines* state that in differentiated product markets (such as automobiles, computers, and other complex consumer goods), an increase in market power is likely "when the product offerings of the merging parties are close substitutes for one another."[154] In *Superior Propane*, this position was presented by the Commissioner's expert and summarized by the Tribunal as follows:

> [T]he potential for a unilateral price increase is high when the merging parties place competitive constraints on each other by virtue of a high degree of substitutability between their products prior to the merger. Prior to a merger, a unilateral price increase by one firm may lead to a loss of sales to its closest competitors. However, a unilateral price increase following a merger among close competitors may lead to a reduced loss of sales when the products of the merging companies are closer substitutes for each other than for the products of other firms in the industry.[155]

152 *Parkland*, above note 104 at para 97.
153 *Merger Enforcement Guidelines*, above note 33 at para 6.10.
154 *Ibid* at para 6.13.
155 *Propane CCT1*, above note 98 at para 247.

The Tribunal cited evidence from the Commissioner's expert of "consumer substitution between the products of ICG and Superior, i.e., that they compete directly and their products are close substitutes for each other in the eyes of consumers."[156] It accepted the expert's conclusion that "average prices would rise by eight percent or more as a result of the merger assuming that propane demand is relatively inelastic."[157] While propane is a homogeneous product, service, reputation, and contractual limits on switching provided a degree of product differentiation.

Using various models of oligopoly market behaviour and depending on the availability of supporting data, economists may be able to simulate the unilateral effects of the merger and make predictions about its effect on future prices, output, and profitability.[158] As noted in Chapter 4, these projections may be possible in some circumstances without the need to define the relevant market.[159]

In markets where the product is homogeneous or undifferentiated (such as for commodities like petroleum, minerals, or grain), the *Merger Enforcement Guidelines* indicate that factors affecting the likelihood of the creation or enhancing of market power post-merger include the share of the market accounted for by the merged firm and whether competitors have any capacity constraints which may limit their ability to respond to a price increase.[160] In *Hillsdown*, the presence of excess capacity throughout the meat rendering industry (due to a contracting supply of renderable material) was a leading factor that led the Tribunal to reject the possibility of a substantial lessening of competition from the two industry leaders in the Toronto area.[161]

ii) *Coordinated Effects*

The *Merger Enforcement Guidelines* explain the nature of the coordinated behaviour which may be affected by the merger:

> Coordinated behaviour may involve tacit understandings that are not explicitly negotiated or communicated among firms. Tacit understandings arise from mutual yet independent recognition that firms can, under certain market conditions, benefit from competing less aggressively with one another. Coordinated behaviour may also involve

156 *Ibid* at para 249.

157 *Ibid* at para 261.

158 Thomas W Ross & Andy Baziliauskas, "Lessening of Competition in Mergers under the Competition Act: Unilateral and Interdependence Effects" (2000) 33:3 *Canadian Business Law Journal* 373 at 380–86 [Ross & Baziliauskas].

159 See Chapter 4, Section B(2).

160 *Merger Enforcement Guidelines*, above note 33 at para 6.20.

161 See Ross & Baziliauskas, above note 158 at 418–20.

> express agreements among firms to compete less vigorously or to refrain from competing.[162]

The Bureau's concern will be raised by a merger that "materially increases the likelihood of coordinated behaviour . . . or materially increases the extent or effectiveness of coordination."[163] An example is the acquisition of a price discounting firm or "maverick" in a market featuring few sellers. This may reduce price competition and leave the remaining players in a position to engage in price leadership or other strategies, which may move prices upward without the need for an express agreement between them.[164]

Certain market conditions affect the likelihood of successful coordination. Large and infrequent transactions increase the profitability of departures from coordinated behaviour and make it less likely. As the number of competitive players increases, coordination becomes more difficult. On the other hand, the ability of firms to monitor the prices and service offerings of competitors facilitates coordination.[165] Ross & Baziliauskas list the following factors as affecting the likelihood of coordinated behaviour: (1) small number of sellers/high levels of concentration; (2) many small buyers making frequent small purchases; (3) inelastic demand; (4) limited excess capacity; (5) barriers to entry; (6) product and cost homogeneity; (7) predictable or stable demand and costs; (8) transparency—good information about prices and customers; (9) history of cooperation/coordination.[166]

Gasoline retailing, for example, features price transparency in the form of publicly posted prices, frequent transactions, and a handful of suppliers, making it an industry potentially susceptible to coordinated behaviour. It features a history, in some geographic markets, of periodic collusion or coordination. As a result, mergers in gasoline retailing markets may give rise to concerns about their impact on coordination.[167] In *Parkland*, for example, the Tribunal accepted the Commissioner's expert's conclusion that the merger of gasoline retailers would likely lead to coordinated effects in certain geographic markets. It held:

> [T]he analysis in the Boyer reports . . . contains an extensive review by Dr. Boyer of the various structural and behavioural factors that are conducive to increased coordination, which demonstrates that these

162 *Ibid* at para 6.23.
163 *Ibid* at para 6.27.
164 *Ibid* at paras 6.37–6.38.
165 *Ibid* at paras 6.31–6.32.
166 See Ross & Baziliauskas, above note 158 at 396–402.
167 *Merger Enforcement Guidelines*, above note 33 at para 6.34.

can be considered present in the various local markets identified by the Bureau and how they apply to them. Dr. Boyer talks about a "reasonable certainty" that coordinated price increases will emerge in the market conditions created by the Proposed Merger.[168]

b) Factors in the Assessment of Competitive Effects

i) *Remaining Competition*

This factor may be decisive against any challenge to a merger. If the merger has little impact on the presence of effective competition remaining in the market, the *Merger Enforcement Guidelines* indicate "this alone generally justifies a decision not to challenge the merger"[169] because the remaining competition will constrain the ability of the merging firm to exercise market power. The effectiveness of remaining competition is assessed based upon evidence of "existing forms of rivalry, such as discounting and other pricing strategies, distribution and marketing methods, product and package positioning, and service offerings."[170]

In *Superior Propane*, the Tribunal examined the evidence of the strength of the remaining competitors and concluded "there is insufficient evidence to demonstrate that there will be effective remaining competition capable of constraining the exercise of market power by the merged entity."[171]

ii) *Removal of a Vigorous and Effective Competitor*

This factor can have significant weight in the competitive assessment carried out by the Bureau and Tribunal. In *Superior Propane*, the respondents argued that the acquired firm, ICG, was not an effective competitor. The Tribunal rejected this, based upon evidence which included ICG's financial performance over time, the company's service offerings and innovative programs, the fact that it was a "strong and aggressive competitor for large volume accounts," and the reliance of customers on ICG as an option for obtaining competitive prices.[172]

This factor alone may not provide a sufficient basis for competitive concerns about a merger. For example, the presence of remaining competition or low entry barriers may supply sufficient competitive discipline post-merger, so that even if an effective competitor is removed, the merging parties still cannot exercise market power. Conversely, the fact

168 *Parkland*, above note 104 at para 98.
169 *Merger Enforcement Guidelines*, above note 33 at para 6.2.
170 *Ibid* at para 6.3.
171 *Propane CCT1*, above note 98 at para 238.
172 *Ibid* at paras 212–19.

that the firm acquired was not vigorous and competitive previously just prior to acquisition is not decisive; it must still be determined whether its pre-merger position might have been caused by temporary financial distress, declining markets, or some other factor that might change in the future.[173]

iii) Change and Innovation

The nature and extent of change and innovation in the relevant market may affect competition in a number of ways. In a dynamic and rapidly changing market, the ability of the merging firm to sustain a price increase may be limited by changes in demand, buyer preferences, and a host of other factors.[174] Any market power may be transient or not sustainable. Changes in technology may also reduce entry barriers as new production methods or novel products permit new entrants to gain a competitive edge on incumbents.

Assessing the effects of a competition-reducing merger on innovation raises the debate between those such as Joseph Schumpeter, who argued that less competition may be a stimulus to the innovation which would drive dynamic markets, and Kenneth Arrow, who argued that vigorous price and product competition stimulates greater innovation in an effort to capture demand.[175] Nonetheless, there are situations in which a merger will clearly negatively affect innovation, for example, when an innovative firm is acquired "with intent to suppress innovation through acquisition."[176] This may "hinder or delay the introduction of new products, processes, marketing approaches, and aggressive research and development initiatives or business methods."[177]

More generally, the European Commission in the assessment of the merger of Dow and DuPont, close competitors in certain markets, concluded that the transaction was likely to negatively affect future innovative

---

173 *Merger Enforcement Guidelines*, above note 33 at para 6.6.

174 See, e.g., the discussion of mature markets, below in this chapter.

175 See Chapter 3, Section D(1)(c)(iii). See also Carl Shapiro, "Competition and Innovation. Did Arrow Hit the Bull's Eye?" in Josh Lerner & Scott Stern, *The Rate and Direction of Inventive Activity Revisited* (Chicago: University of Chicago Press, 2012) at 361–410 and Pieter van Cleynenbreugel, "Innovation in Competition Law Analysis: Making Sense of On-Going Academic and Policy Debates," ch 1 in Paul Nihoil & Pieter van Cleynenbreugel, eds, *The Roles of Innovation in Competition Law Analysis* (Cheltenham: Edward Elgar, 2018).xxx

176 Andrew I Gavil, William E Kovacic & Jonathan B Baker, *Antitrust Law in Perspective: Cases, Concepts and Problems in Competition Policy* (St. Paul: West Group, 2002) at 1072.

177 *Merger Enforcement Guidelines*, above note 33 at para 6.9. See also Collins, Trebilcock & Winter, above note 110 at 143–44.

activity.[178] Given the building evidence of the importance of innovation to competition, this factor may play a significant role in future cases.[179]

iv) *Factors Focused on Digital Markets, Concentration and Tacit Collusion*

FACTORS RELEVANT TO DIGITAL MARKETS

The 2022 amendments introduced three additional factors to the list in section 93. These have been identified in the assessment of rising digital market concentration and concerns for exclusionary practices. Each of these added factors correspond, for example, to matters alleged in the complaint filed in the FTC v Facebook[180] litigation brought by the FTC in the United States:

> (g.1) network effects within the market;
> FTC v Facebook para 4: "[B]ecause a personal social network is more valuable to a user when more of that user's friends and family are already members, a new entrant faces significant difficulties in attracting a sufficient user base to compete with Facebook."
>
> (g.2) whether the merger or proposed merger would contribute to the entrenchment of the market position of leading incumbents;
> *FTC v Facebook* para 7: "Failing to compete on business talent, Facebook developed a plan to maintain its dominant position by acquiring companies that could emerge as or aid competitive threats. By buying up these companies, Facebook eliminated the possibility that rivals might harness the power of the mobile internet to challenge Facebook's dominance.";
>
> (g.3) any effect of the merger or proposed merger on price or non-price competition, including quality, choice or consumer privacy;
> *FTC v Facebook* para 106: In sum, Facebook's acquisition and control of Instagram represents the neutralization of a

---

178 European Commission Decision of 27 March 2017 "Declaring a Concentration to Be Compatible with the Internal Market and the EEA Agreement" (Case M.7932—Dow/DuPont), Annex 4 to the Commission Decision, Implications of the Economic Theory on Mergers, Competition and Innovation in Light of the Features of the Transaction," online: https://ec.europa.eu/competition/mergers/cases/decisions/m7932_13668_3.pdf at para 59.

179 See, e.g., the research cited in Jonathan B. Baker, "Beyond Schumpeter vs. Arrow: How Antitrust Fosters Innovation" (2007) 74 *Antitrust Law Journal* 575 at footnotes 8 & 9 and following.

180 *FTC v Facebook Inc*, "Substituted Amended Complaint for Injunctive and Other Equitable Relief" (September 8, 2021), online: https://www.ftc.gov/system/files/documents/cases/2021-09-08_redacted_substitute_amended_complaint_ecf_no._82.pdf.

> significant threat to Facebook Blue's personal social networking monopoly … This conduct deprives users of the benefits of competition from an independent Instagram … including, among other things: the presence of an additional locus of competitive decision-making and innovation; a check on Facebook Blue's treatment of and level of service offered to users, including ad load and level of privacy."

The Bureau explained network effects in its 2018 *Big Data and Innovation* paper as follows: "[A] social media platform is more valuable to a user when more of her acquaintances use that same platform. Somewhat differently, a user of a search engine may benefit when more users search on that platform to the extent that extra searches can be used to improve the overall search product. The most important implication of network effects for competition law is that they can be both an efficiency that benefits consumers but also a barrier to entry that may limit competition."[181] Summarizing its consultations on digital competition issues the Bureau noted that "the tools and methods used for competition analysis may need to be adapted to account for issues related to, for example, platforms and network effects." It also identified network effects as a feature of emerging AI-related markets.[182]

Network effects arising from the collection of Multiple Listings Service real estate sales data were identified as a source of barriers to entry in the *Toronto Real Estate Board* abuse of dominance case.[183]

The potential for mergers to entrench dominant incumbent firms (g.2), has been identified as a concern arising in digital market by several reports. ISED Canada traced as an influence for this amendment Australia's 2019 "Digital Platforms Inquiry."[184] That report recommended

---

181 Competition Bureau, *Big data and innovation: key themes for competition policy in Canada* (February 19, 2018) at 7; online: http://www.competitionbureau.gc.ca/eic/site/cb-bc.nsf/eng/04342.html [Big Data and Innovation Report].

182 Competition Bureau, *Artificial Intelligence and Competition Discussion Paper* (March 20, 2024) at para 3.1.4; online: https://ised-isde.canada.ca/site/competition-bureau-canada/sites/default/files/documents/AICompetition-Discussion-Paper-240320-ver3-e.pdf

183 *Canada (Commissioner of Competition) v Toronto Real Estate Board*, 2016 Comp Trib 7 at para 264.

184 Canada, Innovation, Science and Economic Development Canada, *The Future of Competition Policy in Canada* (Ottawa: ISED, 2022), online: https://ised-isde.canada.ca/site/strategic-policy-sector/sites/default/files/attachments/2022/The-Future-of-Competition-Policy-eng_0.pdf. The report noted at 22: "Australia's Digital Platforms Inquiry produced the recommendation that certain considerations be made more explicit in the law's merger review provisions, including the likelihood that the acquisition would result in the removal from the market of

certain additional merger factors including "the likelihood that an acquisition would result in the removal from the market of a potential competitor."[185] In Canada, an analysis of digital competition issues noted that "[d]igital markets are prone to disruption and incumbents may seek to stifle innovation through mergers or other conduct. Especially where nascent or potential competition is affected, it may be that this conduct tends to *prevent* competition rather than *lessen* competition."[186] This observation led to the suggestion that "s. 93 could invite the Tribunal to consider whether an acquisition would entrench or enhance the market position of a leading firm, including leading firms in the digital sector."[187] The amendment picks up on this suggestion.

Paragraph (g.3), refers to the effects of the merger on "price *or* non-price competition", and then gives three examples of the latter: "quality, choice or consumer privacy." It is well-established that non-price effects can be relevant to the assessment of a merger. The legislation speaks of the substantial prevention or lessening of competition, and does not restrict effects to those related to higher prices. Non-price factors have been accepted as relevant and formed part of the Tribunal's findings in several decided merger cases.[188] The Supreme Court of Canada noted in *Tervita* that the market power assessment under the section examines "the ability to 'profitably influence price, quality, variety, service, advertising, innovation or other dimensions of competition.'"[189]

Non-price competition has been prominent in examinations of digital competition issues, given that many digital services are offered to consumers at a zero price, and competition thus often focuses on non-price dimensions. In the Competition Bureau's paper *Big Data and Innovation* it is noted that quality "is a leading example of a non-price

a potential competitor, and the nature and significance of assets being acquired, including data and technology" and at footnote 45: "The … amendments partially embraced this approach in Canada, making certain considerations such as network effects and entrenchment of incumbents explicit."

185 Australian Competition & Consumer Commission, *Digital platforms inquiry - final report* (July 26, 2019); see also European Commission, Directorate-General for Competition, Y Montjoye, H Schweitzer, J Crémer, *Competition policy for the digital era* (2019) at 112–23, online: https://data.europa.eu/doi/10.2763/407537.

186 Edward M Iacobucci, "Examining the Canadian Competition Act in the Digital Era" (27 September 2021) at 21 [Iacobucci].

187 *Ibid* at 22–23.

188 See, for example, *Canada (Commissioner of Competition) v Secure Energy Services Inc*, [2023] CCTD No 2 at paras 157–174, 358–368, 536. See also the cases cited in Andy Baziliauskas and Margaret Sanderson, "Should Canada Overhaul the SLPC Test for Mergers?", (2023) 36 CCLR 128 at 145–147.

189 *Tervita*, above note 43 at para 44.

dimension of competition, although what constitutes 'quality' will vary from case to case. It is conceivable, for example, that in some cases consumers may view privacy as an important element of quality."[190]

Measuring or assessing the "material" nature and "substantiality" of quality changes, such as privacy, can pose challenges. Consumer preferences for quality can be highly variable and subjective, and lack the arguably objective measuring stick of a monetary benchmark (price) reached through the process of market negotiation. The legislation merely provides that the Tribunal may consider this element, without providing additional guidance on how it is to be measured or weighed.

v) Concentration/Market Share and Coordination

The 2024 amendments added paragraphs (g.4) and (g.5).[191] The reference in the former to concentration and market share as a factor is consistent with the addition of the structural presumption in s 92(2), given that the presumption places greater emphasis on market structure as at least a *prima facie* measure of competitive impact. The latter refers to the impact of the merger on the likelihood of express or tacit coordination, an important factor identified in the *Merger Guidelines* and the caselaw (see above in this chapter, Section D(4)(a)(ii).

iv) Countervailing Power

Countervailing power is present when buyers are able to constrain the ability of a seller to increase prices or otherwise exercise market power. Large or well-resourced buyers may, for example, be able to threaten vertical integration to bypass a seller, to refuse to purchase other products, or to not purchase the product in question in other geographic areas in which that buyer regularly purchases[192] in order to counteract the seller's market power.

Countervailing power has not been a significant feature in the decided merger cases to date. In *Tervita*, for example, the merging parties argued that their customers possessed countervailing power, but the Tribunal was not convinced that they were able to exercise any significant countervailing power enabling them to resist a price increase.[193]

c) Non-horizontal Mergers: Effects on Competition

Non-horizontal mergers—vertical and conglomerate—involve firms that do not supply competing or potentially competing products. Such

190 Big Data and Innovation Report, above note 181 at 8.

191 *Bill C-59 2024*, above note 30, s 250.

192 *Merger Enforcement Guidelines*, above note 33 at para 8.1.

193 *Tervita CT*, above note 45 at paras 226–28.

mergers may raise issues "if the merged firm is able to limit or eliminate rival firms' access to inputs or markets."[194]

The *Merger Enforcement Guidelines* describe a vertical merger as "a merger between firms that produce products at different levels of a supply chain (e.g., a merger between a supplier and a customer)."[195] The definition of "merger" in section 91 of the *Competition Act* includes acquisitions of a "customer" and "supplier," making it clear that vertical mergers may be reviewed in Canada for their competitive impact.[196] The *Merger Enforcement Guidelines* note that vertical mergers are "less likely to prevent or lessen competition substantially than are horizontal mergers" (mergers between competitors or potential competitors).[197] First, they do not eliminate direct competition as in a horizontal merger. Second, they may create efficiencies. They may "eliminate double marginalization, reduce transaction costs, align incentives, and facilitate product design enhancements. Consumers may benefit from any of these effects."[198] The elimination of double marginalization occurs when the vertically merged firm eliminates or reduces one level of mark-up in the chain of transactions, leading to a lower downstream price.

There have been few merger cases in Canada in which vertical effects have been an issue. In a number of cases, consent resolutions involving divestitures or behavioural remedies have been reached to avoid contested proceedings.[199]

In the United States, the courts have placed a greater burden on those challenging vertical mergers to prove anti-competitive effect:

> [U]nlike horizontal mergers, the government cannot use a short cut to establish a presumption of anticompetitive effect through statistics about the change in market concentration, because vertical mergers produce no immediate change in the relevant market share . . . . Instead, the government must make a "fact-specific" showing that the proposed merger is "likely to be anticompetitive."[200]

A concern with vertical mergers is "foreclosure"—that the acquiring firm may have the ability to limit the access of its rivals to needed sources

194 *Merger Enforcement Guidelines*, above note 33 at para 11.4.

195 *Ibid* at para 11.1.

196 *Tervita CT*, above note 45 at para 354, Crampton CJ concurring.

197 *Merger Enforcement Guidelines*, above note 33 at para 11.2.

198 Jonathan M Jacobson, "Vertical Mergers: Is It Time to Move the Ball?" (2019) 33 *Antitrust* 6 at 8 [Jacobson].

199 *McKesson Canada Corporation and Rexall Pharmacy Group Ltd.—Registered Consent Agreement* 2016-12-14, CT-2016-016; *BCE Inc-Astral Media Inc*—Revised Registered Consent Agreement 2015-01-19 CT-2013-002.

200 *United States v AT&T Inc*, 916 F3d 1029 (DC Cir 2019) at 1032 [*US v AT&T Inc*].

of supply or to customers, raising the rivals' costs and reducing competitive pressure on the merged entity.[201] The Bureau's *Merger Enforcement Guidelines* identify partial or complete input (upstream) and customer (downstream) foreclosure as issues that may arise in the examination of a vertical merger.[202] The following describes the potential issue:

> [A] firm that enjoys market power at one stage may … be able to use vertical integration or vertical contracting practices to enhance its market power—essentially by restricting and/or raising the cost to rivals of access to upstream or downstream resources. By raising costs to rivals, a firm is able to deflect demand to itself and thereby increase its prices and its profitability.[203]

The diagram below (**Figure 5.8**) illustrates the merging parties on the left and downstream rivals on the right.[204]

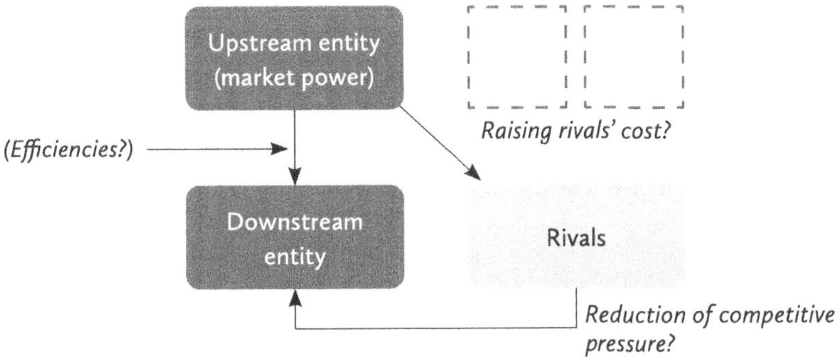

FIGURE 5.8. In input foreclosure, a downstream entity acquires an upstream supplier, and restricts access to, or makes conditions of supply less favourable for its rival(s). Competition concerns are raised when the upstream supplier has substantial market power and the product in question represents a significant cost component of the downstream product

Input (upstream) foreclosure was alleged in the AT&T–Time Warner merger. AT&T, a cable TV distributor through its subsidiary DirectTV (downstream entity), acquired Time Warner, a programming provider

201 See generally: Thomas G Krattenmaker & Steven C Salop, "Anticompetitive Exclusion: Raising Rivals' Costs to Achieve Power over Price" (1986) 96:2 *Yale Law Journal* 209; Michael H Riordan & Steven C Salop, "Evaluating Vertical Mergers: A Post-Chicago Approach" (1995) 63:2 *Antitrust Law Journal* 513.

202 *Merger Enforcement Guidelines*, above note 33 at paras 11.4–11.7.

203 Lawrence J White, "Monopoly and Dominant Firms: Antitrust Economics and Policy Approaches" in Roger D Blair & D Daniel Sokol, eds, *The Oxford Handbook of International Antitrust Economics* (Oxford: Oxford University Press 2014), vol 1 at 20.

204 EC, *Guidelines on the assessment of non-horizontal mergers under the Council Regulation on the control of concentrations between undertakings* (2008/C 265/07), online: https://eur-lex.europa.eu/LexUriServ/LexUriServ.do?uri=OJ:C:2008:265:0006:0025:EN:PDF at para 31, Figure 1 [EC *Guidelines*].

(upstream entity). The US Department of Justice challenged the merger on the basis that "by combining Time Warner's [upstream] programming and DirecTV's [downstream] distribution, the merger would give Time Warner [which already owned upstream programming entities such as Turner Broadcasting] increased bargaining leverage in negotiations with rival [downstream] distributors, leading to higher, supra-competitive prices for millions of consumers."[205] A challenge to the merger was unsuccessful, on the basis, *inter alia*, that the government's case "failed to clear the first hurdle of showing that the proposed merger is likely to increase Turner [Broadcasting]'s bargaining leverage" and therefore to raise rival cable distributors' programming costs.[206]

Downstream foreclosure concerns are illustrated in **Figure 5.9**, below, depicting the merging entities on the left. The competition policy concern is that the merged firm may foreclose access by its upstream rivals to a sufficient customer base in order to reduce those rivals' ability to compete effectively. This reduced upstream competition may also raise the downstream rivals' costs by making it harder for them to obtain supplies of an input at similar prices and under similar conditions to those prevailing before the merger. This may allow the merged entity profitably to raise prices in the downstream market.[207]

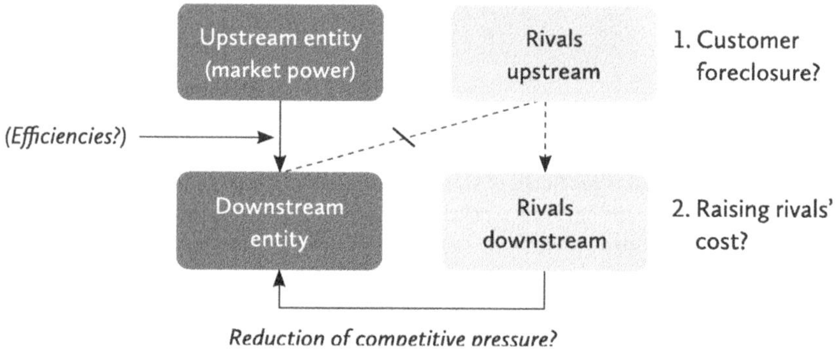

FIGURE 5.9. Downstream or customer foreclosure: a supplier merges with an important customer in the downstream market

An example of a merger challenge based on customer foreclosure was Ford Motor Company's proposed vertical merger with a major spark plug manufacturer, Autolite. The US Supreme Court upheld the US Federal Trade Commission's challenge to the transaction, explaining its effect was to eliminate Ford as the largest customer for independent spark plug manufacturers and "to foreclose to the remaining independent spark

205 *US v AT&T Inc*, above note 200 at 1035.
206 *Ibid* at 1037.
207 EC *Guidelines*, above note 204 at para 58, Figure 2.

plug manufacturers the substantial segment of the market [held by Ford] previously open to competitive selling and to remove the significant pro-competitive effects in the concentrated spark plug market that resulted from Ford's position on the edge of the market as a potential entrant."[208]

Downstream foreclosure was alleged but rejected by the Tribunal in *Canadian Waste Services*.[209]

The Bureau's *Merger Enforcement Guidelines* note that vertical mergers may raise concerns about coordinated effects by, for example, increasing market transparency where the acquiring firm obtains pricing or other sensitive commercial information concerning competitors' products by acquiring a downstream customer.[210] The US *Horizontal Merger Guidelines* also indicate that the acquisition of a disruptive or "maverick" firm in either an upstream or downstream market may facilitate collusion.[211] The EC *Guidelines on the assessment of non-horizontal mergers* similarly address coordination theories of potential anti-competitive effect.[212]

Behavioural remedies, such as firewalls to protect against access to rivals' sensitive competitive information when a supplier acquires a distributor[213] or retailer,[214] or obligations to supply or treat customers in a non-discriminatory fashion, can permit the efficiencies of a vertical merger to be realized while addressing its anti-competitive effects. However, such remedies are controversial, as they place a monitoring burden on competition agencies by requiring ongoing oversight and supervision, a role that some commentators see as at odds with the traditional role of competition authorities.[215]

---

208 *Ford Motor Co v United States*, 405 US 562 (1972) at 574.

209 *Canadian Waste Services*, above note 124 at paras 214–24.

210 *Merger Enforcement Guidelines*, above note 33 at para 11.9.

211 US, Department of Justice, *1984 Merger Guidelines* (14 June 1984), online: www.justice.gov/archives/atr/1984-merger-guidelines, Section 4, Horizontal Effect From Non-Horizontal Mergers; withdrawn 20 January 2020; also US, Department of Justice and the Federal Trade Commission, *Draft Vertical Merger Guidelines*, online: www.ftc.gov/public-statements/2020/01/joint-vertical-merger-guidelines-draft-released-public-comment, released for public comment on 10 January 2020 at 8: "A vertical merger may enhance the market's vulnerability to coordination by eliminating or hobbling a maverick firm that otherwise plays or would play an important role in preventing or limiting anticompetitive coordination in the relevant market."

212 EC *Guidelines*, above note 204 at paras 79–90.

213 *In the Matter of Sycamore Partners II, LP, Staples, Inc and Essendant Inc*, FTC File No 181-0180 (29 January 2019), online: www.ftc.gov/enforcement/cases-proceedings/181-0180/sycamore-partners-ii-lp-staples-inc-essendant-inc-matter.

214 *McKesson Canada Corporation and Rexall Pharmacy Group Ltd. — Registered Consent Agreement* 2016-12-14, CT-2016-016, Section VII Confidentiality.

215 See Jacobson, above note 198 at 10.

A *conglomerate* merger involves the acquisition of a firm that competes in a different product market that does not have a vertical connection to the acquiror. Challenges to such mergers are rare, given the absence of direct or immediate competitive effects. The *Merger Enforcement Guidelines* refer to two potential situations where there may be concern from conglomerate mergers: (1) where the merged firm is able to use the acquired product to engage in tied selling to "foreclose rivals"; and (2) where acquisition of multiple product lines provides the acquiring firm another avenue to punish rivals for price deviations from coordinated behaviour.[216]

5) Potential Failure of a Party to the Merger or Proposed Merger

Section 93(b) provides that, in considering the effects of a merger on competition, the Tribunal "may have regard" to "whether the business, or part of the business, of a party to the merger or proposed merger has failed or is likely to fail." This language makes it clear that the likely failure of the acquired firm is not an absolute "defence," but a consideration in the overall assessment of the merger's effect. In contrast, in the European Union and United States, the likely failure of the acquired firm is elevated to a defence or exemption (as developed in the case law), and considered separately from the assessment of effect of the merger on competition.[217] In practice, the approaches differ little in substance, with the *Merger Enforcement Guidelines* devoting a separate section to this factor, signalling that its analysis by the Bureau is distinct from the others considered under section 93.[218]

Absent case law in Canada on this consideration, the *Merger Enforcement Guidelines* provide the principal source of guidance for how the failing firm factor operates. The issue has played a role in the Bureau's assessment of a number of cleared mergers, such as Canadian Airlines/PWA's acquisition of charter carrier Wardair, Air Canada's takeover of Canadian Airlines, and Rogers's acquisition of wireless competitor Microcell.[219] It also resulted in the Bureau not challenging a merger of

216 *Merger Enforcement Guidelines*, above note 33 at paras 6.33, 11.8 and 11.9. Regarding tied selling, see Chapter 8.

217 Marianela Lopez-Galdos, "Comparing the US & the EU Failing Firm Defense: Reflections from an Economic Perspective" (2016) 28:2/3 *Loyola Consumer Law Review* 297 [Lopez-Galdos].

218 Thomas Mathews, "The Failing Firm: Re-Examining Canada's Approach to Rescue Mergers in Light of the US and EU Experience" (2014) 27:1 *Canadian Competition Law Review* 1 at 8–9 [Mathews].

219 *Ibid* at 11–14.

the two largest scrap metal processors in Quebec, on the basis that the acquired company "was a failing firm and its assets were likely to have exited the market in the absence of the merger."[220]

The central rationale for considering the failure of the acquired firm in the context of merger review is *causation*: "the loss of the actual or future competitive influence of a failing firm is not attributed to the merger if imminent failure is probable and, in the absence of a merger, the assets of the firm are likely to exit the relevant market."[221] The *Merger Enforcement Guidelines* state that a firm will be considered to be failing if:

- it is insolvent or is likely to become insolvent;
- it has initiated or is likely to initiate voluntary bankruptcy proceedings; or
- it has been, or is likely to be, petitioned into bankruptcy or receivership.[222]

The *Merger Enforcement Guidelines* go on to set out the kinds of financial information needed to show that a firm is likely to fail, such as financial statements, auditors' reports, and details of the ability of the firm to pay creditors or service its debt.

In addition to likely failure, the Bureau considers whether alternatives to the merger exist which are "likely to result in a materially greater level of competition than if the proposed merger proceeds." If so, this may form a basis for blocking the acquisition. The alternatives are listed below.[223]

- *Acquisition by a competitively preferable purchaser*: The Bureau must be satisfied that there has been "a thorough search for a competitively preferable purchaser" and may require "involvement of an independent third party (such as an investment dealer, trustee or broker who has no material interest in either of the merging parties or the proposal in question) to conduct such a search before the failing firm rationale is accepted." If such a purchaser is located, "it can generally be expected that, if the proposed merger under review cannot be completed, the target will either seek to merge with that competitively preferable purchaser, or remain in the market."

220 Canada, Competition Bureau, "Competition Bureau statement regarding the acquisition of Total Metal Recovery (TMR) Inc. by American Iron & Metal Company Inc" (29 April 2020), online: www.competitionbureau.gc.ca/eic/site/cb-bc.nsf/eng/04528.html [Bureau Statement Re *American Iron & Metal Company Inc* Merger].

221 *Merger Enforcement Guidelines*, above note 33 at para 13.2.

222 *Ibid* at para 13.3.

223 *Ibid* at paras 13.8–13.10.

- *Retrenchment/restructuring*: Where no purchaser is likely, the Bureau will examine whether the target firm can make changes to its operations "by narrowing the scope of its operations, for instance, by downsizing or withdrawing from the sale of certain products or from certain geographic areas" in order to "prevent failure and enable it to survive as a meaningful competitor."
- *Liquidation*: If neither of the above are possible, the Bureau will still assess whether liquidation—that is, the sale and distribution of the firm's assets to the marketplace—may "facilitate entry into a market by enabling actual or potential competitors to compete for the failing firm's customers or assets to a greater degree than if the failing firm merged with the proposed acquirer." In one transaction, the Bureau acknowledged that resort to the remedy of liquidation may be mitigated by practical considerations: "[b]ecause liquidation is disruptive to all parties involved and may not result in an efficient allocation of resources, there are very limited circumstances under which the Bureau may determine that liquidation is the preferable outcome."[224]

The foregoing requirements are stringent, reflecting the fact that the acquisition of a failing firm by a leading market competitor may fundamentally alter the competitive landscape, and therefore should only be permitted where less anti-competitive options have been thoroughly canvassed.

On the other hand, it has been observed that if permitted acquisitions of failing firms is too circumscribed, this may also have adverse consequences on competition and the public interest. For example, "defining a failing firm very strictly could render the defense itself useless since the assets of the failing firm could be deteriorated to an extent that no company would be willing to buy it, ultimately leading the failing company to exit the market."[225] Permitting the efficient acquisition of ailing or inefficient firms is an essential aspect of a competitive economy.[226] As a result, the application of the failing firm factor may require the careful balancing of conflicting policy considerations.

6) Efficiencies

In 2023, Parliament repealed a statutory "efficiencies defence" in section 96 which had precluded any order against a merger which "brought about or is likely to bring about gains in efficiency that will be greater than, and

224 Bureau Statement Re *American Iron & Metal Company Inc* Merger, above note 220.
225 Lopez-Galdos, above note 217 at 309.
226 Mathews, above note 218 at 33.

will offset, the effects of any prevention or lessening of competition that will result or is likely to result from the merger or proposed merger." The test thus involved the balancing of "gains in efficiency" from a merger against "the effects of any prevention or lessening of competition."

The majority judgment of the Supreme Court in *Tervita* had placed an onus on the Commissioner to quantify alleged anti-competitive effects as part of this balancing test.[227] The dissent of Justice Karakatsanis, however, opined on this quantification requirement that "[t]he statutory language does not require such a result. Nor does the purpose or context of the legislation."[228] Subsequent academic and other expert commentary also critiqued this requirement as unnecessary, given that qualitative assessment of anti-competitive effects is commonplace in merger assessment and noted that requiring quantification made analysis of the defence burdensome and overly complex.[229]

With the repeal of the defence, an interpretative question raised is what role, if any, efficiencies now play in merger review, given that the explicit defence was removed by Parliament without further change or guidance.[230] While at common law "there is a presumption that amendments to the wording of a legislative provision are made for some intelligible purpose, such as to clarify the meaning, to correct a mistake, or to

---

227 *Tervita*, above note 44 at para 90.

228 *Ibid* at para 194.

229 See, e.g., Iacobucci, above note 186 at 29–32; Marcel Boyer, Thomas W Ross & Ralph A Winter, *The Rise of Economics in Competition Policy: A Canadian Perspective, Working Paper 2017s-26* (Montreal: CIRANO, 2017) at 39; CD Howe Institute Competition Policy Council Communique, "Distilled Wisdom: Council Members Agree on the Most-Needed Reforms for the Next Government" (21 September 2021) at 4: "many members of the Council believe the efficiencies defence has become an accounting exercise that narrowly considers the tractable questions of static efficiency but makes it difficult for the Commissioner to challenge mergers on the basis of the harder-to-quantify dynamic effects that mergers may have on the economy. These dynamic factors are perhaps especially relevant in the digital economy." For a description of the pre-amendment defence, see the previous edition, Chapter 5 at 228–40.

230 The Competition Bureau had, for example, proposed initially that section 96 be repealed but that efficiencies be inserted as a factor which the Tribunal could take into account in the assessment of competitive effect in section 93. See Competition Bureau Canada, "Examining the Canadian *Competition Act* in the Digital Era, Submission by the Competition Bureau" (8 February 2022), [Bureau Submissions 2022], online: https://ised-isde.canada.ca/site/competition-bureau-canada/en/how-we-foster-competition/promotion-and-advocacy/regulatory-adviceinterventions-competition-bureau/examining-canadian-competition-act-digital-era.

change the law,"[231] the *Interpretation Act* at the same time cautions that an amendment of itself shall not be deemed to imply that the former law was "different from the law as it is under the enactment as amended."[232] Professor Sullivan has observed that the *Interpretation Act* provisions do not "preclude the court from acknowledging that, in principle at least, the foremost purpose of amendment is to bring about a substantive change in law. They do, however, remind the courts that amendments do not necessarily have that purpose."[233] On balance, these counterbalancing indicators suggest that the courts will search for the usual signals of legislative intent behind such a change, including those found in extrinsic evidence from the legislative process.

The extrinsic evidence provides support for the view that Parliament intended, at minimum, to move away from the complex balancing test provided for in the prior s 96 and *Tervita*. The Minister responsible for the Bill stated during Second Reading that the defence had been subject to criticism during public consultations as being a barrier to effective enforcement. He explained that as a result, "We are proposing to eliminate the efficiencies exception, which would mean that if a proposed merger were considered anti-competitive, it could be reviewed despite any efficiency gains generated for the companies … Of course, if a proposed merger creates efficiencies that strengthen competition in a sector, the [T]ribunal would be able to consider them in its deliberations."[234] Support for such an approach can be found in the purpose clause of the Act. If a merger give rises to significant cost-reducing efficiencies to the point, for example, that post-merger prices are shown to be likely to be lower, or terms or service or quality are improved, permitting the merger to proceed could be consistent with not only the statutory goal of efficiency but also with that of providing consumers with competitive prices and product choices.[235]

a) A Potential Model? Treatment of Efficiencies in the United States

While the foregoing suggests the Bureau and Tribunal may be prepared to integrate efficiencies asserted by the merging parties into the assessment

---

231 *R v Ulybel Enterprises Ltd*, 2001 SCC 56 at para 34, citing R Sullivan, Driedger on the Construction of Statutes, 3rd ed. (Toronto: Butterworths, 1994) at 450.

232 *Interpretation Act*, RSC 1985 c. I-21, s 45(2).

233 R Sullivan, The Construction of Statutes, 7th ed. (Toronto: LexisNexis, 2022) at §23.02.

234 Canada, House of Commons Debates (Hansard), 44th Parl. 1st Sess, No 223 (25 September 2023). The Minister stated during Senate 3rd Reading, "to the extent that the efficiencies would be procompetitive, they would be considered… by the Competition Bureau, and that's a good thing." Canada, Senate Debates (Hansard) 44th Parl. 1st Sess, No 223 (13 December 2023).

235 *Competition Act*, above note 1, s 1.1.

of the competitive effects of a merger in certain circumstances, the statute provides no guidance on how this is to occur. One approach could be drawn from the practice of antitrust authorities in the United States. There, while the US Supreme Court has expressed doubt about the ability of efficiencies to ever provide a defence to an anti-competitive merger,[236] lower courts have held that they may be assessed as part of the overall analysis of anti-competitive effects.[237] This is reflected in the enforcement practice set out in the 2023 FTC/DoJ *Merger Guidelines*, which accept the potential for merging parties to submit that efficiencies counteract any substantial prevention or lessening of competition by way of a "rebuttal argument" which "asserts that the merger would not substantially lessen competition in any relevant market in the first place." The *Guidelines* require that to be cognizable, efficiencies must: (a) not be achievable without the merger (i.e., be "merger-specific"), (b) be verifiable, and (c) "prevent the risk of a substantial lessening of competition in the relevant market."[238]

This is not a balancing test (unlike the repealed s 96, which was); it focuses on the overall impact of efficiencies in individual markets and whether in light of them, the merger will result in benefits which will produce lower consumer prices or improved service. The prior (2010) US *Merger Guidelines* had stated that a merger would not be challenged if "cognizable efficiencies likely would be sufficient to reverse the merger's potential to harm customers in the relevant market, e.g., by preventing price increases in that market."[239] This was termed the "price standard."[240] The 2023 US *Merger Guidelines* continue the same approach but refer more generally to the need to show "substantial competitive benefits" from the merger. They go on to note, consistent with the earlier *Guidelines*, that efficiencies "cannot justify a merger that may tend to create a monopoly."[241]

An example of the prior differing treatment of efficiencies in Canada and the United States can be seen in the 2016 proposed $1 billion merger of Canadian chemical suppliers Superior Plus Corp and Canexus Corp.

---

236 *FTC v Proctor & Gamble Co*, 386 US 568 (1967) at 580; *United States v Philadelphia National Bank*, 374 US 321 (1963) at 370–71.

237 See, e.g., *FTC v HJ Heinz Co*, 246 F3d 709 (DC Cir 2001) at 720; *St Alphonsus Medical Center–Nampa Inc v St Luke's Health Systems, Ltd*, 778 F3d 775 (9th Cir, 2015) at 790.

238 US 2023 *Merger Guidelines*, above note 60 at 33–34.

239 US *Horizontal Merger Guidelines*, above note 145 at 30–31.

240 *Propane FCA1*, above note 8 at para 41. Sometimes referred to as the "consumer welfare" standard: Herbert J Hovenkamp, "Appraising Merger Efficiencies" (2017) 24 *Geo Mason L Rev* 703 at 713.

241 The US 2023 *Merger Guidelines*, above note 60 at 32, 33.

The transaction would have given the merged entity almost half of the North American production capacity in sodium chlorate (a chemical used to bleach the wood pulp that is then processed into paper, tissue, diaper liners, and other products). The Competition Bureau's analysis concluded that the merger would likely result in a substantial lessening of competition for the supply of sodium chlorate in both Eastern and Western Canada, where the merged entity would have been the sole supplier of certain related chemicals. However, the Bureau's assessment of the (then existing) efficiencies defence under section 96 concluded that the anti-competitive effects were "clearly outweighed" by the efficiency gains from the transaction, and therefore the Commissioner decided not to challenge the merger.[242] The US Federal Trade Commission, on the other hand, decided to challenge, stating on the issue of efficiencies that "[r]espondents cannot demonstrate cognizable efficiencies that would be sufficient to rebut the strong presumption and evidence that the Acquisition likely would substantially lessen competition in the North American market for sodium chlorate."[243] The transaction was abandoned as a result.[244] Given the repeal of section 96, the approach in the two jurisdictions is unlikely to be as divergent in future with respect to the efficiencies assessment.

E. EXCEPTIONS FROM SECTION 92

In addition to the efficiencies defence, the Act provides that the Tribunal shall not make an order where approval is given to a merger pursuant to finance and transportation regulatory regimes. An exception is also made for joint ventures. The relevant exceptions are:

1) **Certification by the Minister of Finance:** The Minister may certify that a merger or proposed merger under the *Bank Act*, the *Cooperative Credit Associations Act*, the *Insurance Companies Act* or the *Trust and Loan Companies Act* is in the public interest.[245]

---

242 Canada, Competition Bureau, "Competition Bureau statement regarding Superior's proposed acquisition of Canexus" (28 June 2016), online: www.competitionbureau.gc.ca/eic/site/cb-bc.nsf/eng/04111.html.

243 FTC, Complaint, *In the Matter of Docket No. 9371 Superior Plus Corp. and Canexus Corporation* (27 June 2016), online: www.ftc.gov/system/files/documents/cases/160627superiorcanexuscmpt.pdf at para 59.

244 FTC, Order Dismissing Complaint, *In the Matter of Docket No. 9371 Superior Plus Corp and Canexus Corporation* (2 August, 2016), online: www.ftc.gov/system/files/documents/cases/160803superiorcanexuscmpt.pdf.

245 *Competition Act*, above note 1, s 94(b).

2) **Certification or Approval by the Minister of Transport:** The Minister may certify the names of the parties to an approved merger or proposed merger, or approve an arrangement, pursuant to section 53.2(7) of the *Canada Transportation Act*.[246]
3) **Joint Ventures:** An exempt joint venture consists of a combination (other than through a corporation) undertaking a specific project or research and development program that has met the requirements set out in section 95 of the Act.

Under the *Canada Transportation Act*, certain mergers involving transportation undertakings cannot be completed without approval of the Governor in Council. A "transportation undertaking" under the *Canada Transportation Act* may include an entity that transports goods and/or passengers across provincial or national borders by air, rail, or road. The Commissioner contributes to the Minister of Transport's public interest review through a "report to the Minister and the parties to the transaction on any concerns regarding potential prevention or lessening of competition that may occur as a result of the transaction."[247] The Governor in Council, on recommendation by the Minister, must decide whether to approve the transaction, with any necessary conditions. The Commissioner, for example, issued reports in 2019 and 2020 respectively, indicating competition concerns with the Air North–Canadian North Inc [248] and Air Canada–Air Transat[249] mergers. In the former case, the transaction was nonetheless approved by the Governor in Council.[250]

With respect to joint ventures, the merger provisions will only apply when the definition of "merger" discussed earlier is met—i.e., when there is the acquisition of a "significant interest" of a competitor. If this

246 *Ibid*, s 94(c) & (d). See below in this chapter.

247 *Canada Transportation Act*, SC 1996, c 10, s 53.2(2).

248 Canada, Commissioner of Competition, *Report to the Minister of Transport and the Parties to the Transaction Pursuant to Subsection 53.2(2) of the Canada Transportation Act Proposed Merger of Bradley Air Services Limited, dba First Air, and Canadian North Inc* (25 February 2019), online: www.competitionbureau.gc.ca/eic/site/cb-bc.nsf/eng/04419.html.

249 Canada, Commissioner of Competition, *Report to the Minister of Transport and the Parties to the Transaction Pursuant to Subsection 53.2(2) of the Canada Transportation Act Proposed Acquisition by Air Canada of Transat AT Inc* (27 March 2020), online: www.competitionbureau.gc.ca/eic/site/cb-bc.nsf/eng/04522.html.

250 The latter case has a deadline of 11 December 2020 in the European Union; it is still pending in Canada. See Eric Atkins, "Transat Renews Call for Bailout as Stalled Air Canada Deal Hampers Its Ability to Borrow" *Globe and Mail* (10 September 2020), online: www.theglobeandmail.com/business/article-transat-renews-call-for-bailout-as-stalled-air-canada-deal-hits/.

is so, section 95 exempts from merger review under section 92 certain unincorporated "combinations" for a "specific project or a program of research and development" meeting specified criteria. These criteria are that (1) the project or program would not have occurred without the joint venture; (2) the joint venture does not involve a change of control over any party to the combination; (3) the merger is subject to a written agreement, *inter alia*, to contribute assets and to terminate on completion of the project or program; and (4) any prevention or lessening of competition does not go beyond the degree required to undertake or complete the project or program.[251] The numerous statutory requirements have made the exemption of little practical relevance.[252] In practice, joint ventures are more likely to be subject to the horizontal agreement provisions in section 90.1, canvassed in the next chapter.[253]

F. PROCEDURAL ISSUES AND REMEDIES

1) Limitation Period: Section 97

No application may be made under section 92 to challenge a merger (other than those covered by an advance ruling certificate request or section 114 notification) "more than three years after the merger has been substantially completed."[254] The limitation period had been reduced from three to one year in 2009 for all mergers, after an expert panel appointed by the government said this would foster "more certainty for the Canadian business community and international investors."[255] However, Parliament again adopted a general three-year period in 2024 after consultations in which it was argued by some participants that "one year was too short to determine the true impact of a merger, and some felt that businesses can easily delay the clearest signs of lessened competition, such as higher prices, for a year before leveraging their increased market power."[256] It was also noted that a longer limitation period "would also

251 *Competition Act*, above note 1, s 95(1)(a)–(e).

252 Anthony W Swisher, "Joint Ventures in the United States and Canada" (2014) 10:1 *Competition Law International* 35 at 50.

253 *Competition Act*, above note 1, ss 45 and 90.1; see below Chapter 6, Section 6(B)3 and Section 6(E).

254 *Competition Act*, above note 1, s 97.

255 Canada, Competition Policy Review Panel, *Compete to Win* (Public Works and Government Services Canada, Ottawa, 2008) at 57.

256 Canada, ISED, *Future of Canada's Competition Policy Consultation – What We Heard Report*, 20 Sept 2023 at s 9, IV, online: https://ised-isde.canada.ca/site/strategic-policy-sector/en/marketplace-framework-policy/

allow the Bureau to consider a merger *ex post* with better information about its competitive effects," including to assess the impact of the acquisition of a potential or nascent competitor.[257]

The one-year limitation period was retained for mergers which are the subject of an advance ruling certificate request or section 114 notification. Where the Bureau has been given fulsome notification and an opportunity to review the transaction in advance, the rationale for a longer, after the fact, limitation period is reduced.

2) Final Remedies

Section 92 provides for a number of potential remedies against proposed and completed mergers.

- section 92(1)(e)—**completed merger**: to dissolve the merger, to dispose of assets or shares or with consent, to take any other action
- section 92(1)(f)—**proposed merger**: not to proceed in whole or part with the merger; in addition or in lieu thereof, prohibition of acts or things done (where the merger is completed in whole or part); and with consent, to take any other action

A final remedy is also possible through the general consent order provisions.

- section 105—permitting a consent order, if the transaction could be the subject of an order
- section 106—the Tribunal may rescind or vary a consent order

a) The Remedial Standard

Until 2024, the minimum standard for a merger remedy under the jurisprudence was whether it eliminated the likely substantial prevention or lessening of competition that the merger caused. The remedy did not necessarily need to restore the pre-merger competitive situation.[258] The Commissioner's February, 2022 submission on competition law reform stated, "[t]he remedy standard established in the case law does not restore competition to pre-merger levels, allowing merging parties to

---

competition-policy/consultation-future-competition-policy-canada/future-canadas-competition-policy-consultation-what-we-heard-report.

257 E Iacobucci, CD Howe Institute Commentary No 658 "Uncertainty and the Burden of Proof in Competition Law" (May 2024) at 10.

258 *Canada (Director of Investigation and Research) v Southam Inc*, [1997] 1 SCR 748 at paras 82–85.

accumulate market power and harm the economy."[259] The Commissioner described this standard as "out of step with important foreign counterparts" including the EU, US and UK.[260] In a March 2023 submission in response to the Government of Canada's consultation and discussion paper *The Future of Competition Policy in Canada*, the Commissioner recommended amending the Act "to provide that the Tribunal's remedial order shall restore competition to the level that would have prevailed but for the merger."[261]

Parliament adopted the new standard recommended by the Commissioner in its 2024 amendments to the Act.[262] Section 92(1)(e) now requires that where a merger has been completed, the remedy must "restore competition to the level that would have prevailed but for the merger"; section 92(1)(f) requires that a remedy for proposed mergers must "preserve the level of competition that would prevail but for the merger." The new remedies tests may increase the incentive for parties to propose an up-front remedy which might be accepted by the Commissioner, as if the matter is challenged and results in a remedy, the remedy must not only alleviate any substantial anti-competitive effects but restore competition to its pre-merger level.

b) Completed Mergers

If the Tribunal finds a completed merger is likely to prevent or lessen competition substantially, it has three options. First, under section 92(1)(e)(i), it may "dissolve" the merger, meaning that the parties are put back in the position they were before the merger. The Tribunal has held under a dissolution, "the merger no longer exists and the parties are separated as before the merger."[263]

Second, under section 92(1)(e)(ii), the Tribunal has the power to order the disposal of assets or shares to a third party. This involves "'getting

259 Competition Bureau Canada, "Examining the Canadian *Competition Act* in the Digital Era, Submission by the Competition Bureau" (8 February 2022) [Bureau Submissions 2022] at s 2, online: https://ised-isde.canada.ca/site/competition-bureau-canada/en/how-we-foster-competition/promotion-and-advocacy/regulatory-adviceinterventions-competition-bureau/examining-canadian-competition-act-digital-era,

260 *Ibid*, s 2.4.

261 Competition Bureau Canada, "The Future of Competition Policy in Canada, Submission by the Competition Bureau" (15 March 2023) at s 1.6, online: https://ised-isde.canada.ca/site/competition-bureau-canada/en/how-we-foster-competition/promotion-and-advocacy/regulatory-adviceinterventions-competition-bureau/future-competition-policy-canada [Bureau Submissions 2023].

262 *Bill C-59 2024*, above note 30, ss 249(1.1) and (1.2).

263 *Canada (Commissioner of Competition) v Canadian Waste Services Holdings Inc*, *[2001] CCTD No 32 [Canadian Waste Services* Remedies] at para 37.

rid of' something that is owned" or the "transfer [of] ownership over property." In contrast, "the creation of a contract, post-merger, to provide a service to somebody does not constitute disposal of an asset" and therefore does not fall within the Tribunal's authority under the provision.[264]

Ordering the disposal of assets or shares has been described as a "blunt instrument" given that it involves a divestiture of the substance of the merger against the will of the parties.[265] However, it has the benefit of being simple and not requiring the ongoing supervision or assessment of behaviour. The Tribunal in *Canadian Waste Services* cited the following passage from the US Supreme Court's *DuPont* decision in approving an order for divestiture of a landfill by the acquirer within ninety days, or failing that, through a trustee:

> Divestiture or dissolution has traditionally been the remedy for *Sherman Act* violations whose heart is intercorporate combination and control . . . . Divestiture has been called the most important of antitrust remedies. It is simple, relatively easy to administer, and sure. It should always be in the forefront of a court's mind when a violation of [s] 7 has been found.[266]

The blunt nature of divestiture creates room for the third option under section 92(1)(e)(iii), an order on the consent of the party against whom it is made, and the Commissioner. The Federal Court of Appeal has noted "the all-or-nothing nature of the orders that can be given under subparas (i) and (ii)[,] which no doubt [gives the consent order power in] subpara (iii) its vitality and increase its utility."[267] Consent of the parties opens the potential for behavioural remedies not available under dissolution or divestiture.[268]

c) Proposed Mergers

Section 92(1)(f) provides the Tribunal the authority to order that a proposed merger not proceed, in whole or in part. The Tribunal also has

---

264 *Ibid* at paras 41 and 44–45.

265 *Canada (Director of Investigation and Research) v Air Canada* (1993), 49 CPR (3d) 417 (FCA) at para 21 [*Air Canada*].

266 *Canadian Waste Services* Remedies, above note 277 at para 111, citing *United States v EI Du Pont de Nemours*, 366 US 316 (1961) at para 24.

267 *Air Canada*, above note 279 at para 21.

268 *Canadian Waste Services* Remedies, above note 277 at para 47. See also Canada, Competition Bureau, *Competition Bureau Merger Remedies Study* (11 August 2011), online: www.competitionbureau.gc.ca/eic/site/cb-bc.nsf/vwapj/cb-merger-remedy-study-summary-e.pdf/$FILE/cb-merger-remedy-study-summary-e.pdf at 8. See also Deborah L Feinstein, "Conduct Merger Remedies: Tried but Not Tested" (2011) 26:1 *Antitrust* 5.

authority to prohibit the doing of "any act or thing" which it finds necessary to avoid a substantial prevention or lessening of competition should the merger (in the future) be completed in whole or part. That might, for example, involve a prohibition of the closure or other disposition of a part of a merged business so that it may be available for divestiture to a third party, if necessary to alleviate the effects of the merger on competition.

As with a completed merger, the Tribunal also has the authority to order a "person to take any other action" with the consent of that person and the Commissioner.[269]

d) Consent Order Applications

Section 105 permits "[t]he Commissioner and a person in respect of whom the Commissioner has applied" for, *inter alia*, relief against a merger, to enter into a consent agreement that "may be filed with the Tribunal for immediate registration."[270] Under subsection 105(4), registration gives the agreement binding effect, as an order of the Tribunal:

> Upon registration of the consent agreement, the proceedings, if any, are terminated, and the consent agreement has the same force and effect, and proceedings may be taken, as if it were an order of the Tribunal.

The section permits the Commissioner to obtain an enforceable order to cover settlement agreements, which, for example, provide for the divestiture of assets forming part of a merger when deemed necessary to avoid the potential for a substantial prevention or lessening of competition. Prior to 2002, section 105 provided that the Tribunal could issue a consent order "without hearing such evidence as would ordinarily be placed before the Tribunal had the application been contested or further contested." However, in practice, the process was cumbersome. It was described by the Tribunal itself as "time-consuming, unpredictable and expensive."[271] It had the effect of discouraging settlement by consent order, encouraging more informal settlements supported by undertakings given to the Commissioner. These informal agreements created uncertainty both for the private sector and for law enforcement.[272] As a result, Parliament passed amendments in 2002 to "streamline the

---

269 *Competition Act*, above note 1, s 92(1)(f)(iii)(B).

270 *Ibid*, s 105(2).

271 *Burns Lake Native Development Corp v Canada (Commissioner of Competition), [2006] CCTD No 16 at para 28 [Burns Lake]*.

272 See Neil Campbell, Hudson Janisch & Michael Trebilcock, "Rethinking the Role of the Competition Tribunal" (1997) 76 *Canadian Bar Review* 297 at 313.

settlement process and make it faster and more predictable."[273] The streamlined process does not require any evidence to be filed at the time of registration of a consent agreement.[274]

Subsection 106(2) provides a narrow basis for the Tribunal to vary or rescind the terms of a consent agreement. The subsection requires an application within sixty days after its registration by a "person directly affected by a consent agreement, other than a party to that agreement." The Tribunal may only grant the application "if it finds that the person has established that the terms could not be the subject of an order of the Tribunal." In *Kobo Inc v Canada (Commissioner of Competition)*, the Federal Court of Appeal upheld the Tribunal's conclusions that the review role under section 106(2) is narrow.[275] The Tribunal held that its authority is limited to reviewing whether the agreement registered is "the type of order(s) that the Tribunal has the jurisdiction to make," whether the consent agreement application filed discloses basic information about the agreement and the elements of the reviewable trade practice in question, and "whether one or more of the terms of a consent agreement are unenforceable or would lead to no enforceable obligation, for example, because they are too vague."[276]

e) Changed Circumstances: Varying or Rescinding an Order

Section 106(1) permits the Tribunal to "rescind or vary a consent agreement or an order made," on application by "the Commissioner or the person who consented to the agreement, or the person against whom the order was made." The basis is either consent of the parties to the agreement (or person subject to the order),[277] or a finding by the Tribunal that:

> [106(1)] (a) the circumstances that led to the making of the agreement or order have changed and, in the circumstances that exist at the time the application is made, the agreement or order would not have been made or would have been ineffective in achieving its intended purpose.

---

273 *Kobo Inc v Canada (Commissioner of Competition), [2014] CCTD No 14 at para 71 [Kobo]*, citing *Rona Inc v Canada (Commissioner of Competition)*, [2005] CCTD No 17 at para 71 [*Rona Inc*].

274 *Burns Lake, above note 286 at para 78.*

275 *Rakuten Kobo Inc v Canada (Commissioner of Competition), 2015 FCA 149.*

276 *Kobo, above note 288, Order.*

277 This has occurred in numerous cases. See, e.g., *Canada (Commissioner of Competition) v Pfizer Inc*, [2016] CCTD No 10; *Canada (Commissioner of Competition) v Bank of Montreal, [2003] CCTD No 7; Canada (Commissioner of Competition) v BCE Inc, [2018] CCTD No 1. The subsection applies to orders made under Part VIII of the Act ("Matters Reviewable by the Tribunal"), except interim orders under s 103.3 and consent orders entered into on applications by private parties under section 106.1.*

In *Air Canada*, Hugessen JA of the Federal Court of Appeal held that assessing "the circumstances that led to the making of the order" involves "a simple causal relationship between the circumstances and the order, but no more. It is not necessary . . . to relate the circumstances to the purposes sought to be achieved by the order, although it is of course always legitimate to look to such purposes as a guide to identifying some of the circumstances leading to it."[278]

In *Canadian Waste Services*, the Tribunal made an order of divestiture of the Ridge landfill site after a contested hearing in 2001. In 2003, Canadian Waste sought to vary the divestiture to cover a different landfill on the basis of changed circumstances related to events surrounding expansion of landfills since the order. The Tribunal denied the application on the basis that "it is not open to CWS to raise revised expectations about timing as changes of circumstances when the facts which could reasonably have been expected to impact the timing were known to CWS and not presented at the Section 92 Hearing."[279] In a procedural ruling in *Canadian Waste*, the Tribunal also held that "the present tense suggests that predictions and uncertain future events are not circumstances as that term is used in subsection 106(1)(a) of the Act."[280]

The nature of changed circumstances was also addressed in *Rona Inc v Canada (Commissioner of Competition)*. In that case, Rona Inc acquired Réno-Dépôt's twenty home improvement stores in Ontario and Quebec in 2003. Rona agreed to divest the Réno-Dépôt store in Sherbrooke in order to address the Commissioner's concerns that that portion of the acquisition would substantially lessen competition, and entered into a consent agreement to that effect. In 2005, before the divestiture had been completed, Rona sought to rescind the consent agreement on the basis that a Home Depot store was opening in Sherbrooke which, it argued, constituted a change in circumstances, meaning that "the agreement or order would not have been made" under section 106(1). The Commissioner opposed the application on the basis that the potential entry of Home Depot was known at the time of the agreement and that allowing the rescission would encourage parties to intentionally delay divestitures. The Tribunal disagreed, finding on the evidence that "the arrival of a competitor of such stature addresses the concerns about a substantial

---

278 *Air Canada*, above note 279 at para 14.

279 *Canadian Waste Services Holdings Inc v Commissioner of Competition, [2004] CCTD No 10 at para 37.*

280 *Canadian Waste Services Holdings Inc v Commissioner of Competition, [2003] CCTD No 25 at para 15.*

lessening of competition."[281] It rescinded the agreement, and noted that in the language of section 106(1):

> Parliament has recognized that human predictions are sometimes flawed, and that there can be a change in the status of a market in which the Commissioner sees fit to intervene. Parliament decided that it was not appropriate to insist on the enforcement of a consent agreement or order if the circumstances that prevailed when the remedial measure was adopted later change and it is established that the new circumstances eliminate the need for the measure.[282]

f) Enforcement of Consent Orders

In 2024, Parliament added s 106.2, which provides the Tribunal authority to impose remedies, including a $10,000 a day monetary penalty, on persons who have failed to comply or are likely to fail to comply with a consent agreement registered under section 105.

3) Interim Remedies

The legislation provides for a number of interim remedies in respect of mergers:

- section 100—an interim order may be made against proposed mergers where there is no section 92 application
- section 104—an interim order may be made against a merger based on the common law injunction test where the Commissioner has already filed an application against the merger under section 92
- section 123.1—an interim or final order may be made for failure to comply with merger notification requirements

a) Section 100 Interim Order

Section 100 is a special interim remedy for mergers that recognizes that transactions related to mergers may harm competition or the public interest. It permits the Commissioner to enjoin the cessation of "any act or thing . . . directed toward the completion or implementation of the proposed merger." Its history was described by the Tribunal in *Canada (Commissioner of Competition) v Labatt Brewing Co*:

> Before 1999, section 100 included as a condition of the making of an interim order a finding by the Tribunal that the merger was

281 *Rona Inc*, above note 288 at para 97.

282 *Ibid* at para 109.

> "reasonably likely to prevent or lessen competition substantially." . . . A Consultative Panel appointed by then Minister of Industry, the Honourable John Manley . . . recommended changing the wording of section 100 in order to remove the condition of a finding of a reasonable likelihood of substantial lessening or prevention of competition ("SLC" or "SPC").
>
> [T]he provision retained the requirement for the Tribunal to find that its ability to remedy the effect of the merger on competition would be "substantially" impaired absent the interim order (the "impairment issue").[283]

Under section 100(1)(a), the Tribunal may issue an interim order if (1) the Commissioner certifies that more time is needed to complete an inquiry into a proposed merger; and (2) the Tribunal finds that in the absence of an order, there would be a substantial impairment of its ability to remedy the anti-competitive effects. The order may not exceed thirty days, but may be extended up to a further thirty days.

In *Labatt*, the Commissioner applied for an order to stop steps being taken toward the acquisition of Lakeport Breweries. Labatt argued that a hold separate arrangement was sufficient to avoid the substantial impairment of the Tribunal's ability to remedy the effects of the merger. The Tribunal agreed, finding that the Commissioner had not satisfied the applicable test, which is "that absent an order, the Tribunal's remedies post-merger would not be effective to eliminate the SLC."[284]

Under section 100(1)(b), the Tribunal may also enjoin a proposed merger on the basis l that "its completion would result in a contravention" of the notification requirements under section 114.[285] Pre-merger notification is discussed further below.

In 2024, Parliament added s 100(3.1), which creates an automatic "interim interim" injunction against completion of a merger once an application for an interim order is made, which remains in effect "until the application is disposed of by the Tribunal."

b) Section 104 Injunction

Section 104 provides for an interim order when the Commissioner has already filed an application under section 92 against a merger (or

283 *Canada (Commissioner of Competition) v Labatt Brewing Co, [2007] CCTD No 5 at paras 9 and 11 [Labatt]*.

284 *Ibid* at para 48.

285 The 2022 amendments modified the test to employ the quoted words, which means the test requires only an *anticipated* failure to contravene the notification requirements, permitting the Tribunal to provide a remedy prior to failure to comply.

otherwise under Part VIII of the Act). In considering whether to issue an order, the Tribunal must apply "the principles ordinarily considered by superior courts when granting interlocutory or injunctive relief." This language invokes the Supreme Court's *RJR-MacDonald Inc v Canada (Attorney General)* tripartite test, involving determination of whether there is a serious issue to be tried, an assessment of irreparable harm, and weighing the "balance of convenience." [286]

In *Parkland*, the Commissioner obtained a section 104 order in respect of a 2015 merger of retail gasoline facilities. The Commissioner applied for an order to hold separate the retail assets to be acquired in fourteen local markets. The Tribunal issued an interim order in respect of six markets. It noted in comparing sections 100 and 104:

> [T]he language used in the two provisions is now clearly different, reflecting the different objectives . . . and the fact that they correspond to different stages of the merger investigation process undertaken by the Commissioner. At the stage of a section 100 application, no application has yet been made by the Commissioner, a Commissioner's inquiry is on-going and more time is needed to complete the inquiry. In a section 104 application, the Commissioner has reached a further stage in his merger investigation, he has made the decision to file a section 92 application challenging the merger in whole or in part, and he is evidently further along in his review of the transaction at stake.[287]

With respect to irreparable harm, the Commissioner alleged harm from "the ability of the merged entity to increase prices and otherwise limit competition through coordinated behaviour and unilaterally, further to increases in market power and market concentration." The Tribunal held that it must find "clear and non-speculative evidence from which it can be reasonably and logically inferred that the apprehended harm will be suffered by consumers and the Canadian economy."[288] It found such evidence present in the six markets.

In considering the balance of convenience, the Tribunal cited Crampton CJ in *Canada (Commissioner of Competition) v Pearson Canada Inc* to the effect that "[i]t is now well established that, as a statutory authority responsible for the administration and enforcement of the Act, the Commissioner benefits from a presumption that actions taken pursuant to the

286 *RJR-MacDonald Inc v Canada (Attorney General)*, [1994] 1 SCR 311. See also *Canada (Director of Investigation and Research) v Southam Inc, [1991] CCTD No 6.*

287 *Parkland*, above note 104 at para 35.

288 *Ibid* at para 71.

Act are *bona fide* and in the public interest."[289] It held "the Commissioner's review of the Proposed Merger is a *bona fide* investigation. Significant weight should be given to these public interest considerations by the Tribunal."[290] The Tribunal held that the risk of harm to the public interest was not outweighed by evidence of potential inefficiencies or additional costs from the hold separate; that "the balance of inconvenience weighs in favour of the Commissioner and is not offset by the harm that the Respondents would suffer if the interim relief is granted."[291]

In *Superior Propane*, the Federal Court of Appeal refused to stay an order of the Tribunal permitting the acquired firm to no longer be held separate, where it was unconvinced that the evidence disclosed an inability to remedy the anti-competitive effects of the transaction through a later divestiture. Justice Linden held:

> In my view, the metaphor of scrambled eggs is dramatic, but not entirely apt. When one scrambles eggs it is impossible to unscramble them, but a merged company is not exactly like scrambled eggs. It can be broken up, though it is maybe difficult to do so. Competition can be restored. It is not enough for it to be hard or inconvenient to do so. To obtain a stay, the damage must be truly irreparable and proved to be so.[292]

As in the case of the section 100 interim injunction application, in 2024, Parliament provided for an automatic "interim interim" injunction against the merger once a s 104 application for an interim order is made, which remains in effect so that the "the merger shall not be completed until the application is disposed of by the Tribunal."[293]

c) Section 123.1: Failure to Comply with Merger Notification Requirements

Section 123.1 provides authority to a provincial superior court, the Federal Court, and the Tribunal to make a number of orders, including for injunctive relief, if there is a failure to comply with the merger notification requirements and waiting periods (which are described in the next section). The relief available includes:

- an interim order prohibiting actions to complete or to implement the merger;
- dissolution of a completed merger or sale or disposal of assets; and

289 *Canada (Commissioner of Competition) v Pearson Canada Inc*, [2014] FCJ No 430 at para 43 (FC).

290 *Parkland*, above note 104 at para 108.

291 *Ibid* at para 111.

292 *Propane FCA1, above note 8 at para 13.*

293 *Competition Act*, above note 1, s *104(1.1)*.

- administrative monetary penalties of up to $10,000 for each day there has been a failure to comply.

These quite onerous remedies provide a strong incentive for parties to comply with the merger notification requirement set out below. They are in addition to the criminal penalties of up to $50,000 for failure to provide the information required by the notification regime.[294]

In 2022, Parliament adopted a broadly-worded "anti-avoidance" provision targeted at a transaction "designed to avoid the application of" the merger notification provisions. Where a transaction is designed in this way, the injunctive relief and penalty provisions (sections 114 and 123.1) of the Act nonetheless "apply to the substance of the transaction or proposed transaction."[295] The Bureau's Guide to the 2022 amendments explains that the intent of the provision is "to ensure that the mandatory merger notification requirements will apply to transactions that have been designed to avoid notification."[296]

G. MERGER NOTIFICATION

The 1986 amendments require that information about large mergers be provided before such transactions may be completed. This regulatory regime applies whether or not the transaction has any adverse effect on competition.

1) History and Rationale

The *Guide* to the 1986 amendments cited a 1977 Standing Committee Report on the rationale for adding a new merger notification regime to the legislation, stating: "once consummation occurs, it is often too late to obtain meaningful relief even if the merger is ultimately found to be anti-competitive."[297] The *Guide* went on:

> The purpose of the prenotification is to ensure that a thorough and timely review is made of the relatively small number of mergers that are likely to have an adverse effect on competition. If these mergers

294 *Ibid*, s 65(2).
295 *Bill C-19 2022*, above note 28, s 271.
296 Competition Bureau, *Guide to the 2022 Amendments to the Competition Act* (June 24, 2022), online: https://competition-bureau.canada.ca/how-we-foster-competition/education-and-outreach/publications/guide-2022-amendments-competition-act.
297 *Competition Law Amendments, A Guide*, above note 6 at 19.

were allowed to proceed without prior notification, consumers could be placed at a disadvantage through a reduction in choice and potentially higher prices.[298]

The *Guide* explained that prior notification would also promote greater certainty by permitting the parties to the merger "to make a reasoned decision at an early point in time" concerning the impact of the merger provisions.[299]

2) Notification: Application and Thresholds

The gateway to the notification scheme is section 110 of the *Competition Act*, which describes the kinds of transactions which are notifiable. The trigger for notification is the nature and size of the transaction, not its effect on competition.

a) Transaction Types

With respect to the nature of the transactions, notification is required for certain acquisitions of assets, acquisitions of voting shares, amalgamations, and combinations described in section 110, which involve an "operating business."[300] The latter term is broadly defined as "a business undertaking in Canada to which employees employed in connection with the undertaking ordinarily report for work."[301] The test requires some presence in Canada of an active business operation to which employees report.

b) Size Thresholds

The regime in the *Competition Act* requires prior notification of the Commissioner concerning acquisitions of assets and voting shares, amalgamations, and combinations, based upon two thresholds:

1) **Party Size:** The parties to the transaction, together with their affiliates, have assets in Canada or annual revenues in, from, or into Canada, with an aggregate value which exceeds $400 million.
2) **Transaction Size:** The target entity's assets in Canada or revenues from sales in, from or into Canada generated from those assets exceed a threshold prescribed in the regulations ($93 million in 2024).

---

298 *Ibid.*

299 *Ibid.*

300 *Competition Act*, above note 1, s 110. A helpful flow chart of the transaction types and then-existing thresholds can be found in Paul S Crampton, *Mergers and the Competition Act* (Toronto: Carswell, 1990) at 557.

301 *Competition Act*, above note 1, s 108(1).

The first — the $400 million threshold, covering assets and revenues of the parties — is set out in the statute.[302] The second — the monetary thresholds for the target — are set out in the *Canada Gazette*.[303] The *Notifiable Transactions Regulations*[304] indicate the procedure for calculating the aggregate value of assets and gross revenues from sales for the party and transaction size thresholds.

The table below indicates how the transaction size threshold has changed over time.[305]

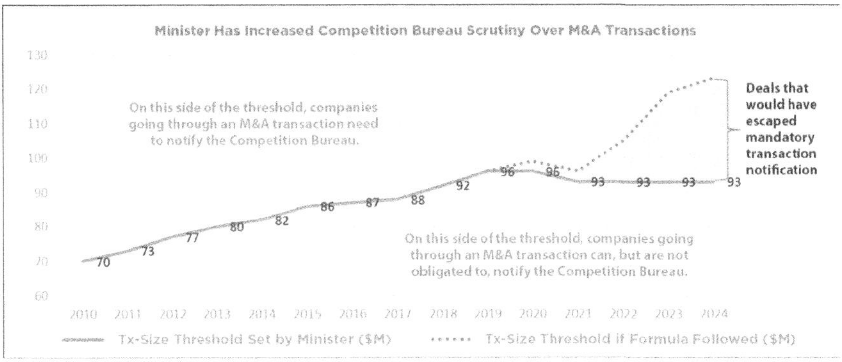

Acquisitions of shares must also exceed certain thresholds relating to the percentage of the voting shares acquired in order for the notification scheme to apply.[306]

c) Notification Applies to All the Parties to the Transaction

The foregoing thresholds apply irrespective of the effect of the transaction on competition. All parties[307] to a proposed transaction meet-

302 *Ibid*, ss 108 and 109; the method of valuation is prescribed in the *Notifiable Transactions Regulations*, SOR 87/348, ss 8 and 9 [*Notifiable Transactions Regulations*]. A greater amount may also be prescribed.

303 See, e.g., *Canada Gazette*, Part I, Volume 155, Number 7 (13 February 2021), online: https://canadagazette.gc.ca/rp-pr/p1/2021/2021-02-13/pdf/g1-15507.pdf.

304 *Notifiable Transactions Regulations*, above note 313.

305 Canada, Innovation, Science and Economic Development, "Backgrounder – Merger Notification Threshold" (27 February 2024), online: https://ised-isde.canada.ca/site/ised/en/backgrounder-merger-notification-threshold: "Line graph showing an upward trend in the merger notification threshold, set by the Minister of Industry, between 2010 and 2024. The threshold in 2010 was $70 million and rose steadily to $96 million in 2019 and 2020 before being set at $93 million from 2021 onwards. The graph also highlights an upward trend in the transactions that would have escaped scrutiny from the Competition Bureau since the threshold freeze in 2020."

306 *Competition Act*, above note 1, s 110(3).

307 In the case of share acquisitions, the parties are the person(s) "who propose to acquire the shares and the corporation the shares of which are to be acquired": RSC 1985, c C-34, as am, s 109(2).

ing the thresholds must submit the prescribed information before the transaction may be completed,[308] although they may do so jointly if so authorized.[309]

In the case of an "unsolicited or hostile take-over bid," if the Commissioner receives prescribed prenotification information from the proponent of the take-over and the entity which is the subject of the bid (the target entity) did not already supply prescribed prenotification information, the Commissioner must immediately notify the target entity of such receipt. Within ten days after that notification, the target entity must supply the Commissioner with the prescribed information.[310] This ensures that a hostile takeover proponent can satisfy requirements to supply the Bureau notification information with or without the target's cooperation.

d) Notification Information and Filing Fee

The information to be provided is set out in the *Notifiable Transactions Regulations*. It must be certified under oath or solemn affirmation that it is correct and complete in all material respects.[311] The information required includes

- "a description of the proposed transaction and the business objectives intended to be achieved as a result of it";
- a copy of legal documents "used to implement the proposed transaction";
- a list of "the foreign competition or antitrust authorities that have been notified of the proposed transaction by the parties" and the date(s) thereof;
- details about the parties to the transaction, their businesses, and products sold; and
- "all studies, surveys, analyses and reports that were prepared or received by an officer or director of [each party and its affiliates in Canada, or analogous individuals if not incorporated] for the purpose of evaluating or analysing the proposed transaction with respect to market shares, competition, competitors, markets [etc.]."[312]

A filing fee must accompany notification information.[313]

308 *Competition Act*, above note 1, s 114(1).

309 *Ibid*, s 114(4).

310 *Ibid*, s 114(3).

311 *Ibid*, s 118.

312 *Notifiable Transactions Regulations*, above note 313, s 16(1).

313 The fee was $73,584 from May 1, 2018, and is adjusted periodically. See Competition Bureau, *Fees and Service Standards Handbook for Mergers and MergerRelated*

e) Supplementary Information Requests

Since 2009,[314] the Bureau has had the authority, similar to that possessed by American antitrust agencies, to send a supplementary information request (SIR) within thirty days after receiving the prescribed merger notification information. The Bureau has stated that such requests apply to "those relatively few transactions that raise a potential substantial lessening or prevention of competition" issue.[315] This additional step was intended to harmonize Canadian with US procedures for merger review.[316] The amendments followed after some criticism of the Commissioner's use of formal power to compel the production of documents,[317] as well as of the time taken for merger review.[318] The SIR request is a powerful tool, because it not only provides valuable information to the Bureau, but also postpones the parties' ability to complete the transaction until thirty days after the SIR information requested has been received by the Commissioner.[319] This gives the Commissioner additional time to determine whether or not to challenge, or to prepare materials to challenge, a transaction, without the need to seek an injunction during that waiting period.

f) Waiting Periods

Notifiable mergers may not be completed until the following waiting periods have elapsed (see section 123 of the *Competition Act*):

1) **Prescribed Information:** 30 days after the day on which the information prescribed in the *Notifiable Transactions Regulations* was received by the Commissioner
2) **SIR Information:** if a supplementary information request (SIR) has been made, 30 days after the day on which the requested information was received by the Commissioner

---

Matters (1 May 2018), online: www.competitionbureau.gc.ca/eic/site/cb-bc.nsf/eng/04358.html.

314 *Budget Implementation Act, 2009*, SC 2009, c 2, s 437.

315 Canada, Competition Bureau, *Merger Review Process Guidelines* (8 September 2015), online: www.competitionbureau.gc.ca/eic/site/cb-bc.nsf/vwapj/merger-review-process-2015-e.pdf/$FILE/merger-review-process-2015-e.pdf at 1 [*Merger Review Process Guidelines*].

316 Canada, Competition Policy Review Panel, *Compete to Win* (Ottawa: Public Works and Government Services Canada, 2008), online: www.ic.gc.ca/eic/site/cprp-gepmc.nsf/vwapj/compete_to_win.pdf/$file/compete_to_win.pdf at 53 and 56.

317 Following from *Canada (Commissioner of Competition) v Labatt Brewing Co, 2008 FC 59*.

318 See, for example, Neil Campbell & Sorcha O'Carroll, "The Americanization of Canada's Competition Act" (2009) 48:3 *Canadian Business Law Journal* 446 at 456, n51.

319 *Competition Act*, above note 1, s 123(b).

The waiting periods can be curtailed if

- pursuant to subsection 123(2), the parties are notified that the Commissioner does not, at that time, intend to make an application under section 92 (in the context of a "No-Action letter"[320]);
- the parties receive an Advance Ruling Certificate (ARC, described below); or
- the Commissioner, pursuant to paragraph 113(c) of the Act, waives, during the year preceding the day on which the transaction was completed, the waiting period because substantially the same information was already provided pursuant an ARC request.

In a hostile takeover, subsection 123(3) of the Act provides that the waiting period is determined "without reference to the day on which the [prescribed] information . . . is received" from the target corporation, to avoid the potential for the target to delay compliance with the notification requirements and hence frustrate the transaction's completion.

g) Bureau Guidance

The Bureau's *Procedures Guide for Notifiable Transactions and Advance Ruling Certificates* provides detailed guidance on the notification thresholds, information requirements, relevant forms, and other details.[321] The Bureau has also issued interpretation guidelines "to assist parties and their counsel in interpreting and applying the provisions of the Act relating to notifiable transactions."[322]

H. THE MERGER REVIEW PROCESS

1) Bureau's Procedures Guide and Service Standards

As noted above, the Bureau has issued practical guidelines for the merger review process, including the waiting periods, information requirements, and steps for negotiation of timing agreements governing the provision of information and transaction closing.[323] More detail on notification and ARCs is available in a separate *Procedures Guide*[324] as well

320 Canada, Competition Bureau, *Procedures Guide for Notifiable Transactions and Advance Ruling Certificates Under the Competition Act* (1 November 2010), online: www.competitionbureau.gc.ca/eic/site/cb-bc.nsf/eng/03302.html, section 2.5 [*Procedures Guide*].

321 *Ibid.*

322 *Ibid* at 11. See Canada, Competition Bureau, *Pre-Merger Notification Interpretation Guidelines*, online: https://www.competitionbureau.gc.ca/eic/site/cb-bc.nsf/eng/03357.html [*Pre-Merger Guidelines*].

323 *Merger Review Process Guidelines*, above note 325.

324 *Procedures Guide*, above note 330.

as in the *Pre-Merger Notification Interpretation Guidelines*.[325] Finally, the Bureau has issued a *Fees and Service Standards Handbook for Mergers and Merger-Related Matters*, which provides further practical information on typical timing for review of complex and non-complex matters, how to seek written opinions from the Bureau, and applicable fees.[326]

Counsel can play a significant role in addressing the Bureau's concerns in respect of a merger through the provision of timely and complete information, and by discussing potential methods of resolution. As noted above, resolution may take the form of consent orders, but it may also take the form of more informal arrangements, such as altering a transaction so that it no longer raises concerns about its effects on competition.

2) Advance Ruling Certificates (ARCs) and No-Action Letters

Section 102 provides that if the Commissioner "is satisfied by a party or parties to a proposed transaction that he would not have sufficient grounds on which to apply to the Tribunal under section 92," an ARC may be issued to that effect. An ARC bars the Commissioner from applying to the Tribunal under section 92 "if the transaction is completed within one year after the certificate is issued."[327] It also exempts the transaction from merger notification.[328] The bar applies to a section 92 application founded on "information that is the same or substantially the same as the information on the basis of which the certificate was issued." In other words, the Commissioner is not precluded from bringing an application if the parties supplied incorrect or incomplete information in the process of requesting an ARC.

Applicable fees and the information required in order to obtain an ARC are described in the Bureau's *Handbook* and in other guidance described above. If the Bureau is not satisfied that the information supplied meets the clear requirements for the issuance of an ARC, the

325 Sixteen separate guidelines are available online: *Pre-Merger Guidelines*, above note 332.

326 Canada, Competition Bureau, *Fees and Service Standards Handbook for Mergers and MergerRelated Matters* (1 May 2018), online: www.competitionbureau.gc.ca/eic/site/cb-bc.nsf/eng/04358.html. On 21 May 2020, the Bureau released a *Model Timing Agreement for Merger Reviews Involving Efficiencies* which addresses, in particular, steps and timelines when parties to a merger assert efficiencies under section 96; see Canada, Competition Bureau, *Model Timing Agreement for Merger Reviews Involving Efficiencies* (21 May 2020), online: www.competitionbureau.gc.ca/eic/site/cb-bc.nsf/eng/04531.html.

327 *Competition Act*, above note 1, s 103.

328 *Ibid*, s 113(b).

Commissioner may still issue a "No-Action Letter," "indicating that the Commissioner does not, *at that time*, intend to make an application under section 92 in respect of the proposed transaction."[329] Such a letter provides the Commissioner the ability to re-open an examination within the one-year limitation period, for example, if new information comes forward. It thus does not provide the level of certainty of an ARC that no application will be forthcoming.

3) Confidentiality

Parliament recognized that information obtained by the Bureau is often commercially sensitive and that its disclosure may cause competitive harm to parties which supply information, whether voluntarily, or under compulsion. The Bureau must be able to protect information obtained from whistleblowers, witnesses, and complainants to ensure their cooperation and protection in the course of enforcement of the Act. For these reasons, the Act provides that all formal inquiries must be carried out in private.[330] Section 29 also prohibits those who enforce the Act from communicating specified information, which includes:

- merger notification information, including that notice of a transaction has been provided
- information obtained with formal powers
- information supplied in support of an ARC request
- information provided voluntarily[331]

The prohibition on disclosure in section 29 is subject to a number of limited exceptions. Information may be disclosed

- to a Canadian law enforcement agency;
- for the purposes of administration or enforcement of the Act;
- when the information has been made public; and
- when it has been authorized by the person who provided the information.[332]

The Bureau has issued a Bulletin which provides a description of its practices with respect to confidentiality, including details of when the foregoing exceptions may apply. The Bulletin notes:

---

329 *Procedures Guide*, above note 329 at 14 [emphasis added].

330 *Competition Act*, above note 1, s 10(3).

331 *Ibid*, s 29(1)(a)–(e).

332 *Ibid*, ss 29(1) and (2).

> The Bureau is committed to treating confidential information responsibly and in accordance with the law because maintaining confidentiality is fundamental to the Bureau's ability to pursue its responsibilities under the Act and to maintain its integrity as a law enforcement agency.[333]

Consistent with the foregoing statement, in 2014, the Bureau issued a further Bulletin to provide greater transparency concerning its disclosure of information about investigations to industry participants and others. The Bulletin specifically addresses its disclosure practices used in the course of examining mergers.[334]

I. CONCLUSION

The *Competition Act* equips the Canadian Competition Bureau with the tools to review whether a merger transaction is likely to permit parties to substantially prevent or lessen competition. Those tools include notification of large transactions in advance of their completion, powers to obtain records and evidence, and the ability to seek injunctive relief and final remedies including divestiture or dissolution.

The substantive test governing merger review is focused on the impact of the transaction on market power. As a result, only transactions which create, maintain, or enhance market power, or give the parties substantial market control, are likely to raise issues under the Act. The vast majority of the cases reviewed by the Competition Bureau do not result in a challenge or the need for a remedy.[335]

With the repeal of the efficiencies defence, efficiencies must be factored into the general assessment of competitive effect under section 92. In the United States, an assessment of efficiencies focused on their consumer welfare impact has been favoured and is one course open to

333 Canada, Competition Bureau, *Information Bulletin on the Communication of Confidential Information under the Competition Act* (30 September 2013), online: www.competitionbureau.gc.ca/eic/site/cb-bc.nsf/eng/03597.html, Preface.

334 Canada, Competition Bureau, *Information Bulletin on the Communication during Inquiries* (26 June 2014), online: www.competitionbureau.gc.ca/eic/site/cb-bc.nsf/eng/03747.html.

335 See the Bureau's "Monthly Report of Concluded Merger Reviews," online at www.competitionbureau.gc.ca/eic/site/cb-bc.nsf/eng/04290.html. In 2019, for example, only one of the 216 concluded reviews was not resolved by a "No Action" letter or ARC. The one case was a consent application in *Commissioner v Thoma Bravo, LLC/Aucerna* CT-2019-002, Registered Consent Agreement (20 August 2019).

the Tribunal as it considers how this factor may or may not apply to the assessment of competitive effects.

Canada's merger review regime has produced only a limited amount of jurisprudence, given that the vast majority of cases pose no issue, and that those which do are often resolved through a negotiation between the parties and the Commissioner. That informal procedure has the advantage of expeditiousness, but it means that guidance from decided cases has not been abundant. This reflects the desire of most merging parties to avoid being subject to a lengthy and costly public hearing process should they contest the Commissioner's decision to challenge a transaction. With the adoption of a structural presumption, the Commissioner may be emboldened to expedite merger review and bring more cases. This would be welcome in providing more jurisprudence and guidance on the meaning of the law, particularly in the context of digital markets.

Canada's merger regime is one of over sixty in the world which require notification of merger transactions. This means that in cases involving large multinational mergers, Canada's enforcement decision may not be decisive, and whether the transaction proceeds, or in what form, may be decided elsewhere, or with Canada's competition authority being merely one of many voices.[336] The reality of a globalized economy is that economic decision making by law-enforcement authorities often affects other jurisdictions. Given the nature of the issues raised in competition law merger review, it seems unlikely that there will be any multilateral agreement creating a binding transnational decision-making body for the review of mergers, as exists pursuant to treaties to certain trade disputes.[337] Cooperation and exchanges of information among competition authorities will thus continue to be important for the effective and timely evaluation of mergers affecting multiple jurisdictions.[338]

---

336 See Eleanor M Fox, *GE/Honeywell: The U.S. Merger that Europe Stopped—A Story of the Politics of Convergence*, 331 at 335 in Eleanor M Fox & Daniel A Crane, eds, *Antitrust Stories* (NY: Thomson/West, 2007).

337 See the history of efforts in this direction summarized in D Daniel Sokol, "Monopolists Without Borders: The Institutional Challenge of International Antitrust in a Global Gilded Age" (2007) 4:1 *Berkeley Business Law Journal* 37 at 50–51: "even with a proposed reduction in scope at the WTO, there remained significant divergence in views, preventing advanced negotiations on binding antitrust WTO rules. By 2003, the Working Group agreed that any binding standards for antitrust law were not feasible or desirable. In 2003, at its Cancun Ministerial, the WTO ended the Working Group on the Interaction Between Trade and Competition Policy and dropped antitrust from the trade agenda. Similarly, by 2006, the OECD, in response to U.S. concerns, had dropped the Joint Group on Trade and Competition."

338 *Ibid* at 121–22; Daniel A Crane, *The Institutional Structure of Antitrust Enforcement* (Oxford: Oxford University Press, 2011) at ch 12, "Toward International Institutions?"

CHAPTER 6

AGREEMENTS BETWEEN COMPETITORS

A. INTRODUCTION

This chapter is focused on "horizontal" collusive and concerted practices—i.e., agreements and other anti-competitive arrangements between competitors (other than mergers and joint dominance). First, the policy concerns surrounding these practices will be discussed. Second, the history of the Canadian provisions will be examined. Finally, their structure and the legal tests will be described.

Agreements among competitors that reduce competition cover a wide spectrum of behaviour, from clearly harmful to potentially beneficial. This is true even for price fixing. At the harmful end of the spectrum are "naked" price agreements; for example, gasoline station operators on opposite corners at a busy city intersection who, on a Thursday night before a long weekend, secretly decide to increase the price of gas five cents a litre for the following four days. Outraged drivers, seeing the prices at the two stations rise simultaneously Friday morning, would have little difficulty viewing such clandestine conduct as worthy of sanction if they were made aware of it.

On the other hand, price fixing may be ancillary to potentially beneficial behaviour. For example, lawyers in a partnership may agree on their fees, including those they will charge for a simple property conveyance, which they post on the firm's website.[1] Cooperation made possible by the partnership on such matters as mentoring junior lawyers, sharing expertise and support staff, choosing areas of specialization, and sharing of risk, provides benefits which must be weighed against the competitive impact of its fee agreement. The partnership permits the operation of an efficient law firm with the resources needed to provide competent services.[2] It is unlikely to create concerns about limiting output, where there are other firms providing legal services in the area.[3]

The foregoing examples illustrate the need for competition law to be capable of screening out harmful behaviour from beneficial horizontal collusive conduct. The *Competition Act* does this in a number of ways. The principal method is by employing two different regimes for the review of anti-competitive agreements. On the one hand, the Act creates criminal offences for conspiracies to fix prices, share markets, and limit production that are not ancillary to a broader agreement. Other kinds of behaviour, such as agreements between financial institutions and bid-rigging, are also subject to criminal prohibitions. On the other hand, anti-competitive agreements that are not prohibited may still be examined by way of a civil review before the Competition Tribunal, to determine whether they are likely to prevent or lessen competition substantially and should be subject to a remedy.

This two-track approach to the review of anti-competitive agreements, criminal and civil came into effect in 2010. It was born from the realization that the previous criminal law regime, which had remained largely unchanged since 1889, was in dire need of reform and replacement. The 2010 reforms greatly simplified and improved the law.

---

1 Such advertising is, for example, permitted in Ontario under s 4.2 of the *Rules of Professional Conduct* adopted by the Law Society of Ontario pursuant to its authority under the *Law Society Act*, RSO 1990, c L.8.

2 Presley L Warner & Michael J Trebilcock, "Re-Thinking Price Fixing Law" (1993) 38 *McGill Law Journal* 679 at n 21 [Warner & Trebilcock]:

> [P]artnership agreements among professionals almost always increase economic welfare. Partners may share administrative and overhead costs and provide a broad range of services to clients which professionals working on their own could not offer. The renowned American judge Oliver Wendell Holmes once remarked that if antitrust laws were interpreted so as to prohibit partnership agreements, this "would make eternal the *bellum omnium contra omnes* [the war of all against all] and disintegrate society so far as it could into individual atoms."

3 Robert Bork, *The Antitrust Paradox* (New York: Basic Books, 1978) at 265.

FIGURE 6.1. The service station: the public's window on price competition

B. THE POLICY CONCERNS WITH CONCERTED PRACTICES BETWEEN COMPETITORS

1) Hard Core Cartels

In 1998, the Organization for Economic Cooperation and Development (OECD), an international organization of thirty-six of the world's leading economies, passed a recommendation that "[m]ember countries should ensure that their competition laws effectively halt and deter hard core cartels." These were defined as agreements or arrangements "by competitors to fix prices, make rigged bids (collusive tenders), establish output restrictions or quotas, or share or divide markets."[4] The Preamble to the recommendation stated:

> [H]ard core cartels are the most egregious violations of competition law and . . . injure consumers in many countries by raising prices and restricting supply, thus making goods and services completely unavailable to some purchasers and unnecessarily expensive for others.

The justification for an outright ban on price fixing and market sharing agreements rests on the view "that they are so clearly anti-competitive in nature, so devoid of any purpose except the stifling of competition that they may be conclusively be presumed to be illegal without

---

4 OECD, *Recommendation of the Council Concerning Effective Action Against Hard Core Cartels* (25 March 1998), online: www.oecd.org/daf/competition/2350130.pdf [OECD *Recommendations Against Hard Core Cartels*].

further enquiry once the Crown has established that such restraint has occurred."[5] This view is anchored in policy concerns which include impacts on consumers, effects on rivalry, harm to efficiency, and moral or ethical concerns.

Cartels can increase prices and transfer income from consumers to producers. The Supreme Court of Canada observed in a case addressing the scope of a civil action for damages from alleged price fixing:

> [T]he purpose of the *Competition Act* is to "maintain and encourage competition in Canada" with a view to providing consumers with "competitive prices and product choices" (s. 1.1). A conspiracy to price-fix is the "very antithesis of the *Competition Act*'s objective."[6]

Background information accompanying proposed amendments to the conspiracy provisions in 1984 explained that "cartel-like agreements involuntarily redistribute income from consumers, or other buyers, to sellers. In effect, the parties to a collusive agreement are imposing a 'tax' on the buyers of the goods and services."[7] The Competition Bureau describes this kind of impact from cartels as follows:

> When suppliers conspire to fix prices, purchasers throughout the supply chain, both businesses and consumers, can be harmed; higher prices will be paid by someone. The ability of small and medium-sized businesses to compete may also be affected by artificial cost increases resulting from a cartel. Bid-rigging targeting private or government procurement increases the cost of goods and services. Where government procurement is affected, the cost increase caused by the cartel means less public money is available for other important needs.[8]

Collusion also has the effect of reducing or eliminating rivalry, whether in respect of pricing, product quality, or innovation: "[a]greements among competitors to fix prices or share markets . . . relax the pressure for firms to be efficient."[9] Rivalry — the independent jockeying

---

5 William T Stanbury, "Legislation to Control Agreements in Restraint of Trade in Canada," ch 6 [Stanbury] in RS Khemani & William T Stanbury, eds, *Historical Perspectives on Canadian Competition Policy* (Halifax: IRPP, 1991) at 80–81 [Khemani & Stanbury].

6 *Pioneer Corp v Godfrey*, 2019 SCC 42 at para 65.

7 Canada, Consumer and Corporate Affairs, *Amendments to the Combines Investigation Act, Background Information and Explanatory Notes* (Ottawa: Minister of Supply and Services, 1984) at 10 [*Background Information and Explanatory Notes 1984*].

8 Canada, Competition Bureau, "About Cartels: Fact Sheet" (20 April 2017), online: www.competitionbureau.gc.ca/eic/site/cb-bc.nsf/eng/02442.html#sec02.

9 *Background Information and Explanatory Notes* 1984, above note 7 at 10.

and striving for superior position and advantage—is a key driver of competitive markets. The economists' paradigm of the perfectly competitive market, and the beneficial results it produces, depends on firms behaving independently in making pricing and other competitive decisions. Rivalry creates competitive pressure on suppliers to lower production costs and to innovate. Competition creates "a kind of Darwinian selection: in competitive environments inefficient firms lose sales and, at the limit, are driven out of business; more efficient and innovative firms gain sales."[10] Competitive markets thus have a tendency to weed out the inefficient firms—a natural process not present where a market has been subject to monopolistic pricing by a cartel. Dulling rivalry can result in productive and dynamic inefficiency.

FIGURE 6.2. Adam Smith

At the economy-wide level, it has been observed that "vigorous domestic rivalry fuels the growth of world-class industries."[11] Economic rivalry can stimulate a strong, dynamic, and robust domestic economy.[12] Conversely, failure to ensure rivalry can lead to a culture of collusion, whether within a country or a corporation.[13] One American multinational became infamous for an internal corporate slogan that "the competitors are our friends, and the customers are our enemies," coined by an executive during participation in the 1990s lysine cartel.[14] This recalls Adam Smith's famous warning from his treatise *The Wealth of Nations* in 1776, that rivalry is by no means the natural state of affairs for many market participants:

> People of the same trade seldom meet together, even for merriment and diversion, but the conversation ends in a conspiracy against the public, or in some contrivance to raise prices. It is impossible indeed

10 Matthew Chiasson & Paul A Johnson, "Canada's (In)Efficiency Defence: Why Section 96 May Do More Harm than Good for Economic Efficiency and Innovation" (2019) 32:1 *Canadian Competition Law Review* 1 at 8.

11 Harry S Gerla, "Restoring Rivalry as a Central Concept in Antitrust Law" (1996) 75 *Nebraska Law Review* 209 at 233 [Gerla].

12 Michael E Porter, "Competition and Antitrust: Toward a Productivity-Based Approach to Evaluating Mergers and Joint Ventures" (2001) 46 *Antitrust Bulletin* 919 at 932: "Unless a firm is forced to compete at home, it will usually quickly lose its competitiveness abroad. Local competition matters for productivity and productivity growth, even in industries whose geographic scope is global."

13 Christopher R Leslie, "Foreign Price-Fixing Conspiracies" (2017) 67 *Duke Law Journal* 557 at 601–3.

14 Kurt Eichenwald, *The Informant* (New York: Broadway Books, 2000). Lysine is used in the production of animal feed.

> to prevent such meetings, by any law which either could be executed, or would be consistent with liberty and justice. But though the law cannot hinder people of the same trade from sometimes assembling together, it ought to do nothing to facilitate such assemblies; much less to render them necessary.[15]

The absence of rivalry can reduce competitive pressure to keep costs in check and result in productive inefficiency. Thus, "the carrot of profits without the stick of competition is not sufficient to guarantee that monopolists will minimize costs, leading to what has been called X-inefficiency."[16] X-inefficiency is a "type of inefficiency which is manifest as excess unit costs of production among firms sheltered from competitive pressure."[17] Efforts to establish and maintain cartels can also result in the inefficient expenditure of resources. This occurs because cartels require policing and monitoring systems necessary to ensure compliance by participants.[18] Richard Posner described this as "the tendency of monopoly rents to be transformed into costs."[19]

Price increases caused by cartels also results in allocative inefficiency: the misallocation of resources that occurs when market power is exercised in the raising of prices above competitive levels.[20] As we saw

---

15 Adam Smith, *The Wealth of Nations* (New York: Dutton & Co, 1910) vol 1 at 117. Figure 6.2. The engraving of Adam Smith is by John Kay, United States, Library of Congress, Digital ID: (b&w film copy neg.) cph 3c01759, online: http://hdl.loc.gov/loc.pnp/cph.3c01759. See also Arthur Austin, "Adam Smith on the Inevitability of Price Fixing" (2005) 55 *Case Western Reserve Law Review* 501.

16 Thomas W Ross, "Proposals for a New Canadian Competition Law on Conspiracy" (1991) 36:4 *Antitrust Bulletin* 851 at 857 [Ross, "Proposals"].

17 Gerla, above note 11 at 224 citing Roger S Frantz, *X-Efficiency: Theory, Evidence and Applications* (Boston: Springer, 1988) at 2–3.

18 Tim Kennish & Thomas W Ross, "Toward a New Canadian Approach to Agreements between Competitors" (1997) 28:1 *Canadian Business Law Journal* 22 at 26 [Kennish & Ross].

19 Richard Posner, "The Social Costs of Monopoly and Regulation" (1975) 83 *Journal of Political Economy* 807 at 808; Patrick Hughes & Margaret Sanderson, "Conspiracy Law and Jurisprudence in Canada: Towards an Economic Approach" (1998) 13:1 *Review of Industrial Organization* 153 at 160, n 26:

> [A] agreement may increase the scope to raise price and restrict output, with a resulting deadweight loss to society. An agreement may also give rise to dynamic costs where the scope to increase price is enhanced by restrictions in nonprice dimensions such as product differentiation, innovation or restrictions on entry by new more efficient rivals. More controversial is the notion of X-inefficiency, i.e., the reduced incentive that conspirators may have to minimize costs. Finally there is the cost of rent seeking.

20 *Canada v Maxzone Auto Parts (Canada) Corp, 2012 FC 1117 at para 86 [Maxzone]*; see also para 55.

in Chapter 3, allocative inefficiency occurs because, as prices rise above competitive levels, consumers turn to less desirable or less efficiently produced substitutes:

> The typical cartel raises price and restricts output. Because this diverts resources to less valued uses, the gain to the cartel in the form of higher profits is not as great as the loss to customers in the form of lost consumers' surplus. This net social loss is referred to as deadweight loss and is quite generally accepted as a significant cost of monopoly.[21]

The same point was made by the Federal Court in a sentencing decision:

> [T]he harm resulting from price fixing . . . includes the wealth transfer from victims to the perpetrators of the offence, as well as the deadweight loss that such agreements bring about for the Canadian economy.[22]

Cartels often employ output restriction to raise prices artificially. The Organization of the Petroleum Exporting Countries (OPEC), the international oil cartel controlling more than a third of the world's production, has repeatedly used this strategy. OPEC members often announce meetings to discuss efforts to cut back on production in order to raise the market price.[23] The US courts have identified output restriction as an indicator of the prejudicial impact of price fixing and other horizontal agreements which restrict competition.[24]

The price increase from a cartel may be significant. For example, two international cartels in the 1990s involved substantial commerce. The citric acid (a food additive and preservative) cartel involved annual world-wide sales during the conspiracy of USD$4.8 billion. Based on an estimated 30 percent price increase during its duration, overcharges amounted to almost USD$1.5 billion. The amino acid lysine (an animal feed additive) cartel reportedly raised prices on more than USD$1.4 billion in global sales, translating into price overcharges of

---

21 Ross, "Proposals," above note 16 at 857.

22 *Maxzone, above note 20 at para 55.*

23 See, e.g., Clifford Krauss, "OPEC and Russia Agree to Cuts in Oil Production to Push Up Prices" *New York Times* (5 December 2019), B4; Jillian Ambrose, "OPEC to Slash Oil Production to Help Prop Up Prices," *The Guardian* (6 December 2019) at 2B2.

24 E Thomas Sullivan & Jeffrey L Harrison, *Understanding Antitrust and its Economic Implications*, 5th ed (Newark: Matthew Bender, 2009) at 107, citing *inter alia*, *FTC v Indiana Federation of Dentists*, 476 US 447 (1986) at 458–59 and *NCAA v Board of Regents*, 468 US 85 (1984) at 104 [*NCAA*].

USD$140 million.[25] In 2005, the OECD reported that research reviewing overcharges in a large number of cartel cases estimated the average overcharge in the range of 20–30 percent, with overcharges for international cartels often higher than those for purely domestic cartels.[26]

While cartels result in allocative inefficiency, they generally do not realize scale economies (which could otherwise lead to the lowering of costs from increased productive efficiency), because each co-conspirator continues to operate separately.[27] As a result, "bare cartels are unambiguously inefficient."[28] For this reason, "most economists favour *per se* prohibition of price-fixing cartels — effectively the rule adopted by US courts from an early date under the *Sherman Act*."[29] That rule was developed in the course of interpreting the broad prohibition in the *Sherman Act* section 1 of "[e]very contract, combination in the form of trust or otherwise, or conspiracy, in restraint of trade or commerce."[30] The rationale for the *per se* rule was described by the US Supreme Court in 1958:

> [T]here are certain agreements or practices which because of their pernicious effect on competition and lack of any redeeming virtue are conclusively presumed to be unreasonable and therefore illegal without elaborate inquiry as to the precise harm they have caused or the business excuse for their use. This principle of *per se* unreasonableness . . . avoids the necessity for an incredibly complicated and prolonged economic investigation into the entire history of the industry involved, as well as related industries, in an effort to determine at large whether a particular restraint has been unreasonable — an inquiry so often wholly fruitless when undertaken. Among the practices which the courts have heretofore deemed to be unlawful in and of themselves are price fixing, division of markets, group boycotts and tying arrangements.[31]

---

25 OECD, *Hard Core Cartels: First Report on the Implementation of the 1998 Recommendation* (2000) at 16 and 23, online: www.oecd.org/competition/cartels/2752129.pdf.

26 OECD, *Hard Core Cartels: Third Report on the Implementation of the 1998 Recommendation* (2005) at 25, online: www.oecd.org/competition/cartels/35863307.pdf.

27 Warner & Trebilcock, above note 2 at 682.

28 Bruce Dunlop, Michael Trebilcock & David McQueen, *Canadian Competition Policy: A Legal and Economic Analysis* (Toronto: Canada Law Book, 1987) at 112 [Dunlop, Trebilcock & McQueen].

29 *Ibid* at 112.

30 15 USC § 1 (1890), as am.

31 *Northern Pacific Railway Co v United States, 356 US 1 (1958) at 8–9 [case citations omitted].*

In addition to the economic objections to hard core cartels are those founded on moral or ethical grounds.[32] Cartels can be seen as undermining "the most fundamental tenets of a market economy, namely that sellers will act independently in seeking competitive advantage."[33] When clandestine, they also create an appearance of dishonesty: "cartels . . . deliberately mislead by pretending to abide by the rules of free competition—in an effort to appropriate a benefit that would not accrue to them if they were open about their intentions."[34]

Along these lines, in an early Canadian bid-rigging case, the trial judge equated the co-conspirators' actions to theft, finding that the parties "took from the public . . . money to which they had no possible claim than any person has when, meeting another in the street, he by force, robs them."[35] Chief Justice Crampton of the Federal Court more recently called price fixing "analogous to fraud and theft," because

> [b]uyers in free market societies are entitled to assume that the prices of the goods and services they purchase have been determined by the forces of competition. When they purchase products that have been the subject of such an agreement, they are effectively defrauded.[36]

In the United States, the Supreme Court has referred to collusion as "the supreme evil of antitrust."[37] A senior official of the US Justice Department's Antitrust Division has described price fixing as "nothing less than theft by well-dressed thieves."[38]

Such strong moral views are not universal; it has been observed that "social norms may typically be weak or sympathetic towards price fixing outside of North America because such practices have historically been treated

---

32 See, generally, Maurice E Stucke, "Morality and Antitrust" [2006] 3 *Columbia Business Law Review* 443 at 498–501.

33 Stanbury, above note 5 at 80.

34 Jennifer A Quaid, "Making Sense of the Shift in Paradigm on Cartel Enforcement: The Case for Applying a Desert Perspective" (2012) 58:1 *McGill Law Journal* 149 at 194.

35 *R v Master Plumbers and Steam Fitters Cooperative Association Limited* (1907), 14 OLR 295 at 304 (CA), commas added.

36 *Maxzone, above* note 20 at para 54.

37 *Verizon Communications v Law Offices of Curtis V Trinko, LLP*, 540 US 398 (2004) at 408.

38 Scott D Hammond, Director of Criminal Enforcement, Antitrust Division, US Department of Justice, "The Fly On The Wall Has Been Bugged—Catching An International Cartel In The Act," EU Competition Law Congress, Dublin (15 May 2001), online: www.justice.gov/atr/speech/fly-wall-has-been-bugged-catching-international-cartel-act.

favourably."[39] In the United Kingdom, for example, coordinated pricing was seen for an extended period as a potentially beneficial and stabilizing practice. It was widespread there in the first half of the twentieth century, and went largely unchallenged under the domestic law until relatively recently.[40] In the rest of Europe, civil rather than criminal enforcement of cartel behaviour is the norm and "the use of incarceration has been virtually unknown."[41] Nonetheless, as reflected in the OECD's 1998 recommendation cited above and other international initiatives, a consensus has developed among the world's leading competition authorities on the need to strengthen laws and make the enforcement of hard core cartel prohibitions (whether civil or criminal) an enforcement priority.[42]

2) Other Agreements Among Competitors Which Lessen Competition

In contrast to hard core cartels, horizontal agreements or other cooperative arrangements affect competition but may have beneficial effects. Sale of businesses, for example, generally occur in conjunction with restrictive covenants that limit the vendor's ability to compete in a defined geographic area and for a fixed period of time. Restrictive covenants protect and enhance the value of a business for both the vendor and the purchaser and may facilitate a transaction which promotes competition by injecting new management, additional resources and fresh energy into the purchased firm. Similarly,

> [p]artnerships, joint ventures and strategic alliances among rivals are ubiquitous and rarely present serious competitive concerns. Quite to the contrary, they often provide a significant source of competitive vigor and product and service innovation.[43]

More difficult to assess are agreements which may resemble price fixing or other arrangements in the "hard core" category, but which

---

39 Andreas Stephan, "Cartel Laws Undermined: Corruption, Social Norms, and Collectivist Business Cultures" (2010) 37:2 *Journal of Law & Society* 345 at 366.

40 Richard Whish & David Bailey, *Competition Law*, 9th ed (Oxford University Press: Oxford, 2018) at 530 [Whish & Bailey].

41 Donald I Baker, "An Enduring Antitrust Divide across the Atlantic over Whether to Incarcerate Conspirators and When to Restrain Abusive Monopolists" (2009) 5:1 *European Competition Journal* 145 at 146.

42 OECD *Recommendations Against Hard Core Cartels*, above note 4 at 521; Whish & Bailey, above note 40.

43 Andrew I Gavil, William E Kovacic & Jonathan B Baker, *Antitrust Law in Perspective: Cases, Concepts and Problems in Competition Policy* (St Paul: West Group, 2002) at 80 [Gavil, Kovacic & Baker].

may have beneficial or efficiency-enhancing features. One example that has created challenges for competition law is the blanket licensing of copyrighted material through non-profit organizations acting on behalf of holders of copyright.[44] Given the large number of copyright holders for music and literary works, an entirely open competitive market is often neither practical, nor desired by prospective licensees.

Broadcast Music Inc (BMI), a non-profit corporation established to negotiate licensing of musical works with parties such as radio and TV broadcasters, was challenged by CBS in the late 1970s on the basis that blanket licensing was illegal price fixing. The US Supreme Court disagreed, finding that blanket licensing had benefits for artists and broadcasters alike. These included "unplanned, rapid, and indemnified access to any and all of the repertory of compositions," and "substantial lowering of costs." As a result, noting that "most users" wanted a blanket licence scheme,[45] the Court refused to treat the agreement as a "naked restraint" subject to *per se* illegality, and instead found "it should be subject to a more discriminating examination under the rule of reason."[46]

The American "rule of reason" doctrine involves "a full-blown discussion of the economic advantages and disadvantages of the agreement"[47] to determine whether it is lawful. An example of its application was the 1984 *NCAA* case, in which the setting of common terms for the broadcasting of college football by the National Collegiate Athletic Association (NCAA) on behalf of member universities was attacked as price fixing. The US Supreme Court found that *per se* condemnation was not appropriate, holding, "despite the fact that this case involves restraints on the ability of member institutions to compete in terms of price and output, a fair evaluation of their competitive character requires consideration of the NCAA's justifications for the restraints."[48]

The Court said in a footnote, "there is often no bright line separating *per se* from rule of reason analysis. *Per se* rules may require considerable inquiry into market conditions before the evidence justifies a presumption of anticompetitive conduct."[49] Analyzing the nature and impact of the agreement at issue, the Court nonetheless found that it had breached the *Sherman Act*. The majority concluded that even though the NCAA

44 For a discussion of the competition law treatment of blanket licensing, see Frederick C Boucher, "Blanket Music Licensing and Local Television: An Historical Accident in Need of Reform" (1987) 44 *Washington & Lee Law Review* 1157.

45 *BMI v CBS Inc*, 441 US 1 (1979) at 120 [*BMI*].

46 *Ibid* at 24.

47 *R v Nova Scotia Pharmaceutical Society, [1992] 2 SCR 606 at para 90 [Nova Scotia Pharmaceutical Society*].

48 *NCAA*, above note 24 at 103.

49 *Ibid*, n 26.

"plays a critical role in the maintenance of a revered tradition of amateurism in college sports," the broadcasting plan was more restrictive than necessary; for example, "more games would be televised in a free market than under the NCAA plan," illustrating the harm produced by the agreement.[50]

BMI and *NCAA* illustrate that, where agreements fall outside the hard core cartel category but restrict competition, there is a need to carry out a broader assessment of their effects, benefits and impacts than a *per se* rule would permit. Kennish & Ross have set out the following examples of kinds of potentially beneficial cooperation and agreements among firms which may require such a case-by-case assessment:

(1) research and development, production and distribution joint ventures (common in high technology industries);
(2) sharing of facilities (e.g., train track, distribution facilities);
(3) agreement on product standards;
(4) buying groups (in many retail trades);
(5) specialization agreements; and
(6) licensing of production and/or distribution.[51]

The authors recommended that the general conspiracy provision in the *Competition Act*, section 45 "[should] be amended to apply only to agreements involving 'naked' restraints and that a second, civil provision be added to the law on horizontal agreements that permits all other agreements to be evaluated by the Tribunal much as it would review a merger."[52] This is the path which the 2009 amendments to section 45 of the *Competition Act* ultimately followed. The section 45 criminal prohibition was narrowed to three *per se* categories (price fixing, market sharing, and restricting production) and a new, flexible civil provision (section 90.1) was created. The latter permits the assessment and weighing of the anti-competitive effects of an agreement against its offsetting efficiencies on a case-by-case basis.

C. HISTORY OF THE CANADIAN PROVISIONS

As we saw in Chapter 2, the first Canadian criminal conspiracy provision in 1889 created a misdemeanour which included a prohibition covering "[e]very person who combines, conspires, agrees or arranges

50 *Ibid* at 119.

51 Kennish & Ross, above note 18 at 28.

52 *Ibid* at 62–63; *Competition Act*, RSC 1985, c C-34, s 45 [*Competition Act* or Act]; see also Ross, "Proposals," above note 16 at 864.

with any other person . . . to unduly prevent or lessen competition."[53] That language proved remarkably resilient, remaining as a criminal offence in more or less the same form for 120 years (in the *Criminal Code*, *Combines Investigation Act*,[54] and *Competition Act*[55]), until overhauled in the 2009 amendments.[56] Attempts to deploy civil law remedies against anti-competitive agreements and pricing had been struck down on constitutional division of powers grounds in 1921[57] and 1936,[58] and the law remained on a criminal foundation, with the prohibition tied to the qualifier "unduly."

The courts initially interpreted the conspiracy prohibition as being directed toward promoting "free competition."[59] While that created a useful framework focused on the effect of the agreement on competition, the statute still required that the competitive restraints be found "undue." The courts' interpretation of the "undueness" test significantly weakened the effectiveness of the Canadian law during the lengthy period that it was present.

The conspiracy provision was the most actively enforced provision over the first century of Canadian combines and competition law. A commentator summarized the numbers to 1976: "[o]f all the cases between 1889 and 1976, 57% involved agreements to restrict trade, 29% resale price maintenance, 6% mergers and monopoly and 4% price discrimination and predatory pricing."[60]

1) "Unduly" and Its Sorry Legacy

Initially the Supreme Court interpreted "unduly" by simply deploying a string of synonyms. The Court held that "improper, inordinate, excessive or oppressive" limits on competition were "undue."[61] The term "undue" affected the outcome in many cases. An analysis of the 145 cases decided

53 *Act for the Prevention and Suppression of Combinations Formed in Restraint of Trade*, 52 Vict, c 41.

54 SC 1892, c 29, s 520 until SC 1960, c 45.

55 *Competition Act*, above note 52.

56 *Budget Implementation Act, 2009*, SC 2009, c 2, s 410 [*Budget Implementation Act, 2009*]. For a comprehensive history of the provision, see Stanbury, above note 5.

57 *Canada (Attorney General) v Alberta (Attorney General)* (1921), 60 *DLR* 513 (UKPC).

58 *Reference re legislative jurisdiction of Parliament of Canada to enact the Dominion Trade and Industry Commission Act, 1935, [1936] SCR 379.*

59 See, e.g., *Stinson-Reeb Builders Supply Company v R*, [1929] SCR 276 at 280.

60 Thomas W Ross, "The Evolution of Competition Law in Canada" (1998) 13 *Review of Industrial Organization* 1 at 6 [Ross, "Evolution"].

61 *Weidman v Shragge* (1912), 46 SCR 1 [*Weidman*], citing *R v Elliott* (1905), 9 CCC 505 (Ont CA) at 520.

in the century after the legislation was enacted in 1889 concluded that the undueness test played a role in more than half of the twenty-two acquittals.[62] One problem was that, while the cases did not establish a bright line for the fixed share of the market which the conspirators needed to possess, the undueness requirement permitted the accused to argue that low market share among the conspirators should vitiate criminality. Acquittals occurred in some cases simply because the accused possessed less than 50 percent of the market.[63]

Confusion about the meaning of "unduly" was fueled when, in 1957, Cartwright SCJ, in a concurring judgment in *R v Howard Smith Paper Mills*, held that an agreement must have "the effect of virtually relieving the conspirators from the influence of competition" to be undue.[64] The suggestion that an effective monopoly was a requirement has been labelled the "Cartwright heresy," because such a high level of control of the market, which had not previously been a requirement for conviction, would render the law essentially unenforceable.[65] While Cartwright J's statement was not consistently applied by trial courts,[66] the uncertainty it spawned led to an amendment of the *Combines Investigation Act* in 1975 providing that, "for greater certainty," a conviction under the conspiracy offence did not require proof that the agreement "eliminate, completely or virtually, competition in the market."[67] However, more confusion was introduced in *Aetna Insurance Co v R* in 1978.

The accused fire insurance underwriters in *Aetna*, representing the vast majority of such companies operating in Nova Scotia, had fixed a common price for fire insurance through a trade association. At trial, they argued that the agreement had beneficial objectives, such as "establishing equitable premium rates" and "avoiding unfair discrimination between risks of essentially the same hazard."[68] Evidence of these benefits was admitted into the trial record, and the trial judge acquitted the accused. On appeal, Ritchie J, for the majority in the Supreme Court of Canada, found no error, on the basis that the evidence of beneficial objectives showed that the agreement "was not for the purpose of

62 Stanbury, above note 5 at 78–79.

63 *Ibid* at 77.

64 *R v Howard Smith Paper Mills*, [1957] SCR 403.

65 Dunlop, Trebilcock & McQueen, above note 28 at 125.

66 Stanbury, above note 5 at 77; Michael J Trebilcock, "The Supreme Court and Strengthening the Conditions for Effective Competition in the Canadian Economy" (2001) 80 *Canadian Bar Review* 542 at 593.

67 SC 1974-75-76, c 76, s 14.

68 *R v Aetna Insurance Co* (1974), 19 CCC (2d) 449 (NS SC).

FIGURE 6.3. A building fire in Halifax: In *Aetna Insurance*, the Supreme Court held that evidence of public benefit from an agreement to fix fire insurance rates was relevant to "undueness," a departure from earlier jurisprudence

lessening competition unduly."[69] In dissent, Laskin CJC noted that under the previous case law, "benefits to the public, either in price or service or otherwise" were not relevant and that "the public interest in free competition" was the sole measure of undueness. (**Figure 6.3**, a building fire in Halifax.[70])

The Supreme Court added to the confusion in *R v Atlantic Sugar* in 1980, which established a low point for the ability to prosecute conspiracies under Canadian competition law. The accused sugar refiners were acquitted at trial of agreeing to share the Canadian market in fixed proportions, following a similar scheme created during the Second World War by the government. The trial judge held that the accused—who collectively held three-quarters of the Canadian sugar market during the relevant period—had reached a "tacit agreement" to maintain fixed market shares, but acquitted them, finding the absence of undueness and

69 *Aetna Insurance Co v R*, [1978] 1 SCR 731 at 751.

70 Nova Scotia Archives, "The Queen Hotel Fire, Hollis Street, Halifax, 2 March 1939," accession no 1995-370 no 6 /neg no: N-9453, online: https://novascotia.ca/archives/halifax/archives.asp?ID=57.

insufficient intent to unduly lessen competition.[71] The Quebec Court of Appeal entered a conviction,[72] but the Supreme Court of Canada overturned the appellate court.

On the issue of undueness, the Supreme Court majority cited Ritchie J in *Aetna* to the effect that "[w]hat is criminal is an agreement that is intended . . . to have the effect of virtually relieving the conspirators from the influence of free competition"—an application of the Cartwright heresy. Justice Pigeon, for the majority, went on to find that "applying this test to the facts found by the trial judge, it is impossible to say that he erred in law when coming to the conclusion that the Crown had failed to prove an agreement to lessen competition unduly."[73] The majority also held that the *mens rea* requirement for the offence obliged the Crown to prove not only the intent to enter into an agreement, but also intent to unduly lessen competition, stating "as was stressed in *Aetna*, the offence lies in the agreement made with the intention to lessen competition unduly, not in the actual result of the agreement."[74]

Requiring "double intent"—both the intention to agree and to lessen competition unduly—made the offence virtually unenforceable. It permitted the accused to argue that their conduct was simply self-interested behaviour, not intended to *unduly* lessen competition. Justice Estey, in dissent in *Atlantic Sugar*, found that the trial judge had erred by imposing a double intent requirement and would have upheld the conviction as found by the Court of Appeal.[75]

Rather than delete the unduly requirement, Parliament responded to *Atlantic Sugar* with another band-aid solution: an amendment to the effect that it was "not necessary to prove that the parties intended that the conspiracy" have the effect of unduly lessening competition in order

---

71 *R v Atlantic Sugar Refineries Co* (1976), 26 CPR (2d) 14 (Que SC).

72 *R v Atlantic Sugar Refineries Co* (1978), 41 CPR (2d) 5 (Que CA).

73 *Atlantic Sugar Refineries Co v Canada (Attorney General), [1980] 2 SCR 644 at 659 [Atlantic Sugar Refineries* SCC].

74 *Ibid* at 660. The trial judge had held:

> [I]n my opinion, it has not been shown that this agreement was arrived at with the intention of unduly preventing or lessening competition. The reason for maintaining traditional market shares was to avoid a price war which would have resulted had the accused taken the only method of increasing them by price cutting through extensive discounts.

Justice Pigeon found no error in this statement.

75 *Ibid* at 672.

to convict.[76] However, problems with enforcement of the conspiracy offence persisted.

2) The Enforcement Record, 1980–2000

The impact of the "unduly" requirement after *Atlantic Sugar* is traced in a comprehensive review of the record of prosecutions from 1980 to 2000 by Chandler & Jackson.[77] The authors concluded that the test played a significant role in the acquittal or discharge of accused conspirators in numerous contested cases:

> Based on our reading of the decisions, of the 17 cases where the accused were acquitted at trial or discharged at a preliminary hearing, just over one-third (6 cases or 35 percent) were lost by the Crown because of insufficient evidence of an agreement, and almost two-thirds (11 cases or 65 percent) because of insufficient evidence of an undue lessening of competition or of the parties' intent that the agreement have that effect.[78]

One of the cases to go to trial in that time period was *R v Nova Scotia Pharmaceutical Society*. In that case, the Supreme Court of Canada ruled on an appeal from a preliminary motion that the undueness test required that the Crown show that the agreement in question created "moderate market power" and involved "some behaviour likely to injure competition."[79] Interpreting the elements of the offence in light of the "principles of fundamental justice" mandated by section 7 of the *Charter of Rights and Freedoms*, the Court found with respect to *mens rea* that the offence required a form of double intent—the intent to agree, plus at least objective knowledge of the undue effects of the agreement on

---

76 *Competition Tribunal Act* SC 1986, c 26; RSC 1985, c 19 (2d Supp), s 30: "For greater certainty . . . it is necessary to prove that the parties thereto intended to and did enter into the conspiracy . . . but it is not necessary to prove that the parties intended that the conspiracy . . . have an effect set out in subsection (1)." See also William T Stanbury, "The New Competition Act and Competition Tribunal Act: Not with a Bang, but a Whimper" (1986) 12 *Canadian Business Law Journal* 2 at 21–22.

77 Harry Chandler & Robert H Jackson, "Beyond Merriment and Diversion: The Treatment of Conspiracies under Canada's Competition Act" (Paper presented at the Roundtable on Competition Act Amendments, Insight Conferences, Toronto, Ontario, 25 May 2000) [Chandler & Jackson].

78 *Ibid*. In this period, there were fifty-one cases brought under the conspiracy provision, s 45. Of those cases, twenty-nine resulted in guilty pleas.

79 *Nova Scotia Pharmaceutical Society*, above note 47 at paras 102 and 109.

competition.[80] At trial after the Supreme Court decision, an acquittal was entered on that very issue. The trial judge found that the Crown had failed to prove that the accused pharmacists' association had the necessary objective intention to lessen competition unduly. Clouding the issue of intent was the fact that the process for setting rates and prices for dispensing fees and prescription drugs between pharmacists and private insurance companies (the subject of the criminal charge) was patterned after that used to set rates under a drug insurance plan mandated by provincial legislation.[81]

Another case illustrating the impact of the undueness requirement was *R v Clarke Transport Inc*. There was clear proof that the accused companies had entered into an agreement to fix prices and allocate the market for the delivery of freight by railway "pool car" to Western Canada from Toronto. However, the trial judge, Moldaver J (as he then was), acquitted the companies on the basis that the Crown had failed to show that the accused possessed market power. He noted that "no matter how nefarious the object of the agreement, absent a showing of some market power, there can be no violation of s. 45(1)(c)."[82] He also concluded that because the accused believed they were competing with other forms of transport such as trucking, the necessary intent to lessen competition unduly, even on an objective standard, had not been shown.[83]

3) The Process of Amending the Conspiracy Provision, 1999–2009

The undueness requirement made the section both too narrow and too broad.[84] Prosecuting hard core cartels had become difficult, and in some

80 *Ibid* at paras 117–119.

81 *R v Nova Scotia Pharmaceutical Society* (1993), 120 NSR (2d) 304 (SC).

82 *R v Clarke Transport Canada Inc* (1995), 130 DLR (4th) 500 (Ont Gen Div) at para 79 [*Clarke Transport*]. See also paras 175 and 184.

83 *Ibid* at para 88.

84 The Canadian Bar Association (CBA) summarized the case for reform as:

- The law is "under-inclusive", because it does not adequately capture "hard-core" cartels; there are too many acquittals in contested cases.
- The law is "over-inclusive", because it criminalizes agreements between competitors that could have pro-competitive effects. This has created a "chill" on pro-competitive business arrangements.

National Competition Law Section, Canadian Bar Association "Submission on Reform of Section 45 of the *Competition Act* (Conspiracy)" (February 2003) at 10, online: www.cba.org/CMSPages/GetFile.aspx?guid=9e7cda88-8569-41a2-8e6a-a2bd01bbeec0.

cases impossible, as seen above, because of the need to show undue effect and prove *mens rea*. Clearly harmful conduct, such as the freight charges conspiracy in *Clarke Transport*, was falling outside the scope of the law. In addition, the broad criminal prohibition of all agreements which "unduly lessen competition" potentially also covered beneficial cooperative conduct.[85] This raised the concern that a criminal law "chill" might be put on desirable commercial cooperation, such as benchmarking agreements, joint ventures, sharing expertise, or exchanging market data and statistics.[86]

In 1999, the House of Commons Standing Committee on Industry, Science and Technology "decided that an in-depth study of the *Competition Act* was warranted."[87] The review came at a time when five different private members' bills were tabled in Parliament, all addressing competition policy-related issues. One of the bills targeted reforms to the conspiracy provisions of the Act.[88] In 2000 and 2002 respectively, the Committee released two reports, both recommending a two-track system: a criminal conspiracy offence for hard core cartels and a new civil provision for other agreements.[89] The 2002 Report stated that "[c]ompetition law experts believe, almost unanimously, that section 45, as

---

85 Ross, "Proposals," above note 16 at 863.

86 Paul S Crampton, "Beyond Bill C-23: A Competition Law for the New Millennium" (2002) 36 *Canadian Business Law Journal* 161 at 170; Kennish & Ross, above note 18 at 52.

87 House of Commons, Standing Committee on Industry, *Interim Report on the Competition Act* (June 2000) (Chair: Susan Whelan), Chairman's Foreword; also Public Policy Forum, *Amendments to the Competition Act and the Competition Tribunal Act: A Report on Consultation, Final Report Submitted to the Commissioner of Competition* (20 December 2000) [unpublished].

88 *Ibid*, Appendix 2: Bill C-472, *An Act to Amend the Competition Act (conspiracy agreements and right to make private applications), the Competition Tribunal Act (costs and summary dispositions) and the Criminal Code as a consequence*, 36th Parl, 2d Sess, 1999–2000, ss 1 and 7 would have created a new offence covering:

> [A] agreement . . . where the person knew, or ought reasonably to have known, that the agreement or arrangement, if implemented, would or would be likely to have the effect of: (a) fixing, establishing, controlling or maintaining the minimum price of the product; (b) allocating any markets, territories, customers or sales for the product between the person and the competitor; (c) boycotting a competitor or a competitor's suppliers or customers; or (d) preventing, eliminating, lessening or otherwise limiting the production or supply of the product.

Bill C-472 died on the Order Paper with the dissolution of Parliament on 22 October 2000.

89 *Ibid*; also House of Commons, Standing Committee on Industry, Science and Technology, *A Plan to Modernize Canada's Competition Regime* (April 2002) (Chair: Walt Lastewka) [*A Plan to Modernize Canada's Competition Regime*].

currently written, is hard to enforce" and recommended the repeal of the "unduly" standard.[90]

In spite of the clear direction from the Committee, and a response that "[t]he Government endorses the basic principle of a two-track approach for conspiracies,"[91] there followed a further slow-moving consultation process. The process began with a 2003 discussion paper,[92] public consultations, and then a 2004 report summarizing the comments received.[93] A government bill was tabled in late 2004,[94] but as had a bill passed in 2002,[95] it dealt with competition policy issues unrelated to the conspiracy provision. In 2005, the Bureau formed an "[e]xternal Working Group of lawyers, economists and academics who possess extensive knowledge of competition law, criminal law, and economics, to assist the Bureau in its consideration of the reform of section 45" and to develop "a proposal to reform section 45."[96]

The process of amending the Act languished until July 2007, when the government appointed a five-member "Competition Policy Review Panel"[97] composed of three business executives, a lawyer, and a retired

90 *Ibid* at 59 and 62.

91 Canada, Competition Bureau, "Government Response to the Report of the House of Commons Standing Committee on Industry, Science and Technology '*A Plan to Modernize Canada's Competition Regime*'" (23 April 2002), online: www.competitionbureau.gc.ca/eic/site/iccat.nsf/eng/03282.html.

92 Canada, Competition Bureau, "Discussion Paper—Options for Amending the Competition Act: Fostering a Competitive Marketplace" (2003).

93 Public Policy Forum, *National Consultation on the Competition Act: Final Report* (27 April 2004).

94 Bill C-19, *An Act to amend the Competition Act and to make consequential amendments to other acts*, 38th Parl, 1st Sess, 2004–2005. The bill died on the Order Paper in the autumn of 2005.

95 Bill C-23, *An Act to amend the Competition Act and the Competition Tribunal Act*, 37th Parl, 1st Sess, 2002 (assented to 4 June 2002) SC 2002, c 16, covered (from the legislative summary) "amendments to facilitate cooperation with foreign competition authorities for the enforcement of civil competition and fair trade practices laws; amendments prohibiting deceptive prize notices; amendments streamlining the Competition Tribunal process by providing for cost awards, summary dispositions and references; amendments broadening the scope under which the Tribunal may issue temporary orders; and—some housekeeping items."

96 Canada, Competition Bureau, Commissioner of Competition, "Submission to the Competition Policy Review Panel" (11 January 2008) at 6, online: www.competitionbureau.gc.ca/eic/site/cb-bc.nsf/eng/02555.html [*Submission to Reform Section 45*].

97 Canada, Competition Policy Review Panel Website, "LR Wilson, Chair of the Competition Policy Review Panel, speaks at the release of *Sharpening Canada's Competitive Edge*, in Montreal on October 30, 2007" (30 October 2007), online: www.ic.gc.ca/eic/site/cprp-gepmc.nsf/eng/00011.html.

politician. It was "mandated to review Canada's competition and foreign investment policies and to make recommendations to the Minister of Industry . . . for making Canada more competitive."[98] The Commissioner of Competition's Submission to the Panel stated the following with respect to the conspiracy prohibition:

> [C]ommentators note that section 45 is overly inclusive because it subjects all strategic alliances and other collaborations among firms to the threat of criminal sanctions even when these agreements may potentially increase economic welfare. At the same time, while Canada has a *per se* prohibition against bid-rigging, section 45 is under-inclusive because it can allow manifestly anti-competitive agreements relating to price fixing, market sharing and output restrictions to escape sanction.[99]

On the issue of anti-competitive agreements, the Panel's final report noted the enforcement problems posed by the qualifier "unduly" in the existing criminal provision[100] and yet again recommended moving to a two-track approach consisting of *per se* criminal and civil agreements provisions.[101]

Amendments to the *Competition Act*, including the recommended two-track approach to anti-competitive agreements, were included as Part 12, sections 407 to 444 of the lengthy *Budget Implementation Act*. The bill was tabled in the House of Commons on 6 February, ten days

---

98 Canada, Competition Policy Review Panel, *Compete to Win, Final Report* (Ottawa: Public Works and Government Services Canada, 2008) at 1, online: www.ic.gc.ca/eic/site/cprp-gepmc.nsf/vwapj/Compete_to_Win.pdf/$FILE/Compete_to_Win.pdf [*Compete to Win*].

99 *Submission to Reform Section 45*, above note 96 at 5.

100 *Compete to Win*, above note 98 at 116, n 64:

> These complications arise largely from the requirement under Canadian law to establish that an agreement prevents or lessens competition *unduly* before it can be considered a criminal offence. It is the combination of market power and behaviour likely to injure competition that makes a lessening of competition undue. . . . This tends to increase the quantity and quality of evidence required to establish an offence to the criminal standard of proof, thereby resulting in longer, more complex investigations and prosecutions in Canada compared with other industrialized countries.

101 *Ibid* at 61: "[R]epeal the existing conspiracy provisions and replace them with a *per se* criminal offence to address hardcore cartels and a civil provision to deal with other types of agreements between competitors that have anti-competitive effects."

after the Federal Budget,[102] passed on 4 March, and given royal assent on 12 March 2009.[103]

The legislative process leading to passage of the bill was severely curtailed. A Senate Report noted "witnesses were concerned about the inclusion of proposed changes to the *Competition Act* in a budget implementation bill and the consequential absence of debate over important issues concerning competition law."[104] However, "[i]n spite of the relative lack of prior debate on the *Competition Act* proposals contained in the legislation . . . the witnesses appearing before the Committee . . . generally agreed that the changes to the *Competition Act* in the *Budget Implementation Act, 2009* were beneficial to competition."[105] The Senate Committee Report made no recommendations given the limited number of witnesses appearing before it and the short time available to complete a review.[106]

Given the limited discussion in Committee and in Parliament, the extrinsic evidence available to assist in interpretation of the new provisions is very sparse. However, the record of previous studies and consultations profiled above does provide considerable insight into the legislative objectives, which were rooted in the ineffectiveness of the undueness standard.

---

102 Bill C-10, *An Act to implement certain provisions of the budget tabled in Parliament on January 27, 2009 and related fiscal measures (Budget Implementation Act 2009)*, 40th Parl, 2d Sess, 2009 (assented to 12 March 2009), SC 2009, c 2.

103 *Budget Implementation Act, 2009*, above note 56. The Hon Jim Flaherty, Minister of Finance, the Bill's sponsor, said in Committee:

> [I]ncluded are initiatives . . . to protect consumers from anti-competitive and unscrupulous business practices by adding new provisions to the *Competition Act*, and more. Colleagues, I can see that at 524 pages, this is a detailed and lengthy bill. We could, as parliamentarians, spend months engaging in debate, some of it abstract or philosophical, and sometimes partisan, I'm sure, about the measures within this large bill, but as I mentioned earlier, we do not have that luxury. The consequences of delay for Canadians are too high. Bill C-10 contains the right measures that we need to implement right now in order to help Canadian families now and to help our overall economy weather the current economic storm. We must pass this bill as soon as we can.

House of Commons, Evidence, Standing Committee on Finance (23 February 2009) (Chair: Julia Munro) at 2–3. During the limited debate of the bill, MP John McCallum stated "Many Canadians, not just big business but small business, object to putting through fundamental changes to the *Competition Act* with essentially no debate. Whatever the merits of the content, the process is egregiously bad." House of Commons Debates, 40th Parl, 2d Sess, No 12 (10 February 2009) at 1170 (Hon John McCallum).

104 Senate of Canada, Standing Senate Committee on Banking, Trade and Commerce, "Recent *Competition Act* Changes: A Work in Progress" (June 2009) at 1, online: https://sencanada.ca/Content/SEN/Committee/402/bank/rep/rep02Jun09-e.pdf.

105 *Ibid* at 2.

106 *Ibid*.

D. CRIMINAL CONSPIRACY PROVISIONS

1) Section 45(1) of the *Competition Act*: Conspiracies to Fix Prices, Allocate Markets, and Limit Production

a) The Offence

The general *per se* conspiracy provision, section 45(1), came into force on 12 March 2010 and applies to agreements formed or continuing as of that date.[107] It provides:

> 45 (1) Every person commits an offence who, with a competitor of that person with respect to a product, conspires, agrees or arranges
>
> (a) to fix, maintain, increase or control the price for the supply of the product;
> (b) to allocate sales, territories, customers or markets for the production or supply of the product; or
> (c) to fix, maintain, control, prevent, lessen or eliminate the production or supply of the product.

The offence as set out in section 45(1) has the following elements:

- *Actus reus*
  - An agreement ("every person who . . . conspires, agrees or arranges")
  - With a "competitor"
  - The subject of the agreement is:
    - to fix prices;
    - to allocate production; or
    - to control output.
- *Mens rea* in the form of the intention to enter into the agreement

Section 45(2) specifies that the foregoing is an indictable offence with a maximum penalty of fourteen years' imprisonment or a fine of $25 million. Of note:

- The section does not require any assessment of the effect of the agreement on competition, or of market power.
- It applies only to the supply, not to the purchase of a product.[108] A more specific *per se* offense dealing with purchase-side employment

---

107 *Budget Implementation Act, 2009*, above note 56, s 444; *Interpretation Act*, RSC 1985, c I-21, s 43 [*Interpretation Act*].

108 See *Mohr v. National Hockey League*, 2021 FC 488 at para.36, affd 2022 FCA 145 at paras 33-42, leave to appeal to SCC refused [2022] SCCA No 392; *Latifi v. The*

agreements was added in 2023 and will be discussed separately below.[109]

- It applies to any "person," which includes both individuals and corporations.[110]
- The word "product" is defined in the Act to include all kinds of real and personal property as well as services.[111]
- A number of defences are available, including that the agreement is merely ancillary to a broader agreement.

The language of the section and the various defences are considered in more detail below.

b) Agreement: The *Actus Reus*

i) *Components of Agreement*

a. A Meeting of the Minds

The *actus reus* of the offence in section 45 is that the accused "conspired, agreed, or arranged" with a competitor in respect of a product and that the agreement falls within one or more of the three categories in paragraphs (a), (b), and/or (c) of the section.[112] The language "conspires, agrees or arranges" is the same as in the predecessor section, however, the word "combines" was removed. The case law under the previous section 45 held that the words all require the reaching of an agreement, a common design, or a "meeting of the minds," analogous to the standard applicable to conspiracy under the *Criminal Code*. Under the general criminal law, "[t]he *actus reus* is the act of agreement."[113] Justice Houlden held in *R v Armco Canada Ltd*, referring to Perdue J in *R v Gage*:[114] "Even if 'arranges' has a different meaning from 'conspires, combines and agrees,' (and I need express no opinion on this point) . . . it still requires "the act of agreeing."[115]

TDL Group Corp, 2021 BCSC 2183 at para 77. Purchase agreements are, however, still subject to s 90.1 of the *Competition Act*, above note 52.

109 *An Act to implement certain provisions of the budget tables in Parliament April 7, 2022 and other measures*, SC 2022, c 10, s 257 [*Bill C-19 2022*]

110 *Interpretation Act*, above note 107, s 35(1).

111 *Competition Act*, above note 52, s 2(1), definitions of "article," "product," and "service."

112 *Watson v Bank of America Corp, 2015 BCCA 362 at para 75 [Watson]*.

113 *R v Papalia; R v Cotroni*, [1979] 2 SCR 256 at 276 [*Papalia*].

114 *R v Gage* (1908), 13 CCC 428 (Ont CA).

115 *R v Armco Canada Ltd* (1976), 30 CCC (2d) 183 at 192 (Ont CA) [*Armco CA*]; followed in *R v Cominco Ltd*, [1980] 2 WWR 693 (Alta SCTD) at para 34 [*Cominco*]. The British Columbia Court of Appeal recently cited this passage with

What constitutes a "meeting of the minds," or a "common design," or "the act of agreeing"? As these words indicate, the essential aspect is the mental state of the accused co-conspirators in adopting a common (unlawful) purpose. A court must be satisfied beyond a reasonable doubt that this mental state of shared purpose exists in order to find the accused culpable.

b. Common Purpose or Design

Conspiracy has been described as "a crime of intention."[116] The Supreme Court in *R v O'Brien* adopted the following definition of conspiracy from the English case of *Mulcahy v The Queen*, which indicated that this intention must be directed at a common purpose:

> A conspiracy consists not merely in the intention of two or more, but in the agreement of two or more to do an unlawful act, or to do a lawful act by unlawful means. So long as such a design rests in intention only, it is not indictable. *When two agree to carry it into effect, the very plot is an act in itself, and the act of each of the parties . . . punishable if for a criminal object.*[117]

The Supreme Court has described the required object alternatively as "an intention to put the common design into effect,"[118] or "the intention to reach the common goal."[119] This requirement means that there is no offence covering a party who does not share the common design: "Where one member of a so-called conspiracy . . . never intends to carry out the common design, there can be no conspiracy involving that person. Nonetheless, a conspiracy can still exist between other parties to the same agreement."[120]

The law does not require that the parties to the conspiracy agree on all the details of how the conspiracy is to be put into effect, as long as they have agreed on the unlawful purpose: "[t]he participants need not know each other, nor need they communicate directly with one another. Each need not know the details of the common scheme, though each

---

approval in considering the previous s 45 in the context of a class action under the Act's civil damages provision: *Watson, above note 112 at para 77.*

116 *R v Root*, 2008 ONCA 869 at para 71 [*Root*].

117 *Mulcahy v The Queen*, (1868) LR 3 HL 306 [emphasis added] cited by *R v O'Brien*, [1954] SCR 666 at 668–69 [*O'Brien*]; cited with approval in *United States v Dynar*, [1997] 2 SCR 462 at para 86 [*Dynar*]. See also *R v Abitibi Power & Paper Co (1960), 131 CCC 201(Que CQ) at paras 21–22 [Abitibi Power & Paper]*.

118 *O'Brien*, above note 117 at 668.

119 *Ibid.*

120 *Dynar*, above note 117 at para 88.

must be aware of the general nature of the common design and be an adherent to it."[121]

c. Implementation Not Required

The offence lies in the agreement between the parties on the matters set out in section 45. The agreement is the key to the offence—the Supreme Court has held that it is not a crime in Canada to attempt to conspire to commit a substantive offence. In the Court's view, given that conspiracy is already a crime of intention, it would not be appropriate to criminalize attempt to conspire, because "an attempt to conspire amounts, at best, to a risk that a risk will materialize."[122]

On the other hand, the offence is complete once there has been a "meeting of the minds": "the essence of the conspiracy is the agreement to carry out an unlawful act and such agreement constitutes the offence, even if nothing is ever done to implement it."[123] The Crown need not show that the accused took steps toward putting into effect the conspiracy: "the focus of the inquiry is on . . . what was agreed, not on what was done, although what was done in furtherance may help to establish the core element of conspiracy—the agreement."[124]

The Supreme Court has observed that "[c]onspiracy is in fact a more 'preliminary' crime than attempt, since the offence is considered to be complete before any acts are taken that go beyond mere preparation to put the common design into effect."[125] The law of conspiracy in this respect has been described as "a pre-emptive strike by the criminal law as soon as the agreement exists, even if it is far from fruition."[126]

In the case of agreements such as price fixing, this position can be justified because the agreement itself reflects an alteration, if not extinguishment, of the rivalry that competition law seeks to protect, even if no steps are actually taken to charge the prices agreed to. Competitors, rather than acting independently as would occur in a competitive market, have agreed upon a common design. In this sense, the "mischief" the *Competition Act* conspiracy offence is directed against is present once an agreement is reached, even if it is never carried into effect.

---

121 *Root*, above note 116 at paras 68 and 70 citing *R v Longworth* (1982), 67 CCC (2d) 554 (Ont CA) at 565–66; followed *Proulx v R, 2016 QCCA 1425 at para 117; R v McNamara* (1981), 56 CCC (2d) 193 (Ont CA) at para 654.

122 *R v Déry, [2006] 2 SCR 669 at para 50.*

123 *Abitibi Power & Paper, above note 117 at para 77; citing Weidman*, above note 61 at 20–21.

124 *Root*, above note 116 at para 67.

125 *Dynar*, above note 117 at para 87.

126 *R v Alexander*, [2005] OJ No 3777 (CA) at para 48.

ii) Proof of Agreement

Proof of criminal conspiracy does not necessitate showing an agreement which is enforceable in contract law; for example, satisfying requirements such as consideration or "*consensus ad idem*."[127] In fact, most of the time, given the clandestine nature of conspiratorial behaviour, the Crown does not possess direct evidence of the agreement. Cartel members seldom commit the terms of their agreement to writing. One trial judge put it cogently as follows:

> There is no ground for surprise that one does not find in the minute books the text of the understandings, agreements or arrangements that may have been made by the defendants. In the case of such offences, one finds rarely, if ever, concrete and precise evidence in black and white of combinations designed to create a monopoly or operate it.
>
> . . .
>
> It is sufficient, as in any other criminal affair, to be able to gather from the total amount of evidence that an agreement, even tacit, has in fact come into existence, that a common plan has been conceived and put into operation to violate the Act, whatever may be the results obtained.[128]

Relying on circumstantial evidence, conspiracy must often be "inferred by proof of a course of conduct."[129] The Supreme Court's decision in *Atlantic Sugar* created some confusion when Pigeon J, speaking for the majority, stated that proof of agreement required "not only . . . a course of conduct from which acceptance may be inferred, [but] there must also be communication of th[e] offer."[130] This suggested that proof of agreement in section 45 depended upon contract law principles such as offer and acceptance. Justice Estey, in dissent, correctly noted that "[t]he four words [conspires, combines, agrees or arranges] describe 'agreement' in the broadest sense accorded to that word in the language and not the narrow term of art from a specialized branch of the law."[131] Consistent with the dissent, section 45(3) was added in 1986 to eliminate any uncertainty created by the majority decision:

> In a prosecution under s (1), the court may infer the existence of a conspiracy, agreement or arrangement from circumstantial evidence, with

127 Morris Manning, Alan W Mewett & Peter J Sankoff, *Manning, Mewett & Sankoff: Criminal Law*, 5th ed (Markham: LexisNexis, 2015) at 373.

128 *R v Eddy Match Company Limited*, [1951] QJ No 8 (KB) at paras 287 and 289 [*Eddy Match Company Limited*].

129 *R v Northern Electric Co*, [1955] 3 DLR 449 (Ont SC) at 453.

130 *Atlantic Sugar Refineries* SCC, above note 73 at 657.

131 *Ibid.*

> or without direct evidence of communication between or among the alleged parties to it, but, for greater certainty, the conspiracy, agreement or arrangement must be proved beyond a reasonable doubt.[132]

The nature of the inference-drawing exercise in conspiracy cases was described as follows by the Supreme Court:

> The actual agreement must be gathered from "several isolated doings" . . . having possibly little or no value taken by themselves, but the bearing of which one upon the other must be interpreted; and their cumulative effect, properly estimated in the light of all the surrounding circumstances, may raise a presumption of concerted purpose entitling the jury to find the existence of the unlawful agreement.[133]

Circumstantial evidence supporting an inference of conspiracy to fix prices, for example, has included

- the existence of uniform, or stable prices or policies, or sustained follow-the-leader behaviour;
- the advance publication of price lists or their circulation to competitors;
- evidence of other communication between competitors or meetings prior to price changes;
- evidence of concerns being expressed at such meetings over the disadvantages of "cut throat" competition or the need to bring prices into line;
- the existence of enforcement activities against non-complying parties;
- accusations that competitors are "guilty" or "not playing by the book" by pricing competitively; or
- acts of repentance or apology by the "guilty" party.[134]

It is the accumulation of several examples of the foregoing kinds of evidence which may tip the scales of proof toward a finding of agreement in the absence of direct evidence. For example, in *R v CGE Co*, the three accused companies, CGE, Westinghouse, and Sylvania, were suppliers of industrial lamps, holding over 90 percent of the market collectively. Following the announcement by CGE of "industry sales plans" in 1959 and 1961 setting out the prices for the sale of its products

---

132 SC 1986, c 26, s 30(3); *Competition Act*, above note 52, s 45(3). See also *Eddy Match Company Limited*, above note 128 at 44; *Abitibi Power & Paper, above note 117 at 238.*

133 *Paradis v The King*, [1934] SCR 165 at 168.

134 See, e.g., *R v Armco Canada Ltd* (1974), 21 CCC (2d) 129 (Ont HC) [*Armco* HC], var'd (1976), 30 CCC (2d) 183 (Ont CA), leave to appeal to SCC refused (1976), 30 CCC (2d) 183 n (SCC); *R v CGE Co* (1976), 34 CCC (2d) 489 (Ont HC) [*CGE*].

on consignment by distributors, well in advance of the implementation date, the other two suppliers put in place substantially similar plans. There was significant uniformity of pricing, including quotes which were the same down to the penny for large and complex tenders. The accused "strictly and closely" monitored their agents to ensure compliance with the plans, and moved their agents to a consignment arrangement which tightened price control.[135] There was some evidence of direct communication between the competitors concerning adherence to the plans and complaints about failures to do so. In one case, for example, the manager of Central Sales (Regina) for CGE wrote a letter to the district manager of Westinghouse after one of the CGE agents applied a discount of 5 percent for cash on a tender instead of the 2 percent specified in the sales plan. The letter indicated that the purchaser had refused to permit the tender's withdrawal, but that the distributor would realize no profit, which would be "donated to charity."[136] Justice Pennell reviewed this evidence and held:

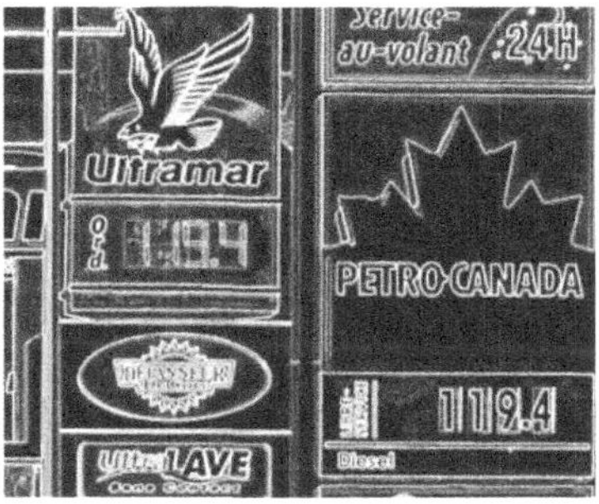

FIGURE 6.4. Uniform gasoline prices: a sign of competition or collusion?

> It is no answer to say that the letter was returned. To my mind it would violate reality to treat the incident as a bona fide mistake. Genuine competitors do not make reports of their business transactions to their rivals . . . This was not the conduct of a competitor but of a sales manager who believed that the accused were united in an agreement, express or implied, to act together and pursue a common purpose.[137]

The defence argued that the price uniformity was not the result of agreement, but that "[t]hrough a sophisticated set of signals, the defendants had the potential to communicate effectively with one another and co-ordinate their activities without conspiratorial meetings."[138] The trial judge disagreed, finding the accumulated evidence disclosed, beyond a reasonable doubt, "an agreement among the accused to introduce and maintain an industry sales plan."[139]

135 *Ibid* at para 118.
136 *Ibid* at para 133.
137 *Ibid* at para 138.
138 *Ibid* at para 158.
139 *Ibid* at para 165.

iii) *Conscious Parallelism or Agreement?*

The accused in *CGE* invoked "conscious parallelism" in their defence. The concept was referred to by the trial judge as "one of the great battlefields of anti-combines litigation."[140] The defence theory was that the industry structure (few sellers and a homogeneous product) created the conditions by which price uniformity could be achieved without agreement, through the independent recognition by the parties that their self-interest justified uniform behaviour. This situation has been explained as follows:

> Producers will be discouraged from charging less by an awareness that major competitors, faced with the threat of market share erosion, will immediately match the lower prices. . . . This type of industrial structure will normally produce identical list prices and virtually identical transactions prices. Price adjustments upward may occur almost simultaneously, without any formal agreement.[141]

The defence of conscious parallelism comes down to proof.[142] If parallel conduct is indeed shown to have been achieved without agreement, it does not constitute an offence. However, in *CGE*, based on the accumulated evidence, including that of communication between the parties, the trial judge held, "I am not able to reconcile the substantial uniformity of action taken by the accused with price conscious parallelism" and convicted the accused. Similarly, the Competition Bureau takes the position that "parallel conduct coupled with facilitating practices, such as sharing competitively sensitive information or activities that assist competitors in monitoring one another's prices, may be sufficient to prove that an agreement was concluded between the parties."[143]

Armco was another case in which the defence argued that Armco's conduct amounted to conscious parallelism and that there was no agreement. The accused were suppliers of metal culverts. The evidence in the case included actions by the accused, both through an industry association and individually, to establish an "open pricing policy" to achieve price uniformity in the market by public disclosure of a price list which contained "every discount and terms of credit" on the "expectation that

140 *Ibid* at para 41.

141 William T Stanbury & GB Reschenthaler, "Oligopoly and Conscious Parallelism: Theory, Policy and the Canadian Cases" (1977) 15:3 *Osgoode Hall Law Journal* 617 at 618.

142 See Russell W Lusk, QC "Conspiracy: From What Evidence Is It Appropriate to Find an Agreement?" ch 7 in Khemani & Stanbury, above note 5.

143 *CGE*, above note 134 at para 164; Canada, Competition Bureau, *Competitor Collaboration Guidelines* (23 December 2009) at para 2.2, online: www.competitionbureau.gc.ca/eic/site/cb-bc.nsf/eng/03177.html.

prices will adjust themselves to the requirements of the individual producer."[144] After some communication among the suppliers to this effect, one of them, Robertsteel, "attempted to establish an open price policy by publishing a price list." This initial attempt was not followed and a price war continued. Six months later, Robertsteel "again tried to establish an open price policy. It published a price list effective December 2, 1963." This time, "the price war came to an end. From December, 1963, until August, 1967, there was price stability in the Ontario market."[145] The defence theory, presented through expert evidence, was as follows:

> Dr. James Sherbaniuk, a consulting economist . . . described the corrugated metal pipe industry as an oligopoly, this being the market condition that exists when an industry has few sellers. According to Dr. Sherbaniuk, where there has been a price war in an oligopoly which sells a homogeneous product to "informed buyers" (i.e., public buyers who are well qualified to judge the goods) a natural upward force is exerted on prices, and prices tend to rise to uniform levels that provide an acceptable margin of profit. This tendency is accentuated by public tendering and delivered pricing. Sellers tend to act in a parallel way out of self-interest, and this "conscious parallelism" explains uniformity of prices in the complete absence of arrangement or agreement.[146]

The trial judge rejected the defence theory, finding significance in evidence such as the industry efforts to establish an open pricing policy, the persistent attempts by Robertsteel at price leadership, and then the sudden success:

> It would offend one's common sense after reviewing the history which I detailed earlier in this judgment, not to arrive at the irresistible conclusion and beyond a reasonable doubt that an arrangement was finally achieved between the members of the Institute to have . . . price "leadership" and "followership." With the difficulty experienced over the first 10 or 11 months of 1963, in "educating" the industry, the sudden achievement of open price policy within two weeks of the publication of the Robertsteel price list on December 2, 1963, could only occur if there was an arrangement or agreement.[147]

The essence of the agreement found was that the industry members would all follow the price set out by the price leader. The accused appealed to the Ontario Court of Appeal, which upheld the conviction

144 *Armco* CA, above note 115 at para 9.
145 *Ibid* at para 14.
146 *Ibid* at para 16.
147 *Armco* HC, above note 134 at 177.

in this respect. The appellate court held that there was "ample evidence to support the theory of the Crown that the identical pricing resulted from an agreement or arrangement."[148]

R v Aluminum Co of Canada Ltd (Alcan) is an example of a case in which the trial judge was not convinced that parallel behaviour or price followership amounted to conspiracy. He concluded that the mere use of Alcan's price lists by its competitors as a guide to their pricing, and the circulation of such lists to them by Alcan, was insufficient to establish an agreement.[149]

Similarly, in *R v Cominco Ltd*, the Crown's theory was that the accused fertilizer manufacturers achieved close similarity of prices by an agreement which included the adoption of mechanisms such as standard terms of sale, zone pricing, and exchanges of product between the manufacturers. It was rejected by the trial judge. He concluded that the close monitoring and surveillance of competitors' actions and "identity or similarity" in prices was a sign of "a highly competitive climate" in this oligopolistic industry, rather than collusion.[150]

The United States Supreme Court also dismissed an action alleging a conspiracy which relied only on allegations of parallel conduct by telecommunications firms not to compete in long distance services. The court held in striking out the claim:

> "[C]onscious parallelism," a common reaction of "firms in a concentrated market [that] recogniz[e] their shared economic interests and their interdependence with respect to price and output decisions" is "not in itself unlawful."[151]

While conscious parallelism involving the independent actions of industry players does not amount to conspiracy, it still raises policy concerns for competition law. Firms in industries with a small number of players (i.e., an oligopoly) are able to coordinate their behaviour simply by observing and anticipating their rivals' pricing moves. They recognize their mutual interdependence. As noted in Chapter 3, game theoretical models used by economists show that firms can raise prices without express agreement through price signalling if certain market conditions such as homogeneous products and public pricing information are present.[152] This can produce increased or uniform prices resembling the

148 *Armco* CA, above note 115 at para 29.

149 *R v Aluminum Co of Canada Ltd* (1975), 29 CPR (2d) 183 at 206 (Que SC).

150 *Cominco*, above note 115 at para 72.

151 *Bell Atlantic Corp v Twombly, 550 US 544 (2007) at 554–55.*

152 Jeffrey R Church & Roger Ware, *Industrial Organization: A Strategic Approach* (Boston: McGraw-Hill, 2000) at 314–15; Gregory J Werden, "Economic Evidence

market results of an agreement or cartel.[153] The effect on the economy may be similar to the inefficiency and loss of social welfare caused by an express conspiracy.[154]

Because the law of conspiracy does not sanction conduct which falls short of an agreement, other mechanisms, such as laws dealing with mergers (in addressing coordinated effects)[155] or joint dominance (with respect to the adoption of "facilitating practices")[156] may be relied upon to address the adverse effects of such conduct. Proposals for reform have also been suggested, such as the adoption of special provisions providing a remedy for forms of coordinated behaviour without the need to show an express agreement,[157] or modifying the test for price fixing to focus on such matters as interdependence[158] or on the impact of the communication and signalling by the parties.[159] Another policy suggestion is to apply other laws, such as merger review, more strictly to reduce the potential for oligopolistic interdependence in the first place.[160]

---

on the Existence of Collusion: Reconciling Antitrust Law with Oligopoly Theory" (2004) 71:3 *Antitrust Law Journal* 719. See Chapter 3, Section D(1)(e)(ii).

153 Milton Moore, *How Much Price Competition?* (Montreal: McGill-Queen's University Press, 1970) at 3:

> Formal collusion is susceptible to regulation, but conscious parallel action is extremely difficult to detect and even more difficult to prove, and it is impossible to prevent independent action on the recognition of mutual dependence. But the effects of all three are similar.

154 Louis Kaplow, "An Economic Approach to Price Fixing" (2011) 77:2 *Antitrust Law Journal* 343 at 353.

155 See Chapter 5, Section D(4)(a).

156 See Chapter 7, Section D(1).

157 William T Stanbury & GB Reschenthaler, "Oligopoly and Conscious Parallelism: Theory, Policy and the Canadian Cases" (1977) 15 *Osgoode Hall Law Journal* 617 at 685–700.

158 Louis Kaplow, "On the Meaning of Horizontal Agreements in Competition Law" (2011) 99:3 *California Law Review* 683.

159 Dennis W Carlton, Robert H Gertner & Andrew M Rosenfield, "Communication among Competitors: Game Theory and Antitrust" (1997) 5 *George Mason Law Review* 423 at 424–25: "Courts (and economists) should analyze how a specific type of communication did in fact affect prices and output in a specific market setting."

160 Joseph Kattan & William R Vigdor, "Game Theory and the Analysis of Collusion in Conspiracy and Merger Cases" (1997) 5 *George Mason Law Review* 441 at 453: "if oligopolistic interdependence is irremediable under Section 1 of the *Sherman Act*, a stringent approach toward incipient oligopolies may be warranted under the merger laws, at least to the extent that theory can reliably predict the non-competitive outcome."

iv) Participants and Parties to the Agreement

A conspiracy is not necessarily a frozen circle confined to a defined group of participants over its entire life. The Supreme Court of Canada stated in this respect:

> The agreement reached by the co-conspirators may contemplate a number of acts or offences. Any number of persons may be privy to it. Additional persons may join the ongoing scheme while others may drop out. So long as there is a continuing overall, dominant plan there may be changes in methods of operation, personnel, or victims, without bringing the conspiracy to an end.[161]

Different parties may therefore participate for shorter periods than the duration of the entire conspiracy, during which they agree to join in pursuing the common design. This is not unusual in cartels, which may continue for long periods but involve a changing group of players.

Aiding and abetting or counselling the formation of an agreement can be the basis for finding that an accused is a party to a conspiracy under sections 21 and 22 of the *Criminal Code*.[162] Thus, even if a party such as a trade or industry association is not a "competitor" (see below), if it aids or counsels the achievement of an agreement covered by section 45, this may give rise to an offence.[163] However, aiding and abetting the mere furtherance of the objects of an existing conspiracy (such as assisting someone to implement an existing price fixing agreement, as opposed to enabling its achievement in the first place) does not constitute an offence.[164]

v) Special Rules of Evidence

Specific rules govern the admissibility of evidence against co-conspirators.[165] For example, as an exception to the hearsay rule, extrajudicial statements, both in oral and documentary form, made by co-conspirators

---

161 *Papalia, above note 113 at 276.*

162 *Criminal Code*, RSC 1985, c C-46, s 21 [*Criminal Code*].

163 Canada, Competition Bureau, *Competitor Collaboration Guidelines* (23 December 2009), online: www.competitionbureau.gc.ca/eic/site/cb-bc.nsf/eng/03177.html at para 2.3.1 [*Collaboration Guidelines*].

164 *R v JF*, [2013] 1 SCR 565 at paras 39–43. However, "where a person, with knowledge of a conspiracy (which by definition includes knowledge of the unlawful object sought to be attained), does (or omits to do) something for the purpose of furthering the unlawful object, with the knowledge and consent of one or more of the existing conspirators, this provides powerful circumstantial evidence from which membership in the conspiracy can be inferred" (para 52).

165 This text cannot purport to provide a comprehensive review of these rules. A reference on the law of evidence should be consulted for same.

in furtherance of the conspiracy, may be admitted against other parties.[166] The *Competition Act*, section 69, also contains rules creating presumptions to the effect that actions taken by agents of an alleged co-conspirator, or records written or received by or in the possession of such an agent, or in the possession of a co-conspirator, are *prima facie* attributable to that co-conspirator.[167] In *R v Durward*, the presumptions in section 69(2) were held to violate the presumption of innocence in section 11(d) and the principles of fundamental justice in section 7 of the *Charter of Rights and Freedoms*.[168] It has been observed that the objectives of the provision within the *Competition Act* are arguably pressing and substantial, and that further appellate reviews will be needed to determine whether the decision is correct that the section cannot be upheld under section 1 of the *Charter*.[169]

c) Agreements Between Competitors

As noted above, section 45 no longer requires an assessment of the effects of the agreement on competition. However, the agreement must be with a *competitor*, which under section 45(7) "includes a person who it is reasonable to believe would be likely to compete with respect to a product" in the absence of the agreement.

Determining who is a competitor does not require the same process as market definition, but it does require some assessment of what products compete with one another and in what territories, in order to determine if the parties to the agreement are or were competing, or likely to compete. Thus, it requires at least a partial assessment of what relevant market competitors operate in.[170]

The Competition Bureau in 2009 released *Competitor Collaboration Guidelines*, representing "the general approach of the Bureau in applying sections 45 and 90.1 of the *Act* to collaborations between competitors." Given the statutory definition above, the Bureau views the term "competitors" as including "potential competitors." [171] The Bureau, however,

---

166 See, e.g., John Sopinka, Sidney N Lederman & Alan W Bryant, *The Law of Evidence in Canada*, 2d ed (Toronto: LexisNexis, 1999) at 303.

167 *Competition Act*, above note 52, s 69.

168 *R v Durward (aka Mancini), 2014 ONSC 4194 [Durward]*.

169 Pierre-Christian Collins Hoffman & Guy Pinsonnault, "The Purpose, Nature and Constitutionality of the Presumptions of Section 69 of the *Competition Act*" (2015) 28 *Canadian Competition Law Review* 1.

170 See Chapter 4.

171 *Collaboration Guidelines*, above note 163 at para 2.3.1, "Interpretation." In 2020, the Bureau released for public consultation during the period 29 July to 28 Sept revised *Competitor Collaboration Guidelines* (29 July 2020), online: www.ic.gc.ca/eic/site/cb-bc.nsf/eng/04543.html.

does not consider parties in a supplier-customer ("dual distribution") or in a franchisor-franchisee relationship to be competitors. This is a narrowing of the concept, given that suppliers may compete for sales and customers with distributors of the product which they themselves supply. The reason for the Bureau's approach is that these relationships "can be pro-competitive [and] not deserving of condemnation without an inquiry into their actual competitive effects."[172] Franchises, for example, may reduce distribution costs, increase franchisees' incentive to compete and increase competition.[173] Agreements of this kind may, however, be subjected by the Bureau to review under the civil provisions of the Act[174] and still may be subject to private civil damages actions under section 36.

Dual distribution and franchise agreements may create the basis for an "ancillary restraints defence," as discussed below. The issue would be whether the competitive restraint in question were merely ancillary, and reasonably necessary for giving effect to, a dual distribution or franchise agreement.[175]

d) *Per se* Categories

Section 45 identifies three categories of agreements which are deemed criminal without any inquiry into their anti-competitive effects: agreements between competitors to fix prices, allocate markets, and restrict output. These are all well-known types of anti-competitive conduct, having been the subject matter of prosecution and guilty pleas prior to the enactment of the amendments creating the *per se* provisions in 2010.[176]

Given that no anti-competitive effects need be proven, even agreements between only two competitors with potentially minor economic impact—such as price fixing by produce vendors at a local farmers' market—could be covered by the section. However, the discretion of both the Bureau in referring matters to the Director of Public Prosecutions (DPP) and the DPP's discretion in laying or withdrawing charges, may be exercised in situations where a *de minimis* effect are encountered. The *Collaboration Guidelines* note, "[t]he respective enforcement and prosecutorial decisions of the Commissioner and the DPP, and the ultimate resolution of issues, will depend on the particular circumstances of the matter in question."[177] The *Collaboration Guidelines* state further: "The Bureau will consider the merits of an alternative case resolution only

172 *Collaboration Guidelines*, above note 163.

173 See Chapter 8.

174 *Competition Act*, above note 52, ss 75–77; also vertical practices under s 79.

175 See below in this chapter at Section D(1)(g)(i).

176 For example, the cases reviewed in Chandler & Jackson, above note 77, Appendix II.

177 *Collaboration Guidelines*, above note 163 at para 2.3.1, "Interpretation."

in cases where, for example, the actual or potential economic harm is negligible, there are no aggravating factors and there are significant mitigating factors."[178] This signals that the Bureau may choose not to take enforcement action in respect of agreements that involve insignificant economic harm.

i) Section 45(1)(a): Price Fixing Agreements

Section 45(1)(a) refers to agreements "to fix, maintain, increase or control the price for the supply of the product." "Price" is defined broadly in section 45(8) to include "any discount, rebate, allowance, price concession or other advantage in relation to the supply of a product." The section thus covers not only agreements to fix the level of prices, but also agreements to reduce discounts, promotional allowances, and other customer advantages; to adopt a common price list or price formula; to apply specific price differentials to different grades of products; or to put in place common surcharges or credit terms.[179] On the other hand, the Bureau does not view section 45(1)(a) as applying to agreements which incidentally increase prices due to the implementation of certain measures, such as those to protect the environment, or to adopt a new industry standard.[180]

Cartels may use varying methods to set prices. Analysis of international cartels, for example, shows that the price-fixing methodology may vary: "In some cases the price is fixed on a worldwide basis, in other cases on a region-by-region basis, in still others on a country-by-country basis. The fixed prices may set a range, may establish a floor, or may be a specific price, fixed down to the penny or the equivalent."[181]

ii) Section 45(1)(b): Market Allocation Agreements

This prohibition covers agreements "to allocate sales, territories, customers or markets for the production or supply of the product." It includes agreements not to compete with respect to customers, whether on an individual, group, category, regional, or market-wide basis.[182]

The anti-competitive concern for geographic market division, for example, is that, "by dividing a market into territories and assigning particular territories exclusively to particular firms, each firm within its own

178 *Ibid* at para 2.7 at 17.

179 *Ibid* at para 2.4.1.

180 *Ibid*.

181 James M Griffin, "An Inside Look at a Cartel at Work: Common Characteristics of International Cartels," (Paper delivered at the ABA Antitrust Section, 48th Annual Spring Meeting, Washington, DC, 6 April 2000) at 10–11, online: www.justice.gov/atr/speech/inside-look-cartel-work-common-characteristics-international-cartels [Griffin].

182 *Collaboration Guidelines*, above note 163 at para 2.4.2.

territory may be able to act as a monopolist."[183] As seen in reported cases, agreements among competitors to divide a market based on customers or market shares are often accompanied by agreements to fix the prices offered to the customers which a particular competitor has been allocated.[184] In the case of an international graphite electrodes cartel implemented in Canada, for example, the parties agreed "to divide markets among themselves, on a region-by-region basis, and in each region to designate a company to fix the price that others in that region would follow," and also "to charge prices of graphite electrodes at certain levels and otherwise to increase and maintain prices in Canada and elsewhere."[185]

Market allocation agreements may be quite intricate and require ongoing monitoring and adjustment. In a volume allocation agreement (such as that used in the 1990s for lysine), "[c]artel members typically meet to determine how much each producer has sold during the preceding year and to calculate the total market size. Next, the cartel members estimate the market growth for the upcoming year and allocate that growth among themselves."[186]

iii) Section 45(1)(c): Production Limitation Agreements

Creating artificial scarcity by limiting output is a method used by cartels to increase the price for a product or service:

> In the case of a multi-party price-fixing cartel, the firms will attempt to act like a single-firm monopolist and reduce output and raise price to the monopoly level.[187]

It is therefore not surprising to find agreements limiting output listed in the *per se* categories found in section 45, since they go hand-in-hand with price fixing. Section 45(1)(c) covers agreements "to fix, maintain, control, prevent, lessen or eliminate the production or supply of the product." The Bureau views the section as including agreements to limit not only the quantity, but also the quality of production, as well as agreements to discontinue supplying products to specific customers or groups of customers.[188]

Production limits may also be part and parcel of volume allocation agreements, whereby the conspirators agree to limit their respective

183 Dunlop, Trebilcock & McQueen, above note 28 at 111.

184 See, e.g., *Atlantic Sugar Refineries* SCC, above note 73; *Clarke Transport*, above note 82.

185 *R v UCAR Inc* (1999), 164 FTR 85 at para 13 [*UCAR*].

186 Griffin, above note 181 at 11.

187 Dunlop, Trebilcock & McQueen, above note 28 at 111.

188 *Collaboration Guidelines*, above note 163 at para 2.4.3.

outputs to defined levels to keep prices up. This was the case with international cartels involving such commodities as lysine, citric acid, and vitamins.[189] Another example of an international output-limiting agreement involved potash.[190]

e) *Mens Rea*: The Intention to Agree

The *mens rea* of agreement was described by the Court in *R v Nova Scotia Pharmaceutical Society*:

> [T]he Crown must prove that the accused had the intention to enter into the agreement and had knowledge of the terms of that agreement. Once that is established, it would ordinarily be reasonable to draw the inference that the accused intended to carry out the terms in the agreement, unless there was evidence that the accused did not intend to carry out the terms of the agreement.[191]

The accused must not only agree to a common design or purpose, but also "to put the common design into effect."[192] The *mens rea* for conspiracy has also been described as "a genuine intention to agree to commit the indictable offence."[193] As the Court noted in *Nova Scotia Pharmaceutical Society*, however, the intention to enter into an agreement, which closely parallels the *actus reus*, creates an inference of the additional component of intent to put the agreement into effect. Thus, the evidence proving the agreement and the *mens rea* may be identical, or closely intertwined.

The Court in *Nova Scotia Pharmaceutical Society* also identified a second *mens rea* requirement: "that on an objective view of the evidence adduced, the accused intended to lessen competition unduly."[194] However, because the amended section 45 no longer involves any element of anti-competitive effect, this is not a component of the current offence.

f) Scope of Section 45: Application to Foreign-Based Conspiracies

The domestic impacts of an international cartel may provide a basis for the jurisdiction of Canadian courts over such activities.[195] Anti-competitive

---

189 Griffin, above note 181 at 14.

190 Christopher R Leslie, "Foreign Price-Fixing Conspiracies" (2017) 67 *Duke Law Journal* 557 at 560.

191 *Nova Scotia Pharmaceutical Society, above note 47 at para 120; see also para 118.*

192 *O'Brien*, above note 117 at 668.

193 *R v Wang*, 2013 BCCA 311 at para 44, leave to appeal to SCC refused [2013] SCCA No 368.

194 *Nova Scotia Pharmaceutical Society, above note 47 at para 119.*

195 The issue has not been definitively decided in a prosecution under s 45; in civil conspiracy actions, see *Vitapharm Canada Ltd v F Hoffmann-La Roche Ltd*, [2002] OJ No 298 (SC) at paras 95 and 101, aff'd [2002] OJ No 1400 (Div Ct); *Fairhurst*

harm in Canada provides the basis for a "real and substantial connection" to Canada and a foundation for jurisdiction by a Canadian court, even where a conspiracy is entered into outside the country.[196]

g) Defences

i) *The Ancillary Restraints Defence*

Section 45(4) provides:

> (4) No person shall be convicted of an offence under subsection (1) in respect of a conspiracy, agreement or arrangement that would otherwise contravene that subsection if
> (a) that person establishes, on a balance of probabilities, that
> (i) it is *ancillary to a broader or separate agreement or arrangement* that includes the same parties, and
> (ii) it is *directly related to, and reasonably necessary for giving effect to, the objective of that broader or separate agreement or arrangement*; and
> (b) the broader or separate agreement or arrangement, considered alone, does not contravene that subsection [emphasis added].

Of note:

- While the Crown carries the onus of proving that the *per se* restraint contravenes section 45(1), the parties to the agreement have the onus of proving the two elements of the defence set out in section 45(4)(a).
- For the defence to apply, the *per se* restraint can be in a separate agreement (such as a separate non-compete agreement rather than a non-compete covenant) as long as it is ancillary to a related agreement.

---

v Anglo American PLC, 2012 BCCA 257 at para 32; *Sun-Rype Products Ltd v Archer Daniels Midland Company*, [2013] 3 SCR 545 at para 46.

196 *Shah v LG Chem Ltd*, 2015 ONSC 2628 at para 83. Re the "real and substantial connection test," see, e.g., *R v Libman*, [1985] 2 SCR 178; *Lapointe Rosenstein Marchand Melançon LLP v Cassels Brock & Blackwell LLP*, [2016] 1 SCR 851. In the case of guilty pleas, courts have assumed jurisdiction over alleged foreign price fixing conspiracies: *R v BASF Aktiengesellschaft*, 1999 CarswellNat 6381 (FCTD); *R v Daicel Chemical Industries, Ltd*, T-1686-00 (2000); Canada, Competition Bureau, News Release, "Japanese Company to Plead Guilty and Pay US$130M Fine for Its Participation in a Bid-Rigging Scheme" (20 July 2016), online: www.canada.ca/en/competition-bureau/news/2016/07/unprecedented-cooperation-with-us-antitrust-enforcement-authority-leads-to-major-cartel-crackdown.html. See the *obiter* discussion of section 45 in *Canada (Commissioner of Competition) v HarperCollins Publishers LLC*, [2017] CCTD No 10 at paras 94–98 [*HarperCollins*], as well as in *Rakuten Kobo Inc v Canada(Commissioner of Competition)*, [2018] 4 FCR 111 (FC) at paras 116–21 [*Rakuten Kobo*].

a. Background

This defence was mentioned in several proposals for reform to the conspiracy provision as a way of distinguishing between "naked" agreements deserving of *per se* prohibition and those which may be anti-competitive but which should be subjected to a case-by-case analysis of their anti-competitive effect.[197] One study explained that the rationale for the defence was that restraints which are simply a minor or incidental part of a desirable broader agreement (such as an innovative joint venture), may be seen as deserving exemption to permit efficiencies and the lowering of costs.[198]

The defence in section 45 has several components which, given the onus being placed on the accused, may make it challenging to rely upon. One commentator concluded, "it will be difficult for competitors or potential competitors to be confident that this defence is available in many legitimate commercial collaborations."[199]

b. The Agreement Is Ancillary to a Broader or Separate Agreement

The dictionary definition of "ancillary" includes "subservient, subordinate to"[200] and "auxiliary."[201] These words suggest that the main thrust, subject matter, or purpose of the overall agreement cannot be the *per se* restraint. The restraint must be a minor or less significant part of a broader agreement or agreements. The Bureau's *Collaboration Guidelines* state that "ancillary" requires that the restraint is "functionally incidental or subordinate to the objective of some broader agreement" or "does not

---

197 See, e.g., Kennish & Ross, above note 18 at 55; *A Plan to Modernize Canada's Competition Regime*, above note 89, Recommendations 12 and 56–61.

198 Because the ancillary restraint on competition is not the principal *object* of the transaction, there is justification for treating such restraints differently, particularly when they are reasonably necessary to give effect to the principal agreement. For the most part, competition authorities approach ancillary restraints with greater leniency than naked restraints on competition because they recognize that the overall impact of the cooperative venture may enhance competition. For example, a research and development joint venture may lead to the creation of innovative new products, such as drugs, while a production joint venture may result in significant efficiencies and a lower cost product.

Al Gourlay, "A Report on Canada's Conspiracy Law: 1889–2001 and Beyond," *Report Commissioned by the Competition Bureau* (August 2001) at 29, online: www.competitionbureau.gc.ca/eic/site/cb-bc.nsf/vwapj/gourleyrep.pdf/$FILE/gourleyrep.pdf [emphasis in original].

199 Neil Campbell & Sorcha O'Carroll, "The Americanization of Canada's Competition Act" (2009) 48:3 *Canadian Business Law Journal* 446 at 451.

200 *The Shorter Oxford English Dictionary* (Oxford: Clarendon Press, 1973) at 68.

201 *Black's Law Dictionary* (St Paul: West Publishing, 1979) at 78.

represent the object of [the] cooperation." Factors which the Bureau takes into account in assessing this are

- the form of the agreement (the Bureau anticipates that ancillary restraints will typically be reduced to writing as part of formal agreements);
- the functional relationship or lack thereof between the restraint and the principal agreement; and
- how the restraint makes the main agreement more effective in accomplishing its purpose.[202]

The *Collaboration Guidelines* provide the following examples of matters which would be considered ancillary:

> (a) A non-compete clause found in an employment agreement, or an agreement for the sale of assets or shares between parties
> (b) An agreement among competitors to charge a common price in a blanket license agreement for artistic works
> (c) An agreement to abstain from making material changes to a business pending the consummation of a merger
> (d) A non-compete obligation between the parent undertakings and a joint venture where such obligations correspond only to the products, services, and territories covered by the joint venture agreement[203]

c. Directly Related to and Reasonably Necessary for the Objective of the Broader or Separate Agreement

This element of the defence requires that the parties establish a connection between restraint and achieving the objective of the broader agreement. This must be grounded in the facts of the subject matter of the broader agreement. For example, a non-compete clause which is of reasonable scope and duration is arguably a necessary component of the sale of an operating business. Without the non-compete clause, the purchaser would be unable to realize the value of the goodwill of the business, as the vendor would be able to poach customers or take advantage of commercial knowledge gained during its operation. Such a restraint is connected to, and necessary for, the objective of the broad agreement, which is to permit the sale of an ongoing and viable business.

The *Collaboration Guidelines* signal that while there is no requirement that the restraint be the *least* restrictive available, the existence of

---

202 *Collaboration Guidelines*, above note 163 at 13–14.

203 *Ibid* at 12–13.

significantly less restrictive alternatives available to achieve the results of the restraint may create a basis for the Bureau looking to the parties to show why those alternatives were impractical. If the Bureau finds less restrictive means were "reasonably available to the parties at the time when the agreement was entered into," it "will conclude that the restraint was not reasonably necessary." Factors taken into account by the Bureau in examining whether the restraint was reasonably necessary include:

- the duration of the ancillary restraint
- the subject matter of the restraint (e.g., whether it applies to products outside of the collaboration)
- the geographic scope of the restraint
- whether, in the absence of the restraint, the broader agreement would likely be implemented
- whether, in the absence of the restraint, the broader agreement could only be implemented under considerably more uncertain conditions, at substantially higher cost or over a significantly longer period[204]

These factors emphasize the need to examine the scope and duration of restrictive covenants or other provisions to measure their importance. The wording of the defence asks about "reasonableness," as opposed to necessity, indicating that some latitude must be given for unknown or uncertain contingencies. In the common law context, the courts employ a test of "reasonableness as between the parties" for restrictive covenants, also framed as "not more than adequate to protect [a] party's interests."[205] Such an assessment may be relevant in determining that the restriction on competition is reasonably needed to further the objectives of the broader agreement, although the differing context within a statute directed at the public interest in advancing competition must be taken into account.

Evidence of how the agreement's objectives played out in the commercial or other negotiations or planning of the parties may be important to establishing the defence. The *Collaboration Guidelines* indicate that the Bureau will take particular interest, for example, in "evidence created during the evaluation and negotiation of the agreement that demonstrates the objectives of the agreement, and any evidence of alternative options considered by the parties at the time the agreement was negotiated."[206]

---

204 *Ibid* at 14–15.

205 *Tank Lining Corp v Dunlop Industrial Ltd* (1982), 140 DLR (3d) 659 at 666 (Ont CA).

206 *Collaboration Guidelines*, above note 163 at 15.

d. The Broader or Separate Agreement, Considered Alone, Does Not Contravene Section 45

This requirement adds little beyond performing a backstop function to ensure that the mere presence of an element that is ancillary does not inadvertently exempt a broader or separate agreement which itself falls within one of the three *per se* categories.

e. Case Law

The issue of the ancillary restraints defence has arisen in civil damage actions relying upon section 45. In a class action by Tim Hortons franchisees against the parent franchisor, it was held in a summary judgment motion that setting the price at which doughnuts could be sold was ancillary to a joint venture agreement to construct a bakery and produce the product, and therefore that the defence applied.[207]

On the other hand, a restriction in a joint venture agreement between Dow Chemicals and NOVA Chemicals on the ability of Dow to competitively purchase ethane, was held at trial not to qualify for the ancillary restraint defence. The Court held that NOVA had not led evidence that the restriction on Dow's ability to compete was related to the broader agreement or that less restrictive arrangements were not available. In addition, the Court found that the restriction's duration, 80 years, far exceeded any period that could be considered reasonably necessary for the protection of NOVA's interests in the plant which was the subject of the joint venture, particularly given that NOVA had expected to recover its investment in the plant in only eight years.[208]

f. American Ancillary Restraint Jurisprudence

The American "ancillary restraint" concept developed not so much as an outright defence to conspiracy, as in the case of section 45(4), but as a way of determining which agreements should be subject to *per se* condemnation as opposed to a more searching assessment of the economic benefits under the rule of reason. As such, its application may sow confusion if directly applied here.[209]

---

207 *Fairview Donut Inc v The TDL Group Corp, 2012 ONSC 1252 at para 633, aff'd on other grounds 2012 ONCA 867.*

208 *Dow Chemical Canada ULC v NOVA Chemicals Corp*, 2018 ABQB 482 at paras 1415–16, aff'd on this point, 2020 ABCA 320 [*Dow Chemical*].

209 The context of the US jurisprudence, interpreting the broad and flexible test of "unreasonable" restraints under the American *Sherman Act*, differs from s 45 of the *Competition Act*, above note 52, which employs very specific statutory language for the defence in Canada. The US judge-made ancillary restraints concept therefore covers a much broader range of anti-competitive agreements than the three *per se* categories found in s 45(1). That scope affects the nature of the test

The ancillary restraint concept was first invoked by the US Supreme Court as *dicta* in 1899[210] as a way to identify agreements which should be viewed as reasonable and not illegal under the *Sherman Act*. It was then employed in the 1970s in jurisprudence distinguishing "naked" anti-competitive agreements which should be subject to *per se* treatment from those subject to a broader assessment of their effects under the rule of reason.[211] The Supreme Court held that the rule of reason applies "as a standard for testing the enforceability of covenants in restraint of trade which are ancillary to a legitimate transaction, such as an employment contract or the sale of a going business."[212] Under the jurisprudence, the anti-competitive restraint must be "no greater than necessary" to facilitate the proffered pro-competitive main purpose of the agreement.[213]

ii) *Export Defence*

a. The Statutory Language

Section 45(5) provides:

> (5) No person shall be convicted of an offence under subsection (1) in respect of a conspiracy, agreement or arrangement that relates only to the export of products from Canada, unless the conspiracy, agreement or arrangement
> (a) has resulted in or is likely to result in a reduction or limitation of the real value of exports of a product;
> (b) has restricted or is likely to restrict any person from entering into or expanding the business of exporting products from Canada; or
> (c) is in respect only of the supply of services that facilitate the export of products from Canada.

The section creates a defence for an agreement which "relates only to the export of products from Canada" but takes the defence away where there are domestic impacts. This reflects an effort to balance the exemption

---

developed by the US courts, given that the US standard has to be flexible enough to permit a potentially broad range of agreements to be susceptible to rule of reason treatment.

210 *United States v Addyston Pipe and Steel Co*, 85 F 271 (6th Cir 1898), aff'd as modified, 175 US 211 (1899).

211 *Broadcast Music, Inc v CBS, Inc*, 441 US 1 (1979).

212 *National Society of Professional Engineers v United States, 435 US 679 (1978) at 688. See Medical Center at Elizabeth Place, LLC v Premier Health Partners, 2017-2 Trade Cas. 80,084 (SD Ohio); Medical Center at Elizabeth Place, LLC v Atrium Health Systems, 922 F3d 713 (Sixth Cir 2019).*

213 Gavil, Kovacic & Baker, above note 43 at 159.

of export agreements against the potential for prejudice to the domestic economy.

The section was first enacted in 1960, and its basic structure has remained the same since then, although the exemption it creates has been broadened somewhat by two rounds of amendment. From the time of its enactment, concerns were expressed that the exemption was ineffective because it contained several restrictive qualifications which severely narrowed its availability.[214] At the time of the 1986 amendments which created the *Competition Act*, the sponsoring department's *Competition Law Amendments, A Guide* stated that it was the view of "many observers" that "the present construction of the exemption is unclear, too restrictive and may inhibit the formation of export consortia."[215] As a result, Parliament made three principal changes.[216] First, it removed the requirement that an export agreement would not qualify for the exemption if it "lessened or is likely to lessen competition unduly in relation to a product in the domestic market." This language had created uncertainty as to the availability of the defence where there were unintended domestic spillover effects.[217]

Second, the requirement that the export agreement not result in a "reduction or limitation of the *volume of exports* of a product" was modified to a "reduction or limitation *of the real value of exports* of a product." This change recognized that an export cartel will often reduce output in order to increase price.[218] Such a reduction is now acceptable as long as the real value of exports is not diminished. That is possible if an increase in price offsets the reduction in output in terms of the net effect on export revenues.[219]

Finally, amendments in 1986 and 2009 reworded the qualifier in section 45(5)(c), which now takes away the exemption for an agreement that "is in respect only of the supply of services that facilitate the export of products from Canada."[220]

---

214 Robert D McIntyre, "The Purpose, Operation and Effect of the Export Exemption Provisions of the Combines Investigation Act (Section 32(4) and (5)" (1964) 3:1 *Osgoode Hall Law Journal* 106 at 110 [McIntyre].

215 Canada, Consumer and Corporate Affairs, *Competition Law Amendments, A Guide* (Ottawa: Minister of Supply and Services, 1985) at 27 [*Competition Law Amendments Guide* 1985].

216 *Competition Tribunal Act*, above note 76, s 30.

217 *Competition Law Amendments Guide* 1985, above note 215 at 28; Frederic Desmarais, "Export Cartels in the Americas and the OAS: Is the Harmonization of National Competition Laws the Solution?" (2009) 33 *Manitoba Law Journal* 41 at 70 [Desmarais].

218 Desmarais, above note 217 at 71.

219 *Competition Law Amendments Guide* 1985, above note 215 at 28.

220 The initial 1986 amendments removed the defence for an agreement that "prevented or lessened or is likely to prevent or lessen competition unduly in the

b. Export Exemptions in Other Jurisdictions

In the United States, exemption from antitrust of export cartels is provided by three pieces of legislation. Under the *Webb-Pomerene Export Trade Act of 1918*,[221] registration can be made with the Federal Trade Commission within thirty days from the date an export agreement comes into effect in order to obtain exemption. Based on the belief that the terms of that exemption were too narrow, the legislation was supplemented by the *Export Trading Company Act*, which, for example, applies to services as well as goods.[222] The Secretary of Commerce, in concurrence with the Attorney General, is given authority under that legislation to issue a certificate to an export association seeking the exemption. Finally, the *Foreign Trade Antitrust Improvements Act* eliminates jurisdiction for antitrust over conduct that occurs in the United States or abroad, where the effects of the conduct are felt only in foreign markets. This legislation did not create an explicit export exemption but it has a similar effect, by removing conduct with only foreign impacts from the scope of American law.

Exemptions in competition laws for export cartels are found in numerous other jurisdictions, including the European Union.[223]

c. Policy Rationale and Concerns

At the time of its first enactment in 1960, the Minister of Justice, E Davie Fulton, made statements in Parliament about the factors motivating the defence. One was a desire to permit Canadian firms to compete globally, particularly in light of the presence of other international cartels.[224] A specific concern was the ability of Canadian firms to compete with state-sponsored enterprises, including those from the then Soviet bloc.[225]

---

supply of services facilitating the export of products from Canada." This was substantially narrowed in 2009 to the current language: *Budget Implementation Act, 2009*, above note 56, s 410.

221 15 USCA §§ 61–65 (1973) s 5.

222 15 USCA §§ 4001–3, 4011–21 (West Supp 1983).

223 See A Paul Victor, "Export Cartels: An Idea Whose Time Has Passed" (1991) 60:2 *Antitrust Law Journal* 571 at 575–77 [Victor].

224 McIntyre, above note 214 at 106.

225 *Ibid* at 107. Fulton stated:

> [I]n international trade we are now coming into a situation where we are faced with the massive communist organization, represented by the Union of Soviet Socialist Republics, as a competitor and increasingly this great force is entering into international trade with the whole weight of the state behind it. This state organization is prepared to do anything to obtain markets for its exports and to eliminate markets for exports from other countries, particularly the western world with which, ideologically, the Soviets are in conflict.

One commentator explained that the export exemption would permit Canadian firms to work together to realize economies of scale unachievable without competitive collaboration:

> [I]t is only by some concerted arrangement that Canadian industries faced by foreign cartelization, as exemplified by the European and Japanese giants, can obtain the larger production runs necessary for competitively priced products; consequently the export exemption provisions are a recognition of economic reality.[226]

The sponsoring Department's *Background Information and Explanatory Notes* (which preceded the 1986 amendments) also justified broadening the defence on the basis of the significance of exports to the Canadian economy and the need to assist "firms combining their efforts to penetrate foreign markets."[227] The OECD similarly described the rationale for exemption of export cartels internationally in terms of the self-interest of the exempting state:

> The rationale for permitting export cartels is that it may facilitate cooperative penetration of foreign markets, transfer income from foreign consumers to domestic producers and result in a favourable balance of trade.[228]

A number of policy concerns have been raised by the exemption. First, it is seen as inconsistent with free trade:

> [E]xport cartels may maintain or create barriers to trade by forcing customers to pay high, non-competitive prices or by limiting the quantity of exports. In such cases they lead to a deliberalisation of international trade, which jeopardises important economic goals, such as increasing economic efficiency and the optimum supply of commodities to consumers.[229]

Second, export cartels may have adverse effects on domestic markets. Export cartels create a platform and domestic culture which may lead to cartelization or tacit collusion in the domestic market. For example, exporting competitors who exchange trade information in support of an export cartel may pattern their domestic competitive behaviour in

---

226 *Ibid.*

227 *Background Information and Explanatory Notes* 1984 above note 7 at 11.

228 RS Khemani & DM Shapiro, OECD Directorate for Financial, Fiscal and Enterprise Affairs, *Glossary of Industrial Organisation Economics and Competition Law* (OECD: Paris, 1993), online: www.oecd.org/regreform/sectors/2376087.pdf.

229 OECD, Committee of Experts on Restrictive Business Practices, *Export Cartels* (Paris: OECD, 1974) at 7.

light of the knowledge gained and the practices occurring in the export context. In explaining a recommendation by an American Bar Association subcommittee to eliminate the export cartels exemption worldwide, one participant noted, "[o]nce competitors are allowed to join for overtly anticompetitive purposes in foreign markets, it is not surprising to find that the attractions of covert collaboration are too great to resist at home."[230]

Third, export cartels are seen as being particularly detrimental to developing economies.[231] Consumers in such countries are often "price takers," lacking the economic power to resist the price increases forced upon them by an international cartel. An example involves potash, a commodity with a significant Canadian dimension.[232] Canada controls more than half of the world's reserves, and domestic firms have participated in export markets outside Canada and the United States through a joint export venture, Canpotex. Noting that "potash is essential in the production of fertiliser used in the agricultural industry," one commentator concluded that price increases from the potash export cartel "had a devastating effect on developing countries" which lack potash reserves.[233]

In 2003, the Canadian Bar Association delivered a submission advocating elimination of the exemption of export cartels as part of a proposed Free Trade Agreement of the Americas, citing the need to remedy the failure to do so in NAFTA, which explicitly preserved the exemptions.[234] Canada has, however, taken no steps to move away from the exemption. The major revision of the conspiracy provision in 2009, in fact, broadened the export exemption somewhat.[235]

Compelling policy arguments against export cartels have, elsewhere, led some jurisdictions to move away from explicit exemptions to tests focused on competitive effects on their domestic market. However, the

---

230 Victor, above note 223 at 577.

231 See, e.g., Margaret C Levenstein & Valerie Y Suslow, "The Changing International Status of Export Cartel Exemptions" (2005) 20:4 *American University International Law Review* 785 at 796 [Levenstein & Suslow].

232 See Frederic Jenny, "Export Cartels in Primary Products: The Potash Case in Perspective" in Simon J Evenett & Frédéric Jenny, eds, *Trade, Competition, and the Pricing of Commodities* (Centre for Economic Policy Research: London, 2012) ch 6 at 99.

233 Tiffany Kwok, "Export Cartels: Analysing the Gap in International Competition Law and Trade" (2015) 2:4 *Edinburgh Student Law Review* 140 at 144.

234 National Competition Law Section, Canadian Bar Association, "Submission Concerning the FTAA Competition Chapter" (April 2003) at 2, online: www.cba.org/CMSPages/GetFile.aspx?guid=09b626cb-8dfa-4d31-ac5c-9a92c555d3f6.

235 *Budget Implementation Act, 2009*, above note 56, s 410.

impact of these changes on export cartels is uncertain at best, given that the modified test still leads these countries not to apply their domestic law to export-focused conduct.[236] The political will has evidently yet to crystallize for meaningful change to be made to the substance of the exemption.[237]

d. Case Law

There have been few cases in Canada considering the export exemption. In *R c Manigo inc*,[238] the accused were fourteen producers of salted cod from the Gaspé region of Quebec. They entered into a consortium, agreeing to sell all their production to an Italian corporation, Canada Fish, for export. The consortium took steps to stop one of its member producers from selling to a competing exporter. The Court found that the export defence was inapplicable because of the qualifier in what is now section 45(5)(b) to the effect that the defence does not apply if the agreement "has restricted or is likely to restrict any person from entering into or expanding the business of exporting products from Canada." In this case, the export agreement kept the domestic complainant firm from expanding its exports. The case highlights that the exemption will not apply if there is a domestic competitive effect.

e. Export Cartels May Be Subject to Foreign Law

While the Canadian statute provides an exemption to domestic conspiracies which relate only to the export of products from Canada, it does not exempt the parties from the potential application of foreign law to any cartel entered into. The United States, for example, has passed legislation which permits the application of the *Sherman Act* to conduct which has "a direct, substantial, and reasonable effect" on US commerce, including imports and exports.[239] The US Supreme Court has confirmed that antitrust claims may be made which address conduct which did not take place in the United States, on the basis that "it is well-established by now that the *Sherman Act* applies to foreign conduct that was meant to produce and did in fact produce some substantial effect in the United States."[240] This potentially exposes Canadian

236 Levenstein & Suslow, above note 231 at 806–12.

237 One commentator concluded in 2009 that there is "no willingness to ban export cartels among the major economies of the world, including the United States": Desmarais, above note 217 at 79.

238 *R c Manigo inc*, [1988] JQ no 101 (CS).

239 *Foreign Trade Antitrust Improvements Act of 1982*, 15 USC § 6a.

240 *Hartford Fire Insurance Co v United States*, 509 US 764 (1993) at 796; see Douglas F Broder, *US Antitrust Law and Enforcement: A Practice Introduction*, 3d ed (New York: Oxford University Press, 2016) at 70–74.

firms to both prosecution and to damages claims in the United States if the impact of a cartel in which they participate is realized there. An action was brought against Canadian and other potash producers in 2008, alleging a potash cartel which affected American purchasers. The action was held to properly state a claim under US antitrust laws,[241] but was then settled with the payment of nearly USD$100 million by the firms implicated.[242]

iii) Regulated Conduct

Section 45(7) provides that existing jurisprudence establishing what has been referred to as the "regulated conduct defence" continues to apply to section 45:

> (7) The rules and principles of the common law that render a requirement or authorization by or under another Act of Parliament or the legislature of a province a defence to a prosecution under subsection 45(1) of this Act, as it read immediately before the coming into force of this section, continue in force and apply in respect of a prosecution under subsection (1).

The application of this defence can be seen in *Canada (Attorney General) v Law Society of British Columbia*.[243] In that case, the Competition Bureau started an investigation into the actions of the Law Society's Discipline Committee to suspend Mr Jabour, a BC lawyer, for advertising his legal services, such as uncontested divorces and incorporations, at fixed fees. The Law Society, in turn, applied for a declaration that the Bureau was without jurisdiction to investigate the conduct. The Supreme Court of Canada upheld the finding of the BC Court of Appeal that the then *Combines Investigation Act* conspiracy provision, section 32 (the predecessor to section 45), did not apply to the Law Society. The Court reviewed the jurisprudence, which it termed the "regulated industries cases," which had held that federal criminal combines prohibitions did not apply to actions authorized by provincial statute, such as in the

---

241 *Minn-Chem, Inc v Agrium Inc, 683 F3d 845 (7th Cir 2012), cert denied 570 US 935 (2013).*

242 Pav Jordan & Jeff Gray, "Three Potash Exporters Settle U.S. Cartel Lawsuit," *The Globe and Mail* (30 January 2013), online: www.theglobeandmail.com/globe-investor/three-potash-exporters-settle-us-cartel-lawsuit/article8003542/#:~:-text=Canada's%20major%20potash%20exporters%20have,.%2C%20and%20Plymouth%2C%20Minn. The firms denied any wrongdoing in reaching the settlement.

243 *Canada (Attorney General) v Law Society of British Columbia*, [1982] 2 SCR 307 [*Jabour*].

context of the regulation of agricultural products.[244] The Supreme Court identified three main reasons for this finding.

First, the use of the word "unduly" in the *Combines Investigation Act* conspiracy prohibition, and its criminal law character, was viewed as introducing a requirement that the conduct in question must operate against the public interest. The Supreme Court held in *Jabour*:

> So long as the [federal conspiracy provision], is styled as a criminal prohibition, proceedings in its implementation and enforcement will require a demonstration of some conduct contrary to the public interest. It is this element of the federal legislation that, these cases all conclude, can be negated by the authority extended by a valid provincial regulatory statute.[245]

Second, provincial actions to regulate an activity, and the actions of a regulatory body to give effect to a regulatory scheme, were found to lack the necessary "intent to breach the federal law."[246]

Third, the Court found that under the cases, provincially mandated conduct lacked the voluntariness which is a hallmark of criminal conspiracy. Justice Estey for the Court held that in the case at hand:

> [T]he provincial statute is "coercive" as applied to members of the provincially regulated group, whereas the federal statute is directed towards "voluntary combinations or agreements." Here the "agreement" was apparently the determination by the Discipline Committee that the appellant Jabour by advertising as he did was guilty of professional misconduct. In so "agreeing," the Benchers are said not only to have been doing that which was permitted by their admittedly valid parent statute but were in fact discharging their assigned duties under that Act.[247]

The Court rejected the suggestion that in order to qualify for the defence, the provincial legislation must expressly require, not merely authorize, the conduct under consideration, and that the provincial

---

244 *Ontario Boys' Wear Ltd v The Advisory Committee*, [1944] SCR 349; *Re The Farm Products Marketing Act*, [1957] SCR 198; *R v Chung Chuck*, [1929] 1 DLR 756 (BC CA); *R v Can Breweries Ltd*, [1960] OR 601 (SC); *R v Simoneau* (1935), 65 CCC 19 (Que CQ); *Cherry v The King ex rel Wood* (1937), 69 CCC 219 (Sask CA) [*Cherry*].

245 *Jabour*, above note 243 at 354.

246 Referring to *Cherry*, above note 244, the Court in *Jabour*, above note 243 at 349, found that "The Court was there concerned with the practical problem of the presence or absence of 'intent' on the part of provincial administrators to breach the federal law."

247 *Jabour*, above note 243 at 355.

scheme must specifically approve regulations controlling the activity in question (as opposed to merely authorizing the regulator to pass them).[248] In the end, the Court held that there was no conflict between the federal and provincial legislation; the federal conspiracy prohibition simply did not apply to the Law Society's conduct.

These principles were applied by the Federal Court in *Industrial Milk Producers Assn v British Columbia (Milk Board)* to strike out a civil damages claim for breach of the conspiracy provision on the basis that the provision was displaced by regulation. In that case, as in some of the earlier agricultural regulated industries cases, the regulated conduct was authorized by a complex joint federal and provincial statutory scheme.[249]

In *Garland v Consumers' Gas Co*, the Supreme Court rejected the application of the regulated industries cases as a defence against an alleged breach by a provincially regulated gas utility of the *Criminal Code* criminal interest rate provisions. The Court noted that the regulated conduct cases depended on the existence of language in the criminal competition law provision which "granted leeway to those acting pursuant to a valid provincial regulatory scheme." Given the absence of such language in the *Criminal Code*, the Court held there was no reason limiting the application of the *Code* to the gas company.[250]

In summary, the following general principles apply to the application "regulated conduct defence" to section 45:

- The defence applies to *conduct* that is regulated; the mere fact that regulation is present does not exempt the actions of an entire industry from section 45.[251]
- To benefit from the defence, the conduct may be required, directed, *or* authorized;[252] it does not have to be specifically mandated under the regulatory scheme.[253]

---

248 The Court held that "in none of these cases so far has there been any requirement in the provincial statute for approval by the province of any regulations adopted by the statutory body for the control of the activities in question." *Jabour*, above note 243 at 350.

249 *Industrial Milk Producers Assn v British Columbia (Milk Board), [1989] 1 FC 463 [Industrial Milk Producers]*.

250 *Garland v Consumers' Gas Co*, [2004] 1 SCR 629 at para 77 [*Garland*].

251 *Industrial Milk Producers*, above note 249 at para 36.

252 *Hughes v Ontario (Liquor Control Board), 2018 ONSC 1723 at para 220 [Hughes]*.

253 *Ibid*; *Jabour*, above note 243; *Fournier Leasing Co v Mercedes-Benz Canada Inc*, 2012 ONSC 2752 at para 58 [*Fournier Leasing*]; in *Hughes*, the Ontario Court of Appeal found that the defence could be established by "[b]oth an express grant of authority and a grant of authority by necessary implication": *Hughes v Ontario (Liquor Control Board)*, 2019 ONCA 305 at para 25.

- The authorization must derive from validly enacted federal or provincial legislation or regulations.[254]
- The statutory or regulatory authority must be exercised; a statute merely providing authority which has not been exercised would not provide a foundation for the defence.
- The use of regulatory authority as a springboard to engage in anti-competitive conduct that is not authorized by the regulatory scheme will not benefit from the defence.[255]

While the common law principles applicable to regulated conduct are preserved by subsection (7), an issue raised is whether those principles may need to be adapted or modified in view of changes in language in the amended section 45. For example, the elimination of the undueness requirement removes one basis for the public interest rationale for the common law defence as developed in the jurisprudence. Nonetheless, the intent and voluntariness aspects arguably still apply, preserving those rationales for the defence as established under the common law.[256]

The Competition Bureau's Bulletin on the regulated conduct defence accepts that the case law has "immunized a regulatory body, exercising its authority under a validly enacted law, from the criminal conspiracy provisions of the prevailing competition law by, effectively, reading down the conspiracy provision."[257] The Bulletin states that where "a validly enacted provincial law authorizes (expressly or impliedly) or requires the impugned conduct . . . the Bureau will not pursue a case under section 45 of the Act."[258] The Bulletin, however, signals uncertainty in the

---

254 Fournier Leasing, above note 253.

255 *Industrial Milk Producers*, above note 249 at para 36.

256 The motions court judge in *Hughes* rejected the submission that the removal of "unduly" changed the availability of the defence:

> I agree with the Defendants' argument that when the conspiracy provisions were amended, Parliament ensured that the Regulated Conduct Defence would continue to apply, despite the removal of any reference to "unduly" lessening or restraining competition. As explained by Parliament's Standing Senate Committee on Banking, Trade and Finance in its Report on the 2010 amendments to the *Competition Act*, s. 45(7) was designed to preserve the Regulated Conduct Defence despite the removal of the word 'unduly' from the statutory language.

Hughes, above note 252 at para 226.

257 Canada, Competition Bureau, "Technical Bulletin on the Regulated Conduct Defence" (27 September 2010), online: www.competitionbureau.gc.ca/eic/site/cb-bc.nsf/vwapj/RegulatedConduct-sept-2010-e.pdf/$FILE/RegulatedConduct-sept-2010-e.pdf at 3 [*Regulated Conduct Defence Bulletin*].

258 *Ibid* at 4.

case law about whether regulated parties, as opposed to the regulators, may be subject to the Act in spite of the regulatory regime.[259]

Where the source of the regulatory authority is federal (as opposed to provincial), the Bulletin is less categorical on the availability of the defence,[260] taking the position that this requires an interpretation of the applicable federal regulatory scheme to determine "whether the provisions can stand together [with the *Competition Act*] and both operate without either interfering with the other, i.e. whether a party may reasonably comply with both the [*Competition*] *Act* and the other federal law(s)." The Bureau takes the view that the *Competition Act* applies "unless it can confidently determine that Parliament intended that the other federal law prevail, either by clear language in the Act or by the other federal law authorizing or requiring the particular conduct or, more generally, providing an exhaustive statement of the law concerning a matter."[261] The presence of a "comprehensive regulatory scheme," however, will be taken by the Bureau as such an "exhaustive statement."[262]

iv) *Affiliates*

a. The Exemption

Pursuant to section 45(6), it is not an offence if the agreement in question "is entered into only by parties each of which is, in respect of every one of the others, an affiliate." Affiliation is defined by sections 2(2) through (4) of the Act.

An entity is an affiliate of another if it is a subsidiary of that entity or if they are both subsidiaries of or controlled by the same entity or individual.[263] An entity is a subsidiary of another if it is controlled by that other entity.[264] "Control" is in turn defined for corporations around direct or indirect holdings of securities that give the right to cast more than 50 percent of the votes to elect directors of the controlled corporation, where such votes are sufficient to elect a majority of those directors.[265] Control of non-corporate entities is tied to the right to receive more than 50 percent of the profits of that entity or more than 50 percent of

---

259 *Ibid* at 6, citing *Waterloo Law Association v Canada (Attorney General of Canada)* (1986), 58 OR (2d) 275 (HC); *R v Charterways Transportation Ltd* (1981), 40 OR (2d) 86 (CA) [*Charterways* CA] and *R v British Columbia Fruit Growers Assn* (1985), 11 CPR (3d) 183 (BC SC).

260 See *Garland*, above note 250.

261 *Regulated Conduct Defence Bulletin*, above note 257 at 7.

262 *Ibid*.

263 *Competition Act*, above note 52, ss 2(2)(a) & (b).

264 *Ibid*, s 2(3).

265 *Ibid*, s 2(4)(a).

its assets on dissolution.[266] Finally, control of corporations by the Crown occurs through either holdings of vote-bearing shares (employing the test set out above) or in the case of a corporation without share capital, by the ability of a Minister or the Governor in Council to nominate a majority of the directors.[267]

b. Rationale for the Exemption

Why are affiliates exempt from the conspiracy offence? First, it is arguable that actions taken by a firm through direction of a subsidiary are in substance not actions of multiple parties but simply the actions of the directing firm; this is not a "true" conspiracy among differing parties. Subsidiaries can simply reflect the corporate form chosen to conduct business, and treating them as separate entities under conspiracy law arguably elevates form over substance. Second, the exemption means that a holding company can provide corporate direction to a controlled subsidiary concerning competitive strategies such as pricing, product development, or marketing, and the subsidiary can follow this direction without fear that this conduct might come afoul of the criminal *per se* conspiracy prohibition in section 45 of the Act. Permitting such behaviour is consistent with governance duties created by corporate law.[268]

Having said that, common ownership of two competitors' stock by an entity which does not control either may raise competition concerns where the common owners become the conduit for collusive behaviour.[269] For example, in examining a significant merger between The Dow Chemical Company (Dow) and EI du Pont de Nemours and Company (DuPont), the European Commission concluded that common shareholding ownership in an industry may lead to higher prices and less innovation.[270] In Canada, such conduct cannot be addressed under section 45, however, unless an agreement can be proven. It was noted in Chapter 5, however, that the merger provisions may apply if,

266 *Ibid*, s 2(4)(c).

267 *Ibid*, s 2(4)(b).

268 See J Anthony VanDuzer, *The Law of Partnerships and Corporations*, 4th ed (Toronto: Irwin, 2018) ch 9.

269 See, e.g., Fiona Scott Morton & Herbert Hovenkamp, "Horizontal Shareholding and Antitrust Policy," (2018) 127 *Yale Law Journal* 2026; Anna Tzanaki, "The Common Ownership Boom—Or: How I Learned to Start Worrying and Love Antitrust" (21 May 2019), *Competition Policy International*—CPI Antitrust Chronicle on "Common Ownership Revisited," online: https://ssrn.com/abstract=340120.9.

270 EC, *Dow/Du Pont*, Case M.7932 (27 March 2017), online: https://ec.europa.eu/competition/mergers/cases/decisions/m7932_13668_3.pdf.

for example, the acquisition of an interlocking directorship creates the ability to materially influence a competitor.[271]

2) Employer Agreements: Section 45(1.1)

Section 45(1.1) came into effect in 2023[272] to address a perceived lacuna in the general conspiracy provision for agreements among employers, given the language of s 45(1) which restricts its application to supply-side agreements.[273] It creates a criminal offence punishable by up to 14 years imprisonment or a fine in the discretion of the court, or both. It provides:

> (1.1) Every person who is an employer commits an offence who, with another employer who is not affiliated with that person, conspires, agrees or arranges
> (a) to fix, maintain, decrease or control salaries, wages or terms and conditions of employment; or
> (b) to not solicit or hire each other's employees.

With respect to section 45(1.1)(a), the Competition Bureau has issued *Guidelines* which state that "terms and conditions of employment" may include "job descriptions, allowances such as *per diem* and mileage reimbursements, non-monetary compensation, working hours, location and non-compete clauses, or other directives that may restrict an individual's job opportunities."[274]

Section 45(1.1) (b) prohibits so-called "no-poach" agreements. Such agreements had become subject to active enforcement in the United States by antitrust authorities.[275] The Bureau's *Guidelines* on the provision states that such agreements "could include, for example, restrictions on the communication of information related to job openings and the adoption of biased hiring mechanisms."[276]

---

271 See Chapter 5, Section B.

272 For background see John Pecman, Chris Margison & Robin Spillette, "No-Poach and Wage-Fixing Agreements - A Canadian Perspective" (2021) 17 *Competition L Int'l* 49.

273 *Bill C-19 2022*, above note, s 257. This provision came into force on June 23, 2023.

274 Competition Bureau, *Enforcement Guidelines on wage-fixing and no poaching agreements* (May 30, 2023) at para 2.1, online: https://ised-isde.canada.ca/site/competition-bureau-canada/en/how-we-foster-competition/education-and-outreach/enforcement-guidelines-wage-fixing-and-no-poaching-agreements [*Wage-Fixing Guidelines*].

275 See, e.g., Michael A Lindsay, "McDonald's and Medicine: Developments in the Law of No-Poaching and Wage-Fixing Agreements" (2019) 33:2 *Antitrust* 18.

276 *Wage-Fixing Guidelines*, above note 274 at para 2.2.

3) Implementation of Foreign Conspiracies: Section 46

Section 46 creates a separate, indictable offence which applies to corporations (not individuals) that implement directives from outside Canada to give effect to a foreign conspiracy:

> 46(1) Any corporation, wherever incorporated, that carries on business in Canada and that implements, in whole or in part in Canada, a directive, instruction, intimation of policy or other communication to the corporation or any person from a person in a country other than Canada who is in a position to direct or influence the policies of the corporation, which communication is for the purpose of giving effect to a conspiracy, combination, agreement or arrangement entered into outside Canada that, if entered into in Canada, would have been in contravention of section 45, is, whether or not any director or officer of the corporation in Canada has knowledge of the conspiracy, combination, agreement or arrangement, guilty of an indictable offence and liable on conviction to a fine in the discretion of the court.

The provision applies to "a directive, instruction, intimation of policy or other communication" coming from a foreign-based person "who is in a position to direct or influence the policies of the corporation." The directive must give effect to an agreement which, had it been entered into in Canada, would be in contravention of section 45. The section explicitly applies whether or not any directors or officials of the corporation in Canada knew of the agreement.

A corporation convicted under section 46 is liable to a fine at the discretion of the court. For example, fines of up to $12.5 million were entered for convictions under the section, in a case involving a foreign-based conspiracy to fix the price of graphite electrodes.[277]

The section allows competition enforcement authorities "to target subsidiaries operating in Canada that implement a foreign communication, whether or not [the subsidiaries] know they are implementing a conspiracy and despite the fact that they are not immediate parties to the conspiracy."[278] In this sense, the section is broader than section 45, which applies only to those immediate parties.[279]

Section 46 addresses the problem, sometimes present in Canada's "branch plant" economy (where Canadian companies are often subsidiaries of foreign companies), of not being able to assign criminal

277 *R v Mitsubishi Corp* (2005), 40 CPR (4th) 333 (Ont SC) at para 16 [*Mitsubishi Corp*]; *UCAR*, above note 185.

278 *HarperCollins*, above note 196 at para 90.

279 *Ibid* at para 91.

culpability to a Canadian corporation because there is no directing mind[280] in Canada to whom liability may otherwise attach, because the conspiracy was entered into beyond Canada's borders, or because the officials in Canada who are implicated are not sufficiently high in the corporate hierarchy to be considered "directing minds." Section 46 resolves this problem by creating an offence for which the *actus reus* consists only of implementing the conspiracy within Canada, and the *mens rea* the mere intent to implement, without the need to prove knowledge of the underlying foreign agreement. The *Background Papers* prepared for the 1976 amendments which added the provision stated that it was "the only effective way of attacking combines formed abroad which are deliberately projected into Canada through Canadian subsidiaries and harmful to the Canadian economy."[281]

Section 83 of the *Competition Act* creates a civil provision governing foreign directives. Section 46(2) provides a limitation against double jeopardy by barring a prosecution under section 46 where civil proceedings based on substantially the same facts have already been initiated under section 83.

4) Bid-Rigging: Section 47

a) Background and History

Section 47 creates an indictable offence, carrying as a penalty a fine in the discretion of the court, or imprisonment for up to fourteen years, or both, for agreements surrounding bidding and tendering. Such agreements may also fall within section 45 to the extent that they involve the *per se* conduct found in that section.

The separate bid-rigging offence was created in 1976 and removed the requirement to prove any effect—undue or otherwise— as required in the conspiracy provision at the time.[282] The problems created by the presence of the qualifier "unduly" were illustrated by *R v Beamish Construction*. The accused were road paving contractors who reached a secret agreement to rotate the successful bidder on tenders, which agreement was implemented in numerous public procurements. The trial judge

---

280 Regarding the directing mind concept, see *R v Canadian Dredge & Dock Co*, [1985] 1 SCR 662; *R v Shell Canada Products Ltd (1990), 63 Man R (2d) 1 (CA) [Shell Canada]*.

281 Canada, Bureau of Competition Policy, *Background Papers. Stage 1 Competition Policy* (April 1976) at 29.

282 *An Act to amend the Combines Investigation Act and the Bank Act and to repeal an Act to amend an Act to amend the Combines Investigation Act and the Criminal Code*, SC 1974-75-76, c 76, s 15.

acquitted the accused companies, finding that while eleven of them had been parties to a conspiracy, the effect of which was to lessen competition in road surfacing materials and services, the conspiracy did not do so unduly. The reasons included that the accused firms represented less than one-third of the total number of road paving companies, and that this was insufficient market control.[283] The unduly requirement thus meant that the statute was not capable of rendering a conviction of accused when they controlled only part of a market, even though there had clearly been bid-rigging.

On appeal, the Ontario Court of Appeal stated that the firm's bid-rigging scheme was "completely devoid of business ethics," "reprehensible in the highest degree" and that "one must deplore the conduct of the respondents in hoodwinking the Department of Highways and the municipalities with which they dealt."[284] Nonetheless, the Court upheld the acquittal, given the language of the section. The situation cried out for reform. In 1976, a new, separate offence of bid-rigging was created, which removed the undueness requirement for that conduct. Parliament recognized that for bid-rigging, the undueness requirement was superfluous and no further case-specific assessment was needed for there to be prejudice to the public.[285]

b) Nature of the Conduct

Quebec's Charbonneau Commission Report in 2015 found that bid-rigging was among the corrupt practices which were a recurring problem in provincial and municipal public procurement, citing "rampant collusion in the field of asphalting and the acquisition of materials and licensed products."[286] The public injury from bid-rigging includes higher costs for establishing and running a tendering process and for the products or services acquired, costs which are often borne by consumers and

---

283 *R v JJ Beamish Construction Co Ltd (and eleven other corporations), [1966] 2 OR 867 (HC)*.

284 *R v JJ Beamish Construction Co* (1967), 65 DLR (2d) 260 (Ont CA) at paras 15, 20, and 21, leave to appeal to SCC refused (1967), 65 DLR (2d) 260 at 286n (SCC).

285 *Charterways* CA, above note 259.

286 Sarah Chaster, "Public Procurement and the Charbonneau Commission: Challenges in Preventing and Controlling Corruption" (2018) 23 *Appeal: Review of Current Law and Law Reform* 121 at 134, citing Quebec, Commission d'enquête sur l'octroi et la gestion des contrats publics dans l'industrie de la construction, France Charbonneau & Renaud Lachance, *Rapport final de la Commission d'enquête sur l'octroi et la gestion des contrats publics dans l'industrie de la construction* (November 2015) at 99–101, online: www.ceic.gouv.qc.ca/fileadmin/Fichiers_client/fichiers/Rapport_final/Rapport_final_CEIC_Integral_c.pdf.

taxpayers.[287] Testimony from the Charbonneau Commission indicated that bid-rigging raised the costs of municipal procurement by 20 to 25 percent or more in some cases.[288]

The Competition Bureau has identified four common types of agreements that may occur in the context of procurement:

- **Cover bidding**: The impression of competitive bidding when, in reality, suppliers have agreed to submit token bids and let an agreed-upon firm succeed.
- **Bid suppression and withdrawal**: An agreement among suppliers to abstain from bidding and to withdraw bids made.
- **Bid rotation**: An agreement whereby a preselected supplier submits the lowest bid on a rotating basis.
- **Market division**: An agreement not to compete in designated geographic regions or for specific customers.[289]

c) Elements of Bid-Rigging

The operative provisions state:

> 47(1) In this section, bid-rigging means
>
> (a) an agreement or arrangement between or among two or more persons whereby one or more of those persons agrees or undertakes not to submit a bid or tender in response to a call or request for bids or tenders, or agrees or undertakes to withdraw a bid or tender submitted in response to such a call or request, or
>
> (b) the submission, in response to a call or request for bids or tenders, of bids or tenders that are arrived at by agreement or arrangement between or among two or more bidders or tenderers,
>
> where the agreement or arrangement is not made known to the person calling for or requesting the bids or tenders at or before the time when any bid or tender is submitted or withdrawn, as the case may be, by any person who is a party to the agreement or arrangement.

---

287 Canada, Competition Bureau, "Bid Rigging" (22 February 2018), online: www.competitionbureau.gc.ca/eic/site/cb-bc.nsf/eng/h_00110.html.

288 Matthew Boswell, Senior Deputy Commissioner of Competition, "Bid-rigging Detection and Prevention: Ensuring a Competitive and Innovative Procurement Process" (Speech delivered at the Canadian Public Procurement Council Forum 2017: Innovation in Public Procurement, Ottawa, Ontario, 7 November 2017), online: www.canada.ca/en/competition-bureau/news/2017/11/bid-rigging_detectionandpreventionensuringacompetitiveandinnovat.html.

289 Canada, Competition Bureau, "Bid Rigging Pamphlet" (5 November 2015), online: www.competitionbureau.gc.ca/eic/site/cb-bc.nsf/vwapj/cb-pam-bid-rigging-e.pdf/$FILE/cb-pam-bid-rigging-e.pdf.

> (2) Every person who is a party to bid-rigging is guilty of an indictable offence and liable on conviction to a fine in the discretion of the court or to imprisonment for a term not exceeding 14 years, or to both.

i) Agreement

Section 47 addresses the following kinds of agreements:

- agreements not to submit a bid or tender (section 47(1)(a))
- agreements to withdraw a bid or tender already made (section 47(1)(a))[290]
- agreements on the content of bids or tenders which have been submitted (section 47(1)(b))

The agreement element places the same onus on the Crown and requires the same burden of proof discussed above with respect to section 45. While an agreement can be inferred from circumstantial evidence, for example, in *R v Durward* the trial judge entered a directed verdict of acquittal against a co-accused on the basis that the proffered evidence from emails showing knowledge and participation by the accused was insufficient. The Court held that the email exchanges were consistent with cooperation by bidders which the Crown had accepted was necessary to respond to the tender and not illegal.[291]

ii) Call or Request for Tenders: Formalities of the Tendering Process

In all three categories of agreement covered by section 47, there must have been a call or request for tenders. What degree of formality does this require? Merely requesting price quotes from several firms without a defined process or rules for receiving bids would likely not satisfy this requirement. In *R v York-Hanover Hotels*, it was held that the section was intended to cover "a system which is designed and intended to take advantage of the competitive factor in the market by inviting offers to provide a service or product at a price to be stipulated by the individual making the offer and rewarding those who submit the lowest, or lower, offers."[292] The Court found that a practice by the tendering authority of seeking selective revisions to prices supplied by hotels for inclusion in a government travel directory, had "destroyed the very essence of the bid process upon which the system was based," taking it outside the scope of section 47.[293]

290 This particular conduct was covered by an amendment made in 2009: *Budget Implementation Act, 2009*, above note 56, s 411.

291 *Durward*, above note 168.

292 *R v York-Hanover Hotels*, [1986] OJ No 3063 (Prov Ct) at para 2.

293 *Ibid* at para 5.

Similarly, where a procuring party called for bids complying with certain construction requirements but reserved the right to accept non-compliant bids, the process was held to fall outside section 47.[294] In another case, bids made by subcontractors which were not in response to a specific direction or call made to the general contractors were held not to apply to the section because what is required is "a direct relationship, or nexus, between the person calling for the bids and tenders and the person submitting the tenders."[295]

On the other hand, a tendering process which merely sought to establish a list of suppliers based on a standing offer,[296] and one whereby negotiations occurred after the opening of the bids,[297] were both found to have involved a "call or request" within the meaning of the section.

The cases demonstrate that there is a degree of flexibility surrounding the processes used to take advantage of a competitive market and which may be found to fall within section 47, even where they do not comply with the strict formalities of contract law, such that the acceptance of the bids received would create a binding contract. This flexibility furthers the purpose of the Act to promote the benefits of competition for the public, rather than having the Act serve other interests, such as certainty of contracting. When parties reach an agreement to collude in providing quotations which are relied upon by the recipient in negotiations or contracting, the mischief to which the Act is directed, the subverting of the competitive process, is arguably present. That those parties agreed on an offer incapable of being accepted to create a binding contract does not take away from this prejudice, as long as the bid or tender process in question has created the appearance of a competitive system.

iii) Bids or Tenders

A similar issue is raised with respect to the characteristics of the bid or tender which has been submitted. For example, is a bid or tender something which has sufficient detail or responsiveness that its acceptance by the tendering authority creates a binding contract? In *R v Charterways Transportation Ltd*, the Ontario court held that this was not required. The trial judge considered the entirety of the conduct of the parties,

---

294 *R v Rousseau*, 2018 QCCS 640.

295 *R v Coastal Glass and Aluminum* (1986), 27 CCC (3d) 289 (BC CA), aff'g (1984), 17 CCC (3d) 313 (BC SC).

296 *R v Dowdall*, 2013 ONCA 196 at para 6, leave to appeal to SCC refused, [2013] SCCA No 244.

297 *R v Charterways Transportation Ltd* (1981), 123 DLR (3d) 159 (HC) at para 40 [*Charterways* HC]. The Court rejected the argument that this involved the mere "invitation to commence negotiations."

concluding that the intention of the parties to treat the process as tendering is the decisive factor:

> The procedure followed by the board in inviting, advertising for tenders, the detailed conditions of tendering and the general conditions enclosed in the invitation for tender forwarded to each accused, considered in the light of the general understanding between the parties from past practice and procedure, leads me to the conclusion that the submissions of each accused was a tender or bid.[298]

iv) "Made Known" Defence

There is no offence under section 47 if the agreement in question was "made known to the person calling for or requesting the bids or tenders at or before the time when any bid or tender is submitted or withdrawn."[299] To benefit from this defence, it has been held that an accused must demonstrate under the section that there was clear notice of the existence of an agreement among the bidding parties. It is not sufficient to show the mere ability on the part of the party seeking bids to infer an agreement's existence from the parties' conduct. The higher standard was held to create greater certainty, consistent with the requirements of a penal statute. Justice Osler held:

> I agree with the submission of the Crown that there is an affirmative obligation upon those who join in such an agreement not just to make it possible for the recipient of their bids to become aware that they had made an agreement but to affirmatively notify such persons in some manner other than the mere production of identical bids.[300]

This reasoning was adopted even though the tendering official who opened identical bids testified that this had led her to conclude an agreement had been reached. The Court held that the identical bids themselves, without more corroboration, did not satisfy the "made known" requirement because of the lack of an affirmative notification of the agreement.[301]

v) Mens Rea

The *mens rea* required by section 47 is, like that in section 45, the intention to enter into the agreement in question. The court in one case described the *mens rea* requirement as "that the accused intentionally

---

298 *Ibid* at para 46.

299 *Competition Act*, above note 52, s 47(1).

300 *R v Travelways School Transit Ltd* (1980), 52 CCC (2d) 399 at 405 (Ont SC).

301 *Charterways* HC, above note 297 at paras 53–57.

and advertently entered into an agreement or arrangement with one or more bidders pursuant to which a bid or tender is arrived at."[302]

5) Agreements Relating to Professional Sport: Section 48

Section 48 of the *Competition Act* creates a separate criminal offence, which replaces the general conspiracy provision, for agreements or arrangements relating to the granting and operation of professional sport franchises and to the terms and conditions applied to players and competitors.[303] The focus of the provision is the ability of players to participate in professional sport without the imposition of "unreasonable" terms and conditions. The offence is as follows:

> 48 (1) Every one who conspires, combines, agrees or arranges with another person
> (a) to limit unreasonably the opportunities for any other person to participate, as a player or competitor, in professional sport or to impose unreasonable terms or conditions on those persons who so participate, or
> (b) to limit unreasonably the opportunity for any other person to negotiate with and, if agreement is reached, to play for the team or club of his choice in a professional league
>
> is guilty of an indictable offence and liable on conviction to a fine in the discretion of the court or to imprisonment for a term not exceeding five years or to both.
>
> (2) In determining whether or not an agreement or arrangement contravenes subsection (1), the court before which the contravention is alleged shall have regard to
> (a) whether the sport in relation to which the contravention is alleged is organized on an international basis and, if so, whether any limitations, terms or conditions alleged should, for that reason, be accepted in Canada; and

---

302 *Ibid* at para 74.

303 *Competition Act*, above note 52, s 48(3) provides:

> This section applies, and section 45 does not apply, to agreements and arrangements and to provisions of agreements and arrangements between or among teams and clubs engaged in professional sport as members of the same league and between or among directors, officers or employees of those teams and clubs where the agreements, arrangements and provisions relate exclusively to matters described in subsection (1) or to the granting and operation of franchises in the league, and section 45 applies and this section does not apply to all other agreements, arrangements and provisions thereof between or among those teams, clubs and persons.

(b) the desirability of maintaining a reasonable balance among the teams or clubs participating in the same league.[304]

The background to the provision is described in the 1973 *Proposals for a New Competition Policy for Canada*,[305] which led to the so-called First Stage amendments. Those amendments came into force in 1976, and included the predecessor to section 48, which has been unchanged since then.[306] Several developments influenced the addition of this provision, according to the report.

First, the Economic Council had recommended that all recreational activities be brought under the legislation, which was accomplished when the legislation was amended in 1976 to apply to services.[307] Given the expanded application of the general conspiracy provision to services, a new section was deemed necessary to address the unique circumstances of professional sport, which raise different issues than those arising for other collusive agreements. The undueness test in the general conspiracy provision was seen as potentially applicable to agreements to create professional sports leagues. The responsible Minister stated to the legislative committee that the section was intended "to permit professional leagues to exist."[308]

Second, there had been two public inquiries, in 1966 and 1969, "where serious concern about restrictive practices in hockey was brought to light." These concerns included the conduct of National Hockey League (NHL) clubs in the "acquisition and retention of players."[309]

Third, at the time of the advent and operation of the rival World Hockey Association (WHA), antitrust litigation in the United States had challenged certain provisions in the contracts imposed by the NHL on its players.[310] There was thus a perceived need to address such issues in Canadian law.

---

304 The language used is "conspires, combines, agrees or arranges," language which in the context of section 45 has been interpreted as requiring agreement. See above in this chapter, Section D(1)(b)(i)a.

305 Canada, Consumer and Corporate Affairs, *Proposals for a New Competition Policy for Canada, First Stage* (Ottawa: CCAC, 1973) at 49–52 [*First Stage*].

306 *An Act to amend the Combines Investigation Act and the Bank Act and to repeal an Act to amend an Act to amend the Combines Investigation Act and the Criminal Code*, SC 1975-75-76, c 76, s 15 (adding s 32.3).

307 *Ibid*, s 1.

308 Senate of Canada, *Proceedings of the Standing Senate Committee on Banking Trade and Commerce*, 30th Parl, 1st Sess (19 November 1975) at 61:5 (Hon André Ouellet).

309 *First Stage*, above note 305 at 50–51.

310 *Ibid* at 51. See, e.g., *Philadelphia World Hockey Club v Philadelphia Hockey Club*, 351 F Supp 462 (ED Pa 1972) at 509.

The reference to agreements that create unreasonable limits on players and competitors can be contrasted to the prohibition of undue agreements, as present in the general conspiracy provision at the time of its enactment (the latter provision being amended to remove "unduly" in 2009). The undueness standard involved an assessment of the effect of the practice on competition, without a wholesale examination of the private or public benefits which the agreement may have brought about.[311]

In contrast, the use of the word "unreasonably" suggests introducing a somewhat different inquiry, permitting the parties to justify their conduct based on a potentially broader range of considerations than simply anti-competitive effect.[312] Given the word "unreasonable" is also employed in the common law of restraint of trade, jurisprudence in that area may assist its interpretation.[313] The section itself gives guidance that concerns for competitive balance among teams, as well as the impacts of leagues organized on an international basis, are factors at play, among others. These factors may provide a basis to argue that restraints on terms and conditions applicable to players, such as caps placed on teams' expenditures for salaries, are reasonable. At the same time, the section opens the way to attack anti-competitive agreements which are not linked to structural and other considerations needed to permit a professional sports league to function. For example, "unreasonable" terms and conditions would likely include those "that do not relate to anything unique about sports, but simply serve to further the same sort of private commercial interests that any Canadian firm might have."[314]

---

311 *Nova Scotia Pharmaceutical Society*, above note 47 at para 90: s 45 "does allow for discussion of the anti-competitive effects of the agreement [but] does not permit a full-blown discussion of the economic advantages and disadvantages of the agreement, like a rule of reason would. Since 'unduly' . . . leads to a discussion of the seriousness of the competitive effects, but not of all relevant economic matters, one may say that this section creates a partial rule of reason."

312 J Kevin Wright & Jonathan Gilhen, "A Note on US Antitrust Law and Professional Sport: *American Needle* and the Implications for Canadian Competition Law" (2010), 23 *Canadian Competition Record* 66 at 72.

313 Stephen F Ross, "The NHL Labour Dispute and the Common Law, the Competition Law, and Public Policy" (2004) 37:2 *University of British Columbia Law Review* 343 at 373: "the statutory standard of 'unreasonableness' is judicially interpreted to permit consideration of goals deemed essential to the vitality and survival of professional sport leagues. However, as the long Anglo-Canadian common law tradition demonstrates, in spite of this flexibility, restraints broader than necessary to achieve goals such as competitive balance are 'unreasonable' and thus under the statute remain illegal."

314 *Ibid* at 376; see also J Colin H Jones & Duncan K Davies, "Not Even Semi Tough: Professional Sport and Canadian Antitrust," (1978) 23 *Antitrust Bulletin* 713.

There has been little jurisprudence under the provision. In *Yashin v National Hockey League*, it was ruled that the section does not apply to agreements and arrangements achieved as a result of collective bargaining, by virtue of the exemption created for such activities in section 4 of the Act.[315] Given that various professional sport leagues in addition to hockey leagues have in recent years employed collective bargaining extensively to negotiate terms and conditions between clubs and players,[316] a process that has seen players make substantial gains in compensation, there may be less room for application of section 48. Jurisprudence relating to the provision may remain undeveloped for some time. Nonetheless, section 48 provides a backstop for players should recourse to collective bargaining prove unsuccessful.

While the focus of the section is the terms and conditions of participation by players, section 48(1)(a) also applies to limits placed on the ability of a "competitor" to participate in professional sport. The scope of this avenue remains to be explored judicially. It potentially opens the section to addressing such issues as barriers to entry created by leagues to new franchises, including limits on expansion of, for example, the NHL to other Canadian cities. However, recent complaints in this area have been considered by the Competition Bureau under the abuse of dominance provisions, rather than section 48. Abuse of dominance remains an alternative basis upon which to consider competitive practices in this area, given the evident market power of major sports leagues in North America.[317]

6) Agreements Between Federal Financial Institutions: Section 49

By virtue of section 45(6), the general conspiracy prohibition does not apply to federal financial institutions—that is, banks governed by the *Bank Act*, as well as federal trust and loan and insurance companies.[318]

---

315 *Ibid* at 379; *Yashin v National Hockey League, [2000] OJ No 3306 (SC) [Yashin]*.

316 Gabriel Feldman, "Brady v. NFL and Anthony v. NBA: The Shifting Dynamics in Labor-Management Relations in Professional Sports" (2012) 86 *Tulane Law Review* 831.

317 See Chapter 7.

318 *Bank Act*, SC 1991, c 46 [*Bank Act*]; *Competition Act*, above note 52, ss 45(6)(b) and 49(3): "In this section and section 45, federal financial institution means a bank or an authorized foreign bank within the meaning of section 2 of the *Bank Act*, a company to which the *Trust and Loan Companies Act* applies or a company or society to which the *Insurance Companies Act* applies." It has been argued that "the failure to repeal section 49 in 2009 was a legislative oversight and it is not reasonable to apply a different and higher standard to federal financial institutions than to

Instead, section 49 applies to "agreements and arrangements" between federal financial institutions.

This offence-creating provision was moved to the *Competition Act* in 1986 from the *Bank Act*,[319] transferring responsibility of investigating such agreements to the competition authorities from financial regulators because the *Competition Act* is a "law of general application" to which financial institutions should be subject.[320] By the 1980s, the chartered banks had grown significantly, increasing their importance as sources of financing for corporations, making it "essential that the banks be subject to competition policy legislation to ensure they operate independently and efficiently and that rates they charge borrowers and pay to lenders are determined fairly by the forces of competition."[321]

Section 49(1) provides:

> 49 (1) Subject to subsection (2), every federal financial institution that makes an agreement or arrangement with another federal financial institution with respect to
> (a) the rate of interest on a deposit,
> (b) the rate of interest or the charges on a loan,
> (c) the amount or kind of any charge for a service provided to a customer,
> (d) the amount or kind of a loan to a customer,
> (e) the kind of service to be provided to a customer, or
> (f) the person or classes of persons to whom a loan or other service will be made or provided or from whom a loan or other service will be withheld,
>
> and every director, officer or employee of the federal financial institution who knowingly makes such an agreement or arrangement on behalf of the federal financial institution is guilty of an indictable offence and liable to a fine not exceeding ten million dollars or to imprisonment for a term not exceeding five years or to both.

The offence, like that in section 45, is *per se*: the prohibition applies to agreements of these kinds, without any inquiry into their anti-competitive effects. This reflects Parliament's judgment that such agreements, given the critical role of the financial sector in the economy, are so harmful that no case-specific inquiry into their anti-competitive effect is required.

---

other businesses." Canadian Bar Association Competition Law Section, "Submission on the Revised *Competitor Collaboration Guidelines*" (October 2020) at 10.

319 *Competition Act*, SC 1986, c 26, ss 34 and 50.

320 *Background Information and Explanatory Notes* 1984, above note 7 at 13.

321 *Ibid*. See also *Competition Law Amendments Guide* 1985, above note 215 at 30–31.

Section 49(2) contains a list of nine exemptions from the application of section 49(1). The rationale for this lengthy list is that, given the nature of financial transactions, "a certain amount of cooperation is necessary between" federal financial institutions.[322] The exemptions include agreements concerning loans paid or payable outside Canada, underwriting of securities, exchange of statistics and credit information,[323] and participation in loan guarantee programs authorized by legislation. In addition, the Minister of Finance may approve an agreement "for the purposes of financial policy" and exempt it from section 49 by certifying this approval to the Commissioner.[324] Finally, agreements between financial institutions which are affiliates are also exempt.[325]

Double jeopardy under civil agreement provisions and section 49 is precluded by section 49(4). Proceedings may not be taken under section 49 when they have been taken under any of the civil merger, abuse of dominance, civil agreements, or price maintenance provisions based on substantially the same set of facts.

7) Criminal Penalties, Other Remedies, and the Bureau's Leniency Policy

a) Penalties—Fines and Imprisonment

The offences under sections 45 to 48 carry maximum penalties of imprisonment of from five to fourteen years, and fines set "in the discretion of the court." Section 49 carries maximums of 5 years and $10 million. While the Competition Bureau is responsible for investigating alleged wrongdoing and making recommendations on sentencing, the Public Prosecution Service of Canada (PPSC) under the direction of the Director of Public Prosecutions has ultimate responsibility for laying charges and is responsible for the decision on sentencing positions and whether to enter plea agreements.[326]

---

322 Calvin S Goldman & JD Bolrug, eds, *Competition Law of Canada* (Huntington, NY: Juris, 2013) at 8–95. See 8–87 to 8–89 for a history of this provision in the *Bank Act*, above note 318.

323 The exemption for the exchange of credit information was applied as a defence to a civil action for damages, *Greenspan v Canada Trust Co*, [1998] OJ No 5240 (Gen Div) at para 15, aff'd [1999] OJ No 2783 (CA).

324 *Competition Act*, above note 52, s 49(2)(h).

325 *Ibid*, s 49(2)(i).

326 Canada, Competition Bureau *Immunity and Leniency Programs under the Competition Act* (15 March 2019), "Preface," online: www.competitionbureau.gc.ca/eic/site/cb-bc.nsf/eng/04391.html [*Immunity and Leniency Programs*]. See also "Consensual Resolutions—Criminal Cases" in Canada, Competition Bureau, *Competition and Compliance Framework* (Gatineau: Industry Canada, 2015), online:

Imprisonment has seldom been imposed on individuals convicted under these provisions.[327] Conditional sentences involving terms of house arrest and curfew have, however, been imposed on individuals in numerous cases.[328] In *Maxzone*, the Federal Court, in reviewing a joint submission to impose a fine of $1.5 million for price fixing of aftermarket auto parts, commented that in future cases the Court would expect to receive submissions on why prison sentences should not apply to individuals who are officials of companies who are not the first to disclose conspiratorial conduct to the prosecution, given the need for deterrence and other sentencing values.[329]

The likelihood and scale of punishment may play a role not only in the deterrence of behaviour, but it may also affect the stability and likelihood of cartel behaviour being successful in the first place. Understanding these dynamics has been assisted by the application of game theory. Stiff penalties can alter the payoffs available from conspiratorial conduct, and affect the incentive to cheat. Sentencing policies such as offering immunity to the first to report illegal behaviour can increase the incentives for disclosure of conspiratorial behaviour by co-conspirators, making collusion a less stable or likely state of affairs (see the discussion of leniency, below).[330]

With respect to fines, the Bureau has set out a methodology for calculating a base fine in its Bulletin *Immunity and Leniency Programs under the Competition Act*, applying the volume of commerce affected by the conduct and other factors.[331] In *Maxzone*, the Federal Court expressed concern that more evidence was needed to assess whether the fine recommended to the court on a joint submission satisfied sentencing principles, including the need to disgorge expected profits and create deterrence.[332]

---

www.competitionbureau.gc.ca/eic/site/cb-bc.nsf/eng/03982.html and Public Prosecution Service of Canada, *Deskbook*, Section 5.2, *Competition Act* (1 March 2014), online: www.ppsc-sppc.gc.ca/eng/pub/fpsd-sfpg/fps-sfp/tpd/d-g-eng.pdf [PPSC *Deskbook*].

327 An exception was the Sherbrooke driving schools prosecution, in which the accused was sentenced to one year in prison after a contested sentencing hearing: *R v Perreault*, [1996] RJQ 2565 (SC) at para 84.

328 Canada, Competition Bureau, "Penalties Imposed by the Courts," online: www.competitionbureau.gc.ca/eic/site/cb-bc.nsf/eng/01863.html#sec2019.

329 *Maxzone*, above note 20.

330 Christopher R Leslie, "Trust, Distrust, and Antitrust" (2004) 82:3 *Texas Law Review* 515 at 639–40.

331 *Immunity and Leniency Programs*, above note 325 at paras 124 and following.

332 *Maxzone*, above note 20 at paras 90–108.

Substantial fines have been imposed for conspiratorial behaviour in recent cases. Examples of guilty pleas in the last decade are: a total of $86 million in fines obtained from several parties involved in bid-rigging of auto parts contracts;[333] more than $2 million for price fixing of gasoline in the Kingston-Brockville area;[334] $650,000 for fixing surcharges for ocean freight;[335] $1.25 million for participation in an international conspiracy in potassium sorbate, a food preservative;[336] $4.5 million for bid-rigging in wheel bearings;[337] more than $25 million for fixing air cargo rates;[338] $2.5 million in respect of an international hydrogen peroxide cartel;[339] and $12.5 million for a polyurethane foam cartel.[340] A fine of $1 million was imposed after trial for gas price fixing by Pétroles Global Inc in Magog, Quebec.[341] Three employees of the company pled guilty.

The courts have held the factors applicable to sentencing in *Competition Act* prosecutions center on denunciation and general and specific deterrence (as reflected in the general sentencing principles in the

333 Canada, Competition Bureau, News Release, "Thirteenth Guilty Plea Concludes Auto Parts Bid Rigging Investigations With Fines Totalling Over $86 Million" (19 October 2018), online: www.canada.ca/en/competition-bureau/news/2018/10/thirteenth-guilty-plea-concludes-auto-parts-bid-rigging-investigations-with-fines-totalling-over-86-million.html.

334 Canada, Competition Bureau, "List of Charges and Sentences for Gasoline Price-Fixing," online: www.competitionbureau.gc.ca/eic/site/cb-bc.nsf/eng/03079.html.

335 Canada, Competition Bureau, News Release, "Fourth Guilty Plea in the Competition Bureau's Investigation in Ocean Freight Industry" (9 April 2014), online: www.competitionbureau.gc.ca/eic/site/cb-bc.nsf/eng/03720.html.

336 *R c Ueno Fine Chemicals Industry Ltd, 2001 CanLII 25122 (Que CS).*

337 Canada, Competition Bureau, News Release, "Japanese Bearings Manufacturer Fined $4.5 Million" (30 January 2014), online: www.competitionbureau.gc.ca/eic/site/cb-bc.nsf/eng/03652.html.

338 Canada, Competition Bureau, News Release, "South American Company Pleads Guilty to Air Cargo Price Fixing Conspiracy" (20 August 2013), online: www.competitionbureau.gc.ca/eic/site/cb-bc.nsf/eng/03590.html.

339 Canada, Competition Bureau, News Release, "Solvay Chemicals Fined $2.5 Million for Its Role in a Price Fixing Conspiracy" (12 May 2010), online: www.competitionbureau.gc.ca/eic/site/cb-bc.nsf/eng/03228.html.

340 *R v Domfoam Inc, 2012 CarswellOnt 17498 (SCJ) [Domfoam]*; Canada, Competition Bureau, News Release, "Competition Bureau Sends Signal to Price-Fixers with $12.5 Million Fine" (6 January 2012), online: www.competitionbureau.gc.ca/eic/site/cb-bc.nsf/eng/01353.html.

341 *R c Pétroles Global Inc, 2015 QCCS 1618; Canada, Competition Bureau, News Release,* "Les Pétroles Global Inc. Fined $1 Million For Gasoline Price-Fixing in Quebec" (17 April 2015), online: www.competitionbureau.gc.ca/eic/site/cb-bc.nsf/eng/03908.html.

Criminal Code[342]) and that the fine should be much more than a cost of doing business illegally or a "licence fee." Other factors include:[343]

- the seriousness of the offences, which carry significant public prejudice
- prior conduct, convictions or criminal record
- the duration of the conduct
- its geographic scope
- the volume of commerce affected
- the scale of the price increase realized by the conspiracy or other economic harm
- the profits obtained and the need to disgorge same
- the likelihood of detection versus the benefits obtained
- efforts to conceal the behaviour
- whether the accused was an instigator
- whether the conduct was planned and deliberate
- in the case of individual accused, the role in the offence, and seniority in the company in question, including whether that person was a directing mind of a corporate accused
- the value of imprisonment as a deterrent to this kind of behaviour

Mitigating factors include:

- cooperation
- guilty plea
- recognition of wrongdoing
- regret or remorse
- playing a lesser or passive role in the conspiracy
- restitution provided
- institution of remedial measures such as a corporate compliance program

---

342 The objectives and principles of sentencing are codified in ss 718 to 718.21 of the *Criminal Code*, above note 162.

343 See, e.g., *R c Darby, 2012 QCCS 26; Domfoam, above note 340; Maxzone*, above note 20; *R v Kason Industries Inc, 2011 FC 281; R v Hart, 2005 CarswellNat 573 (FC); Mitsubishi Corp*, above note 277 at para 16; *UCAR*, above note 185; *R v Kanzaki Specialty Papers Inc (1994), 82 FTR 63; R v Ocean Construction Supplies Ltd* (1974), 15 CPR (2d) 224 at 229 (BC SC); *Shell Canada*, above note 28-; *R v Rolex Watch Co of Canada Ltd* (1980), 50 CPR (2d) 222 at 228 (Ont CA); *R v A&M Records of Canada Ltd* (1980), 51 CPR (2d) 225 at 230 (Ont Co Ct); *R v Kito Canada Ltd* (1976), 25 CPR (2d) 145 at 146 (Man CA); *R v Superior Electronics Inc* (1979), 45 CPR (2d) 234 at 236 (BC CA); *R v Northern Electric Company Limited* (1957), 26 CPR 73 at 74–75 (Ont HC); *R v Goodyear Tire & Rubber*, [1956] SCR 303 at 311; and *R v Dominion Steel* (1957), 27 CPR 57 at 76 (Ont HC).

b) Other Remedies

Section 34(1) of the *Competition Act* provides authority for the court, at the time of a conviction, to impose an order prohibiting "the continuation or repetition of the offence or . . . the doing of any act or thing" directed to its continuation or repetition. The order may apply to corporations and individuals. The Bureau has stated that it will "typically" recommend requesting such an order to the PPSC when there is a finding of guilt.[344]

A prohibition order can also be issued under section 34(2) without any prosecution for a substantive offence, conviction, or admission of guilt. These are commonly issued on consent as a form of alternative case resolution. In *Canada v Chambre d'immeuble du Saguenay-Lac St Jean Inc*, the Federal Court found that a prohibition order against the Canadian Real Estate Association and member organizations was terminated after an amendment to add section 34(2.2), which created a maximum duration of ten years for such orders.[345]

The Act also provides for the issuance of an interim injunction pending the commencement or completion of a proceeding, if there is injury to competition "that cannot be remedied under any other provisions of this Act" or "serious harm is likely to ensue . . . and the balance of convenience favours issuing the injunction."[346] In *AG Canada v David Oppenheimer & Associates*, the Federal Court was satisfied that the requirements for an injunction had been met in respect of a price fixing conspiracy concerning imported mandarin oranges, but did not issue an order given the lack of a defined timetable for the pending prosecution.[347]

In addition to public enforcement, parties subject to prosecution, whether that prosecution is contested or resolved by guilty pleas, must also be conscious of the potential for civil damages actions under section 36 of the Act, an increasingly common feature given the increase in recourse to class actions under provisions in provincial law.[348]

c) Leniency and Immunity

The Bureau has indicated that its approach to the recommendation of remedies in criminal matters involves consideration of a continuum of relief, from a warning letter on the one hand, to a contested fine or

---

344 *Collaboration Guidelines*, above note 163 at s 2.7.

345 *Canada v Chambre d'immeuble du Saguenay-Lac St Jean Inc* (1999), 174 FTR 235.

346 *Competition Act*, above note 52, s 33(1).

347 *Canada (Attorney General) v David Oppenheimer & Associates* (1994), 57 CPR (3d) 101 (FC TD).

348 See Chapter 2 at Section C(2)(b)(ii)(d).

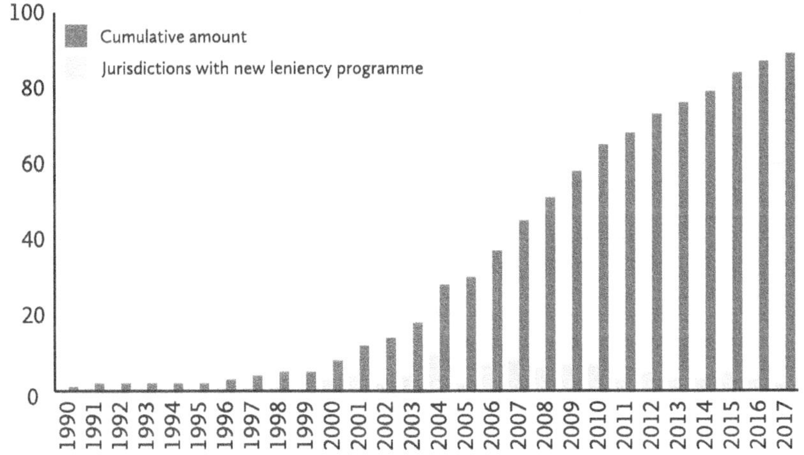

FIGURE 6.5. According to the OECD, the number of leniency programs in place grew from ten jurisdictions worldwide in 1990 to eighty-nine in 2017

sentencing application on the other.[349] Its policy toward leniency is set out in its Bulletin *Immunity and Leniency Programs under the Competition Act*.[350] Leniency involves the Crown seeking a reduced sentence or remedy in view of factors such as a party's cooperation, acceptance of wrongdoing, or restitution of damage. Immunity, on the other hand, removes any potential for a prosecution or a penalty from a party. An OECD study concluded in 2019 that "[t]he most notable development in cartel enforcement in the last 20 years . . . is the introduction of leniency programmes in numerous jurisdictions." The study noted that eighty-nine jurisdictions had adopted such programs worldwide. (See **Figure 6.5** depicting the number of leniency programs worldwide, 1999–2017.)[351]

An important element of the Bureau's immunity policy is that immunity is offered to the first party to report conspiratorial conduct to the Crown. This creates a substantial incentive for the "first in" to reveal such conduct, and is a potentially powerful tool to undermine planned and ongoing cartels. As noted earlier, this can erode the stability of a cartel. Furthermore, given the difficulty of proof of conspiratorial conduct, and its generally clandestine nature, obtaining evidence from a

349 *Collaboration Guidelines*, above note 163 at s 2.7.

350 See *Immunity and Leniency Programs* and PPSC *Deskbook*, above note 326.

351 OECD, *Review of the 1998 OECD Recommendation concerning Effective Action against Hard Core Cartels* (2019) at 24, online: www.oecd.org/daf/competition/oecd-review-1998-hard-core-cartels-recommendation.pdf. See Figure 6.5, drawn from OECD (2020), OECD Competition Trends at 30, Figure 2.2, "Leniency Programs by Year of Introduction 1990–2017," online: www.oecd.org/competition/oecd-competition-trends.htm.

co-conspirator is an invaluable method of advancing the enforcement of those provisions. The various factors, conditions, and steps for seeking and obtaining immunity are set out in detail in the Bureau's *Immunity and Leniency Programs* Bulletin and PPSC *Deskbook*.

E. THE CIVIL TRACK FOR REVIEW OF AGREEMENTS: SECTION 90.1

1) Introduction and Background

Section 90.1 creates a civil law track for the review of agreements. The section dates to the 2009 amendments, when it was restricted to agreements between competitors. In 2023, new section 90.1(1.1) was added, which enlarges its potential application to agreements between non-competitors where "a significant purpose of the agreement … is to prevent or lessen competition in any market."[352] In 2024, private enforcement of the section was provided for, and remedies were broadened to include recoupment of benefits derived and monetary penalties.[353]

As noted above, the 2009 amendments creating the provision reflected the view, which can be traced to the Economic Council's *Interim Report on Competition Policy* in 1969, that the criminal law should be reserved for matters subjected to categorical prohibitions, while those matters requiring a case-by-case assessment of competitive effect should be adjudicated by an expert civil tribunal. Section 90.1 follows this approach with a broad category of agreements that are now subject to review before the Competition Tribunal.

Of note:

- The Commissioner is no longer the sole "gatekeeper" for applications under section 90.1; private parties were given the right to apply for a remedy in 2024, and the remedies available were expanded to include divestiture, administrative monetary penalties and recovery of any benefit derived from the conduct.[354]
- As with the merger provisions, the efficiency defence to the provision was repealed in the 2023 amendments.[355]

352 *An Act to amend the Excise Act and the Competition Act*, SC 2023, c 31, s. 8 [*Bill C-56 2023*].

353 *Fall Economic Statement Implementation Act, 2023*, SC 2024, c 15, s 248 [*Bill C-59 2024*]. These provisions come into effect in June, 2025.

354 *Ibid*.

355 *Bill C-56 2023*, above note 352, s 8(1.1).

- There is a close similarity between the structure and language of the merger provision of the Act and section 90.1 in respect of the operative test for anti-competitive effect. It is therefore not surprising that the Competition Bureau reviews agreements under section 90.1 "in a manner consistent with the approach outlined in the Bureau's *Merger Enforcement Guidelines*."[356]

2) Elements of Section 90.1(1) – Agreements Between Competitors

Section 90.1 provides:

> 90.1 (1) If, on application by the Commissioner or a person granted leave under section 103.1,[357] the Tribunal finds that an agreement or arrangement, or a proposed agreement or arrangement between persons of whom two or more are competitors prevents or lessens, has prevented or lessened, or is likely to prevent or lessen, competition substantially in a market, the Tribunal may make an order
> (a) prohibiting any person—whether or not a party to the agreement or arrangement—from doing anything under the agreement or arrangement; or
> (b) requiring any person—whether or not a party to the agreement or arrangement—with the consent of that person and the Commissioner, to take any other action.

The section involves the following elements:[358]

- an agreement or arrangement;
- past, existing or proposed;
- between two or more "persons" who are competitors (like section 45, this includes both individuals and corporations); and
- that prevents or lessens, has prevented or lessened, or is likely to prevent or lessen, competition substantially in a market.

a) Agreement or Arrangement

As noted above, section 45, the criminal conspiracy provision, applies to anyone who "conspires, agrees or arranges," and has been interpreted to require proof of the "act of agreeing."[359] Section 90.1, as do several

356 *Collaboration Guidelines*, above note 163 at para 3.1.

357 *Bill C-59 2024*, above note 353, s 248(2); the language permitting private applications under s 90.1 comes into effect June 20, 2025.

358 *Rakuten Kobo*, above note 196 at para 126.

359 The word "combines" was dropped from the *Competition Act*, above note 52, s 45 in 2009.

other provisions in the Act, uses the words "agreement or arrangement." Do those two words invoke a different standard from section 45—for example, can an arrangement involve conduct which falls short of agreement, such as price leadership?

While the interpretative indicators point in different directions,[360] the Competition Bureau's *Collaboration Guidelines* take the view, consistent with the interpretation of the criminal conspiracy prohibition, that some element of agreement is required by section 90.1, stating "the mere act of adopting a course of action" or "conscious parallelism" is not covered by the section,[361] although the section can apply "to all forms of agreements and arrangements between competitors, regardless of the degree of formality."[362]

b) Agreements Between Competitors

The word "competitor" includes new or future entrants: those "who it is reasonable to believe would be likely to compete with respect to a product in the absence of the agreement or arrangement."[363] As in the case of section 45, determining who is a competitor may involve an assessment of factors similar to those considered in market definition, to gauge what products are substitutes and what geographic areas are served by competing suppliers.

---

360 On the one hand, it is a presumption of statutory interpretation that the use of the same words, "agrees or arranges," should have the same meaning in the same statute: "Giving the same words the same meaning throughout a statute is a basic principle of statutory interpretation": *R v Zeolkowski*, [1989] 1 SCR 1378 at 1387. On the other hand, the presumption can be rebutted if the words have a different context: "Identical words may not have identical meanings once they are placed in different contexts and used for different purposes": Ruth Sullivan, *Sullivan on the Construction of Statutes*, 6th ed (Toronto: LexisNexis, 2014). Given the different and non-criminal context of s 90.1, it is arguable that the words "agreement or arrangement" may have a relaxed meaning to cover less explicit forms of parallel behaviour which may fall short of agreement. A supportive point is that the adjacent words in s 90.1 are different than those in s 45, and that the word "conspires," which more clearly invokes the criminal law concept of meeting of the minds, is not present in s 90.1. See Sullivan at para 8.58: "When two or more words which are susceptible of analogous meanings are coupled together they are understood to be used in their cognate sense. They take their colour from each other, the meaning of the more general being restricted to a sense analogous to the less general." The Tribunal has held, "the meaning of the words can only be established by considering their context": *HarperCollins, above note 196 at para 102*.

361 *Collaboration Guidelines*, above note 163 at para 3.2.

362 *Ibid*. This is consistent with a purposive interpretation of the section, which suggests that it is the substance of the horizontal agreement and its effect on competition to which Parliament was directed, not the formalities, such as the requirements of contract law for consideration.

363 *Competition Act*, above note 52, s 90.1(11).

c) Existing, Past and Proposed Agreements

The section as originally worded did not cover past conduct.[364] This gave rise to challenges to a consent agreement entered into by the Commissioner with ebook publishers. The consent agreement addressed an arrangement whereby ebook publishers were alleged to have agreed, *inter alia*, to move from a wholesale to an agency model to distribute ebooks in Canada, allegedly resulting in greater price control by publishers. Both the Tribunal[365] and the Federal Court[366] dismissed this challenge on the basis, *inter alia*, that evidence on the record supported the Commissioner's position that the agreement or arrangement was "existing or proposed."

This issue was removed when the section was amended in 2024 to cover past agreements.[367]

d) The Agreement Is "Likely to Prevent or Lessen Competition Substantially"

The test for anti-competitive effect under section 90.1 is the same as that applicable to mergers: whether the agreement "prevents or lessens, or is likely to prevent or lessen, competition substantially in a market."[368] Consistent with the jurisprudence under the merger provisions, the *Collaboration Guidelines* focus on the impact of the agreement in question on market power:

> A substantial lessening or prevention of competition results from agreements that are likely to create, maintain or enhance the ability of the parties to the agreement to exercise market power.[369]

Market power involves the ability to raise prices or alter terms of trade prevailing in a competitive market.[370] The *Collaboration Guidelines* take the same approach as the *Merger Enforcement Guidelines* to the assessment of an agreement's effects on market power.[371] The elements of that assessment were described above in Chapter 5.[372] The

---

364 *HarperCollins*, above note 196 at para 179.

365 *Ibid*.

366 *Rakuten Kobo, above note 196 at paras 166–83.*

367 *Bill C-59 2024*, above note 353, s. 248.

368 *Competition Act*, above note 52, s 90.1(1); compare to s 92(1).

369 *Collaboration Guidelines*, above note 163 at para 3.4.1.

370 See Chapter 4, Section B; Chapter 5, Section C(1).

371 *Collaboration Guidelines*, above note 163 at para 3.4.1; Canada, Competition Bureau, *Merger Enforcement Guidelines* (6 October 2011), online: www.competitionbureau.gc.ca/eic/site/cb-bc.nsf/eng/03420.html.

372 See Chapter 5, Section C(1).

elements of section 90.1 closely parallel those applicable to mergers, consisting of:[373]

1) Market Definition
2) Market Shares and Concentration
3) Barriers to Entry
4) Effects of the Agreement on Competition

i) Market Definition

Chapter 4 has provided a detailed discussion of market definition. In the case of an agreement under section 90.1, it is the products of the parties to the agreement which are assessed, and the geographic areas those parties operate in which are considered, to determine the appropriate scope of the market. Once a market has been defined, it is possible to identify existing and potential competitors within the market, and consider other structural issues, such as barriers to entry.

In the case of an ongoing agreement, the base price used to project the impact of a small but significant and non-transitory increase in price (SSNIP) may have to be adjusted downward if the parties to the agreement already have market power. The reasons for this adjustment were discussed in Chapter 4 in respect of the "cellophane fallacy."[374]

ii) Market Shares and Concentration

The *Collaboration Guidelines* set out certain safe harbours under section 90.1 based on market share, stating:

> Consistent with the MEGs, as a general rule, the Commissioner will not challenge an agreement under section 90.1 on the basis of:
>
> i. a concern related to the exercise of market power by the parties to the agreement where the market share held by the parties represents less than 35% of the relevant market; or
>
> ii. a concern related to a coordinated exercise of market power by firms in the relevant market where the share of the four largest firms in the relevant market is less than 65%, or the share of the parties to the agreement is less than 10% of the relevant market.[375]

As in the case of the merger provisions, this factor is not decisive. The Act provides that the Tribunal cannot make any finding of substantial prevention or lessening "solely on the basis of evidence of concentration or market share."[376] On the other hand, market share can provide

373 Except there is no "failing firm" defence.

374 See Chapter 4, Section C.

375 *Collaboration Guidelines*, above note 163, s 3.4.2.

376 *Competition Act*, above note 52, s 90.1(3).

at least a "*prima facie* indication of market power."[377] For any issue to arise under the section, some level of market power is required from the combined market presence of the parties to the agreement. The Tribunal held in *Canada (Competition Act, Director of Investigation and Research) v The D&B Companies of Canada Ltd*, "[i]f the share is very large, the firm will likely have market power although, of course, other considerations must be taken into account."[378] A critical further consideration is barriers to entry.

iii) Barriers to Entry

As in the case of the assessment of the competitive effects of mergers, barriers to entry play a key role in assessing the potential effects of anti-competitive agreements.[379] Where entry barriers are low and markets are easily contestable, the parties to an agreement are unlikely to have the ability to raise prices or otherwise exercise significant market power. As the Tribunal stated in *Canada (Commissioner of Competition) v Canada Pipe*, "[w]here barriers to entry are non-existent, even a very large market share will not support a finding of market power."[380] In assessing barriers, the Bureau examines entry by existing, poised, or potential competitors.[381] The nature of barriers to entry and their assessment were discussed in detail in Chapter 5.[382]

iv) Effects of the Agreement on Competition

Section 90.1(2) contains a list of factors which the Tribunal "may have regard to" in considering the competitive effects in an application under section 90.1(1). These are identical to those applicable to the merger provision and include factors relevant to emerging digital competition issues introduced in the 2022 amendments (e.g., network effects and impacts on non-price competition, including consumer privacy.)[383]

The *Collaboration Guidelines* examine several categories of agreements that may affect competition. These are:

---

377 *Canada (Director of Investigation and Research, Competition Act) v Laidlaw Waste Systems Ltd*, [1992] CCTD No 1 at para 118; *Canada (Commissioner of Competition) v Visa Canada Corp*, [2013] CCTD No 10 at paras 252–53.

378 *Canada (Competition Act, Director of Investigation and Research) v The D&B Companies of Canada Ltd, 1995 CarswellNat 2684, [1995] CCTD No 20 at para 115.*

379 See Chapter 5, Section D(3).

380 *Canada (Commissioner of Competition) v Canada Pipe, [2005] CCTD No 3 at para 138.*

381 *Collaboration Guidelines*, above note 163, s 3.4.3.

382 See Chapter 5, Section D(3).

383 *Bill C-19 2022*, above note s 263. See discussion of these new factors in Chapter 5.

- Commercialization and joint selling agreements: The parties agree to share a common distribution network, warehouse facilities, or sales agent for efficiency reasons.
- Information sharing agreements: Trade associations and others exchange information on production, distribution, or management techniques. Such information may assist in raising overall industry efficiency by sharing know-how, or permitting better planning and decision-making.
- Research and development agreements: Parties agree to share technology, knowledge, or resources to accelerate innovation, new product development, or production.
- Joint production agreements: Parties agree to produce a product, in whole or part, in one plant, or in a common or jointly controlled facility, in order to realize scale or other economies.[384]
- Joint purchasing agreements or buying groups: Parties agree to combine their purchases to increase discounts and realize efficiencies.

Until further case law is developed under the section, there is little guidance available beyond the Act and the *Collaboration Guidelines* on the treatment of these kinds of agreements. Factors that affect whether the foregoing kinds of agreements raise issues under the Act include those discussed below.

a. Competition Outside the Agreement: Remaining Competition

As in the assessment of the impact of a merger, the size and competitive strength of parties in the industry outside the agreement must be considered, because they may be able to constrain or counteract any anti-competitive effects the agreement may produce. This includes examining "the extent to which effective competition remains or would remain in the market."[385]

b. Effects Internal to the Agreement

COMPETITION BETWEEN THE PARTIES

A key question is the impact of the agreement on the competitive vitality of the parties. For example, were the parties strong competitors in respect of the subject matter of the agreement prior to its commencement? In the absence of the agreement, would "the parties . . . otherwise be likely to independently develop competing products"?[386] Will the

384 A joint production agreement may qualify as a specialization agreement that can be exempted from s 90.1 under s 86 if registered. *Competition Act*, above note 52, s 90.

385 *Ibid*, s 90.1(2)(e).

386 *Collaboration Guidelines*, above note 163, s 3.8.2.

agreement likely cause the removal of a vigorous and effective competitor?[387] An additional factor is whether the agreement would "contribute to the entrenchment of the market position of leading incumbents"[388] — perhaps by restraining an emerging competitor who might have challenged the incumbent in the absence of the agreement. Examining the subject matter of the agreement is central to these questions.

COMPETITIVE IMPORTANCE OF THE CONDUCT INCLUDED OR LEFT OUTSIDE THE AGREEMENT

What potentially competitive conduct does the agreement cover? Agreements which relate to central features of competition such as marketing, sales, production, output levels, product development decisions, or other "key aspects of competitive rivalry between the participants"[389] are more likely to raise issues. Conversely, if the parties are free to make independent decisions about such matters in spite of collaboration on distribution, production, or research, such concerns are reduced.

DURATION AND SCOPE

The duration and scope of the agreement may colour its assessment, particularly when it is broader than necessary to achieve efficiencies or gain other benefits of cooperation or if it extends to matters central to healthy competition. For example, in terms of duration, concerns are raised by "restraints on competition . . . imposed for a period of time that extends beyond that which is reasonably necessary to achieve the objectives of [an] R&D agreement."[390] In terms of scope, competitive concerns are heightened, for example, "where [a] joint production agreement relates to the use of key production facilities of the parties, thereby reducing the individual participants' capacity or control over assets necessary to compete independently."[391]

NATURE AND IMPACT OF ANY EXCHANGE OF INFORMATION

The exchange of sensitive commercial information such as "pricing information, costs, trading terms, strategic plans, marketing strategies or other significant competitive variables" is likely to raise concerns under the Act.[392] Information about future pricing and marketing decisions is viewed as particularly sensitive.[393] On the other hand, the aggregation of data and its collection and exchange by an independent third party

387 *Competition Act*, above note 52, s 90.1(2)(f).

388 *Ibid*, s 90.1(2)(g.2).

389 *Collaboration Guidelines*, above note 163, s 3.6.2.

390 *Ibid*, s 3.8.4.

391 *Ibid*, s 3.9.3.

392 *Ibid*, s 3.7.1.

393 *Ibid*, s 3.7.2.

reduces its sensitivity and the potential for stimulating concerns about collusive or coordinated behaviour.[394]

c. Change and Innovation

Another factor is the extent to which the market is growing or being affected by changes such as innovation[395] and other forms of non-price competition.[396] Market growth may make entry easier or provide opportunities for expansion. Conversely, a contracting market may magnify the anti-competitive effects of an agreement among industry players, because new entry may be less likely and the market power of incumbents may be enhanced. Where excess capacity is created by a contracting market, however, this may stimulate competition among incumbents as they seek to find a market for their spare capacity.

d. Foreign Agreements, Domestic Effects

The Tribunal has held that section 90.1 applies to agreements entered into outside Canada which have domestic anti-competitive effects.[397] The scope of a Canadian court's or tribunal's authority to address conduct by foreign corporations or individuals is governed by the law defining the subject matter and personal jurisdiction of the court or tribunal in question.[398]

3) Elements of Section 90.1(1.1) – Agreements Between Non-Competitors

Section 90.1(1.1) provides:

> (1.1) If the Tribunal finds that a significant purpose of the agreement or arrangement, or any part of it, is to prevent or lessen competition in any market, it may make an order under subsection (1) even if none of the persons referred to in that subsection are competitors.

This subsection, introduced in the 2023 amendments,[399] changed the potential scope of section 90.1 by permitting its application to agreements other than those made between competitors. The immediate mischief to which the amendment was addressed was what the Bureau has

394 *Ibid*, s 3.7.4.
395 *Competition Act*, above note 52, s 90.1(2)(g).
396 *Ibid*, s 90.1(2)(g.3).
397 *Rakuten Kobo, above note 196* at paras 116–22; *HarperCollins, above note 196*.
398 See, e.g., Jean-Gabriel Castel & Janet Walker, *Canadian Conflict of Laws*, 6th ed (Toronto: LexisNexis, 2005) ch 10, §10.1 Juridical Jurisdiction.
399 *Bill C-56 2023*, above note 352, s 8(1).

described as "competitor property controls," such as shopping centre and other lease agreements which may restrict the ability of grocers (and other retailers) to enter a market and compete against an incumbent store.[400] In such circumstances, the shopping centre owner is not a competitor of the incumbent grocery who insists on the restriction, yet the agreement clearly affects the ability of new entrants to compete in the grocery market.[401]

This provision may also cover agreements between retailers and suppliers to impose terms which limit competition in the retail market. For example, such agreements between Loblaws and its suppliers were subject of an inquiry by the Bureau which was discontinued after Loblaws withdrew its policies which led to such agreements. Under these agreements, Loblaws obtained compensation where suppliers provided competitors discounts which reduced Loblaws' return. The Bureau concluded that "may have caused suppliers to implement various strategies, which would impact rivalry among retailers."[402] Concerns

400 The Finance Minister said in introducing the Bill: Canada, House of Commons Debates (Hansard), 44th Parl. 1st Sess, No 223, Sept 25, 2023: "It would also enable the Competition Bureau to ensure that big grocery stores cannot prevent smaller competitors from opening stores nearby." Minister Champagne, the Minister responsible for the Bill stated in the same debate " As identified in the bureau›s recent retail grocery market study, cases have emerged about property controls made between commercial landlords and tenants to exclude potential competitors from a rental property, sometimes even after the tenant has left. … controls like these have prevented independent grocers from moving into the only shopping centre in a community. In other cases, discount retailers were prevented from selling certain products near large supermarket chains renting from the same landlord." See also Canada, House of Commons, Standing Committee on Finance, Evidence, 44th Parl. 1st Sess, No 223, March 19, 2024: "Mark Schaan: [Senior Assistant Deputy Minister, Innovation, Science and Economic Development Canada] … We know that one of the factors potentially reducing competition is access to retail space. There are restrictions between, for example, land owners and grocery stores that prohibit the entry of new players within the retail footprint of the broader developer." The Bureau has released draft guidelines on how it will address such agreements: Competition Bureau, "Competitor Property Controls and the Competition Act" (7 August 2024), online: https://competition-bureau.canada.ca/how-we-foster-competition/education-and-outreach/competitor-property-controls-and-competition-act.

401 See Competition Bureau Canada, *Canada Needs More Grocery Competition: Competition Bureau*

Retail Grocery Market Study Report (Ottawa: ISEDC, 27 June 2023) at 28–9 and 38, online: https://ised-isde.canada.ca/site/competition-bureau-canada/sites/default/files/attachments/2023/CB-Retail-Grocery-Market-Study-Report-EN-2023-06-23.pdf.

402 Canada, Competition Bureau, *Position Statement, Alleged Anti-Competitive Conduct by Loblaw* (Gatineau: Competition Bureau, 2017), "Summary

raised by the Bureau included raising rivals' costs and reducing rivalry because of penalties extracted when suppliers reduced prices or introduced new products. Such agreements may arguably lessen competition substantially when implemented in concentrated markets (such as the grocery business).

4) Defences and Exceptions

a) Efficiencies

As noted above, the efficiencies defence for this provision was repealed alongside that defence for the merger provisions.[403] Having efficiencies dealt with identically in the merger provisions has the benefit of ensuring that parties do not seek to structure a transaction as a section 92 merger or section 90.1 civil agreement simply based on the availability of an efficiencies defence.

In the absence of a formal defence, parties to an agreement may still argue that efficiencies bring about cost savings which avoids the potential for the transaction to harm consumers (e.g., with higher prices). The *Collaboration Guidelines* recognize the potential for efficiencies to be achievable by competitor agreements falling within section 90.1:

> [R]eductions in fixed and variable costs owing to rationalization of distribution, sales and advertising functions; improved utilization of distribution and warehousing; increased specialization in distribution, sales and marketing functions; more intensive use of a network infrastructure; and improvements to product quality.[404]

On the other hand, parties will be faced with the counter-argument that Parliament intended in repealing the efficiencies defence that efficiencies should no longer provide any basis to justify a substantial prevention or lessening of competition. Until such arguments are evaluated in the context of the facts from a specific case, this will remain an area of uncertainty.

b) Regulated Conduct Defence

Does the presence of legislation or regulations requiring or authorizing the conduct in question create a defence to section 90.1? In enacting

---

of Bureau Conclusions," online: https://competition-bureau.canada.ca/how-we-foster-competition/education-and-outreach/position-statements/alleged-anti-competitive-conduct-loblaw-companies-limited.

403 *Bill C-56 2023*, above note 352, s 8(1.1).

404 *Collaboration Guidelines*, above note 163, s 3.5.1.

section 90.1, Parliament did not include a "grandfathering provision" like section 45(7), applicable to criminal conspiracy, making it clear that the existing case law governing the regulated conduct defence should continue to apply to the section.[405] The absence of such a parallel provision in section 90.1 strongly suggests that Parliament did not intend the defence to apply to this provision. That was the *obiter* view expressed by the Tribunal in *Canada (Commissioner of Competition) v Vancouver Airport Authority*, in considering the application of the defence to the abuse of dominance provision:

> If Parliament had intended to extend the RCD to the civil agreements between competitors governed by section 90.1, it would have said so expressly by adding language similar to s 45(7) in structuring this new civil provision. It did not. The plain wording and structure of section 90.1 speak for themselves. Under the implied exclusion rule of statutory interpretation, and even under the plain meaning rule, it is apparent that Parliament's intent was not to extend the RCD to this most recent civil provision and to make it available for this reviewable matter.[406]

If the defence is found to have some application to section 90.1, the Tribunal's consideration of the defence to abuse of dominance provides a framework which may be applied to section 90.1. The Tribunal's approach was to ask whether, applying the ordinary principles of statutory interpretation, there is any conflict between the *Competition Act* and the statutory or regulatory scheme in question.[407] The interface between a regulatory scheme and the civil *Competition Act* is discussed further in Chapter 7.[408]

Even if the regulated conduct defence is not applicable, the existence of a regulatory regime which establishes prices, limits entry, or regulates quality pursuant to validly enacted legislation or regulations nonetheless may affect the extent to which there is "room" as a factual matter for competition law to apply under a "substantial prevention or lessening of competition" standard. An agreement under section 90.1 must still have a "substantial" effect, and if the dimensions of competitive activity have been narrowed by the impact of a valid regulatory scheme, this may affect the ability to establish the necessary effect.

---

405 See above in this chapter at Section D(1)(g)(iii).

406 *Canada (Commissioner of Competition) v Vancouver Airport Authority, [2019] CCTD No 6 at para 244.*

407 *Ibid* at paras 248–58.

408 See Chapter 7, Section D(3).

c) Other Defences and Exceptions

Sections 90.1(7) and 90.1(8) exclude agreements between affiliates and relate to exports, respectively. The language is identical to that for the affiliate exception and largely the same as the export exception to the criminal agreements provision, section 45; the discussion above of those provisions is thus substantially applicable here.[409] The different criminal burden means that the accused in section 45 need only raise the possibility that a defence exists to shift the burden on the Crown to disprove the defence beyond a reasonable doubt.[410] The onus is on the parties to an agreement examined under section 90.1 to show that the exceptions in question apply, on a balance of probabilities.[411]

In common with other agreement-related provisions, section 90.1(10) limits bringing multiple proceedings based on substantially the same facts, under section 90.1 and under the merger, abuse of dominance, conspiracy, and price maintenance provisions.

Other exemptions from the Act which may be applicable to section 90.1 are described in section F, below in this chapter.

5) Remedies and Limitation Period

Section 90.1 empowers the Tribunal to issue an order of prohibiting the parties to an agreement or other person "from doing anything under the agreement or arrangement" and with consent, to require them "to take any other action."

As part of amendments passed in 2024 to encourage private enforcement and to bolster the teeth of the civil practices provisions, the remedies available under section 90.1 were broadened to include divestiture of assets or shares and administrative monetary penalties.[412] In the case of private enforcement, the Tribunal was given the power to require the payment of "the benefit derived from the conduct" to the private applicant and "any other person affected by the conduct."[413]

---

409 See above in this chapter, Section D(1)(g). With respect to the export exception, there is a difference in the language of s 90.1(8)(c) and s 45(5)(c), which suggests the export defence may be narrower under section 45 and inapplicable where there are any effects on the supply of services in Canada.

410 Morris Manning, Alan W Mewett & Peter J Sankoff, *Criminal Law*, 5th ed (Markham: LexisNexis, 2015) at 397.

411 *Tervita Corp v Canada (Commissioner of Competition)*, [2015] 1 SCR 161 at para 122.

412 *Bill C-59 2024*, above note, s 353, s 248.

413 *Competition Act*, above note 52, ss 90.1(10.1) and (10.2). The Tribunal's authority to grant leave to bring a private application under s 90.1 and to make an award which covers the benefits derived from the conduct comes into force June 20, 2025.

The 2024 amendments also added a limitation period whereby applications under s 90.1 may only be made within three years after the agreement or arrangement under review has been terminated.[414]

6) Cases

As noted above, there has been limited jurisprudence under the provision to date. As a result, the case law interpreting similar legislative language in the merger and abuse of dominance provisions provides the most direct source of case authority.

An application filed in 2011 in respect of an arrangement entered into between Air Canada and United Continental illustrates the potential for overlap between section 90.1 and the merger provisions. The application related to coordination agreements and a joint venture entered into between the airlines which involved cooperation on pricing, capacity setting (route planning), scheduling, frequent-flyer programs, and sales, as well as on revenue and cost-sharing. The joint venture was challenged under the merger provisions and the coordination agreements under section 90.1. The application alleged that the agreements would create a monopoly in ten cross-border routes between Calgary, Montreal, Toronto, Ottawa, and US destinations, and market shares of 70 per cent or more for four other such routes serving Calgary, Montreal, and Vancouver. The Commissioner alleged that the agreements gave the parties the power "to charge passengers inflated fares."[415]

In 2012, the Commissioner settled with the parties in a consent agreement that prohibited Air Canada and United Continental from certain activities, including joint pricing, revenue or cost sharing, and sharing sensitive commercial information about the fourteen transborder routes featuring the highest market shares.[416]

As noted above, the Commissioner also filed section 90.1 applications in respect of pricing agreements reached between ebook publishers and Apple Inc. Four publishers agreed in 2014 "to remove or amend clauses in . . . distribution agreements with individual eBook

---

414 *Competition Act*, above note 52, s 90.1(9.1).

415 Canada, Competition Bureau, News Release, "Competition Bureau Seeks to Block Joint Venture between Air Canada and United Continental" (27 June 2011), online: www.ic.gc.ca/eic/site/cb-bc.nsf/eng/03387.html.

416 *The Commissioner of Competition v Air Canada, United Continental Holdings, Inc, United Airlines, Inc and Continental Airlines Inc*, Consent Agreement (24 October 2012), online: https://decisions.ct-tc.gc.ca/ct-tc/cd/en/item/462548/index.do?q=CT-2012-001. In 2018, the Minister of Transport was given the authority to approve similar arrangements and create an exemption from competition law, including s 90.1: s 53.73(8) of the *Canada Transportation Act*, SC 1996, c 10 [*CTA*].

retailers that the Bureau believes have the effect of restricting retail price competition, which will allow retailers to offer discounts on eBooks."[417] The consent agreements were ultimately registered in 2017 and 2018 after certain preliminary motions and interventions were addressed.[418]

Section 90.1 was raised in a common law civil action between Dow Chemical and Nova Chemical. An issue (among many others raised in the complex litigation) arose over certain provisions in an agreement governing the operation of a petrochemical complex in Joffrey, Alberta by those parties, which restricted Dow's ability to independently purchase ethane. Dow argued that the provisions were contrary to section 90.1 and therefore void and unenforceable under contract law. The Alberta Court of Queen's Bench heard expert economic testimony and concluded that "[t]he implementation of these restrictions vis-à-vis Dow would have removed one of only two major purchasers of ethane in Alberta, and would have had the effect of preventing or lessening competition significantly in the purchase of ethane in Alberta,"[419] rendering the provision void. The case illustrates that an agreement between the two main competing purchasers of a product like ethane, with the potential for creating market power, may create the basis for a remedy under section 90.1.

F. EXEMPT AGREEMENTS AND ARRANGEMENTS

There are several provisions in Part I of the *Competition Act* that create exemptions for types of horizontal agreements and arrangements from the entire Act, from section 45, or from other specific provisions. Other exemptions are created by other federal statutory schemes.

---

417 Canada, Competition Bureau, News Release, "Four major publishers agree to take steps that are expected to lower ebook prices in Canada" (7 February 2014), online: www.competitionbureau.gc.ca/eic/site/cb-bc.nsf/eng/03658.html.

418 *The Commissioner of Competition v HarperCollins Publishers LLC and HarperCollins Canada Limited* (9 January 2018); *The Commissioner of Competition v Simon & Schuster Canada, a division of CBS Canada Holdings Co*; *The Commissioner of Competition v Apple Inc, and Apple Canada Inc*; *The Commissioner of Competition v Hachette Book Group Canada Ltd, Hachette Book Group, Inc, and Hachette Digital, Inc*; *The Commissioner of Competition v Holtzbrinck Publishers, LLC* (19 January 2017), online: https://decisions.ct-tc.gc.ca/ct-tc/cd/en/item/462492/index.do?q=CT-2017-002.

419 *Dow Chemical*, above note 208 at para 1417.

1) Collective Bargaining

Section 4 exempts from the entire Act certain coordinated actions by "workmen and employees"[420] and by "employers in a trade, industry or profession."[421] The former exemption is linked to actions taken by employees "for their own reasonable protection," while the latter is more specific to matters "pertaining to collective bargaining with their employees in respect of salary or wages and terms and conditions of employment." These exemptions are directed toward resolving what might otherwise be a conflict between competition law and federal and provincial labour legislation. The latter is designed to permit labour interests to act in combination in negotiating wages and other terms governing employment.[422] The exemptions have a slightly different scope than labour law, given the reference to "workmen," which is potentially broader than "employees," and the exemption of certain fishing activities, which potentially covers more than wages and other working conditions.[423]

Notwithstanding section 4, in one case a labour arbitrator held that he had the jurisdiction to consider whether or not the terms of a collective agreement were consistent with criminal and civil provisions of the *Competition Act*. He decided to exercise his discretion not to do so, however, given the complexity of the issues raised and the relative expertise of the Competition Tribunal to consider such issues.[424] While the decision was upheld on appeal, the appeal court did not comment on whether the arbitrator should simply have determined that the presence of the collective agreement ousted the *Competition Act*.[425]

In the case of employers, section 4(2) removes the exemption for collective actions to withhold a product, or to refrain from acquiring a product, other than the services of workers or employees. Group

420 *Competition Act*, above note 52, s 4(a). The language is that "Nothing in this Act" applies to such matters.

421 *Ibid*, s 4(c).

422 "The intention of Parliament in enacting s 4(1)(a) was to recognize as legitimate the formation of trade unions (combinations of workers) and to exempt their activities from the operation of anti-combines legislation." *British Columbia (Restrictive Trade Practices Commission, Member) v Hewison* (1979), 17 BCLR 124 (SC) at para 6, aff'd (1982), 41 BCLR 233 (CA) [*Hewison*]; see also *Yashin, above note 315 at para 44*.

423 *Canada Post Corporation*, 87 CLLC para 16,029.

424 *Universal Workers Union, Local 183 v Metropolitan Toronto Apartment Builders' Assn (Collective Agreement Grievance), [2013] OLAA No 477.*

425 *Metropolitan Toronto Apartment Builders Assn v Labourers' International Union of North America, Local 183, 2014 ONSC 5775 (Div Ct).*

boycotts by employers covering the purchase of a particular product are therefore not exempt, for example.

If the actions of both employers and employees go beyond what may be considered collective bargaining activities, the exemption may also not apply. For example, boycotts of a particular price-discounting firm organized by workers, even if used as a strategy to raise wages, may not fall within the exemption.[426]

Section 4(b) covers negotiations and collective action in matters relating to fishing. It exempts "contracts, agreements or arrangements" between or among fishers on the one hand and "persons or associations of persons engaged in the buying or processing of fish" on the other. The exemption covers matters "relating to the prices, remuneration or other like conditions under which fish will be caught or supplied to those persons by fishermen." This language covers not only collective action with respect to work terms and conditions but also the pricing of the commodity. Fishers are also covered by the collective bargaining exemption given that they are also "workers."[427]

2) Underwriting Activities

Section 5 provides an exemption from section 45 for activities relating to the underwriting of securities that financial institutions and investment houses issue to raise capital for a new venture or ongoing operation. The exemption applies to agreements and arrangements between securities dealers and securities issuers or vendors, which have "a reasonable relationship to the underwriting of a specific security." "Underwriting" is defined as the primary or secondary distribution of a security pursuant to the rules established under a domestic or foreign securities law

---

426 See, e.g., Restrictive Trade Practices Commission, *Report re Bread and Other Bakery Products in the Winnipeg Area* (Ottawa: Queen's Printer, 1952):

> If the present situation were held to be exempt from the provisions of the *Combines Investigation Act*, such exemption would have to be upon the principle that, so long as Union members are motivated by a desire to protect their wages, they may combine to dictate the prices and other conditions of sale of their employers' goods and to forbid such employers, upon pain of a stoppage of work, to enter into price competition with each other. The implications of admitting such a principle are obvious. The situation created for suppliers acting in good faith would be intolerable and any who were disposed to seek means to avoid the *Combines Investigation Act* would have a new expedient at their disposal. All in all, the effect would tend to be subversive of the anti-combines legislation in important respects.

427 *Hewison*, above note 425.

involving the filing of a prospectus or to which an exemption from filing a prospectus applies.[428]

In the United States, the Supreme Court has held that the actions of parties related to an initial public offering of securities are regulated and exempt from the application of antitrust laws. The Supreme Court noted that "the activities in question here — the underwriters' efforts jointly to promote and to sell newly issued securities — [are] central to the proper functioning of well-regulated capital markets."[429] The statutory exemption in the *Competition Act* appears to be based on the same logic — that securities underwriting involves coordinated behaviour governed by a securities regulatory scheme which protects the public interest, and which removes the rationale for the application of competition law.

3) Amateur Sport

By virtue of section 6 of the Act, "agreements and arrangements between or among teams, clubs and leagues pertaining to participation in amateur sport" (those involving participants who are not compensated)[430] are exempt from the entire Act. The meaning of "compensation" may raise issues in certain circumstances, such as those of young players who are nominally unpaid, receive a stipend and may play for a for-profit club under the hope or expectation of gaining a position in a professional league.[431]

4) Cooperative Action by Artists and Holders of Copyright

The federal *Status of the Artist Act* provides artists' associations certified under that legislation with the exemption provided employees in section 4 of the *Competition Act* "for the purpose of providing appropriate protection for the professional interests of the artists they represent."[432] The same exemption is provided to producers' collective actions "pertaining

428 *Competition Act*, above note 52, s 5(2).

429 *Credit Suisse Sec (USA) LLC v Billing*, 551 US 264 (2017) at 276.

430 *Ibid*, s 6(2).

431 See, e.g., the issues raised in the class action certified in *Berg v Canadian Hockey League*, 2019 ONSC 2106 (Div Ct). The plaintiffs and defendants in related actions in Ontario (Court File No CV-14-511423-00CP), Alberta (Court File No 1401-11912), and Québec (Court File No 500-06-000716-148) reached a $30-million settlement on 20 May 2020, subject to court approval.

432 SC 1992, c 33, s 9(2)(a).

to bargaining in respect of remuneration and the terms and conditions of engagement of artists."[433]

The *Copyright Act* similarly exempts from the application of section 45 of the *Competition Act* agreements for the licensing of copyrighted material filed by a collective society permitted under that legislation.[434] The exemption applies "in respect of any royalties or related terms and conditions arising under" such agreements, meaning that other competitive aspects are not exempt.[435] Anti-competitive conduct which goes beyond the refusal to license copyrighted material, and does not involve the mere exercise of copyright rights, may be subject to the Act.[436]

5) Agreements and Arrangement Related to Protecting the Environment

The 2024 amendments added authority for the Commissioner to issue a certificate exempting an agreement or arrangement "that is for the purpose of protecting of the environment" from the application of the criminal and civil agreement provisions of the Act. Such agreements may only be certified when the Commissioner is satisfied "that it is not likely to prevent or lessen competition substantially in a market."[437] The practical effect of this language is that the certificate is most likely to be available and useful for exemption from the criminal conspiracy provisions (ss 45, 46, 47 and 49), given that the civil provisions would not be applicable in any case if the agreement in question does not give rise to a likely substantial prevention or lessening of competition.

The certificate process was added in spite of recommendations from the Commissioner against its addition to the Act. The Commissioner argued that it was unnecessary (given that various means, including the "ancillary restraints" defence are already available to avoid the application of the Act to environmentally beneficial agreements already), and that it might lead to certain "unintended consequences," including confusion about what the criminal conspiracy provisions may cover.[438]

---

433 *Ibid*, s 9(2)(b). A "producer" is defined in s 5 to mean government institutions and broadcast undertakings. On the relationship between this scheme and copyright see *Canadian Artists' Representation v National Gallery of Canada, [2014] 2 SCR 197*.

434 *Copyright Act*, RSC 1985, c C-42, ss 67 and 76.

435 *Ibid*, s 76(3).

436 Canada, Competition Bureau, "Intellectual Property Enforcement Guidelines" (13 March 2019), online: https://www.ic.gc.ca/eic/site/cb-bc.nsf/eng/04421.html.

437 *Competition Act*, above note 52, ss 124.3–124.7.

438 M Boswell, Letter to the Chair and Members of the House of Commons Standing Committee on Finance (March 1, 2024) at 11-12.

6) Miscellaneous Exemptions

The *Shipping Conferences Exemption Act, 1987* creates a scheme which exempts agreements reached as part of ocean shipping conferences, in respect of tariffs and other terms and conditions, from the application of the entire *Competition Act*.[439] The exemption does not apply to predatory pricing,[440] or to aspects of shipping conference agreements that purport to apply to non-party ocean carriers or to the inland transportation of goods.[441]

Statutory exemptions from the *Competition Act* are also provided for agreements entered into between producers of federally regulated farm products and the agencies created under a supply management scheme,[442] as well as for agreements exempted by order under the federal emergency supplies regime.[443] A less explicit exemption applies to "an international agreement or convention respecting air services to which Canada is a party," which are simply stated to "prevail to the extent of the inconsistency or conflict" over the *Competition Act*.[444]

Other sector-specific exemptions from section 45 found in the *Competition Act* itself are for agreements between federal financial institutions covered by section 49[445] and arrangements between airlines approved by the Minister of Transport under the *Canada Transportation Act*.[446]

Finally, the *Competition Act* creates a civil regime for the registration of agreements by the Competition Tribunal that allow parties to specialize in the production of a product. For example, under such agreements, two firms might agree that each will discontinue output of a particular product line and concentrate on producing the product discontinued by the other in order to take advantage of economies of scale. The section is triggered by an application to the Tribunal by a

439 RSC 1985, c 17 (3d Supp), s 4.
440 *Ibid*, s 4(4).
441 *Ibid*, s 5.
442 *Farm Products Agencies Act, RSC 1985, c F-4, s 32.*
443 *Energy Supplies Emergency Act, RSC 1985, c E-9, s 33.*
444 *CTA*, above note 419, s 4(3).
445 *Ibid*, s 45(6)(b); see above in this chapter for a discussion of s 49.
446 *Ibid*, s 45(6)(c) and the *Transportation Modernization Act*, SC 2018, c 10, ss 14 and 85, referring to the authority of the Minister to approve arrangements as provided for in the new s 53.73(8) of the *CTA*, above note 419. "Arrangement" is defined in s 53.7 of the *CTA* to mean "an agreement or arrangement, other than a transaction referred to in subsection 53.1(1), involving two or more transportation undertakings providing air services, as defined in subsection 55(1), to, from or within Canada, to coordinate on any aspect of the operation or marketing of such services, including prices, routes, schedules, capacity or ancillary services and to share costs or revenues or other resources or benefits."

party to the specialization agreement. The Commissioner is afforded an opportunity to be heard in the consideration of any such application. The purpose of this provision, which has not been used to date, has been described as follows:

> The specialization agreement provisions were added with the idea that the Canadian economy needed a certain amount of restructuring to compete internationally and that the *Competition Act* should not stand in the way of this process.[447]

Where registered, sections 45, 77 (in respect of exclusive dealing) and 90.1 do not apply to such agreements.[448]

G. CONCLUSION

This chapter has reviewed the criminal and civil provisions in the *Competition Act* focused on horizontal agreements. Central to these provisions is section 45, the criminal prohibition of price fixing, market allocation, and limits on production. Its origins can be traced to Canada's first combines law in 1889. Section 45 remained largely unchanged until the substantial amendments of 2009 (in effect in 2010). The amendments removed the requirement to prove any lessening of competition (undue or otherwise) and focused on "hard core" anti-competitive practices. The issues under the section are now narrowed to questions, such as the existence of an agreement, which the criminal courts are well suited to evaluate.

The conspiracy provision remains a key component in ensuring an efficiently functioning domestic economy. Deterrence of cartels and collusion promotes rivalry, competitive prices, and product choices for

---

447 Thomas W Ross, "The Evolution of Competition Law in Canada" (1998) 13 *Review of Industrial Organization* 1 at 15:

> A hypothetical example involves two companies that each produce cars and trucks for the small Canadian market and that agree that Company 1 will discontinue producing cars while Company 2 discontinues the production of trucks. Each will then benefit from longer production runs and lower costs. They may further agree to sell their products to each other so that both can continue to sell at retail a full line of products.

For a further discussion, see also HE English, "Specialization and Export Agreements in Canada: Retrospect and Prospect," ch 19, and K Stegemann, "The European Experience with Exempting Specialization Agreements and Recent Proposals," ch 20 in J Robert S Pritchard, William T Stanbury & Thomas A Wilson, *Canadian Competition Law, Essays in Law and Economics* (Toronto: Butterworths, 1979).

448 *Competition Act*, above note 52, ss 85–90.

consumers, and provides a stimulus to innovation. A competitive and efficient domestic economy in turn enhances Canada's international competitiveness. The Supreme Court reflected on these considerations when it said about the predecessor provision:

> [I]t remains at the core of the criminal part of the Act. The prohibition of conspiracies in restraint of trade is the epitome of competition law, finding its place in every competition law, from para. 1 of the *Sherman Act* to Article 85 of the *Treaty establishing the European Economic Community*.[449]

Another key criminal provision is the prohibition of bid-rigging, particularly given the substantial resources devoted to the process and outcomes of tendering and public procurement. The *Competition Act* also contains criminal provisions dealing with foreign conspiracies, agreements among financial institutions, and agreements involving professional sports associations.

Section 90.1(1) permits the Commissioner, and as of June 20, 2025, private parties, to apply to the Competition Tribunal to examine agreements between competitors. The provision applies the same standard as that used to review mergers. It permits the review of agreements, such as joint ventures, and research and development arrangements, which may affect competition. At the same time, the section removes the criminal law "chill," present under the previous provision, over beneficial cooperative behaviour. The combination of a *per se* criminal provision and a flexible civil provision permitting a case-by-case assessment of agreements before an expert tribunal implements policy recommendations from decades of reports and legislative deliberations commencing in the 1960s.

With the addition of private enforcement and various monetary remedies coming into effect in 2025, there may be more activity under this provision, for which there had been few cases prior to these changes.

Collusive behaviour which does not involve an express agreement poses challenging issues for competition law. With changes in economic theory, there is a consensus among economists that such behaviour can be as harmful to consumers and to the economy as many forms of explicit collusion. Businesses increasingly rely upon computerized pricing and other digital tools, creating the potential for algorithmic collusion, signalling, and other coordinated conduct. Detecting and assessing these practices can be difficult. On the one hand, enhanced dissemination of pricing and other data can make markets more efficient and competitive.

449 *Nova Scotia Pharmaceutical Society*, above note 47 at para 87.

On the other, it can lead to parallel conduct, higher prices and reduced rivalry. The challenge for competition law is to discern the differences between beneficial and harmful cooperative conduct, and to develop appropriate remedies.[450] Some forms of cooperative behaviour can be dealt with as a classical conspiracy under section 45.[451] Other practices that facilitate collusion or parallel behaviour can also be addressed under the abuse of dominance provisions of the *Competition Act*. Those provisions are the subject of the next chapter.

---

450 See, e.g., Stefan Thomas, "Harmful Signals: Cartel Prohibition and Oligopoly Theory in the Age of Machine Learning" (2019) 15 *Journal of Competition Law and Economics* 159 at 161: "Information can be used by competitors to collude or to compete, and the challenge of competition law is being able to detect the differences."

451 ABA Antitrust Law Section, Report of the International Developments and Comments Task Force, "Common Issues Relating to the Digital Economy and Competition" (27 February 2020), online: www.americanbar.org/content/dam/aba/administrative/antitrust_law/lp-files/sal-report-on-common-sssues-relating-to-the-digital-economy-and-competition-final-4162020.pdf at 46–47.

CHAPTER 7

ABUSE OF DOMINANCE

A. INTRODUCTION: THE POLICY APPROACH TO DOMINANT FIRM BEHAVIOUR

Possession of monopoly or market power[1] by a dominant firm can produce allocative, productive and dynamic inefficiency, result in social welfare losses and impose a transfer of income from consumers to producers.[2] Dominant firms may also use their power to exclude competitors or increase barriers to entry through such tactics as signing customers to long-term exclusive contracts, selective price cutting to deter entry, intimidating and acquiring emerging competitors, engaging in sham litigation, or refusals to supply. These practices often carry a sense of unfairness in addition to their impacts on efficiency and consumer welfare.

While such concerns provide a basis for competition law to address the behaviour of dominant firms, there are a number of factors that support the need for caution in a policy approach that would see bigness *per se* as a basis for sanctioning or breaking up dominant entities. These include:

---

1 See the discussion of market definition and market power in Chapter 4.

2 See Chapter 3.

FIGURE 7.1. The match factory at the foot of the tall smoke stack, Hull, after 1867[3]

- Large firms may have obtained or maintained their position due to economies of scale or scope, or from efficiencies derived from vertical integration.[4] Breaking them up, or limiting their competitive actions, may increase costs and reduce social welfare.
- Attacking firms that have become industry leaders through "superior skill, foresight and industry" may have an adverse effect on their incentives to expand by legitimate competitive means; in short, it may dissuade competition, the very thing competition policy strives to promote.[5]
- Large firm size may be essential to the ability to compete on an international level.[6]
- The returns derived from a monopoly position may provide the incentive that fuels critical expenditures on innovation, a key driver of competition. Economist Joseph Schumpeter opined that monopoly returns would unleash the forces of "creative destruction," resulting in novel products, better service, or cheaper production

3 The *Encyclopedia of French Cultural Heritage in North America*, online: www.ameriquefrancaise.org/en/article-719/Chaudi%C3%A8re_Falls_in_the_Outaouais_Region.html.

4 Bruce Dunlop, Michael Trebilcock & David McQueen, *Canadian Competition Policy: A Legal and Economic Analysis* (Toronto: Canada Law Book, 1987) at 156–58; Lawrence A Skeoch & Bruce C McDonald, *Dynamic Change and Accountability in a Canadian Market Economy* (Ottawa: Consumer and Corporate Affairs, 1976) at 148 [*Skeoch-McDonald Report*].

5 Maurice E Stucke, "Should the Government Prosecute Monopolies?" [2009] 2009 *University of Illinois Law Review* 497 at 517 [Stucke], citing the US jurisprudence, including *United States v Aluminum Co of America*, 148 F2d 416 (2d Cir 1945) at 430; *Verizon Communications Inc v Law Offices of Curtis V Trinko, LLP*, 540 US 398 (2004) at 406 [*Verizon*].

6 *Skeoch-McDonald Report*, above note 4 at 149.

methods.[7] Schumpeter's hypothesis has been widely cited and even endorsed by the US Supreme Court in its antitrust jurisprudence.[8] At the same time, there remains a solid theoretical and empirical foundation for believing that competition is a key driver of innovation in many circumstances.[9]

Given such factors, the abuse of dominance provisions in the *Competition Act* may sanction monopolistic practices that are predatory, exclusionary, or disciplinary, but do not provide relief against the mere possession of a dominant market position.[10] If a firm gains a dominant position by legitimate competitive means such as better products, superior services, innovation, lower costs, or efficient practices, economic theory suggests caution toward intervention.[11] Successful competitive behaviour is what competition law is intended to encourage; "monopoly can sometimes result from competition."[12]

Once a firm gains a substantial share of the market, however, market power may give it the economic clout and leverage that can be used against competitors by employing means that do not involve the mere exercise of superior competitive performance. Obtaining and maintaining a dominant position by anti-competitive means rather than competition raises policy concerns. Sanctioning dominant behaviour that creates exclusionary barriers to entry is consistent not only with

---

7 Joseph Schumpeter, *Capitalism, Socialism, and Democracy* (New York: Routledge, 2003) at ch VII.

8 *Verizon, above note 5 at 407:*

> The mere possession of monopoly power, and the concomitant charging of monopoly prices, is not only not unlawful; it is an important element of the free-market system. The opportunity to charge monopoly prices—at least for a short period—is what attracts "business acumen" in the first place; it induces risk taking that produces innovation and economic growth. To safeguard the incentive to innovate, the possession of monopoly power will not be found unlawful unless it is accompanied by an element of anticompetitive *conduct*.

9 See, e.g., Jonathan B Baker, "Beyond Schumpeter vs. Arrow: How Antitrust Fosters Innovation" (2007) 74 *Antitrust Law Journal* 575; Stucke, above note 5 at 509–13.

10 *Competition Act*, RSC 1985, c C-34, ss 78 & 79 [*Competition Act* or Act]; *Canada (Commissioner of Competition) v Vancouver Airport Authority, [2019] CCTD No 6 at para 625 [VAA]*: "As the Tribunal has previously observed, '[. . .] section 79 is not intended to condemn a firm merely for having market power. Instead, it is directed at ensuring that dominant firms compete with other firms on merit and not through abusing their market power' (*Canada (Director of Investigation and Research) v Tele-Direct (Publications) Inc et al*, [1997] CCTD No 8, 73 CPR (3d) 1 (Comp Trib) at 179)."

11 Stephen Martin, *Industrial Economics* (New York: Macmillan, 1988) at 86.

12 *Ibid.*

dynamic and innovative markets, but also serves the interest of promoting the economic freedom to participate in commerce.[13] In *Canada (Director of Investigation and Research, Competition Act) v Laidlaw Waste Systems Ltd*, for example, the Competition Tribunal found that the dominant waste disposal company on central Vancouver Island had signed customers to long-term restrictive contracts, intimidated or acquired numerous fledgling competitors, and engaged in sham litigation, all as a way of raising entry barriers, discouraging or eliminating emerging competition, and maintaining its market position. These were found to be anti-competitive practices aimed at preserving or adding to the dominant firm's position and were made subject to a remedial order.[14]

This chapter will examine the elements of the law after a brief discussion of its historical origins.

B. BACKGROUND AND HISTORY

Monopoly was subject to a criminal prohibition in Canada beginning in 1910.[15] The operative test was the same as that applicable to mergers; it was a criminal offence for a monopoly to operate "to the detriment of or against the interests of the public."[16] Under the case law as it developed, this required that the firm in question not only possess total market control, but also that there be demonstrated public prejudice in the form of excess prices or profits.[17] There was only one criminal conviction for the offence of monopoly[18] and as a result of the stringent test applied by the courts, the provision "was widely perceived as ineffective in dealing with

13 Eleanor M Fox, "Competition Policy at the Intersection of Equity and Efficiency: The Developed and Developing Worlds" (2018) 63 *Antitrust Bulletin* 3 at 5.

14 *Canada (Director of Investigation and Research, Competition Act) v Laidlaw Waste Systems Ltd (1992), 40 CPR (3d) 289 (CCT) [Laidlaw]*.

15 *Combines Investigation Act*, SC 1910, c 9, s 2 defined a "combine" as "any contract, agreement, arrangement or combination which has, or is designed to have, the effect of . . . restricting competition . . . to the detriment of consumers or producers of such article of trade or commerce, and includes the acquisition. . . or obtaining by any person to the end aforesaid, of any control over or interest in the business, or any portion of the business, of any other person, and also includes what is known as a trust, monopoly or merger." Combines were only subject to criminal prosecution after an order of prohibition of an *ad hoc* Board was made and the practices continued.

16 This language dates to 1923: SC 1923, c 9, ss 2(a) (definition of "combine"), 26(a) (offence).

17 See, e.g., *R v KC Irving Ltd*, [1978] 1 SCR 408 [*KC Irving*].

18 *R v Eddy Match Company Limited*, [1953] QJ No 8 (CA) [*Eddy* CA].

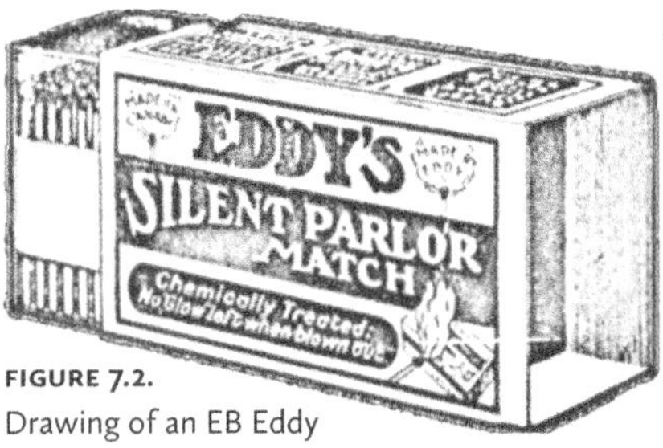

FIGURE 7.2.
Drawing of an EB Eddy Silent Parlor match box in 1919

anti-competitive conduct by dominant firms."[19]

The conviction came in 1951 in *R v Eddy Match Co Ltd.* Eddy Match was a maker of wooden matches.[20] It was incorporated in 1927 from an amalgamation of Canada's three leading match producers, leaving the company as "practically the only producer of wooden matches in Canada," permitting it to increase prices.[21] This was followed by numerous acquisitions of competitors in conjunction with predatory practices.

The Crown charged the company and several of its affiliates with operating "a merger, trust or monopoly which . . . substantially or completely controlled throughout Canada, excluding Newfoundland, the class or species of business in which they were engaged, to wit: the business of producing, manufacturing, supplying or dealing in wooden matches" during the period 1927 to 1950.

The trial judge convicted, finding that the company and its accused affiliates had operated a combine during the relevant period, through their market control and anti-competitive practices. The latter included the acquisition of competitors, the closure after acquisition of competing plants, and the use of "fighting brands"—low-cost regional match brands—as a temporary competitive response to new entry, designed to drive entrants out of business or force them into acquisition by one of Eddy Match's affiliates.[22] On appeal, the conviction was upheld, the appeal court holding:

> There is uncontradicted evidence that the leading actor—Eddy Match—deliberately set out to eliminate competition as it arose; that because of its strength and resources it was able to do so; that each new subsidiary was given its role and played its part in the general plan and finally, that the five appellants, all competition eliminated, were able to give to the public the products that they chose to make available, at the price they chose to fix and through the channels they chose to use.[23]

---

19 D Jeffrey Brown, ed, *Competition Act and Commentary* (LexisNexis: Markham, 2016) at 123.

20 Outaouais Forest History, online: www.histoireforestiereoutaouais.ca/en/c18/#10.

21 *R c Eddy Match Company Limited, [1951] JQ no 8 (KB)* at paras 193 and 195 [*Eddy* KB].

22 *Eddy* CA, above note 18 at paras 68 and 71–76.

23 *Ibid* at para 68.

The Court sentenced Eddy Match and its four affiliated corporations to relatively modest fines, ranging from $10,000 to $25,000 per company. These were a tiny fraction of the more than $10 million in dividends paid out by Eddy Match alone to its shareholders in the period 1928 to 1946.[24]

While the Quebec court entered a conviction for this particularly egregious behaviour, the frailties in the "detriment to the public" test again were evident in 1976 in the Supreme Court of Canada's decision in *R v KC Irving*. The case was a prosecution for both merger and monopolization of the New Brunswick English newspaper market. As noted earlier, Bora Laskin CJ, for the unanimous Court, rejected the Crown's contention that a presumption of public detriment arose from Irving's acquisition of complete control of the New Brunswick English newspaper market or from the absence of competition.[25] Professor Trebilcock wrote that the case represented "[t]he final straw for Canadian merger and monopolization law."[26] The provision had become virtually unenforceable, given the need to show detriment above and beyond monopolistic competitive impact. Subsequent attempts to enforce the monopoly provision were frustrated by the high standard set by the Supreme Court, and no further contested prosecutions were successful, with two acquittals and a discharge at a preliminary hearing entered.[27]

The path toward reform of the criminal provisions was laid out in the Economic Council of Canada's 1969 *Interim Report on Competition Policy*

---

24 *Eddy* KB at paras 255 and 335.

25 *KC Irving, above note 17 at 424–25.*

26 Michael J Trebilcock, "The Supreme Court and Strengthening the Conditions for Effective Competition in the Canadian Economy" (2001) 80 *Canadian Bar Review* 542 at 587.

27 In the period 1976–86, monopoly charges were "the subject of five court proceedings resulting in two acquittals, a discharge at preliminary hearing and an order of prohibition issued pursuant to subsection 30(2) of the Act." See Gordon E Kaiser & Ian Nielsen-Jones, "Recent Developments in Canadian Law: Competition Law" (1986) 18 *Ottawa Law Review* 401 at 428:

> In . . . *R. v. Thomson Newspapers Ltd* (28 October 1983), [unreported] . . . the Court was faced with monopoly offences relating to the Montreal and Winnipeg markets. The Court declined to accept that an absence of competition can support the element of operating a monopoly to the detriment or against the interest of the public. In so finding, it held: "The framing of the offence of monopoly in the Act tacitly acknowledges there may be monopoly without detriment. *Proof of detriment must, therefore, go beyond the consequences which flow purely and simply from the fact of monopoly, to some abuse in its operation.* The Crown did not submit that Southam had abused or was abusing the monopoly; in other words, there was no evidence of present detriment" [emphasis in original].

and in the 1976 *Skeoch-McDonald Report* (both discussed in Chapter 3).[28] The reports recommended that competition law address abusive behaviour by dominant firms rather than monopoly market position *per se*. The former suggested the appropriate approach for competition policy was that

> [t]here would be no barrier to the achievement of market dominance or monopoly via the route of internal company expansion and superior efficiency. But the achievement of dominance or monopoly via merger or via the employment of "exclusionary" trade practices would be open to examination and question.[29]

The latter report recommended "that dominant firms be prohibited from engaging in forms of conduct which constitute the abusive use of monopoly power."[30]

The background materials for what became the 1986 amendments enacting the *Competition Act* took the position that the criminal law was incapable of addressing monopolistic practices. At the same time, it was recognized that such practices "may, in different circumstances, be pro-competitive,"[31] and that the new provisions should not "create an impediment to aggressive, competitive behaviour."[32] On this basis, Parliament adopted a provision involving a case-by-case assessment of competitive effect, adjudicated before the specialized Competition Tribunal on a civil, balance of probabilities standard.[33]

The substantive abuse of dominance provisions remained unchanged from those adopted in 1986 until 2022. Prompted by the rise of dominant players in digital markets, evidence of increasing market concentration and other factors, proposals for reform from Parliament and the Bureau in 2021 stimulated what has been described as "a flurry of work from academics, think tanks, interest groups and others providing suggestions for changes (or arguing against certain changes) in Canada's competition law, policy and institutions."[34] The process led to amendments in

---

28 See Economic Council of Canada, *Interim Report on Competition Policy* (Ottawa: Queen's Printer, 1969) [*Interim Report* 1969] and *Skeoch-McDonald Report*, above note 4.

29 *Interim Report* 1969, above note 28 at 129.

30 *Skeoch-MacDonald Report*, above note 4 at 150.

31 Canada, Consumer and Corporate Affairs, *Amendments to the Combines Investigation Act, Background Information and Explanatory Notes* (Ottawa: Minister of Supply and Services, 1984) at 20.

32 Canada, Consumer and Corporate Affairs, *Competition Law Amendments, A Guide* (Ottawa: Minister of Supply and Services, 1985) at 22, online: www.competitionbureau.gc.ca/eic/site/cb-bc.nsf/eng/03045.html.

33 Sections 78 & 79 of the *Competition Act*, above note 10.

34 Thomas Ross, "Canada's Competition Act: The Reform Process Continues," CPI Columns, US & Canada, November 2023 at 2.

2022 and in 2023 which modified the substantive test, permitted private parties to seek relief from the Tribunal for abuse of dominance, and increased penalties available from the Tribunal.[35]

In 2024, remedies for private applications under section 79 were broadened to include recovery of "the value of the benefit derived from the conduct that is the subject of the order."[36] As with other civil provisions subject to private enforcement, this amount may be "distributed among the applicant and any other person affected by the conduct, in any manner that the Tribunal considers appropriate."[37]

C. ABUSE OF DOMINANCE ELEMENTS

Section 79 of the *Competition Act* provides that the Competition Tribunal, on application by the Commissioner of Competition, may impose a remedy where the following elements are proven on a balance of probabilities:

- I. Control of a class or species of business: "one or more persons substantially or completely control class or species of business throughout Canada or any area thereof" and
- II. Anti-competitive practices or conduct: "that person or those persons have engaged in or are engaging in" either
  - A practice of anti-competitive acts as defined in section 78; or
  - Conduct having a substantial effect on competition.[38]

These main elements are discussed below.

1) Control of a Class or Species of Business in an Area of Canada

Section 79(1) refers to the need for substantial or complete control of a class or species of business in Canada. What does that require? As we will see below, "control" is the equivalent of market power, and is assessed

35 *An Act to implement certain provisions of the budget tables in Parliament April 7, 2022 and other measures*, SC 2022, c 10 [*Bill C-19 2022*]; *An Act to amend the Excise Act and the Competition Act*, SC 2023, c 31 [*Bill C-56 2023*].

36 *Fall Economic Statement Implementation Act, 2023*, s 247.

37 *Competition Act*, above note 10, s 79(4.1). This provision comes into effect on June 25, 2025.

38 The substantive elements as they existed prior to the 2022-23 amendments were discussed in *Canada (Commissioner of Competition) v Toronto Real Estate Board*, 2017 FCA 236 at paras 11 and 48 [*TREB* FCA2].

by examining the product market ("class or species of business") and geographic market ("throughout Canada or any area thereof").

a) The Framework for Assessing Market Power: The Relevant Product and Geographic Markets

Section 79(1) requires that market power be assessed in the two dimensions applicable to the assessment of any relevant market: product and geography. The Tribunal held in *Canada (Competition Act, Director of Investigation and Research) v The D&B Companies of Canada Ltd*, after considering the statutory language and extrinsic evidence from the legislative record:

> [Section 79] divides the two dimensions of a market: "class or species of business" refers to the relevant product market and "throughout Canada or any area thereof" to the relevant geographic market. Parliament has made clear that, although the section may from time to time address powerful international firms, for the section to apply they must have market power in parts of, or all of, Canada. I conclude that "class or species of business" is synonymous with the relevant product market and "control" is synonymous with market power.[39]

Given that the geographic ambit of "control" under section 79 is limited to Canada, the extraterritorial scope of the provision is limited. For example, "the Canadian statute cannot be used to stop an American firm that is dominant in the world market, but has a small Canadian market share, from taking anti-competitive action against a Canadian company in Europe."[40] At the same time, anti-competitive practices by a firm based outside Canada that have a real and substantial connection to Canada (by, for example, lessening competition substantially in Canada) could be subject to the jurisdiction of the Competition Tribunal.[41]

The process of market definition as a step toward assessing market power was discussed in Chapter 4. In examining markets occupied by dominant firms, the hypothetical monopolist test used in market definition must take into account any market power already possessed by

---

39 *Canada (Director of Investigation and Research) v D&B Companies of Canada Ltd* (1995), 64 CPR (3d) 216 (CCT) at para 38 [*D&B*].

40 *Ibid* at para 36, referring to RJ Roberts, "Abuse of Dominant Position: From Bork to Bain and Back Again (But This Time with Extraterritoriality)" in RS Khemani & William T Stanbury, *Canadian Competition Law and Policy at the Centenary* (Halifax: Institute for Research on Public Policy, 1991) 337 at 344–48, who opined that an amendment would be needed to extend the section's territorial reach.

41 *Rakuten Kobo Inc v Canada (Commissioner of Competition), [2018] 4 FCR 111 (FC) at paras 116–22; Canada (Commissioner of Competition) v HarperCollins Publishers LLC, [2017] CCTD No 10.*

the incumbent firm. The base price used in that test must be adjusted to remove any monopoly premium above competitive pricing levels.[42]

b) "Control" Means Market Power

The Tribunal has held that "control" is "synonymous with market power."[43] Market power was discussed in detail in Chapter 4.[44] In summary, it was described by the Federal Court of Appeal in *Canada (Commissioner of Competition) v Toronto Real Estate Board* (*TREB*) as "the ability to control either price or non-price dimensions of competition for a significant period of time. Non-price dimensions of competition include innovation and quality of service, among others."[45] This statement mirrors the reasoning of the Supreme Court in *Tervita Corp v Canada (Commissioner of Competition)* on the meaning of "market power" under the merger provisions.[46]

c) The Degree and Nature of Market Power Required

In *R v Nova Scotia Pharmaceutical Society*, the Supreme Court contrasted the degree of market power required under the undueness standard in what was then section 45 with that in section 79. It held that the former involved "the capacity to behave independently of the market, in a passive way," or "a moderate degree of market power," while section 79 involves a greater degree of market power: that required to "influence the market."[47] In view of this authority, the use of the word "dominance" in the statute, and the internal context, the Tribunal concluded in *TREB* that the subparagraph requires "a substantial degree of market power," which it described as:

> [A] degree of market power that confers upon an entity considerable latitude to determine or influence price or non-price dimensions of competition in a market, including the terms upon which it or others carry on business in the market. This roughly approximates . . . an ability to behave to an appreciable extent independently of its competitors.[48]

---

42 See Chapter 4, Section C, regarding the cellophane fallacy.

43 *Canada (Commissioner of Competition) v Canada Pipe, [2005] CCTD No 3 at para 65* [*Canada Pipe* CCT], overturned on other grounds, 2006 FCA 233 [*Canada Pipe* FCA].

44 See Chapter 4, Section B.

45 *TREB* FCA2, above note 38 at para 89, citing the Tribunal's decision at [2016] CCTD No 7 [*TREB* CCT].

46 *Tervita Corp v Canada (Commissioner of Competition)*, [2015] 1 SCR 161 at para 44 [*Tervita*].

47 *R v Nova Scotia Pharmaceutical Society*, [1992] 2 SCR 60 at paras 101–2 [*Nova Scotia Pharmaceutical Society*].

48 *TREB* CCT, above note 45 at para 174.

d) Indirect and Direct Measures of Market Power

Market definition permits identification of the competitors in the defined market and an indirect assessment of market power, from such indicators as market shares and barriers to entry.[49] In *TREB* it was noted that "the Tribunal has suggested that a *prima facie* finding of substantial control of a market will be made with a large market share exceeding 50 percent. Such a presumption would become stronger as the disparity between the market share of the respondent and the market shares of the other firms in the market increases, or if the respondent's share is fairly stable over time."[50] The Tribunal held in *Canada (Director of Investigation and Research) v Tele-Direct (Publications) Inc*, "[a] large market share can support an initial determination that a firm likely has market power, absent other extenuating circumstances, in general, ease of entry."[51] In *Canada Pipe* it referred to additional factors:

> [A] large market share leads to a *prima facie* conclusion that the firm likely has market power. In order to establish market power, this conclusion must be supported by other findings on issues such as the existence of barriers to entry, the number of other competitors, excess capacity and the state of the market. Where barriers to entry are non-existent, even a very large market share will not support a finding of market power.[52]

In *TREB*, the Tribunal noted "it has invariably assessed market shares and barriers to entry and has sometimes concluded that the respondent substantially or completely controlled a market largely on the basis of those two factors." It identified other indirect evidence of market power, including "the excess capacity of other firms," "the limited penetration of competitors," and "the limited growth potential of the market."[53]

The Bureau's *Abuse of Dominance Enforcement Guidelines* set out a range of indirect factors used to assess market power, including "structural characteristics of a market (including market shares and any barriers to entry), the extent of technological change, the effects of a practice of anti-competitive acts, and customer or supplier countervailing power."[54] With respect to market shares, its general approach is as follows:

---

49 Chapter 4, Section B(3).

50 *TREB* CCT, above note 45 at para 194 [citations omitted].

51 *Canada (Competition Act, Director of Investigation and Research) v Tele-Direct (Publications) Inc*, (1997), 73 CPR (3d) 1 (CCT) at para 227 [*Tele-Direct*].

52 *Canada Pipe* CCT, above note 43 at para 138.

53 *TREB* CCT, above note 45 at para 193 [citations omitted].

54 Canada, Competition Bureau, "Abuse of Dominance Provisions Enforcement Guidelines" (Gatineau, QC: Industry, Science and Economic Development, 2019)

- A market share below 50 percent will generally only prompt further examination if other evidence indicates the firm possesses a substantial degree of market power, or that it appears the firm is likely to realize the ability to exercise a substantial degree of market power through the alleged anti-competitive conduct within a reasonable period of time while that conduct is ongoing;
- A market share of 50 percent or more will generally prompt further examination; and
- In the case of a group of firms alleged to be jointly dominant, a combined market share equal to or exceeding 65 percent will generally prompt further examination.[55]

The Bureau's assessment of indicators of market power such as barriers to entry, technological change, and countervailing power parallels the approach and factors considered with respect to mergers.[56]

As noted in Chapter 4, market power can also be assessed directly. Direct indicators of market power include such factors as "performance results (e.g., profits) or observed patterns of conduct (e.g., pricing policy),"[57] which reflect the possession of market power. The Tribunal in *Canada Pipe* reviewed the direct and indirect approaches as follows:

> Market power is defined as the ability to set prices above competitive levels for a considerable period. The direct approach involves showing that prices are indeed above the competitive level. In *Tele-Direct*, for example, the Tribunal found that the very large accounting profits were a direct indication of market power. However, as was the case in *Laidlaw, Nielsen* and *NutraSweet*, this approach is not always feasible. If a market is monopolized or not perfectly competitive because of a trade restraint imposed by a major supplier, it may be difficult to determine what would be the relevant competitive benchmark. In such a case, an indirect approach can be taken, which will consider such indicia as market share, barriers to entry and customer countervailing power.[58]

e) Control and Market Power: By Whom, in What Market?

In *TREB*, the Tribunal initially dismissed the case, finding that section 79(1) did not apply to the respondent Toronto Real Estate Board (TREB),

---

at para 26, online: www.competitionbureau.gc.ca/eic/site/cb-bc.nsf/eng/04420.html [*Abuse Guidelines*].

55 *Ibid* at para 34.

56 *Ibid* at paras 39–40 and 45.

57 *Tele-Direct*, above note 51 at para 226.

58 *Canada Pipe CCT, above note 43 at para 122.*

because it did not compete in the market for real estate services, where a lessening of competition was alleged to have occurred. This was overruled by the Federal Court of Appeal, on the basis that the competitive effect of the alleged conduct could be in a market in which the respondent did not compete.[59] This ruling provides important clarification of how the elements within section 79 interact.

By way of background, the respondent TREB, a not-for-profit corporation, had approximately 46,000 members who were licensed real estate brokers.[60] TREB provided various services to those members, including access to and use of the Multiple Listing Service (MLS system), which included a database of information on properties, including addresses, list prices, interior and exterior photographs, length of time for sale, etc. To obtain access to the MLS system, TREB members had to execute, and agree to be bound by, TREB's MLS rules and policies. Those rules placed restrictions on the ability of members to share certain MLS data (the "disputed data") from the board's database with clients through online means. This restriction was alleged to create barriers to entry by excluding brokers from using novel "virtual office websites," which barriers caused or were likely to cause a substantial prevention of competition in the market for real estate brokerage services.

In overruling the Tribunal's initial decision, the Court of Appeal held that the language of the section could "reasonably bear" the applicant's case theory that a person (the Board, a trade association) that is not a competitor in a particular market nevertheless "may control that market within the meaning of [section 79(1)] by, for example, controlling a significant input to competitors in the market, or by making rules that effectively control the business conduct of those competitors."[61] The Court of Appeal sent the case back to the Tribunal. In its re-hearing decision,[62] the Tribunal found that the elements of section 79 were satisfied. At the first stage, it held that "the focus is upon the existence of dominance and whether the respondent substantially or completely controls throughout Canada or any area thereof, any class or species of business." In the Tribunal's view, the conduct and the market in which the anti-competitive effect is alleged to have occurred "is not necessarily relevant" at this stage.[63]

59 *Canada (Commissioner of Competition) v Toronto Real Estate Board*, 2014 FCA 29 [*TREB* FCA1].

60 Licensed pursuant to the *Real Estate and Business Brokers Act, 2002*, SO 2002, c 30.

61 *TREB* FCA1, above note 59 at para 13.

62 *TREB* CCT, above note 45.

63 *Ibid* at para 202.

On the facts, the Tribunal held that the board had market power, and therefore control, of both the upstream market for the supply of the disputed data to real estate brokers, as well as the downstream market for the supply of MLS-based residential real estate brokerage services.[64] It was in the latter market that anti-competitive acts were alleged to have prevented competition substantially. .[65]

The Federal Court of Appeal upheld the Tribunal's re-hearing decision.[66] The issue of control was not contested by the appellant board.[67] The decision makes it clear that the respondent in an abuse of dominance case may control a class or species of business in a market (such as an upstream market), which is not the same as the market in which the effect on competition is alleged.

2) A Practice of Anti-competitive Acts or Conduct Having a Substantial Effect on Competition

The second main element of section 79 is that the alleged dominant firm(s) "have engaged in or are engaging in" either "a practice of anti-competitive acts" or "conduct … that had, is having or is likely to have the effect of preventing or lessening competition substantially in a market." Prior to the amendments of 2022-23, a likely substantial prevention lessening of competition was a required element; it is now an alternative path to a remedy under the section. Government discussion papers identified a desire to lower the standard for finding abusive conduct by large firms, particularly in view of developments in the EU and elsewhere showing a more aggressive approach to enforcement in digital markets.[68]

---

64 *Ibid* at para 205.

65 *Ibid* at para 207.

66 *TREB* FCA2, above note 38.

67 *Ibid* at para 50.

68 Canada, Innovation, Science and Economic Development, *The Future of Competition Policy in Canada* (2022) at 37, citing Vass Bednar, Ana Qarri and Robin Shaban, *Study of Competition Issues in Data-Driven Markets in Canada*, Vivic Research, January 2022, at 24: "it may be difficult to establish anti-competitive effects from some behaviours given the high evidentiary standards needed to establish a substantial lessening or prevention of competition. …At present, the Commissioner is required to show, on a balance of probabilities, that the abusive conduct has led to specific negative outcomes (the consequentialist approach). The effects that are typically considered include higher prices, lower quality, or less innovation. However, the law in other jurisdictions, particularly the EU, requires that authorities show primarily that the conduct in question has taken place, and there is less emphasis on demonstrating that the conduct has caused

a) Practice of Anti-Competitive Acts

A *practice* of anti-competitive acts encompasses "more than an isolated act but may be one occurrence that is sustained and systemic, or that has had a lasting impact on competition."[69] At the same time, "different individual anti-competitive acts taken together may constitute a practice."[70]

The section covers a past or present practice, but not one anticipated in the future, given the words "have engaged in or are engaging in." In contrast, for example, the UK *Competition Act* abuse of dominance provision applies to "any conduct."[71]

b) Anti-competitive Acts

i) Section 78's Definition and Non-exhaustive List

This section prior to the 2022 amendments provided simply a non-restrictive list of anti-competitive acts. Those amendments added the following definition of "practice of anti-competitive acts":

> any act intended to have a predatory, exclusionary or disciplinary negative effect on a competitor, or to have an adverse effect on competition[72]

The definition is followed by a list of anti-competitive acts, which "without restricting the generality of the term, includes" the following eleven examples:

> (a) squeezing, by a vertically integrated supplier, of the margin available to an unintegrated customer who competes with the supplier, for the purpose of impeding or preventing the customer's entry into, or expansion in, a market;
>
> (b) acquisition by a supplier of a customer who would otherwise be available to a competitor of the supplier, or acquisition by a customer of a supplier who would otherwise be available to a competitor of the customer, for the purpose of impeding or preventing the competitor's entry into, or eliminating the competitor from, a market;
>
> (c) freight equalization on the plant of a competitor for the purpose of impeding or preventing the competitor's entry into, or eliminating the competitor from, a market;

---

certain harms (the deontological approach, or what some in Canada call a *per se* approach)."

69 *Canada Pipe CCT, above note 43 at para 171.*

70 *Canada (Director of Investigation and Research) v NutraSweet Co* (1990), 32 CPR (3d) 1 at para 92 [*NutraSweet*].

71 *Competition Act 1998* (UK), c 41, s 18(1).

72 *Bill C-19 2022,* above note 35, s 261.

(d) use of fighting brands introduced selectively on a temporary basis to discipline or eliminate a competitor;
(e) pre-emption of scarce facilities or resources required by a competitor for the operation of a business, with the object of withholding the facilities or resources from a market;
(f) buying up of products to prevent the erosion of existing price levels;
(g) adoption of product specifications that are incompatible with products produced by any other company and are designed to prevent entry into, or to eliminate the company from, a market;
(h) requiring or inducing a supplier to sell only or primarily to certain customers, or to refrain from selling to a competitor, with the object of preventing a competitor's entry into, or expansion in, a market;
(i) selling articles at a price lower than the acquisition cost for the purpose of disciplining or eliminating a competitor;
(j) a selective or discriminatory response to an actual or potential competitor for the purpose of impeding or preventing the competitor's entry into, or expansion in, a market or eliminating the competitor from a market;[73] and
(k) directly or indirectly imposing excessive and unfair selling prices.[74]

Practices outside this list have frequently been addressed in the case law. In *NutraSweet*, eight anti-competitive acts were alleged, none of which exactly matched the examples in section 78. The Tribunal concluded that several of these had been proven to fall within the section.[75] At the same time, the Court of Appeal noted that section 78 "provides direction as to the type of conduct that is intended to be captured . . . by analogy, a non-enumerated anti-competitive act will exhibit the shared essential characteristics of the examples listed in section 78."[76]

73 *Ibid.*

74 *Bill C-56 2023*, above note 35, s 7.1.

75 *NutraSweet*, above note 65 at para 155 stated that the practices were:

> use in its supply contracts of exclusive supply and use clauses, logo display allowances, cooperative marketing allowances, meet-or-release clauses, and most-favoured-nation clauses. . . . [T]he use of its United States patent to foreclose competition by a system of rebates on exports from the United States to induce Canadian importers to have only NSC aspartame used in products purchased by them in Canada.

76 *Canada Pipe* FCA, above note 43 at para 63.

Practices covered by other sections of the Act, such as exclusive dealing[77] and mergers constituting a practice of acquisitions[78] may also fall within the abuse of dominance provision.

ii) Anti-competitive Purpose: Intention and Effect

A required element for finding that a practice falls within the section is an anti-competitive purpose. The Federal Court of Appeal in *Canada Pipe* endorsed the following statement from *NutraSweet*:

> A number of the acts [mentioned in section 78] share common features but . . . only one feature is common to all: an anti-competitive act must be performed for a purpose, and evidence of this purpose is a necessary ingredient. *The purpose common to all acts, save that found in paragraph 78(f), is an intended negative effect on a competitor that is predatory, exclusionary or disciplinary.*[79]

The definition of anti-competitive act added in the 2022 amendments essentially adopted this jurisprudential language, to the effect that such an act must be "intended to have a predatory, exclusionary or disciplinary negative effect on a competitor."[80] In addition, Parliament added the words "or to have an adverse effect on competition." The latter language is consistent with of subsequent jurisprudence and commentary which pointed out that a test focused solely on competitive effects directed toward *a competitor* is both bad policy and at odds with the statutory language.

From a policy perspective, narrowing the assessment of anti-competitive act to those directed against a competitor would overlook a practice that reduces competition but potentially benefits other competitors (for example, a practice by a supplier that facilitates express or tacit collusion on the wholesale prices charged by suppliers to retailers).[81]

Furthermore, competitive practices directed against a competitor will often be beneficial to competition and increase consumer welfare.

---

77 *Canada Pipe* CCT, above note 43 at paras 200–3 and 279–82.

78 *Laidlaw*, above note 14 at paras 134–40.

79 *Canada Pipe* FCA, above note 43 at para 64 [emphasis added by court], citing *NutraSweet*, above note 70.

80 "This drew from, and broadened, prior caselaw, while continuing to list illustrative examples in s. 78. Both subjective intent and reasonably foreseeable consequences are relevant, and distinguish truly anti-competitive behaviour from justifiable business decisions that nevertheless may prejudice a competitor." Canada, Innovation, Science and Economic Development, *The Future of Competition Policy in Canada* (2022) at 33.

81 *Ibid*; see Ralph A Winter, "The Gap in Canadian Competition Law following Canada Pipe" (2014) 27 *Canadian Competition Law Review* 293.

For example, vigorously reducing prices or introducing innovative products to gain greater market share at the expense of competitors has a foreseeable negative effect on them, suggesting it could be characterized as anti-competitive if the test were focused only on adverse effects on competitors. However, to view the practices in this way would be inconsistent with the Act's emphasis on the protection of competition rather than the protection of competitors.[82] To be consistent with the purpose clause of the Act and to promote competition. the words "predatory, exclusionary or disciplinary" should be read to require a focus only on behaviour which is anti-competitive,

A test directed solely on competitor effects is also inconsistent with the statute, in which not all enumerated anti-competitive acts are competitor-directed.[83] For example, section 78(1)(f) refers to "buying up of products to prevent the erosion of existing price levels." The Federal Court of Appeal noted in *TREB* that "requiring a predatory, exclusionary, or disciplinary negative effect on a competitor in all cases would render paragraph 78(1)(*f*) meaningless."[84]

What then of the words in the newly added definition section "intended to"? The concept of intent was discussed in the pre-amendment case law, which had held that a consideration of a practice's intent or purpose should not be a search for the subjective intent of the dominant firm or its principals; rather, but rather an assessment of the *overall character* of the act in question. The Court of Appeal held in *Canada Pipe*:

> As the Tribunal observed in *Tele-Direct, supra* at p. 180, "'purpose' is used in this context in a broader sense than merely subjective intent on the part of the respondent . . . it might be more apt to speak of the *overall character* of the act in question" (emphasis added). . . . the purpose or character of the impugned conduct must therefore be

82 Marcel Boyer, Thomas W Ross & Ralph A Winter, *The Rise of Economics in Competition Policy: A Canadian Perspective*, Working Paper 2017s-26 (Montreal: CIRANO, 2017) at 37, online: https://cirano.qc.ca/files/publications/2017s-26.pdf, citing Michael J Trebilcock, "Abuse of Dominance: A Critique of Canada Pipe" (2007) 22 *Canadian Competition Record* 1 at 7:

> The decision runs against the principle that the purpose of competition law is not the protection of competitors but rather protection of the competitive process so that the ultimate goal of competition policy, the efficient allocation of resources, is achieved—a principle that Trebilcock (2007) calls "the single greatest advance in thinking in the competition policy field over the past 30 years."

See also Michael J Trebilcock & Francesco Ducci, "The Evolution of Canadian Competition Policy: A Retrospective" (2018) 60 *Canadian Business Law Journal* 171 at 191 [Trebilcock & Ducci].

83 *TREB* FCA1, above note 59 at para 20; *TREB* FCA2, above note 38 at para 54.

84 *TREB* FCA2, above note 38 at para 54.

> determined. Relevant factors to be considered and weighed to determine this overarching "purpose" include the reasonably foreseeable or expected objective effects of the act (from which intention may be deemed, as I explain further below), any business justification, and any evidence of subjective intent, if available (see *Tele-Direct*, *supra* at p. 180).[85]

The assessment of the overall character of the practice is thus flexible; it is intended to screen out benign or pro-competitive actions from those worthy of sanction. It reflects the overall objective of section 79, which as noted at the outset of the chapter, is to permit dominant firms to compete on their merits, and to provide a remedy where they use anti-competitive practices to exclude or discipline actual or potential competitors. Often, as the Tribunal noted in *Tele-Direct* "distinguishing between competition on the merits and anti-competitive conduct . . . is not an easy task."[86]

The assessment of anti-competitive character involves the weighing of all the relevant evidence. For example, in *Commissioner v Vancouver Airport Authority*, evidence that officials of the respondent VAA intended to exclude competitors and that this exclusion was the reasonably foreseeable effect of their conduct was held by the Tribunal not to be decisive in terms of anti-competitive character of VAA's practices. It was weighed against the respondent's business justification, including the efficiency or pro-competitive rationales they identified.[87]

In the assessment of the overall character of the practice, there must be "sufficiently clear, convincing and cogent evidence . . . to demonstrate that the overriding purpose of the impugned practice was anti-competitive."[88]

a. Predatory, Exclusionary, or Disciplinary Purpose

As noted above, the 2022 amendments codified the Tribunal's statement that "[t]he purpose common to all acts [in s 78] . . . is an intended negative effect on a competitor that is predatory, exclusionary or disciplinary."[89] Examples of conduct that have been found to fall into these categories in the decided cases are:

---

85 *Canada Pipe* FCA, above note 43 at para 67, citing *Tele-Direct*, above note 51 at 180.

86 *Tele-Direct*, above note 51 at 179–80.

87 *VAA*, above note 10 at paras 535–36 and 623.

88 *TREB* CCT, above note 45 at para 289.

89 *Canada Pipe* FCA, above note 43 at para 64; except s 78(f) of the *Competition Act*, above note 10.

- **Predatory**[90]
  - » Selling products at a price lower than acquisition cost,[91] and predatory pricing more generally, was alleged in *NutraSweet*, but rejected by the Tribunal as not made out on the facts, given the lack of reliable or comprehensive cost data.[92]
  - » Predatory pricing was accepted as a potential anti-competitive act under section 79 in *Canada (Commissioner of Competition) v Air Canada* in respect of the airline's competitive response to entry in Atlantic Canada.[93] The case was discontinued after an initial costs assessment phase.
- **Exclusionary**[94]
  - » In *TREB*, the Tribunal accepted that rules limiting access by competing real estate brokers and customers to electronic MLS data constituted an exclusionary practice, characterized by the Commissioner as "preventing rivals from introducing products to the market."[95] The Tribunal found that the rules "were primarily to limit or at least restrict a potentially disruptive form of competition" and "for an exclusionary purpose."[96]
  - » In *NutraSweet*, the Tribunal found that rebates granted to food processors were used to exclude competing artificial sweetener suppliers from gaining customers and to prevent their expansion.[97]
- **Disciplinary**[98]
  - » "Use of fighting brands introduced selectively on a temporary basis to discipline or eliminate a competitor" was among the anti-competitive practices identified in *R v Eddy Match*[99] and is one of those listed in section 78;[100]
  - » The use of sham litigation against competitors as a form of disciplinary conduct was an anti-competitive practice found in *Laidlaw*. The Tribunal held that Laidlaw had used "spurious litigation

90 See *Abuse Guidelines*, above note 54 at paras 59–61.

91 Under the *Competition Act*, above note 10, s 78(1)(i).

92 *NutraSweet*, above note 70 at paras 124–29.

93 *Canada (Commissioner of Competition) v Air Canada, [2003] CCTD No 9 at* paras 46–55. It was also considered within the (now-repealed) airline-specific regime then in place in the Act.

94 *Abuse Guidelines*, above note 54 at paras 62–74.

95 *TREB* CCT, above note 45 at para 175 [citations omitted].

96 *Ibid* at paras 390 and 392.

97 *NutraSweet*, above note 70.

98 *Abuse Guidelines*, above note 54 at paras 75–79.

99 *Eddy* CA, above note 18 at paras 68 and 71–76.

100 *Competition Act*, above note 10, s 78(d).

and threatened litigation against its competitors to drive or attempt to drive them out of business by raising their costs of doing business."[101]

In determining whether a practice is predatory, exclusionary or disciplinary, its anti-competitive effects are a relevant, but not necessary, consideration.[102]

b. Subjective Intent Is Relevant, but Not Required

Based on a review of the legislative history of the 1986 amendments, the Federal Court of Appeal in *Canada Pipe* concluded that "that evidence of subjective intent, although certainly probative if available, is not required in order to find that a given act is anti-competitive within the meaning of [section 79]."[103]

In *D&B*, for example, the respondent market research firm was alleged to have signed both retailers supplying scanner-based raw data and manufacturers who purchased compiled data, to long-term contracts to exclude competitors from both these sources of supply and from customers. The evidence examined by the Tribunal included "[a] number of [D&B] documents [that] refer to a strategy of trying to 'lock up' as much business as possible in the face of possible entry."[104] It concluded that D&B "intended its long-term manufacturer contracts, along with the exclusives and inducements to exclusivity, to exclude potential competitors . . . . All three actions constitute anti-competitive acts under section 78 of the Act."[105]

c. Purpose or Intent Can Be Inferred from a Practice's Effects

As noted above, while the 2022 amendments define a practice of anti-competitive act as "any act intended to" have an anti-competitive impact, consistent with the existing case law, purpose or intent can be inferred from "the reasonably foreseeable or expected objective effects

---

101 *Laidlaw*, above note 14, paras 156–58.

102 *Canada Pipe* FCA, above note 43 at para 68: although this was qualified: "some types of effects on competition in the market might be irrelevant for the purposes of paragraph 79(1)(*b*), if these effects do not manifest through a negative effect on a competitor." But see *TREB CCT, above note 41 at para 275: "While adverse effects on competition can be relevant in determining the overall character or objective purpose of an impugned practice, it is not necessary to ascertain an actual negative impact on competition in order to conclude that the practice is anti-competitive."*

103 *Canada Pipe FCA, above note 43 at paras* 70–72, citing *Laidlaw*, above note 14 at paras 127 and 153.

104 *D&B*, above note 39 at para 147.

105 *Ibid* at para 154.

of the act."[106] Actual effects may be relevant to foreseeability. In *Laidlaw*, an alleged anti-competitive practice was the signing of customers for waste disposal services to long-term and restrictive contracts, which made market entry by smaller competitors impossible due to the latter's inability to achieve economies of scale and to build a sustainable customer base. The Tribunal found that the effects of the contracts were exclusionary: "three-year term, the automatic roll-over provisions, the inability to cancel the contract after 60 days before the end of each three years, the liquidated damages clauses and the exclusivity provision bind the customer tightly to Laidlaw for a long period of time."[107] After examining the nature of these provisions the Tribunal concluded:

> [T]here is no doubt that they have anti-competitive effects. It is no answer to say that they were designed for a different market and therefore not intended to have anticompetitive effects in the smaller market. As has been noted, actions will be presumed to have been intended to have the effects which actually occur in the absence of convincing evidence to the contrary. The argument that Laidlaw lacked the requisite intention because the contracts were designed to counter B.F.I. and W.M.I. contracting practices is not convincing.[108]

d. Legitimate Business Justification

In determining whether a given practice is to be considered anti-competitive under section 79(1)(a), a respondent may put forward "a credible efficiency or pro-competitive rationale for the conduct in question, attributable to the respondent, which relates to and counterbalances the anti-competitive effects and/or subjective intent of the acts."[109] The party advancing this "legitimate business justification" bears the onus of establishing it on a balance of probabilities, and that it outweighs the evidence of foreseeable anti-competitive effects.[110]

---

106 *Canada Pipe FCA, above note 43 at paras 67 and 72; see also TREB FCA2*, above note 38 at para 56:

> The Tribunal correctly noted that subjective or objective intent could be used to demonstrate the requisite intent (TR at paras 274, 283; *Canada Pipe* at para 72). It closely scrutinized the evidence of TREB's subjective intent (TR at paras 319–431). The Tribunal also looked to the "reasonably foreseeable or expected objective effects of the act (from which intention may be deemed . . .)" (TR at paras 432–51) as instructed by *Canada Pipe* at para 67.

107 *Laidlaw, above note 14 at para 148.*

108 *Ibid* at para 154.

109 *TREB* FCA2, above note 38 at para 148, citing *Canada Pipe* FCA, above note 43 at para 73.

110 *VAA*, above note 10 at para 520; *TREB* FCA2, above note 38 at paras 146–47.

Examples of legitimate business practices set out by the Bureau in their *Abuse of Dominance Guidelines* are "cost reductions in production or other aspects of a firm's operations, improvements in technology or production processes that result in innovative new products, and improvements in product quality or service."[111]

This factor assists in screening legitimate competitive behaviour from actions that should be sanctioned. It ensures that pro-competitive or efficiency-motivated practices will not be discouraged or prohibited under section 79. The main elements required for a business justification are as follows:

- Two facts must be proven:
  - "First, there must be a credible efficiency or pro-competitive rationale for the practice";
  - "Second, the efficiencies or competitive advantages, whether on price or non-price issues, must accrue to the appellant. Put otherwise, the evidence must demonstrate how the practice generates benefits which allow it to better compete in the relevant market."[112] Where the dominant player does not compete in the relevant market, as was the case with the Vancouver Airport Authority, it may demonstrate how the practice was nonetheless driven by legitimate business concerns and not anti-competitive purposes.
- A valid business justification must be weighed against other evidence of the motivation of the dominant party, including its subjective intent and the reasonably foreseeable effects of its conduct, to determine its "overriding purpose."[113] A business justification therefore does not provide an "absolute defence."[114] The Court of Appeal stated in *Canada Pipe*:

  > As the Tribunal observed in *D & B*, *supra*, a business justification proffered by a respondent must . . . be "weigh[ed] . . . in light of any anti-competitive effects to establish the overriding purpose" of the impugned act.[115]

---

111 *Abuse Guidelines*, above note 54 at s 3.2. The tribunal agreed with this list as examples in *TREB CCT, above note* 45 at para 295.

112 *TREB* FCA2, above note 38 at para 149.

113 *VAA*, above note 10 at para 626.

114 *TREB* FCA2, above note 38 at para 148; *Canada Pipe* FCA, above note 43 at para 87:

> [B]y demonstrating that such anti-competitive effects are not in fact the overriding purpose of the conduct in question . . . a valid business justification essentially provides an alternative explanation as to why the impugned act was performed, which in the right circumstances might be sufficient to counterbalance the evidence of negative effects on competitors or subjective intent.

115 *Ibid* at para 88 [citations omitted].

The weighing exercise permits the Tribunal to open the practice to further scrutiny where, for example, on balance, the business rationale put forward is not sufficiently compelling to overcome evidence of seriously prejudicial anti-competitive effects.[116]

Other considerations noted in the case law include:

- the proffered business justification must be unrelated to the anti-competitive purpose[117]
- a party's self-interest is not a legitimate business justification[118]
- there must an actual link between the business justification and the respondent's action,[119] i.e., it must not be merely theoretical
- statutory or regulatory requirement for specific conduct can provide a business justification

On the latter point, in *TREB* FCA2, the Court of Appeal upheld the Tribunal's rejection of the proffered business justification that the Toronto Real Estate Board had restricted access to multiple listing data because of privacy law concerns. The Court found that the Tribunal made no reviewable error when it concluded, "TREB was motivated by a desire to maintain control over the disputed data in an effort to forestall new forms of competition, and not by any efficiency, pro-competition, or genuine privacy concerns."[120] However, the Court accepted that if "a business practice or policy exists as a matter of a statutory or regulatory requirement," that could provide a justification for the conduct.[121]

e. "Or intended … to have an adverse effect on competition"

This new phrase was added to the definition of anti-competitive act in section 78 in the 2022 amendments.[122] As noted above, purpose or intent can be inferred from the actual or reasonably foreseeable anti-competitive effects of a practice. This phrase makes it clear that a practice of anti-competitive acts can encompass behaviour which is

---

116 *D&B*, above note 39 at para 141:

> Even if Nielsen had been able to establish that there was some justification for the exclusives in the early stages of development, it would have been necessary to weigh the justification in light of any anti-competitive effects to establish the overriding purpose of the exclusives. Moreover, any such justification for exclusives in the early stages of development would not have been applicable to the current exclusives.

117 *Ibid* at paras 90–91; *D&B*, above note 39 at para 136.

118 *Canada Pipe FCA, above note 43 at para 91; TREB CCT, above note 45* at para 294.

119 *Ibid.*

120 *TREB* FCA2, above note 38 at para 150.

121 *Ibid* at para 146.

122 *Bill C-19 2022*, above note 35, s 261.

not targeted at a competitor. The Bureau's *Guidelines* on the amended section note that the section covers "conduct that softens competition, benefitting one or more competitors." Examples given are as follows:

a. *Agreements Between Competitors*: Agreements among competitors may reduce their ability or incentive to compete;
b. *Information Sharing*: Making competitively sensitive information more transparent may increase the risk of conscious parallelism, a form of coordination between firms without an agreement between them;
c. *Contracts that Reference Rivals*: Where contractual terms depend on competitors in some way, such as MFN clauses, they may reduce incentives for competitors to compete as vigorously as they otherwise would, facilitate conscious parallelism or exclude competitors; and
d. *Serial Acquisitions*: Dominant firms may render a market less competitive by making a series of acquisitions.[123]

The words "adverse effect on competition" are also found in the refusal to supply and price maintenance provisions of the Act. They have been interpreted as involving a lesser standard than "substantial" effect but still requiring some element of market power.[124] The Tribunal held in a refusal to supply case, *B-Filer*:

> Adverse effects in a market are generally likely to manifest themselves in the form of an increase in price, the preservation of a price that would otherwise have been lower, a decrease in the quality of products sold in the market (including such product features as warranties, quality of service and product innovation) or a decrease in the variety of products made available to buyers.[125]

f. Acquiring Dominance Through an Anti-competitive Practice

An anti-competitive practice that permits a firm to obtain market power may fall within the section even if the firm did not have market power before the practice. A firm must have "control" at the time the application is filed given that section 79(1) is framed in the present tense, but the anti-competitive practice may occur in the past or present under

123 Canada, Competition Bureau, "*Bulletin on the Amendments to the Abuse of Dominance Provisions*" (25 October 2023) at para 18.

124 *Nadeau Poultry Farm Ltd v Groupe Westco Inc*, [2009] CCTD No 6 at para 366, affd 2011 FCA 188 (Fed. C.A.); *B-Filer Inc v Bank of Nova Scotia*, [2006] CCTD No 36 at para 208; *Canada (Commissioner of Competition) v Visa Canada Corp, [2013] CCTD No 10* at paras 350-353.

125 *B-Filer, ibid* at para 206.

section 79(1)(a) or (b).[126] In *Laidlaw*, for example, the Tribunal accepted the theory that the respondent's pattern of acquiring competitors in the waste disposal business "was *for the purpose of initially acquiring a monopolistic position* in the markets in question and then eliminating competitors from those markets."[127] In *D&B*, the practice of signing retailers who supplied scanner data to long-term exclusive contracts for the purposes of "retaining *or obtaining* a dominant position" was found to be a practice of anti-competitive acts.[128] In *VAA*, the Tribunal stated the test of anti-competitive effect in terms of whether the practice "has facilitated, is facilitating or is likely to facilitate the exercise *of new* or increased market power by the respondent(s)."[129]

On the other hand, the section requires that a firm must already have control when the application is filed, not have the mere potential for, or have taken steps toward, obtaining it in the future.[130] In this sense it is narrower than section 2 of the US *Sherman Act*, which covers an "attempt to monopolize . . . any part of the trade or commerce among the several States, or with foreign nations."[131]

g. A Respondent That Is a Non-competitor Must Have a "Plausible Competitive Interest" in the Market

The requirement of a "plausible competitive interest" was codified in section 79(1)(b) in the 2023 amendments to the section.[132] While it (somewhat oddly) only applies to section 79(1)(b) "conduct," the above case law suggests it also will continue to apply to a "practice of anti-competitive acts" under section 79(1)(a), given that it is a logical requirement for any practice to be anti-competitive.

In *TREB*, as noted above, the respondent trade association was not a competitor of the real estate agents who were allegedly excluded by its rules governing sharing of multiple listing data. The Tribunal held:

> [B]efore a practice engaged in by a respondent who does not compete in the relevant market can be found to be *anti-competitive*, the

126 The subparagraph reads "have engaged in or are engaging in a practice of anti-competitive acts."

127 *Laidlaw*, above note 14 at para 125 [emphasis added].

128 *D&B*, above note 39 at para 138 [emphasis added].

129 *VAA*, above note 10 at paras 636–37 [emphasis added].

130 George Addy, John Bodrug & Charles Tingley, "Abuse of Dominance in Canada: Reflections on 25 Years of Section 79 Enforcement" (2012) 25:2 *Canadian Competition Law Review* 276 at 300–1.

131 15 USC § 2 (2000).

132 *Bill C-56 2023*, above note 35, s 7.2.

> Commissioner will be required to satisfy the Tribunal that the respondent has a plausible *competitive interest* in the market.[133]

In the case of a trade association such as TREB, the Tribunal considered the satisfaction of this requirement "as straightforward as demonstrating that it has a plausible interest in protecting some or all of its members from new entrants or from smaller disruptive competitors in the market."[134]In *VAA*, the respondent Vancouver Airport Authority also did not compete in the airline catering markets that were the subject of the exclusionary practices in question. The Tribunal therefore required this factor to be demonstrated by the Commissioner. On the facts, it was held that the Authority had a sufficient interest in the catering market that a plausible competitive interest (PCI) had been demonstrated.[135] The Tribunal clarified that "the PCI test is conducted *prior to* the assessment of the overall character, or overriding purpose, of the impugned conduct. It is not conducted together with that assessment."[136]

h. The Mere Exercise of Intellectual Property Rights Is Not an Anti-competitive Act

Section 79(5) provides:

> For the purpose of this section, an act engaged in pursuant only to the exercise of any right or enjoyment of any interest derived under the *Copyright Act*, *Industrial Design Act*, *Integrated Circuit Topography Act*, *Patent Act*, *Trademarks Act* or any other Act of Parliament pertaining to intellectual or industrial property is not an anti-competitive act.

The subsection permits holders of intellectual property rights under applicable Acts of Parliament pertaining to intellectual or industrial property to exercise those rights without risk of application of the abuse of dominance provisions. The subsection exempts "an act engaged in pursuant only to the exercise of any right or enjoyment of any interest derived under" these statutes.

Where an owner of intellectual property rights permits use to a third party, imposing anti-competitive restrictions or conditions on such use is not an act "engaged in pursuant only to the exercise" of such rights. In *Toronto Real Estate Board*, one of the issues raised was whether the respondent Board had copyright in certain real estate listing data and if so whether its policy on the use of that data (which

---

133 *TREB CCT*, *above note* 45 at para 279 [emphasis in original].

134 *Ibid* at para 280.

135 *VAA*, above note 10 at paras 478–510.

136 *Ibid* at para 480.

restricted distribution to online customers by certain real estate agents) was an anti-competitive act. The Tribunal concluded it was; that "where a respondent attaches anti-competitive conditions to the use of its intellectual property, subsection 79(5) will not immunize it from scrutiny."[137] The conditions in question were limitations placed by the Board on agents' ability to display and distribute certain real estate listing data on agents' websites.

On appeal, the Federal Court of Appeal held that the Board did not possess copyright in the data, but even if it had, it agreed with the Tribunal that the Board's actions were not the mere exercise of copyright pursuant to section 79(5). The Court focused on the fact that the practice must be pursuant "only" to the exercise of intellectual property rights:

> Parliament clearly signaled, through the use of the word "only," to insulate intellectual property rights from allegations of anti-competitive conduct in circumstances where the right granted by Parliament, in this case, copyright, is the sole purpose of exercise or use. Put otherwise, *anti-competitive behaviour cannot shelter behind a claim of copyright unless the use or protection of the copyright is the sole justification for the practice.*
>
> TREB attached conditions to the use of its claimed copyright rights in the disputed data. For the reasons given earlier, we see no error in the Tribunal's findings as to the anti-competitive purpose or effect of the VOW Policy. The Tribunal found that the purpose and effect of those conditions was to insulate members from new entrants and new forms of competition. *The purpose, therefore, of any asserted copyright was not "only" to exercise a copyright interest.*[138]

Another case that considered the exercise of copyright was *Canada (Director of Investigation and Research) v Warner Music Canada Ltd.* Warner refused to grant copyright licences to BMG Canada to permit BMG to make sound recordings. The Bureau alleged that this was a refusal to deal contrary to section 75 of the Act. Warner possessed copyright over the master recordings in Canada. Although the case did not allege abuse of dominance, the Tribunal referred to section 79(5) in concluding:

> The right granted by Parliament to exclude others is fundamental to intellectual property rights and cannot be considered to be anti-competitive, and there is nothing in the legislative history of section 75 of

137 *TREB CCT, above* note 45 at para 754.

138 *TREB* FCA2, above note 38 at paras 180–81 [emphasis added].

the Act which would reveal an intention to have section 75 operate as a compulsory licensing provision for intellectual property.[139]

The Tribunal made a similar finding in respect of the exercise of trademark rights in *Tele-Direct*. In that case, one of the anti-competitive acts alleged was that Tele-Direct, the publisher of telephone directories on behalf of affiliated phone companies, had selectively refused to license its trade-marks, such as the words "Yellow Pages" and the "walking fingers" logo, to competing suppliers of advertising services. The Tribunal held that "there may be instances where a trade-mark may be misused. However, in the Tribunal's view, something more than the mere exercise of statutory rights, even if exclusionary in effect, must be present before there can be a finding of misuse of a trade-mark. Subsection 79(5) explicitly recognizes this."[140] The Tribunal found that the refusal to license fell "squarely within [the] prerogative" to determine to where or not, and to whom, to grant a licence, and was distinguishable from a situation in which anti-competitive conditions are attached to a licence granted.[141] The mere fact that Tele-Direct was motivated in part by competitive considerations in its licensing decision was found to be immaterial because the licensing right under the *Trade-marks Act* did not place any limits on the exercise of the right.[142]

The Competition Bureau has published *Intellectual Property Enforcement Guidelines* (IPEGs), which provide guidance on the interface between rights granted under intellectual property statutes and the *Competition Act*.[143] The IPEGs recognize that those statutes grant to the owners of intellectual property the right to unilaterally exclude others from the use of such property.[144] They note that such unilateral exclusion generally raises no issues under competition laws (not just the exemption in section 79(5) for abuse of dominance) because "[t]o hold otherwise could effectively nullify IP [intellectual property] rights, impair or remove the economic, cultural, social and educational benefits created by them."[145] The exception is section 32 of the Act, which permits the attorney general to seek a special remedy from the Federal Court when

139 *Canada (Director of Investigation and Research) v Warner Music Canada Ltd, [1997] CCTD No 53 at para 30. Applied in Stargrove Entertainment Inc v Universal Music Publishing Group Canada, [2015] CCTD No 26 at paras 24–26.*

140 *Tele-Direct*, above note 51 at para 65.

141 *Ibid* at para 66.

142 *Ibid* at para 68.

143 Canada, Competition Bureau, "Intellectual Property Enforcement Guidelines" (13 March 2019), online: www.ic.gc.ca/eic/site/cb-bc.nsf/eng/04421.html [IPEGs].

144 *Ibid* at paras 26–28.

145 *Ibid* at para 37.

there has been an undue exercise of IP rights. The Bureau describes the circumstances in which that remedy would be employed as limited, and only where the remedies available under the relevant IP legislation are inadequate.[146]

On the other hand, the IPEGs recognize that, as occurred in *TREB*, anti-competitive practices that go beyond the mere exercise of IP rights may be subject to the Act. Thus, the *Competition Act* may apply "when IP rights form the basis of agreements or arrangements between independent entities, whether in the form of a transfer, licensing arrangement or agreement to use or enforce IP rights, and when the alleged competitive harm stems from such an agreement or arrangement and not just from the mere exercise of the IP right."[147] Thus TREB's restriction on its members' ability to share data with third parties that excluded the potential entry of innovative "virtual office websites" was an arrangement that went beyond the mere exercise of IP rights in that data (had any existed).

c) Conduct Having the Effect of Lessening or Prevention of Competition Substantially

Under the 2023 amendments, the Commissioner no longer needs to show a likely substantial lessening or prevention of competition to obtain a remedy in an abuse of dominance case. Instead, it is an alternative path to a remedy but still a requirement to obtain an order other than prohibition, including a divestiture of assets or shares under section 79(2).[148] What follows examines the test for an "effect of preventing or lessening competition substantially in a market" in section 79(1)(b) based upon the case law which had interpreted the words as found in the section prior to this amendment, when this was a required, rather than alternative, element.

i) The Core Test: Likely to Create, Maintain, or Enhance Market Power

The requirement that conduct "has had, is having or is likely to have the effect of preventing or lessening competition substantially in a market" involves an assessment of whether it is "likely to create, maintain or enhance the ability of the [dominant firm] to exercise market power."[149]

146 *Ibid.*

147 *Ibid* at para 38.

148 *Bill C-56 2023*, above note 35, s 7.2.

149 *TREB* FCA2, above note 38 at para 83, referring to *Tervita*, above note 46 at para 44.

To this end, the Tribunal has asked whether "the anti-competitive acts engaged in by [the dominant firm] preserve or add to [its] market power."[150]

ii) The "But For" Test

The Court of Appeal in *Canada Pipe* described the assessment under section 79 as a "but for" test, which compares the market conditions in the presence of the anti-competitive practice to those that would have prevailed in its absence. It described the test in the following terms:

> [T]he Tribunal must compare the level of competitiveness in the presence of the impugned practice with that which would exist in the absence of the practice, and then determine whether the preventing or lessening of competition, if any, is "substantial." This comparison must be done with reference to actual effects in the past and present, as well as likely future effects.[151]

The "but for" approach was adopted by the Supreme Court in *Tervita* in the context of merger assessment and has been applied by the Court of Appeal and Tribunal in subsequent cases.[152]

While the Court in *Canada Pipe* held that the "but for" test must be applied in all cases, it left open the possibility that the Tribunal may develop other tests in future cases as well.[153] In the instant case, it found that the Tribunal had erred in using in an "absolute evaluation" of the state of competition for the product under scrutiny, rather than considering a relative or comparative assessment. The Court observed that the Tribunal did not address the question of what the state of competition and market entry conditions would have been, in the past, present, or future, in the absence of the practice, which is the relevant test.[154] The Court considered that the "but for" test may include the following factors in comparing the current state of competition with the past, present, or future "but for" world:

- whether entry or expansion might be substantially faster, more frequent, or more significant without the anti-competitive practice
- whether switching between products and suppliers might be substantially more frequent

---

150 *NutraSweet*, above note 70 at para 138; *D&B*, above note 39 at para 155; *Canada Pipe* FCA, above note 43 at para 43.

151 *Canada Pipe* FCA, above note 43 at para 37.

152 *Tervita*, above note 46 at paras 50–51; *TREB* FCA2, above note 38 at paras 86 and 90; *TREB* CCT, above note 45 at para 633.

153 *Canada Pipe* FCA, above note 43 at para 44.

154 *Ibid* at para 53.

- whether prices might be substantially lower
- whether the quality of products might be substantially higher[155]

iii) Assessment of Substantial Effect

The "but for" framework seeks to determine whether the difference between (1) the level of competition in the presence of the practice at issue; and (2) the level of competition that would have existed in its absence is substantial.[156] This determination has the following components:

- The assessment of "substantiality" turns on the impact on market power,[157] not a wholescale weighing of the welfare effects of the practice.[158]
- Market power "is the ability to control either prices or non-price dimensions of competition for a significant time. Non-price dimensions of competition include innovation and quality of service, among others."[159]
- In assessing the impact on market power, the appropriate question is whether "either price is materially higher, or one or more non-price dimensions are materially lower than in the absence of the practices."[160]
- The materiality of the effect is assessed by reference to both its size and duration to determine whether it is substantial.[161]
- This determination may involve either a prevention or lessening of competition:
  - » Under the prevention branch, the question is "whether the impugned practice has preserved, is preserving or is likely to preserve any existing market power enjoyed by the respondent(s), by preventing or impeding new competition that otherwise likely would have materialized in the absence of the impugned practice";

---

155 *Ibid* at para 58.

156 As noted by the Supreme Court, the test applicable to mergers under s 92 employs essentially the same language and conveys the same ideas: *Tervita*, above note 46 at para 50.

157 *TREB* FCA2, above note 38 at para 89; *Tervita*, above note 46 at para 45.

158 As concluded by Jeffrey Church & Roger Ware, "Abuse of Dominance under the 1986 Competition *Act*" (1998) 13 *Review of Industrial Organization* 85 at 126 [Church & Ware]: "no attempt has been made (at least in the cases so far) to impose a threshold for the magnitude of the loss in efficiency caused by the anti-competitive practices."

159 *TREB* FCA2, above note 38 at para 89.

160 *Ibid* at para 90.

161 *Ibid* at para 91.

- » Under the lessening branch it is "whether the impugned practice has facilitated, is facilitating or is likely to facilitate the exercise of new or increased market power by the respondent(s)."[162]
- The burden to demonstrate both the substantial nature of the alleged prevention or lessening of competition, and the basic facts of the "but for" scenario that are required to make that demonstration, lies with the Commissioner.[163]

The Tribunal has not applied rigid criteria to the assessment of whether there is "materially" greater market power, noting that this will vary from case to case.[164] With respect to the duration of any material price increase or reduction in non-price dimensions, it has asked whether this effect has or will last for "approximately two years."[165] The Court of Appeal has confirmed that a duration of two years will "usually be sufficient" to establish the necessary substantial effect.[166]

In *Tele-Direct*, the Tribunal observed that "[w]here a firm with a high degree of market power is found to have engaged in anti-competitive conduct, smaller impacts on competition resulting from that conduct will meet the test of being 'substantial' than where the market situation was less uncompetitive to begin with."[167] This is similar to the approach the Supreme Court of Canada took to the assessment of the market power and behaviour combination required to meet the now-repealed undueness standard under the conspiracy provision. The Court found, for example, that when market power was possessed independently of the subject agreement, "any anti-competitive effect of the agreement will be suspicious." [168]

iv) Case Examples

In *TREB*, the Tribunal concluded that the Board's restrictions on the distribution of the real estate listing data substantially prevented competition for residential real estate brokerage services in the Greater Toronto Area (GTA). Applying the "but for" test, it found that the impact of the restrictions included increasing market entry and expansion barriers for real estate brokers offering innovative virtual office websites.

---

162 *VAA*, above note 10 at paras 636–37.

163 *Ibid* at para 644.

164 *Ibid* at para 641.

165 *Ibid*, citing *Tervita*, above note 42 at para 80 and *Canada (Commissioner of Competition) v CCS Corp*, 2012 CCTD No 14 at para 123.

166 *TREB* FCA2, above note 38 at para 64.

167 *Tele-Direct*, above note 51 at para 758.

168 *Nova Scotia Pharmaceutical Society, above note 47 at para 109.*

The Tribunal cited several examples of firms that would have entered or expanded their innovative and competitive services, but for the restrictions on their ability to use the disputed data on their websites.[169] Other effects included reducing the range of brokerage services in the market, service quality, and innovation.[170]

In assessing whether the impact of the restrictions was substantial, the Tribunal set out the various ways in which the lack of access to the disputed data had limited the ability of internet-based brokerages to compete.[171] For example, it found that information such as "sold" and "pending sold" data as well as cooperating broker commissions was "very important, if not critical, in assisting Internet-based brokerages to distinguish themselves from incumbent traditional brokerages."[172] It found the impact of not having access to this data substantial in view of the aggregate adverse impact on non-price competition, the range of brokerage services offered, the quality of services, and innovation.[173] This was reinforced given the duration of the impact (the practice was in place since 2011, and its impact was likely to continue) and its scope (it covered the entire GTA).[174] The Tribunal reached the following conclusion on the impact of the data restrictions on market power of TREB's member brokers:

> [T]hose restrictions are maintaining what is in essence the collective market power that TREB's Members are able to exercise through their control of TREB and its rule-making functions. This collective market power is manifested in the form of materially less brokerage service offerings, innovation, quality and variety than would exist "but for" the VOW Restrictions.[175]

As noted earlier, TREB controlled both the upstream market for the supply of the disputed data to real estate agents, as well as the downstream market for the supply of MLS-based residential real estate brokerage services. Although TREB did not compete in the latter market, the Tribunal found that its anti-competitive restrictions on the use of data by its members in that market could provide the foundation for a remedy against TREB.

---

169 *TREB CCT, above* note 45 at paras 505–51.

170 *Ibid* at paras 552–619.

171 *Ibid* at paras 666–90.

172 *Ibid* at para 691.

173 *Ibid* at para 702.

174 *Ibid* at paras 703–4.

175 *Ibid* at para 709.

The Court of Appeal upheld the decision, rejecting, *inter alia*, the appellate board's suggestion that the Tribunal had erred by finding a substantial effect in the absence of quantitative evidence of the effects on competition. The Court rejected the proposition that such quantification was required under section 79.[176]

In contrast, the Tribunal in *VAA* was unable to find that the practice by the Vancouver Airport Authority of restricting entry of airline catering services at the airport had substantially lessened competition. The evidence the Tribunal considered included that airlines typically possessed long-term (three- to five-year) contracts with incumbent in-flight caterers, suggesting that new entrants could not have readily displaced them or competed on a scale that would have had material price and non-price impacts in the market.[177] The Tribunal was also not convinced that the restriction on entry had caused price effects on catering services for airlines, finding the evidence put forward by the Commissioner "unpersuasive and insufficient."[178] Finally, the Tribunal rejected the Commissioner's suggestion that new entrants would have provided additional dynamic competition, innovation, or a higher quality of service.[179]

v) "The Effect is not the Result of Superior Competitive Performance"

Section 79(1)(b)(ii) requires that for a remedy to be available, even where the conduct has had the effect of substantially preventing or lessening competition, the Tribunal must find that "the effect is not a result of superior competitive performance."[180]

This is not an "efficiency defence." Bill C-29 of 1984 had proposed that no order could be made under the abuse of dominance provision where competition was prevented or lessened substantially "as a result of the superior economic efficiency" of the party against whom an order

176 *TREB* FCA2, above note 38 at para 100.

177 *VAA*, above note 10 at paras 666–69.

178 *Ibid* at 775.

179 *Ibid* at 777–97.

180 In the 2022 and 2023 amendments (*Bill C-19 2022*, above note 35, s. 260; *Bill C-56 2023*, above note 35, s 7.2) Parliament replaced the previous subsection 79(4), which was to similar effect:

> In determining, for the purposes of subsection (1), whether a practice has had, is having or is likely to have the effect of preventing or lessening competition substantially in a market, the Tribunal shall consider whether the practice is a result of superior competitive performance.

was sought.[181] The language was changed to "superior economic performance" in a subsequent version.[182] Subsection 79(4) was inserted in legislative committee, which thus moved away from an "absolute defence" and opted for the "superior competitive performance" language, making it only a factor in the assessment of competitive effect.[183]

The subsection was referred to,[184] but was not subject to any extensive interpretation, in the jurisprudence.

The "legitimate business justification" element discussed above provides an avenue for a respondent to put forward "a credible efficiency or pro-competitive rationale for the conduct in question."[185] As a result, it is unclear what the "superior competitive performance" element adds because a dominant firm could already argue that its practice was merely intended to be legitimate, non-exclusionary competitive behaviour.

It has been suggested that the previous section 79(4) could have been intended as a way of introducing into the assessment of an alleged abusive practice by a dominant firm a trade-off between "any efficiency gains from the anticompetitive practice against its exclusionary effects on competitors."[186] However, the legislative history referenced above reveals that Parliament chose not to adopt such an explicit efficiency defence in initially adopting the "superior competitive performance" element.

vi) Factors in Assessing Competitive Effect

The 2023 amendments[187] added a list of factors that the Tribunal "may consider" in determining "whether conduct has had, is having or is likely

---

181 Bill C-29, *An Act to amend the Combines Investigation Act and the Bank Act and other Acts in consequence thereof*, 32d Parl, 2d Sess, 1983–83, s 31.41(4).

182 Bill C-91, *An Act to establish the Competition Tribunal and to amend the Combines Investigation Act and the Bank Act and other Acts in consequence thereof*, 33d Parl, 1st Sess, 1984–85, s 51(4). See *Canada (Commissioner of Competition) v Superior Propane Inc*, [2002] CCTD No 10 at para 70.

183 House of Commons, *Minutes of Proceedings and Evidence of the Legislative Committee on Bill C-91*, 33d Parl, 1st Sess, No 11 (21 May 1986) at 11:33 and 11:35.

184 *TREB* FCA1, above note 59 at para 22; *Canada Pipe FCA, above note 43 at para 17.*

185 *TREB* FCA2, above note 38 at para 148, citing *Canada Pipe* FCA, above note 43 at para 73.

186 Church & Ware, above note 158 at 96. The authors concede, however:

> While it is fine in theory to suggest this interpretation of the abuse provisions based on accepted welfare economics, it is quite another thing to implement such a rule of reason. Successful implementation will require that the Tribunal determine the "correct" economic model of the behavior in question and apply it appropriately.

187 *Bill C-56 2023*, above note 35, s 7.2.

to have the effect of preventing or lessening competition substantially in a market." These are:

(a) the effect of the conduct on barriers to entry in the market, including network effects;
(b) the effect of the conduct on price or non-price competition, including quality, choice or consumer privacy;
(c) the nature and extent of change and innovation in a relevant market; and
(d) any other factor that is relevant to competition in the market that is or would be affected by the conduct.

These factors reflect some of the considerations or conditions identified as raising concerns in digital markets and were also added to the mergers and civil agreements provisions. They are unlikely to have a significant impact, given that the Bureau has stated that "where appropriate we considered each of these factors, which were already referenced in the Guidelines. Consequently, these additions do not change our enforcement approach."[188]

D. OTHER ABUSE OF DOMINANCE ISSUES

1) Joint Dominance

Section 79 refers to situations in which "*one or more persons* substantially or completely control" a market. This language has the potential to apply to a spectrum of behaviour, from explicit agreements between competitors to control essential facilities or a market,[189] to joint exclusionary conduct,[190] to facilitating practices that have the effect of eliminating

188 Competition Bureau, "*Bulletin on the Amendments to the Abuse of Dominance Provisions*"(25 October 2023) at para 58. See also Canada, Innovation, Science and Economic Development, *The Future of Competition Policy in Canada* (2022) at 33: "In order to emphasize their increasing importance, the BIA Amendments enshrined the notion of non-price elements of competition as factors for the Competition Tribunal to consider, including the emerging dimension of competing on the basis of protecting consumer privacy. This makes it no less a challenge to measure or appraise them, however."

189 *Canada (Director of Investigation and Research) v AGT Directory Limited*, [1994] CCTD No 24 (consent order); *Canada (Director of Investigation and Research) v Bank of Montreal*, [1996] CCTD No 12 (approving consent order) [*Bank of Montreal*]. Sections 90.1 (civil review of agreements) and 45 (criminal conspiracy) may also apply to such agreements.

190 *Canada (Commissioner of Competition) and Waste Services (CA) Inc and Waste Management of Canada Corporation* (16 June 2009), CT-2009-003 (CCT), online:

competition between rivals.[191] Given that the cases before the Tribunal that have alleged this kind of conduct in Canada have come only in the context of consent proceedings,[192] there has been little jurisprudential guidance in this area.

Examples of facilitating practices in concentrated markets that may raise competitive concerns when a group of firms act in a parallel fashion include:

- pre-announcing price increases or publishing price lists (which facilitates coordinated pricing)
- the joint adoption of meet-or-release clauses, which oblige a supplier to either match an offer received by a customer or release the customer from its obligation to purchase under the contract (this can make price cutting transparent, permit price matching, and discourage discounting)
- the joint adoption of most favoured nation clauses, which commit a seller to offer a buyer the most favourable terms offered to any of its customers (this can deter the seller from cutting prices to avoid having to offer the cut to all its customers)[193]

These kinds of practices can, for example, increase the likelihood of coordinated or collusive behaviour being successful by reducing the incentives for firms to cheat on an arrangement, increasing the probability that cheating is detected or increasing the punishment associated with cheating.[194]

Academic commentary has supported the need for competition law to address joint collusive conduct in concentrated or oligopolistic markets that does not involve explicit agreement or a formal

---

https://decisions.ct-tc.gc.ca/ct-tc/cd/en/item/462579/index.do?q=CT-2009-003. A registered consent agreement followed the Commissioner's allegations of joint dominance in the imposition of various contractual terms on customers that excluded competitors, such as long contract and renewal terms, limits on termination, rights of first refusal, requirement to reveal information on offers, and liquidated damages.

191 Edward M Iacobucci & Ralph A Winter, "Abuse of Joint Dominance in Canadian Competition Policy" (2010) 60 *University of Toronto Law Journal* 219 at 237 [Iacobucci & Winter]: "Given that . . . facilitating practices can allow jointly dominant firms to substantially lessen competition, it would be preferable to interpret s. 79 in a more purposeful, substantive way that would address facilitating practices."

192 See, e.g., cases cited above at note 188.

193 Michael Trebilcock et al, *The Law and Economics of Canadian Competition Policy* (Toronto: University of Toronto Press, 2003) at 513–14 [Trebilcock et al].

194 Church & Ware, above note 158 at 94.

arrangement.[195] Section 79 has the potential to address such conduct, although existing case law finding that a "predatory, exclusionary or disciplinary" purpose[196] may need to be distinguished or modified to permit the section to apply to matters such as facilitating practices that bring about coordination intended to benefit, or that has the effect of benefitting, competitors.[197]

The Bureau's *Abuse of Dominance Enforcement Guidelines*[198] take the position that merely "similar or parallel" conduct by firms is insufficient to constitute joint dominance under section 79. On the other hand, they state that "evidence of coordinated behaviour by firms in the allegedly jointly dominant group may be probative" of why the "allegedly dominant group" are not competing (without enumeration of what this behaviour may consist of).[199] The *Abuse Guidelines* focus on the aggregate market power of the allegedly dominant firms and whether it is constrained by existing or potential competition in order to determine whether issues are raised under section 79.[200] They provide little additional guidance on the nature or degree of coordinated activity necessary to constitute joint control. Further case law is likely to be needed to test the content and boundaries of the provision in this respect.

2) Essential Facilities and Refusals to Deal

In the United States, these two closely related concepts have developed in the jurisprudence to address situations in which, for example, competitors are denied access by a dominant firm to inputs or facilities that are essential to being able to compete. Both are subject to numerous qualifications and limitations in their application.[201] Their role in the future development of the law in the United States remains unclear. In the context of digital markets, for example, some commentators have questioned whether access to essential data could provide the basis for a claim founded on the essential facility concept.[202] However, reliance

---

195 *Ibid* at 93–94; Trebilcock et al, above note 192; see also Trebilcock & Ducci, above note 110 at 192; C Scott Hemphill & Tim Wu, "Parallel Exclusion" (2013) 122 *Yale Law Journal* 1182.

196 *Canada Pipe* FCA, above note 43 at para 64.

197 Iacobucci & Winter, above note 190.

198 *Abuse Guidelines*, above note 54.

199 *Ibid* at para 49.

200 *Ibid* at para 47.

201 For an excellent overview, see Congressional Research Service, "Antitrust and 'Big Tech'" (11 September 2019) at 13–15, online: https://fas.org/sgp/crs/misc/R45910.pdf.

202 See, e.g., Zachary Abrahamson, "Essential Data" (2014) 124:3 *The Yale Law Journal* 867 at 870–71.

on the idea of "essential facilities" has been controversial in the United States, and has not yet been fully embraced by the Supreme Court.[203] Canadian authors have described the concept as "problematic," summarizing the sources of controversy in the American jurisprudence by stating that (1) "it requires price regulation"; (2) "duties to deal with competitors themselves discourage provision of facilities in the first place"; and (3) "courts can assess antitrust liability without it."[204]

In Canada, section 75 of the Act provides a specific provision addressing refusals to supply, which adopts a multi-faceted test.[205] This provision does not limit the availability of abuse of dominance as a remedy if denial of access can also be characterized as a practice of anti-competitive acts, but all three elements discussed above would have to be established on the facts to make out a case. It is likely that a key issue would be whether a legitimate business purpose, such as increased cost or efficiency, may be raised in response to the question of whether such conduct may be characterized as an anti-competitive act.

The concept of essential facilities was raised by the respondent in *TREB*, but the Tribunal rejected the suggestion that it applied. The Tribunal held that, because TREB had provided access to the disputed and other data, but imposed restrictions on its use, the case did not involve a denial of access typical of an essential facilities matter.[206] In another case involving the electronic payment organization Interac, it has been observed that the elements of the essential facility concept may have been met, but the case went forward as a consent order and there was no comment by the Tribunal on the substance of that issue.[207] Thus, as yet there has been no Canadian jurisprudence that has considered the concept in detail.

3) Regulated Conduct

Unlike the criminal conspiracy provision, section 79 contains no provision incorporating the jurisprudential "regulated conduct defence" (the

---

203 *Verizon*, above note 5. The US House of Representatives, Subcommittee on Antitrust Commercial and Administrative Law of the Committee on the Judiciary, *Investigation of Competition in Digital Markets Majority Staff Report and Recommendations* (6 October 2020) at 397 called for legislative reform: "Congress should consider overriding judicial decisions that have treated unfavorably essential facilities- and refusal to deal-based theories of harm."

204 TJ Brennan & Alan Gunderson, "2003 in Competition Law Enforcement: An Economic Perspective" (2007) 22 *Canadian Competition Record* 54 at 81.

205 Discussed in more detail in Chapter 8.

206 *TREB* CCT, above note 45, paras 212–13.

207 Church & Ware, above note 157 at 124–25; *Bank of Montreal*, above note 188 at para 79.

"doctrine"). In *VAA*, the Tribunal considered the Airport Authority's argument that aspects of its authorizing legislation and mandate created a defence to the allegations of abuse of dominance by the Commissioner. The VAA's authorizing legal regime was grounded in federal law. The conclusions of the Tribunal were as follows:

- The regulated conduct jurisprudence is inapplicable to section 79 because
  - » the section lacks the "leeway language" used to find the conspiracy provision of the *Competition Act* inapplicable to regulatory regimes in the case law;
  - » the section is not criminal law and lacks the kind of public interest standard that provided a supporting rationale for the development of the regulated conduct defence in the decided cases.[208]
- Even if the jurisprudence governing the doctrine were applicable, in the instant case, the authority relied upon by the *VAA* "can be interpreted in a manner that gives VAA broad latitude to fulfill its mandate, without conflicting with section 79."[209] In assessing this aspect, the Tribunal asked whether, applying the ordinary principles of statutory interpretation, there was any conflict between the *Competition Act* and the statutory or regulatory scheme in question. That approach has two components:
  - » determine whether, applying interpretative rules, there is any conflict
  - » if a conflict exists, seek to resolve it, applying rules such as the primacy of an Act of Parliament (such as the *Competition Act*) over subordinate legislation[210]
- The Tribunal did not need to address the last step, given that its interpretation of VAA's authorizing scheme resolved the conflict, and that it had determined that in any case (as noted above) the doctrine "is not available in respect of section 79."[211]

The approach taken to regulated conduct may be different where the abuse of dominance provisions are applied to *provincial* authority or regulatory schemes, because the interpretative rules governing conflicting actions of the same legislature would not apply. The Competition Bureau takes the position that it "will not refrain from pursuing regulated conduct . . . because [a] provincial law may be interpreted as

208 *VAA*, above note 10 at paras 215–45.
209 *Ibid* at para 291.
210 *Ibid* at paras 248–58.
211 *Ibid* at para 259.

authorizing the conduct or is more specific than the Act given that the Bureau's mandate is to enforce the law as directed by Parliament not a provincial legislature or its delegate."[212] The Bureau references authority supporting the constitutionality of federal competition laws, presumably invoking the constitutional principle of federal paramountcy applicable to situations of conflict between federal and provincial legislation.[213] However, a conflict may not arise where compliance with a provincial regulatory scheme provides a business justification.[214] Furthermore, as a factual matter, the existence of provincial regulation mandating, requiring, or otherwise affecting the competitive conduct in a particular industry (such as by creating barriers to entry) may have a bearing on whether the applicable tests, such as prevention or lessening of competition substantially, have been satisfied.[215]

4) Remedies

a) Limitation Period

The section is subject to a limitation period of three years after the anti-competitive practice or conduct has ceased.[216] Where the alleged anti-competitive acts are acquisitions, this may be a way of reviewing a series of mergers that, individually, would otherwise be subject to the one-year limitation period in the merger provisions.[217] In *Laidlaw*, the Tribunal found that a practice of acquisitions and related behaviour by the respondent fell within section 79,[218] and made an order prohibiting

---

212 Canada, Competition Bureau, *Technical Bulletin on the Regulated Conduct Defence*, 27 September 2010 at 5, online: www.competitionbureau.gc.ca/eic/site/cb-bc.nsf/vwapj/RegulatedConduct-sept-2010-e.pdf/$FILE/RegulatedConduct-sept-2010-e.pdf.

213 See *ibid*, n 23, citing Article 91(2) of the *Constitution Act, 1867*; *General Motors of Canada Ltd v City National Leasing Ltd*, [1989] 1 SCR 641; *Alex Couture Inc v Canada (Attorney General)* (1991), 83 DLR (4th) 577 (Que CA), leave to appeal to SCC ref'd (1992), 91 DLR (4th) vii (SCC); and *Thomson Newspapers Ltd v Canada (Director of Investigation and Research, Restrictive Trade Practices Commission)*, [1990] 1 SCR 425.

214 See above in this chapter, Section C(2)(b)(ii)(e).

215 See above in this chapter, Section C(3).

216 *Competition Act*, above note 10, s 79(6): "No application may be made under this section in respect of a practice of anti-competitive acts or conduct more than three years after the practice or conduct has ceased."

217 *Ibid*, s 97, which provides that a merger cannot be subject to an application "more than one year after the merger has been substantially completed."

218 *Laidlaw*, above note 14 at para 140, where the tribunal agreed with the following interpretation of the provisions:

Laidlaw from acquiring any competitor in the market for a period of three years.[219]

b) Interim Remedies

Section 103.3 permits the Tribunal to make an interim order of ten days' duration (which can be extended twice for thirty-five-day periods) to "prevent the continuation of conduct" contrary to section 79, where it finds that in the absence of the order

> (a) injury to competition that cannot adequately be remedied by the Tribunal is likely to occur;
> (b) a person is likely to be eliminated as a competitor; or
> (c) a person is likely to suffer a significant loss of market share, a significant loss of revenue or other harm that cannot be adequately remedied by the Tribunal.[220]

The Tribunal may also make an interim order under section 104 "that it considers appropriate" when a section 79 application has been filed, founded on the normal principles governing interlocutory and injunctive relief in the superior courts.[221] In such an order, the Tribunal has broad discretion to provide terms it "considers necessary and sufficient to meet the circumstances of the case."[222] The section permits the Tribunal to provide interim relief, for example, against the practices of a dominant firm causing competitive harm that may be irreparable and where the balance of convenience favours an order restraining the conduct.

c) Final Orders

Section 79(1) provides that where the Tribunal finds the elements of abuse of dominance proven, "it may make an order prohibiting the person or persons from engaging in a practice or conduct if it finds that the person or persons have engaged in or are engaging in" the relevant practice(s). Section 79(2) provides the Tribunal broad discretion to go

---

> The choice between the merger and abuse of dominance provisions could arise, for example, in situations involving a series of acquisitions in an industry by a dominant firm. In such situations it may be the cumulative effect of such actions (i.e., the practice of anti-competitive acts) rather than any single purchase which lessens competition substantially. In these circumstances, the abuse provisions may be more readily applicable than the merger provision.

219 *Ibid* at para 180.
220 *Competition Act*, above note 10, s 103.3(2).
221 *Ibid*, s 104.
222 *Ibid*, s 104(2).

beyond mere prohibition orders but only where the conduct is found to have a substantial effect on competition:

> 79(2) If, on an application under subsection (1), the Tribunal finds that a practice of anti-competitive acts amounts to conduct that has had or is having the effect of preventing or lessening competition substantially in a market in which the person or persons have a plausible competitive interest and that an order under subsection (1) is not likely to restore competition in that market, the Tribunal may, in addition to or in lieu of making an order under subsection (1), make an order directing any or all persons against whom an order is sought to take actions, including the divestiture of assets or shares, that are reasonable and necessary to overcome the effects of the practice in that market.

The purpose of a remedial order is to "restore competition in the relevant markets"[223] or in the language of section 79(2), to "overcome the effects of such practices as may have already occurred."[224] This requires an assessment of the effects of the anti-competitive acts on the relevant markets and a determination of the remedies needed to restore competition.[225]

In *Laidlaw*, as well as prohibiting acquisitions for three years (pursuant to section 79(1)), the Tribunal ordered Laidlaw to remove from its existing contracts anti-competitive clauses such as rights of first refusal, requirements to reveal bids or competitive quotes and to liquidate damages, and prohibited enforcing these aspects of existing contracts. Laidlaw was also required to shorten the duration of existing contracts to one year and to eliminate exclusivity requirements.[226] Orders forbidding certain behaviours and requiring certain actions have been issued in several other cases.[227]

Divestiture, while a common remedy in the context of mergers, has not been used to date under section 79. Section 79(3) provides an indication that such relief must be resorted to only to restore competition:

> In making an order under subsection (2), the Tribunal shall make the order in such terms as will in its opinion interfere with the rights of

223 *Laidlaw*, above note 14 at paras 179–80 and 187 and *D&B*, above note 39 at paras 202, 204, 211, and 220.

224 *NutraSweet*, above note 70 at 57.

225 *Laidlaw*, above note 14 at paras 179–80 and 187.

226 *Canada (Director of Investigation and Research) v Laidlaw Waste Systems Ltd*, CT-1991-002, Order Pursuant to Reasons Dated January 20, 1992 (11 February 1992), online: https://decisions.ct-tc.gc.ca/ct-tc/cdo/en/item/465022/index.do.

227 *Tele-Direct*, above note 51 at para 767; *D&B*, above note 39.

> any person to whom the order is directed or any other person affected by it only to the extent necessary to achieve the purpose of the order.

In the United States, divestiture has been used on occasion in monopolization cases. The 1982 *AT&T* consent decree is a well-documented example, by which, *inter alia*, AT&T relinquished control of the Bell local services companies across the United States and separated its long distance, local, and product development arms.[228] While competition flourished in most of the markets touched by the decree, the use of the remedy spawned a debate about the effectiveness of divestiture versus behavioural alternatives.[229]

In *Microsoft*, the trial judge issued an order to break the company into two entities, in order to separate the personal computer applications business from that dealing with the operating system. However, this was overturned on appeal.[230] The appellate court cited *United States v ALCOA* to the effect that "a corporation, designed to operate effectively as a single entity, cannot readily be dismembered of parts of its various operations without a marked loss of efficiency."[231] On remand to a remedies hearing, the Department of Justice no longer sought divestiture, and the court accepted a set of behavioural remedies.[232]

The Tribunal also has the authority, to issue administrative monetary penalties (AMPs). They are only available "[i]f the Tribunal finds that a person has engaged in or is engaging in a practice of anti-competitive acts that amounts to conduct that has had or is having the effect of preventing or lessening competition substantially in a market," and the Tribunal has made a prohibition order against that practice. The penalties available were increased in the 2022-23 amendments to the *greater of* $25 million ($35 million for subsequent orders) and the "value of the benefit derived from the anti-competitive practice, or, if that amount cannot be reasonably determined, 3% of the person's annual worldwide gross revenues."[233]. The Act provides guidance on determining the amount of penalty as follows:

> (3.2) In determining the amount of an administrative monetary penalty, the Tribunal shall take into account any evidence of the following:

228 *United States v AT&T Co*, 552 F Supp 131 (DDC 1982) at 224.

229 See, e.g., Philip J Weiser, "Regulating Interoperability: Lessons from AT&T, Microsoft, and Beyond" (2009) 76 *Antitrust Law Journal* 271 at 274–79.

230 *United States v Microsoft Corp*, 97 F Supp 2d 59, 64 (DDC 2000), rev'd, 253 F 3d 34, 48 (DCC 2001).

231 *Ibid*, (DC Cir) at 106, citing *United States v ALCOA* (1950), 91 F Supp 333, 416 (SDNY 1950).

232 *New York v Microsoft Corp*, 224 F Supp 2d 76, 184 (DDC 2002).

233 *Bill C-19 2022*, above note 35, s 260; *Bill C-56 2023*, above note 35, s 7.2.

> (a) the effect on competition in the relevant market;
> (b) the gross revenue from sales affected by the practice;
> (c) any actual or anticipated profits affected by the practice;
> (d) the financial position of the person against whom the order is made;
> (e) the history of compliance with this Act by the person against whom the order is made; and
> (f) any other relevant factor.
>
> (3.3) The purpose of an order made against a person under subsection (3.1) is to promote practices by that person that are in conformity with the purposes of this section and not to punish that person.

The Bureau's *Abuse Guidelines* say in respect of the decision-making criteria in section 79(3.2):

> When assessing whether an AMP is appropriate, the Bureau will consider factors such as: (i) the respondent's willingness to collaborate in a timely manner with the Bureau in the context of the investigation or inquiry, including to immediately cease the impugned conduct when the Bureau raises competition concerns; (ii) the respondent's history of compliance with the Act; and (iii) whether the evidence suggests the respondent intended not to comply with the Act, or showed a wanton or reckless disregard for the Act.[234]

The Bureau also takes the position that AMPs should be set at sufficiently high levels such that they do not become a "cost of doing business."[235]

In *Canada (Commissioner of Competition) v Direct Energy Marketing Ltd*, the Tribunal was faced with a preliminary motion to dismiss an application seeking administrative monetary penalties for abuse of dominance in the Ontario water heater rental market. The respondent argued, *inter alia*, that the remedy was punitive, given that the respondent firm had already exited the market. The Tribunal held that the order may still have remedial effect and dismissed the motion.[236] The parties ultimately settled the matter and a consent agreement was registered, providing for a monetary penalty of $1 million.[237]

---

234 *Abuse Guidelines*, above note 54 at para 105.

235 *Ibid* at para 108.

236 *Canada (Commissioner of Competition) v Direct Energy Marketing Ltd, [2015] CCTD No 2 at paras 53–59.*

237 *Canada (Commissioner of Competition) v Direct Energy Marketing Ltd*, Registered Consent Agreement, CT-2012-003 (30 October 2015) at para 4, online: https://decisions.ct-tc.gc.ca/ct-tc/cdo/en/item/463069/index.do.

Finally, in the case of private applications brought under section 79, the Tribunal was given the authority in the 2024 amendments to require the payment of "the benefit derived from the conduct" to the private applicant and "any other person affected by the conduct."[238]

d) Consent Orders

As illustrated by the *Direct Energy* case, section 105 permits summary registration of consent orders with the Tribunal. The scope of the provision, and the companion provision for the rescission and variation of consent orders, was discussed in Chapter 5.[239]

The Bureau's *Abuse Guidelines* state a willingness to explore consensual remedies even in the absence of a remedial order.[240] However, they indicate that when the Bureau decides the requirements of section 79 have been met, it will not "typically" discontinue an inquiry or withdraw an application without a registered consent agreement, to ensure that the anti-competitive conduct will not be resumed.[241]

E. CONCLUSION

For abuse of dominance under the *Competition Act* to result in a remedy by the Competition Tribunal, it is not sufficient for a dominant firm merely to possess market power—there must be some predatory, exclusionary, or disciplinary practice or conduct. The examination of an alleged "practice of anti-competitive acts" permits an inquiry into whether there was a legitimate business purpose for conduct that has had an anti-competitive effect. This is a critical aspect of the law, needed to avoid competition-based rules inadvertently discouraging efficient competitive behaviour by firms that have acquired dominance through meritorious competition.

The list of anti-competitive practices and conduct that may fall within abuse of dominance is open-ended. The next two chapters address vertical restraints and pricing practices, both of which are among those which can, and have been, raised under the abuse of dominance

---

238 *Competition Act*, above note 10, ss 79(4.1), 79(4.2).

239 See Chapter 5, Section F(2)(c) & (d).

240 *Abuse Guidelines*, above note 54 at para 97, referring to Canada, Competition Bureau, *Competition and Compliance Framework* (Gatineau: Industry Canada, 2015), online: www.competitionbureau.gc.ca/eic/site/cb-bc.nsf/vwapj/Competition-Compliance-Framework-Bulletin-e.pdf/$file/Competition-Compliance-Framework-Bulletin-e.pdf.

241 *Ibid* at para 98.

provisions. As Chapter 8 notes, there is substantial overlap between the elements of abuse of dominance and those of the vertical restraint provisions, which (in the case of exclusive dealing, for example) are some of the most common examples of exclusionary conduct that have been dealt with in the abuse of dominance jurisprudence. Chapter 9 includes a discussion of predatory pricing, which has arisen in various forms in previous abuse of dominance cases. Those chapters examine the economic benefits and anti-competitive effects of these practices in greater detail, as well as the considerations the law balances to determine whether a remedy is appropriate.

CHAPTER 8

VERTICAL PRACTICES: EXCLUSIVE DEALING, MARKET RESTRICTION, TIED SELLING, AND REFUSALS TO SUPPLY

A. INTRODUCTION

"Vertical" practices occur between players performing different functions in the chain of supply. The various functions in that chain include resource extraction, manufacturing, distribution, wholesaling, retailing, and end consumption.

Vertical practices by a given firm may be directed at firms "upstream" (e.g., applied by a customer to a supply source) or "downstream" (e.g., applied by a manufacturer to a consumer or supplier further down the chain of supply), or both. These practices can be contrasted with "horizontal" conduct (such as mergers between competitors or price fixing), which occurs between players at the same competitive level in the supply chain.

Vertical practices are widespread in the economy and are often not anti-competitive. Examples include franchise agreements restricting competition between food and beverage outlets of a particular brand, exclusive arrangements requiring car or farm equipment retailers to sell only the supplier's branded product, or telecommunications services offered to customers at discounts tied to the customer taking a bundle of services from the same firm.

Such arrangements may have varying effects on competition and efficiency depending on the context, which means that they require a case-by-case assessment to determine their anti-competitive effect. In general, unless the firm imposing the vertical restraint is a major supplier or possesses market power in a properly defined market, the practices are unlikely to raise issues under the *Competition Act*.[1]

There is a high degree of overlap between the vertical practices and abuse of dominance provisions, given that each of the vertical practices described below may also be assessed as an anti-competitive practice under section 79 when engaged in by a dominant firm. Indeed, several of the cases reviewed below, such as *Canada (Commissioner of Competition) v Canada Pipe*[2] and *Tele-Direct*,[3] were brought under both the abuse of dominance and vertical practices provisions. A tabular comparison of the main elements of abuse of dominance and of vertical practices falling within section 77 is set out below in **Table 8.1**. Several differences can be seen in comparing the elements set out there: under section 77, the respondent firm need only be a "major supplier"; the practice of anti-competitive acts is narrowed under section 77 and must have an "exclusionary effect"; and there is no "adverse effect on competition" or "prevention of competition" branch under section 77, which in all cases requires a "likely substantial lessening of competition."

Table 8.1. Comparison of the Elements of Sections 78–79 and 77

	Abuse of Dominance (Sections 78–79)	Vertical Practices[4] (Section 77)
Market Definition, Structure, Control	79(1)(a): substantial or complete control of a class or species of business	77(2) & (3): major supplier of a product in a market or widespread in a market
Conduct	78 and 79(1)(a): practice of anti-competitive acts that are intended to have a "predatory, exclusionary or disciplinary" effect on a competitor or adverse effect on competition or (b) "conduct" likely to prevent or lessen competition substantially	77(1): practice of tied selling, exclusive dealing, and market restriction as defined

1 RSC 1985, c C-34 [*Competition Act* or Act].

2 *Canada (Commissioner of Competition) v Canada Pipe*, [2005] CCTD No 3 [*Canada Pipe* CCT], overturned on other grounds 2006 FCA 233 [*Canada Pipe* FCA], based on finding that the Tribunal erred in its consideration of the anti-competitive effects of the practice.

3 *Canada (Competition Act, Director of Investigation and Research) v Tele-Direct (Publications) Inc* (1997), 73 CPR (3d) 1 (CCT) [*Tele-Direct*].

4 Except refusal to supply, s 75.

Table 8.1. Comparison of the Elements of Sections 78–79 and 77 (*Continued*)

	Abuse of Dominance (Sections 78–79)	Vertical Practices[4] (Section 77)
Effect	79(1)(a): practice of anti-competitive acts are not required to have an effect on competition if there is a predatory/exclusionary/disciplinary purpose (see above) but can also be shown by an intended "adverse effect on competition" (some market power) 79(1)(b) conduct which is likely to substantially prevent or lessen competition (SPLC), i.e., "likely to create, maintain or enhance" market power	77(2) & (3): practice is likely to have an "exclusionary effect," including impeding entry or expansion of a firm or the introduction of a product to a market, resulting in a likely substantial lessening of competition

It is important to draw a distinction, when discussing vertical practices, between "intrabrand" and "interbrand" competition. Intrabrand competition occurs among suppliers of the same branded product, such as among Petro-Canada gas stations. Interbrand competition is that between rival suppliers' products and outlets: e.g., between those of Petro-Canada, Shell, Ultramar, etc.

Vertical restraints can affect both intrabrand and interbrand competition. In most cases, intrabrand restraints, such as limitations on the ability of the same branded franchises to compete against each other, are not a concern for competition law as long as there is sufficient interbrand competition.[5] For example, if Petro-Canada were to limit the geographic territory within which its service stations could market their branded motor oil (reducing intrabrand competition in oil between those stations), that would pose few concerns, as consumers can purchase oil from many different competing sources (i.e., there are plenty of interbrand competitors in motor oil).

B. BACKGROUND AND HISTORY

These provisions were added in the Stage I amendments of 1976.[6] The genesis of the amendments was a research inquiry conducted by the

5 See, however, the discussion of the importance of intrabrand competition in Stephen Martin & John T Scott, "GTE Sylvania and Interbrand Competition as the Primary Concern of Antitrust Law" (2017) 51 *Review of Industrial Organization* 217.

6 *An Act to amend the Combines Investigation Act and the Bank Act and to repeal an Act to amend an Act to amend the Combines Investigation Act and the Criminal Code*, SC 1974-75-76, c 76, s 12.

Restrictive Trade Practices Commission (RTPC) in the early 1960s into the distribution practices of the major oil companies of products such as motor oil, anti-freeze, tires, batteries, and other products.[7]

Its 1962 *TBA Report* concluded that most of the oil companies required their branded service station operators[8] to carry only the products supplied by that company—a form of exclusive dealing.[9] It found that the effect of this and other practices, such as tied selling, was to create barriers to entry for competing suppliers of oil and other products by excluding their products from distribution via outlets covering a significant portion of the market.[10] The RTPC recommended that these practices be prohibited by making them criminal offences.

When the Economic Council was tasked to conduct a wholesale review of competition law in 1966, part of its mandate was to examine the RTPC's recommendations.[11] The Council recommended that the practices examined in the *TBA Report* be added to the law as civilly reviewable matters, given the need to assess their competitive effect on a case-by-case basis.[12]

The 1976 amendments added refusals to deal, exclusive dealing, tied selling, market restriction, foreign suppliers' refusal to supply, and consignment selling. The provisions have undergone few significant changes over the years.[13] Amendments in 2002 added a requirement for an adverse effect on competition to the refusal to deal provision and introduced private party applications (i.e., in addition to that of the Commissioner of Competition) for several of the provisions.[14] In 2009, the prohibition of consignment selling was repealed.[15]

---

7 Canada, Restrictive Trade Practices Commission, *Report on the Distribution and Sale of Automotive Oils, Greases, Anti-Freeze, Additives, Tires, Batteries and Accessories and Related Products* (Queen's Printer: Ottawa, 1962)—the so-called *TBA Report* [*TBA Report*].

8 Operators of non-company owned stations, which made up the bulk of the stations in that era.

9 *TBA Report*, above note 7 at 40–48.

10 *Ibid* at 75.

11 Economic Council of Canada, *Interim Report on Competition Policy* (Ottawa: Queen's Printer, 1969) at 124 [*Interim Report* 1969].

12 *Ibid* at 121–22 and 125.

13 A minor amendment was made in 1999 to s 77 to change the article "*a* market" to "*the* market" in the test for anti-competitive effect: *An Act to amend the Competition Act and to make consequential and related amendments to other Acts*, SC 1999, c 2.

14 *An Act to amend the Competition Act and the Competition Tribunal Act*, SC 2002, c 16, s 11.1. Private applications were permitted for refusals to supply, exclusive dealing, market restriction, tied selling, and a new provision discussed in Chapter 9, Section E, Civil Price Maintenance.

15 *Budget Implementation Act, 2009*, SC 2009, c 2, s 426.

The RTPC was given the authority in 1976 to make final decisions and issue binding orders about these new "civilly reviewable matters." It had hitherto been tasked with making policy recommendations and carrying out "research inquiries," rather than conducting trial-like proceedings and issuing final orders and remedies. Its mandate was extended to implement the Economic Council's 1969 recommendation that a specialized tribunal make case-by-case assessments of economic effects. The RTPC heard and decided several vertical restraint applications. In 1986, the Competition Tribunal took over responsibility for the adjudication of these provisions.[16]

The economic thinking on vertical restraints has evolved over time. In the United States, for example, the approach to vertical non-price restraints was substantially revised in 1977, consistent with the direction of the 1976 Canadian amendments. The US Supreme Court in *Continental TV Inc v GTE Sylvania Inc*[17] addressed agreements limiting the geographic territories in which franchised dealers of televisions could sell their products (termed "market restriction" in Canada). The Court overruled its decision in *United States v Arnold, Schwinn & Co*, decided only ten years earlier, which had held such restraints to be *per se* unlawful.[18] The Court in *Sylvania* found that market restriction could have sufficient "redeeming virtues" in terms of stimulating interbrand competition and that it should be subject to a case-by-case assessment of anti-competitive effect under the rule of reason. The decision "initiated a major change of course for the law of vertical restraints" in the United States.[19] It reflects that the economic analysis of vertical restraints involves more controversy, and less consensus, both in terms of differing international legal treatment and approaches to their economic analysis, than other areas of competition law, such as mergers or price fixing.

Private enforcement of the vertical restraints provisions was first made available in 2002. In 2024, to encourage increased private enforcement and permit a form of restitution, remedies available on private applications were broadened to include recovery of "the value of the

---

16 *Competition Act*, above note 1; *Competition Tribunal Act*, RSC 1985, c 19 (2d Supp).

17 *Continental TV Inc v GTE Sylvania Inc*, 433 US 36 (1977) [*Sylvania*]. For a discussion, see, e.g., D Daniel Sokol, "The Transformation of Vertical Restraints: Per Se Illegality, the Rule of Reason, and Per Se Legality" (2014) 79 *Antitrust Law Journal* 1003; William H Rooney, Timothy G Fleming & Sruti Swaminathan, "Amex in Context: Tracing the Application of the Rule of Reason to Vertical Restraints" (2019) *Columbia Business Law Review* 1.

18 *United States v Arnold, Schwinn & Co*, 388 US 365 (1967).

19 Andrew I Gavil, William E Kovacic & Jonathan B Baker, *Antitrust Law in Perspective: Cases, Concepts and Problems in Competition Policy* (St Paul: West, 2002) at 357.

benefit derived from the conduct that is the subject of the order."[20] This amount may be "distributed among the applicant and any other person affected by the conduct, in any manner that the Tribunal considers appropriate."[21]

C. EXCLUSIVE DEALING AND MARKET RESTRICTION

These practices are two common forms of vertical restraint. They both fall within section 77; their elements under the legislation will be discussed further below.

1) Nature of the Practices

Exclusive dealing involves a practice whereby dealers (distributors, wholesalers, or retailers) of a product agree, or are induced, to deal only or primarily in the products of a particular supplier or manufacturer. As a result, as depicted in **Figure 8.1**, competing Manufacturer B cannot sell its product through the dealers who are subject to the restraint.

An example of exclusive dealing was the Stocking Distributor Program (SDP) considered by the Tribunal in *Canada Pipe*. Under the Program, distributors of the respondent Bibby's[22] cast iron drain, waste, and vent (DWV) products obtained rebates and discounts (often amounting to more than 50 percent of the list price) in return for stocking only cast-iron products produced by the company. Distributors were permitted to stock other companies' DWV products not made of cast iron (such as plastic pipe). The Tribunal found that cast iron pipe constituted the relevant market. It concluded that the SDP was a

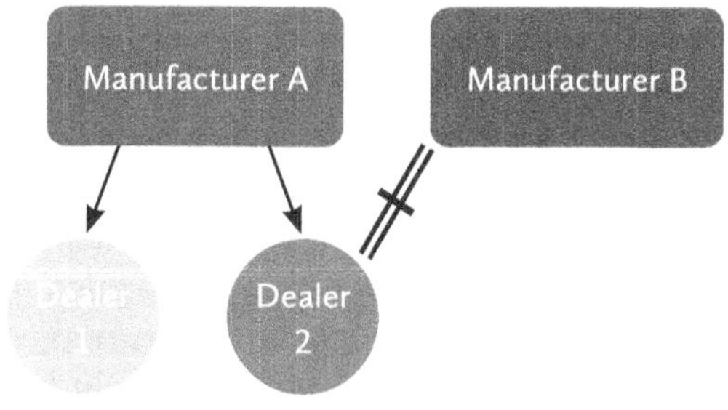

FIGURE 8.1. Exclusive dealing places limits on the ability of downstream firms to deal in the products of competing suppliers

20 *Fall Economic Statement Implementation Act, 2023*, SC 2024, c 15, s 244 [*Bill C-59 2024*]

21 *Ibid*, s. 75(2.1).

22 Bibby Ste-Croix was a division of Canada Pipe Company Ltd.

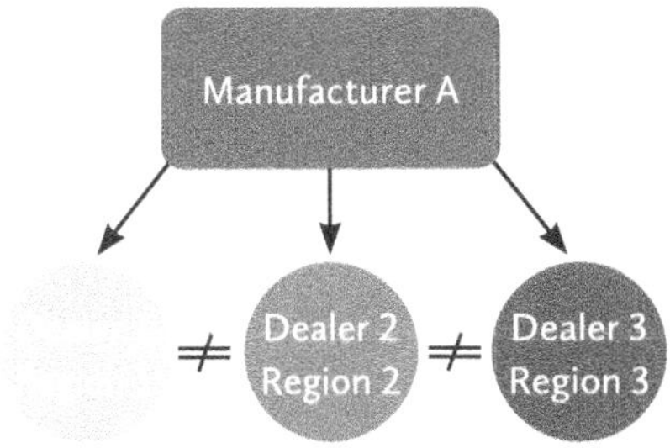

FIGURE 8.2. Market (or territorial) restriction means a supplier limits the territories that may be served by dealers

practice of exclusive dealing in cast iron DWV products within section 77 of the Act.[23]

In **market restriction** (see **Figure 8.2**—also referred to as territorial restriction), dealers agree, or are induced, to devote their sale efforts to an assigned "territory"; either a geographic region, or a specific segment of the market (for example, retail versus online sales) and not to sell the manufacturer's product outside that territory. The manufacturer may or may not agree to appoint additional dealers within that territory, depending on whether it has agreed to make each dealer's territorial arrangement exclusive.

Market restriction may be put in place by a supplier as part of a franchise arrangement, as a *quid pro quo* for a dealer's willingness to deal only in the products of the supplier.[24] It provides a dealer some protection against competition by the supplier's other franchisees; this protection may make the limit imposed on sourcing from other suppliers more palatable to the dealer and align its interests more closely with those of the franchisor.

An example of market restriction cited in the background materials in support of the 1976 amendments came from a complaint to the Competition Bureau involving a European car manufacturer that allocated defined geographic territories to its car dealers. Any dealer selling outside the allotted territory was required to reimburse the dealer in whose territory the customer resided with a "substantial part of his profit margin." The territorial restraint had the effect of discouraging the manufacturer's dealers from seeking business outside their assigned franchise area.[25]

Market restriction may also occur when a supplier refuses to distribute its products through retailers that only have an online presence (i.e., that do not operate bricks-and-mortar stores) or when a supplier requires that retailers not conduct internet sales.

---

23 *Canada Pipe CCT, above note 2 at para 14 (re discounts) and para 279 (re the practice).*

24 Frederic M Scherer, *Industrial Market Structure and Economic Performance* (Boston: Houghton Mifflin, 1980) at 586 [Scherer].

25 Canada, Competition Bureau, Consumer and Corporate Affairs Canada, *Background Papers, Stage I Competition Policy* (1976) at 10 [*Stage I Competition Policy*].

2) Economic Effects of Exclusive Dealing and Market Restriction

Three main sets of interests can be identified which are affected by these practices: those of the manufacturer, those of a dealer, and those of the consumer/buyer.[26] These will be examined below in regard to their respective benefits and competitive concerns.

a) Benefits

Benefits to the **manufacturer** may include the following:

- Exclusivity and market restriction may produce greater returns to dealers and result in increased devotion of selling effort and enthusiasm; they "encourage a more dedicated sales, service, and quality effort by the affected distributor or retailer."[27] The higher returns can permit dealers to, for example, carry larger inventories, spend more time and money on promotion, service, maintenance, and repair.
- The supplier can reduce monitoring costs and more easily manage or enforce compliance with franchise rules and standards when only the supplier's product line is being offered.
- Restricting supply to "full service" dealers avoids those who are not prepared to devote the necessary effort and resources to the product from "free-riding" on the franchised operators' superior product reputation or services or on the manufacturer's marketing efforts, innovation, or costly advertising.
- Prospects for larger returns may also attract dealers with greater resources, skill, or ability.
- If dealers perform more services, such as carrying larger inventories, this may reduce the supplier's selling costs.

Benefits to the **dealer** include:

- If the foregoing factors enhance a product's reputation for quality or superior service, more customers will be drawn to purchase it from the dealer.
- If the dealer is granted an exclusive territory, it will be insulated from other dealers handling the same product, permitting a greater return.
- Retailers "can use exclusives to induce more price competition among their suppliers."[28] For example, the potential for exclusive access to

---

26 This discussion follows many of the points made in Scherer, above note 24.

27 Jonathan M Jacobson, "Exclusive Dealing, Foreclosure, and Consumer Harm" (2002) 70 *Antitrust Law Journal* 311 at 354 [Jacobson].

28 Steven C Salop, "The Raising Rivals' Cost Foreclosure Paradigm, Conditional Pricing Practices, and the Flawed Incremental Price-Cost Test" (2017) 81 *Antitrust Law Journal* 371 at 395.

shelf space at the retail level (such as at supermarkets) may increase supplier competition for retail shelf space, and this may induce discounts or other concessions granted by suppliers to retailers (to the ultimate benefit of consumers).[29]

Benefits to the **consumer or buyer** include:

- Dealers subject to these restrictions may be capable of providing greater service, information, and customer support. This increased level of service can increase product differentiation, quality, and inter-brand competition.
- Territorial exclusivity may envigorate new competitors if, for example, it permits them to access capable dealers quickly or to build a favourable brand image.
- Suppliers may be willing to ensure that a buyer is provided reliable and secure supply when there is an exclusive purchase commitment.[30] For example, a long-term exclusive contract may justify a supplier investing in production and transportation facilities to ensure that a buyer's needs are met.

In *Canada Pipe*, the respondent manufacturer of cast iron drain pipe cited several of the foregoing factors as a justification for its exclusive dealing practice, including the central rationale, that it permitted it to carry a full line of products of varying sizes and types, to the benefit of distributors and customers alike. The Tribunal held:

> [H]igh volumes allow Bibby to maintain in inventory smaller, less profitable but nevertheless important products. As a result, items that are used less often remain available in the market. This availability serves the interests of distributors and contractors, whether or not they belong to the SDP, and ultimately benefits the consumer. . . .
>
> The Respondent's business argument that Bibby needs to sell a certain volume in all three products to be able to maintain full production of all product lines is valid. There are certainly recognizable advantages in having a reliable source able to manufacture and supply a full line of cast iron pipe DWV products for the Canadian market.[31]

On appeal, the Court of Appeal held that the necessary efficiency-related connection to Bibby's operations had not been established to

---

29 Benjamin Klein & Kevin M Murphy, "Exclusive Dealing Intensifies Competition for Distribution" (2008) 75 *Antitrust Law Journal* 433 at 465–66.

30 Jacobson, above note 27 at 359.

31 *Canada Pipe CCT, above note 2 at paras 212 and 259.*

support a defence.[32] This conclusion has been criticized on the basis that a practice which promotes consumer welfare should be permitted under the business justification defence to abuse of dominance, even if a connection to the respondent's business is not shown.[33] The case nonetheless illustrates how exclusive dealing has the potential to create benefits to all players in the supply chain.

b) Competition Policy Concerns

Where it involves exclusive territories for franchised dealers, **market restriction** reduces or eliminates intrabrand competition—competition between dealers of the same branded product who would otherwise seek customers in each other's territories. Intrabrand effects may be of concern when the product is sold by a dominant supplier possessing market power. As one author put it, "intrabrand competition can be the only game in town. For a unique product like a Harry Potter novel, intrabrand competition can be the primary discipline that keeps consumer prices down."[34] Competition in distribution, for example, can reduce cost and promote efficiency.

Exclusive territories may also increase costs: "costs may be increased if distributors are confined to exclusive territories, as they were in the U.S. soft drink bottling industry, much too small to support operations of minimum optimal scale."[35]

---

32 *Canada Pipe* FCA, above note 2 at para 91:

> [T]he Tribunal's reasons do not establish the requisite efficiency-related link between the SDP and the respondent, and hence do not supply a legitimate explanation for the latter's choice to engage in the impugned conduct, unrelated to an anti-competitive purpose. Without such a link, self-interest remains as the only justification for the SDP which is attributable to the respondent for the purposes of paragraph 79(1)(*b*). The Tribunal thus erred in concluding, on the basis of the reasoning provided in its decision, that the respondent had established a valid business justification for the SDP.

33 See Michael J Trebilcock, "Abuse of Dominance: A Critique of *Canada Pipe*" (2007) *Canadian Competition Record* 1; George Addy, John Bodrug & Charles Tingley, "Abuse of Dominance in Canada: Reflections on 25 Years of Section 79 Enforcement" (2012) 25 *Canadian Competition Law Review* 276 at 289–90; but see Donald G McFetridge, "Economics and Canadian Competition Policy" (2012) 25 *Canadian Competition Law Review* 540 at 580–81.

34 Warren S Grimes, "The Path Forward After Leegin: Seeking Consensus Reform of the Antitrust Law of Vertical Restraints" (2008) 75 *Antitrust Law Journal* 467 at 473.

35 Scherer, above note 24 at 587. Note, however, that the bottling industry has undergone significant consolidation, suggesting this example may no longer apply: US, Federal Trade Commission, *Transformation and Continuity: The U.S. Carbonated Soft Drink Bottling Industry and Antitrust Policy Since 1980* (November

The reduction in intrabrand competition is unlikely to raise competition policy concerns, on the other hand, where interbrand competition is vigorous and capable of influencing price and quality in the intrabrand market. In such circumstances, consumers can move to other products which offer the price or service options that they prefer, creating competitive discipline on the practice in question.

In the European Union, where an objective of its foundational *Treaty* is market integration, reductions in intrabrand competition are given weight even when they may increase interbrand competition.[36] A case dealing with market restriction of internet sales was *Ping Europe Ltd v Competition and Markets Authority*.[37] Ping, the leading manufacturer and distributor of high-end golf clubs in the United Kingdom, placed restrictions on the marketing of its products online. The UK Court of Appeal upheld the finding that the practice was contrary to both Article 101 of the *Treaty on the Functioning of the European Union* and section 2(1) of the UK *Competition Act 1998*.[38] The Court rejected Ping's arguments that, *inter alia*, the restriction on intrabrand competition was necessary to protect the brand image of its products by ensuring proper in-store fitting of clubs and that interbrand competition by other club manufacturers eliminated any competitive prejudice from the practice.

In Canada, in contrast, the Competition Bureau takes the view that restrictions on internet sales may be imposed for pro-competitive reasons, such as to ensure that retailers provide an appropriate level and quality of service that cannot be offered through an online sales channel, or to avoid free-riding. The Bureau's experience is that "when these types of restraints apply to products in respect of which effective competition remains at the supplier and/or retailer level, it is unlikely a restraint will create, preserve or enhance market power . . . or [result in] a substantial prevention or lessening of competition in a market."[39]

1999), online: www.ftc.gov/reports/transformation-continuity-us-carbonated-soft-drink-bottling-industry-antitrust-policy-1980.

36 See Ben Van Rompuy, *Economic Efficiency: The Sole Concern of Modern Antitrust Policy? Nonefficiency Considerations within Article 101* (The Hague: Kluwer Law International; Kluwer Law International, 2012) at 190.

37 *Ping Europe Ltd v Competition and Markets Authority*, [2020] EWCA Civ 13 (CA).

38 *Treaty on the Functioning of the European Union* (25 March 1957), OJ C 326 (entered into force 1 January 1958); *Competition Act 1998* (UK), c 41.

39 Submission by the Competition Bureau of Canada to OECD Directorate for Financial and Enterprise Affairs Competition Committee, *Policy Roundtables: Vertical Restrains for Online Sales* (13 February 2013), DAF/COMP13 at 65, online: www.oecd.org/competition/VerticalRestraintsForOnlineSales2013.pdf.

In the case of **exclusive dealing**, competition concerns arise, for example, when competitors or new entrants have difficulty finding or establishing distributors or dealerships allowing them to maintain or to create their own distribution or retail network: "If distribution systems were unavailable to an entrant, the entrant or potential entrant would have to enter on both the supplier and distribution levels, thus incurring significant extra costs."[40] If entrants are excluded, consumer welfare is reduced as a result of a combination of the reduction of product choice and increased retail prices.[41] While the likelihood of such exclusionary effects has been debated,[42] it has been noted that "most economists recognize that exclusive dealing has the potential to cut off current or potential competitors' access to vital downstream customers to the point of impeding them from competing effectively in the market."[43] These effects suggest a need to carefully scrutinize efficiency-based rationales for exclusivity put forward by suppliers with market power:

> [B]old claims of increased "dealer loyalty" may amount to nothing more than creation of barriers to entry that maintain monopoly prices, rather than leading to product or service improvements that increase total market output and benefit consumers. Thus, it is important to

---

40 Daniel J Gifford & Robert T Kudrle, "Towards a Coherent and Workable Antitrust Policy on Vertical Restraints" (2017) 13 *Journal of Law, Economics & Policy* 55 at 62 [Gifford & Kudrle], citing Thomas G Krattenmaker & Steven C Salop, "Anticompetitive Exclusion: Raising Rivals' Costs to Achieve Power Over Price" (1986) 96 *Yale Law Journal* 209.

41 Bruce Dunlop, Michael Trebilcock & David McQueen, *Canadian Competition Policy: A Legal and Economic Analysis* (Toronto: Canada Law Book, 1987) at 260 [Dunlop, Trebilcock & McQueen].

42 See, e.g., the summary of these arguments, *ibid* at 260–62.

43 A Neil Campbell, "Distribution Freedom: The Evolution of Vertical Distribution Practices under the Competition Act" (2012) 25 *Canadian Competition Law Review* 377 [Campbell], referring to Ilya R Segal & Michael D Whinston, "Naked Exclusion: A Comment" (2000) 90 *American Economic Review* 296. See also Christopher R Leslie, "Antitrust Made (Too) Simple" (2014) 79 *Antitrust Law Journal* 917, referring to the following example from *United States v Dentsply International, Inc*, 399 F3d 181 (3d Cir 2005):

> The *Dentsply* case, however, shows how a monopolist may use exclusive dealing to exclude rivals and to raise price, which . . . necessarily reduces output. In *Dentsply*, a monopolist in the market for artificial teeth precluded dealers from distributing the products of Dentsply's competitors. The Third Circuit held that Dentsply's policy violated Section 2 of the Sherman Act as it artificially excluded rivals, thereby rendering them too small to price discipline Dentsply and allowing the monopolist to raise prices aggressively.

> analyze the efficiency claims on a case-by-case basis, taking market structure into account, rather than assuming their existence.[44]

Such exclusionary effects remain the rationale for these provisions in the *Competition Act*.[45]

A reduction in welfare may also occur from both exclusive dealing and market restriction for those consumers who prefer lower prices over the increased service levels or information that both exclusive dealing and territorial restrictions may permit. This may reduce overall welfare if the loss to those consumers is greater than the welfare increase to consumers who do value the improvement in services which the practice may bring about.[46]

3) Elements of the Practices

a) Exclusive Dealing

The conduct has several components, as set out in sections 77(1) and (2) of the Act:

> (1) For the purposes of this section,
>
> **exclusive dealing** means
>
> (a) any practice whereby a supplier of a product, as a condition of supplying the product to a customer, requires that customer to
>
> (i) deal only or primarily in products supplied by or designated by the supplier or the supplier's nominee, or
>
> (ii) refrain from dealing in a specified class or kind of product except as supplied by the supplier or the nominee, and
>
> (b) any practice whereby a supplier of a product induces a customer to meet a condition set out in subparagraph (a)(i) or (ii) by offering to supply the product to the customer on more favourable terms or conditions if the customer agrees to meet the condition set out in either of those subparagraphs; . . .
>
> (2) Where, on application by the Commissioner or a person granted leave under section 103.1, the Tribunal finds that exclusive dealing . . .

---

44 Steven C Salop, "The Raising Rivals' Cost Foreclosure Paradigm, Conditional Pricing Practices, and the Flawed Incremental Price-Cost Test" (2017) 81 *Antitrust Law Journal* 371 at 396.

45 See the Restrictive Trade Practices Commission's *TBA Report*, above note 7.

46 See Stephen Martin, *Industrial Economics, Economic Analysis and Public Policy* (MacMillan: New York, 1988) at 460 [Martin]; William S Comanor, "Vertical Price-Fixing, Vertical Market Restrictions, and the New Antitrust Policy" (1985) 98 *Harvard Law Review* 983 at 990–92.

> because it is engaged in by a major supplier of a product in a market or because it is widespread in a market, is likely to
> (a) impede entry into or expansion of a firm in a market,
> (b) impede introduction of a product into or expansion of sales of a product in a market, or
> (c) have any other exclusionary effect in a market,
>
> with the result that competition is or is likely to be lessened substantially, the Tribunal may make an order directed to all or any of the suppliers against whom an order is sought prohibiting them from continuing to engage in that exclusive dealing or tied selling and containing any other requirement that, in its opinion, is necessary to overcome the effects thereof in the market or to restore or stimulate competition in the market.

The five main elements set out in the section are discussed in turn below.

i) Practice

As in the case of abuse of dominance, there must be a "practice," i.e., not an isolated act.[47]

ii) Requirement or Inducement

Under section 77(1)(a) and (b), exclusive dealing is defined as a practice whereby a supplier of a product

- "requires" a customer to fulfill certain conditions for supplying the product; or
- "induces" a customer to meet those conditions by offering to supply the product "on more favourable terms and conditions."

iii) Conditions

The conditions in question are either

- to "deal only or primarily in" the supplier's products or designated products; or
- to "refrain from dealing in" a class or kind of product except as supplied by the supplier or the supplier's nominee.[48]

---

47 *Canada (Director of Investigation and Research) v NutraSweet Co* (1990), 32 CPR (3d) 1 (CCT) at para 163 [*NutraSweet*]: "The Director submits that the same definition of 'practice' as holds for sections 78 and 79 should apply here (something other than an isolated act). The Tribunal accepts that this is an appropriate approach."

48 *Competition Act*, above note 1, ss 77(1)(a)(i) & (ii).

In *NutraSweet*, the Tribunal held that the mere presence of an exclusivity clause in a contract did not make this a condition of supply. It held that in "an allegation of exclusive dealing it is the circumstances in which the particular terms of supply were agreed upon that are critical"; given the use of the term "requires," the supplier must have refused to supply the product unless the exclusivity clause was agreed to. It found "that there is no evidence on the record that customers were refused or threatened with a refusal of aspartame supply if they did not enter into an exclusive contract."[49] On the other hand, with respect to reference in the section to a supplier who "induces" a buyer, the respondent NutraSweet (NSC) conceded that it had provided inducements to exclusivity in the form of various financial incentives. The Tribunal held "the customers clearly agreed to deal only or primarily in the products of NSC and in return received various rebates whose existence depends on exclusive use of NutraSweet brand aspartame."[50] This was held to satisfy the inducement requirement of section 77.

Similarly, the inducement provided by discounts tied to exclusive sourcing of cast iron pipe from the respondent led the Tribunal in *Canada Pipe* to find that section 77(1) had been satisfied.[51]

The requirements that the customer "*deal* only" or "refrain from *dealing*" in certain products means that the customer must be someone who "deals" in the market — i.e., supplies products to another person (for example, a distributor, wholesaler, or retailer). The section therefore does not apply to exclusive arrangements between suppliers and end consumers or end users.[52] Such exclusive practices may, however, be considered under the abuse of dominance provisions.[53]

iv) Market Structure

For the section to apply, exclusive dealing must be "engaged in by a major supplier" or be "widespread in a market."[54]

In *Canada (Director of Investigation and Research) v Bombardier Ltd*, the respondent manufacturer required its dealers to sell only its brand of snowmobile and admitted to having terminated the contracts of dealers who had breached this requirement. The RTPC heard the application,

49 *NutraSweet*, above note 47 at para 160.

50 *Ibid* at para 162.

51 *Canada Pipe CCT, above note 2 at para 279.*

52 The section therefore does not apply, for example, to "requirements contracts." See Michael J Trebilcock et al, *The Law and Economics of Canadian Competition Policy* (Toronto: University of Toronto Press, 2003) at 444–45 and n 16.

53 See, e.g., *Canada (Competition Act, Director of Investigation and Research) v The D&B Companies of Canada Ltd* (1995), 64 CPR (3d) 216 (CCT).

54 *Competition Act*, above note 1, s 77(2).

and had little difficulty finding that Bombardier was a major supplier. The company had a North American market share at the manufacturing level of 30 percent. It had a 60 percent share at the distribution level in Quebec and the Maritimes, 40 percent in Ontario, and a "strong presence" in markets at the retail level in numerous local areas. The Tribunal set out the test for major supplier which has been applied in subsequent cases:[55]

> A major or important supplier is one whose actions are taken to have an appreciable or significant impact on the markets where it sells.[56]

The RTPC held further that a firm's market share is a good indicator of its importance, along with characteristics such as its "financial strength and record as an innovator," and noted that other factors will "vary from industry to industry."[57]

The reference to the practice being "widespread in a market" opens the door to applying the section simultaneously to several firms which adopt exclusive dealing as a common practice even if none of them have significant market share individually. The section does not require that such adoption be the subject of an explicit or tacit agreement—simply that it be "widespread." This suggests the section could be used to address the application of parallel exclusive arrangements as a "facilitating practice" in concentrated markets, where it has the effect of excluding competitors or limiting new entry.[58]

v) Effects on Competition

Anti-competitive practices are evaluated on their ability to

1) impede entry into or expansion of a firm in a market;
2) impede introduction of a product into or expansion of sales of a product in a market; or
3) have any other exclusionary effect in a market.

For a remedy, the result of the practice must be that competition is or is likely to be lessened substantially.[59]

In *Bombardier*, the foregoing elements were considered together, on the basis that:

> Whether exclusive dealing by a supplier impedes expansion or entry of competitors in the market is most easily and meaningfully considered

55 See, e.g., *NutraSweet*, above note 47 at para 165.

56 *Canada (Director of Investigation and Research) v Bombardier Ltd* (1980), 53 CPR (2d) 47 at 223 (RPTC) [*Bombardier*].

57 *Ibid.*

58 See the discussion of this issue under "Joint Dominance" in Chapter 7, Section D(1).

59 *Competition Act*, above note 1, s 77(2).

as part of the determination of whether there is or is likely to be a substantial lessening of competition as a result of the practice.[60]

On the facts, the RTPC concluded that Bombardier's exclusive dealing had not substantially lessened competition. Competing snowmobile manufacturers such as Yamaha had been able to increase their market shares over time, and "overcome any barriers to expansion . . . created by Bombardier's exclusive dealing policy."[61] This finding was bolstered by evidence that entry at the retail level was easy, that other firms had been able to recruit snowmobile dealers, and that, as there was a high turnover rate among dealers, competing suppliers had a choice among them.[62]

The test for "substantially lessening of competition" is the same as that for the abuse of dominance provisions.[63] The test under those provisions employs a "but for" framework, to compare the level of competition in the presence of the practice with the level of competition that would have existed (in the past, present, or future) in its absence, and then to determine whether the lessening of competition, if any, is "substantial."[64] The measure of substantiality is the impact of the practice on preserving or adding to the market power of the major supplier whose practice is at issue.

In the United States, the degree of competitive foreclosure — the percentage of the market subject to the exclusivity restriction in question — screens whether a case is viable, but "[a]bsent a viable theory, supported by evidence, that customer or supplier foreclosure will affect price, output, quality, or choice, even the highest levels of foreclosure provide no basis for a claim."[65] This suggests that the law in both

60 *Bombardier*, above note 56 at 224.

61 *Ibid* at 229.

62 *Ibid* at 227–29.

63 *NutraSweet*, above note 47 at para 169.

64 *Canada Pipe FCA, above note 2 at para 37; Tervita Corp v Canada (Commissioner of Competition)*, [2015] 1 SCR 161 at para 50.

65 Jacobson, above note 27 at 362; *McWane, Inc v FTC*, 783 F3d 814, 840 (11th Cir 2015). Jonathan M Jacobson, "Vertical Mergers: Is It Time to Move the Ball?" (2019) 33 *Antitrust* 6 at 8: "one would expect to see at least 40 percent of the secondary market foreclosed before inferring competitive harm, with potentially lower shares if the acquiring primary market firm is a monopolist; and, even then, consumers would not be harmed absent barriers to entry into, and limited choices available in, the secondary market." Gifford & Kudrle, above note 40 at 61: "Some cases have indicated that foreclosure will become unlawful when, *inter alia*, the foreclosure denies entrants or other rivals the minimum viable scale required to operate in a concentrated market."

jurisdictions has substantially converged, given that the Canadian test similarly turns on the impact on market power.

b) Market Restriction

Sections 77(1) and (3) define market restriction and remedy.

> (1) For the purposes of this section,
>
> **market restriction** means any practice whereby a supplier of a product, as a condition of supplying the product to a customer, requires that customer to supply any product only in a defined market, or exacts a penalty of any kind from the customer if he supplies any product outside a defined market; . . .
>
> (3) Where, on application by the Commissioner or a person granted leave under section 103.1, the Tribunal finds that market restriction, because it is engaged in by a major supplier of a product or because it is widespread in relation to a product, is likely to substantially lessen competition in relation to the product, the Tribunal may make an order directed to all or any of the suppliers against whom an order is sought prohibiting them from continuing to engage in market restriction and containing any other requirement that, in its opinion, is necessary to restore or stimulate competition in relation to the product.

Market restriction is thus a practice whereby a supplier, as a condition of supplying the product, requires the customer to supply the product only in a defined market, or exacts a penalty for supply outside a defined market.[66] The condition is different from exclusive dealing, and there is no inducement aspect.

The other elements are similar to exclusive dealing. The major supplier/widespread in a market requirements are the same, and the anti-competitive effect element is identical, except there is no reference to the three exclusionary effects. This makes sense, given that market restriction limits the firm from selling outside a geographic territory and thus limits intrabrand competition, but it does not stop that firm from selling other firms' branded products. It therefore cannot have a direct exclusionary effect on interbrand competition. Consistent with the economic view of the practice discussed above, the section only applies where a single supplier is so dominant that there is potential for market power to be affected by interbrand competition.

Perhaps because of its limited scope, there have been few applications before the Tribunal alleging the practice, and no applications by

66 *Competition Act*, above note 1, s 77(1).

the Commissioner. In *Coretti v Bureau de la Sécurité Privée and Garda World Security Corporation*,[67] a private application for leave under section 103.1, the applicant alleged he had been unable to enter the Quebec market for security services due to, *inter alia*, a practice of market restriction whereby he could not supply security services unless he joined Garda. The Tribunal held that the supporting affidavit material was "silent as to the alleged requirement or penalty exacted" in respect of the alleged market restriction and dismissed the application for leave.[68]

c) Defences and Exceptions

Sections 77(4), (5), and (6) create a number of exceptions, some very specific and targeted:

> (4) The Tribunal shall not make an order under this section where, in its opinion,
>
> (a) exclusive dealing or market restriction is or will be engaged in only for a reasonable period of time to facilitate entry of a new supplier of a product into a market or of a new product into a market, . . . and
>
> No order made under this section applies in respect of exclusive dealing, market restriction or tied selling between or among entities that are affiliated.
>
> (5) For the purposes of subsection (4), in addition to the circumstances specified in paragraph 2(2)(a) or (b) under which two entities are affiliated, an entity is affiliated with another entity in respect of any agreement between them in which one of them grants to the other the right to use a trademark or trade name to identify the business of the grantee, if
>
> (a) the business is related to the sale or distribution, in accordance with a marketing plan or system prescribed substantially by the grantor, of a multiplicity of products obtained from competing sources of supply and a multiplicity of suppliers; and
>
> (b) no one product dominates the business.
>
> (6) For the purposes of subsection (4) in its application to market restriction, where there is an agreement whereby one person (the "first" person) supplies or causes to be supplied to another person (the "second" person) an ingredient or ingredients that the second person processes by the addition of labour and material into an article of food

67 *Coretti v Bureau de la Sécurité Privée and Garda World Security Corporation*, [2019] CCTD No 4 [*Coretti*].

68 *Ibid* at para 13.

> or drink that he then sells in association with a trademark that the first person owns or in respect of which the first person is a registered user, the first person and the second person are deemed, in respect of the agreement, to be affiliated.

In summary, these provisions provide that the section does not apply to

- new entrants who rely on exclusive dealing or market restriction for a reasonable period of time to permit their entry or to assist in introducing a new product (section 77(4));
- affiliates (within the meaning of sections 2(2)(a) and (b) of the Act) that engage in the practice among themselves (section 77(4), trailing phrase);
- arrangements for product distribution of multiple products collectively under a common trademark or trade name (section 77(5) has been termed the "Canadian Tire exemption"[69]); or
- for market restriction only, arrangements for product distribution such as those used by soft drink bottlers (section 77(6) has been termed the "soft drink bottlers' exemption"[70]).

d) Remedies for Exclusive Dealing and Market Restriction

If the elements of the section are satisfied, the Tribunal has the discretionary power to prohibit the practices (it "may"), and to issue an order "containing any other requirement that, in its opinion, is necessary to overcome the effects thereof in the market or to restore or stimulate competition in the market." In *NutraSweet*, which was also brought as an abuse of dominance case, the Tribunal issued an order prohibiting exclusivity contracts with Canadian customers for the supply of aspartame.[71] The boundaries of the other remedial authority available to the Tribunal under the section have yet to be tested.

The same interim order authority available under abuse of dominance pursuant to section 103.3 is available under section 77. The provision requires that the Commissioner show that a person is likely to be eliminated as a competitor, or that a person is likely to suffer a significant loss of market share, revenue, or other irremediable harm.[72] The order is for short duration—ten days—but can be extended for up to two

---

69 Gordon Kaiser, "The New Competition Law: Stage One" (1976) 1 *Canadian Business Law Journal* 147 at 163.

70 Bruce C McDonald, "Reviewable Marketing Practices in Canada" (1977) 22 *Antitrust Bulletin* 801 at 819.

71 *NutraSweet*, above note 47 at para 227; *Competition Act*, above note 1, s 77(2) & (3).

72 *Ibid*, s 103.3(2).

periods of thirty-five days on application of the Commissioner.[73] Finally, again as in the case of abuse of dominance, pursuant to section 104, the Tribunal "may issue any interim order that it considers appropriate" where an application has been made under section 77. The common law injunction test applies to the making of such orders.[74]

D. TIED SELLING

1) Nature of the Practice

Tied selling involves a seller requiring or inducing a customer to take, use, or distribute an additional product or products (the "tied product(s)") along with another product (the "tying product") that the customer wants (**Figure 8.4**). An example from an early case was a practice by United Shoe Machinery Company of leasing shoe manufacturing equipment only if lessees leased the company's complete range of shoe manufacturing equipment. The practice became the subject of an inquiry, but no enforcement proceedings.[75]

FIGURE 8.3. Under tied selling, a supplier requires or induces a customer of the tying product to take the tied product as well

Tied selling is another practice that is prevalent in the economy, but that seldom raises competition policy issues. Shoes are sold with laces, automobiles with tires and engines, and computers with an operating system already installed. In these situations, the tied product is a complement, i.e., something used in conjunction with the tying product. However, that need not be the case—the tied product may be an unrelated product. Telecommunications companies, for example, offer "bundles" of services—e.g., cable TV, wireless, home phone—at lower prices if they are acquired together.

73 *Ibid*, s 103.3(5).

74 *Ibid*, s 104(1).

75 *United Shoe Machinery Co v Laurendeau* (1912), 2 DLR 77 (Que KB (AD)); see Gordon E Kaiser & Ian Nielsen-Jones, "Recent Developments in Canadian Law: Competition Law" (1986) 18 *Ottawa Law Review* 401 at 453.

Vertical or Horizontal?

While tying is "vertical" in the sense that it is typically imposed by a supplier on market participants, such as distributors or end customers, further down the chain of supply, its anti-competitive impact, if any, is felt in a market in which the supplier competes: that is, the market for the tied product. Thus, unlike other vertical practices, such as territorial restraints and exclusive dealing arrangements that result in vertical foreclosure, "[t]ying arrangements . . . can create horizontal foreclosure" in a market in which the supplier or manufacturer directly competes. [Kurt A Strasser, "An Antitrust Policy for Tying Arrangements" (1985) 34 *Emory LJ* 253 at 268.]

2) Economic Effects of the Practice

Tied selling has been the subject of a prodigious body of economic and legal literature, principally in the United States, authored since the 1950s. The Chicago School proponents have vigorously argued that tying cannot be motivated by monopolistic purposes, and in fact is usually pro-competitive or efficiency enhancing.[76] Leading Chicago thinker Robert Bork even wrote that "there is no viable theory of a means by which tying arrangements injure competition" in a scathing critique of the American law's treatment of the practice as *per se* illegal.[77] On the other hand, the proponents of the view that tied selling can permit a monopolist to extend its market power into the tied product market—the so-called leveraging theory—argued that the Chicago approach made simplistic or unrealistic assumptions and was too static or incomplete. Those Post-Chicago theorists concluded that tied selling is, in fact, anti-competitive in certain circumstances.[78] The Chicago critique succeeded, however, in convincing the US Supreme Court to moderate the *per se* treatment. The controversy surrounding the economics, and the

---

76 See, e.g., Ward S Bowman Jr, "Tying Arrangements and the Leverage Problem" (1957) 67 *Yale Law Journal* 19 [Bowman].

77 Robert H Bork, *The Antitrust Paradox: A Policy at War with Itself* (New York: Basic Books, 1978) at 372 [Bork].

78 See, e.g., Louis Kaplow, "Extension of Monopoly Power through Leverage" (1985) 85 *Columbia Law Review* 515; Kurt A Strasser, "An Antitrust Policy for Tying Arrangements" (1985) 34 *Emory Law Journal* 253 [Strasser]; Michael D Whinston, "Tying, Foreclosure and Exclusion" (1990) 80 *American Economic Review* 837; Christopher R Leslie, "Cutting through Tying Theory with Occam's Razor: A Simple Explanation of Tying Arrangements" (2004) 78 *Tulane Law Review* 727 [Leslie].

appropriate legal treatment, of the practice is likely to continue as long as the *per se* rule endures.[79]

What follows provides an overview of some of the major arguments or theories on both sides of the debate concerning the character of this practice. In Canada, we have adopted a more flexible test than the US *per se* rule,[80] one that permits parties to bring their arguments and theories forward in the context of a particular case to justify why the practice does or does not lessen competition. Thus, there remains latitude in Canada to examine the pros and cons of the practice on the facts of any case brought forward.

a) Benefits of Tied Selling

Complementary products are usually sold together because it is efficient to do so, and/or because such sales satisfy consumer preferences. Selling cars without engines would increase manufacturing and transactions costs, delay production, and reduce consumer satisfaction. Tied sales may also promote economies of scale in joint production, distribution, and marketing. For example, tying repair contracts to the sale of a product can reduce the costs of marketing and negotiating them separately.[81]

Tied selling may also protect product brand name and reputation where the use of two products together—e.g., truck gear boxes and specialized gear fluid—is necessary to ensure the proper performance of the product. It may be more costly to monitor a customer's correct use of two separate products than to impose a tying requirement.[82]

Franchise tie-ins—the requirement that a franchisee buy all of its products from the franchisor—can similarly be connected to product quality and reputation. For example, Tim Hortons franchisees are required to source all of their supplies and ingredients from Tim Hortons or its designated suppliers, as well as to adhere to certain quality standards.[83] As well as ensuring quality, such requirements create

---

79 "Despite decades of scholarship and hundreds of published opinions, tying law remains a confusing and controversial area of antitrust jurisprudence." Leslie, above note 78 at 2136.

80 As will be seen below, the *per se* rule has been narrowed by more recent jurisprudence in the United States.

81 Dunlop, Trebilcock & McQueen, above note 41 at 257.

82 The validity of this rationale has been questioned: "A court should accept this justification for tying only when there is true technological interdependence and good reason to believe that buyers will be unable or unwilling to perceive it and act in their own self-interest. In other cases, the justification is more likely offered as a smokescreen for other motives or effects." Strasser, above note 78 at 262.

83 *Fairview Donut Inc v The TDL Group Corp, 2012 ONSC 1252 at para 28, aff'd on other grounds, 2012 ONCA 867:*

product uniformity across all the franchised outlets so that customers are offered an identical experience wherever the product is purchased. Requiring franchisees to purchase non-interchangeable product-specific assets also enhances a franchisee's financial commitment to the brand and may reduce the franchisor's costs of enforcing product standards.[84]

Firms may use tying to implement price discrimination—charging different customers different prices with different markups—in a manner that expands output of the tying product (which can be beneficial). In certain circumstances, the tied product can be used as a "metering device" to measure consumer demand and gain a higher return from valued consumers. For example, if the vendor of a copying machine (the tying product) charges a supracompetitive price for the tied product (the ink or paper required to be used with the copier), "the subsequent purchases of the tied product measure the intensity of use of the tying product. Because the tied product is supracompetitively priced, high-volume users are effectively charged a higher price for the tying product."[85] Such price discrimination is, however, ambiguous in terms of its welfare implications and thus this rationale remains controversial.[86]

b) Competition Concerns

Tying can reduce consumer choice when it forces a purchaser to take a product they do not want or would have preferred to source elsewhere. This economic coercion has been cited as a concern by the US Supreme Court:

> Our cases have concluded that the essential characteristic of an invalid tying arrangement lies in the seller's exploitation of its control over the tying product to force the buyer into the purchase of a tied product that the buyer either did not want at all, or might have preferred to purchase elsewhere on different terms. When such "forcing" is present, competition on the merits in the market for the tied item is restrained and the *Sherman Act* is violated.[87]

> [L]ike most franchise operations—the franchisee is required to abide by a set of rules and procedures, to purchase all supplies and ingredients from Tim Hortons or from its designated suppliers, and to offer for sale only products that have been approved by Tim Hortons. As one might expect, the franchise agreement provides that the franchisee must adhere to rigorous standards designed to protect and enhance the Tim Hortons brand.

84 Dunlop, Trebilcock & McQueen, above note 41 at 257.

85 Christopher R Leslie, "Patent Tying, Price Discrimination, and Innovation" (2011) 77 *Antitrust Law Journal* 811 at 814.

86 Dunlop, Trebilcock & McQueen, above note 41 at 255–57.

87 *Jefferson Parish Hospital District No 2 v Hyde, 466 US 2 (1984) at 12 [Jefferson Parish]*.

A central objection to tying, supporting its *per se* treatment as anti-competitive under American law, is the so-called leveraging theory (**Figure 8.4**). Under this theory, tying permits a seller with substantial market power in the tying good (e.g., patented dispensing machines for salt) to extend its monopoly power into the tied good market (e.g., salt[88]) by requiring that the purchasers of the former acquire all supplies of the latter from the vendor as well. The US Supreme Court held in *International Salt Co v US* that it is "unreasonable, *per se*, to foreclose competitors from any substantial market."[89]

FIGURE 8.4. The leveraging theory of tying: the seller of a tying product with market uses its market power to induce the customer to take a second product in a market where the former does not, but for the tying, possess such power

As noted above, the *per se* rule against tying came under attack from the American Chicago School proponents starting in the late 1950s.[90] A purported weakness in the leveraging theory—the "single monopoly profit" view—was cited by the Supreme Court in *Jefferson Parish Hospital District No 2 v Hyde* in 1984. This view holds that, at least in some circumstances (such as where the products are complements used in fixed proportions), tying cannot permit a greater overall return for the supplier possessing market power in the tying product market if the tied product market is competitive. The Supreme Court held:

> The existence of a tied product normally does not increase the profit that the seller power can extract from sales of the *tying* product. A seller with a monopoly on flour, for example, cannot increase the profit it can extract from flour consumers simply by forcing them to buy sugar along with their flour. Counterintuitive though that assertion may seem, it is easily demonstrated and widely accepted.[91]

While the Court maintained the view that tied selling was *per se* unlawful, it imposed three conditions on the application of the *per se* rule: "First, the seller must have power in the tying-product

88 *International Salt Co v United States*, 332 US 392 (1947).
89 *Ibid* at 396.
90 See, e.g., Bowman, above note 76.
91 *Jefferson Parish*, above note 87 at 35 citing Bork, above note 77 at 372–74, and Phillip Areeda, *Antitrust Analysis*, 3d ed (Boston: Little Brown, 1981) at 735. Re fixed proportions, see *Tele-Direct*, above note 3 at paras 427–31.

market. . . . Second, there must be a substantial threat that the tying seller will acquire market power in the tied-product market. . . . Third, there must be a coherent economic basis for treating the tying and tied products as distinct." We will examine the third requirement below in the context of section 77, as it has been largely adopted in Canada. The effect of these three requirements was to substantially soften the *per se* rule. Nonetheless, the US Supreme Court has retained the leveraging rationale for tying.[92] It has been pointed out that the "single monopoly profit" objection does not address the possibility of exclusion of competitors in the market for the tied product by cutting those competitors off from potential customers who are forced to take the product by the practice:

> The removal of a significant proportion of end user sales from the [tied product] market [due to tying] can seriously impair the ability of others to make competitive sales in the market. As the unrestricted proportion of the tied market shrinks, sellers have fewer potential buyers to pursue, and the markets may become so thin that they cease to function competitively.[93]

The Court in *Jefferson Parrish* held:

> The antitrust law is properly concerned with tying when, for example, the flour monopolist threatens to use its market power to acquire additional power in the sugar market, perhaps by driving out competing sellers of sugar, or by making it more difficult for new sellers to enter the sugar market.[94]

It has been noted that the American test "retains the harshest element of *per se* rules in antitrust: it assumes an anticompetitive effect without proof that the actual tie-in before the court has, in fact, diminished competition."[95] In contrast, while the leveraging theory is reflected in the language of section 77 of the *Competition Act*, which refers to the potential exclusion of competition by virtue of the practice, the section employs a competitive effects test rather than treating tied selling as *per se* unlawful.

---

92 See, e.g.: "The Court has held many times that power gained through some natural and legal advantage such as a patent, copyright or business acumen can give rise to liability if a seller exploits his dominant position in one market to expand his empire into the next." *Eastman Kodak Co v Image Technical Services, Inc*, 504 US 451 (1992) at 479, n 29 [*Eastman Kodak*] (quoting *Times-Picayune Publishing Co v United States*, 345 US 594 (1953) at 611).

93 Strasser, above note 78 at 269.

94 *Jefferson Parish*, above note 87 at 36–37.

95 Leslie, above note 78 at 735.

A final concern about tying, albeit one that is seldom observed in practice, is that it can be used to avoid governmental price regulation. If a regulatory agency has jurisdiction over the tying product, but not the tied product, and does not prevent the tie, the regulated company can exploit its market power in the unregulated product market by imposing a tie and raising the price of that product. It has been opined however that "[s]upervision in the regulatory process more effectively addresses this problem than does tying law."[96]

c) Elements of the Practice

Tied selling has several components similar to those for exclusive dealing which are set out in subsections 77(1) and (2) of the Act:

> . . . **tied selling** means
>
> (a) any practice whereby a supplier of a product, as a condition of supplying the product (the "tying" product) to a customer, requires that customer to
>
> (i) acquire any other product from the supplier or the supplier's nominee, or
>
> (ii) refrain from using or distributing, in conjunction with the tying product, another product that is not of a brand or manufacture designated by the supplier or the nominee, and
>
> (b) any practice whereby a supplier of a product induces a customer to meet a condition set out in subparagraph (a)(i) or (ii) by offering to supply the tying product to the customer on more favourable terms or conditions if the customer agrees to meet the condition set out in either of those subparagraphs.
>
> (2) Where, on application by the Commissioner or a person granted leave under section 103.1, the Tribunal finds that exclusive dealing or tied selling, because it is engaged in by a major supplier of a product in a market or because it is widespread in a market, is likely to
>
> (a) impede entry into or expansion of a firm in a market,
>
> (b) impede introduction of a product into or expansion of sales of a product in a market, or
>
> (c) have any other exclusionary effect in a market,
>
> with the result that competition is or is likely to be lessened substantially, the Tribunal may make an order directed to all or any of the suppliers against whom an order is sought prohibiting them from continuing to engage in that exclusive dealing or tied selling and containing any other requirement that, in its opinion, is necessary to

96 Strasser, above note 78 at 281.

overcome the effects thereof in the market or to restore or stimulate competition in the market.

i) Practice

As in the case of exclusive dealing and market restriction, there must be a "practice," i.e., not an isolated act.

ii) Requirement or Inducement

A "supplier of a product, as a condition of supplying the product" (the **tying product**) "to a customer"

- **requires**, or
- "**induces** a customer . . . by offering to supply the **tying product** to the customer on more favourable terms and conditions."

iii) Conditions

The conditions in question are either

- to "**acquire** any other product" (the **tied product**) "from the supplier or the supplier's nominee"; or
- to "**refrain from using or distributing**, in conjunction with the tying product, another product that is not of a brand or manufacture designated by the supplier or the nominee."

In *Canada (Director of Investigation and Research) v BBM Bureau of Measurement*, both a requirement and an inducement were found. BBM compiled data from audience surveys of radio listeners and television viewers which it used to calculate the audience shares or ratings of radio and television stations and programming. The customers for this information were advertisers and advertising agencies, who used it in making decisions on media purchases. BBM was the sole supplier of radio data, and the dominant provider of television data. The only competitor for the latter product was Nielsen. The RTPC found that BBM had tied the sale of radio data (the tying product) to television data (the tied product). Initially, the tie was via a *requirement*—both products were *only* made available together for one fee. BBM then changed its policy to permit separate acquisition of the two types of data, but provided steep discounts if both products were taken together. This was found to involve tied selling as an *inducement*.[97]

In *BBM*, there were clearly two separate products: radio and television data. In tied selling, distinguishing the two products is not always so clear. In *Tele-Direct*, the question of what constitutes one product or

97 *Canada (Director of Investigation and Research) v BBM Bureau of Measurement* (1981), 60 CPR (2d) 26 (RTPC) [*BBM*].

separate products was at issue. This is a key question, because if there is only one product, there can be no tying.

Tele-Direct published Yellow Pages telephone directories on behalf of the major phone companies. Businesses placing ads and listings in the directories could receive free services from Tele-Direct's own staff (such as advice, guidance, and artwork—advertising services) if they placed an ad (i.e., acquired advertising space). Some businesses, especially those such as banks or restaurant chains, placed ads in numerous directories in major centres across the country, and used advertising agencies to provide advice on when and how to place ads. These advertisers did not use Tele-Direct's in-house salespeople. The customers would receive a discount from Tele-Direct (of 15 to 25 percent) if they used an agency, but only if their advertising order qualified under certain criteria based on the number of directories and size of ads. When Tele-Direct narrowed the criteria by increasing the number of directories required to obtain a commission discount, advertising agencies complained that they were being squeezed out of the market because customers would not hire the agencies when Tele-Direct's services were free. They argued that non-commissionable customers going to agencies were being forced to pay twice for services by paying the agency fee plus the full Tele-Direct ad price, which included the "free" service component. They said that those customers would not choose agencies' services in such circumstances.

An application was filed with the Tribunal, alleging that Tele-Direct was tying space to service by offering free services if a customer took both products together, at least for non-commissionable accounts. Tele-Direct argued that space and service were simply one product: advertising in a directory.

The Tribunal found that advertising space and advertising services were separate products, at least in some circumstances. In doing so, it adopted the following test developed by the majority of the US Supreme Court in *Jefferson Parish*:

> [N]o tying arrangement can exist unless there is a sufficient demand for the purchase of anesthesiological services separate from hospital services to identify a distinct product market in which it is efficient to offer anesthesiological services separately from hospital services.[98]

The Tribunal held that this test involved two questions:

1) Is there a significant set of advertisers who actually want the items separated?
2) If so, is it efficient to separate the products?[99]

---

98 *Jefferson Parish, above note 87 at 21–22.*

99 *Tele-Direct*, above note 3 at para 353.

On the facts in *Tele-Direct*, the Tribunal found that larger, multi-directory advertisers did demand advertising services as a separate product, and often used advertising agencies, given that their needs were more complex, including not only advice and creative services, but also "help in administration and in assuring uniformity of message."[100] On the other hand, smaller advertisers with an ad in only one, or a handful of directories did not demand separate services.

Turning to the second question, efficiency of unbundling, the Tribunal found that advertising agencies lack interest in customers billing less than $10,000 to $50,000 in annual orders in directories, suggesting Tele-Direct's internal sales force was more efficient in serving those clients with fewer advertising needs. The Tribunal found that determining a "dividing line" was difficult, but concluded: "we find that space and services constitute two products down to the six-market level and a single product below that level."[101] In other words, for customers placing ads in six or more "markets" (corresponding to certain geographic areas defined by Tele-Direct[102]), space and service were separate products.

The Tribunal also concluded that offering free services constituted a tie for customers at or over the six-market or "local" threshold. It held that a "condition" did not need to be an express contractual term to create coercion; this may "also be equally present where there is a discount or other advantage that constitutes an inducement to acquire the two from the same source."[103] It found that "the lack of commission . . . operated as a powerful inducement to acquire both space and services from Tele-Direct."[104]

A final point on these elements of the practice is that tied selling, unlike exclusive dealing and market restriction, can apply to "conditions and inducements" for tying imposed on end customers, not just distributors or retailers. That is because the section refers to a "customer" rather than using the word "dealer" (as for the other two practices under section 77). *BBM* was an example of tying being imposed upon end users of radio and TV data: advertisers and advertising agencies.

---

100 *Ibid* at para 499.

101 *Ibid* at para 506.

102 "Canada was divided into 19 markets, with six in Quebec and seven in Ontario. The entire United States constituted a single 20th market. If the account qualified and the agency provided completed artwork, Tele-Direct would pay a 15 percent commission on the account." *Ibid* at para 326.

103 *Ibid* at para 519.

104 *Ibid* at para 522.

iv) Market Structure

For the section to apply, tied selling must be "engaged in by a **major supplier**" or be "**widespread in a market**."[105]

The test from Bombardier is again applicable:

> A major or important supplier is one whose actions are taken to have an appreciable or significant impact on the markets where it sells.[106]

This requirement was easily satisfied in *BBM* and *Tele-Direct*. BBM was the only supplier of radio data and the dominant supplier of TV data; hence clearly a major supplier in both markets.[107] Similarly, *Tele-Direct* had more than 96 percent of telephone directory revenues in Ontario and Quebec and more than 80 percent even in markets where it faced its most significant competition.[108]

v) Effects on Competition

For a remedy to be available, the practice must be likely to: (1) impede entry into or expansion of a firm in a market, (2) impede introduction of a product into or expansion of sales of a product in a market, or (3) have any other exclusionary effect in a market. The result is that competition is or is likely to be lessened substantially.[109]

In *BBM*, the RTPC found that the tie between radio and TV data created an "insurmountable" barrier to entry in the data market because of the "severe competitive disadvantage" Nielsen was under[110] given that any customer needing both kinds of data was likely to go to BBM for both and take advantage of the substantial discount. The facts bore this out: among customers who purchased both kinds of data, BBM had an 88.5 percent market share.[111] The case provides an illustration of leveraging in practice: BBM (using its monopoly in radio data) was able to raise the barriers for Nielsen and others seeking to enter the TV data market by locking in a large share of available customers using tying. The RTPC found that producing broadcast data involves high fixed costs, and that Nielsen's financial records revealed that it was unable to break even, and could not continue in the TV data market, without a greater share of sales.[112] The suggestion that Nielsen should simply enter the radio data market was rejected by the RTPC:

---

105 *Competition Act*, above note 1, s 77(2).
106 *Bombardier*, above note 56 at 223.
107 *BBM*, above note 97 at 34.
108 *Tele-Direct*, above note 3 at paras 229–31.
109 *Competition Act*, above note 1, s 77(2).
110 *BBM*, above note 97 at 36–37.
111 *Ibid* at 34.
112 *Ibid* at 32 and 36.

> It is no answer to say that Nielsen is able and free to enter radio data service and challenge BBM's monopoly position in that market. The intention of the statute is to free the market so that the producer of any one product has opportunity to enter and compete on a fair basis.[113]

The need to enter two markets instead of one is, in fact, one of the "textbook" ways in which tied selling is seen as anti-competitive, by raising barriers to entry.[114] *BBM* illustrates how barriers to entry are raised in a market characterized by high fixed costs and featuring a supplier with market power in both the tying and tied product markets.

In *Tele-Direct*, the Tribunal found the nature of demand for advertising space and service meant that Tele-Direct could augment its monopoly power by also controlling service, because dispensing its advice through its own salesforce (rather than permitting agencies to provide advice) could manipulate the customer's relative lack of information and increase the amount of advertising space sold.[115] The Tribunal held that the lack of commission for large accounts had created a tie which affected approximately $30 million worth of advertising business coming from directory advertisers. This was about 50 percent of the value of the market which was then available to advertising agencies. The Tribunal

---

113 *Ibid* at 36.

114 Strasser, above note 78 at 269.

115 The Tribunal held:

> [A]gents tend, compared to Tele-Direct representatives, to be less likely to promote increased expenditures on space, the additional expenditures on advertising services by agency clients (through the purchase of extra advertising, foregoing monthly billing) lead to the substitution of advertising services for advertising space. Furthermore, once it is recognized that there is an issue of the quality and content of advertising services, as indicated by the evidence of advertisers and their willingness to pay more for agents than it would cost them to use Tele-Direct's representatives, even assuming the same expenditure on space using an agent or Tele-Direct, it is difficult to see how advertising services are being consumed in fixed proportions with advertising space.

Tele-Direct, above note 3 at para 429. See also para 430:

> The evidence regarding the activities of consultants also suggests that advertising services and advertising space are not used in fixed proportions, and that they are partial substitutes. The purchase of services from a supplier other than Tele-Direct results in reduced expenditures on space. An example provided by a consultant concerned a very large and apparently inappropriate existing advertisement for a taxi company in the Hamilton area. The existing full page advertisement included a large picture of an airplane and reference to airport service. The consultant (Serge Brouillet of Ad-Vice Communications) determined from his marketing needs analysis for the client that he actually did very little airport business. The changes proposed by the consultant were both less costly and appeared to be more effective.

concluded, "[b]oth in relative and absolute dollar terms, the amount of revenue affected by the tie is undoubtedly sufficient to conclude that there is a substantial lessening of competition."[116] Thus, the Tribunal's assessment of the impact on competition of the practice was focused on the share of the market affected by the tie, rather than on a broader trade-off between the efficiencies or benefits of tying and anti-competitive effect.[117]

d) Defences and Exceptions

Sections 77(4), (5), and (6) create a number of exceptions, some of which are common to exclusive dealing and market restriction and were discussed above.[118] The following two exceptions are, however, only applicable to tied selling:

> (4) The Tribunal shall not make an order under this section where, in its opinion, . . .
>
> (b) tied selling that is engaged in is reasonable having regard to the technological relationship between or among the products to which it applies, or
>
> (c) tied selling that is engaged in by a person in the business of lending money is for the purpose of better securing loans made by that person and is reasonably necessary for that purpose.

Both these exceptions are examples of a pro-competitive or efficiency-enhancing use of tied selling, and the bundling of products serving legitimate business purposes.

---

116 *Ibid* at para 524.

117 Jeffrey Church & Roger Ware, "Abuse of Dominance under the 1986 *Competition Act*" (1998) 13 *Review of Industrial Organization* 85 at 115:

> The economic theory of tying is subtle and complex, but many of those subtleties were not clearly articulated in this case. . . . If space and advertising services are used in fixed proportions to produce a yellow pages ad, then a monopolist in space (TeleDirect) cannot improve their profits by tying. But if space and advertising services are either *imperfect* complements, or substitutes in production, then a monopolist in space (the directory publisher) may increase profits through tying. In the absence of a tie, charging the monopoly price for space will lead the non-integrated sector to substitute advertising services for space. Tying ensures that production is efficient, however it also excludes competing providers of advertising services. The effect on total surplus or welfare is ambiguous. On the one hand production of advertisements is now efficient, but on the other hand, competition has been reduced.

118 Affiliates, including those defined in the "Canadian Tire exemption" are not subject to the section. See above in this chapter at Section C(3)(c).

Section 77(4)(b) was considered in *BBM*. The RTPC rejected BBM's suggestion that radio and TV data were bundled due to a technological relationship, finding:

> Undoubtedly, cost efficiencies and useful technological exchange can be expected to flow from producing two similar products under one roof. However [para](4)(b) applies to the reasonable requirement of the sale of two products together for technological reasons, not to their production. In effect, the section provides a defence or justification of a tied sale on the basis that the reputation of the tying product might be injured or destroyed if the supplier cannot insist on a purchaser using only the tied product in conjunction with it.
>
> In the present instance, there is no suggestion that the reputation or goodwill of either of BBM's reporting services would be damaged by the purchaser not using the other service. Section [77](4)(b) has no application.[119]

In this passage, the RTPC outlines an exception to tying, and that is when it is used to protect the reputation or goodwill of its product. This is one of the well-accepted justifications for tying put forward by economists,[120] and represents a useful extrapolation of the meaning of the exemption, which refers only to the question of a technological relationship.

e) Remedies for Tied Selling

The Tribunal's authority for remedial orders is the same under tied selling as under exclusive dealing and market restriction. The Tribunal may issue an order prohibiting the practices "and containing any other requirement that, in its opinion, is necessary to overcome the effects thereof in the market or to restore or stimulate competition in the market."[121] In *Tele-Direct*, the Tribunal issued an order under which the respondent was "prohibited from continuing to engage in tied selling, namely tying the supply of advertising space by them to the acquisition of advertising services from them, for customers advertising in six, seven and eight markets."[122] The order did not specify how the tie was to be broken; the reasons indicated that either separate pricing of space and service, or a commission of 15 percent for the markets in

---

119 *BBM*, above note 97 at paras 26–27.

120 See, e.g., Bowman, above note 76 at 27–28; Bork, above note 77 at 379–80.

121 See *Competition Act*, above note 1, s 77(2) and above in this chapter at Section C(3)(d).

122 *Tele-Direct*, above note 3 at para 767.

question, would be satisfactory, but left the matter for further direction, if needed.[123]

In *BBM*, the Tribunal simply made an order "prohibiting BBM from continuing to engage in tied selling of both radio audience measurement service and television audience measurement service."[124]

E. REFUSAL TO SUPPLY

1) Background and Nature of the Practice

The Economic Council recommended in 1969 that "refusals to deal, including refusals under franchise arrangements," should be one of the new civil trade practices subject to review on a case-by-case basis by an expert tribunal.[125] No further rationale was provided for including this practice at that time. The *Background Papers* to the 1976 amendments explained that the practice had been the subject of many complaints to the Competition Bureau by businesses which were, in some cases, new entrants, and in others, established players "whose supply lines have been disrupted after developing the market for the product involved."[126] They went on to note that there was no remedy under the previous legislation even though "the withdrawal may have resulted in the ruin of the complaining firm or in a serious reduction in competition in the market."[127]

The section as initially drafted was clearly more concerned with providing a remedy for businesses cut off from supplies than addressing any broader anti-competitive effect. In *Canada (Director of Investigation & Research) v Xerox Canada Inc*, decided under the original section, the Tribunal noted that a purpose listed in section 1.1 of the *Competition Act*, "to ensure that small and medium-sized enterprises have an equitable opportunity to participate in the Canadian economy," was consistent with providing a remedy in the intermediate market being considered, the supply to independent repair services of photocopier parts.[128] This

123 *Ibid* at paras 533–34.

124 *BBM*, above note 97 at para 46.

125 *Interim Report* 1969, above note 11 at 122.

126 Canada, Competition Bureau, Consumer and Corporate Affairs Canada, *Background Papers, Stage I Competition Policy* (1976) at 4.

127 *Ibid*.

128 *Canada (Director of Investigation & Research) v Xerox Canada Inc* (1990), 33 CPR (3d) 83 (CCT) at para 63 [*Xerox Canada*].

focus was criticized by some commentators as inconsistent with the promotion of competition.[129]

In 2002, section 75 was amended to add the requirement that a refusal to supply must have an "adverse effect on competition," a lesser test than the "substantial" effect required for other vertical practices, abuse of dominance, mergers, and anti-competitive agreements.[130] The amendments also provided for a private right of access to the Tribunal in section 75 cases.[131] The reason for the different competition test in the amended section 75 was addressed in the 2000 House Standing Committee Report which preceded the amendments:

> The use of the "adverse effects" test in section 75 is to permit small and medium-sized enterprises the opportunity to have their cases heard in the new private access regime. In the case of a firm with a small market share, a refusal to deal might not "substantially lessen" but still "adversely affect" competition. The requirement to show a "substantial lessening of competition" in a market would be likely to exclude [a remedy] in all but the largest cases.[132]

The creation of private right of action resulted in an increase in litigation under the section. During the twenty-six-year period between 1976 and 2002 only three refusal to supply applications by the Commissioner were considered by the Competition Tribunal in substance,[133] while in the next fifteen years there were more than twenty applications for leave to file refusal to deal cases brought by private parties under section 75. Leave, however, was denied by the Tribunal in a majority of cases.[134] The number of applications filed has slowed over time, perhaps due to the lack of success of applicants in meeting the threshold for leave. The applicable leave test required that they show: (1) that the applicant may have been directly and substantially affected in his business by the

---

129 Zhiqi Chen, Thomas Ross & William T Stanbury, "Refusals to Deal and Aftermarkets" (1998) 13 *Review of Industrial Organization* 131.

130 *An Act to amend the Competition Act and the Competition Tribunal Act*, SC 2002, c 16, s 11.1.

131 *Ibid*, s 12.

132 House of Commons, Standing Committee on Industry, Science and Technology, *A Plan to Modernize Canada's Competition Regime* (April 2002) (Chair: Walt Lastewka) at 3 [*A Plan to Modernize Canada's Competition Regime*].

133 *Xerox Canada*, above note 128; *Chrysler Canada Ltd v Canada (Competition Tribunal)*, [1989] CCTD No 49 [*Chrysler Canada*]; *Canada (Director of Investigation & Research) v Warner Music Canada Ltd*, [1997] CCTD No 53 [*Warner Music Canada*].

134 D Jeffrey Brown, ed, *Competition Act and Commentary* (Markham: LexisNexis, 2016) at 96, reviewing the data to 2016.

alleged practice, and (2) that the practice in question could be subject to an order under the applicable section.[135] One private application that did go to a final hearing, *B-Filer Inc v Bank of Nova Scotia*, resulted in a dismissal of the applicant's case.[136]

In 2024 section 75 was amended as part of certain "right of repair" initiatives from the government[137] to permit the Tribunal to order a supplier to make the "means of diagnosis and repair" available to a person seeking them to support the operation of their business.[138]

2) Economic Effects of the Practice

Refusals to deal can often arise in the context of a supplier enforcing other vertical restraints such as exclusive dealing, tied selling, or market restriction. For example, a franchisor may refuse to supply the franchised product, ingredients, or necessary equipment based upon a franchisee breaching a term of the franchise agreement.[139] When refusals arise in the course of those practices, the discussion above of the benefits and competition concerns would apply to the practices.

Refusals to supply also may be a consequence of a firm weighing the pros and cons of vertical integration. For example, a supplier which initially decided to use distributors may determine that in order to compete more effectively or reduce costs, it should internalize the distribution function and sell directly to retailers. It has been observed that "refusals to deal can play an important role in enabling companies to implement efficient distribution systems."[140] The economic incentive to vertically integrate may include the desire to reduce the transaction costs involved in negotiating contracts with firms at another vertical level, or to obtain greater management control over a transaction which is critical to the business. However, vertical integration may also be strategic, including raising rivals' input costs or to increase the absolute capital costs of entry.[141] Given these different scenarios, it is difficult to generalize about the competitive nature of the practice; the facts and circumstances of each case must be considered.

---

135 See, e.g., *Coretti*, above note 67 at paras 9–14.

136 *B-Filer Inc v Bank of Nova Scotia*, 2006 CCTD No 36 [*B-Filer* 2006].

137 See Canada, *Budget 2024*, 16 April 2024 at 153, "A Right to Repair Your Devices," online: https://budget.canada.ca/2024/home-accueil-en.html#pdf.

138 *Bill C-59 2024*, above note 20, s 244.

139 For example, in *Bombardier*, above note 56, the supplier admitted having terminated dealers for breaches of contract requiring exclusive dealing.

140 Campbell, above note 43 at 386.

141 Martin, above note 46 at 231.

In the United States, the law recognizes the ability of a firm to make decisions related to vertical integration. There is no free-standing obligation in antitrust law to supply a competitor. However, a firm possessing market power or motivated by a monopolistic purpose may be under an obligation to supply. The US Supreme Court has held:

> In the absence of any purpose to create or maintain a monopoly, the [law] does not restrict the long recognized right of trader or manufacturer engaged in an entirely private business, freely to exercise his own independent discretion as to parties with whom he will deal.[142]

More recently, the Court held, "[i]t is true that as a general matter a firm can refuse to deal with its competitors. But such a right is not absolute; it exists only if there are legitimate competitive reasons for the refusal."[143]

3) Elements of Section 75

Section 75 contains five separate subparagraphs of criteria that have to be met by an applicant to obtain an order for supply. Some of the criteria contain more than one element. The sheer number of these elements reflects the substantial onus placed on an applicant in order to obtain a remedy.

> 75(1) The Tribunal may, on application by the Commissioner or a person granted leave under section 103.1, order one or more suppliers of a product, including a means of diagnosis or repair, in a market to accept a person as a customer, or to make the means of diagnosis or repair available to a person, within a specified period and on the terms that the Tribunal considers appropriate if the Tribunal finds that
>
> (a) a person is substantially affected in in the whole or part of their business or is precluded from carrying on business due to their inability to obtain adequate supplies of the product anywhere in a market on usual trade terms,
>
> (b) the person is unable to obtain adequate supplies of the product because of insufficient competition among suppliers of the product in the market,
>
> (c) the person is willing and able to meet the usual trade terms of the supplier or suppliers of the product,

142 *United States v Colgate & Co*, 250 US 300 (1919) at 307; cited with approval in *Aspen Skiing Co v Aspen Highlands Skiing Corp*, 472 US 585 (1985) at 601.

143 *Eastman Kodak, above note 92, n 32.*

(d) the product is in ample supply or, in the case of a means of diagnosis or repair, can be readily supplied, and
(e) the refusal to deal is having or is likely to have an adverse effect on competition in a market.

Section 75(3) defines "means of diagnosis and repair" as including "diagnostic, maintenance, repair and calibration information, technical updates, diagnostic software or tools and any related documentation and service parts."[144] At the same time, in order to protect confidential commercial information, section 75(2.1) states that "[n]othing in this section is to be interpreted as requiring the disclosure of any information that is a trade secret."

What follows identifies issues raised by the elements of the section and discussed in the case law.

a) The Product Market Under Section 75(1)(a)

An initial question is the scope of the "product market" for the determination of the impact on the applicant's business based on whether there are "adequate supplies of *a product anywhere in a market*." In the first two cases to come before the Tribunal under the section, the refusal involved the branded products of a particular supplier. In *Chrysler Canada*,[145] the products were auto parts supplied by Chrysler, and in *Xerox Canada*,[146] they were photocopier replacement parts supplied by that company. In both cases, the respondents argued that branded products were not the appropriate market. In *Xerox Canada*, for example, the respondent's expert took the position that the appropriate market was the one Xerox competed in with other copier manufacturers: "the provision of a package of services which leads to the creation of an imaged piece of paper." He opined that was the *relevant* market for competition law purposes, because competition in that market provided the competitive discipline which protected consumers of Xerox products.[147]

In *Xerox Canada*, the Tribunal concluded, as it had in *Chrysler Canada*, that a product market under section 75 can consist of one supplier's product, when the facts indicate that those products are a relevant market from the standpoint of the company refused supply. The Tribunal

144 In moving second reading of Bill C-59, Senator Mancion explained that the House Committee studying the Bill amended it to "strengthen the definition of 'means of diagnosis and repair' at … by including 'maintenance' and 'calibration' given that these services and activities are central to proper repair in the aftermarket." Canada, Senate Debates (Hansard) 44th Parl. 1st Sess, No 223 (30 May 2024).

145 *Chrysler Canada*, above note 133.

146 *Xerox Canada*, above note 128.

147 *Ibid* at para 61.

adopted the following passage from *Chrysler Canada*, which had found that the market definition was affected by the context of section 75 itself:

> Products and markets can only be meaningfully defined in a particular context and for a particular purpose. The approach to defining these terms may be entirely different where, as in the case of a merger, the ultimate test is whether the merger will substantially lessen competition and the definition must be consistent with the attempt to determine whether the merger will result in an increase in prices or in other effects consistent with a lessening of competition. In the case of paragraph 75(1)(a), the ultimate test concerns the effect on the business of the person refused supplies. Where products are purchased for resale, the effect on the business of the person refused supply will depend on the demand of the person's customers and whether substitutes are acceptable to them. Therefore, the starting point for the definition of "product" under section 75 is the buyer's customers.[148]

From the standpoint of Xerox's customers, who were small companies that repaired Xerox copiers, other suppliers' replacement parts were not adequate substitutes. They did not work in Xerox machines. Therefore, the Tribunal held that branded Xerox proprietary parts were a relevant market. The Tribunal further noted that even if one examined the issue from the perspective of the end customer market, users of Xerox machines "cannot easily, during the economic life of that machine, switch to another manufacturer's brand of copier." Therefore, the market for photocopy services did not adequately discipline competition issues facing customers "locked in" to a Xerox machine.[149]

In *B-Filer* 2006, the Tribunal had to determine whether the test from *Chrysler Canada*, focused on the standpoint of the buyer's customers, was still applicable given the fact that the section had been amended to add a competitive effects test in section 75(1)(e). The Tribunal considered that the test was driven by the language of section 75(1)(a), and still governed:

> In our view, while the addition of paragraph 75(1)(*e*) changes the context and purpose of section 75 to the extent that there is now a focus on determining whether refusals to deal result in adverse effects on competition, this amendment does not change the ultimate concern

---

148 *Ibid* at para 54.

149 *Ibid* at para 62. See also re "aftermarkets," or markets for parts and other products used by an installed market base, Carl Shapiro, "Aftermarkets and Consumer Welfare: Making Sense of *Kodak*" (1994) 63 *Antitrust Law Journal* 483.

> of 75(1)(*a*). That concern, as stated in *Chrysler*, is the effect on the business of the person refused supply.[150]

Section 75(2) must be considered in the context of product market definition under section 75. It provides that "an article is not a separate product in a market only because it is differentiated from other articles in its class by a trademark, proprietary name or the like, unless the article so differentiated occupies such a dominant position in that market as to substantially affect the ability of a person to carry on business in that class of articles unless that person has access to the article so differentiated." The mere lack of availability of product because it is of a particular brand or trade name is thus not a foundation for a refusal to supply application. However, the Tribunal in *Xerox Canada* inferred from this provision that if a branded product *does* hold such a dominant position that it affects the ability of the refused party to carry on business, it may be considered a separate product.[151]

b) Substantial Effect on Business Due to Inability to Obtain Adequate Supplies: Section 75(1)(a)

This issue involves largely a financial and accounting assessment of the refusal's impact, as well as an explanation of how the financial impact affects the company's ability to operate. A business has been "substantially affected," for example, if its inability to obtain supplies has resulted in a "significant and important" reduction in earnings. The Tribunal also stated "the Applicant need not demonstrate that it is affected by the refusal to the point of it being unable to carry on business. Rather, it is required to establish on a balance of probabilities that it is affected in an important or significant way." [152]

The business impact was held to be insufficient if it affects only part of the applicant's business.[153] This has been criticized as being "a somewhat formalistic approach which ignores the possibility that a firm may have several distinct businesses."[154] This was corrected by the amendment of the section in 2024 to provide that only "part" of the business need be affected substantially.[155]

---

150 *B-Filer* 2006, above note 136 at para 78.

151 *Xerox Canada*, above note 128 at para 87.

152 *Nadeau Poultry Farm Ltd v Groupe Westco Inc*, [2009] CCTD No 6 at paras 131 and 221 [*Nadeau* CCT]; aff'd on other grounds, *Nadeau Poultry Farm Ltd v Groupe Westco Inc*, 2011 FCA 188 [*Nadeau* FCA].

153 *Sears Canada Inc v Parfums Christian Dior Canada Inc*, [2007] CCTD No 3 at paras 16–21.

154 Campbell, above note 43 at 387.

155 *Bill C-59 2024*, above note 20, s 244.

c) No Adequate Supplies Anywhere in a Market on Usual Trade Terms: Section 75(1)(a)

This element involves the largely fact-driven exercise of the applicant providing an explanation of why alternative sources are not adequate, why other trade terms are usual or not usual, and what searches or efforts have taken place to obtain supplies.[156]

d) Unable to Obtain Adequate Supplies Due to Insufficient Competition Among Suppliers: Section 75(1)(b)

This element means that insufficient competition among suppliers must be the causal reason for the supply limit, not other factors. In *Nadeau Poultry Farm Ltd v Groupe Westco Inc*, the Federal Court of Appeal found no reviewable error when "the Tribunal found that insufficient competition among producers was not the cause of Nadeau's supply difficulties." The cause in question was the supply management regulatory system for chicken, which set limits on production.[157]

The Tribunal held in *Xerox Canada* that a market composed of numerous suppliers acting independently would not be considered a market in which there was insufficient competition.[158]

e) Willing and Able to Meet the Usual Trade Terms of the Supplier(s): Section 75(1)(c)

Section 75(3) defines "trade terms" as "terms in respect of payment, units of purchase and reasonable technical and servicing requirements." In *Nadeau*, the Tribunal held "that usual trade terms are not the specific terms in effect between the parties prior to the refusal to deal, but rather those terms which are considered usual from the perspective of all processors competing for the product in the relevant market."[159] It has been noted that

> [i]f there are other customers buying the product in the market, it should not be problematic to ascertain usual trade terms[;] when there is no such benchmark (e.g., because the customer was an exclusive distributor or retailer) . . . the terms in place before supply was terminated are a potential point of reference if the parties have had a prior business relationship.[160]

---

156 See, e.g., *Nadeau* CCT, above note 152 at paras 146–82.

157 *Nadeau* FCA, above note 152 at para 69.

158 *Xerox Canada*, above note 128 at para 82 (in *obiter*).

159 *Nadeau* CCT, above note 152 at para 24.

160 Campbell, above note 43 at 387, citing on the latter point, *B-Filer Inc v Bank of Nova Scotia* (2005), 44 CPR (4th) 214 (CCT) at paras 56–57.

In the context of markets for data, such as information on customer browsing patterns collected by a dominant entity like Google, competitors may seek to obtain access to supplies of such data to "level the playing field" and lower barriers to entry.[161] A challenge for such competitors may be establishing what the "usual trade terms" for supply might be, where the data have not been supplied previously. For example, it may be difficult to fashion a remedy, or the Tribunal might have little reference point so that "reasonable" terms can be established, where a supplier has not previously supplied the product in question.

f) The Product Is in Ample Supply: Section 75(1)(d)

A product is not in ample supply in "[a] market in which increased demand of a product can only be accommodated by diverting supplies from one customer to another." Producers must have "capacity to increase production in a timely way to meet increases in demand for the product."[162] That was not the case in *Nadeau*, due to the supply management regime, which restricted poultry production.

In 2002, the House Committee expressed concern that this requirement might mean that the section could not apply to a market characterized by supply shortages. It noted:

> [A]n unscrupulous and dominant supplier could profit by the shortage to promote his own retail network and discipline independent retailers by selectively rationing their supply in a discriminatory manner. The current wording of the section might suggest that Parliament simply did not anticipate selective rationing being used in this way; or perhaps it was aware that such a practice might occur, but that it could be better addressed under the abuse of dominance provisions in section 79.[163]

The committee proposed only that a guideline be issued by the Bureau on the topic, and did not propose an amendment. The abuse of dominance provisions thus may be the only way to deal with refusals in the context of an industry characterized by chronic shortages. However, for

---

161 See, e.g., UK, HM Treasury, *Unlocking Digital Competition, Report of the Digital Competition Expert Panel* (March 2019), online: https://doi.org/10.17639/wjcs-jc14. See, e.g., at 57:

> Secure access to non-personal and anonymised data: tackling the data barrier to entry for smaller and newer firms, while protecting privacy. The power of bulk data driving economies of scale and scope is a key reason new firms struggle to compete and bring innovative services to consumers. Overcoming this barrier will allow the digital economy to remain dynamic.

162 *Nadeau* CCT, above note 152 at paras 88 and 91.

163 *A Plan to Modernize Canada's Competition* Regime, above note 132 at 106.

those provisions to apply, the dominant firm would have to engage in a refusal to supply for an anti-competitive purpose.[164]

It has been held that intellectual property such as a copyright licence is not a product that can be in "ample supply" under section 75 given the right of the copyright holder to withhold access to such a licence.[165] With respect to the "means of diagnosis and repair," the paragraph was amended in 2024 to make it clear that these need only be in a position to be "readily supplied."[166] This additional language should make available such things as specifications, repair instructions or manuals, subject to the limitation in section 75(2.1) that the section is not to be interpreted as requiring the disclosure of trade secrets.

g) The Refusal Is Having or Is Likely to Have an Adverse Effect on Competition in a Market: Section 75(1)(e)

The Federal Court of Appeal in *Nadeau* noted that section 75(1)(e) was introduced at the same time as the expansion of private applications to cover refusals to deal. Given this context, the Court concluded the section was "designed to avoid private [applications] based on injury to an individual market participant without any impact on the relevant markets themselves."[167]

The Court also held that the market affected in section 75(1)(e) need not be the market in which the refusal had occurred, i.e., the upstream market from which supply is sourced (i.e., live chickens), but it could be the "downstream" market in which the product is refused (i.e., processed chicken). The Court held "the statutory reference to 'a' market is a reference to any relevant product or geographical market into which the complainant sells."[168] This is consistent with the view that the subparagraph is concerned with broader impacts on competition and consumers in a *final* product market.

164 See Chapter 7, Sections C(2)(b) and D(2).

165 *Warner Music Canada*, above note 133 at para 30:

> Although a copyright licence can be a product under the Act, it is clear that the word "product" . . . must be read in context. The requirements in section 75 that there be an "ample supply" of a "product" and usual trade terms for a product show that . . . there cannot be an "ample supply" of legal rights over intellectual property which are exclusive by their very nature and there cannot be usual trade terms when licences may be withheld. The right granted by Parliament to exclude others is fundamental to intellectual property rights and cannot be considered to be anti-competitive, and there is nothing in the legislative history of section 75 of the Act which would reveal an intention to have section 75 operate as a compulsory licensing provision for intellectual property.

166 *Bill C-59 2024*, above note 20, s 244.

167 *Nadeau* FCA, above note 152 at para 98.

168 *Ibid* at para 97.

The Tribunal in *Nadeau* adopted the following test from *B-Filer* 2006 of the nature of the adverse effect required under section 75(1)(e):

> [For] a refusal to supply to have an adverse effect on a market, the remaining market participants must be placed in a position, as a result of the refusal, of created, enhanced or preserved market power.[169]

The Tribunal in *B-Filer* 2006 noted that "adverse" is a lesser standard than "substantial." It applied the comparative "but for" framework developed in *Canada Pipe*, examining the conditions in the market with the refusal to deal with the likely competitive conditions if supply were affected, to determine whether the difference was an adverse effect. The Tribunal also applied the same approach to measure the impact of the practice on market power used under abuse of dominance.[170]

The Tribunal in *Nadeau* applied the same framework. It found that given the number of competitors in the chicken processing market, the likelihood that Nadeau could replace some of its supply from other sources, no adverse effect on competition in the processing market had been demonstrated from the refusal to supply the company live chickens.[171] The Court of Appeal held that this finding was reasonable.[172]

The fact that a market power assessment must occur means that a second product market definition may be required for section 75(1)(e), unless market power can be inferred from direct evidence.[173] In *Nadeau*, the Court of Appeal found no error in the Tribunal's conclusion that the relevant market under section 75(1)(e) was processed chicken.[174]

4) Remedies for Refusal to Supply

The only final remedy available under section 75 is an order for supply; "the Tribunal may order that one or more suppliers of the product in the market accept the person as a customer within a specified time on usual trade terms." As in the section 77 practices above, damages are not available; a private applicant with a breach of contract or tort claim would be required to bring a civil damages action. A potential difficulty is that (unlike the deceptive marketing provisions which permit actions in the superior courts), the Tribunal does not have jurisdiction for such

169 *Nadeau* CCT, above note 152 at para 366; *B-Filer* 2006, above note 136 at para 208.

170 *B-Filer* 2006, *ibid* at paras 197 and 213.

171 *Nadeau* CCT, above note 152 at paras 468–77.

172 *Nadeau* FCA, above note 152 at para 116.

173 See Chapter 4, Section B(2).

174 *Nadeau* FCA, above note 152 at paras 100–7.

civil damages claims, and actions in two separate fora may be required if common law claims are asserted.[175]

In *Chrysler Canada*, the Tribunal identified the following factors relevant to exercising its discretion (derived from the word "may" in the section) to issue a section 75 order: (1) the reasons behind the respondent's decision to discontinue supply; (2) the market position of the respondent, including whether it possessed market power and the changes that it was making in its distribution system; (3) the length of the association between the parties to the refusal; (4) encouragement by the supplier to the refused party; and (5) the manner in which the cut-off was implemented.[176]

An applicant under section 75 may seek an interim order of supply under section 104. One such order was entered on consent, providing for supply to be effected "[u]ntil the disposition of the . . . application under section 75 of the Act by the Tribunal, or the withdrawal, cessation, settlement or termination of that application by other means."[177] Shortly after the consent order was issued, it was challenged on the basis of changed circumstances. In rejecting the challenge, the Tribunal commented that "[i]nterim supply orders are relatively common in cases such as these to ensure that a Tribunal's final order is not rendered moot or ineffective."[178]

In *Nadeau*, the Tribunal found that the common law injunction test had been met and issued a contested order that the respondent "continue to supply the Applicant with live chickens on the usual trade terms at the current level of weekly supply . . . until a final decision is made on the merits of the application under section 75 of the Act."[179]

F. REFUSAL TO SUPPLY BY FOREIGN SUPPLIERS

Section 84 provides the Tribunal authority to review refusals to supply by foreign suppliers.

> 84. Where, on application by the Commissioner, the Tribunal finds that a supplier outside Canada has refused to supply a product or

175 Campbell, above note 43 at 389.

176 *Chrysler Canada*, above note 133 at para 68.

177 *Used Car Dealers Assn of Ontario v Insurance Bureau of Canada, [2012] CCTD No 11 at para 12.*

178 *Ibid* at para 48. The Commissioner may also apply for an interim order of short duration under s 103.3. See above notes 72 & 73.

179 *Nadeau Poultry Farm Ltd v Groupe Westco Inc, [2008] CCTD No 16 at paras 57–58. See also Quinlan's of Huntsville Inc v Fred Deeley Imports Ltd, [2004] CCTD No 26.*

> otherwise discriminated in the supply of a product to a person in Canada (the "first" person) at the instance of and by reason of the exertion of buying power outside Canada by another person, the Tribunal may order any person in Canada (the "second" person) by whom or on whose behalf or for whose benefit the buying power was exerted
>
> (a) to sell any such product of the supplier that the second person has obtained or obtains to the first person at the laid-down cost in Canada to the second person of the product and on the same terms and conditions as the second person obtained or obtains from the supplier; or
>
> (b) not to deal or to cease to deal, in Canada, in that product of the supplier.

The provision is targeted at the particular and rather narrow situation of the exertion of buying power outside Canada causing another supplier (again outside Canada) to refuse to supply a purchaser within Canada. According to the *Background Papers, Stage I Competition Policy* at the time of the 1976 amendments, the section was motivated by a particular case involving an American distributor of Japanese drums which put pressure on the Japanese supplier of that product not to supply Canadian distributors, but to supply the American company's Canadian affiliate, the "beneficiary" of the practice.[180] The "buying power" referred to was, in that scenario, that of the American company, which put pressure on the Japanese manufacturer to refuse to supply. The section provides a remedy to permit Canadian distributors to gain access to the product through a supply order made against the beneficiary firm in Canada. Two requirements must be proven under this section:

1) a supplier outside Canada *refused* to supply a product or otherwise *discriminated* in the supply of a product to a person in Canada (the "first" person); and
2) the refusal or discrimination resulted from the exertion of buying power outside Canada by another person on behalf of a second party in Canada.

If these requirements are met, the Tribunal may order the Canadian beneficiary itself to sell the product in question to the affected Canadian purchaser at the former's "laid-down" cost and on the same terms and conditions as it secured from the foreign supplier. Alternatively, it may order the second party to cease dealing in the product in Canada.

---

180 *Stage I Competition Policy*, above note 25 at 15–16.

G. CONCLUSION

Vertical restraints are commonplace commercial practices. Used widely in franchising, distribution, and supply contracts, they often reduce costs, increase efficiency, and facilitate interbrand competition. They can provide benefits to all players in the supply chain, from manufacturers to end consumers. The *Competition Act* reflects these considerations by providing remedies against such practices only when they are likely to have an exclusionary effect, raise barriers to entry, or otherwise substantially lessen competition (with the exception of refusal to supply, which requires only an adverse effect on competition). The provisions require a case-by-case assessment to determine their competitive effect. The Canadian law, however, focuses on the effects of vertical restraints on competition, and does not weigh the benefits and costs of these practices on social welfare.

The understanding of vertical restraints in competition law and policy has evolved. Such practices are now known to have advantages as well as disadvantages and therefore require case-specific analyses. This remains an area where economic analysis is evolving and where international rules and practices diverge in certain respects. Cases in this area thus present fertile ground for the use of economic evidence to assess the advantages and disadvantages of vertical restraints in a particular case.

CHAPTER 9

PRICING PRACTICES: PREDATORY PRICING, PRICE MAINTENANCE, AND PRICE DISCRIMINATION

> Predatory pricing is rare and very difficult to identify in practice because low prices are what competition is all about.
>
> —House of Commons, Standing Committee on Industry, *Interim Report on the Competition Act* (Ottawa: House of Commons, 2000), ch 3

A. INTRODUCTION

By 2009, the criminal laws against predatory pricing, price discrimination, and price maintenance had not been enforced for some time. These practices were regarded by many economists as often benign or even beneficial. The Competition Bureau had issued enforcement guidelines for price discrimination and predatory pricing which reduced their scope.[1] Criminal law enforcement was recognized as an ineffective method for addressing such conduct and had created concerns about the risk of a "chill" over pro-competitive pricing.[2] To make matters worse,

1 Canada, Competition Bureau, *Price Discrimination Enforcement Guidelines* (Ottawa: Consumer and Corporate Affairs Canada, 1992); Canada, Competition Bureau, *Predatory Pricing Enforcement Guidelines* (Ottawa: Consumer and Corporate Affairs Canada, 1992) [*Predatory Pricing Enforcement Guidelines* 1992].

2 See, e.g., Canadian Bar Association, Competition Law Section, "Submission to the Competition Policy Review Panel" (January 2008): "It is harmful to the

the law carried with it the potential for statutory civil damage actions,[3] making an often costly and time-consuming legal risk assessment necessary for some competitive business conduct.

That year, the criminal provisions were repealed. The law against price maintenance was retained, but revised as a civilly reviewable practice. Predatory pricing and price discrimination were left to be addressed under the abuse of dominance provision. All of these practices are now subject to civil enforcement before the Competition Tribunal. These changes reflect the increased focus in the legislation on the protection of competition and efficiency as the primary goals of Canadian competition law.

The treatment of these practices in this separate chapter has more to do with their common historical evolution than their economic character. Under the current law, predatory pricing and price discrimination are practices which may fall within abuse of dominance and the framework set out in Chapter 7. Resale price maintenance, now dealt with separately as a civilly reviewable practice, shares many characteristics with the vertical restraints discussed in Chapter 8. Given the foregoing, what follows draws on the discussion in earlier chapters and focuses on the distinct or unique elements of this conduct.

B. HISTORY AND BACKGROUND

1) Price Discrimination and Predatory Pricing

a) Origins

As noted in Chapter 3,[4] the criminal price discrimination and predatory pricing provisions were both part of a legislative reaction to the effects of the Great Depression of the early 1930s. In 1934, Parliament appointed a Special Committee of members of the House "to inquire into and investigate the causes of the large spread between the prices received for commodities by the producer thereof, and the price paid by the consumers therefor."[5] Its mandate was also to examine "the effect of mass

---

competitiveness of the Canadian economy to continue to have criminal provisions prohibiting such conduct." See also Lawson A Hunter & Susan M Hutton, "Is the Price Right?: Comments on the *Predatory Pricing Enforcement Guidelines* and *Price Discrimination Enforcement Guidelines* of the Bureau of Competition Policy" (1993) 38 *McGill Law Journal* 830 at 847 [Hunter & Hutton].

3 Section 36 of the *Competition Act*, RSC 1985, c C-34 [*Competition Act* or Act].

4 See Chapter 3, Section C(3)(a).

5 Figure 9.1, Canada, *Report of the Royal Commission on Price Spreads* (Ottawa: King's Printer, 1935) at xxvi.

buying by department and chain store organizations upon the regular retail trade of the country, as well as upon the business of manufacturers and producers,"[6] reflecting concerns with the plight of small businesses. The Committee was unable to complete its work by the deadline, and its mandate was rolled into that of a Royal Commission on Price Spreads. The Commissioners were members of Parliament, and thus their recommendations reflected a political and populist focus.

The *Report of the Royal Commission on Price Spreads* was released in 1935. It recommended that a Federal Trade and Industry Commission be appointed with the power to prohibit certain "unfair competitive practices," including "discriminatory discounts, rebates and allowances, territorial price discrimination and predatory price-cutting."[7] While the *Report* recognized that many of its concerns with individual businesses' competitive survival were the product of the forces at play during the Great Depression, the authors held fast to the need for remedies for the future.[8] The House of Commons debate on the draft legislation flowing from these recommendations has been described as showing "confusion . . . as to what were its objectives."[9] Some legislators viewed the legislation as promoting competition, others as a way of protecting both labour and small business interests.[10] The provisions themselves, enacted as section 498A of the *Criminal Code*, reflected these differing objectives, creating, *inter alia*, criminal prohibitions (a) against discriminating between competitors of a purchaser, and (b) against low pricing designed to eliminate a competitor.[11] These provisions were sustained as constitutional under

---

6 *Ibid*.

7 *Ibid* at xxiv–xxv.

8 *Ibid* at 8:

> It is not enough to say, as many contend, that these problems are the result of depression and will vanish with the depression. It may be true that when recovery is achieved, competition will become less predatory, discrimination less general, and exploitation less obvious. But it is equally true that, while unfair competition and unequal bargaining are intensified by depression, they will not be absent in prosperity, especially in a prosperity characterized by the increasing substitution of imperfect for free competition.

9 See Paul Gorecki & William T Stanbury, *The Objectives of Canadian Competition Policy 1888-1983* (Montreal: IRPP, 1984) at 123–26.

10 *Ibid*. See also Bruce Dunlop, "Price Discrimination, Predatory Pricing and Systematic Delivered Pricing," ch 17 in J Robert S Pritchard, William T Stanbury & Thomas A Wilson, eds, *Canadian Competition Law, Essays in Law and Economics* (Toronto: Butterworths, 1979) at 406–7 [Dunlop].

11 Section 489A of the *Criminal Code*, SC 1935, c 56, s 9; SC 1952, c 39, s 11 [*Criminal Code* 1952]. The provision became s 412 in SC 1953–54, c 51. It was transferred to the *Combines Investigation Act*, RSC 1970, c C-23 as s 33A. See *An*

the federal criminal law power in 1937.[12] They were incorporated into the *Combines Investigation Act* in 1960, and certain additions and adjustments were made to the provisions then, and over the ensuing decades.[13]

The formulation of the criminal predatory pricing offence from 1976 onward was: "Every one engaged in a business who . . . engages in a policy of selling products at prices unreasonably low, having the effect or tendency of substantially lessening competition or eliminating a competitor, or designed to have such effect, is guilty of an indictable offence."[14] Reflecting the initial legislative intent to protect small business, it became an offence for low pricing to target a competitor. Such conduct is, however, often a feature of healthy price competition, suggesting an awkward fit within a law supposedly designed to promote competition.

The price discrimination provision made it an offence for suppliers to grant price concessions to one purchaser but not to competing purchasers of the same articles.[15] Large customers could lawfully receive discounts based on volume, suggesting that the section did not necessarily serve the original intent of protecting smaller purchasers.[16] Another sub-

---

Act to Amend the Combines Investigation Act and the Criminal Code, SC 1960, c 45, s 13 [*An Act to Amend the Combines Investigation Act and the Criminal Code*].

12 *British Columbia (Attorney General) v Canada (Attorney General) sub nom Reference Re Criminal Code of Canada, s 498*, [1937] AC 368 (UK PC).

13 *Combines Investigation Act*, RSC 1952, c 314, as amended by *An Act to Amend the Combines Investigation Act and the Criminal Code*, above note 11. See Donald G McFetridge & Stanley Wong, "Predatory Pricing in Canada: The Law and the Economics" (1985) 63 *Canadian Bar Review* 685 at 686–87. Re price discrimination, see Michelle Lally & Kaeleigh Kuzma, "The Treatment of Vertical Price Restraints under the Competition Act: A Retrospective" (2012) 25 *Canadian Competition Law Review* 326 at 327–29 [Lally & Kuzma]. An offence for discriminatory promotional allowances was also added in 1960: SC 1960, c 45, s 13, adding s 33B based upon recommendations of reports in 1958 and 1959 addressing the impact of discounts afforded large grocery chains: Canada, Restrictive Trade Practices Commission, *Report Re a Study of Certain Discriminatory Pricing Practices in the Grocery Trade* (Ottawa : Queen's Printer, 1958); Canada, Royal Commission on Price Spreads of Food Products, *Report of the Royal Commission on Price Spreads of Food Products*, by Andrew Stewart (Ottawa: Queen's Printer, 1959).

14 See, e.g., *Competition Act*, RSC 1985, c C-34, s 50(1)(c).

15 *Ibid*, ss 50(1)(a) & (b).

16 Dunlop, above note 10 at 409. Canada, Consultative Panel on Amendments to the Competition Act, *Report of the Consultative Panel on Amendments to the Competition Act to the Director of Investigation and Research, Competition Act*, by Ed Ratushny & George N Addy (Hull: Industry Canada, 1996) [*1996 Consultative Panel Report*] at 29–30:

> [T]he existing provisions do not prevent a supplier from granting a discount or a rebate to a purchaser who buys more, and so have done very little to

paragraph, addressing "geographic price discrimination," applied to selling products at different prices in different areas of Canada, that has "the effect or tendency of substantially lessening competition or eliminating a competitor . . . or designed to have that effect."[17] One commentator examined the convoluted language in these provisions and concluded, "[i]t would not be exaggerating too much to say that [the price discrimination provision] as presently drafted might as well not exist."[18]

There was little enforcement of these provisions during their lifespan. Between their enactment in the *Criminal Code* in 1935 and 1976, only six cases involving price discrimination or predatory pricing were brought, with one conviction.[19] Charges were laid in only three cases in the decade 1980–1990,[20] and few in the two decades before the repeal. At the same time, the provisions generated hundreds of compliance requests, as businesses tried to steer clear of the law's opaque language.[21]

b) Process of Reform

Over the period 1995–2009, there was a slow-moving process of proposals for and consultations on repealing these provisions:

- In 1995 the Competition Bureau released a discussion paper proposing the repeal of the price discrimination provisions, noting that they "focus on the impact on individual competitors, rather than the overall level of competition."[22]
- The Minister of Industry appointed a consultative panel which also recommended repeal.[23] After concerns were expressed by the small

protect small retailers from the exertion of buying power on the part of large buyers. Rather, they have had the perverse effect of discriminating against dynamic small businesses by permitting suppliers to make price concessions solely on the basis of volume.

17 *Competition Act*, above note 3, s 50(1)(a) & (b).

18 Dunlop, above note 10 at 412.

19 Paul Gorecki & William T Stanbury "Canada's *Combines Investigation Act*: The Record of Public Enforcement, 1889–1976," in J Robert S Pritchard, William T Stanbury & Thomas A Wilson, eds, *Canadian Competition Policy: Essays in Law and Economics* (Toronto: Butterworth & Co, 1979) at 190, Table 8 [Gorecki & Stanbury].

20 *Predatory Pricing Enforcement Guidelines* 1992, above note 1 at 1.2.

21 Gorecki & Stanbury, above note 20 at 193. In the period 1960–76, predatory pricing and price discrimination generated 436 compliance requests by the Bureau, more than conspiracy, merger, and monopoly put together.

22 Canada, Competition Bureau, *Discussion Paper, Competition Act Amendments* (Ottawa: Industry Canada, 1995). It also proposed repeal of the promotional allowances offence.

23 *1996 Consultative Panel Report*, above note 17.

business sector, the proposal was withdrawn. Amendments proceeded in 1999, but without the recommended changes.[24]

- The comprehensive 1999 VanDuzer/Paquet study by two University of Ottawa professors, commissioned by the Bureau, recommended that both price discrimination and predatory pricing be decriminalized and addressed under abuse of dominance.[25]
- The House Standing Committee on Industry examined the study and recommended a two-track approach to predatory pricing rather than outright decriminalization,[26] and that the government "consider repealing the price discrimination provisions" and replacing them with either a new civil provision or reliance on the abuse of dominance provisions.[27]
- In 2002, a House of Commons Standing Committee Report recommended decriminalization of *both* provisions. Regarding the former, the Report stated: "a consensus has formed on the use of the abuse of dominant position provision as a vehicle for bringing a predatory pricing case."[28]
- The Bureau was opposed to decriminalization at that time.[29] The government stated that it would review the provisions in the context of proposals to amend the conspiracy, and potentially, the abuse of dominance provision.[30]

---

24 Calvin S Goldman & JD Bodrug, *Competition Law of Canada* (New York: Juris, 2013) at 4–5, citing a 10 May 1996 speech by George N Addy, then Director of Investigation and Research; *An Act to amend the Competition Act and to make consequential and related amendments to other Acts*, SC 1999, c 2.

25 Canada, Commissioner of Competition, "Anticompetitive Pricing Practices and the Competition Act Theory, Law and Practice" by J Anthony VanDuzer & Gilles Paquet (22 October 1999) [VanDuzer & Paquet].

26 House of Commons, Standing Committee on Industry, *Interim Report on the Competition Act* (June 2000) (Chair: Susan Whelan), ch 3 [*Interim Report on the Competition Act*].

27 *Ibid*, ch 5.

28 Canada, Standing Committee on Industry, Science and Technology, *A Plan to Modernize Canada's Competition Regime* (April 2002) (Chair: Walt Lastewka) at 72 [*A Plan to Modernize Canada's Competition Regime*]; see the same page re price discrimination.

29 See Lally & Kuzma, above note 13 at 351–52.

30 Canada, Competition Bureau, "Government Response to the Report of the House of Commons Standing Committee on Industry, Science and Technology '*A Plan to Modernize Canada's Competition Regime*'" (1 October 2002), online: www.competitionbureau.gc.ca/eic/site/113.nsf/eng/h_07647.html [Government Response to *A Plan to Modernize Canada's Competition Regime*]:

> The Government is mindful that amendments to the conspiracy and abuse of dominance provisions may have significant consequences on other pricing

- A 2003 discussion paper again proposed decriminalization and reliance on the abuse of dominance provision.[31]
- This was followed by a further consultation process that continued into 2004. The *Final Report* from the consultations proposed, yet again, repealing the criminal price discrimination and predatory pricing provisions.[32]
- The government introduced Bill C-19 in late 2004 to put into effect the repeal as recommended in the *Final Report*. The bill was, however, removed from the parliamentary agenda in 2005.[33]
- The impetus for repeal finally came from the 2008 five-member "Competition Policy Review Panel" following which, with little fanfare, the repealing provision was buried as section 413 of the omnibus *Budget Implementation Act, 2009*.[34]

---

provisions in the *Competition Act*. Consequently it will be crucial for the Government to carefully study the proposed amendments in order to ensure the overall cohesion of the Act's pricing provisions. The Government of Canada will consider the Committee's recommendations concerning sections 50(1)(a), (b) and (c) and 51 in the consultation process for the next round of amendments. The possibility of adding these provisions to the abuse of dominance provisions will necessarily also address the desirability of amending 79(1)(a).

31 Canada, Competition Bureau, *Options for Amending the Competition Act: Fostering a Competitive Marketplace* (Ottawa, Government of Canada, 2003).

32 Public Policy Forum, *National Consultation on the Competition Act: Final Report* by George Kourakos, Geneviève Lépine & Anita Mayer (Ottawa: Public Policy Forum, 2004): "A large majority of the intervenors supported these proposals to reform the pricing provisions and agreed that the current provisions can discourage pro-competitive interactions." The forum was an independent non-profit organization.

33 Andrew Kitching, Law and Government Division, in the Legislative Summary of Canada, Bill C-19, *An Act to amend the Competition Act and to make consequential amendments to other Acts*, 38th Parl, 1st Sess, (2004) at 10, online: https://lop.parl.ca/sites/PublicWebsite/default/en_CA/ResearchPublications/LegislativeSummaries/381LS494E: "It was not universally agreed that the abuse of dominance section would adequately address all issues related to price discrimination. Some submissions stated that repeal of the pricing provisions should be accompanied by a new civil provision or amendments to the section on abuse of dominant position."

34 Canada, Competition Policy Review Panel, *Compete to Win, Final Report* (Ottawa: Public Works and Government Services Canada, 2008), online: www.ic.gc.ca/eic/site/cprp-gepmc.nsf/vwapj/Compete_to_Win.pdf/$FILE/Compete_to_Win.pdf [*Compete to Win*]; *An Act to implement certain provisions of the budget tabled in Parliament on January 27, 2009 and related fiscal measures*, SC, c 2, s 413. See the discussion in Chapter 6, Section C(3).

2) Resale Price Maintenance

a) Origins

Resale price maintenance whereby a supplier requires a dealer of its products to charge a specified price or range of prices was the subject of several *Combines Investigation Act* inquiries over the period 1927–1948.[35] A post-war Royal Commission report in 1949 expressed concern that the practice was a source of price increases and recommended further study.[36] In 1950, the so-called MacQuarrie Committee was appointed by the Minister of Justice. Its appointment occurred following a controversy surrounding delay by the government in releasing a report disclosing wartime price fixing by the flour milling industry, but its mandate was broader: "to recommend what amendments, if any, should be made to our Canadian legislation in order to make it a more effective instrument for the encouraging and safeguarding of our free economy."[37] The committee, composed of a judge of the Supreme Court of Nova Scotia, a law faculty dean, and two economists, issued an *Interim Report* on resale price maintenance in 1951. The report recommended that a new offence be enacted "for a manufacturer or other supplier: 1. To recommend or prescribe minimum resale prices for his products: 2. To refuse to sell, to withdraw a franchise or to take any other form of action as a means of enforcing minimum resale prices."[38] Following these recommendations,

---

35 For example, Canada, Department of Labour, *Report of the Commissioner, Investigation into the Proprietary Articles Trade Association* (Ottawa: King's Printer, 1927). See William J Waldron, "Resale Price Maintenance" (1965) *Electronic Theses and Dissertations* 6410, online: https://scholar.uwindsor.ca/etd/6410:

> It was the only issue in one inquiry involving the Proprietary Articles Trade Association, an offshoot of a druggists' trade organization of the same name in Great Britain. In two reports published in 1926 and 1927 the conclusion was expressed that the public interest was detrimentally affected. The Proprietary Articles Trade Association was dissolved shortly after the final report was published. A similar conclusion was reached in four other investigations under the *Combines Investigation Act*, tobacco 1938, dental supplies 1947, optical goods 1948, and bread in western Canada 1948.

36 Canada, *Report of the Royal Commission on Prices I*, by CA Curtis (Ottawa: King's Printer, 1949) at 41.

37 Maxwell Cohen, "The Background, Main Features and Problems: The MacQuarrie Report (1952) 30:6 *Canadian Bar Review* 551 at 551. The report "was partly a response to the considerable public reaction to the dispute between the former Commissioner, Mr. F. A. McGregor, and the government over the delay in publishing his report in the Flour Milling case."

38 Canada, Department of Justice, Committee to Study Combines Legislation ("MacQuarrie Committee"), *Report of the Committee to Study Combines Legislation and Interim Report on Resale Price Maintenance* (Ottawa: King's Printer, 1951) at 71.

in December 1951, Canada enacted the world's first prohibition of resale price maintenance.[39]

The resale price maintenance provisions contained in the *Combines Investigation Act* and subsequently in the *Competition Act* went through several rounds of amendments (principally in 1960 and 1976) both to broaden the offence, and to expand the defences available.[40] Notable among the changes in 1976 was the removal of the word "resale" from the section so that it could apply "to a situation where one supplier of a product sought by agreement to influence upward the price at which his competitor supplied the same or similar products";[41] i.e., horizontal (competitor to competitor) price maintenance.

In contrast to the price discrimination and predatory pricing provisions of the Act, price maintenance was the subject of fairly consistent enforcement activity. However, prosecutions peaked in the 1970s and 1980s, and dropped off significantly thereafter.

Table 9.1. Price Maintenance (Criminal) Cases 1966–2007[42]

Period	Number of cases
1966–1975	22
1976–1985	105
1986–1995	48
1996–2007	17

b) Process of Reform

Proposals to amend the provision followed a similar path to those for price discrimination and predatory pricing, although the case for reform initially stalled when the Competition Bureau expressed reluctance to jettison the provision, which had some popular support and for which there had been a substantial level of enforcement success. Some key events in the chronology:

39 *An Act to Amend the Combines Investigation Act*, SC 1951, c 30, s 1.

40 *Criminal Code* 1952, above note 11, s 4; *Criminal Code*, SC 1960, c 34, s 14 (adding the "loss leader," bait and switch, insufficient servicing, and other defences); *Combines Investigation Act*, SC 1974-75-76, c 76 (applying the section to services and intellectual property and adding, *inter alia*, attempts to influence upward or discourage the reduction of prices, as well as horizontal price maintenance, and certain rules of proof of elements of the offence); *Competition Tribunal Act*, SC 1986, c 26, s 38 (amending the definition of affiliates subject to an exemption).

41 Canada, Bureau of Competition Policy, *Stage 1—Competition Policy Background Papers* (Ottawa: Consumer and Corporate Affairs, 1976) at 55.

42 Ralph A Winter, "Antitrust Restrictions on Single-Firm Strategies" (2009) 42 *Canadian Journal of* Economics 1207, compiled from Table 3.

- The 1999 VanDuzer/Paquet study recommended that "vertical price maintenance should not be a criminal offence but should be subject to civil review."[43]
- The House Standing Committee's 2000 *Interim Report on the Competition Act* was equivocal: "Price maintenance agreements between a manufacturer and its distributors might best be moved to the reviewable civil section, possibly to be made applicable to abuse of dominant position."[44]
- The 2002 House of Commons Standing Committee Report, *A Plan to Modernize Canada's Competition Regime*, was more categorical, adopting the VanDuzer/Paquet recommendations for repeal and civil law treatment of vertical price maintenance under abuse of dominance.[45]
- The Bureau opposed decriminalization in its comments to the Committee.[46] The government stated in response to its report in 2002 that "it would be more appropriate to wait until the consultation process on" the conspiracy provision was completed.[47]
- The 2008 *Consultative Panel* Report recommended that the government "repeal the existing resale price maintenance provisions and replace them with a new civil provision to address this practice when it has an anti-competitive effect. This new provision should be subject

43 VanDuzer & Paquet, above note 26 at 84, recommendation 11. The authors (at 52–53) noted that abuse of dominance was not necessarily well adapted to deal with the practice.

44 *Interim Report on the Competition Act*, above note 27, ch 4.

45 *A Plan to Modernize Canada's Competition Regime*, above note 29 at 75:

> All witnesses, except Bureau officials, who commented on price maintenance had a recurring theme: vertical price maintenance should be decriminalized and horizontal price maintenance should be moved to the conspiracy provision. The Bureau, the lone dissenter, could only offer a higher success rate when prosecuting under a per se offence as its reason for departing from expert opinion. The Committee, however, must remind everyone that competition policy is not about winning and losing cases; it is about designing a framework whereby an efficient business sector can deliver products and services at competitive prices. Moreover, the Committee sees no social benefit in risking convictions of, and a "chilling effect" on, pro-competitive vertical price maintenance under the criminal section of the Act, when the civil section offers a more reasonable approach and a better result. In decriminalizing vertical price maintenance, competition experts suggested that shifting this act under the abuse of dominant position provision (section 79) would be the preferred route.

46 *Ibid*.

47 Government Response to *A Plan to Modernize Canada's Competition Regime*, above note 31.

to the private access rights before the Competition Tribunal."[48] That recommendation was followed in the 2009 amendments.

The elimination of a *per se* prohibition of resale price maintenance in Canada and substitution of a provision permitting an assessment of its competitive effect was consistent with jurisprudential developments in the United States. In 2007, the United States Supreme Court determined that agreements to set minimum resale prices should no longer be deemed illegal under a *per se* standard, but subject to a case-by-case assessment using the rule of reason.[49]

C. PREDATORY PRICING

1) Introduction: Basic Practice and Economics

As discussed above, since the repeal of the criminal prohibition in 2009, predatory pricing is addressed under the abuse of dominance provision of the Act. The Competition Bureau's 2019 *Abuse of Dominance Guidelines* provide the following definition of predatory pricing:

> Predatory conduct involves a firm deliberately setting the price of a product(s) below an appropriate measure of its own cost to incur losses on the sale of product(s) in the market(s) for a period of time sufficient to eliminate, discipline, or deter entry or expansion of a competitor, in the expectation that the firm will thereafter recoup its losses by charging higher prices than would have prevailed in the absence of the impugned conduct.[50]

The various elements of this definition will be discussed in more detail below. It is worth noting by way of introduction that predatory

---

48 *Compete to Win*, above note 35 at 61. See also at 58:

> The resale price maintenance provisions of the *Competition Act*, broadly speaking, address pricing issues that can arise between suppliers and resellers of a product, but do so as a criminal offence under the legislation. This is an area of Canadian competition law that is more restrictive than comparable US law. Other provisions of the *Competition Act*, such as those relating to refusal to deal and exclusive dealing, address competition issues between suppliers and resellers as civil matters. The Panel believes that resale price maintenance should also be treated as a civil matter.

49 *Leegin Creative Leather Products Inc v PSKS Inc*, 551 US 877 (2007).

50 Canada, Competition Bureau, *Abuse of Dominance Provisions Enforcement Guidelines* (7 March 2019), online: www.competitionbureau.gc.ca/eic/site/cb-bc.nsf/eng/04420.html at para 59 [*Abuse Guidelines*].

pricing is only one predatory tactic that may be used to drive out or exclude rivals from a market. Others include such behaviour as increasing capacity, exclusionary agreements, and raising rivals' costs.[51] *Canada (Director of Investigation and Research, Competition Act) v NutraSweet Co* illustrates the point. Although the Tribunal was not satisfied that predatory pricing had been demonstrated, it was only one of the tactics the respondent manufacturer of aspartame was alleged to have used. Among the exclusionary tactics found by the Tribunal to have been proven were customer exclusivity and other exclusionary contract provisions, which were used to extend the incumbent's market power beyond the expiry of its patent for the artificial sweetener.[52]

Economists highlight the many requirements a practice needs to meet before being characterized as predatory and anti-competitive.[53] A predatory firm is viewed as unlikely to be successful without, for example: (1) pockets sufficiently deep to financially outlast its opponent and (2) barriers to entry in the relevant market sufficiently high to permit a sustainable post-predation price increase to allow it to recoup losses incurred during predation.[54] However, there are several economic models of predation showing it could be rational and likely:

- Predatory pricing can be a way of establishing a reputation for disciplinary price-cutting that drives out recent entrants or deters future entrants.[55]

---

51 Jeffrey R Church & Roger Ware, *Industrial Organization: A Strategic Approach* (Boston: McGraw-Hill, 2000) at 662 [Church & Ware]: "Firms use a variety of predatory tactics to drive out rivals, including increasing capacity, exclusionary agreements, raising rivals' costs, etc. Predatory pricing is just one of these available instruments, and may not be the most important."

52 *Canada (Director of Investigation and Research, Competition Act) v NutraSweet Co (1990), 32 CPR (3d) 1 (CCT) at para 174 [NutraSweet]*, for example. The Tribunal concluded "NSC has induced exclusive dealing with its aspartame customers through its financial incentives or fidelity rebates, and its exclusivity clauses."

53 Michael D Noel, "The 2012 Abuse of Dominance Guidelines: An Economic Review" (2013) 26 *Canadian Competition Law Review* 59 at 72 [Noel] takes a particularly skeptical view: "most economists doubt the existence of predatory pricing strategies in practice except, if at all, in very rare cases."

54 Phillip Areeda & Donald F Turner, "Predatory Pricing and Related Practices under Section 2 of the Sherman Act" (1975) 88 *Harvard Law Review* 697 at 698–99 [Areeda & Turner].

55 See, e.g., Church & Ware, above note 52 at 651, citing David M Kreps & Robert Wilson, "Reputation and Imperfect Information" (1982) 27 *Journal of Economic Theory* 253; US, Department of Justice, "Competition and Monopoly: Single Firm Conduct and Section 2 of the *Sherman Act*" (September 2008), online: www.justice.gov/atr/competition-and-monopoly-single-firm-conduct-under-section-2-sherman-act, citing Paul Milgrom & John Roberts, "Predation,

- A firm participating in multiple markets, by predating in one, may be able to use the reputation or uncertainty this generates to discourage entry in other markets, increasing the profit from predation in the single market.[56]
- Due to imperfect information, a predator may use predatory pricing to lead potential entrants to believe that market conditions are unfavourable when they are not, or to signal false information to the effect that the predator's costs are lower than they actually are, discouraging those rivals from entering at all.[57]
- Predators with a "long purse" may exploit imperfect information about the decline of a new entrant so that it is misinterpreted by banks or investors as poor performance, leading to financial default by the entrant or a withdrawal of financing or investor support from it.[58]
- A dominant firm also may engage in predation to drive away innovative small competitors before they can become efficient.[59]

Two of these scenarios rely on the notion of "incomplete information." For example, a predated firm may not know with certainty some relevant aspect of the industry in which it operates. The predated firm may not know the predator's costs. Such information is germane if a contemplated exit decision is affected by the predator's costs (i.e., exit if the predator's costs are low, remain if the predator's costs are high). In this context, the predator's actions convey a signal to the predated. Those actions may be used strategically to encourage exit or discourage new entry.

One American commentator summarized the legal concern about rational predation and concluded, "[t]he problem for antitrust tribunals does not lie in the plausibility of such scenarios, or even in proof that actual conditions exist under which they occur. Rather, the difficulty lies in developing antitrust rules that are sufficiently reliable that they do not

---

Reputation and Entry Deterrence" (1982) 27 *Journal of Economic Theory* 280 at 303.

56 See Jonathan B Baker, "Predatory Pricing after Brooke Group: An Economic Perspective" (1994) 62 *Antitrust Law Journal* at 585 and 590.

57 Patrick Bolton, Joseph F Brodley & Michael H Riordan, "Predatory Pricing: Strategic Theory and Legal Policy" (2000) 88 *Georgetown Law Journal* 2239 at 2311–20.

58 *Ibid* at 2285–90.

59 International Competition Network, ICN Unilateral Conduct Working Group, "Predatory Pricing Analysis Pursuant to Unilateral Conduct Laws: Recommended Practices" (2014), online: www.internationalcompetitionnetwork.org/wp-content/uploads/2018/07/UCWG_RP_PredPricing-1.pdf at para 4.

do more harm than good to the competitive process."[60] In the absence of a developed jurisprudence under the abuse of dominance provision in Canada, the most readily available framework to assess predatory pricing is provided by the Bureau's *Abuse of Dominance Enforcement Guidelines*, and they will be discussed after a review of the elements of abuse of dominance.

2) The Abuse of Dominance Framework

The main elements of abuse of dominance were set out in Chapter 7 and consist of:

I. Control of a class or species of business: "one or more persons substantially or completely control class or species of business throughout Canada or any area thereof"; and
II. Anti-competitive practices or conduct: "that person or those persons have engaged in or are engaging in" either
   - A practice of anti-competitive acts as defined in section 78; or
   - Conduct having a substantial effect on competition.[61]

Predatory pricing has been held to be an anti-competitive act falling within sections 78 and 79. Section 78 contains a non-exclusive list of anti-competitive acts, which includes in section 78(i), "selling articles at a price lower than the acquisition cost for the purpose of disciplining or eliminating a competitor." The Tribunal in *NutraSweet* held that "the term 'anti-competitive act' in section 78 is broad enough to cover other [forms of] predatory pricing." [62]

3) The Bureau's *Abuse of Dominance Enforcement Guidelines*

The Bureau's *Abuse of Dominance Enforcement Guidelines* apply an approach that provides enforcement clarity. It is worth keeping in mind, however, that the approach taken is not the only way to assess or to prove predation. The *Competition Act* in section 78 contains an open-ended list of anti-competitive acts and does not mandate a particular definition of, or approach to, what constitutes predatory pricing. Given the limited guidance from the jurisprudence in Canada, that treatment

60 Herbert Hovenkamp, "Post-Chicago Antitrust: A Review and Critique" (2001) 2001 *Columbia Business Law Review* 257 at 313.

61 See Chapter 7, Section C.

62 *NutraSweet*, above note 52 at para 124.

and understanding of this practice remains open to interpretation and will likely evolve.

The Bureau's definition of predatory pricing cited above has two essential elements:

1) pricing below a firm's own cost
2) post-predation market power, which is the ability to recoup the losses from predatory pricing by later raising prices

A third factor is relevant to the assessment of whether the conduct can be characterized as an anti-competitive act:

3) anti-competitive purpose/business justification

Finally, to satisfy the requirements of section 79(1)(c), an anti-competitive effect must be shown:

4) substantial prevention or lessening of competition

These elements will be considered in turn below.

a) Below-Cost Pricing

Low pricing is by no means an indicator of predatory behaviour on its own. It is both a rational competitive strategy to gain market share and the kind of conduct competition law seeks to encourage, even when prices are below a competitor's costs:

> [P]ricing below the competitor's cost (but above [the alleged predating firm's] own) drives that competitor out of business, but only because the competitor is less efficient and cannot compete in its own right under fair terms. Rather than being anti-competitive, this is the purest example of meeting and beating the competition and should not be confused with predation. The alleged predator has attained the position of a dominant firm by being the most efficient, the most innovative, or both.[63]

In *Canada (Director of Investigation and Research) v Tele-Direct*, the Tribunal addressed allegations that the respondent, which was dominant in the market for telephone directory publication, had used targeted price reductions and other strategies to deter entry. In concluding that these practices were not anti-competitive on the evidence, the Tribunal expressed concern that an overly aggressive approach to sanctioning predatory behaviour and the lack an objective standard of what

63 Noel, above note 54 at 73.

constitutes a predatory versus "normal" competitive response, might run the risk of chilling healthy competitive behaviour:

> Decisions by the Tribunal restricting competitive action on the grounds that the action is of overwhelming intensity would send a chilling message about competition that is, in our view, not consistent with the purpose of the Act, as set forth in section 1.1. We are concerned that, in the absence of some objective test, firms can have no idea what constitutes a "competitive" versus an "anti-competitive" response when responses like those used by Tele-Direct in this case are involved (e.g., price freezing or cutting, incentives, product improvements, increased advertising).[64]

The advantage of a cost-based standard is that it provides an objective measure of what constitutes predation. Absent a future return from recoupment, a firm that prices below its own marginal cost (the cost of producing an additional unit of output) is not behaving rationally. The firm could save money, and societal resources, by shutting down production and reducing the loss it incurs. For this reason, below-marginal cost pricing is seen as a *prima facie* indicator of predation: "pricing below marginal cost greatly increases the possibility that rivalry will be extinguished or prevented for reasons unrelated to the efficiency of the monopolist."[65] Based on the foregoing logic, Areeda and Turner proposed that below-marginal cost pricing should be regarded as indicative of predation.[66] They provided the following definitions of the relevant cost benchmarks:

> **Fixed costs** are costs that do not vary with changes in output . . . fixed costs are costs that would continue even if the firm produced no output at all.

---

64 *Canada (Competition Act, Director of Investigation and Research) v Tele-Direct (Publications) Inc* (1997), 73 CPR (3d) 1 at para 610 (CCT) [*Tele-Direct*].

65 Areeda & Turner, above note 55 at 711–12:

> If a monopolist produces to a point where price equals marginal cost, only less efficient firms will suffer larger losses per unit of output; more efficient firms will be losing less or even operating profitably. Admittedly, the destruction of an equally efficient rival, and the deterrence of entry of firms which are equally efficient, poses some threat to competition in the long run; if demand increases to its former level, only the monopolist will occupy the market which he formerly shared with the rival. However, we see no satisfactory method of eliminating this risk. Establishing a price floor above marginal cost would permit survival not only of equally efficient firms, but less efficient ones as well. And in the short run, at least, entry even by equally efficient firms will be undesirable since excess capacity already exists.

66 *Ibid.*

> **Variable costs**, as the name implies, are costs that vary with changes in output. . . . The average variable cost is the sum of all variable costs divided by output.
>
> **Marginal cost** is the increment to total cost that results from producing an additional increment of output . . . .
>
> **Average [total] cost** is the sum of fixed cost and total variable cost, divided by output. It is, by definition, higher than average variable cost at all outputs, but will typically be below marginal cost at very high levels of output, when the plant is strained beyond efficient operating capacity.[67]

Areeda and Turner advocated the following standard for predation, based on average variable cost being a proxy for hard-to-measure marginal cost:

> Recognizing that marginal cost data are typically unavailable, we conclude that:
>
> (a) A price at or above reasonably anticipated average variable cost should be conclusively presumed lawful.
> (b) A price below reasonably anticipated average variable cost should be conclusively presumed unlawful.[68]

The Areeda-Turner proposal has generated criticism based on the view that pricing below cost is not necessarily anti-competitive predation. The general critique is that the trade-off between the sacrifice of current profit and the gain from monopolization is what is important—not whether price is above or below marginal cost.[69] Nonetheless, the Areeda-Turner standard has been adopted in the jurisprudence as an indicator of predation.

In *NutraSweet*, in assessing alleged predation under the abuse of dominance provisions, the Tribunal accepted the Areeda-Turner standard "for present purposes," to evaluate the allegation that the respondent had priced below cost. The Tribunal agreed that marginal cost "is so difficult to determine, a proxy for it is normally average variable cost ('AVC'), that is the average cost per unit of production taking into account only the cost components that vary with output."[70] An exception, the Tribunal noted, is a firm operating at capacity, in which case the better proxy

67 *Ibid* at 700–1 [emphasis added].
68 *Ibid* at 733.
69 See Paul L Joskow & Alvin K Klevorick, "A Framework for Analyzing Predatory Pricing" (1979) 89 *Yale Law Journal* 213 [Joskow & Klevorick].
70 *NutraSweet*, above note 52 at para 125.

is average total cost (ATC). In the case at hand, the evidence was that NutraSweet operated its aspartame plant at capacity—"24 hours a day, seven days a week" for at least part of the relevant period.[71] The Tribunal concluded that ATC was the appropriate measure of marginal cost for that period and average variable cost (AVC) the proxy during periods when the plant was operating below capacity. In the former case, the Tribunal had insufficient cost data; in the latter, it was satisfied "its prices were above AVC."[72] The Tribunal thus did not find predatory pricing on the evidence before it.

In *R v Consumers Glass Co*, a prosecution brought under the previous criminal predation provision, the accused firm had reduced the price of its plastic cup lids substantially (more than 16 percent) to counter the entry of a firm run by ex-employees. The court acquitted, finding that at no time had the accused charged prices which were unreasonably low under the applicable prohibition, given that the prices charged were merely intended to retain as much of the market as possible in the face of entry and were loss-minimizing. The court held that while "[i]t is not necessary . . . to decide whether the Areeda and Turner proposal is an appropriate one for the Court to accept in all predatory pricing cases," the accused firm had not priced below AVC, which was the appropriate measure of cost under the Areeda-Turner standard, given the presence of significant excess capacity.[73] The court did not express a view on whether a presumption of predation should apply when prices are below cost.

In *R v Hoffman-La Roche*, the accused were charged with predatory pricing in respect of the sale and supply of the branded prescription medications Librium and Valium, in response to the entry of a competitor (Horner) into the market for those medications. They were convicted on one count out of three, in respect of the supply of Valium to hospitals and governments at no cost over a six-month period. During that period, Roche gave away 174 million capsules to hospitals and governments, while selling them only 41 million.[74] The court considered that the test of "unreasonably low" prices involved a flexible standard, one element of which was "the actual difference between the production cost or accounting cost and the sale price."[75] The court also considered the duration of the price reductions, whether the price cutting was

71 *Ibid* at para 126.

72 *Ibid* at para 127.

73 *R v Consumers Glass Co* (1981), 124 DLR (3d) 274 (Ont HC) at para 69 [*Consumers Glass*].

74 *R v Hoffman-La Roche* (1980), 109 DLR (3d) 5 (Ont CA) at para 47 [*Hoffman-La Roche*], aff'd (1981), 125 DLR (3d) 607 (Ont CA).

75 *Ibid* at para 132.

defensive, and whether legitimate benefits such as retaining a particular market were behind the low pricing. Considering all these factors, the court found that "officials of Roche had the design of eliminating competitors and substantially lessening competition during the entire year that it gave Valium to hospitals."[76] Evidence before the court included correspondence between Roche employees to the effect that offering free product "will not only abort [new entrant] Horner's efforts but serve as a warning to others who seem to be showing an interest in this product."[77] Such evidence is consistent with the creation of a reputational barrier to entry through predatory behaviour.

In 2019, the Bureau discontinued an inquiry into alleged predatory pricing in another pharmaceutical case. It involved the supply by a subsidiary of Johnson & Johnson, Janssen, of the product Remicade, which is used to treat arthritis, psoriasis, Crohn's disease, and other ailments. The product was Johnson & Johnson's top earning pharmaceutical product in 2017, with sales revenue exceeding USD$6.3 billion worldwide and approximately CDN$1 billion in Canada. It was alleged, *inter alia*, that the product was being supplied to hospitals throughout Canada for 1 cent per vial, and for free to a large number of patients without insurance coverage for the drug. Although the Bureau concluded that this constituted below cost pricing, it found that the practice was not sufficiently widespread to cause a substantial prevention or lessening of competition.[78]

The cost standard for predatory pricing which is applied by the Bureau under the *Abuse of Dominance Guidelines* is "average avoidable cost."

76 *Ibid* at para 177.

77 *Ibid* at para 158.

78 Kelly Grant, "How a Blockbuster Drug Tells the Story of Why Canada's Spending on Prescriptions Is Sky High" *Globe and Mail* (20 October 2018), online: www.theglobeandmail.com/canada/article-how-a-blockbuster-drug-tells-the-story-of-why-canadas-spending-on. See also Canada, Competition Bureau, News Release, "Competition Bureau Statement Regarding Its Inquiry into Alleged Anti-competitive Conduct by Janssen" (20 February 2019), online: www.competitionbureau.gc.ca/eic/site/cb-bc.nsf/eng/04418.html [*Janssen Inquiry Discontinuance Statement by Bureau*]:

> In this case, the Bureau's review confirmed that Janssen was offering Remicade at a price below cost to certain hospitals and patients. However, the Bureau did not find credible evidence that Janssen's low pricing strategy was sufficiently widespread that it was likely to eliminate, discipline or deter entry by one or more competitors, so as to substantially prevent or lessen competition in the relevant market. In particular, while Janssen's low prices may have shifted demand from biosimilar products to Remicade, the Bureau did not find that the practice was likely to induce competitors to exit the market or otherwise substantially affect competition at this time.

In *Canada (Commissioner of Competition) v Air Canada*, an application was filed by the Commissioner alleging predation by the respondent airline in Atlantic Canada directed against WestJet and CanJet. At the time the (now repealed) airline-specific abuse of dominance regime identified one anti-competitive act as "operating capacity on a route or routes at fares that do not cover the avoidable cost of providing the service."[79] The Tribunal addressed the cost question in the first phase of the proceeding. The following definition of avoidable cost was put forward by the Commissioner's expert:

> Avoidable costs refer to all costs that can be avoided by not producing the good or service in question. In general, the avoidable cost of offering a service will consist of the variable costs and the product-specific fixed costs of offering the service. Where a particular input is used in the production of multiple products or services, the product-specific cost of the input will be a component of the avoidable cost for that product.[80]

The difference between average avoidable cost and average variable cost is "product-specific fixed costs"—fixed costs which, for example, can be reassigned to another product or service in a multi-product/service firm when the product or service in question is not produced. Even though these are fixed costs (and cannot be eliminated in the short run), they are "avoidable" because they can be shifted or deployed to generate revenue for another product/service of the firm (such as another travel routing, in the case of an airline). Because these costs can be deployed elsewhere to generate income, if the firm's prices do not cover them, that is an indicator that the firm is losing money for a reason, which is inferred to be predatory.[81]

The time period during which a cost adjustment can occur must be defined in order to determine whether a particular cost is avoidable. Definition of that time period can be a key issue. It was a central area of controversy, for example, in the *Air Canada* case.[82] The Bureau's *Guidelines*

---

79 *Canada (Commissioner of Competition) v Air Canada*, [2003] CCTD No 9 at para 25 [*Air Canada*].

80 *Ibid* at para 70.

81 In the *Intel* case, EC, *Commission Decision relating to a proceeding under Article 82 of the EC Treaty and Article 54 of the EEA Agreement* (D (2009) 3726, COMP/C-3 /37.990—Intel) the European Commission noted at para 1060:

> A correct measure of average avoidable cost should in principle take into account the most profitable alternative use of the production inputs Intel (or an as efficient competitor) uses to produce the units in question. If an employee dedicated to producing x86 CPUs can be redeployed to another type of production (for instance chipsets or flash memory), it would not be correct to treat his salary as unavoidable.

82 *Air Canada*, above note 79 at paras 186–92.

take the view that the period of "avoidability" should be determined by the duration of the alleged predation, which was the position adopted by the Tribunal in *Air Canada*.[83]

If pricing is found by the Bureau to be below the average avoidable cost, this is a *prima facie* indication of predation. However, other facts are then examined to determine whether the below-cost pricing may have another, benign explanation:

> Where the firm's pricing of the product(s) does not cover its own average avoidable costs, the Bureau will consider the pricing to be predatory in the absence of evidence that the overriding purpose of the conduct was in furtherance of a credible efficiency or pro-competitive rationale. For example, it may be reasonable for a firm to sell excess, obsolete or perishable products at below-cost prices. Similarly, companies may use below-cost promotional pricing to induce customers to try a new product.[84]

As will be seen below, these kinds of rationales may also be used to assess whether a proffered business purpose is legitimate act under the abuse of dominance provisions.

The ability of the predated firm to cover its costs at the allegedly predatory prices is another indicator of possible predation. The *Guidelines* indicated that, as an initial screen, "the Bureau will examine whether the alleged predatory price can be matched by competitors without incurring losses (suggesting that discipline or exclusion, and subsequent recoupment, is unlikely to occur)."[85]

b) Market Power: The Potential for Recoupment

Pricing below cost is often not anti-competitive. As the United States Supreme Court stated in *Brooke Group v Brown & Williamson Tobacco Corp*:

> Recoupment is the ultimate object of an unlawful predatory pricing scheme; it is the means by which a predator profits from predation. Without it, predatory pricing produces lower aggregate prices in the market, and consumer welfare is enhanced. Although unsuccessful predatory pricing may encourage some inefficient substitution toward the product being sold at less than its cost, unsuccessful predation is in general a boon to consumers.[86]

---

83 *Abuse Guidelines*, above note 51 at para 60.

84 *Ibid*.

85 *Ibid* at para 61.

86 *Brooke Group v Brown & Williamson Tobacco Corp*, 509 US 209 (1993) at 224 [*Brooke Group*].

Recoupment was described as follows in *Hoffman-La Roche*:

> One company, the predator, decides to sell its product at a very low price in order to put his competitor out of business, because they cannot or will not sell at such a low price. If the competitor goes out of business, the predator may then increase his prices, make back any loss as a result of the predatory campaign and continue to reap the benefits of greater profits, because his former competitor has now departed from the scene.[87]

The recoupment scenario is depicted graphically below (**Figure 9.1**). Prior to predation, the price level is cost plus a reasonable return. The predatory firm then drops prices below cost for a sufficient period to drive the entrant out of the market. Having deterred entry or raised barriers by creating a reputation for predation, prices can be raised to recoup losses during the post-predation period.

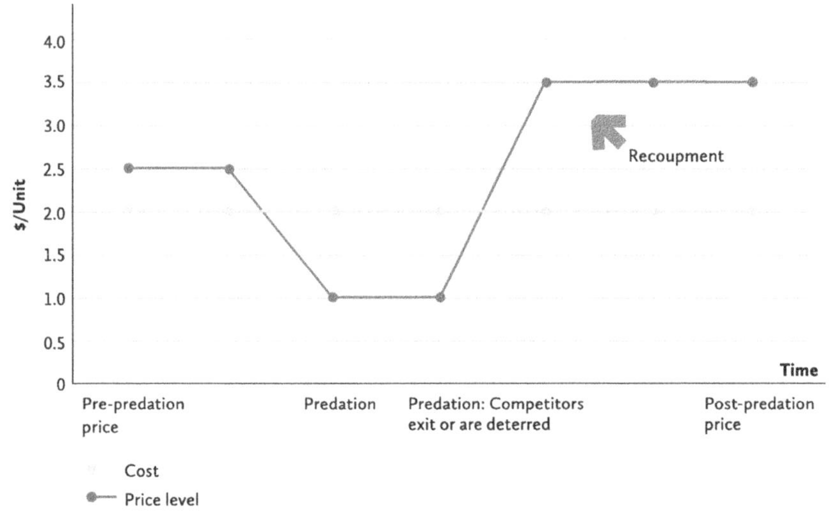

FIGURE 9.1. Predation theory: Recoupment may occur if a firm can raise prices for a sufficiently long period after driving out or deterring competitors with below-cost prices

87 *Hoffman-La Roche*, above note 75 at para 90. See also *Tele-Direct*, above note 65 at para 609:

> The essence of an allegation of predatory pricing is that the firm foregoes short-run revenues by cutting prices, driving out rivals and thus providing itself with the opportunity to recoup more than its short-term losses through higher profits earned in the longer term in the absence of competition. A predatory pricing allegation is difficult because, at least in the short-run, consumers apparently benefit from lower prices. In addition, predation can only succeed if the predator has greater staying power than its rivals and a reasonable prospect of recouping its losses. In order to distinguish competitive pricing action from predation, therefore, the "Areeda-Turner test" for predatory pricing was developed and has been adopted by the courts.

That low pricing may have driven a firm out of business does not necessarily signal predation unless the predator has the capacity to entrench or to enhance its market power. As the court held in *Brooke Group*, "[t]hat below-cost pricing may impose painful losses on its target is of no moment to the antitrust laws if competition is not injured. It is axiomatic that the antitrust laws were passed for 'the protection of *competition*, not *competitors*.'"[88] If competition laws were to sanction low pricing that did not have the potential for preserving or enhancing market power, they could backfire by deterring healthy competitive behaviour.

Under the *Abuse of Dominance Enforcement Guidelines*, the Bureau considers the ability to recoup losses from predation as an indication of whether the practice is likely to prevent or lessen competition substantially. Under the earlier *Predatory Pricing Enforcement Guidelines*,[89] this factor was applied as part of stage one of its assessment to determine whether predation was even possible.[90] While the current *Guidelines* do not use this screen, the approach taken is similar, because the Bureau takes the position that unless this element is satisfied, predation is unlikely:

> In many cases the ability to recoup losses from predation will depend on barriers to entry that prevent new entry in response to supra-competitive prices, or re-entry by predated firms. In the absence of recoupment in the past, present, or likely recoupment in the future, the Bureau would not typically consider paragraph 79(1)(c) to be satisfied.[91]

Market power is necessary for recoupment in order for the predator to be in a position to raise prices above competitive levels. As discussed in Chapter 7, market power may be assessed directly by indicators such

---

88 *Brooke Group*, above note 86 at 244, citing *Brown Shoe Co v United States*, 370 US 294 at 320 [emphasis in original].

89 Canada, Competition Bureau, *Predatory Pricing Enforcement Guidelines* (21 July 2008), s 3.1, online: www.competitionbureau.gc.ca/eic/site/cb-bc.nsf/eng/02713.html [*Predatory Pricing Enforcement Guidelines* 2008].

90 See Joskow & Klevorick, above note 70 at 244:

> In the first stage, we would examine both the structural characteristics of the market in question and the market power of the alleged predator firm to find out if they generate a reasonable expectation that predatory pricing could occur and impose significant economic losses on society.
>
> . . .
>
> We believe that this first-stage "structural" requirement, using generally accepted definitions of monopoly power, would discourage frivolous predatory pricing cases.

91 *Abuse Guidelines*, above note 51 at 20, footnote 39.

as existing price levels, or indirectly, by inferring from high market share in a properly defined market and other structural indicators such as high barriers to entry.[92]

Recoupment is not an explicit requirement in the *Competition Act* and the American requirement of recoupment in *Brooke Group* has not been adopted by any Canadian case to date. Indeed, a rigorous application of the recoupment standard developed in *Brooke Group* has been criticized by some American commentators as making any allegation of predation "literally impossible to satisfy," suggesting a need to scrutinize the evidence closely to see if the conduct in question satisfies alternative models of how predation might occur.[93] In the 2008 *Guidelines*, the Bureau identified a number of additional considerations which were seen as relevant to the issue of whether a firm had created barriers to entry through reputation. These reflect the fact that there are various models of predation which economists have identified. The Bureau's list of factors provides a useful checklist of the kind of evidence that indicates the potential for rational predation, and the potential for recoupment:

> In evaluating whether a firm has a reputation for predation, or whether market conditions exist that make predatory behaviour more likely to be successful such that a potential entrant would be deterred, the Bureau considers whether one or more of the following non-exhaustive list of market conditions are present:
>
> - the firm competes against smaller rivals in more than one geographic or product market or faces a succession of potential entrants over time;
> - the firm has priced below cost in response to actual or potential entry in the past, and there is a rational belief on the part of actual or potential competitors that it is likely to repeat this action in response to future entry;
> - the financing of an entrant is reliant on outside sources or is conditional on its ongoing profitability; and

92 See Chapter 7, Section C(1)(d).

93 Christopher R Leslie, "Predatory Pricing and Recoupment" (2013) 113 *Columbia Law Review* 1695 at 1700; Patrick Bolton, Joseph F Brodley & Michael H Riordan, "Predatory Pricing: Strategic Theory and Legal Policy" (2000) 88 *Georgetown Law Journal* 2239; Michael Funk & Christian Jaag, "The More Economic Approach to Predatory Pricing" (2018) 14 *Journal of Competition Law & Economics* 292 at 293: "the current legal practice in Europe and other constituencies, which requires *ex ante* dominance to pursue predatory pricing, makes the prosecution of predatory pricing virtually impossible because it overlooks the basic economic rationale for predatory pricing"; C Scott Hemphill & Philip J Weiser, "Beyond Brooke Group: Bringing Reality to the Law of Predatory Pricing" (2018) 127 *Yale Law Journal* 2048.

- actual or potential entrants are aware of the exit or other adverse competitive effects experienced by other rival firms.[94]

c) Purpose: Anti-competitive Versus Legitimate Business Purposes and Subjective Intent

As noted in Chapter 7, for any practice, including predatory pricing, to be an abuse of dominance, it must be found to be either a "practice of anti-competitive acts" or conduct which has had, is having or is likely to prevent or lessen competition substantially.. Determining a practice's anti-competitive character under the existing case law involves a flexible consideration of its purpose, including its foreseeable impact on competition. A respondent may put forward "a credible efficiency or pro-competitive rationale for the conduct in question, attributable to the respondent, which relates to and counterbalances the anti-competitive effects and/or subjective intent of the acts."[95] The respondent bears the onus of showing this rationale. Rationales that may be put forward in an attempt to satisfy this requirement in the context of a predatory pricing allegation include:

- selling excess, obsolete, or perishable products at below-cost prices[96]
- below-cost promotional pricing to induce customers to try a new product[97]
- reducing prices below cost in order to retain a sufficient share of the market to support efficient operations, particularly in the presence of chronic excess capacity[98]
- price reductions to meet lower prices already being charged by a competitor[99]

---

94 *Predatory Pricing Enforcement Guidelines* 2008, above note 89, section 3.4.1.

95 *Canada (Commissioner of Competition) v Toronto Real Estate Board*, 2017 FCA 236 at para 148 [*TREB* FCA], citing *Canada (Commissioner of Competition) v Canada Pipe*, 2006 FCA 233 at para 73 [*Canada Pipe* FCA].

96 *Abuse Guidelines*, above note 51 at para 60.

97 *Ibid*.

98 *Consumers Glass*, above note 74 at paras 68 and 74.

99 *Boehringer Ingelheim (Canada) Inc v Bristol-Myers Squibb Canada Inc*, [1998] OJ No 4007 (Gen Div); *Hoffman-La Roche*, above note 75 at para 179; *Canada (Commissioner of Competition) v Toronto Real Estate Board, [2016] CCTD No 7* at para 308 [*TREB* CCT]: "targeted practices that merely 'meet' the competition, as opposed to 'beating' it, typically will be considered to constitute 'competition on the merits,' and be legitimately justified." See also *Tele-Direct*, above note 65 at para 593: "Targeting, in the sense of a differentiated response to competitors, is a decidedly normal competitive reaction. An incumbent can be expected to behave differently where it faces entry than where it does not. One competes where there is competition. Similarly there may be gradations of reaction depending on the nature of the competitive threats."

- a manufacturer wishing to keep its business alive, its customers supplied, and its employees working during a difficult economic period selling products at less than cost for a time in the hope of recouping those losses when conditions improve[100]
- for prestige reasons, a supplier wishes to be represented in a particular market, for example, to maintain well-regarded retail outlets, and reduces prices for that purpose[101]

Evidence of an anti-competitive purpose for the pricing practice is also relevant to its characterization under abuse of dominance, particularly given the 2022 amendments, which included "any act intended to have a predatory, exclusionary or disciplinary negative effect on a competitor" in the definition of "anti-competitive act" in section 78.[102] In *Tele-Direct*, the Tribunal held:

> [T]he Tribunal must decide . . . whether, once all relevant factors have been taken into account and weighed, the act in question is, on balance, "exclusionary, predatory or disciplinary". Relevant factors include evidence of the effects of the act, of any business justification and of subjective intent which, while not necessary, may be informative in assessing the totality of the evidence.[103]

The Tribunal found evidence of subjective intent in the incumbent's response to entry by a well-funded new entrant, Southam. For example, Tele-Direct stated that it wished to "make the cost of carrying on business against [Tele-Direct] market-by-market exceptionally high" and to "make competition an expensive proposition."[104] The Tribunal found "that Tele-Direct intended, in a subjective sense, to convey a warning about future entry as well as protecting its position in the individual markets subject to entry."[105] However, balancing all of the available evidence, the Tribunal was unable to conclude that Tele-Direct's response was anti-competitive or predatory. Even in the face of evidence of subjective intent, the Tribunal was reluctant to brand as anti-competitive the response to entry which was not measured against an "objective" benchmark such as costs. As noted above, its concern was discouraging legitimate competitive behaviour. The application of economic models such as raising rivals' costs and the potential creation of reputational

---

100 *Hoffman-La Roche*, above note 75 at para 135.

101 *Ibid.*

102 *An Act to implement certain provisions of the budget tabled in Parliament April 7, 2022 and other measures*, SC 2022, c 10, s 261.

103 *Tele-Direct*, above note 65 at para 542.

104 *Ibid* at paras 602–3.

105 *Ibid* at para 605.

barriers to entry, discussed above,[106] may provide at least a theoretical rationale to question this finding.

In *Toronto Real Estate Board*, the Tribunal noted that evidence of predatory intent may play a key role in determining the anti-competitive character of the conduct at issue:

> Where any predatory, exclusionary or disciplinary motivations are found to have played a more important role in the respondent's overall subjective intentions than one or more asserted legitimate business justifications, the overall character of the impugned practice typically will be found to have the anti-competitive purpose contemplated by paragraph 79(1)(*b*). Likewise, where it is determined that any predatory, exclusionary or disciplinary effects that are objectively deemed to have been intended outweigh one or more legitimate business justifications, the impugned practice typically will be found to have an anti-competitive purpose.[107]

The fact that a firm has a dominant position itself may have an impact on the characterization of conduct as predatory. Anti-competitive conduct considered competition on the merits when engaged in by a non-dominant firm may be seen in a different light if engaged in by a dominant player.[108]

d) Substantial Prevention or Lessening of Competition

As noted in Chapter 7, the last element of abuse of dominance under section 79(1)(c), competitive effect, comes down to whether the anti-competitive acts engaged in by the dominant firm create, preserve, or add to its market power.[109] In the case of predatory pricing, the anti-competitive effect turns on the potential success of the alleged predation in driving out existing firms and deterring new entrants by reinforcing or raising reputational and other barriers to entry. Thus, in the Bureau's *Janssen* inquiry into alleged predation by the Johnson & Johnson subsidiary through low-cost or free supply of the pharmaceutical Remicade,

---

106 See above in this chapter, Section C(1).

107 *TREB CCT, above note 99* at para 287, aff'd *TREB* FCA, above note 95.

108 *TREB* CCT, above note 99 at para 310: "any conduct that is subjectively intended or deemed to have been intended to have a predatory, exclusionary or disciplinary negative effect on a competitor can be found to be anti-competitive within the meaning of section 79, even if the same conduct would be considered to constitute 'competition on the merits' if pursued by a non-dominant firm (*Tele-Direct*, above at pp. 180–181)."

109 *NutraSweet*, above note 52 at para 138; *Canada (Competition Act, Director of Investigation and Research) v The D&B Companies of Canada Ltd (1995), 64 CPR (3d) 216 (CCT) at para 155; Canada Pipe* FCA, above note 95 at para 43.

it was determined that a substantial prevention or lessening of competition was unlikely because of the lack of substantial impact on competing firms. The Bureau concluded that while Janssen's low prices may have shifted demand from the two competing pharmaceutical products to Remicade, it was not likely to induce competitors to exit the market or otherwise to affect competition substantially.[110]

Central to the assessment of whether predatory pricing may have a substantial impact on competition is the question of the potential for recoupment of losses from predation. Of relevance are high barriers to entry, whether those barriers have increased due to predation, and the amount of remaining competition in the market.[111] Those are among the key considerations in establishing whether a firm has or will likely have the market power necessary to engage in recoupment and thus in satisfying the competitive effects element of abuse of dominance. Given the requirement for enhancing or preserving market power, only firms with a substantial share of a relevant market are likely to be found to have engaged in predation.[112]

D. PRICE DISCRIMINATION

Over the decades since the 1930s, when the criminal price discrimination prohibition in the Canadian competition legislation was initially passed with the (unrealized, as it turned out) intent of protecting small businesses, the provision found an increasingly uneasy home in the statute, as the objective of the legislation evolved in favour of protecting competition, rather than individual competitors. With the repeal of the prohibition in 2009, the practice in some form may still fall under abuse of dominance. The limited circumstances in which it is likely to generate a "substantial prevention or lessening of competition," however, suggest this will be rare.

1) What Is Price Discrimination?

What do we mean by price discrimination? A definition is needed for any discussion to be meaningful. The House of Commons Standing Committee on Industry in 2000 provided the following summary description of the practice:

---

110 *Janssen Inquiry Discontinuance Statement by Bureau*, above note 79.

111 See *Predatory Pricing Enforcement Guidelines* 2008, above note 89 at s 5.1.

112 See Chapter 7, Section C(3)(c).

> Price discrimination is a marketing practice whereby a supplier of goods or services charges different prices to different customers (whether other businesses or final consumers) and these price differentials do not accurately reflect differences in costs of serving the different customers. Three conditions are necessary for a firm to be found to discriminate on the basis of price: (1) the firm must have market power to set prices (otherwise consumers can choose to purchase from a competing supplier); (2) the firm must be able to identify classes of consumers with different price sensitivities; and (3) there is limited opportunity for consumers to resell to each other (otherwise consumers would arbitrate these prices to the lower price offered).[113]

To the foregoing definition should be added that price discrimination may also involve the sale of identical units of a product at a common price in markets that are served at different costs per unit.[114]

It can be a challenge to determine whether underlying costs justify differing prices and to calculate what the appropriate differential may be. This is a reason for caution when intervening in this area in the absence of identification of a clear policy concern arising from this behaviour. In most circumstances, such concerns are not apparent; indeed price discrimination is commonplace and often pro-competitive.

Price discrimination can be found throughout the economy. Electricity rates differ between commercial and residential users for the same amount of energy consumption. Airlines charge different fares for first-class and economy seats, or depending on how far in advance a ticket is purchased, even though the underlying cost differences in these situations often do not justify the price differentials charged.

Even where price discrimination (in the sense defined above) clearly occurs, it is not in many cases harmful to social welfare. If a supplier is able to discriminate by adjusting the prices based on each customer's willingness to pay (for example, a vendor haggling with each buyer in a bazaar),[115] this may raise prices and transfer wealth from consumers to the seller, but it does not necessarily result in the loss of social welfare

---

113 *Interim Report on the Competition Act*, above note 27, ch 3, citing VanDuzer & Paquet, above note 26 at 5.

114 Stephen Martin, *Industrial Economics, Economic Analysis and Public Policy* (MacMillan: New York, 1988) at 374, defining price discrimination generally: "The act of selling the same article, produced under a single control, at different prices to different buyers."

115 "First degree price discrimination." However, due to transaction costs, perfect discrimination is likely to be impossible: Richard A Posner, *Economic Analysis of Law* (Chicago: Little Brown, 1977) at 206 [Posner].

that occurs with simple monopoly pricing.[116] Similarly, if a supplier, such as an airline, segments customers according to their different demand characteristics (e.g., first- and economy-class passengers), this may lead to a loss of wealth for those charged a higher price (e.g., first-class passengers), but a benefit for those charged a lower price (e.g., economy passengers). It may permit the airline to offer more economy seats than would have been the case without price discrimination, meaning economy passengers are better off. However, the net effect on the overall welfare of all passenger groups will vary depending on a number of variables, such as demand elasticity.[117]

2) Application of the Abuse of Dominance Provisions to Price Discrimination

Where price discrimination involves an exercise of market power[118] and results in "excessive" prices for some consumers, such conduct may create a sense of unfairness or inequity. This does not alone, however, supply a basis for intervention under Canadian competition law.[119] As discussed in Chapter 7, the mere possession of a dominant position is not a ground for a remedy: "section 79 is not intended to condemn a firm merely for having market power."[120] Abuse of dominance under section 79 can only be found where there has been a practice of anti-competitive acts (e.g., involving an exclusionary,

116 See Michael J Trebilcock et al, *The Law and Economics of Canadian Competition Policy* (Toronto: University of Toronto Press, 2003) at 344–45 [Trebilcock et al]. Such discrimination produces the same output as in a perfectly competitive market, but all customer surplus is captured by the seller. Furthermore, the seller may expend resources in trying to obtain a monopoly, resulting in a loss of welfare: Posner, above note 115.

117 "Second and third degree discrimination"; *ibid.*

118 But see Michael E Levine, "Price Discrimination without Market Power" (2002) 19 *Yale Journal on Regulation* 1.

119 Generally, see Dennis Carlton & Mark Israel, "Should Competition Policy Prohibit Price Discrimination?" *The Handbook of Competition Economics* (June 2009) at 13, online: www.compasslexecon.com/wp-content/uploads/2018/04/Price_Discrimination.pdf:

> Allowing a firm to set the simple monopoly price or to price discriminate to maximise its profits increases the "prize" associated with successful competition in the marketplace and thus increases the incentives for competitors to capture that prize. Prohibiting these practices, then, has the perverse effect of lessening incentives for competitors to compete, the exact opposite of the aim of competition policy.

120 *Canada (Commissioner of Competition) v Vancouver Airport Authority, [2019] CCTD No 6 at para 625.*

predatory, or disciplinary purpose) or the anti-competitive conduct in question has substantially prevented or lessened competition (i.e., created, preserved, or added to market power). The mere use of price discrimination, even by a dominant firm, "is not inherently anticompetitive."[121] The circumstances must be analyzed to determine its impact on competition.

Price discrimination can be assessed for its effect on competition in the seller's market (referred to as "primary line" effects) or in the buyer's market[122] ("secondary line" effects). The latter are not generally seen by economists as likely to generate competition policy concerns and a basis for intervention. Price differences between different purchases may well be cost-justified and therefore a reflection of the operation of an efficient market. If true price discrimination by a seller is occurring and favours certain large buyers, smaller buyers may form groups to obtain volume discounts to counter the power of their larger rivals. Sellers also have incentives to guard against dependence on monopsonist buyers by offering lower prices to other customers to prevent that state of affairs.[123]

Furthermore, price discrimination is often pro-competitive in the sellers' market. For example:

- It is often an important component of healthy rivalry. Competition is enhanced when prices offered to buyers vary, making it harder for competitors to keep track of rivals' pricing.[124] Further, price discrimination can also be an important tool which can fuel rivalrous responses to changes in price by competitors.[125]

---

121 VanDuzer & Paquet, above note 26 at 6.

122 Hunter & Hutton, above note 2 at footnote 93: "[Section] 79 is a potentially effective weapon against anti-competitive price discrimination, a practice whose competitive effects are felt in the purchaser's, rather than the seller's, market."

123 Trebilcock et al, above note 116 at 350.

124 United States, Antitrust Modernization Commission, *Report and Recommendations* (April 2007) at 320, online: https://govinfo.library.unt.edu/amc/report_recommendation/toc.htm [*Antitrust Modernization Report and Recommendations*].

125 OECD Competition Committee, "Roundtable on 'Price Discrimination'—Note by the United States," DAF/COMP/WD(2016)69 (November 2016) at para 6, online: https://one.oecd.org/document/DAF/COMP/WD(2016)69/en/pdf [*Roundtable on 'Price Discrimination' – Note by the United States*], citing Jacques-Francois Thisse & Xavier Vives, "On the Strategic Choice of Spatial Price Policy" (1988) 78 *American Economic Review* 122 at 134: "[D]enying a firm the right to meet the price of a competitor on a discriminatory price provides the [competitor] with some protection against price attacks . . . [and] weaken[s] competition."

- Price discrimination may facilitate the breakdown of collusion by providing an avenue for cartel members to cheat on arranged or tacit prices.[126]
- Finally, it can also be an important tool for new entrants seeking to distinguish their products from those of incumbents.[127]

In the United States, the foregoing were among the considerations which led the Antitrust Modernization Commission in 2007 to conclude that the *Robinson-Patman Act*,[128] which restricts forms of price discrimination, "potentially harms competition and consumers." The commission recommended that the statute be repealed in its entirety.[129]

It is necessary to identify what specific practices are at issue to assess whether there is any concern from forms of price discrimination on lessening competition in the seller's market. Three are examined below: predatory pricing, loyalty rebates, and a margin squeeze.[130]

Price discrimination in the form of predatory pricing can occur, for example, when a competitor selectively reduces prices in response to a rival's entry in particular markets, such as by using "fighting brands" as in *R v Eddy Match Co Ltd*.[131] Whether such conduct may involve an abuse of dominance will depend on the application of the factors, such as the price–cost relationship and whether the market structure permits recoupment of price reductions, discussed above in this chapter.[132]

The 2022 amendments increase the potential for selective price reductions to be found anti-competitive by adding to the practices listed in section 78 the following:

> (j) a selective or discriminatory response to an actual or potential competitor for the purpose of impeding or preventing the competitor's entry into, or expansion in, a market or eliminating the competitor from a market;

Another potential application of the section is to loyalty rebates, which involve a supplier charging a customer a price that reduces as the customer's purchases increase. Thus, "the same customer is effectively charged different prices on different units purchased, with the highest

---

126 See Trebilcock et al, above note 116 at 349.

127 *Antitrust Modernization Report and Recommendations*, above note 124 at 320.

128 15 USC ¶ 13.

129 *Ibid* at iii, 20, and 311–26. The statute has not been repealed to date but has not been subject to significant public enforcement. See Daniel Sokol, "Analysing Robinson-Patman" (2015) 83 *Geo Wash LR* 2064 at 2067.

130 As identified in the *Roundtable on 'Price Discrimination'—Note by the United States*, above note 125 at 4–6.

131 *R v Eddy Match Co Ltd* (1951), 104 CCC 39, aff'd (1953), 109 CCC 1 (Que CA).

132 See above in this chapter, Section C(3)(b).

price charged on the first units. Hence, the practice can be considered a form of price discrimination."[133] The effects of loyalty rebates are similar to exclusive dealing, in that they align the interests of supplier and customer and may assist efficient distribution, and enhance interbrand competition. Their impact thus depends on considerations such as the potential creation of barriers to the entry of competing suppliers.[134]

A margin squeeze occurs when a vertically integrated firm sets a high price for an essential input, squeezing the profitability of a downstream rival. The margin squeeze can involve price discrimination if higher input prices are charged only to the downstream rival. The list of anti-competitive practices under the abuse of dominance provisions in the *Competition Act* includes:

> (a) squeezing, by a vertically integrated supplier, of the margin available to an unintegrated customer who competes with the supplier, for the purpose of impeding or preventing the customer's entry into, or expansion in, a market.[135]

Whether this practice may lead to a remedy would turn on the elements of abuse of dominance; i.e., whether there is an anti-competitive purpose and the potential for preserving or adding to the market power of the supplier.[136] Thus, squeezing, like the other practices featuring a form of price discrimination, would be assessed in light of its particular impacts on competition and market power.

In summary, price discrimination is often pro-competitive and potentially efficiency- and welfare-enhancing. The circumstances in which the abuse of dominance provisions may apply to this practice appear quite limited.

3) Delivered Pricing

A form of geographic price discrimination in the form of "delivered pricing" is covered in sections 80 and 81:

> 80(1) For the purposes of section 81, ***delivered pricing*** means the practice of refusing a customer, or a person seeking to become a customer, delivery of an article at any place in which the supplier engages in a practice of making delivery of the article to any other of the

---

133 *Roundtable on 'Price Discrimination'—Note by the United States*, above note 125 at para 15.

134 See Chapter 8 at Section C(2)(b).

135 *Competition Act*, above note 3, s 78(a).

136 See Chapter 7, Section C.

> supplier's customers on the same trade terms that would be available to the first-mentioned customer if his place of business were located in that place. . . .
>
> 81 (1) Where, on application by the Commissioner, the Tribunal finds that delivered pricing is engaged in by a major supplier of an article in a market or is widespread in a market with the result that a customer, or a person seeking to become a customer, is denied an advantage that would otherwise be available to him in the market, the Tribunal may make an order prohibiting all or any of such suppliers from engaging in delivered pricing.

Delivered pricing thus involves refusing to deliver articles to a particular location on the same trade terms as those applicable when the supplier delivers them to other customers at that same location. A supplier who supplies goods in Regina and Winnipeg would, for example, engage in delivered pricing if that supplier refused delivery in Winnipeg to a Regina-located customer on the same terms the supplier offers other Winnipeg-located customers.

This provision was added in the 1986 amendments.[137] The background materials explained that it was intended to address a practice by suppliers of charging higher prices in an area featuring less competition and then inhibiting their customers in that area from obtaining and transporting lower-priced goods from another area to side-step the higher prices. A concern about the practice was that it may permit the supplier to maintain price coordination in the higher-priced market.[138]

While the practice must be engaged in by a major supplier or be widespread, section 81 does not require any prevention or lessening of competition. The *Guide* to the 1986 amendments explained that this is because delivered pricing "is usually an indication of lack of vigorous competition rather than a practice whereby competition is itself lessened."[139] In other words, it was seen as involving the exercise of market power, rather than its enhancement.

137 SC 1986, c 26, s 47 (originally ss 52 & 53).

138 Canada, Consumer and Corporate Affairs, *Amendments to the Combines Investigation Act, Background Information and Explanatory Notes* (Ottawa: Minister of Supply and Services, 1984) at 22: "[T]he suppliers will not permit [customers from another region to take delivery elsewhere] because it would tend to break down their oligopolistic pricing system." See also Roy Davidson, "Delivered Pricing Under the New *Competition Act*" (1986) 7 *Canadian Competition Policy Record* 59 at 63: the section "will be encouraging more and more customers to breach basing-point-pricing systems by buying at points where prices are low, particularly where they are free to backhaul with their own trucks."

139 Canada, Consumer and Corporate Affairs, *Competition Law Amendments, A Guide* (Ottawa: Minister of Supply and Services, 1985) at 24.

The section provides exceptions for situations where delivery to the customer would require significant capital investments or affect the maintenance of the quality of a branded product.[140] No applications have been made to date under the provision, which may only be enforced by the Commissioner.

E. PRICE MAINTENANCE

1) Introduction

The civil price maintenance provision introduced in 2009[141] applies to three different practices.

- **Resale price maintenance**: A supplier influences upward, or discourages the reduction of the price at which a customer advertises, supplies, or offers for supply a product for resale within Canada (section 76(1)(a)(i)).
- **Refusal to supply due to low pricing**: A supplier refuses to supply a product or otherwise discriminates against a person or class of persons engaged in business in Canada because of the low pricing policy of that person or class of persons (section 76(1)(a)(ii)).
- **Inducing refusal to supply**: A person induces a supplier, as a condition of doing business with the supplier, to refuse to supply a product to a person or class of persons because of the low pricing policy of the latter person or class of persons (section 76(8)).

Noteworthy aspects:

- All of the foregoing practices require an "adverse effect on competition in a market," and thus are not subject to *per se* treatment, as under the previous law.
- A private application for a remedy for these practice may be made, with leave of the Tribunal, by a person who is "directly affected."[142] However, because the practice was decriminalized, damages are no longer available.
- Section 76 is restricted to *vertical* or *resale* price maintenance, not horizontal or competitor-to-competitor price maintenance, which had been covered by the previous criminal prohibition.

---

140 *Competition Act*, above note 3, ss 81(2) & (3).

141 *Budget Implementation Act, 2009*, SC 2009, c 2, s 426.

142 *Competition Act*, above note 3, s 103.1 (7.1).

2) Resale Price Maintenance: The Elements

> 76(1) On application by the Commissioner or a person granted leave under section 103.1, the Tribunal may make an order under subsection (2) if the Tribunal finds that
>
> (a) a person referred to in subsection (3) directly or indirectly
> (i) by agreement, threat, promise or any like means, has influenced upward, or has discouraged the reduction of, the price at which the person's customer or any other person to whom the product comes for resale supplies or offers to supply or advertises a product within Canada . . . and
>
> (b) the conduct has had, is having or is likely to have an adverse effect on competition in a market.

The section covers what was a prevalent practice of suppliers prior to its being subject to a *per se* criminal prohibition in 1952: dictating the selling price to retailers in many consumer goods markets, such as "clothing (jeans, shoes, socks, underwear, shirts), jewelry, sports equipment, candy, biscuits, automobiles, gasoline, small and large appliances (stereos, shavers, washing machines)."[143] Now the practice is subject to a civil application to the Tribunal, which may result only in an order prohibiting its continuation where there is an adverse effect on competition.

a) Person Subject to an Order

The "person" subject to an order is anyone who is in the business of supplying or producing a product, extends credit or otherwise is engaged in a business which relates to credit cards, or has rights or privileges conferred by a patent or other intellectual property.[144] Section 76(4) on the other hand removes the application of the section from suppliers with specified relationships to the person supplied, which include principal and agent, common employment, or corporate affiliation.

The Bureau has issued *Price Maintenance Guidelines* which take the view that the section "may apply to more than one person," for example, "where several competing suppliers each engage in price maintenance conduct within the scope of paragraph 76(1)(a) of the Act."[145] This scenario reflects a traditional area of concern about price maintenance: that it

---

143 Frank Mathewson & Ralph Winter, "The Law and Economics of Resale Price Maintenance" (1998) 13 *Review of Industrial Organization* 57 at 59 [Matthewson & Winter].

144 *Ibid*, s 76(3).

145 Canada, Competition Bureau, *Enforcement Guidelines: Price Maintenance (Section 76 of the Competition Act)* (15 September 2014) at 3 [*Price Maintenance Guidelines*].

may be the product of collusion among suppliers, who seek to "enhance cartel stability by eliminating . . . retail price variation."[146] While a criminal prosecution of the supplier under section 45 for price fixing might be possible if the evidence exists, section 76 also affords a potential remedy against the impact of a cartel in downstream markets.

b) Articles *and* Services Covered

The word "product" in the Act includes articles and services. The fact that the section only applies to resale (as discussed below) may, however, limit its scope given the more limited circumstances in which a service, as opposed to an article, can be said to be subject to resale.[147]

c) Resale Requirement

In *Canada (Commissioner of Competition) v Visa Canada Corp*, the Commissioner alleged that certain rules imposed on merchants by the respondent credit card network operators involved price maintenance under section 76. The central conduct at issue was a so-called no surcharge rule imposed by Visa and Mastercard, which required that merchants accept credit cards for payment without imposing any additional charges over the advertising price.[148] The rule was imposed contractually by Visa and Mastercard through firms called "acquirers," which provide the technology and hardware permitting merchants to process consumers' credit card payments.

The Tribunal first held that the section "requires a resale of a product." It noted that Parliament removed the resale requirement from the criminal prohibition in 1976, but then specifically reinstated it in the 2009 amendments.[149] It addition to this legislative history, the Tribunal considered that the wording of the section can apply only to *vertical* price maintenance: it covers influencing "the price at which the person's customer or any other person *to whom the product comes for resale* supplies or offers to supply."[150]

---

146 Mathewson & Winter, above note 143 at 65.

147 David Feldman, "The Redemption of S. 76: Finding Meaning for Resale Price Maintenance in the Service Context after *Visa Mastercard*" (2016) 27 *Canadian Competition Law Review* 425 [Feldman].

148 For example, Visa's regulations stated: "Visa merchants agree to accept Visa cards for payment of goods or services without charging any amount over the advertised price as a condition of Visa card acceptance, unless local law requires that merchants be permitted to engage in such practice."

149 *Canada (Commissioner of Competition) v Visa Canada Corp, [2013] CCTD No 10* at paras 119–27 [*Visa/Mastercard*].

150 *Ibid* at para 116 [emphasis in original]. It held that "the word 'resale' applies to both 'customer' and 'other person' given the presence of the word 'other.'"

The Tribunal then considered whether the circumstances of the case involved the resale of a service. The difficulty was that Visa and Mastercard did not provide a service (like a portfolio of financial advice) which was simply resold in the same or similar form by acquirers. The Tribunal found that Visa and Mastercard provided "Credit Card Network Services" to acquirers, but that acquirers provided a different service to merchants ("Credit Card Acceptance Services"). The Tribunal therefore concluded that "the requirement that a product comes for resale to a customer has not been established."[151] (See **Figure 9.2**, below.)

The Tribunal held that a product for resale did not have to be identical to the product supplied to the reseller, but at least "substantially similar on the important characteristics of the product."[152] The Bureau's approach to this requirement in its *Price Maintenance Guidelines* is potentially broader: "where the product resold is repackaged, reapportioned, processed or transformed from the product supplied, or is bundled with products other than the product supplied" the Bureau considers that this could satisfy the requirement that the product resold is "substantially similar."[153]

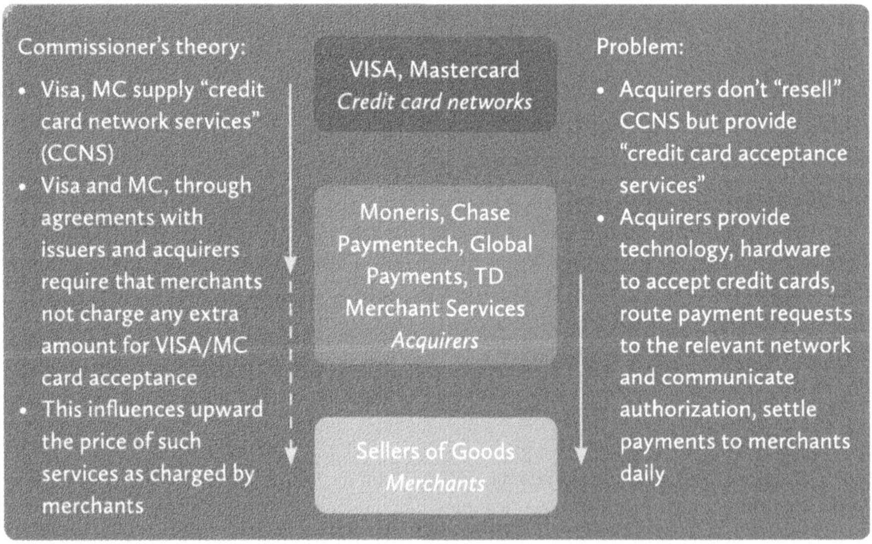

FIGURE 9.2. Visa/MC case (2013): Resale issue. The "credit card acceptance services" provided by Visa and Mastercard were not resold and hence the resale price maintenance provisions were held not to apply.

151 *Ibid* at paras 147–48 and 157.

152 *Ibid* at para 134.

153 *Price Maintenance Guidelines*, above note 145 at 6.

d) Influence Upward or Discourage the Reduction of the Resale Price

The supplier must influence upward or discourage the reduction of the price[154] of the customer, or some other person who, in the vertical chain of supply, resells the product. Unlike the previous criminal offence, the section no longer applies to *attempts* to influence the price—the price effect must have actually occurred.

The mere exercise of market power by a supplier, by raising the wholesale price of a product, is insufficient to constitute price maintenance.[155] The Tribunal in *Visa/Mastercard* noted, however, that the influence in question could be indirect. While the Tribunal dismissed the case on the basis of the lack of a resale, it considered this issue and held that the effect of the "no-surcharge" rule had been to increase the card acceptance fees that acquirers charged merchants, because the rule "reduces the discipline on the Respondents' pricing that would otherwise come from substitution or threatened substitution in favour of other means of payment."[156]

e) By Agreement, Threat, Promise, or Like Means

Given that the language of the section in this respect is unchanged from the former criminal provisions, the extensive jurisprudence on these words may guide the interpretation of section 76.[157] The Bureau takes the view that this language covers "any conduct by which a supplier implicitly or explicitly purports to either confer a benefit on a retailer who adheres to the supplier's influence on the retailer's selling or advertised prices, or to impose a penalty on a retailer if the retailer disregards the supplier's influence on its prices."[158]

f) Presumptions Governing Suggested Retail Prices and Related Matters

Sections 76(5), (6), and (7) set out a number of rules which govern situations where suggested and advertised retail prices are deemed to have

---

154 Price maintenance as dealt with in the United States has also covered "maximum" prices: e.g., *Atlantic Richfield Co v USA Petroleum Co*, 495 US 328 (1990).

155 *Visa/Mastercard*, above note 149 at para 162: "the 'influencing-upward' condition must mean something other than the consequences that flow from a company's exercise of market power which results in adverse effects on competition in the form of an increase in prices in the downstream market. If not, section 76 would turn into an open-ended provision." See also *Price Maintenance Guidelines*, above note 145 at 4.

156 *Visa/Mastercard*, above note 149 at para 321.

157 See, e.g., the case law cited in D Jeffrey Brown, ed, *Competition Act and Commentary* (Markham: LexisNexis, 2016) at 102–103.

158 *Price Maintenance Guidelines*, above note 145 at 4.

influenced the retail price. These correspond to those applicable under the previous criminal provision and include aspects such as suggested resale prices and advertised resale prices.[159]

g) Adverse Effect on Competition

In *CarGurus, Inc v Trader Corp*, the Tribunal stated, "[t]he primary purpose of the price maintenance provisions contained in section 76 of the Act is to allow greater price competition among retailers/dealers by freeing them from pricing restraints which would otherwise be imposed by their suppliers."[160] However, the section is far from a "charter of pricing freedom" for retailers from such restraints, given resale price maintenance must have "an adverse effect on competition in a market." This requirement, which was not present in the previous criminal provision, is a reflection of the view that while resale price maintenance reduces intrabrand competition among retailers supplying the same branded product, it can also enhance interbrand competition and therefore should be subject to case-by-case assessment.[161] This view was reflected in the 2002 House of Commons Standing Committee Report, which provides an indication of the legislative intent, given the lack of debate or scrutiny surrounding the 2009 amendments:[162]

---

159 These sections of the *Competition Act*, above note 3, provide:

> 76(5) For the purposes of this section, a suggestion by a producer or supplier of a product of a resale price or minimum resale price for the product, however arrived at, is proof that the person to whom the suggestion is made is influenced in accordance with the suggestion, in the absence of proof that the producer or supplier, in so doing, also made it clear to the person that they were under no obligation to accept the suggestion and would in no way suffer in their business relations with the producer or supplier or with any other person if they failed to accept the suggestion;
>
> (6) For the purposes of this section, the publication by a producer or supplier of a product, other than a retailer, of an advertisement that mentions a resale price for the product is proof that the producer or supplier is influencing upward the selling price of any person to whom the product comes for resale, unless the price is expressed in a way that makes it clear to any person whose attention the advertisement comes to that the product may be sold at a lower price;
>
> (7) Subsections (5) and (6) do not apply to a price that is affixed or applied to a product or its package or container.

160 *CarGurus, Inc v Trader Corp*, [2016] CCTD No 15 [*CarGurus*].

161 See Chapter 8, Sections A and C(2)(b) for a discussion of interbrand versus intrabrand competition.

162 See Feldman, above note 147.

> From the consumer's perspective, vertical price maintenance results in more services, which we would regard as good, but higher prices, which we would view as bad. The Committee was told that, on balance, the decision of how to market a product and how to design a distribution system should be left up to the manufacturer. Prohibiting resale price maintenance under the *per se* rule is effectively regulating the manufacturer's decisions on how best to maximize the sale of his products. By way of an analogy, we do not prohibit by law high levels of advertising even when such advertising raises prices; for the same reason we should not prohibit vertical price maintenance under a *per se* rule.[163]

Examples of how resale price maintenance may generate more services, and stimulate interbrand competition, are provided in the Bureau's *Price Maintenance Guidelines*:

- Resale price maintenance prevents price discounting and thereby guards against "free riding" by discounting retailers on the quality and product reputation established by full service retailers. It thus preserves incentives to offer higher levels of services.
- It can also provide retailers with a higher margin which can support increased promotion, service, inventory, or other competitive offerings which may enhance the product's success against rivals' products.[164]

On the other hand, the *Price Maintenance Guidelines* describe (as well as implementation of a suppliers' cartel, discussed earlier) how resale price maintenance may be anti-competitive.

> **Supplier exclusion:** An incumbent supplier may use price maintenance conduct to guarantee margins for retailers to make them unwilling to carry the products of rival or new entrant competitors to the supplier. To the extent this results in the foreclosure of downstream distribution channels to competing suppliers, it may limit or reduce the ability of such suppliers to discipline the supplier's wholesale pricing, so as to enable the supplier to charge a price that is higher than could be sustained absent the conduct.[165]

The requirement that the practice must have an "adverse effect on competition" has been interpreted to involve "created, enhanced or preserved market power."[166] This requires a consideration of such factors

163 *A Plan to Modernize Canada's Competition Regime*, above note 29 at 74.
164 *Ibid* at 15.
165 *Price Maintenance Guidelines*, above note 145 at 16.
166 *B-Filer Inc v Bank of Nova Scotia*, [2006] CCTD No 36 at para 208.

as market definition, market shares and concentration, barriers to entry, price and quality impacts and the level of remaining competition in the market.[167] It also requires the same "but for" assessment applicable to abuse of dominance and vertical restraints:

> The Tribunal must thus compare the level of competitiveness of the market in the presence of the conduct with that which would exist in its absence, and then determine whether the effect on competition, if any, is adverse. This comparison must be done with reference to actual effects in the past and present, as well as likely future effects.[168]

It remains to be seen in what circumstances a practice of resale price maintenance may affect competition "adversely." There is little evidence that the practice is often used in the exclusionary fashion suggested by the Bureau's *Price Maintenance Guidelines*. Time will tell whether the 2009 amendment results in any significant jurisprudence surrounding resale price maintenance in Canada. Even if does not, many economists would not likely shed tears of regret, given their view of the beneficial or neutral effect of the practice in most cases.

3) Refusal to Supply Due to Low Pricing

> 76(1) On application by the Commissioner or a person granted leave under section 103.1, the Tribunal may make an order under subsection (2) if the Tribunal finds that
>
> (a) a person referred to in subsection (3) directly or indirectly . . .
>
> (ii) has refused to supply a product to or has otherwise discriminated against any person or class of persons engaged in business in Canada because of the low pricing policy of that other person or class of persons; and
>
> (b) the conduct has had, is having or is likely to have an adverse effect on competition in a market.

As is the case for resale price maintenance, this provision applies to a "person" (as defined in section 76(3)), to the supply (or refusal to supply in this case) of services as well as articles, and requires that there be an "adverse effect on competition in a market" in order for an order to be made. The practice involves several additional elements reviewed below.

167 *Nadeau Poultry Farm Ltd v Groupe Westco Inc*, [2009] CCTD No 6.

168 *Visa/Mastercard*, above note 149 at para 353.

a) Refusal to Supply a Product or Discrimination in the Supply of a Product

The refusal may be direct or indirect; hence it can occur through a wide array of mechanisms which amount to a constructive refusal. The *Price Maintenance Guidelines* take the view that a refusal occurs when a supplier charges excessive wholesale prices, or through delays filling orders or filling them in an incomplete manner. Discrimination may occur through a supplier imposing differing prices or non-price terms on customers. Non-price discrimination may include supplying a product on less favourable terms or conditions than those provided to other customers, or withholding benefits such as marketing or advertising support, from customers that have a low pricing policy.[169]

b) To or Against a Person or Class of Persons Engaged in Business in Canada

A "class of person" in this context may, in the Bureau's view, include a "group of firms that share common distinguishing attributes or characteristics."[170]

c) Due to That Person's or Class of Persons' Low Pricing Policy

This requirement introduces a causation element and raises the question: did the low pricing policy of the firm cause refusal to supply? Where there are several reasons at play, the Bureau takes the view that low pricing policy need only be "the proximate cause" of the supplier's refusal or discrimination; that "a person's low pricing policy need not be the only or even the primary reason for the refusal or discrimination, but rather a factor informing the supplier's decision."[171] This is consistent with the case law under the previous criminal provision, which used the same language.[172]

d) Exceptions to Refusal to Supply

The Tribunal may not make a remedial order against a supplier where the retailer refused supply was engaged in any of the following practices in respect of the product:

- selling the product at a low price for the purpose of advertising, rather than for the purpose of making a profit (i.e., as a loss leader)

---

169 *Ibid.*

170 *Ibid.*

171 *Ibid* at 9.

172 See, e.g., *R v 41813 Alberta Ltd* (February 4, 1994), No 9201-13366 (Alta QB); *R v Royal LePage Real Estate Services Ltd* (October 28, 1994), No 9201-14125 (Alta QB)); also *CarGurus, above note 160* at para 118.

- using the product not for the purpose of selling it at a profit, but for the purpose of attracting customers to sell them other products (bait and switch selling)
- misleading advertising
- not providing the level of service that purchasers of the products might reasonably expect[173]

For the exceptions to apply, the conduct in question must have constituted a "practice" by the retailer (more than one isolated act, but also a single act that is sustained and systemic or that has a lasting impact in a market).[174] The Bureau also takes the position that a supplier relying on one of these exceptions bears the burden of proving that they apply.[175]

4) Inducing Refusal to Supply

Section 76(8) creates a separate reviewable matter relating to requests by persons (usually retailers or wholesalers) to a supplier to cut off a discounting retailer or wholesaler.

> If, on application by the Commissioner or a person granted leave under section 103.1, the Tribunal finds that any person, by agreement, threat, promise or any like means, has induced a supplier, whether within or outside Canada, as a condition of doing business with the supplier, to refuse to supply a product to a particular person or class of persons because of the low pricing policy of that person or class of persons, and that the conduct of inducement has had, is having or is likely to have an adverse effect on competition in a market, the Tribunal may make an order prohibiting the person from continuing to engage in the conduct or requiring the person to do business with the supplier on usual trade terms.

This practice may support or facilitate collusion at the retail or wholesale level by providing an avenue to remove from the market a competitor who refuses to engage in collusion or is cheating on a price fixing arrangement. Enforcement of the provision can thus support or supplement section 45, the criminal prohibition against price fixing.

Section 76(8) requires an inducement of the seller to refuse to supply, which is causally connected to the low pricing of the discounting retailer. The inducement can be made by any person (it need not be another retailer or wholesaler) who uses an "agreement, threat, promise

173 *Competition Act*, above note 3, s 76(9).

174 *Price Maintenance Guidelines*, above note 145 at 10.

175 *Ibid*.

or like means" to induce the refusal. The section applies to inducements carried out by a company which is an affiliate of the company refused supply (i.e., the exclusion available to affiliates for resale price maintenance is not applicable here).

5) Remedies

Section 76(2) provides that where the elements of the practices covered by section 76(1) are satisfied, the Tribunal may prohibit a supplier from continuing to engage in resale price maintenance, or in the case of refusal to supply, order the supplier to accept a customer on usual trade terms. Similarly, section 76(8) dealing with inducements to refuse to supply provides for both prohibition and an order to supply on usual trade terms. Usual trade terms are "terms in respect of payment, units of purchase and reasonable service requirements."[176]

As in the case of the vertical practice provisions, in 2024, to encourage increased private enforcement and permit a form of restitution, remedies available on private applications under section 76 were broadened to include recovery of "the value of the benefit derived from the conduct that is the subject of the order."[177] This amount may be "distributed among the applicant and any other person affected by the conduct, in any manner that the Tribunal considers appropriate."[178]

Section 76 gives the Tribunal discretionary power to make an order. In the case of Visa/Mastercard, the Tribunal dismissed the application given its finding that there was no resale, but went on to consider whether it would have issued an order in any case if the elements of the provision were satisfied. It concluded that it would not have, because of the need for ongoing supervision of the parties, the need for further stakeholder consultation, and the potential for unintended consequences. The Tribunal observed that some form of (non-competition law) regulatory supervision appeared preferable.[179]

F. CONCLUSION

Only a handful of contested criminal price discrimination and predatory pricing cases were brought in the almost seventy-five years that these provisions were in place. Nonetheless, they raised significant legal and

176 *Competition Act*, above note 3, s 76(12).
177 *Fall Economic Statement Implementation Act, 2023*, SC 2024, c 15, s 245,
178 *Competition Act*, above note 3, s 76(11.1) and (11.2).
179 *Visa/Mastercard, above note 149* at paras 393–401.

compliance issues, potentially creating a chill on vigorous and often pro-competitive pricing practices as well as (since 1976) exposure to civil damages. A process of amendment that began in the 1960s gathered momentum in the late 1990s and finally culminated in the repeal of these offences and of resale price maintenance in 2009. Only resale price maintenance was replaced, with a new civilly reviewable offence for practices that have an "adverse effect on competition." Predatory pricing and price discrimination are now among the other potential anti-competitive acts falling within abuse of dominance and subject to a remedy before the Competition Tribunal, where they prevent or lessen competition substantially.

As noted in Chapter 3, the criminal provisions were put in place in part, if not predominantly, for the promotion and protection of individual businesses, a purpose that may clash with the modern conception of competition law as promoting competition and fostering greater efficiency and social welfare. The 2009 amendments thus harmonized these provisions with the increased focus of the legislation on economics and efficiency.

Among the practices reviewed above, predatory pricing is perhaps the most likely to generate significant enforcement activity. The circumstances in which economists envisage the practice raising competition issues are fairly limited, and concerns remain due to the potential for the law to discourage competitive pricing behaviour. However, Post-Chicago scholarship has identified several ways in which predatory pricing may stifle healthy competition when practised by a firm with market power, how it may sustain or heighten barriers to entry, or how it may cause price increases.

On the other hand, price discrimination and price maintenance seldom raise competition issues, and in many situations, they may foster efficient distribution, dissuade collusion, and increase interbrand rivalry. Given the requirement that these practices show some preservation or enhancement of market power, it is most likely that any issues that arise will be in respect of firms with a significant market presence.

CHAPTER 10

DECEPTIVE MARKETING PRACTICES

A. INTRODUCTION

The *Competition Act*[1] contains an extensive scheme of deceptive practices provisions. The core provisions, with the longest lineage in the legislation, are the prohibitions (criminal and civil) of misleading representations. Other criminal provisions address deceptive telemarketing, the awarding of prizes, double ticketing, and pyramid selling. Civil deceptive practices provisions include those dealing with representations on tests and testimonials, bait and switch advertising, sale at above advertised prices, and ordinary price claims.

These provisions may seem at first blush more suited to provincial consumer protection or trade practices than competition legislation. However, laws addressing misrepresentations and deceptive marketing promote competitive markets. Accurate information disclosure is one of the conditions for "workable competition." The prescriptions for workable competition from economists include that there be no "unfair, exclusionary, predatory or coercive tactics," and that sales promotion be informative, or not misleading.[2]

Promoting competitive markets and efficiency was cited as a rationale for the amendments which expanded the misleading trade promotion

1 *Competition Act*, RSC 1985, c C-34 [*Competition Act* or Act].

2 Frederic M Scherer, *Industrial Market Structure and Economic Performance* (Boston: Houghton Mifflin, 1980) at 42. See also Chapter 3, Section C(2)(c) and Section D(1)(e)(i).

prohibitions in the Act in 1976.[3] The Competition Bureau noted in its supporting material for the amendments that promoting accurate disclosure and information about products reduces distortions that can lead markets to function less efficiently.[4] The Federal Court of Appeal in *Canada (Commissioner of Competition) v Premier Career Management Group Corp* echoed this view. Citing the purpose clause, the court noted that "the objective of the deceptive marketing provisions in section 74.01 is to incent firms to compete based on lower prices and higher quality, in order 'to provide consumers with competitive prices and product choices.'"[5] The court went on to observe that when "a firm feeds misinformation to potential consumers, the proper functioning of the market is necessarily harmed, and the Act is rightly engaged."[6] The court noted that "a focus on the consumer is not indicative of the objective of the scheme, but is a consideration antecedent to the ultimate objective: maintaining the proper functioning of the market in order to preserve product choice and quality."[7]

The Federal Court saw an elevated role for consumer protection in the provisions in *Lin v Airbnb*. Citing the purpose clause reference to the objective of competitive prices and product choices, Gascon J stated that the *Competition Act* "has been recognized as a consumer protection legislation . . . to be interpreted . . . in favour of the consumer."[8] He relied on Supreme Court authority to the effect that "consumer protection laws are to be interpreted generously in favour of the consumers" and gave a liberal interpretation of the double ticketing provisions that supported the certification of a class action founded on their breach.[9]

As noted in Chapter 3,[10] the deceptive marketing provisions have also been viewed from time to time as advancing marketplace fairness and honesty. This rationale was referred to when Parliament was considering amendments which became the deceptive practice offences covering such matters as misleading performance guarantees, bait and switch advertising, pyramid schemes, misleading promotional contests, and sale above advertising prices.[11] It was envisioned that these provisions would

---

3 Canada, Bureau of Competition Policy, *Stage I Competition Policy, Background Papers* (Ottawa, Consumer and Corporate Affairs, 1976) at 38.

4 *Ibid.*

5 *Canada (Commissioner of Competition) v Premier Career Management Group Corp*, 2009 FCA 295 at para 61 [*Premier Career Management*].

6 *Ibid* at para 62.

7 *Ibid* at para 63.

8 *Lin v Airbnb, Inc, 2019 FC 1563 at para 57* [*Lin v Airbnb*].

9 *Ibid*, citing *Seidel v TELUS Communications Inc*, [2011] 1 SCR 531 at para 37.

10 See Chapter 3, Section C(2)(c).

11 *An Act to amend the Combines Investigation Act and the Bank Act and to repeal an Act to amend the Combines Investigation Act and the Criminal Code*, SC 1974-75-76, c 76 [*An Act to amend the Combines Investigation Act* 1976].

raise the level of confidence of market participants, and hence stimulate economic activity. The minister (André Ouellet) noted that the amendments would establish rules to encourage the private sector to conduct business in an orderly fashion and stimulate "public confidence in the effectiveness of the market system."[12]

As the legislative material and jurisprudence indicates, these provisions have thus been linked to several of the objectives found in the purpose clause, and form part of the fabric of the *Competition Act*.

In the United States, deceptive marketing prohibitions are similarly enforced alongside antitrust laws. Section 5(a) of the *Federal Trade Commission Act* provides that "**unfair or deceptive acts or practices** in or affecting commerce are . . . declared unlawful."[13] While this covers a wide scope of behaviour, "deceptive" practices were defined in the commission's *Policy Statement on Deception* as "likely to mislead consumers acting reasonably under the circumstances and . . . material to consumers—that is, it would likely affect the consumer's conduct or decisions with regard to a product or service."[14]

B. HISTORY

While the *Criminal Code* contained certain prohibitions against misleading representations as early as 1914,[15] it was only in 1960 that the first offence for misleading advertising was added to the *Combines Investigation Act*.[16] The Code provisions were consolidated into the *Combines Act* in 1969, and in 1976 they were substantially overhauled, with the addition of several new offences, as noted above.[17] For the following twenty-three years, the provisions relied solely on criminal enforcement, in spite of several policy recommendations and legislative proposals to move, in whole or part, to a civil basis and to enlarge remedies in order to facilitate enforcement.[18]

---

12 Paul Gorecki & William T Stanbury, *The Objectives of Canadian Competition Policy 1888-1983* (Montreal: IRPP, 1984) at 137.

13 15 USC § 45(a)(1).

14 US, Federal Trade Commission, *FTC Policy Statement on Deception*, 103 FTC 174 at 175 (1984).

15 Brian R Fraser, "Misleading Advertising and Deceptive Marketing Practices Under the Federal *Competition Act*: A Review of the Last 25 Years and Recent Developments" (2012) 25 *Canadian Competition Law Review* 485 at 496–97 [Fraser]; *An Act to amend the Criminal Code*, SC 1914, c 24, s 1.

16 *An Act to amend the Combines Investigation Act and the Criminal Code*, SC 1960, c 45, s 13.

17 *An Act to amend the Combines Investigation Act* 1976, above note 11, s 18(1).

18 Michael J Trebilcock et al, *Proposed Policy Directions for the Reform of the Regulation of Unfair Trade Practices in Canada* (Ottawa: Information Canada, 1976);

In 1999, the legislation was substantially overhauled to create the core of the current "hybrid" regime of criminal and civil provisions, with a broad range of civil remedies available before the Competition Tribunal, the Federal Court, and provincial superior courts.[19] Criminal enforcement was retained, but in the case of misleading advertising, the offence was restricted to misrepresentations made "knowingly" or "recklessly." A parallel civil provision was created which did not require that mental element. A new criminal telemarketing offence was added, and several of the previous criminal offences were repealed and made solely subject to civil enforcement.

In amendments made in 2009, civil administrative monetary penalties available against individuals were increased to a maximum of $1 million, and against corporations to $15 million. Imprisonment for the criminal offence of misleading advertising was increased to a maximum of fourteen years for most offences. The amendments gave the Competition Tribunal the power to require companies to pay restitution to victims of deceptive marketing practices. The Tribunal was also given interim powers to freeze assets and to prevent the disposal of property.[20]

In 2004, Canada's Anti-Spam Legislation (CASL) amended the Act to prohibit false or misleading representations made in commercial electronic messages, by creating a new offence and a reviewable practice.[21]

In 2024, private enforcement of the civil deceptive market practices provisions was provided for. Leave to bring such applications was permitted where the Competition Tribunal is "satisfied that it is in the public interest to do so."[22]

Over the course of the last several decades, the civil deceptive practices have thus been substantially expanded alongside the development of an arsenal of interim and final civil remedies.

Ed Ratushny et al, *Effective and Equitable Enforcement: Report of the Working Group on Amendments to the Misleading Advertising and Deceptive Marketing Practices Provisions of the Competition Act* (Ottawa: Bureau of Competition Policy, 1991); Canada, Bill C-20, *An Act to amend the Competition Act and to make consequential and related amendments to other Acts*, 36th Parl, 1st Sess, 1998.

19 *An act to amend the Competition Act and to make consequential and related amendments to other acts*, SC 1999, c 2, ss 12–17.1.

20 *Budget Implementation Act, 2009*, SC 2009, c 2, ss 414–16 and 423–25.

21 *An Act to promote the efficiency and adaptability of the Canadian Economy by regulating certain activities that discourage reliance on electronic means of carrying out commercial activities, and to amend the Canadian Radio-television and Telecommunications Commission Act, the Competition Act, the Personal Information Protection and Electronic Documents Act and the Telecommunications Act*, SC 2010, c 23, ss 70–81.

22 *Fall Economic Statement Implementation Act, 2023, SC 2024, c 15*, section 254 *[Bill C-59 2024]*. This provision comes into effect June 20, 2025.

C. MISLEADING REPRESENTATIONS AND DECEPTIVE PRACTICES

The Act contains a number of provisions which focus on misleading representations. The discussion below begins with the general criminal and civil prohibitions in this area and turns to others addressing misleading representations as well as deceptive practices of various kinds.

1) False and Misleading Representations

a) The Criminal and Civil Provisions

The core elements of the parallel criminal and civil provisions addressing misleading representations are set out in **Table 10.1**.

Table 10.1. Criminal and Civil Misleading Representation Provisions

Criminal Offence	**Reviewable Conduct**
52(1) No person shall, for the purpose of promoting, directly or indirectly, the supply or use of a product or for the purpose of promoting, directly or indirectly, any business interest, by any means whatever, ***knowingly or recklessly*** make a representation to the public that is false or misleading in a material respect. (1.1) For greater certainty, in establishing that subsection (1) was contravened, it is not necessary to prove that (a) any person was deceived or misled; (b) any member of the public to whom the representation was made was within Canada; or (c) the representation was made in a place to which the public had access. . . . (4) In a prosecution for a contravention of this section, the general impression conveyed by a representation as well as its literal meaning shall be taken into account in determining whether or not the representation is false or misleading in a material respect.	74.01(1) A person engages in reviewable conduct who, for the purpose of promoting, directly or indirectly, the supply or use of a product or for the purpose of promoting, directly or indirectly, any business interest, by any means whatever, (a) makes a representation to the public that is false or misleading in a material respect; . . . 74.03 (4) For greater certainty, in proceedings under sections 74.01 and 74.02, it is not necessary to establish that (a) any person was deceived or misled; (b) any member of the public to whom the representation was made was within Canada; or (c) the representation was made in a place to which the public had access. (5) In proceedings under sections 74.01 and 74.02, the general impression conveyed by a representation as well as its literal meaning shall be taken into account in determining whether or not the person who made the representation engaged in the reviewable conduct.

As the bold italicized words in the left-hand column above indicate, the sole difference in the required elements of these provisions is the additional mental element of the criminal offence. The Bureau has stated in its *Information Bulletin, Misleading Representations and Deceptive Marketing Practices: Choice of Criminal or Civil Track under the Act* that it will choose the civil law reviewable practices route unless certain criteria are satisfied indicating that the conduct involves the necessary criminal mental element, and that a prosecution would be in the public interest.[23] The factors relevant to the latter determination include the level of harm caused, whether the conduct targeted vulnerable groups, and past conduct.

The Act contains a "double jeopardy" limitation against both criminal and civil proceedings being commenced against the same person on the basis of the same or substantially the same facts.[24]

b) Elements of the Provisions

The misleading representation provisions have the following elements:

- There must be a "representation to the public."
- The representation must be for the purpose of promoting a product (a good or a service) or a business interest.
- The representation must be misleading. To determine this, there are two steps:
  - First, the general impression conveyed to consumers must be examined.
  - Second, it must be determined whether the general impression is false or misleading in a material respect.[25]

Any manner of "representations," including printed or broadcast advertisements, online communications or social media posts, written or oral statements, audio-visual promotions, and illustrations are within the scope of that term. Sections 52(2) and 73.01(1) deem certain delivery mechanisms such as packaging, containers, displays, and door-to-door sales to be representations made to the public. In *Premier Career Management*, the Federal Court of Appeal found that representations made in private to individual members of the public were nonetheless

---

23 Canada, Competition Bureau, "Information Bulletin, Misleading Representation and Deceptive Marketing Practices: Choice of Criminal or Civil Track Under the Competition Act" (22 September 1999), online: www.competitionbureau.gc.ca/eic/site/cb-bc.nsf/eng/01223.html.

24 *Competition Act*, above note 1, ss 52(7) and 74.16.

25 *Bell Mobility Inc v Telus Communications Company*, 2006 BCCA 578 at paras 16–19.

made to the "public" where members of the public were solicited by public advertisements.[26]

In *Apotex Inc v Hoffman La-Roche Ltd*, Rosenberg J addressed the issue of materiality in the context of section 52 of the Act as follows: "[a] representation is material for the purposes of section 52(1) if it is so pertinent, germane or essential that it could affect the decision to purchase."[27]

With respect to the "general impression" test, the Nova Scotia Supreme Court in *Maritime Travel Inc v Go Travel Direct.Com Inc* summarized the principles from the jurisprudence as follows:

1. The general impression of the advertisement must be determined. In doing so, the nature of the particular portion of the public to whom it is directed must be considered.
2. The literal meaning of the advertisement is to be considered as well.
3. In determining if the advertisement is false or misleading in a material respect, extraneous evidence may be considered but not for the purpose of altering the general impression already arrived at.
4. Misleading advertising must be misleading in a material respect. Materiality is defined in terms of the effect it would have upon a consumer's buying decision. It must be "so pertinent, germane or essential" (quoting from *Apotex*) that it would have an effect upon that decision. Mere "puffery" is not sufficient to constitute misleading advertising.
5. Aggressive advertising is not circumscribed by the *Competition Act* unless it is an "untruthful disparagement" of the goods or services of a competitor . . .
6. The court should not interfere with competition in the workplace unless the advertisements are "clearly unfair" . . .
7. Even advertisements which "push the bounds of what is fair" are not misleading in a material way.[28]

The standard applicable to the general impression test was addressed in the context of provincial legislation by the Supreme Court of Canada in *Richard v Time Inc*. The Court found that "[t]he words 'credulous and inexperienced' . . . describe the average consumer for the purposes of"

26 *Premier Career Management*, above note 5 at para 66.

27 *Apotex Inc v Hoffman La-Roche Ltd* (2000), 195 DLR (4th) 244 (Ont CA) at para 16.

28 *Maritime Travel Inc v Go Travel Direct.Com Inc* (2008), 66 CPR (4th) 61 at para 39, aff'd 2009 NSCA 42.

the test as applied in the false and misleading representation provisions of the Quebec *Consumer Protection Act*.[29] Justice Marrocco in *Canada (Commissioner of Competition) v Chatr Wireless Inc* adapted this test to the context of the *Competition Act* provisions, in light of their slightly differing purposes. He held that the "credulous and inexperienced" consumer is a starting point, but that consumers must be taken to have some knowledge of and experience with the service they are seeking. He applied a modified standard of a "credulous and technically inexperienced consumer of wireless services."[30] In an injunction application in *Bell Canada v Cogeco Cable Canada GP Inc, the court referred to Chatr* and held that "[t]he advertisement must be looked at as a whole, from the perspective of an average consumer."[31]

c) Drip Pricing

The criminal and civil misleading representation provisions include a section (added in 2022[32]) which states that "for greater certainty":

> the making of a representation of a price that is not attainable due to fixed obligatory charges or fees constitutes a false or misleading representation, unless the obligatory charges or fees represent only an amount imposed on a purchaser of the product … by or under an Act of Parliament or the legislature of a province.[33]

An example of this kind of conduct was that addressed in an application by the Commissioner concerning rental car companies' pricing representations in websites, mobile apps and emails. The prices represented were unattainable because they did not include certain additional

---

29 *Richard v Time Inc*, [2012] 1 SCR 265 at para 72. See also *TELUS Communications Co v Data & Audio-Visual Enterprises Wireless Inc (cob as Mobilicity)*, 2012 BCSC 1933, applying the "credulous and inexperienced" consumer test to an application for an interlocutory injunction due to an alleged breach of s 52 of the *Competition Act*, above note 1.

30 *Canada (Commissioner of Competition) v Chatr Wireless Inc*, 2013 ONSC 5315 at paras 128–32 [*Chatr Wireless*].

31 *Bell Canada v Cogeco Cable Canada GP Inc*, 2016 ONSC 6044 at para 25. See also Anita Banicevic, "Assessing General Impression under the Competition Act: The Credulous Man Who Was Never There" (2016) 29 *Canadian Competition Law Review* 57.

32 *An Act to implement certain provisions of the budget tables in Parliament April 7, 2022 and other measures*, SC 2022, c 10, ss 258, 259 [*Bill C-19 2022*]; modified to add the reference to "imposed on a purchaser of the product" by *Bill C-59 2024*, above note 22, ss 233.1 and 237.

33 *Competition Act*, above note 1, ss 52(1.3) and 74.01(1.1). Also see ss 52.01(4.1) and 74.011(3.1) concerning electronic messages.

charges which consumers had to pay to rent a vehicle.[34] These non-optional additional charges increased the cost of a car rental for certain firms from 10% to 57%.[35] The rental car companies paid over $4 million in administrative monetary penalties and agreed to compliance measures as part of a consent order settling the matter before the Tribunal.[36] In *Cineplex*, the Tribunal found drip pricing in the provision of cinema tickets because "represented ticket prices were not attainable on the website and the mobile application due to the requirement to pay Online Booking Fees."[37] In addition to a prohibition order, the Tribunal ordered Cineplex to pay an administrative monetary penalty of over $38 million under s 74.1(1)(c) of the Competition Act, representing "the amount Cineplex collected from consumers from the introduction of the Online Booking Fees on June 15, 2022, until December 31, 2023.

d) Persons Liable for Misleading Representations

Section 52(1.2) enlarges the circle of liability by providing that *permitting* a representation to be made or sent falls within the prohibitions of *making or sending* a representation in the deceptive marketing provisions of the Act.[38]

Both the criminal and civil misleading representations provisions also provide that the following types of persons are included:

- an importer, where the person making a deemed representation on packaging or other specified delivery mechanism is outside Canada[39]
- a supplier of "a wholesaler, retailer or other distributor of a product [with] any material or thing that contains a representation of a nature" that is misleading within the provisions[40]

The latter means that a manufacturer or other supplier may be liable even when another party sold the product to consumers. The wholesaler,

---

34 See, eg, *Commissioner v Hertz Canada Limited and Dollar Thrifty Automotive Group Canada Inc*, Registered Consent Agreement, File CT-2017-009, 24 April 2017.

35 *Ibid*, preamble.

36 See also Competition Bureau, Press Release, "Hertz and Dollar Thrifty to pay $1.25 million penalty for advertising unattainable prices and discounts," 24 April 2017. Other examples are *Commissioner v Ticket Network Inc*, Registered Consent Agreement, File CT-2023-009, 21 November 2023 and *Commissioner v Ticketmaster LLC*, Registered Consent Agreement, File CT-2018-005, 27 June 2019.

37 Competition Tribunal, "Information Note," *Commissioner of Competition v Cineplex Inc* CT-2023-003 (24 Sept 2024). Cineplex appealed the decision - FCA File No. A-364-24.

38 Referring to the *Competition Act*, above note 1, ss 52, 52.01, 52.1, 74.01, 74.011, and 74.02.

39 *Ibid*, ss 52(2.1) and 74.03(2).

40 *Ibid*, ss 52(3) and 74.03(3).

retailer, or distributor will not be liable unless it had sufficient involvement in making the representations, or it were the importer. For example, a retailer adapting a manufacturer's representation into its own advertising or promotional material could be liable for such a modified representation.

e) Marketing Areas Raising Issues for Misleading Representations

The Competition Bureau's various bulletins and digests provide guidance on issues and best practices in various areas that may lend themselves to misleading representations:

- consumer rebate promotions[41]
- "made in Canada" and other product origin claims[42]
- disclaimers, or the use of "fine print" in advertisements[43]
- online reviews[44]
- "unlimited" claims in telecommunications advertising[45]
- online "influencer" marketing[46]

---

41 Canada, Competition Bureau, "Enforcement Guidelines—The Application of the Competition Act, the Consumer Packaging and Labelling Act and the Textile Labelling Act to Consumer Rebate Promotions" (21 September 2009), online: www.competitionbureau.gc.ca/eic/site/cb-bc.nsf/eng/03136.html.

42 Canada, Competition Bureau, "'Product of Canada' and 'Made in Canada' Claims," Enforcement Guidelines" (22 December 2009), online: www.competitionbureau.gc.ca/eic/site/cb-bc.nsf/eng/03169.html.

43 Canada, Competition Bureau, "Disclaimers Demystified," ch 2 in "The Deceptive Marketing Practices Digest, Vol 1" (10 June 2015), online: www.competitionbureau.gc.ca/eic/site/cb-bc.nsf/eng/03946.html#s2_0.

44 *Ibid*, ch 3, "Online Reviews."

45 Canada, Competition Bureau, "Unlimited Claims—Marketing 'All You Can Eat' Telecom Services" ch 4 in "Deceptive Marketing Practice Digest, Vol 3" (2 May 2017) at 15, online: www.competitionbureau.gc.ca/eic/site/cb-bc.nsf/eng/04205.html.

46 Canada, Competition Bureau, "Influencer Marketing—A Competition Bureau Perspective," ch 1 in "Deceptive Marketing Practice Digest, Vol 4" (5 June 2018), online: www.competitionbureau.gc.ca/eic/site/cb-bc.nsf/eng/04372.html. Section 74.02 also addresses testimonials:

> 74.02 A person engages in reviewable conduct who, for the purpose of promoting, directly or indirectly, the supply or use of any product, or for the purpose of promoting, directly or indirectly, any business interest, makes a representation to the public that a test has been made as to the performance, efficacy or length of life of a product by any person, or publishes a testimonial with respect to a product, unless the person making the representation or publishing the testimonial can establish that (a) such a representation or testimonial was previously made or published by the person by whom the test was made or the testimonial was given, or (b) such a representation or testimonial was, before being made or published, approved and permission to make or publish it was given in writing by the person by whom the test was made or

- misleading online statements with the aim of collecting consumer data[47]

2) Performance Claims

The following provision requiring adequate and proper testing to support performance claims was, until 1999, a criminal offence (albeit in a different form). Like many of the provisions reviewed below, it is now "reviewable conduct" which may be made the subject of an application before the Tribunal or courts:

> 74.01 (1) A person engages in reviewable conduct who, for the purpose of promoting, directly or indirectly, the supply or use of a product or for the purpose of promoting, directly or indirectly, any business interest, by any means whatever, . . .
>
> (b) makes a representation to the public in the form of a statement, warranty or guarantee of the performance, efficacy or length of life of a product that is not based on an adequate and proper test thereof, the proof of which lies on the person making the representation.

Where a performance or similar claim is made for a product, the burden of proving adequate and proper testing lies upon the respondent by virtue of the express wording of section 74.01(1)(b). A challenge to the provision in *Chatr Wireless* on the basis that it violated section 2(b) of the *Charter of Rights and Freedoms* was rejected. The court upheld the provision under section 1 of the *Charter*.[48] It held that, given the nature of the "adequate and proper test" requirement, the section does not impose an onerous "substantiation burden" on those making performance representations and hence found that it was a reasonable limit on freedom of expression.[49]

Whether a particular test is "adequate and proper" depends on the nature of the representation made or the impression conveyed. The test must objectively establish the claimed performance. The testing need

---

the testimonial was given, and the representation or testimonial accords with the representation or testimonial previously made, published or approved.

See also Canada, Competition Bureau, "Untrue, Misleading or Unauthorized Use of Tests and Testimonials" (22 February 2018), online: www.competitionbureau.gc.ca/eic/site/cb-bc.nsf/eng/00527.html.

47 Canada, Competition Bureau, "Big Data and the Hidden Costs of 'Free' Products and Services," ch 3 in "Deceptive Marketing Practice Digest, Vol 5" (4 March 2020), online: www.competitionbureau.gc.ca/eic/site/cb-bc.nsf/eng/04520.html#sec03.

48 *Chatr Wireless*, above note 30 at para 545.

49 *Ibid* at paras 536–44.

not be as exacting as that required by a scholarly journal, but it should demonstrate that the result claimed is not a chance result.[50]

The phrase "adequate and proper" has been held to be synonymous with sufficient and appropriate. Scientific testing or third-party validation of the test is not required; a flexible and contextual analysis may be applied when assessing whether a representation is based on an adequate and proper test.[51]

The adequate and proper test must be made prior to the making of the representation to the public.[52]

A high-profile settlement of a performance claim case was *Canada (Commissioner of Competition) v Volkswagen Group Canada Inc and Audi Canada Inc*. The case involved representations that diesel engines in approximately 105,000 vehicles produced fewer emissions than equivalent gasoline engines. The consent agreement required the respondents to pay a penalty of $15 million, in the context of a $2.1 billion class action settlement to compensate Canadian consumers.[53]

In 2024, amendments directed at so-called "greenwashing" practices were added to section 74.01(1). They cover promotional practices by a person which:

> (b.1) makes a representation to the public in the form of a statement, warranty or guarantee of a product's benefits for protecting or restoring the environment or mitigating the environmental, social and ecological causes or effects of climate change that is not based on an adequate and proper test, the proof of which lies on the person making the representation;
>
> (b.2) makes a representation to the public with respect to the benefits of a business or business activity for protecting or restoring the

50 *Ibid* at para 295, citing *Canada (Commissioner of Competition) v Imperial Brush Co*, [2008] CCTD No 2 at paras 122, 124, 126, and 127 [*Imperial Brush*].

51 *Ibid* at para 122; *Chatr Wireless*, above note 30 at para 455, citing *R v Big Mac Investments Ltd* (1988), 24 CPR (3d) 39 (Man QB) at 45.

52 *Imperial Brush*, above note 50 at para 125.

53 Canada, Competition Bureau, Press Release, "Volkswagen and Audi to Pay up to $2.1 Billion to Consumers and $15 Million Penalty for Environmental Marketing Claims" (19 December 2016), online: www.canada.ca/en/competition-bureau/news/2016/12/volkswagen-audi-pay-up-2-1-billion-consumers-15-million-penalty-environmental-marketing-claims.html; *Canada (Commissioner of Competition) v Volkswagen Group Canada Inc and Audi Canada Inc*, Registered Consent Agreement, CT-2016-017 (19 December 2016). See also Competition Bureau, Press Release, "Up To $290.5 Million in Compensation for Canadians in Volkswagen, Audi and Porsche Emissions Case" (12 January 2018); *Commissioner of Competition v Volkswagen Group Canada Inc and Audi Canada Inc*, Registered Consent Agreement, CT-2018-009 (12 June 2018).

environment or mitigating the environmental and ecological causes or effects of climate change that is not based on adequate and proper substantiation in accordance with internationally recognized methodology, the proof of which lies on the person making the representation

This conduct was identified as problematic in a report summarizing consultations on potential amendments to the *Competition Act* prepared in 2022 by the sponsoring department. It noted that concerns had been raised about" the inability of individual consumers to identify the false or misleading nature of most sustainability claims following a purchase … necessitating more protective rules." The report also identified concerns about "allowing companies to profit from sustainability related claims that are not backed by sufficient evidence, misleading well-intentioned consumers into thinking their choices help the environment and disadvantaging companies who are more scrupulous about their publicity, or who truly have undertaken pro-sustainability measures."[54]

With respect to the kinds of representations covered by section 74.01(1)(b.2), the Commissioner noted in a letter to Parliamentarians during the 2023-24 amendments process that "a significant portion of the greenwashing complaints the Bureau receives do not involve claims about products, but rather more general or forward-looking environmental claims about a business or brand as a whole (e.g. claims about being 'net zero' or 'carbon neutral by 2030')."[55] That provision is thus more broadly worded to cover more general promotional statements intended to alter public perception of a company or an industry's performance or conduct in respect of environmental matters.[56]

---

54 Innovation, Science and Economic Development Canada, *Future of Canada's Competition Policy Consultation: What We Heard Report* (Ottawa: ISED, 2022), section 8. See also Competition Bureau Canada, "Environmental Claims and Greenwashing" (20 January 2022), online: https://www.competitionbureau.gc.ca/eic/site/cb-bc.nsf/eng/04607.html; Robin Spillette, Huy Do & Antonio Di Domenico, "Greenwashing: What It Is and Why It Matters" (2022) 1 Can Comp L Rev 83.

55 M Boswell, Letter to the Chair and Members of the House of Commons Standing Committee on Finance (March 1, 2024) at 5.

56 See, e.g., Canadian Association of Physicians for the Environment and Greenpeace, "Greenwashing Big Oil and Gas: The Fossil Fuel Deception Playbook" (2023), online: https://cape.ca/wp-content/uploads/2023/12/Greenwashing-Toolkit-Part-1.pdf ; Susan Koswan, "Let's use our Canadian superpower to battle fossil-fuel greenwashing," *Waterloo Region Record* (28 February 2024), online:. https://www.therecord.com/opinion/columnists/let-s-use-our-canadian-superpower-to-battle-fossil-fuel-greenwashing/article_fc787ae1-7d16-549f-886b-49a8572b76d3.html.

3) "Ordinary Price" Claims

Sections 74.01(2) and (3) address requirements governing the making of claims concerning the price at which products have been, are, or will be "ordinarily supplied." The provisions address a marketing strategy of advertising "sale" prices for products which have not, in fact, been sold at a higher price in any substantial volumes or over any period of time. Section 74.01(2) refers to advertising concerning the ordinary selling prices of products of suppliers generally in a geographic market; section 74.01(3) concerns the prices of the supplier making the representation:

> (2) Subject to subsection (3), a person engages in reviewable conduct who, for the purpose of promoting, directly or indirectly, the supply or use of a product or for the purpose of promoting, directly or indirectly, any business interest, by any means whatever, makes a representation to the public concerning the price at which a product or like products have been, are or will be ordinarily supplied where suppliers generally in the relevant geographic market, having regard to the nature of the product,
>
> (a) have not sold a substantial volume of the product at that price or a higher price within a reasonable period of time before or after the making of the representation, as the case may be; and
>
> (b) have not offered the product at that price or a higher price in good faith for a substantial period of time recently before or immediately after the making of the representation, as the case may be.
>
> (3) A person engages in reviewable conduct who, for the purpose of promoting, directly or indirectly, the supply or use of a product or for the purpose of promoting, directly or indirectly, any business interest, by any means, makes a representation to the public as to the price at which a product or like products have been, are or will be ordinarily supplied by the person making the representation unless that person, having regard to the nature of the product and the relevant geographic market, establishes that
>
> (a) they have sold a substantial volume of the product at that price or a higher price within a reasonable period of time before or after the making of the representation, as the case may be; or
>
> (b) they have offered the product at that price or a higher price in good faith for a substantial period of time recently before or immediately after the making of the representation, as the case may be.
>
> (4) For greater certainty, whether the period of time to be considered in paragraphs (2)(a) and (b) and (3)(a) and (b) is before or

after the making of the representation depends on whether the representation relates to

(a) the price at which products have been or are supplied; or

(b) the price at which products will be supplied.

(5) Subsections (2) and (3) do not apply to a person who establishes that, in the circumstances, a representation as to price is not false or misleading in a material respect.

Section 74.01(3) was amended in 2024 to create a reverse onus for price representations after the Bureau noted that the lack of such onus "places a heavy burden on the Commissioner to prove that savings claims are deceptive." It was noted that "[f]or the Bureau to evaluate the truthfulness of a single advertisement, it is required to gather and analyze large volumes of sales and marketing data." As a result, it recommended that "advertisers bear the burden of proving that advertised discounts are, in fact, truthful."[57]

Marketing will run afoul of the section 74.01 provisions when it represents regular or ordinary selling prices that do not pass either the volume or the time tests set out in paragraphs (a) or (b) of sections 74.01(2) or (3). As with the misleading representation provision, section 74.01(5) provides that the general impression conveyed by a representation, as well as its literal meaning, must be taken into account when determining whether it is misleading. It is similarly not necessary to demonstrate that any person was deceived or misled, that any member of the public to whom the representation was made was within Canada, or that the representation was made in a place to which the public had access.[58]

A summary by the Bureau providing practical guidance on section 74.01(2) states:

A person can make a price comparison about a product if the reference price reflects the price at which suppliers generally in the relevant market area have either:

(a) sold a substantial volume of the product within a reasonable period of time before or after making the representation (volume test); or

---

57 Competition Bureau Canada, "Examining the Canadian *Competition Act* in the Digital Era, Submission by the Competition Bureau" (8 February 2022), [Bureau Submissions 2022] at s. 6.2, online: https://ised-isde.canada.ca/site/competition-bureau-canada/en/how-we-foster-competition/promotion-and-advocacy/regulatory-adviceinterventions-competition-bureau/examining-canadian-competition-act-digital-era.

58 *Competition Act*, above note 1, s 74.03(4).

(b) offered the product for sale in good faith for a substantial period of time recently before or immediately after making the representation (time test).[59]

The legislation does not define the terms "substantial volume" or "reasonable period of time" for the volume test, or "good faith" or "substantial period of time" for the time test. The Bureau has published *Enforcement Guidelines*, which give some clarifications.

- **Volume**: More than 50 percent of sales must be at or above the reference price. The time period to be considered for such volumes will be the twelve months prior to (or following) the making of the representation. However, this period may be shorter having regard to the nature of the product.[60]
- **Time**: The product must be offered in good faith at or above the reference price for more than 50 per cent of the time period considered. The time period to be considered will be the six months prior to (or following) the making of the representation. However, this period may be shorter having regard to the nature of the product.[61] A six month period was accepted by the Tribunal in *Canada (Commissioner of Competition) v Sears Canada Inc* and reflected evidence of time periods used internally by the company in assessing their sales of tires.[62]

In *Sears*, the Tribunal rejected a challenge to the constitutionality of the ordinary selling price provisions of the *Competition Act* as contravening the constitutional right to freedom of commercial expression.[63] The case also addressed the "good faith" requirement in section 74.02(2)(b) and held that whether a product was offered in good faith is to be determined on the subjective basis of whether the respondent believed that its prices were "genuine." The Tribunal also held that objective factors such as comparability of the reference price to prices offered by other competitors, and number of sales at the reference price, may provide evidence that is relevant to making this determination.[64]

Ordinary price claims have frequently been settled and an order issued on consent. For example, *Canada (Commissioner of Competition)*

---

59 Canada, Competition Bureau, "Enforcement Guidelines, Ordinary Price Claims—Subsections 74.01(2) and 74.01(3) of the Competition Act" (16 October 2009) at 4.1.1.1.

60 *Ibid* at 4.2.1.2.

61 *Ibid* at 4.2.2.2.

62 *Canada (Commissioner of Competition) v Sears Canada Inc*, [2005] CCTD No 1 at para 310 [*Sears*].

63 *Ibid* at paras 31–127.

64 *Ibid* at paras 238–39.

v Hudson Bay Company dealt with mattresses advertised at discounted prices but allegedly rarely, if ever, sold at their "ordinary" price. The respondent agreed to pay an administrative monetary penalty of $4 million plus costs and to enter into a corporate compliance program.[65]

Canada (Commissioner of Competition) v Amazon involved allegations that the respondent's price comparisons created the general impression that prices for products offered on www.amazon.ca were lower than prevailing market prices. The Bureau concluded that a sample of twelve Bluray movies did not meet the requirements of the time and volume tests set out in the Act and *Guidelines*. An example was given by the Bureau in its position statement on the settlement.

List Price: ~~CDN$ 39.99~~
Price: CDN$ 29.99 **& FREE Shipping on orders over CDN$ 35**. Details
You Save: CDN$ 10.00 (25%)

FIGURE 10.1. Amazon ad example cited by Competition Bureau

The Bureau noted that "Amazon relied on its corporate suppliers without independently validating the regular price against suppliers generally in the market to determine whether these prices were accurate."[66] Under the settlement, Amazon agreed to pay a penalty of $1 million, costs, and to enter into a compliance program.[67] The case illustrates that the operators of internet commerce platforms may be subject to claims under these provisions.

4) Bait and Switch Pricing

Section 74.04 deals with what is commonly known as "bait and switch" pricing: offering a product for sale as an enticement, but then not having the product available when the customer visits the store, enticing the customer toward purchasing another product at a regular or elevated price:

> 74.04(1) For the purposes of this section, bargain price means
> (a) a price that is represented in an advertisement to be a bargain price by reference to an ordinary price or otherwise; or

---

65 *Canada (Commissioner of Competition) v Hudson Bay Company*, Registered Consent Agreement, CT-2017-008 (8 May 2019).

66 Canada, Competition Bureau, "Statement Regarding Its Inquiry into Amazon's Price Advertising in Canada" (11 January, 2017), online: www.competitionbureau.gc.ca/eic/site/cb-bc.nsf/eng/04187.html.

67 *Canada (Commissioner of Competition) v Amazon*, Registered Consent Agreement, CT-2017-001 (11 January 2017).

(b) a price that a person who reads, hears or sees the advertisement would reasonably understand to be a bargain price by reason of the prices at which the product advertised or like products are ordinarily supplied.

(2) A person engages in reviewable conduct who advertises at a bargain price a product that the person does not supply in reasonable quantities having regard to the nature of the market in which the person carries on business, the nature and size of the person's business and the nature of the advertisement.

(3) Subsection (2) does not apply to a person who establishes that

(a) the person took reasonable steps to obtain in adequate time a quantity of the product that would have been reasonable having regard to the nature of the advertisement, but was unable to obtain such a quantity by reason of events beyond the person's control that could not reasonably have been anticipated;

(b) the person obtained a quantity of the product that was reasonable having regard to the nature of the advertisement, but was unable to meet the demand therefor because that demand surpassed the person's reasonable expectations; or

(c) after becoming unable to supply the product in accordance with the advertisement, the person undertook to supply the same product or an equivalent product of equal or better quality at the bargain price and within a reasonable time to all persons who requested the product and who were not supplied with it during the time when the bargain price applied, and the person fulfilled the undertaking.

The provision is not triggered simply because adequate supplies of an advertised product are unavailable. The product must have been advertised at a bargain price, defined as such in an advertisement, or in such a way that a consumer would reasonably understand it as being a bargain price in light of prices at which it or like products are ordinarily supplied.

What about sale products for which there is limited supply? The Bureau's view is that a supplier may sell off old stock that would not normally be considered a reasonable quantity without contravening the section if it clearly specifies in the advertisement the number of items available. However, the Bureau notes that use of disclaimers such as "quantities are limited," would not be an absolute defence under this section, "although it may reduce the quantity that would otherwise be required for a reasonable supply in a given situation."[68]

68 Canada, Competition Bureau, "Price-related Representations, Bait and Switch Selling" (22 February 2018), online: www.competitionbureau.gc.ca/eic/site/cb-bc.nsf/eng/00522.html#sec02.

Section 74.04(3) creates a number of largely self-explanatory defences. The last-mentioned is the familiar practice of offering a "rain check" to customers to obtain the same or an equivalent product within a reasonable time when supplies are not available at the time the customers visits the store.

5) Sale Above Advertised Price

Section 74.05 prohibits suppliers from advertising a price for a product and then simultaneously selling it at a higher price or at a price that adds unjustified fees, effectively changing the price charged:

> 74.05(1) A person engages in reviewable conduct who advertises a product for sale or rent in a market and, during the period and in the market to which the advertisement relates, supplies the product at a price that is higher than the price advertised.
>
> (2) This section does not apply
>
> (a) in respect of an advertisement that appears in a catalogue in which it is prominently stated that the prices contained in it are subject to error if the person establishes that the price advertised is in error;
>
> (b) in respect of an advertisement that is immediately followed by another advertisement correcting the price mentioned in the first advertisement;
>
> (c) in respect of the supply of a security obtained on the open market during a period when the prospectus relating to that security is still current; or
>
> (d) in respect of the supply of a product by or on behalf of a person who is not engaged in the business of dealing in that product.
>
> (3) For the purpose of this section, the market to which an advertisement relates is the market that the advertisement could reasonably be expected to reach, unless the advertisement defines the market more narrowly by reference to a geographical area, store, department of a store, sale by catalogue or otherwise.

Under section 74.05(3) the "market" in which the advertised price must be available is determined by the area the advertisement could reasonably be expected to reach, unless the advertisement itself defines that market more narrowly.

The Bureau's earlier *Misleading Advertising Guidelines* stated that, given the reference to an "advertisement" for products, the prohibition does not apply to oral representations or representations made on product labels, and that manufacturers' "suggested retail prices" do not constitute advertised prices.[69]

---

69 Canada, Competition Bureau, *Misleading Advertising Guidelines* (2001) at 6.C.

In *R v Steinberg's Ltd*, brought under the previous criminal prohibition, a supermarket chain was convicted of selling products to an investigator which were above the prices represented in newspaper advertisements. The evidence showed that prices marked on the shelf and charged at checkout did not reflect advertised prices. The Ontario Court of Appeal held that the accused "was rightly convicted on the eight charges where the prices had not been changed and the sales were made at the higher unchanged price."[70]

6) Double Ticketing

Related to the sale above advertised price provision is the criminal summary conviction offence in section 54 applying to so-called double ticketing, which dates to the 1976 amendments.[71] The legislative history discloses that the prohibition arose during a time of high inflation, out of concerns about high food prices and the practice of some in the grocery industry of increasing the price of existing inventory in response to increased procurement costs without proper labelling.[72] The offence prohibits selling a product at the higher of the prices that appear on its wrapping, container, promotional material, or in-store displays:

> 54 (1) No person shall supply a product at a price that exceeds the lowest of two or more prices clearly expressed by him or on his behalf, in respect of the product in the quantity in which it is so supplied and at the time at which it is so supplied,
>
> (a) on the product, its wrapper or container;
> (b) on anything attached to, inserted in or accompanying the product, its wrapper or container or anything on which the product is mounted for display or sale; or
> (c) on an in-store or other point-of-purchase display or advertisement.

Retailers may wish to sell older stock labelled with lower prices alongside new stock of identical merchandise which has a higher labelled price. The Bureau takes the position that this does not raise an issue as long as each product is clearly priced:

70 *R v Steinberg's Ltd* (1977), 13 OR (2d) 293 (CA).
71 *Combines Investigation Act*, SC 1974-75-76, c 76, then s 36.2.
72 *Lin v Airbnb*, above note 8 at para 38, citing *House of Commons Debates*, 29th Parl, 2d Sess, v 1 (13, 20, and 27 March 1974) at 489, 708, and 918; *House of Commons Debates*, 30th Parl, 1st Sess, v 1 (22 October 1974) at 624-625 and 627; *House of Commons Debates*, 30th Parl, 1st Sess, v 8 (21 October 1975) at 8419; *Senate Debates*, 30th Parl, 1st Sess, v 2 (13 November 1974) at 1295.

> [T]he Bureau would not take enforcement action under this section where a price of $X was marked on one unit of a product and a price of $Y was marked on another, so long as each was sold at its marked price. This view is also based on the assumption that only one price is clearly expressed on each unit and that there are no other prices displayed at point-of-purchase.[73]

The Bureau has also noted that prosecutions under this provision have "rarely occurred."[74] A novel application of the provision was made in *Lin v Airbnb*. In that case, the plaintiff in a class action used the Airbnb website to book accommodation. He claimed that the per night room price changed between the search results phase, and the booking phase on the website. The plaintiff claimed that as a result, the price of Airbnb's accommodation booking services (the "product" in question) changed within the website. The Federal Court certified the claim. It held that on a generous reading of the pleadings, a reasonable cause of action was made out, based on the above claim of two different prices for the same product and that the prices were clearly expressed at the point-of-purchase display on the Airbnb platform.[75]

The court also rejected Airbnb's reliance on the so-called publisher's defence found in section 60. The court held that the provision, which is analogous to section 74.07(1)[76] is intended "to exempt publishers and advertisers (such as newspapers, media or other innocent bystanders) who are only displaying the prices of others, and not their own prices."[77] On the facts of the case, the court decided that Airbnb was not merely

73 Canada, Competition Bureau, "Price-related Representations, Double Ticketing" (22 February 2018), online: www.competitionbureau.gc.ca/eic/site/cb-bc.nsf/eng/00522.html#sec04.

74 See the cases cited in *Lin v Airbnb*, above note 8 at para 39.

75 *Ibid* at para 55.

76 The two provisions of the *Competition Act*, above note 1, provide:

> 60. Section 54 does not apply to a person who prints or publishes or otherwise distributes a representation or an advertisement on behalf of another person in Canada if he or she establishes that he or she obtained and recorded the name and address of that other person and accepted the representation or advertisement in good faith for printing, publishing or other distribution in the ordinary course of his or her business. . . .
>
> 74.07(1) Sections 74.01 to 74.06 do not apply to a person who prints or publishes or otherwise disseminates a representation, including an advertisement, on behalf of another person in Canada, where the person establishes that the person obtained and recorded the name and address of that other person and accepted the representation in good faith for printing, publishing or other dissemination in the ordinary course of that person's business.

77 *Lin v Airbnb*, above note 8 at para 65.

displaying others' prices, but providing "comprehensive accommodation booking services."[78]

7) Promotional Contests and Prize Notices

Section 74.06 prohibits holding a promotional contest without disclosing the number and approximate value of prizes, the area or areas to which they relate, and important information relating to the chances of winning, such as the odds of winning. The section also requires that the distribution of prizes cannot be unduly delayed and that participants be selected or prizes distributed on a skill-testing or random basis. It provides:

> 74.06 A person engages in reviewable conduct who, for the purpose of promoting, directly or indirectly, the supply or use of a product, or for the purpose of promoting, directly or indirectly, any business interest, conducts any contest, lottery, game of chance or skill, or mixed chance and skill, or otherwise disposes of any product or other benefit by any mode of chance, skill or mixed chance and skill whatever, where
> (a) adequate and fair disclosure is not made of the number and approximate value of the prizes, of the area or areas to which they relate and of any fact within the knowledge of the person that affects materially the chances of winning;
> (b) distribution of the prizes is unduly delayed; or
> (c) selection of participants or distribution of prizes is not made on the basis of skill or on a random basis in any area to which prizes have been allocated.

The Competition Bureau takes the view that in order to comply with the disclosure requirements, such disclosure should be made in a "reasonably conspicuous manner" prior to the potential entrant committing to the advertiser's product or to the contest, and this does not involve putting the onus on consumers to obtain the required details. This means, for example, that the manufacturer should ensure disclosure of a short list of the contest rules on the outside of each package of the product.[79]

In *Canada (Commissioner of Competition) v Tristar Distribution Centre (932552 Ontario Ltd)*, it was alleged that a "scratch and win" promotion

---

78 *Ibid* at para 66.

79 Canada, Competition Bureau, *Enforcement Guidelines, Promotional Contests* (16 October 2009), online: www.competitionbureau.gc.ca/eic/site/cb-bc.nsf/vwapj/20100409_PromotionalContests-e.pdf/$FILE/20100409_PromotionalContests-e.pdf at 4–5.

gave the impression that the consumer had won a prize when in fact an in-home demonstration was required. A consent order was entered, whereby the respondent published a corrected advertisement, paid a penalty, and took compliance measures.[80]

Other provisions applying to contests are the general prohibition against false and misleading representations discussed earlier, and the offence created by section 53 of the Act. The latter applies to a promotion "by electronic or regular mail or by any other means a document or notice in any form" which gives the general impression that the recipient has won or will win a prize or other benefit, if the recipient "is asked or given the option to pay money, incur a cost or do anything that will incur a cost."[81] There is no corresponding civil practice covering this conduct. The Bureau has summarized this criminal provision as follows:

> It prohibits the sending of a notice that gives the recipient the general impression he or she has won a prize or other benefit and asks or gives the option to pay money or incur a cost in order to obtain the prize or benefit. The provision applies to notices sent by any means, including but not limited to regular or electronic mail. No offence would arise if the recipient actually receives the prize or benefit.[82]

Other forms of regulation apply to contests such as lotteries.[83] Section 206 of the *Criminal Code* also applies to contests. It prohibits a requirement that a product or service be purchased as the sole condition of contest participation involving "a game of chance or mixed chance and skill" (it is not violated when there are other ways to enter).[84]

Section 74.06 of the Act does not directly prohibit a requirement for an entry fee or other consideration in order to participate in a contest involving skill, but the Bureau takes the view that where a purchase is necessary in order to participate, this fact should be prominently disclosed.[85]

---

80 *Canada (Commissioner of Competition) v Tristar Distribution Centre (932552 Ontario Ltd)*, Consent Agreement, CT-2003-010 (2 December 2003).

81 *Competition Act*, above note 1, s 53(1).

82 Canada, Competition Bureau, "Enforcement Guidelines, Deceptive Notices of Winning a Prize" (16 October 2009), online: www.competitionbureau.gc.ca/eic/site/cb-bc.nsf/vwapj/20100409_WinningaPrize-e.pdf/$FILE/20100409_WinningaPrize-e.pdf [*Enforcement Guidelines, Promotional Contests*].

83 See Fraser, above note 15 at 488–89.

84 See *Enforcement Guidelines, Promotional Contests*, above note 79 at 6, citing *Criminal Code*, RSC 1985, c C-46, s 206(1)(f).

85 *Ibid.*

D. UNFAIR TRADE PRACTICES

In addition to the foregoing provisions, which focus on the misleading character of representations, are provisions which are also directed at nature of the delivery or marketing mechanism used, which may be inherently unfair or susceptible to abuses. The provisions discussed below address telemarketing, digital communications, and pyramid schemes/multilevel marketing.

1) Deceptive Telemarketing

Section 52.1 creates a scheme of criminal offences relating to misleading telemarketing, and the failure to disclose certain required information during the course of telemarketing:

> 52.1 (1) In this section, "telemarketing" means the practice of using interactive telephone communications for the purpose of promoting, directly or indirectly, the supply or use of a product or for the purpose of promoting, directly or indirectly, any business interest.
>
> (2) No person shall engage in telemarketing unless
>
> (a) disclosure is made, in a fair and reasonable manner at the beginning of each telephone communication, of the identity of the person on behalf of whom the communication is made, the nature of the product or business interest being promoted and the purposes of the communication;
>
> (b) disclosure is made, in a fair, reasonable and timely manner, of the price of any product whose supply or use is being promoted and any material restrictions, terms or conditions applicable to its delivery; and
>
> (c) disclosure is made, in a fair, reasonable and timely manner, of such other information in relation to the product as may be prescribed by the regulations.
>
> (3) No person who engages in telemarketing shall
>
> (a) make a representation that is false or misleading in a material respect;
>
> (b) conduct or purport to conduct a contest, lottery or game of chance, skill or mixed chance and skill, where
>
> (i) the delivery of a prize or other benefit to a participant in the contest, lottery or game is, or is represented to be, conditional on the prior payment of any amount by the participant, or
>
> (ii) adequate and fair disclosure is not made of the number and approximate value of the prizes, of the area or areas to which

they relate and of any fact within the person's knowledge, that affects materially the chances of winning;

(c) offer a product at no cost, or at a price less than the fair market value of the product, in consideration of the supply or use of another product, unless fair, reasonable and timely disclosure is made of the fair market value of the first product and of any restrictions, terms or conditions applicable to its supply to the purchaser; or

(d) offer a product for sale at a price grossly in excess of its fair market value, where delivery of the product is, or is represented to be, conditional on prior payment by the purchaser.

(4) In a prosecution for a contravention of paragraph (3)(a), the general impression conveyed by a representation as well as its literal meaning shall be taken into account in determining whether or not the representation is false or misleading in a material respect.

(5) The disclosure of information referred to in paragraph (2)(b) or (c) or (3)(b) or (c) must be made during the course of a telephone communication unless it is established by the accused that the information was disclosed within a reasonable time before the communication, by any means, and the information was not requested during the telephone communication.

The provision was added in order to cover telemarketing conduct which was not encompassed by the general misleading advertising offence. The minister of industry said, in introducing the legislation in 1999:

> At present the *Competition Act* prohibits the use of materially false or misleading representations to promote the supply or use of a product or the promotion of any business interest. The Act also contains provisions relating to promotional contests. However it does not specifically forbid certain practices associated with deceptive telemarketing. The current law is also not specific enough to nail con artists who do not actually make any representations over the telephone. These inadequacies needed to be addressed.[86]

A difference between this provision and the general misleading representation offence is that for this offence, "it is sufficient if the representation is false or misleading in a material way and it is not necessary that it be made to the public."[87]

---

86 *R v Cheung, 2011 ABQB 225 at para 97, citing House of Common Debates*, 36th Parl, 1st Sess (16 March 1998) at 1255 (Hon John Manley).

87 *Ibid* at para 99.

Section 52.1(3) prohibits the making of certain misrepresentations, and failing to make certain disclosures, in promoting the supply of a product or a business interest during "interactive telephone communications." That phrase is interpreted by the Competition Bureau as "live voice communications between two or more persons."[88] The Bureau takes the view that this does not include communications by fax, internet, and automated pre-recorded messages, which are, however, subject to the general prohibition against misleading communications in sections 52 and 74.01(1)(a) of the Act.

Prohibited by section 52.1(3) are

- making materially false or misleading representations;
- requiring payment as a condition for receiving a prize in a contest or game;
- failing to provide adequate disclosure of the number and value of the "prizes";
- offering a "gift" to induce the purchase of another product, without disclosing the value of the gift; or
- offering a product at a grossly inflated price and requiring payment in advance.

The general impression test applies (as it does to the other misleading representation provisions) to the assessment of misleading communication by virtue of section 52.1(4).

It is also an offence under section 52.1(2) for telemarketers to fail to disclose

- the name of the company or person they are working for;
- the type of product or business interest they are promoting;
- the purpose of the call; or
- the price of any product being sold and any restrictions or conditions that must be met before the product will be delivered.

Given that telemarketing may be carried out in "sweatshops" by numerous individuals reading from a script supplied to them by others, and the difficulty in identifying the callers' identity, there are a number of provisions which assist holding corporations, directors, and officers responsible. Section 52.1(7) facilitates prosecution of the responsible corporation. It provides that "it is sufficient proof of the offence to establish that it was committed by an employee or agent of the corporation, whether or not the employee or agent is identified." Section 52.1(8)

---

88 Canada, Competition Bureau, *Enforcement Guidelines: Telemarketing* (16 October 2009), online: www.competitionbureau.gc.ca/eic/site/cb-bc.nsf/vwapj/20100409_Telemarketing-e.pdf/$FILE/20100409_Telemarketing-e.pdf at 5.

also expands the liability of directors and officers by providing that "any officer or director of the corporation who is in a position to direct or influence the policies of the corporation in respect of conduct prohibited by this section is a party to and guilty of the offence" committed by the corporation, whether or not the corporation has been prosecuted or convicted, unless that director or officer can prove its due diligence to avoid liability. Finally, the general expansion of liability provided in section 52(1.2) applies to this section to cover "permitting a representation to be made."[89]

As a result of the fact that this conduct may occur across international borders, individuals alleged to have engaged in fraudulent telemarketing directed at foreign nationals have been subject to extradition from Canada.[90] Various enforcement methods and agreements have also addressed the multi-jurisdictional nature of this conduct. The Centre of Operations Linked to Telemarketing Fraud (COLT), a cross-border partnership of Canadian and American police and government agencies, has been used to investigate such matters.[91] For example, the partnership was used to combat telemarketing operations in Montreal. Under the scam, the callers falsely claimed that they were calling from a business that had an existing relationship with the victim's company, that certain products or services were required under government rules, or that the call was being made on behalf of a government agency. The investigation led to five individuals pleading guilty and to twenty-eight counts of deceptive telemarketing, four counts of fraud, and one count of false or misleading representations.[92]

89 The full language of section 52(1.2) reads: "For greater certainty, in this section and in sections 52.01, 52.1, 74.01, 74.011 and 74.02, the making or sending of a representation includes permitting a representation to be made or sent."

90 See, e.g., *United States v Costanzo*, 2008 BCSC 300, aff'd 2009 BCCA 120, leave to appeal to SCC refused [2009] SCCA No 196; *United States v Anekwu*, [2009] 3 SCR 3.

91 Members include the Competition Bureau, the Royal Canadian Mounted Police, the Sûreté du Québec, the Service de police de la Ville de Montréal, and the Canada Border Services Agency as well as the Federal Bureau of Investigation, the Department of Homeland Security (Immigration & Customs Enforcement), the United States Postal Inspection Service, and the United States Federal Trade Commission. COLT also works closely with Canada Post, the Canada Revenue Agency, and the Canadian Anti-Fraud Centre. See Canada, Competition Bureau, News Release, "Jail Sentence Ends Bureau Case on Fraudulent, Misleading Telemarketing Calls" (26 March 2018), online: www.canada.ca/en/competition-bureau/news/2018/03/jail-sentence-ends-bureau-case-on-fraudulent-misleading-telemarketing-calls.html.

92 *Ibid.*

2) Deceptive Digital Communications

As noted earlier, deception using electronic messages was made a criminal offence and civil reviewable practice in the *Competition Act* in 2014 as part of other so-called anti-spam legislation. The relevant provisions are below.

Table 10.2. Criminal and Civil Deceptive Digital Communications Provisions

Criminal Deceptive Digital Communications	**Reviewable Deceptive Digital Communications**
52.01(1) No person shall, for the purpose of promoting, directly or indirectly, any business interest or the supply or use of a product, ***knowingly or recklessly*** send or cause to be sent a false or misleading representation in the sender information or subject matter information of an electronic message.	74.011(1) A person engages in reviewable conduct who, for the purpose of promoting, directly or indirectly, any business interest or the supply or use of a product, sends or causes to be sent a false or misleading representation in the sender information or subject matter information of an electronic message.
(2) No person shall, for the purpose of promoting, directly or indirectly, any business interest or the supply or use of a product, ***knowingly or recklessly*** send or cause to be sent in an electronic message a representation that is false or misleading in a material respect.	(2) A person engages in reviewable conduct who, for the purpose of promoting, directly or indirectly, any business interest or the supply or use of a product, sends or causes to be sent in an electronic message a representation that is false or misleading in a material respect.
(3) No person shall, for the purpose of promoting, directly or indirectly, any business interest or the supply or use of a product, ***knowingly or recklessly*** make or cause to be made a false or misleading representation in a locator.	(3) A person engages in reviewable conduct who, for the purpose of promoting, directly or indirectly, any business interest or the supply or use of a product, makes or causes to be made a false or misleading representation in a locator.
(4) For greater certainty, in establishing that any of subsections (1) to (3) was contravened, it is not necessary to prove that any person was deceived or misled. (4.1) For greater certainty, the making of a representation of a price that is not attainable due to fixed obligatory charges or fees constitutes a false or misleading representation, unless the	(3.1) For greater certainty, the making of a representation of a price that is not attainable due to fixed obligatory charges or fees constitutes a false or misleading representation, unless the obligatory charges or fees represent only an amount imposed on a purchaser of the product referred to in subsections (1) to (3) by or under an Act of Parliament or the legislature of a province.

Table 10.2. Criminal and Civil Deceptive Digital Communications Provisions (*Continued*)

Criminal Deceptive Digital Communications	**Reviewable Deceptive Digital Communications**
obligatory charges or fees represent only an amount imposed on a purchaser of the product referred to in subsections (1) to (3) by or under an Act of Parliament or the legislature of a province. (5) In a prosecution for a contravention of any of subsections (1) to (3), the general impression conveyed by a representation as well as its literal meaning are to be taken into account.	(3.2) For greater certainty, in determining whether or not the person who made the representation engaged in the reviewable conduct, it is not necessary to establish that any person was deceived or misled.(4) In proceedings under this section, the general impression conveyed by a representation as well as its literal meaning shall be taken into account in determining whether or not the person who made the representation engaged in the reviewable conduct. (5) For the purposes of this section, (a) an electronic message is considered to have been sent once its transmission has been initiated; and (b) it is immaterial whether the electronic address to which an electronic message is sent exists or whether an electronic message reaches its intended destination.

The foregoing came into force in July 2014. As the bold, italicized language in the left-hand column above indicates, the difference in the operative provisions is the mental element requirement for the criminal provision.

Section 52.01(2) and section 74.011(2) mirror those in the general prohibitions of false or misleading representations but apply to the sender or subject matter information of the electronic message. Sections (1) and (3) of both sections 52.01 and 74.011, on the other hand, create new requirements with respect to representations in the locator, sender information, and subject matter of an electronic message. There is no requirement that the representations be misleading "in a material respect." This means there is no need to gauge the impact of the representation on the recipient in determining whether a violation has occurred. Once it is shown that the representation is false or misleading, that is sufficient (subject to showing intent in the case of the criminal provision). For example, a misleading statement in the subject line of an email intended to "hook" the recipient into opening the email would satisfy the provision.

For the civil provision, the electronic message does not have to reach its intended destination; it is also immaterial whether the destination email address exists for the elements of the offence to be satisfied.

Like the general misleading representation provisions, charges under the criminal deceptive electronic message provision may not be brought against a person on the basis of the same or substantially the same facts alleged in a proceeding already brought pursuant to the analagous civil provision (and vice-versa).[93]

3) Pyramid Selling and Multi-level Marketing

Sections 55 and 55.1 create criminal offences relating to multi-level marketing plans and pyramid selling. While the former are permitted, subject to certain disclosure requirements, the latter are prohibited.

> 55(1) For the purposes of this section and section 55.1, **multi-level marketing plan** means a plan for the supply of a product whereby a participant in the plan receives compensation for the supply of the product to another participant in the plan who, in turn, receives compensation for the supply of the same or another product to other participants in the plan.
>
> (2) No person who operates or participates in a multi-level marketing plan shall make any representations relating to compensation under the plan to a prospective participant in the plan unless the representations constitute or include fair, reasonable and timely disclosure of the information within the knowledge of the person making the representations relating to
>
> (a) compensation actually received by typical participants in the plan; or
>
> (b) compensation likely to be received by typical participants in the plan, having regard to any relevant considerations, including
>
> (i) the nature of the product, including its price and availability,
>
> (ii) the nature of the relevant market for the product,
>
> (iii) the nature of the plan and similar plans, and
>
> (iv) whether the person who operates the plan is a corporation, partnership, sole proprietorship or other form of business organization.

93 *Competition Act*, above note 1, s 52.01(8) and 74.16.

(2.1) A person who operates a multi-level marketing plan shall ensure that any representations relating to compensation under the plan that are made to a prospective participant in the plan by a participant in the plan or by a representative of the person who operates the plan constitute or include fair, reasonable and timely disclosure of the information within the knowledge of the person who operates the plan relating to

(a) compensation actually received by typical participants in the plan; or
(b) compensation likely to be received by typical participants in the plan, having regard to any relevant considerations, including those specified in paragraph (2)(b)

(2.2) A person accused of an offence under subsection (2.1) shall not be convicted of the offence if the accused establishes that he or she took reasonable precautions and exercised due diligence to ensure

(a) that no representations relating to compensation under the plan were made by participants in the plan or by representatives of the accused; or
(b) that any representations relating to compensation under the plan that were made by participants in the plan or by representatives of the accused constituted or included fair, reasonable and timely disclosure of the information referred to in that subsection. . . .

55.1 (1) For the purposes of this section, **scheme of pyramid selling** means a multi-level marketing plan whereby

(a) a participant in the plan gives consideration for the right to receive compensation by reason of the recruitment into the plan of another participant in the plan who gives consideration for the same right;
(b) a participant in the plan gives consideration, as a condition of participating in the plan, for a specified amount of the product, other than a specified amount of the product that is bought at the seller's cost price for the purpose only of facilitating sales;
(c) a person knowingly supplies the product to a participant in the plan in an amount that is commercially unreasonable; or
(d) a participant in the plan who is supplied with the product
    (i) does not have a buy-back guarantee that is exercisable on reasonable commercial terms or a right to return the product in saleable condition on reasonable commercial terms, or
    (ii) is not informed of the existence of the guarantee or right and the manner in which it can be exercised.

(2) No person shall establish, operate, advertise or promote a scheme of pyramid selling.

Multi-level marketing (MLM) plans are permissible if participants are given fair, reasonable, and timely disclosure concerning compensation as required by sections 55(2) and (3). Section 55(1) defines a multi-level marketing plan as the supply of a product "whereby a participant in the plan receives compensation for the supply of the product to another participant in the plan who, in turn, receives compensation for the supply of the same or another product to other participants in the plan." This chain of compensation among participants creates policy concerns about the incentives to recruit new participants and to generate inflated or inaccurate expectations about compensation. Hence the provisions require fair and timely disclosure.

Under section 55.1(2), it is an offence to "establish, operate, advertise or promote a scheme of pyramid selling." Section 55.1(1) defines a "scheme of pyramid selling" as an MLM plan with one or more of the following features:

- a payment is required for the right to receive compensation for recruiting others into the MLM plan
- purchases of product are required as a condition of participation (other than a specified amount of product at the seller's cost for the purpose of facilitating sales)
- inventory loading—a person knowingly supplying a commercially unreasonable amount of product to participants
- no buy-back guarantee (no right to return products on reasonable commercial terms) or no information about a guarantee

The Bureau's Enforcement Guidelines, *Multi-level Marketing and Scheme of Pyramid Selling*, provides detailed guidance.[94] It explains the differences between MLM plans and pyramid selling schemes and provides commentary and illustrative examples.

The policy concern with pyramid selling is that paying commissions for recruiting new distributors can create great wealth for a few of the earlier participants (at the "top of the pyramid"), but such schemes tend to collapse when no new distributors can be recruited, resulting in many people losing the money they have invested in the scheme. The recruitment plans may also mislead the participants. For example:

> These schemes may offer products, however the products may have very little value or the plan may offer limited incentives for their sale. Income in the scheme is derived primarily from the money prospective participants pay to join the scheme and not from the sale of product.[95]

---

94 Canada, Competition Bureau, *Enforcement Guidelines, Multi-level Marketing and Scheme of Pyramid Selling* (29 April 2009), online: www.competitionbureau.gc.ca/eic/site/cb-bc.nsf/eng/03035.html.

95 *Ibid* at 4.2.

E. REMEDIES FOR DECEPTIVE MARKETING

As noted above, the Commissioner has the choice of a criminal or a civil track with respect to the core misleading representation provisions, and certain other provisions such as deceptive electronic communications.

Criminal penalties available under the provisions for false and misleading misrepresentations (section 52), deceptive electronic messages (section 52.01), telemarketing offences (section 52.1), and prize awards (section53) are the same. On indictment, the maximum penalties are a fine at the discretion of the court, imprisonment for fourteen years, or both; on summary conviction, $200,000, imprisonment for one year, or both. The multi-level marketing and pyramid selling offences (sections 55 and 55.1) are the same as the above, except for the imprisonment on indictment, which is three years. Double ticketing (section 54) provides for summary conviction only and a fine of $10,000, a year's imprisonment, or both.

Section 36 provides a private right of action for private parties to seek damages for breaches of these provisions; class actions may be available as a vehicle to pursue such claims.[96]

With respect to the civil reviewable practices, the Commissioner must file an application before the Competition Tribunal, the Federal Court, or the superior court of a province. As a civil matter, the elements of the provisions must be proven on a balance of probabilities. Under section 74.11, a temporary order may be issued against a person engaging in reviewable conduct restraining that conduct or restraining the supply of a product used to engage in that conduct if "(a) serious harm is likely to ensue unless the order is issued; and (b) the balance of convenience favours issuing the order."[97] The issuance of an order obliges the Commissioner to complete the inquiry into the conduct in question as expeditiously as possible.

An injunction may also be issued, where a strong *prima facie* case is demonstrated of breach of the misleading representation provision in section 74.01(1)(a), to restrain the disposal of articles where the disposal may impair restitution of sums paid by purchasers who were subject to the misleading representations.[98]

With respect to final orders, section 74.1(1) sets out a range of remedies: prohibition of the conduct, orders requiring advertisers to publish corrective notices, administrative monetary penalties, and restitution to consumers.[99] The authority to issue administrative

---

96 See Chapter 2, Section C(2)(b).

97 *Competition Act*, above note 1, ss 74.11(1) & (2).

98 *Ibid*, s 74.111.

99 *Ibid*, s 74.1(1).

monetary penalties was upheld in *Chatr Wireless*.[100] An example of a case involving restitution to harmed consumers involved alleged misleading representations by Bell, Rogers, Telus, and the Canadian Wireless Telecommunications Alliance concerning text messaging services billed by the companies on consumers' bills. As part of a settlement, the companies agreed to make a total of up to $24 million in rebates available to consumers and pay more than $1 million to fund consumer advocacy and research groups.[101]

In 2022, section 74.1 was amended to provide for monetary penalties up to "three times the value of the benefit derived from the deceptive conduct" and in the case of corporations, "if that amount cannot be determined, 3% of the corporation's annual worldwide gross revenues."[102]

The Bureau's approach to remedies is based upon a "compliance continuum," which it has summarized as follows:

> When the Bureau becomes aware of alleged non-compliance, the appropriate instrument is selected from the range of available responses. When appropriate, the Bureau will use a blended approach, which involves the selection and use of more than one instrument. The choice will depend on the particular circumstances of the case at hand. A variety of factors will be assessed, including the gravity and the impact of the alleged non-compliance, previous anti-competitive conduct and the willingness of the parties to resolve the matter.[103]

Finally, the deceptive marketing provisions contain consent order provisions that parallel those applicable to other civil proceedings under the Act.[104] Private applicants may also enter into consent agreements for

100 See *Chatr Wireless*, above note 30 at paras 546–58.

101 Competition Bureau, News Release, "Bell Customers to Receive up to $11.82 Million as Part of Competition Bureau Agreement" (27 May 2016), online: www.canada.ca/en/competition-bureau/news/2016/05/bell-customers-to-receive-up-to-11-82-million-as-part-of-competition-bureau-agreement.html; *Commissioner v Bell Mobility Inc*, CT-2016-007, Registered Consent Agreement (27 May 2016).

102 *Bill C-19 2022*, above note 32, s 260.

103 Canada, Competition Bureau, "Competition and Compliance Framework" (10 Nov 2015), online: https://competition-bureau.canada.ca/how-we-foster-competition/education-and-outreach/competition-and-compliance-framework#section3_1_1).

104 *Competition Act*, above note 1, ss 74.12 and 74.13.

filing and registration as enforceable orders of the Tribunal.[105] As some of the examples given above have indicated, consent orders, usually involving the payment of penalties and agreement to a compliance program, have been used extensively to resolve these issues.

In 2024, Parliament added provisions which permit the Commissioner to apply for remedies relating to an alleged failure to comply with a registered consent agreement.[106] Available remedies include administrative monetary penalties of up to $10,000 for each day of non-compliance.

The 2024 amendments also provided (in changes coming into force June 20, 2025) for private enforcement of the civil misleading representation provisions by adding section 74.1 to the provisions for which leave to bring an application may be granted by the Tribunal under section 103.1.[107]

F. CONCLUSION

The deceptive offences and reviewable conduct covered in this chapter are among the practices most visible to consumers included in the *Competition Act*. Most people have received a call from a telemarketer, an email seeking money, or a deceptive "prize" award. Those affected by these practices are harmed directly and visibly. Often consumers feel a sense of invasion, unfairness, or outrage. Given the foregoing, the value of the provisions lies in improving consumers' trust for markets and the efficiency of the economy, and they are part of the core of competition law enforcement in Canada.

The deceptive marketing provisions are another example of an area of Canadian competition law in which there has been a transition over time from criminal to civil enforcement. Criminal enforcement has been retained for certain matters which feature a level of criminal culpability, where prosecution is in the public interest. On the other hand, civil resolution has become the norm in this area, with numerous cases resolved by consent order, requiring the payment of monetary penalties and restitution, as well as other relief, and contested matters proceeding to the Competition Tribunal or civil courts. This transition to civil enforcement has made available a range of flexible interim and final remedies better suited to the nature of the conduct involved.

---

105 *Ibid*, s 74.131.

106 *Bill C-59 2024*, above note 22, ss 242 and 243.

107 *Bill C-59 2024*, above note 22, s 254.

Transborder deceptive conduct has become an increasing part of the marketplace. Electronic and online misrepresentation is another evolving area. Such measures as enforcement cooperation between agencies, as well as periodic modification of the law, have been critical to addressing this kind of behaviour. These and other measures will be needed to ensure that the legislative scheme can address the ways in which deceptive conduct continues to adapt to new methods of communication and to ways of doing business in the economy.

TABLE OF CASES

INDEX

ABOUT THE AUTHOR

John Tyhurst is currently an adjunct professor at the University of Ottawa Faculty of Law, Common Law Section (English), where he teaches competition law and supervises directed research. He practiced civil litigation, including competition law, at the Department of Justice in Ottawa for over thirty-two years. Since retiring from Justice, he has been continued to practice law, and was lead counsel for the Commissioner of Competition in the *Rogers/Shaw* merger case before the Competition Tribunal. Born in Montreal and raised in Vancouver, he completed his BA in economics at the University of British Columbia, his LLB at the University of Toronto, and his LLM at McGill University as a recipient of a Duff-Rinfret Scholarship. He articled in Vancouver and then moved to Ottawa to practice with a consumer organization that intervened before various regulatory tribunals, including the CRTC and CITT. He participated in the process leading to amendments to Canadian competition legislation in 1986. He then joined the Department of Justice, providing advice and litigation support to the Competition Bureau at the Departmental Legal Services Unit, where he practiced for ten years. He prosecuted criminal price fixing and bid-rigging cases, and appeared before the Competition Tribunal in civil merger, abuse of dominance, and vertical restraints cases. He moved to the Civil Litigation Section in 1997 to work on the first NAFTA Chapter 11 investor-state proceeding, and thereafter litigated trade, telecommunications, judicial review, and Indigenous law matters. As a member of Department of Justice's Supreme Court Practice Group, he appeared before the Supreme Court in competition law, tort, and Indigenous law cases. He appeared before other appellate courts, including the Federal and Ontario courts of appeal and conducted civil trials, arbitrations, and interventions as counsel for the Attorney General of Canada. In 2020 he was awarded the J Edward (Ted) Thompson, QC award for excellence in trial advocacy.